With these multimedia tools, studying music is a **memorable experience**

◀ Interactive eBook

Included with every new book, access to the eBook enables students to take notes, highlight, and search; access Active Listening Guides, streaming music, YouTube and iTunes playlists; and much more.

"Having the music integrated with the eBook . . . awesome . . ."

Samantha Williams, student, Metropolitan State College

Active Listening Guides ▶

These interactive features enable students to listen actively by guiding them through and pointing out the key aspects of each piece of music as it plays. Students can pause and replay at any point, click on a Profile for a summary of the elements of music in that piece, check the Key Points for its key features, or take an interactive quiz to check their comprehension.

If students want a printout of the listening guide, they simply click ▶ on Export PDF to print out a PDF version for their study.

"By making [Active Listening Guides] visual AND aural (especially color-associated), I think students are much more likely to make connections between the two."

Kyle Sutton, student, Northeastern University

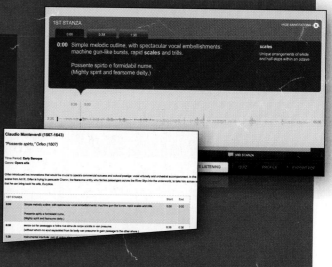

▼ MUSIC CONCEPT CHECKS

In the printed book, these features present mini-reviews of key concepts. Red icons in the eBook link directly to online music demos and iTunes and YouTube playlists.

"Very easy to navigate through . . . I like how it caters to non-majors."

Shaan Duggal, student, Boston University

Music Concept Check
Review and listen to all the instrument families in Britten's *Young Person's Guide to the Orchestra*, on the text website.

TURN THE PAGE ▶
for **MUSIC**'s interactive student resources

MUSIC focuses on **successful learning outcomes** and careful listening

Learning Outcomes

After reading this unit, you will be able to do the following:

LO1 Understand what opera is, the particular challenge of setting drama to music, and the usefulness of developing musical gestures that can depict feelings and moods.

LO2 Understand the revolutionary impact of the first operas in Europe.

LO3 Recognize the importance of Claudio Monteverdi and the sound and vocal style of his opera *Orfeo*.

LO4 Recognize a large ensemble, as well as new ways of composing for instruments.

LO5 Understand the growth of opera, including musical and dramatic changes, during the seventeenth century.

LO6 Recognize an early example of the use of recitative and aria, as well as the expressive capabilities of common practice harmony, in Henry Purcell's "Dido's Lament."

◀ Unit Learning Outcomes

MUSIC's short chapters and modern design present content accessibly without minimizing coverage. *Unit Learning Outcomes*, keyed to heads within each chapter, are reinforced in the *Unit in Review Cards* at the end of the book.

▼ Listen Up!

These cues throughout the printed book offer convenient checklists of features for specific music selections. In the eBook, clicking on the *Listen Up's* icons links students directly to online Active Listening Guides and streaming music.

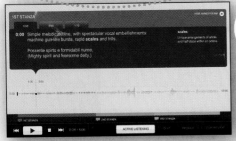

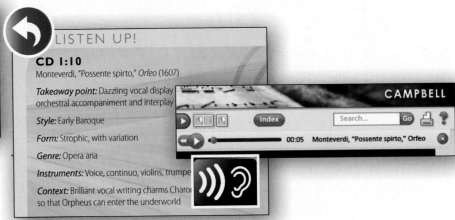

LISTEN UP!

CD 1:10

Monteverdi, "Possente spirto," *Orfeo* (1607)

Takeaway point: Dazzling vocal display orchestral accompaniment and interplay

Style: Early Baroque

Form: Strophic, with variation

Genre: Opera aria

Instruments: Voice, continuo, violins, trumpe

Context: Brilliant vocal writing charms Charo so that Orpheus can enter the underworld

EACH of these music selections is available on CD, streaming, and in an online Active Listening Guide:

Hildegard of Bingen, "Nunc aperuit nobis"
Machaut, "Puis qu'en oubli"
Anonymous, "La uitime estampie real"
Anonymous, "L'homme armé" tune
Josquin, Kyrie, from *Missa l'homme armé sexti toni*
Luther, "Ein' feste Burg ist unser Gott"
Luther/Walter, "Ein' feste Burg ist unser Gott"
Bach, Chorale, from *Ein' feste Burg ist unser Gott*
Wilbye, "Adew, Sweet Amarillis"
Morley, "O Mistresse Mine" (vocal)
Morley, "O Mistresse Mine" (instrumental)
Monteverdi, "Possente spirto," *Orfeo*
Purcell, "Thy Hand, Belinda," *Dido and Aeneas*
Purcell, "When I Am Laid in Earth," *Dido and Aeneas*
Plains Indians War Dance
Anonymous, Song for Odudua

Anonymous, "Barbara Allen"
Guinchard, "Boston Laddie"
Corelli, Sonata in C major, 1st & 2nd movements
Bach, Gigue, from Orchestral Suite No. 3
Vivaldi, Violin Concerto in E major ("Spring"), 1st movement
Bach, Brandenburg Concerto No. 3, 1st movement
Handel, "E pur così" and "Piangerò," *Giulio Cesare in Egitto*
Gay/Pepusch, "I'm Bubbled," "Cease Your Funning," and "How Now, Madam Flirt?" *The Beggar's Opera*
Bach, "Und wenn die Welt voll Teufel wär," from Cantata No. 80, *Ein' feste Burg ist unser Gott*
Handel, Hallelujah Chorus, from *Messiah*
Anonymous, "God Save the King"
Haydn, "Gott erhalte Franz den Kaiser"
Billings, "Chester"

Mozart, Sonata in F major, 1st movement
Haydn, String Quartet in C major ("Bird"), 1st movement
Haydn, Symphony No. 94 in G major, 1st movement
Mozart, "Là ci darem la mano," *Don Giovanni*
Mozart, "A cenar teco," *Don Giovanni*
Mozart, Concerto in C minor, 1st movement
Beethoven, Sonata No. C minor ("Pathétique"), 1st movement
Beethoven, Symphony No. 5 in C minor, 1st–4th movements
Schubert, *Erlkönig*
Schubert, *Gretchen am Spinnrade*
Foster, "Jeanie with the Light Brown Hair"
Foster, "De Camptown Races"
The Duhks, "Camptown Races"
Brahms, "Wie lieblich sind deine Wohnungen," from *Ein deutsches Requiem*

Study anywhere/anytime with **MUSIC's** tear-out
Unit in Review cards

These easy-to-use study essentials are located at the back of the book. There is a perforated review card for each of the book's 23 units. Each review card includes summaries of *Learning Outcomes*, a timeline that puts the chronology of the unit in perspective, terms and definitions keyed to the unit's *Learning Outcomes*, and *Applying Unit Concepts* exercises that encourage students to relate music they've just studied to the popular music they already know.

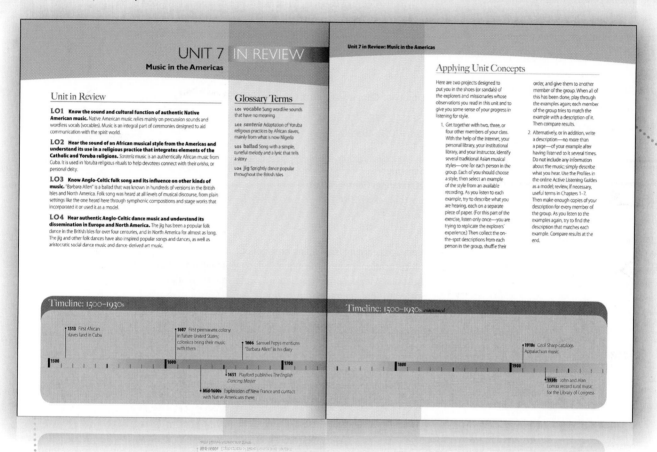

Adams/Mason, "Nearer, My God, to Thee"
Newton, "Amazing Grace"
Gilbert/Sullivan, "I Am the Very Model of a Modern Major-General," *The Pirates of Penzance*
Bizet, "L'amour est un oiseau rebelle," *Carmen*
Verdi, "Dite alla giovine," *La traviata*
Wagner, Act 1 conclusion, *Die Walküre*
C. Schumann, Romance in G minor
R. Schumann, "Aufschwung," from *Fantasiestücke*
Chopin, Etude in C minor ("Revolutionary")
Chopin, Prelude No. 3 in G major
Chopin, Prelude No. 4 in E minor
Berlioz, "Songe d'une nuit de sabbat," *Symphonie fantastique*, 5th movement
Brahms, Symphony No. 2 in D major, 3rd movement
Tchaikovsky, Violin Concerto in D major, 3rd movement
Strauss, *The Emperor Waltz*
Tchaikovsky, Waltz, from *The Sleeping Beauty*
Dvořák, Slavonic Dance in G minor
Schoenberg, "Nacht," *Pierrot lunaire*

Debussy, "Voiles," from *Preludes*
Debussy, "Minstrels," from *Preludes*
Stravinsky, "Introduction," "The Augurs of Spring," and "Mock Abduction," from *The Rite of Spring*
Sousa, "The Stars and Stripes Forever"
Joplin, "The Entertainer"
Ives, "Putnam's Camp, Redding, Connecticut," from *Three Places in New England*
Hayes, "Lord, I Can't Stay Away"
Smith, "Empty Bed Blues"
Armstrong, "Hotter Than That"
Gershwin, *Rhapsody in Blue*
Kern/Hammerstein, "Can't Help Lovin' Dat Man," *Show Boat*
Webern, Concerto for Nine Instruments, 2nd movement
Stravinsky, *Symphony of Psalms*, 1st movement
Chavez, *Sinfonia India*, excerpt
Copland, *Appalachian Spring*, 1st & 2nd sections
Bartók, *Music for Strings, Percussion, and Celesta*, 2nd movement

Prokofiev, "Peregrinus expectavi," from *Alexander Nevsky*
Cage, Sonata V from *Sonatas and Interludes*
Babbitt, *Ensembles for Synthesizer*, excerpt
Penderecki, *Tren (Threnody for the Victims of Hiroshima)*, excerpt
Parker/Gillespie, "Salt Peanuts"
Bernstein/Sondheim, "Cool," *West Side Story*
Machito, "Carambola"
Piazzolla, "Oblivion"
Berry, "Sweet Little 16"
Wilson, "Surfin' U.S.A."
Dylan, "Subterranean Homesick Blues"
Tower, *Fanfare for the Uncommon Woman*
Zwilich, Concerto Grosso 1985, 1st movement
Williams, "Main Title/Rebel Blockade Runner," *Star Wars Episode IV*
Tan, "Farewell," *Crouching Tiger, Hidden Dragon*
Reich, *Music for 18 Musicians*, Section IIIA
Pärt, Kyrie, from *Berlin Mass*

SCHIRMER
CENGAGE Learning

MUSIC
Michael Campbell

Publisher: Clark Baxter

Senior Development Editor: Sue Gleason

Senior Development Editor, Market Strategies: Liz Kendall

Assistant Editor: Nell Pepper

Editorial Assistant: Ashley Bargende

Senior Media Editor: Wendy Constantine

Marketing Manager: Mark T. Haynes

Marketing Coordinator: Josh Hendrick

Marketing Communications Manager: Heather Baxley

Senior Content Project Manager: Lianne Ames

Senior Art Director: Stacy Shirley

Print Buyer: Justin Palmiero

Rights Acquisition Specialist: Mandy Groszko

Production Service: Bill Smith Group

Text Designer: KeDesign, Mason, OH

Cover Designer: KeDesign, Mason, OH

Cover Image: © Getty Images/Clint Spencer

Compositor: Bill Smith Group

For product information and technology assistance, contact us at
Cengage Learning Customer & Sales Support, 1-800-354-9706
For permission to use material from this text or product,
submit all requests online at **cengage.com/permissions**
Further permissions questions can be emailed to
permissionrequest@cengage.com

Library of Congress Control Number: 2010935346

ISBN-13: 978-0-495-00468-4
ISBN-10: 0-495-00468-5

Schirmer
20 Channel Center Street
Boston, MA 02210
USA

Cengage Learning is a leading provider of customized learning solutions with office locations around the globe, including Singapore, the United Kingdom, Australia, Mexico, Brazil, and Japan. Locate your local office at:
international.cengage.com/region

Cengage Learning products are represented in Canada by Nelson Education, Ltd.

For your course and learning solutions, visit **www.cengage.com.**
Purchase any of our products at your local college store
or at our preferred online store **www.cengagebrain.com.**

Printed in the United States of America
1 2 3 4 5 6 7 14 13 12 11 10

Brief Contents

Contents

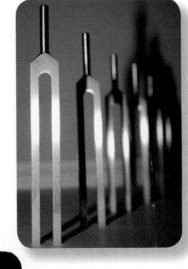

PART 2 SEVEN CENTURIES OF MUSIC

PART 3 THE EIGHTEENTH CENTURY

PART 4 THE NINETEENTH CENTURY

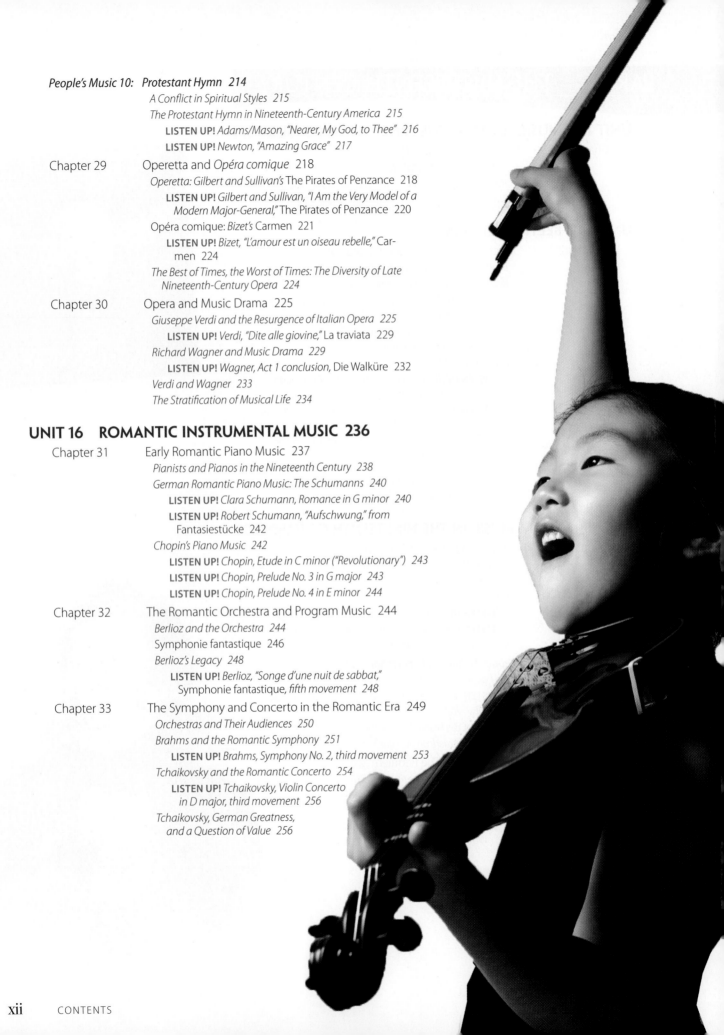

PART 5   THE TWENTIETH CENTURY AND BEYOND

UNIT I
POINTS OF ENTRY

Learning Outcomes

After reading this unit, you will be able to do the following:

LO1 Describe and recognize the basic properties of musical sound.

LO2 Identify the elements of music.

LO3 Define dynamics in detail.

LO4 In the context of understanding instrumentation, compare the tone color of a piano with that of an orchestra.

LO5 Learn the musical meanings of rhythm, beat, and tempo.

LO6 Understand the relationships between beat and meter.

LO7 Define melody and describe how to construct one.

LO8 Understand the uses of scale and tonality.

LO9 Describe the use of phrase in melody.

© iStockphoto.com/Zemdega

CHAPTER 1

Sound and Silence

"We 'play' musical instruments, not 'work' them."

On August 29, 1952, pianist David Tudor walked onstage at the Maverick Concert Hall in Woodstock, New York, sat down at a grand piano, placed a musical score on the piano rack, and pulled out a stopwatch. He started the watch, then closed the lid to cover the piano keys. After thirty seconds, he raised the lid. He closed it again and then lifted it two minutes and twenty-three seconds later. He closed the lid a third time and lifted it for the last time after one minute and forty seconds. During the intervals between lowering and raising the lid, Tudor sat quietly, moving only to shift pages in the music. After lifting the lid over the keys for the third time, Tudor stopped the watch, then stood up to signal the end of the work.

Most of the audience were outraged. Some left before the end of the performance. For them, Tudor had violated the most basic assumption about musical composition and performance: that musicians actually *do* something with sound in performance—that they make sounds with intention. To the audience, it must have seemed like a musical emperor's new clothes.

Tudor's performance was the premiere of *4'33"*, a composition by the American composer and thinker John Cage (1912–1992). Cage called it his "silent piece," but he composed *4'33"* to demonstrate that no environment is truly silent. In this respect, Woodstock's Maverick Concert Hall, the back of which was open to the forest, was an ideal venue. The audience at the first performance could have heard wind rustling through the trees and rain splattering on the roof if they hadn't

Did You Know?

The "trumpets" in the biblical story in which the Israelites sounded trumpets to blow down the walls of Jericho were shofars, or rams' horns.

been so irritated at Cage's seeming violation of musical sensibility. They missed the point. Cage's composition *4'33"* was—and is—an invitation to tune in to the surrounding sound world with heightened awareness and without judgment.

Music is about structuring sound and silence in particular ways. The traditional definition of **music** is the organization of sound in time. The composition *4'33"* represents one extreme of the musical experience—unstructured ambient sound within Cage's temporal frame.

LO1 The Properties of Musical Sound

Given that music involves the intentional manipulation of sounds, what specific properties of sound does a musician control? There are four:

1. How loud the sound is
2. How long it lasts
3. How high or low it is
4. Its distinctive tonal quality

DYNAMICS

We use the word **dynamics** to refer to the relative loudness or softness of musical sound. We measure the volume of sound in **decibels (dB)**, units that range from 0 dB (the minimum that you can

music
Organization of sound in time

dynamics
Relative loudness or softness of musical sound

decibel (dB)
Unit that measures the volume of sound

hear), to 60 dB (the ordinary speaking voice), to 110 dB (heard at the front rows at a rock concert), to 130 dB (the pain threshold), to 160 db (resulting in a perforated eardrum). However, in musical contexts, we typically describe dynamics in more general terms: very loud, very soft, or somewhere in between.

DURATION

We use the word **duration** to refer to the length of time that a musical sound or silence lasts. In many instances, we measure the duration of a sound or intended silence simply by noting when it begins and when it ends. However, when we encounter a series of sounds separated by silence, such as the audible space between strokes in a drum solo, we tend to measure the duration of the sound as the length of time between one impact and the next rather than the actual duration of the sound, which dies away quickly.

PITCH

We use the word **pitch** to refer to the relative highness or lowness of a sound. The pitch of a sound is determined by its frequency, which is measured as the number of vibrations or cycles per second: the highest-pitched string of a conventionally tuned guitar vibrates at 330 cycles per second, while the lowest-pitched string vibrates at one-fourth of that speed, 82.5 cycles per second. We typically use words like *high* and *low* to describe the speed of the vibration: for example, we would say that the top string of the guitar (closest to the performer's leg) produces a higher pitch than the bottom string does. We also distinguish between sounds with *definite pitch*, because they have a consistent frequency, and sounds with *indefinite pitch*, which do not. Many percussion sounds, including those made on a drum set, convey only a general sense of high and low. Sounds such as the crash of a cymbal or the white noise (the complete range of audible frequencies heard at the same time) heard between radio stations may have duration; but, because they have no consistent frequency, they lack definite pitch.

A tuning fork that vibrates at 440 cycles per second produces a definite pitch in the midrange of a woman's voice.

© iStockphoto.com/ CWLawrence

TIMBRE

We use the word **timbre** (TAM-ber) to refer to the distinctive tonal properties of a sound. Timbre is the uniqueness of sound that distinguishes the sound of your voice from the sound of a friend's and, in music, the sound of an electric guitar from the sound of a violin. Timbre is the only property of musical sound that does not fall on a continuum. Differences in duration, pitch, and dynamics do, because they involve matters of degree: longer or shorter, higher or lower, louder or softer. By contrast, distinctions in timbre are not measurable by degree but by the shapes and frequencies of the sound waves produced by a voice or instrument. A single instrument playing a single tone creates a complex and distinctive waveform. Why? Because almost all musical sounds contain several frequencies sounding simultaneously. When you hear a tone, one frequency dominates, but the tone contains other frequencies vibrating faster, and sometimes slower, in varying strengths. The resulting waveform— a synthesis of these various frequencies—produces the

> *Timbre is the property that distinguishes the sound of your voice from the sound of a friend's.*

distinctive timbre of a musical sound. The timbre of a piano is different from the timbre of a flute or a violin, or of the shofar that you will hear shortly, because their waveforms are different.

SOUND BITES

The desire to manipulate sound is a basic human impulse dating back to prehistoric times. While manipulating sound can be playful—indeed, we *play* musical instruments, not "work" them, it can also be functional. In other words, it can aid in other activities, such as dancing or marching, selling products, or supporting the action in a film or television show.

Among the most ancient reasons for manipulating sound is connecting to the spiritual, even altering consciousness. We will explore the essence of musical sound in three audio selections, which present the sounds of the shofar, chanting, and shamanic drumming. All date from prehistory; all have profound significance for their participants; all lie at the simplest end of the musical spectrum; and all derive their power from the basic properties of sound.

Focus on Dynamics and Timbre: The Sound of the Shofar. The shofar is a trumpetlike instrument made from the horn of a ram or goat. In contemporary Judaism, the shofar is essential to the proper celebration of Rosh Hashanah, the Jewish New Year, and Yom Kippur. We also know from drawings and other visual images from the Middle East that the practice of making shofarlike instruments from animal horns is well over 3,000 years old. In the biblical account of the fall of Jericho, the "trumpets of rams' horns," mentioned in God's specific instructions for bringing down the walls of the city, were shofars.

In addition to using the shofar in battle and religious ceremonies, ancient peoples used it to signal the coming of the new moon or to suggest the voice of God. What about the sound of the shofar makes it so suitable for such occasions? First, it's loud: it can be heard at great distances, which makes it use-

> *Shofars could be heard above the shouting of an army.*

ful in battle. Far louder than the human voice, shofars could be heard above the shouting of an army. Second, the shofar has a distinctive timbre, far different from and more piercing than the human voice. The shofar sounds strident, even abrasive. It is used not to create a pleasant sound but to signal something significant across great distances. Although the pitch and rhythm of shofar blasts have symbolic significance, the power of the sounds comes mainly from their musical dynamics and timbre: they are very loud, and they are strident.

Focus on Pitch: Chanting Om. Chanting the syllable *om* (aum) is a spiritual practice well over 3,000 years old that is still practiced today, not only in India, where it originated in the Hindu religion, but also all over the world.

Come with us into a modern-day yurt, a small, circular, domed structure made of wood. Light comes in through a skylight at the top of the dome and a few small windows. A shrine sits against one wall, and a carpet covers the floor; there is no furniture. You join a group of people sitting in a circle, each of them in the lotus position. Their wrists rest on their knees; their palms are open and facing upward; their thumbs and index fingers

Music Concept Check

Hear the blast of the shofar online.

touch lightly. One person begins to sing the vowel *a* on a single pitch, a particular tone emanating at a specific frequency. As the leader moves from *a* to *u* to *m*, she maintains the same pitch. You and the others join in, singing the same letters to the same pitch. Soon the room is filled with the sound of the group chanting

Music Concept Check

Hear the mind-altering sound of *om* online.

a single sound—*om*. Although individual members stop occasionally to breathe, the sound is continuous, going on for several minutes. As you chant, your mind quiets, distractions fade away, and you forget yourself. Through the sound of *om*, your consciousness merges with those of the others in the yurt.

The chanting of *om* is at once an extremely concentrated experience—because the pitch never changes—and a seemingly timeless one, because there

are no interruptions or modifications of the sound. The experience can alter consciousness. We know this not only from countless anecdotal accounts but also from the results of scientific research, which provide clear evidence of profound changes in brain activity during chanting.

Focus on Duration: Shamanic Drumming. Shamans were the first doctors and priests. Since well before recorded history, they were the members of the community who healed others and communicated with the spirit world.

In order to access their powers, shamans enter an altered state, almost always aided by the kind of drumming heard in our recording. The only sound you hear is a steady beat created by two drummers striking single-headed, round-frame drums in unison. In the complete track, they will maintain the drumbeat for about thirty minutes, stop, then shift to a slow intermittent rhythm, and shift again to a very fast drumbeat designed to call the shaman back from his journey.

This drumming sends two messages about time.

Yurt

On one level, it measures time with great precision: the drumbeats mark off identical segments of time. On another level, it seems endless, because nothing in the drumming marks off larger units of time. Essentially, shamanic drumming distills and concentrates the experience of a repetitive beat. It is similar to what one might experience in a dance club, but faster and without other rhythms that add variety and interest and mark off shorter and longer units of time.

Music Concept Check

Hear the relentless drumbeat of shamanic drumming online.

From Sounds to Music. These three short audio selections are more than random sounds or even happy accidents of technology, such as the clickety-clack of a train or the distinctive ring of a cell phone. As is the case with virtually all music, they demonstrate the meaningful control of sound. They seem to be less than music mainly because they lack the kinds of variety and interest that we expect from music.

It is a big step from the minimalist sounds that you just heard to the kinds of music that you hear every day and that you will hear in this course. But consider for a moment the idea that the loud, abrasive sound of the shofar, the sustained *om* of the chanters, and the repetitive drumming of the shaman's assistants represent the seeds of musical experience.

The loudness of a shofar blast lies at one end of the spectrum of sounds available to us in music. Especially in our electronic age when we can control volume with technology, entire musical styles are defined most fundamentally by how loud they are: hip-hop is loud; New Age is soft. If we invert the volume levels for these styles—play hip-hop very softly or New Age very loudly—we distort the context of their musical messages.

The timbre of the shofar is distinctive and memorable but contrasts sharply with the dazzling array of sounds available in our musical world. Anyone who has channel-surfed a radio, sampling a few seconds of several stations before settling on one, knows how to use timbre as a point of entry. For many, timbre is the first filter in their musical decision making, determining what they will or won't listen to. The sweet sounds of a string quartet, the nasal twang of a country singer, the halo of distortion surrounding heavy metal guitar riffs: some love them; others hate them.

The chanting of a single pitch on a single syllable is far removed from melodies that can get you singing along with the radio. However, many melodies use a single tone not only as a melodic point of departure and return but also as an ever-present point of reference throughout. You will hear this explicitly in a medieval chant by abbess and seer Hildegard von Bingen and implicitly in many of the musical examples discussed later in this book. From this perspective, you might hear such melodies as elaborations on a single pitch.

Similarly, the "pure" beat of shamanic drumming is distant from the buoyant rhythms of a Baroque concerto or the toe-tapping groove of a swing band. However, at the center of all this rhythmic activity is the beat; when surrounded by other rhythms, it comes to life.

A distinctive timbre, a focal pitch, an insistent beat: these are the most familiar and accessible points of entry into a musical work, the sounds, the tune, the beat. We encounter these in their most elemental form in these examples and in more elaborate and individualized form in musical works. That they are so widely separated in time, function, and sound should not obscure their underlying connection.

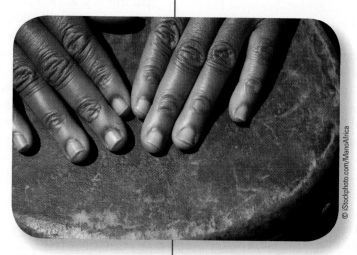

© iStockphoto.com/ManoAfrica

LO2 The Elements of Music

To this point we have introduced the properties of sound and illustrated them with sounds so basic that they may be far from what you expect music to be. Nevertheless, the properties of sound are the most useful starting point for perceiving, understanding, and describing the events in a musical work. Another term for them is **elements of music**, music's basic building blocks. In this chapter we have reviewed dynamics, duration, pitch, and timbre, but even more elements emerge from their interaction. Here are some of the connections: Dynamics describes loudness and changes in it. Timbre is determined by instrumentation—the selection and combination of instruments and voices used in the performance of a musical work. Variations in duration become rhythm. Successions and combinations of pitches become melody and harmony. From timbre, rhythm, melody, and harmony comes texture, the fabric of sound created by the interaction of all the parts of a musical performance. From the sequence of events, as shaped by all of these elements, comes form—the organization of music in time. We will discuss each element in turn in the chapters ahead.

element of music
One of music's basic building blocks: dynamics, rhythm, timbre, melody, harmony, texture, and form

CHAPTER 2

Dynamics and Timbre

"Only a university marching band is likely to be larger than the modern symphony orchestra."

As the Chicago Symphony begins the last movement of Beethoven's Fifth Symphony, all sixty-three string players sound out a stirring melody and the harmony that supports it. At the same time, only seven members of the orchestra's brass section play the same melody and harmony. Despite their disadvantage in numbers, the brass instruments dominate, while the other instruments remain in the background.

This stunning discrepancy between sheer numbers and power demonstrates that how an instrument is designed and the manner in which it is played are inextricably linked to how loud it sounds. Accordingly, in this chapter we consider dynamics and timbre together and experience them in the contrast between the sounds of the solo piano and the full symphony orchestra.

LO3 Dynamics

Terms associated with dynamics (see The Language of Music on page 9) describe either a level of loudness or a change in loudness. Dynamics is the easiest element to discern: no specialized musical training is needed to hear contrasts between loud and soft or even to hear loud gradually becoming soft, or vice versa.

Dynamics, more immediately than any other element, can help communicate the character of a musical work or of a section within a work. Before we process anything else in a piece of music—the shape of the melody, the rhythm, the instruments—we respond to its dynamic level. We are most responsive to dynamics when the dynamic levels approach the extreme in either direction or when there are strong contrasts, either sudden or gradual.

The ear-splitting loudness of heavy-metal groups is a big part of their musical message; conversely, the gentle synthesizer sounds of New Age music are integral to its message.

Did You Know?

The oldest playable musical instruments are Chinese bone flutes. These instruments, unearthed in 1999, date back nine thousand years.

instrumentation
Selection and combination of instruments and voices used in the performance of a musical work

LO4 Timbre and Instrumentation

Timbre is most fundamentally realized in **instrumentation**, the selection and combination of instruments and voices used in the performance of a musical work. A performance may require only singers, only instruments, or singers and instruments together. It may require only a single musician, such as a pianist—even no musician at all, as is the case in purely electronic compositions—or it may require the massed resources of a hundred-member orchestra and a 200-voice choir.

In the course of our survey, you will hear instruments from many times and places, from medieval rebecs and recorders to the rhythm instruments of rock bands. In

LISTEN UP!

CD 3:4-8
Beethoven, Symphony No. 5, fourth movement

Takeaway point: Stirring melody, with harmony

Instruments: Full orchestra, but largely strings and brasses here

this chapter, we introduce the symphony orchestra to present many of the instruments that you will hear in the musical examples and to explore the expressive potential of tone color.

THE SYMPHONY ORCHESTRA

The most established and iconic instrumental ensemble in Western culture is the **symphony orchestra**.

Music Concept Check

Review and listen to all the instrument families in Britten's *Young Person's Guide to the Orchestra*, online.

Many major cities in the world have a resident symphony orchestra. Enjoying more widespread support than any other musical group, orchestras perform the most familiar instrumental music in the classical tradition, accompany operas and musicals, and have become a popular medium for film scores, such as John Williams's music for the Star Wars series. A large symphony orchestra, such as the Chicago Symphony Orchestra or the New York Philharmonic, has a roster of about a hundred musicians. Among large instrumental ensembles, only a university marching band is likely to be larger than the modern symphony orchestra.

Today's orchestra is built around four major sections, or families,

THE LANGUAGE OF MUSIC

In part because the composer's practice of indicating dynamics in a musical score began in Italy, the terms commonly used for dynamics are Italian. The two basic terms for indicating dynamic levels are the Italian words for *loud* and *soft*: *forte* (FOR-tay) means "loud," and *piano* (pee-AH-noh) means "soft." By attaching the superlative suffix *–issimo* (EE-see-moh) or adding the word *mezzo* (MEHD-soh), which means "middle" or "medium," composers could easily indicate six levels of dynamics. Here are the terms for the six most commonly used dynamic levels, from loudest to softest, along with their abbreviations:

fortissimo, *ff* (for-TEE-see-moh)	the superlative of forte: very loud
forte, *f* (FOR-tay)	loud
mezzo forte, *mf* (MEHD-soh FOR-tay)	medium loud: softer than forte but louder than mezzo piano
mezzo piano, *mp* (MEHD-soh pee-AH-noh)	medium soft: louder than piano but softer than mezzo forte
piano, *p* (pee-AH-noh)	soft
pianissimo, *pp* (pee-ah-NEE-see-moh)	very soft

Just as the ups and downs of inflection are intrinsic to speech, dynamic change—raising or lowering the level of sound—occurs in music making. Here, too, musicians use Italian words to describe dynamic change. Here are the three most common:

crescendo, < (creh-SHEN-doh)	growing louder
decrescendo or **diminuendo**, > (dih-min-yoo-EN-doh)	growing softer
sforzando, *sf* (ssfort-SAHN-doh)	a strong accent on a single note or chord

Dynamic indications like the abbreviations shown here began to appear in musical scores around 1600. However, it wasn't until the late eighteenth century that dynamic indications appeared routinely in composers' scores and that the markings indicated both dynamic level and dynamic change.

symphony orchestra Large (100 musicians or more) musical ensemble containing strings, woodwinds, brass, and percussion

fortissimo, *ff* Very loud

forte, *f* Loud

mezzo forte, *mf* Medium loud

mezzo piano, *mp* Medium soft

piano, *p* Soft

pianissimo, *pp* Very soft

crescendo, < Growing louder

decrescendo (diminuendo), > Growing softer

sforzando, *sf* Strong accent on a single note or chord

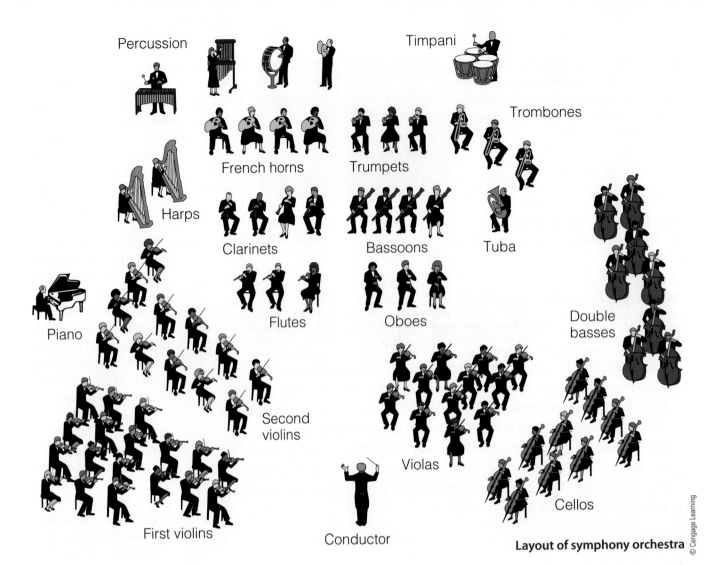

Percussion

Timpani

Trombones

French horns

Trumpets

Harps

Clarinets

Bassoons

Tuba

Double basses

Piano

Flutes

Oboes

Second violins

Violas

Cellos

First violins

Conductor

Layout of symphony orchestra

© Cengage Learning

of instruments: bowed strings, woodwinds, brass, and percussion.

String Instruments. The bowed string family, or **strings**, is the core of the orchestra. There are four orchestral string instruments: the violin, the viola, the violoncello (or simply cello), and the double bass. The violin is the highest-pitched member of the string family, and it has the most brilliant sound. The viola is slightly larger and proportionally wider than the violin. It is somewhat lower in range and has a richer, mellower sound. In orchestral playing, both the violin and the viola are played by placing the instrument under the chin, so that the left hand is free to move up and down the neck of the instrument and the right hand can draw the bow across the strings.

The cello is significantly larger than the viola and is tuned lower. The double bass, or simply bass, is the largest and lowest-pitched of the four orchestral strings.

In a modern major symphony orchestra, the strings comprise almost two-thirds of the entire roster. Even though there are four different string instruments that make up the string section of the symphony orchestra as described above, there are five string sections, each with multiple players: The violins are divided into two sections; first violins and second violins. Usually there are sixteen to nineteen first violins, thirteen to sixteen second violins, eleven or twelve violas, ten or eleven cellos, and eight or nine basses. Typically, all of the players within a section play the same part: the first violinists play the first violin part, the second violinists the second violin part, and so on. The most common exception to this is the bass part, which often **doubles** (plays the same part as) the cello part, an octave lower. Multiple performers on each string part are necessary in most of the orchestral

strings Musical instruments that produce sound when the musician draws a bow across or plucks the strings

double Having the same line of music played by more than one instrument simultaneously

The family of string instruments. These musicians represent the relative sizes of some of the string sections of the orchestra. From left to right: viola, first and second violins, and cello. Note the pronounced difference in size among the instruments and that the viola is slightly larger and wider than the violin.

repertoire to create a rich string sound and to balance the power and brilliance of the rest of the orchestra, particularly the brass and percussion instruments.

In orchestral music, the most common way of producing sound on a string instrument is to draw a bow across a string, which is stretched over the bridge, a small piece of wood held in place to the instrument's body by the tension of the strings themselves. Skilled performers can use the bow to produce a remarkable range of sounds, from melodies that flow smoothly to sharp, clipped notes. A common alternative playing technique is **pizzicato**, in which the performer plucks the string instead of bowing it. In both cases, the resulting vibrations are transmitted to a resonating cavity, then out through sound holes carved in the front of the instrument.

Woodwind Instruments.

There are four **woodwind** sections in all major orchestras: flutes (piccolo, flute); oboes (oboe, English horn); clarinets (clarinet, bass clarinet); and bassoons (bassoon, contrabassoon). Each group of instruments has a distinctive shape and method of tone production. Indeed, the flute is no longer made of *wood*, although it once was; today it is usually made from precious metals. However, it is still considered a woodwind instrument.

Flutists (sometimes referred to as flautists) produce sound by blowing across a mouth hole; they hold the instrument horizontally. Oboists blow into a double reed, two slightly curved pieces of cane that have been bound together and scraped to almost nothing at the tip. Oboists hold the instrument out from their body. Clarinetists attach a reed made from a single piece of cane to a mouthpiece that connects to the body of the instrument. They also hold the instrument out from their body. Bassoonists also use a double reed attached to a long, thin tube, which connects to the body of the instrument. They usually play sitting down. Due to the length of the bassoon, the performer must hold the instrument out to the right side of their body.

The other instruments in each section, such as the piccolo and English horn, are similar enough in shape and playing technique that performers can move between them much more easily than they could move between instruments in different groups. A flutist playing the piccolo need only adapt her basic technique to a smaller instrument; a flutist attempting to play the oboe would have to learn an entirely new instrument.

Not surprisingly, these instruments have quite distinct timbres, which nineteenth-century French composer Hector Berlioz discussed in considerable depth in *Grand Traité d'Instrumentation et d'Orchestration Modernes,* his landmark treatise on orchestration.

The flute: The sonority of this instrument is gentle in the middle range, fairly penetrating in the upper range.

> **pizzicato** Technique of plucking a string instead of bowing it
>
> **woodwind** Musical instrument that produces sound by blowing air through a reed or across an open hole causing air to vibrate within a tube

Clarinet

Flute

brass Musical instrument that produces sound when the musician's lips vibrate against a mouthpiece that has been inserted into a coiled tube ending in a flared bell

mute Device that can change the timbre of an instrument when it is inserted in or applied to the instrument; instruments that most frequently use mutes are those of the brass and string families

percussion instrument Musical instrument that produces sound by striking one object against another

The oboe: The oboe is principally a melodic instrument; it has a rustic character, full of tenderness, I would say even of shyness.

The clarinet: The clarinet is … an epic instrument…. It is the voice of heroic love.

The bassoon: The bassoon … has a propensity towards the grotesque… [its] upper notes have a somewhat painful and suffering character, I might call it almost pitiful.

If you listen to the woodwinds one after the other, you will hear sharp timbral contrasts; by contrast, the members of the string family provide a relatively smooth timbral continuum.

Brass Instruments. Brass

instruments produce sound when musicians' lips vibrate against a mouthpiece that has been inserted into a coiled metal tube ending in a flared bell. The most widely used brass instruments in a modern symphony orchestra are, from highest- to lowest-pitched, the trumpet, horn (also called the French horn), trombone, and tuba. All four descend from ancient trumpets, which were also long, conical metal tubes with a mouthpiece at one end and a bell at the other.

Like the modern-day bugle, these early instruments were limited to only a few notes due to the fixed length of the tube. So instrument makers later developed mechanisms that enabled brass instruments to play all of the available pitches over the range of the instrument. The trombone was the first to assume its modern form. The slide, which enables trombonists to change pitch by temporarily lengthening the tubing, first appeared in the fifteenth century in the *sackbut*, an anteced-

Trombone

Trumpet

French horn

Tuba

ent of the modern trombone. Valves and pistons first appeared around 1800, on trumpets and horns. The tuba is a much more modern instrument, invented during the 1830s.

The most characteristic sound of brass instruments is produced with an open bell. However, brass players occasionally change the timbre of their instruments by inserting a **mute** in the bell. A mute for brass instruments is any device placed in the bell of the brass instrument that alters the character of the sound produced. It is typically a hollow, conical-shaped device made of metal, cardboard, fiberboard, wood, or similar material.

Percussion Instruments. The percussion fam-
ily is potentially the largest and most diverse family of

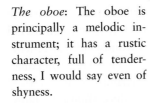

Bassoon

orchestral instruments. Their common feature is the method of sound production: percussionists play their instruments by striking one object against another—for example, a drumstick against a cymbal or drum, or mallets against the bars of a xylophone.

Percussion instruments are distinguished by two criteria. One pertains to the final result: percussion instruments that produce *definite pitches*, such as tympani and xylophones, and those that produce *indefinite pitches*, such as cymbals and drums. The other pertains to the part of the instrument that is struck: some instruments, such as drums and tympani, have a membrane made of animal skin or synthetic material, which is stretched over a frame; others feature thicker materials: metal (cymbals, triangle, xylophone) or wood (marimba, wood block).

The extensive use of percussion in orchestral composition is a relatively recent development. During the eighteenth century, the only frequently used percussion instrument in symphonic music was the timpani. Drums, triangle, and cymbals, used occasionally in the eighteenth century, became more common in the nineteenth. Xylophones, marimbas, and other similar instruments were still a novelty in the nineteenth century but became more widely used in the twentieth. Twentieth-century orchestral music generally features percussion, including ethnic percussion instruments

such as the maracas, more prominently than did early orchestral pieces.

Other Instruments.

A few instruments, most commonly the harp, piano, organ, and saxophone, are used infrequently in the symphony orchestra, and thus are not discussed in detail here. The harp has the longest orchestral history (and the longest history overall). Mozart composed a concerto for flute and harp, and his contemporaries occasionally used it in opera orchestras. However, the harp was not used as often in the orchestra until the nineteenth century, when it was most prominently used in ballet music. But as such, it was still not used frequently. The piano has been used as an orchestral instrument mostly in the twentieth century. The pipe organ has been a less popular member of the orchestra because many concert halls do not have one installed.

The saxophone, a member of the woodwind family, is more common in jazz ensembles than in the symphony orchestra. It has a mouthpiece onto which a single reed is attached, similar to the clarinet. But unlike most woodwinds, the saxophone is—and always has been—made of metal.

orchestration The technique and artistry of assigning musical parts for instruments in various combinations

tone color A distinctive timbre

Orchestration

In the 1980s, Ted Turner scandalized the film establishment by adding color to old black-and-white films. An analogous practice in music—arranging works originally composed for piano or organ to be played by a symphony orchestra—was well established. We use the term **orchestration** to identify the technique and artistry of assigning musical parts for instruments in various combinations. Although orchestration typically refers to the symphony orchestra, the term applies to assigning musical parts for combinations of instruments found in any instrumental ensemble.

One purpose of orchestration is to add a variety of timbres, or **tone colors**. If we compare the timbre of a work for a single instrument, such as the piano, with a black-and-white film, then arranging that work for an orchestra, with its dozens of timbres and countless timbral combinations, is akin to "colorizing" it. We illustrate this point by presenting a hybrid version of Wolfgang Amadeus Mozart's (1756–1791) variations on a theme composed earlier by Christoph Willibald

Cymbals

Timpani

Snare drum

© iStockphoto.com/vhsrt-just

© IdeeFixes by Comstock

© iStockphoto.com/ pixhook

Gluck (1714–1787): "Unser dummer Pöbel meint." Mozart originally composed his version of the work for piano. In 1887, about a century later, the Russian composer Pyotr Ilyich Tchaikovsky (chy-KOFF-skee; 1840–1893), a lifelong admirer of Mozart's music, arranged it for full orchestra as part of his *Mozartiana* suite.

In a conventional piano performance of Mozart's original work, one hears almost every section twice. In our sampling from both works, we have replaced the repetition of each section on the piano with Tchaikovsky's orchestral remake, so that you can hear piano and orchestral versions of the same material one after the other.

This hybrid example illustrates how orchestral timbres can transform the sound of a musical work. The personalities of the many instruments in effect reshape the work. Tchaikovsky's orchestration of Mozart's sparkling variations enriches them with tone color. Instead of using the sound of only one instrument—the piano—Tchaikovsky drew on the varied timbres of a full orchestra: combinations of strings, woodwinds, and brass, along with a battery of percussion instruments. Tchaikovsky varies both instrument choice and the number of instruments as a way of highlighting differences in dynamics and providing timbral interest.

LISTEN UP!

Mozart/Tchaikovsky, hybrid compilation of "Unser dummer Pöbel meint" and *Mozartiana*

Takeaway point: Contrast between "black-and-white" piano timbre and the "colors" of the orchestra

Style: Mozart's original belongs to the late eighteenth century; Tchaikovsky's orchestration gives it a nineteenth-century sound.

Instruments: Piano/symphony orchestra

The two versions acquaint us with two of the important sound worlds of classical music: the piano and the orchestra, a single instrument versus a hundred. It is important to keep in mind that although the timbral variety of Tchaikovsky's orchestration adds immediate appeal, more tone color isn't necessarily better; it's just different. For listeners, it isn't as much about choosing one over the other as it is about appreciating what both versions have to offer.

CHAPTER 3

Rhythm

"We may find a 'good beat' hard to define, but we know it when we hear it."

In the summer of 1979, Sylvia Robinson, head of the newly founded Sugar Hill Records in Englewood, New Jersey, sensed that rap was ready for the masses. She had witnessed firsthand the response to the hot, new underground sound from New York's Bronx when she saw a couple of

Did You Know?

Seventeenth-century conducting could be hazardous to your health. Jean-Baptiste Lully conducted by thumping a staff on the floor but died of gangrenous complications after hitting his toe instead.

rappers perform at a birthday party. Wanting to be the first to capitalize on what she saw as a coming trend, she urged her son Joey to put together a rap group. Joey sought out Henry "Big Bank Hank" Jackson, Michael "Wonder Mike" Wright, and Guy "Master Gee" O'Brien, who became the members of a group called the Sugarhill Gang. Sylvia brought the three rappers into her studio to record what would become Sugar Hill's first recording and rap's first Top 40 hit: "Rapper's Delight."

"Rapper's Delight" begins with the house band laying down a Latin-flavored introduction, followed by their version of the background to Chic's disco party hit "Good Times." The first voice belongs to Michael "Wonder Mike" Wright, who begins:

> I said a hip hop the hippie the hippie
> to the hip hip hop, a you don't stop
> the rock it to the bang bang boogie say up jumped
> the boogie
> to the rhythm of the boogie, the beat

 LISTEN FURTHER

Sugarhill Gang, "Rapper's Delight"

Takeaway point: Listen for the beat in the iTunes and Rhapsody playlists.

LO5 Rhythm

In this lyric, *rhythm* and *beat* mean much the same thing. Both words communicate two meanings. One meaning is specific. "Beat" and "rhythm" refer to a steady pulse, which is measurable: in "Rapper's Delight," the beat moves at about 110 beats per minute. The other meaning, which refers to the qualities that make us want to move to this steady beat, eludes easy definition. In describing a "good beat," listeners face a dilemma similar to former Supreme Court Justice Potter Stewart's famous encounter with hard-core pornography: we may find pornography hard to define, but we know it when we see it. For our purpose, we can adapt Justice Stewart's line: we may find a "good beat" hard to define, but we know it when we hear it.

Rhythm is a multifaceted element of music. Rhythms can be simple or complex. They can be fast or slow, measured or unmeasured. Rhythms can be presented in a single layer in a piece of music or in simultaneous multilayers. The rhythm of a work may include obvious points of entry, such as those accents and patterns that establish the qualities that make you want to move to the steady beat. But rhythms may also conflict with the beat; create irregular, even intermittent patterns; or dart in and out in a seemingly random fashion.

We will encounter a remarkably broad range of rhythmic approaches in our survey, from a chant that does not have a steady beat and an electronic composition in which no beat is discernible to the propulsive

Rhythm is that irresistible element of music that makes you want to move in time to the beat.

rhythms heard in music by J. S. Bach, Béla Bartók, and Chuck Berry. In this comprehensive sense, **rhythm** is the pattern or patterns of musical movement in time: every musical event that happens in time contributes to the rhythm of a musical work.

This comprehensive definition of rhythm contrasts sharply with other connotations of rhythm, both in and out of music. When we speak of the rhythm of our breathing or our heartbeat, or label a musical work "rhythmic," we are referring to rhythmic events with a regular, easily discernible pulse. But this more limited view of rhythm cannot account for the richness and variety in the rhythms of the music that we will encounter. But it is most often at the center of rhythmic activity and is typically our point of entry into the rhythmic flow of a musical work.

LO6 Beat, Tempo, and Meter

Rhythm begins with the beat. However, we will encounter music that does not have a steady pulse, because the style is built on free, unmeasured rhythm or because the composer chose to obscure or suspend the pulse, either for effect or as an aesthetic principle. However, the vast majority of works that we will hear in our survey will feature rhythm organized around a regularly recurring pulse. We call this pulse the **beat**, and the organizational framework, meter.

BEAT

Unlike "Wonder Mike," we will most often use "beat" to refer only to the pulse. In most situations, beat can be described as simply the regular division of time at a speed that matches up with large-scale physical movement: walking, running, marching, dancing, exercising, tapping our foot, or conducting an orchestra.

rhythm Pattern or patterns of musical movement in time

beat Regularly recurring pulse associated with music

tempo Speed of the beat in a piece of music

We can hear how the beat tends to line up with movement in our comfort zone by listening to an excerpt from the sixth variation of Mozart's variation set "Ah, vous dirai-je Maman." It features a simple theme, which the English-speaking world knows as "Twinkle, Twinkle, Little Star," supported by a busy pattern that moves four times as fast. You should find it easy to tap your foot to the rhythm of the familiar melody, which lines up easily with the beat, but unless you possess superhuman powers, you will find it all but impossible to match your foot tapping to the faster rhythm.

TEMPO

We use the word **tempo** to describe the speed of the beat—fast, slow, or somewhere in between—and we measure it in beats per minute. Typically, the tempo of a musical work will fall somewhere between 70 and 140 beats per minute. For example, a march and a disco song typically have a fast tempo—about 120 beats per minute—energetic enough that you can march or dance in time to the music but not so fast that you're exhausted after a few minutes.

Tempo contributes heavily to the mood of a musical composition, in part because we can so easily relate it to such basic pulses as our heartbeat and the speed at which we walk. This is especially the case at the upper and lower boundaries of our comfort zone. For example, the supercharged tempos of a punk song or a circus march convey manic energy, while the extremely slow tempo of a funeral march—so slow that we have to hesitate between steps—helps convey the solemnity of the occasion.

METER

The excerpt from the sixth variation features several regular rhythms. The most obvious are the rhythm of the melody and the busy line underneath. However, there is also a slower

© iStockphoto.com/Cimmerian

The supercharged tempo of a punk song conveys manic energy.

> **Music Concept Check**
>
> Listen to the beat in Mozart, Twelve Variations on "Ah, vous dirai-je Maman," Variation 6, online.

THE LANGUAGE OF MUSIC

Like dynamic markings, the most widely used tempo indications are in Italian. Although there is general agreement as to their relative speeds—presto is faster than allegro; largo is slower than adagio—none represents a specific range of speeds measured in beats per minute. Here are the eight most common terms with their English translations, ordered from fast to slow:

presto	(PRESS-toe):	very fast
vivace	(vih-VAH-chay):	lively and fast
allegro	(ah-LEG-grow):	cheerful, lively
moderato	(mod-air-AH-toe):	moderate
andante	(ahn-DAHN-tay):	walking speed
adagio	(ah-DAH-gee-oh):	slow and stately
lento	(LEN-toe):	very slow
largo	(LAR-go):	broad

Interestingly, only moderato and lento refer specifically to tempo. The others originally indicated the character of the work rather than a specific speed. Two final notes: First, like dynamic markings, these eight tempo markings are occasionally modified by superlatives (-issimo) and diminutives (-etto; -ino). Second, tempo indications were often modified with further clues to the character of the work: "allegro con brio," Beethoven's tempo indication for the first movement of his Fifth Symphony, translates as "cheerfully lively with brilliance."

rhythm created by the regular change from one pitch to the next. The graphic below shows the connection between the beat and this slower rhythm, using the familiar version of the melody as a reference.

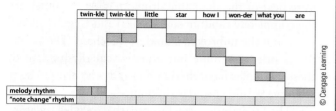

twin-kle	twin-kle	little	star	how I	won-der	what you	are

melody rhythm
"note change" rhythm

© Cengage Learning

The gray boxes represent the rhythm of the melody, which almost always marks off the beat. The yellow boxes represent the slower rhythm created by the change in pitch every two beats.

This "note change" rhythm establishes and maintains a slower regular rhythm that groups beats by twos; it also creates the expectation that this grouping will continue, as it does in this variation. As you can hear, the "note change" rhythm and the rhythm of the accompaniment surround the beat with regular rhythms that move in simple ratios, 1:2 and 4:1. Because of these rhythms, we are aware of not only the beat but also the meter.

Meter is the organization of beats into regular recurring patterns. We label meters both by the grouping of beats and by the characteristic division of the beat. However, in this chapter, we are concerned almost exclusively with the grouping of beats and the terminology associated with it.

A meter in which the beats are grouped by twos is a **duple meter**: "Twinkle, Twinkle" has a duple meter. A meter in which beats are grouped by threes is a **triple meter,** as is evident in "The Star-Spangled Banner." A meter in which the beats are grouped by fours is a **quadruple meter**. "Joyful, Joyful, We Adore Thee," also known as "Ode to Joy," from the finale of Beethoven's Ninth Symphony, is written in quadruple meter. We use the words **measure** or **bar** to identify a consistent grouping of beats. The first section of "Twinkle, Twinkle" (shown in the graphic on page 16) has sixteen beats, and eight measures, because each measure has two beats. Because they encompass a longer but still regular time span, measures or bars often offer a more convenient measurement of musical time: we refer to a twelve-bar blues, not a forty-

eight-beat blues.

The second and twelfth (and final) variations clearly illustrate the difference between duple and triple meter. In both, the melody is stated simply, and the accompanying figures are closely related. The theme as presented in the second variation uses the familiar duple meter; we could sing along without any rhythmic adjustment:

> | Twin - kle |
> twin - kle | lit -
> tle | star |

However, in the final variation, Mozart interpolates silence or an extra note in each note pair to create groups of three beats. If we were to add words to this new version of the melody, they might read something like this:

> | Twin - (wait) - kle | twin - (wait) - kle | my
> lit - tle | star |

To describe this difference in rhythmic organization, we would note that Mozart shifts from a duple meter to a triple meter.

RECOGNIZING METER

We recognize the meter of a musical work mainly through two rhythmic features, pattern repetition and accent. Patterns can be regular, like the "note change" rhythm, or irregular, as we'll hear in subsequent excerpts. In either case, the *repetition* of the pattern must be regular in order to confirm the meter.

Accent most often involves *more* of some musical element: a sound is accented if it is louder, longer, higher, thicker (a chord versus a single note), or more prominent in any way. The two most common forms of accent are loudness and duration. In "Twinkle, Twinkle" there is an accent implicit in the text; the first syllable of each word is stressed. Performers typically confirm this verbal accentuation in the melody by singing or playing the first note of each pair a little louder than the second.

Music Concept Check

Listen to the difference between duple and triple meter in Mozart, Twelve Variations on "Ah, vous dirai-je Maman," Variations 2 and 12, online.

meter Organization of beats into regular recurring patterns

duple meter Meter whose beats are grouped by two

triple meter Meter whose beats are grouped by three

quadruple meter Meter whose beats are grouped by four

measure (bar) Consistent grouping of beats in a work

accent *More* of some musical element

As "Twinkle, Twinkle" and countless other musical works evidence, accent and pattern generally work together to establish meter. Typically, it can be observed that a discernible emphasis is placed on the first beat of each measure, thus making it easier to recognize a particular meter. It is possible to have accents and patterns that do not line up with the metrical structure; we will encounter examples shortly. But the preponderance of accent and pattern must confirm the metrical structure if it is to be projected clearly and unambiguously.

BEAT, METER, AND RHYTHM

The three Mozart variations highlight five features of rhythm and meter characteristic of much of the music that we will encounter:

1. Change in any aspect of the music contributes to rhythm.

2. Rhythms that occur faster and slower than the beat are inevitable.

3. Regularly recurring accent and pattern repetition help create rhythms that establish and maintain meter.

4. Metrical relationships are likely to involve simple ratios, for example, 2:1 or 3:1.

5. Once established, these regular rhythms create the expectation that they will continue.

Especially in music for movement, meter is not only

Meter	Beats per measure	Heard in
Duple meter	Two	The march (one beat per leg)
Triple meter	Three	The minuet and the waltz, the most popular social dances of the eighteenth and nineteenth centuries, respectively
Quadruple meter	Four	Just about any rock-era song or dance track

obvious but also integral to the identity of the genre. The table on page 19 lists the three most common metrical groupings and identifies familiar genres defined in part by their characteristic meter.

THE RANGE OF RHYTHMIC EXPERIENCE

To this point in our survey, we have encountered the extremes of rhythmic experience. At one extreme is the pure beat of the shamanic drumming. At the other are the completely random sounds heard in Cage's "silent" piece and the unbroken sound of the chant. The shofar blasts offer a definite but nonmetrical rhythm. All of these examples have rhythm, but only the drumming is what we would consider rhythmic.

The remaining tracks on the playlist feature rhythms that align along a continuum that ranges from "nothing but beat" to "no beat at all." Indeed, the first track on our historical survey is a twelfth-century chant characterized by unmeasured rhythm.

Even in measured music, there is a continuum between music in which the rhythmic events explicitly establish the meter and music in which the metrical structure is more implicit. Toward one end are the Mozart variations we have heard so far. All have rhythms that establish and maintain a clear beat and meter through accent and pattern repetition.

By contrast, the slow variation in Mozart's "Twinkle, Twinkle" variations presents a much more varied and individual rhythmic profile. In this variation, the confirmation of the beat and meter is more subtle because of several rhythmic strategies that play off our expectations regarding beat and meter. We present these strategies here in order of appearance:

1. *A tempo outside the "comfort zone" of the beat.* The tempo of the slow variation is less than half the speed of the preceding variations. In these instances, the slower tempo invests the music with a sense of dignity: it's as if royalty suddenly entered the room.

2. *Irregular division of the beat.* Unlike the preceding variations, which mostly feature even division of the beat, the slow variations offer strong contrasts between long and short durations and irregular alternations between silence and sound. This rhythmic approach gives the rhythmic flow a more distinctive profile.

Music Concept Check

Listen to Mozart, Twelve Variations on "Ah, vous dirai-je Maman," Variation 11, an alternative version that removes strategies for rhythmic play, online.

THE LANGUAGE OF MUSIC

THE LANGUAGE OF MUSIC

The most common symbols for notating rhythm serve one of four functions:

1. Indicate the duration of sound
2. Indicate the duration of silence
3. Identify or clarify the meter
4. Indicate tempo

The notation of duration begins with a set of symbols that shows rhythmic relationships in a 2:1 ratio. This durational pyramid shows the relative durations of the most commonly used durational values.

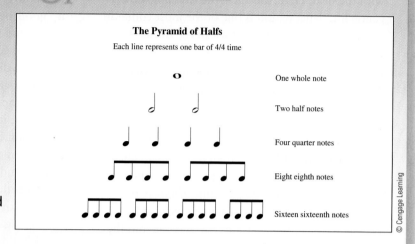

The Pyramid of Halfs

Each line represents one bar of 4/4 time

One whole note

Two half notes

Four quarter notes

Eight eighth notes

Sixteen sixteenth notes

© Cengage Learning

The following symbols indicate the duration of sound. A comparable set of symbols exists to notate silences within a musical work. These symbols, called rests, are shown here, to the far right, with their sound equivalents.

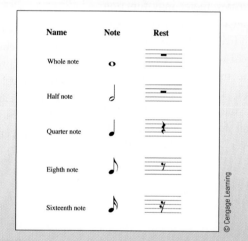

Name	Note	Rest
Whole note		
Half note		
Quarter note		
Eighth note		
Sixteenth note		

© Cengage Learning

The **time (meter) signature**, which appears at the beginning of a musical score (or at any point in the score where the meter changes), identifies the meter. In this short example, the top number tells the user that there are two beats per measure (duple meter); the bottom number indicates that the quarter note is assigned to represent the beat. *Barlines* mark off measures or bars with a vertical line. The line runs from the top to the bottom of the staff, the set of five horizontal lines.

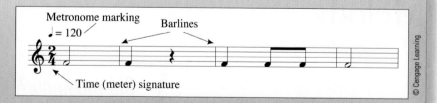

Metronome marking

♩ = 120

Barlines

Time (meter) signature

© Cengage Learning

Since the early 1800s, composers have had the option of including a metronome marking to indicate the tempo, or speed of the beat. The marking is written as: (duration representing the beat) = (speed of the beat in beats per minute). In this illustration, the beat is represented by the quarter note, and the tempo is 120 beats per minute.

3. *Syncopation.* A **syncopation** is an accent that conflicts with the beat or meter instead of confirming it. In this variation, the syncopations are long notes that come between beats instead of aligning with the beat. Here, they give the rhythmic flow a gentle lift. Syncopation is one of the most common forms of rhythmic play in most of the music that we will encounter.

4. *Held notes and pauses that interrupt the pulse.* Throughout much of the variation, the music proceeds steadily, if slowly. However, just before the return of the opening material, Mozart arrests the rhythmic flow, first with a high note that the performer can hold longer than its notated value, then with a silence whose length is also at the discretion of the performer. In this instance, the purpose of the pause is to delay the inevitable. Listeners expect the return of the opening, but the performer controls when the return occurs.

As this variation demonstrates, meter may function as a kind of aural graph paper onto which composers and improvisers can inscribe individual designs. The metrical structure is in place in the mind of the composer and the performer(s), but it may serve as simply a foil for rhythms that soar over or conflict with it

syncopation Accent that conflicts with the beat or meter instead of confirming it

rather than as a grid onto which relentless rhythms snap into place.

To return to the notion of a "good" beat, the elegant, stately flow of this variation is a world away from the groove of "Rapper's Delight." It does not have a "good beat" in the sense that it will inspire you to get up and move to the beat. Nevertheless, the relationship between rhythm and meter is similar in principle, if wildly different in result, in that both use the beat and metrical framework as a springboard for rhythmic play. In rap, there are active rhythms and persistent syncopation: it is this interplay between beat and rhythms that conflicts with it that is most responsible for the groove. In the slow variation, there is interplay of a different kind: there is also syncopation, but it is much more gentle, and the rhythm is more subtle and elastic. What both pieces have in common is playing with time by playing off the meter.

Rhythmic play makes the rhythms of a musical work interesting and inviting. Pure beat is maddening or mind-altering, as we have noted. Pure meter would be worse, if only because there would be at least three layers of relentlessly regular rhythms. Still, without a metrical structure in place, the other rhythms would have no consistent frame of reference. In the course of our survey, we will hear the extraordinarily varied ways in which the relationship between rhythm and meter has been realized over the centuries.

CHAPTER 4

Melody

"Melody is the face of music."

Among the biggest hits of 1920 was "Avalon." The songwriters of record were Vincent Rose, a popular bandleader and songwriter, and Al Jolson, arguably the most celebrated entertainer of the era. (Jolson would go

Did You Know?

That ballpark staple "Take Me Out to the Ball Game" has a long introductory melody that hardly anyone knows. The part we all remember is a relatively small piece of the melody that is the most memorable and rousing.

on to star in the first talking film, *The Jazz Singer.*) Jerome Remick, the publisher, identified the song as a fox-trot, the most popular dance of the 1920s and 1930s. However, Remick, Jolson, and Rose soon found themselves in court. Shortly after the song was published, G. Ricordi, an Italian music publisher whose clients included the famed opera composer Giacomo Puccini, sued Remick and the songwriters for copyright violation. Ricordi argued that Rose and Jolson had flagrantly borrowed the melody from "E lucevan le stelle," a famous aria from Puccini's opera *Tosca*, which had been produced in 1900. The court awarded Ricordi $25,000 (at least $280,000 in 2011) and the rights to all future royalties.

Forty-two years later, Brian Wilson, the mastermind of the Beach Boys, also found himself in court. Soon after "Surfin' U.S.A." climbed the charts, Chuck Berry sued the Beach Boys, claiming that Wilson had simply put new words to his 1958 hit "Sweet Little Sixteen." Berry is now listed as the sole composer of the song.

Tosca is an opera; "Avalon" is a popular song. "E lucevan le stelle" is sung by an operatic tenor with orchestral accompaniment, with clarinet featured prominently. It moves along at a slow, flexible tempo. Jolson belts out "Avalon" while a band provides a bouncy accompaniment. Despite these and other big differences—language, function, mood—the court found for Ricordi. The reason: the first ten notes of the melody. For the court, this opening phrase, the most memorable melodic fragment in both aria and song, trumped every other difference between the two works: the almost note-for-note similarity was the basis of the favorable decision for Ricordi.

These two lawsuits and numerous others about musical borrowing and copyright infringement remind us that melody is the face of music, its most distinctive and individual element. It is a rare musical work whose most identifiable feature is something other than the melodic material. In this chapter, we explore the nature of melody, its raw materials, and the various forms that it can take.

LO7 Melody

A **melody** is an organized succession of pitches that completes a musical idea. In a melody, we expect to hear the pitches one after the other—that is, in a series. However, not all series of pitches can be considered melody. In most musical styles, a random string of notes, such as those produced by a toddler plunking away on a piano, is not a melody. We expect an organized melody to have a beginning, an end, and a middle connecting the two. And we expect it to have a distinctive enough rhythm and **contour** (the pattern of rise and fall) that make it unique, or almost unique.

PITCH AND INTERVAL

Recall that a (definite) pitch is a sound that has a specific frequency. We hear the chanted *om* as a definite pitch because the vibrations creating the sound are at a specific frequency for its entire duration. We use the word **interval** to describe the relationship or distance between two consecutive or simultaneously heard pitches. The most basic interval is that between any pitch and itself, or the same pitch, performed in succession or simultaneously: we call that interval a **unison**. The next most basic interval is the relationship between two pitches that vibrate in a 2:1 ratio; that is, the frequency of the higher pitch is twice as fast as that of the lower one. We call that interval an **octave**. Notes that are an octave apart share the same note name. If you want to capture the sound of an octave in your mind, think of the lyrics "Take me out to the ball game" or "Somewhere, over the rainbow"; both begin with the same octave interval.

For other intervals, we differentiate between *step* and *leap*. A **step** is a small interval between two adjacent pitches; a **leap** is anything larger. In the opening section of "Twinkle, Twinkle" only the first interval (from the first "twinkle" to the second) is a leap; the others are steps.

Steps come in two sizes: we call the smaller step a *half-step* and the larger step a *whole step* (because it is equivalent to two half-steps). A **half-step** is the smallest interval possible between any two pitches (immediately adjacent keys) on a piano. In the opening section of "Twinkle, Twinkle," we hear a half-step between "I" and

melody Organized succession of pitches that completes a musical idea

contour Pattern of rise and fall in a melody

interval Relationship or distance between two consecutive or simultaneously heard pitches

unison The most basic interval: that between any pitch and itself; the same pitch, performed in succession or simultaneously

octave Relationship between two pitches that vibrate in a 2:1 ratio, with the higher pitch vibrating twice as fast as the lower; notes that are an octave apart share the same note name

step The small interval between two adjacent pitches

leap Any interval larger than a step

half-step The smallest interval possible between any two pitches (immediately adjacent keys) on a piano

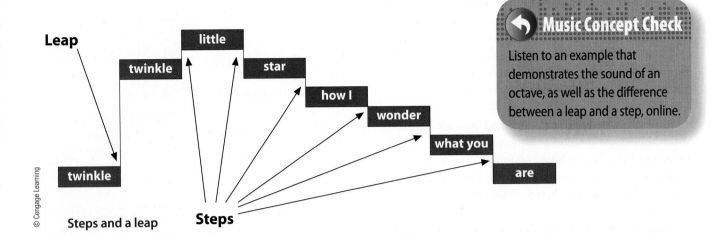

Leap

little

twinkle | star

how I

wonder

what you

twinkle | | are

© Cengage Learning

Steps and a leap   **Steps**

Music Concept Check

Listen to an example that demonstrates the sound of an octave, as well as the difference between a leap and a step, online.

"won-" (How I won-der), and whole steps everywhere else after the initial leap. Leaps are much more variable, ranging from just larger than a step to the distance between the lowest and highest audible pitches (although it is very unlikely that we would find such a large leap in any melody).

Two familiar images, the guitar fretboard and the piano keyboard, provide ways to visualize whole and half-steps. On the guitar fretboard, each fret marks off a half-step; the white dots span a whole step (two frets). The blue dots on the piano keyboard mark off half-steps. A half-step is the interval between two adjacent keys, white or black. The orange dots mark off whole steps: in each case, there is a key between adjacent dots.

In virtually all of the music that we will encounter, the half-step serves as the fundamental measurement unit for pitch. In the most widely used system of pitch organization, half-steps divide the octave into twelve equal parts. We can measure the intervals in melodies (and harmonies) precisely by simply counting the num-

ber of half-steps that they include. For example, the pitches sung to the first two "twinkles" are separated by seven half-steps. However, we will generally describe melodic contour using just "step" and "leap": "twinkle" rises quickly with a leap and a step, then descends gently by step.

LO8 Scales

Scales are the raw material of melody, serving as a pitch bank on which musicians draw to create melodies. Composers, songwriters, and improvisers can use some or all of the scale tones in any sequence to create distinctive, memorable melodic ideas. The

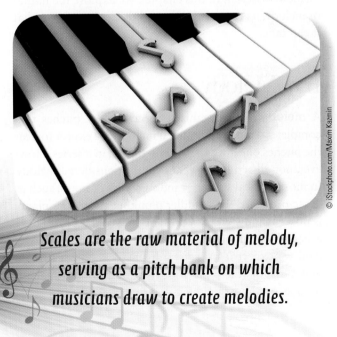

Scales are the raw material of melody, serving as a pitch bank on which musicians draw to create melodies.

THE LANGUAGE OF MUSIC

THE LANGUAGE OF MUSIC

The word *scale* comes from the Latin word *scala*, meaning "stairs" or "ladder." The word *diatonic*, which came into use during the fifteenth century to describe scales, derives from two Greek words: *dia* (through) and *tonos* (tones); diatonic means, roughly, "through the tones."

Mozart variation themes bear this out. Both closely follow the outline of a scale. But by slight changes in rhythm and some embellishment, each projects a distinct identity.

Scales are typically unique arrangements of whole and half-steps within an octave (a few scales also include small leaps of three half-steps). The pattern of whole and half-steps is understood in relation to a focal pitch, most often called the **tonic** or **keynote**: both variation themes begin and end on the tonic pitch. Most of the scales that we will

Music Concept Check

Listen to a demo of the difference between major and minor scales online.

encounter are **diatonic scales**, scales with seven notes per octave. The two most common scales are the major scale and the minor scale.

MAJOR AND MINOR SCALES

The scale that we hear in the themes of the Mozart variations is a major scale. A **major scale** is a diatonic scale with half-steps only between the third and fourth and seventh and eighth notes. (The eighth note is an octave higher than the tonic and shares the same note name.) Major scales are often contrasted with minor scales. The **minor scale** is also a diatonic scale, but it has a different arrangement of the seven tones. Melodies derived from the major scale are said to be in *major mode*; melodies derived from the minor scale are said to be in *minor mode*.

Since the time of ancient Greece, musicians and commentators have presumed a connection between mode and mood. In the *Republic*, Plato advised soldiers to listen to music using certain modes to gain strength and to avoid other modes that caused weakness. Ancient Greek music made use of several modes; so did European music during the Middle Ages and the Renaissance. By the eighteenth century, however, most composers used only two modes: major and minor. As in ancient Greece, there was a strong connection with mood. During the eighteenth and nineteenth centuries, when composers wanted to write a work that conveyed an upbeat, happy message, they generally used major mode. When they wanted to convey sadness, sorrow, anxiety, and other similar emotions, they used minor mode.

scale Unique arrangement of whole and half-steps within an octave

tonic (keynote) Focal pitch of a scale, to which the other pitches are related

diatonic scale Specific sequence of seven pitches within each octave

major scale One kind of diatonic scale, containing a specific sequence of seven pitches within each octave; considered "happy" sounding

minor scale One kind of diatonic scale, containing a specific sequence of seven pitches within each octave; considered "sad" sounding

© Perry Mastrovito/Corbis

Like a boomerang or a roller coaster, a melody often has a point of both departure and return: the tonic.

Plato advised soldiers to listen to music using certain modes to gain strength and to avoid other modes that caused weakness.

© iStockphoto.com/Keith Binns

© Ancient Greek theatre scene, after an antique vase (colour engraving) by French School (19th century) Bibliotheque des Arts Decoratifs, Paris, France/ Archives Charmet/ The Bridgeman Art Library

OTHER SCALES

Although we encounter major and minor scales more frequently than any others, they are far from the only possible scales. Other diatonic scales, called **modes** or **modal scales**, predate the major and minor scales by several centuries. There are scales containing five pitches per octave (**pentatonic scales**), which come down to us mainly in folk music. A scale containing all twelve possible pitches within the octave is called a **chromatic scale**; other scales are also possible. We will discuss these in more detail as we encounter them.

NOTATION OF PITCH

The most widely used method for identifying pitch typically involves just ten specific labels: the first seven letters of the alphabet (A to G) and three modifiers—sharp, flat, and natural. The pitches A through G account for seven of the

mode (modal scale) A diatonic scale that predates major and minor scales

pentatonic scale Scale containing five pitches per octave

chromatic scale Scale containing all twelve possible pitches within the octave

sharp (♯) Musical symbol that raises a pitch by a half-step

flat (♭) Musical symbol that lowers a pitch by a half-step

staff Set of five horizontal lines used for music notation

clef Symbol placed on a staff to indicate specific pitches; treble and bass clefs are the two most common

twelve pitches within each octave; they correspond to the white keys on a piano keyboard. They are identified as natural notes. If we **sharp** a letter-name pitch, we raise it one half-step: an F sharp is a half-step above the note F (natural). Similarly, if we **flat** a pitch, we lower it one half-step: an F flat is a half-step below F. By using sharps and flats we are able to account for all twelve pitches within an octave. Pitches an octave apart use the same letter name. So, on a conventional piano keyboard, which contains eighty-eight pitches, there are more than seven complete octaves.

The system of pitch notation, developed over almost a millennium, enables musicians to notate all eighty-eight pitches on a piano (and more) by using a relatively small set of symbols. Here are the most common, and most essential. The common feature of the symbols used to notate duration is the *note head*. It can be open or closed and with or without a stem and other components. The note head is placed on, above, or below a *staff* with a clef to indicate a specific pitch.

© Cengage Learning

The **staff** is a set of five horizontal lines used for music notation.

THE STAFF

Pitches are notated on both the lines of the staff and the spaces between the lines. However, a plain staff, such as the one pictured here, cannot be used to indicate specific pitches because there is no symbol to indicate what pitch a particular line or space represents. To use the staff to indicate a specific range of pitches, musicians use **clefs**.

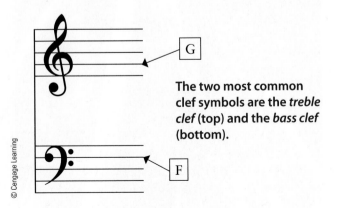

© Cengage Learning

The two most common clef symbols are the *treble clef* (top) and the *bass clef* (bottom).

Each designates a series of midrange pitches. The shape of the clef sign and its placement on the staff designate a specific pitch. The treble clef is also called a *G clef* because the inner curl circles the second line up from the bottom of the staff, which is a G.

Similarly, the bass clef is also known as an *F clef* because the symbol begins on the fourth line and the two dots to the right of the curved line are on each side of the fourth line, which is F.

The following graphic shows an octave's worth of pitches in both treble and bass clef. Each pitch is assigned a particular place on, above, or below the staff. Ledger lines are note-specific extensions of the staff, to notate pitches that lie beyond the range of the staff. The highest of the four A's (notated below) requires a ledger line.

The symbols for sharps (♯) and flats (♭) are placed to the left of the note head.

Note: We use the words *high* and *low* to describe pitch relationships. For instance, we might say that the second pair of pitches in "Twinkle, Twinkle" is higher than the first pair. Technically this means that the second pair is at a faster frequency than the first. Notation reinforces the impression of high and low: higher pitches above lower pitches in the same clef, and clefs specifying a higher range of pitches, generally appear above those spanning a lower range.

SCALE AND KEY

When a scale has a tonic pitch or keynote, we say that it is in the **key** of that pitch. A **tonic** pitch, or **keynote**, is the principal tone of a scale. Almost all of the music that we will hear has a tonic pitch. The scales that surround a given tonic may differ, but the fact that each scale's tones relate in a specific way to a tonic pitch (either higher or lower) is constant. The tonic can be any one of the twelve pitches, within an octave.

In the same way that we label a pitch, we label a

key by using the alphabetic symbol identifying its keynote—A, B♭, C♯, and so on. For example, if we say a melody is in the key of E major, we mean that it is using a major scale that has E as the tonic pitch.

Music can be in any key. We stay in the key by preserving the relationship of all the other pitches to the keynote. Some music stays in one key throughout. More extended works often begin in one key and move to others before returning to the initial key.

TONAL MUSIC

The idea of using a tonic pitch as the primary point of reference is central to the music of many cultures. In European culture, it dates back to the very first preserved examples. Music that uses one note of a scale as a reference pitch is said to be **tonal**. Most of the music that we will hear is tonal.

It is also possible to compose **atonal** music: that is, music that does not use one pitch as a reference point with the other pitches arranged hierarchically around it. However, the fact that there is neither a tonic pitch nor a scale related to that tonic typically makes the music more difficult to process.

Scales such as the major scale have familiar sounds—sounds that we have heard in countless musical examples. When we hear a new melody formed from the notes of a scale that we know, we are often able to grasp it more easily because we hear its close relationship with the scale. Your experience with the Mozart variations should bear this out.

To this point, we have discussed the foundations of melody: pitch and interval, scale and tonic. The choice of definite pitches and their arrangement into scales are preconditions for any kind of pitch organization. We consider another more specific aspect of melody next.

LO9 Melodic Organization: The Phrase

Please read the following sentence out loud: melodylikelanguageisoftenorganizedhierarchically. Now read it again: Melody, like language, is often organized hierarchically. As we read such a

key Indication of the tonic or keynote of a scale

tonic (keynote) Focal pitch of a scale to which the other pitches are related

tonal Used to describe music that uses one note of a scale as a reference pitch

atonal Used to describe music that does not use one pitch as a reference point

sentence in its normal form, we respond to visual cues that clarify its organization: the spaces between words, the commas, the capital letter, and period. These cues typically reflect the flow of the words as spoken: some separation between words, small pauses at the commas, and a longer pause at the period.

We are able to process a statement in a familiar language because the sounds are meaningful (we know the vocabulary); because we are able to organize the sounds into successively larger units (letters, syllables, words, phrases, clauses, sentences); and because we periodically interrupt the flow of sounds to indicate boundaries between units (pauses indicated by commas, colons, periods).

Our experience with pitch organization, and especially with melody, is analogous in many respects to our experience with language. We group sounds together into larger units, using scales and other familiar musical material as references and relying on periodic punctuation of the musical flow to define the units.

The succession of pitches that eventually form melodies can range from musical molecules, such as the repeated note that grows into the melody of "Twinkle, Twinkle," to long streams of notes, such as those we will soon hear in a chant by Hildegard of Bingen. Most melodies have some kind of internal punctuation to mark off sections of melody. Here we consider the most common unit created by this internal punctuation, the phrase.

We might define a musical **phrase** this way: a substantial but incomplete melodic idea that is separated from adjacent melodic material with clear musical punctuation. That's a long definition; let's clarify each part of it in turn.

Consider the opening section of "Twinkle, Twinkle." It consists of two short phrases, each punctuated by a long note. The long note on "star" functions much like a comma; the long note on "are" is comparable to a period.

Neither phrase can stand alone as a complete musical thought. However, together they form a musical sentence. (By contrast, Mozart's version of the melody has no musical comma—no internal punctuation. It forms a short but complete musical unit.)

Melody: An Expanded View

We recognize melody most easily when it has words, as in "Twinkle, Twinkle," or at least when we can imagine words set to it that move at a pace no faster than everyday speech. But if you've listened to both variation sets, you've heard individual variations where the most individual and distinctive part moves at a pace that would challenge the most skilled rapper, if the part had lyrics, and whose contour and range would challenge the vocal agility of the most skilled singer. Although these fast-moving lines are not melody in the familiar sense of the term, they are melody in the sense that they are a coherent series of pitches with an individual character. All have these characteristics:

- They have a beginning, middle, and end.
- They unfold as a series of pitches, one after the other.
- They are the most interesting, prominent, and appealing of the several parts heard at that particular time.

They are also typically—although not always—performed on instruments rather than sung.

For much of this chapter we have discussed melody in its most familiar form: the part of a musical work that we sing. But a fuller understanding of melody can include melodic lines written for instruments rather than the voice; melody-like parts in a musical passage that are not the main melody; and musical works that include several melodies, which may contrast with each other. We will encounter all of these in our survey.

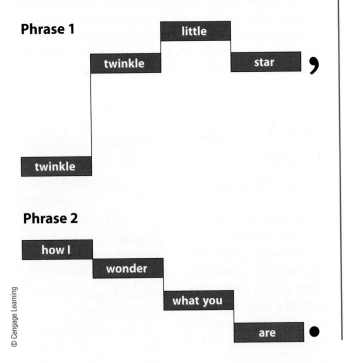

Phrase 1

little

twinkle   star ,

twinkle

Phrase 2

how I

wonder

what you

are •

{ More Bang for Your Buck }

MUSIC has it all, and you can too. Between the text, eBook, and our online offerings, you have everything at your fingertips. Make sure you check out all that MUSIC has to offer:

- Unit in Review cards
- Online quizzing with feedback
- Robust eBook
- Streaming music

- Active Listening Guides
- Flashcards
- And more!

Visit CourseMate at **www.cengagebrain.com** to find the resources you need today!

UNIT 2
ORGANIZING
MUSIC

Learning Outcomes
After reading this unit, you will be able to do the following:

LO1 Understand harmony as the complement of melody, and describe a chord progression.

LO2 Discuss the meaning and function of a cadence.

LO3 Define texture and the roles of part, line, and voice in texture; and distinguish between density and independence in texture.

LO4 Define musical form and describe how we recognize musical form through musical punctuation (cadences) and pattern.

LO5 Describe the use of repetition, contrast, and variation in music.

LO6 Differentiate some basic musical forms.

LO7 Describe what we mean by musical style and important considerations in identifying it.

CHAPTER 5

Harmony and Texture

"When several people with different things to say talk at the same time, the result is gibberish. But in music, several interesting and intelligible lines can weave together and make perfect sense."

The clangorous sound that begins The Beatles' "A Hard Day's Night" is arguably the most famous single chord in the history of rock. George Martin, The Beatles' producer, remarked, "We knew it would open both the film and the soundtrack LP, so we wanted a particularly strong and effective beginning."

For forty years, that chord remained one of rock's great unsolved mysteries: what were the notes in it, and who was playing them? Those who tried to replicate it knew that George Harrison had played it on a Rickenbacker twelve-string guitar and that the other Beatles were somehow involved, but their attempts to reproduce the chord never sounded quite right. However, in 2004, Jason Brown, a Canadian mathematics professor and an enthusiastic amateur guitarist, decoded the chord through a computer-aided mathematical procedure called the Fourier transform. He was able to identify all of the pitches in the chord and determine their relative strength. From that he deduced that pitched sounds were played not only by Harrison, Lennon (on six-string guitar), and McCartney (on bass) but also by Martin on the piano.

This famous chord spotlights two elements that are most often in the background: harmony and texture. The reason: harmony and texture seldom offer easy points of entry, such as we may experience with dynamics, instrumentation, rhythm, and melody. In this regard, Harrison's clangorous chord is exceptional. And as the song continues, our attention goes to the words and melody, the brash sound of The Beatles' voices, the instruments that they are playing, and the propulsive rock rhythm that they generate.

However, underneath a memorable melody may well be striking chords (harmony) woven into a rich accompaniment (texture). And even in music without a prominent melody, we may hear a compelling beat formed from the interplay among several layers of activity (texture).

Harmony and texture provide complementary perspectives on pitches that sound at the same time.

Did You Know?

The power chords of rock guitarists revive an ancient harmonic practice. A riff harmonized in power chords could be compared to a similar compositional technique used by tenth-century monks, who sang chants with all parts moving in tandem.

LO1 Harmony

Harmony is the study of chords and how they work together with the other elements of music. We tend to think of chords and harmony as taking a subordinate role, for instance when we think of the "harmony" parts that backup singers perform or the strummed guitar accompaniment that "harmonizes" with the melody sung by a folk artist. But we can also hear chords within melody.

Chords

A **chord** is a group of three or more pitches sounded together or a series of pitches that are heard and understood as if they were sounded together.

> **harmony** The study of chords and how they work with the other elements
>
> **chord** Group of three or more pitches sounded together, or a series of pitches heard and understood as if sounded together

Block chord   Arpeggio   Melody

From chord to melody

When we hear a group of pitches sounded all at once, we have no trouble identifying it as a chord. However, we can also recognize chords when we hear the individual notes of the chord played one after another rather than at the same time. We call a chord whose pitches are presented as a series an **arpeggio** or a **broken chord**. The graphic above presents the same chord in three forms: as a **block chord**, where the notes are sounded simultaneously; as an arpeggio; and as the beginning of a familiar melody.

CHORDS AS HARMONY, CHORDS IN MELODY

The straightforward example above helps us perceive three important points about the relationship between harmony and melody.

- *Melody and harmony.* In most of our musical examples that include harmony, the composers have typically derived both melody and harmony from the same set of pitches. In this case, a major scale provides both the chord and the beginning of the melody.

- *Melody versus harmony.* While it is easy to distinguish harmony from melody when we hear harmony as block chords and melodies as individual pitches, the boundary becomes fuzzier when we hear the pitches of a chord one after the other. As our example demonstrates, John Stafford Smith (who composed the melody of "The Star-Spangled Banner") had only to tweak the rhythm a little to turn a simple arpeggio into the beginning of his melody.

- *Melody or harmony.* Whether we hear a series of pitches as melody or harmony depends on what we are listening for. If we listen for the contour and rhythm of an arpeggio, then we are hearing it melodically. However, if we group each oscillation of the contour into the chord that it is outlining, then we are hearing harmonically. Whether we decide to listen for melody or for harmony will probably depend on the source of the musical interest:

> ### Music Concept Check
> A chord can be heard in three ways: as pitches played all at once, in a series, or in a melody. Listen to an arpeggio and a chord online.

a simply oscillating arpeggio does not make for a very interesting melody. The important point, however, is that we have the option.

CHORD PROGRESSIONS

A **chord progression** is a series of chords that proceeds—or progresses—toward a harmonic goal. In the sense that we will use the term here, a chord progression not only progresses toward a goal—for example, toward the **tonic chord** (the single chord that represents the definite center or "home" in relationship to other chords that are used in the composition)—but often does so by following well-traveled paths. Particularly as the chords approach the goal, their sequence becomes more predictable. Such progressions mark off units of musical thought more powerfully than any other aspect of the music.

Harmony enables us to hear the key even more strongly than melody does, for two reasons. First, the tonic chord confirms the tonic note as the focal pitch. Second, chord progressions that depart from and ultimately return to the tonic chord by a predictable path create a sense of expectation, which is fulfilled upon arrival at the tonic chord. The path may include one or more intermediate stops but ultimately completes the round-trip from tonic to tonic. Next we examine harmonic stopping points, which are called cadences.

LO2
Cadences

A **cadence** is a short series of chords (typically two or three) that defines and achieves a

> **arpeggio (broken chord)** Chord whose pitches are presented as a series
>
> **block chord** Chord whose notes are sounded simultaneously
>
> **chord progression** Series of chords that proceed toward a harmonic goal
>
> **tonic chord** The single chord that represents the definite center or "home" in relationship to other chords that are used in the composition
>
> **cadence** A short series of chords (typically two or three) that defines and achieves a harmonic goal

> *A chord progression not only progresses toward a goal ... but often does so by following well-traveled paths.*

© iStockphoto.com/Jeremiah Deasey

harmonic goal. Cadences punctuate the musical flow, much as commas and periods punctuate the flow of words in sentences. To emphasize a cadence, composers often coordinate reaching the harmonic goal with a lull in activity. This drop in activity helps signal arrival at a cadence; the particular chord progression determines the degree to which the cadence punctuates the musical flow.

A progression that ends decisively on the tonic chord functions like a red light. It brings the music to a complete stop, thus delineating a complete musical statement. One reason that we feel such clear separation between variations in the Mozart variation set is that the original theme and almost all of the variations end with a strong cadence on the tonic chord. In effect, they are musical paragraphs containing two sentences.

By contrast, cadences that do not end decisively on the tonic function more like yellow lights in that they slow down the musical flow momentarily but do not bring it to a final stop. It is precisely this capability—to determine through chord choice how emphatically a cadence punctuates the musical flow—that makes possible the large-scale hierarchical organization heard in the concertos of Mozart, the symphonies of Beethoven, and virtually all of the music of the eighteenth and nineteenth centuries.

Music Concept Check

Listen to various cadences online.

© iStockphoto.com/Daniel Halvorson

Some cadences are yellow lights or red lights; some are commas, semicolons, or periods.

LO3 Texture

We have introduced three basic elements of harmony: the chord, chord progression, and cadence. When we observe several simultaneous pitches as harmony, we hear "vertically"; that is, we hear several pitches as a single event, even if the individual pitches are heard consecutively. By contrast, we tend to hear texture more "horizontally." In texture, we are concerned more with the relationship between parts through a block of time.

Texture is the fabric of sound created by the interaction of all the parts of a piece of music. When we listen for texture, we observe everything that is going on—melody, harmony, and rhythm—and consider how the separate strands of activity relate to each other.

In the previous chapter, we argued that melody was the face of music, its most distinctive feature. Our Mozart excerpts would seem to contradict that because each variation has a very distinct identity, yet the melody remains much the same. However, this is a special case, the exception that proves the rule. Variation sets require variation, and Mozart employs two complementary strategies: either vary the melody (as in the first variation) or vary the setting of the melody.

We use the word *texture* to identify the relationship between the melody and the setting that surrounds it—or more generally, the relationship among all parts. For melody, texture is "the rest of the story" with regard to overall musical activity, just as harmony is the rest of the story with regard to pitch organization.

We may often find that although melody draws us into a musical work, texture keeps us listening. The variations demonstrate this convincingly. They begin with a tuneful melody that catches our ear. However, in the variations that follow, the main source of interest is texture, because it is the source of the greatest contrasts and variety. No other aspect of the music changes as clearly and decisively from variation to variation.

PARTS

Our point of reference in hearing and describing texture is the *part*. We seek to discover how many parts there are, what their roles are (melody, accompaniment, rhythmic support), and how they interrelate.

Part refers to the music that an individual performer sings or plays. (We also use **line** or **voice** to refer to the same thing.) For example, in the theme to Tchaikovsky's orchestral version of "Unser dummer Pöbel meint," we can speak of the first violin *part* or the clarinet and bassoon *parts*. A part typically unfolds one pitch or note at a time. We can associate a part—for example, the melody—with a voice or an instrument because voices and most orchestral instruments are able to sing or play only one pitch at a time. When we cannot make the association, as in the case of instruments that are capable of playing more than one pitch at a time, we identify the part by referring to the sequence of pitches that belong together—a melody line or an accompaniment—as the *melody line* or *upper part*, and the *bass line* or *lower part*.

In two common situations, both called **doubling**, two or more instruments share the same line. One kind of doubling occurs when two or more instruments play the same part in the same octave; the other kind, when two instruments (or hands at the piano) play a line one or more octaves apart. We heard the first kind of doubling in the string parts of the orchestral version of *Mozartiana*; we heard the second kind in both the piano and the orchestral versions of the opening measures.

DENSITY AND INDEPENDENCE

In observing texture, we consider two aspects of the relationship among two or more parts: the *density* of the texture and the *independence* of the parts. Although both contribute to our impression of texture, density and independence are largely independent of each other, as we discover next.

Textural Density.

Density refers to the thickness of the texture. Our impression of textural density emerges mainly from the interrelationship of three variables: the *number* of parts, the *spacing* of the parts (how widely separated they are from each other), and the *register*, or range of pitches lowest to highest, in which the parts operate. We will hear a denser texture if there are more rather than fewer instruments or voices, if the parts are closely spaced rather than widely separated, and if the parts lie in a low rather than a high register. In general, we will use descriptive words to characterize textural density: *thick* or *thin*, *dense* or *transparent*, and other words that evoke strongly contrasting sound images.

Textural Independence.

Textural independence measures the degree to which a musical line stands apart from those around it. We observe textural independence by looking at how *different* a part is from those around it in melodic contour and rhythm, and how *distinctive and memorable*, or melody-like, it is. Typically, we use the melody—generally the most dominant line—as our primary point of reference. There are good reasons for this. Our ear tends to go to the melody first, and the style of the melody (simple or elaborate, vocal or instrumental) provides a useful benchmark for observing the other parts.

Textural independence can range from completely dependent to completely independent. A part is *completely dependent* when it follows the contour and rhythm of another part, such as the melody. This is analogous to children following the lead of the teacher as they recite a familiar text. At the other end of the spectrum are textures whose every part has a distinctive rhythm and contour, and all parts are of comparable melodic interest. We have noted the parallels between melody and spoken language: the notion of phrases and sentences and differing degrees of punctuation that clarify them. Texture reveals a significant difference; it is where music and spoken language part company. When several people with different things to say talk at the same time, the result is gibberish. But in music, several interesting and intelligible lines can weave together and make perfect sense. It is one of the miraculous things about music.

Describing Textural Independence.

We can view textural independence on a continuum. On one end of the continuum is the simplest texture of all: a single line, or **monophonic** (meaning "one voice") texture. In this book, and in everyday experience, this texture is exceptional: we have only one instance of it among our musical examples. At the other end of the continuum is a multipart texture in which every part is of comparable interest and moves with

---

part (line; voice) Music that an individual performer sings or plays

doubling Two or more instruments sharing the same line, or part

density A measure of the thickness of texture

textural independence Degree to which a musical line stands apart from those around it

monophonic (*n.* monophony) Used to describe texture with a single line, or voice

distinct rhythm and contour. We call such textures **polyphonic** (meaning "many voices") or **contrapuntal** (based on the term *counterpoint*—literally, "point against point"). We can easily move from one extreme to the other by starting a song such as "Frère Jacques" in unison, then continuing as a **round** (staggered entrances of a melody by different voices or instruments at predetermined points in a composition). It is monophonic when everyone sings the melody at the same time; it becomes polyphonic when sung as a round, with three entrances of the melody.

Most textures that we will encounter lie between these two extremes. Commentators who talk or write about music often use the term **homophonic** (meaning "same or similar voice") and **melody and accompaniment** more or less interchangeably to describe the wide range of textures that include more than one part, with one part a clearly dominant melody and the others subordinate. This is by far the most common and most variable range of textures. For example, almost all of the variations we have heard are homophonic, although there are considerable differences from one to the next.

Music Concept Check

See and hear familiar examples of monophony, homophony, and polyphony online.

For this reason, we will use "homophonic" more often to refer to those textures in which the parts move in the same rhythm (as in a hymn) or when the rhythm of the subordinate parts is less active than the melody (as in the first variation of either set), and "melody and accompaniment" more frequently to refer to those textures in which the subordinate parts are more active, as is the case in the "Twinkle, Twinkle" variations. In addition, we will encounter many style-specific textures, such as the predominant melody and bass line heard in Baroque music and jazz.

polyphonic (*n.* polyphony; contrapuntal, *n.* counterpoint) Used to describe multipart texture in which every part is of comparable interest and moves with distinct rhythm and contour

round Staggered entrances of a melody by different voices or instruments at predetermined points in a composition

homophonic (melody and accompaniment; *n.* homophony) Used to describe a wide range of textures that include more than one part, with one part a clearly dominant melody and the others subordinate

---

CHAPTER 6

Form

"When we sense form, it's like looking out a train window at the slowly passing countryside."

Did You Know?

Music is one of the few art forms that unfolds in time rather than space.

A lean, loose-jointed Negro had commenced plunking a guitar beside me while I slept. His clothes were rags; his feet peeped out of his shoes. His face had on it some of the sadness of the ages. As he played, he pressed a knife on the strings of the guitar in a manner popularized by Hawaiian guitarists who used steel bars. The effect was unforgettable. His song, too, struck me instantly.
"Goin' where the Southern cross' the Dog."
The singer repeated the line three times, accompanying himself on the guitar with the weirdest music I had ever heard.

In his 1941 autobiography, *Father of the Blues*, W. C. Handy (1873–1958) tells of his first contact with the blues, which took place in 1903 at a train station in Tutwiler, Mississippi.

The musician whom Handy heard was a predecessor of bluesmen like Blind Lemon Jefferson, Robert Johnson, and Muddy Waters, and his use of the knife on the guitar strings anticipates the bottleneck style of Delta bluesmen.

By the time of this encounter, Handy was well into a professional career as a bandmaster. Growing up in Alabama, he received formal musical training while largely ignoring black folk music. However, as a result of this and other similar experiences, Handy began to study the blues, noting the words and notating the melodies of the songs that he heard.

Handy was not the "father of the blues," but he was the father of blues as commercial music. He played a leading role not only in popularizing the blues but also in shaping its now-classic form. It is in his songs from the early twentieth century that many Americans first encountered what has come to be known as the "twelve-bar blues" form. Like the variation themes of Mozart, the twelve-bar blues is a short but complete musical statement that can be used as a building block for a larger musical work. We will revisit the twelve-bar blues in People's Music 13. In this chapter, we introduce the idea of musical form, provide guidelines for recognizing form, and show the relationship between conventional forms and specific examples of the form, using the variation sets as examples.

LO4 Form

Form is the organization of musical elements in time. It is concerned principally with the structure and coherence of a musical work. *Structure* in this sense means the relationship of various sections of a musical work to each other. *Coherence* refers to those qualities that make a musical work a purposefully unified creative effort rather than a random assemblage of sounds.

Music unfolds in time. New events continually replace old; we hear something, and then it is gone. Listening to a live performance of a musical work, we cannot absorb it all at once or even examine it at our own pace, as we can a painting or sculpture. For this reason, most successful composers have provided musical cues that help listeners hear a work as a single coherent statement. These cues help us assemble the stream of sounds

form Organization of musical elements in time; concerned principally with the structure and coherence of a musical work

that we hear into larger segments, which can ultimately evolve into a pattern that we can understand as a unified whole. That has been the case in the Mozart variations, and it will be our experience in virtually all of the music that we will listen to from this point on. Our first goal in this chapter is to identify the kinds of musical cues that enable us to recognize the boundaries of and relationships among forms.

© Iain Crockart/Digital Vision/Getty Images

Listening to a live performance of a musical work, we cannot absorb it all at once or even examine it at our own pace, as we can a painting or sculpture.

Recognizing Form

Recognizing the form of a musical work can be approached in three steps. The first step is to identify the boundaries within the work. The second is to compare the music on either side of these boundaries. The third is to recognize the relationships between sections as a larger pattern. We begin this process at a local level, then assemble the work into progressively larger sections until we can view it as a whole.

PUNCTUATION AND FORMAL BOUNDARIES

Punctuation in music is a decisive change in the musical flow that marks a boundary between two sections of music. Typically, punctuation results from a reduction of musical activity or an interruption of the musical flow. The drop in musical activity can—and usually does—come from coordinated change in several elements; for instance, a long note and a melodic descent to the tonic, confirmed by a cadence. We hear these changes as a decisive punctuation, like the period at the end of a sentence, because several elements send much the same signal: stop. Some musical signals are more or less universal: the descent of the melody or a long note following shorter notes. (These are like the drop in your voice at the end of a declarative sentence and the short pause you take before continuing.) Others are specific to the pitch organization: a cadence on the tonic may define a complete musical unit. (This parallels completing the grammatical requirements for a complete sentence.) All work together to punctuate the musical flow.

Our impression of the strength of a musical punctuation comes both from the events that lead up to the punctuation and from what follows. As a rule, the greater the contrast between sections, the more decisive the punctuation seems to be. Typically, there is a correlation between the strength of the punctuation and the amount of music that it marks off: the stronger the punctuation, the more music it delineates.

Punctuations outline the shape of the musical work in time. The musical material between punctuations fills in the outline. We explore this aspect of form next.

LO5 Comparing Sections

The relationship between two sections of music falls somewhere on a continuum that ranges from rote repetition to strong contrast. **Repetition** is exactly that, a verbatim restatement of something heard earlier in the work. **Contrast** involves substantial change, usually in more than one element. For example, dynamics could change from soft to loud, harmony could shift to a new key or mode, rhythm could become more or less active, or register could shift from low to high. Our sense of contrast grows out of three variables: the number of elements that change, the degree of change in each element, and the prominence of the elements that are changed. The greater the cumulative change, the stronger the contrast. Musical works seldom have complete contrast—that is, completely new rhythms, meters, instruments, themes, tempos, and the like—because some element of connection is necessary to lend coherence to the work. Still, strong contrasts are possible, particularly between major sections.

Repetition and contrast are at either end of the continuum. Between them lies variation. **Variation** involves a balanced mix of continuity and change in the work. It is the compositional technique of applying changes to one or more elements of a musical work. The new material is enough like material in an earlier section that we hear a clear connection, but altered enough that we hear a discernible difference between the two sections.

> **repetition** Verbatim restatement of something heard earlier in a work
>
> **contrast** Substantial change in a work, usually in more than one element
>
> **variation** The compositional technique of applying changes to one or more elements of a musical work

LO6 Examples of Form

A variety of forms have become common through popular usage. From the most basic binary and ternary (two- and three-part) to more complex forms like sonata form and rondo, form is fundamentally the organization of musical elements in time. Forms are not rigid molds into which composers must pour their ideas but a concept of how to organize the material into a coherent work. In this chapter we will explore examples of binary, rounded binary, variation, and strophic form. In later chapters we will discuss sonata form, minuet, rondo, and other forms within the historical context during which they were developed.

To this point, our discussion of form has been conceptual—necessarily so, because form is infinitely variable. However, the conceptual becomes concrete when we encounter form in a musical work. Conceptually, form is abstract; structurally, *the* form of a musical work is specific. Let's explore this point by looking at the form of the two variation themes.

THE FORM OF "TWINKLE, TWINKLE, LITTLE STAR"

The lyrics of "Twinkle, Twinkle" offer a guide to the form of the theme: a complete sentence set to the first part of the melody, followed by two short phrases, which are in turn followed by a restatement of the opening sentence. The punctuation in the music matches up with the period after "are" because "are" is set to a long note, the melody returns to the tonic pitch after a steady descent, and the harmonic progression arrives at a cadence that says "stop." Here melody, rhythm, and harmony work together to punctuate the musical flow at the completion of a musical thought, to match the complete sentence in the lyrics. The following graphic shows the sequence of events in the melody as they relate to the lyrics.

First section	Second section	Third section
Twinkle, twinkle, little star; how I wonder what you are. **Statement**	Up above the world so high, like a diamond in the sky **Variation**	Twinkle, twinkle, little star; how I wonder what you are. **Return**
Punctuation: Long note on "are," descent to tonic, cadence that says "stop"	**Lighter punctuation:** Long note, but no return to tonic pitch, plus "yellow light" cadence	**Punctuation:** Long note on "are," descent to tonic, cadence that says "stop"

Mozart's Setting of "Ah, vous dirai-je Maman" and "Unser dummer Pöbel meint"

Mozart's setting of "Ah, vous dirai-je Maman" differs only cosmetically from the melody we know as "Twinkle, Twinkle." The most significant difference by far is that Mozart repeats the first section, then combines the second and third sections into a larger unit and repeats that. If we were to sing the words to "Twinkle, Twinkle" using Mozart's version of the melody ("Ah, vous dirai-je Maman"), here is the sequence of events.

First part (first section)	First part, repeated	Second part (second and third sections combined)	Second part, repeated
Twinkle…..are	Twinkle…..are	Up above…are	Up above…are
Statement	**Statement**	**Change and return**	**Change and return**

The Gluck theme ("Unser dummer Pöbel meint") follows the same outline.

First part (first section)	First part, repeated	Second part (second and third sections combined)	Second part, repeated
Statement	**Statement**	**Change and return**	**Change and return**

In their basic structure, the two themes are identical; the differences in form have mainly to do with the relationship between sections. In "Ah, vous dirai-je Maman," the different section is a variation; only the melody has changed. The last section exactly matches the opening section; it is literal repetition. In Mozart's version of Gluck's "Unser dummer Pöbel meint," the situation is different. The "something different" section contrasts with what has come before: there are abrupt changes in dynamics, melody, rhythm, harmony, and texture. (However, notice the deeper continuity produced by retaining tempo, meter, key, and instrumentation.) The final section returns to the opening melody, but it is recast in a higher register and with slightly different harmony at the end. This we might label "varied repetition."

Music Concept Check
Hear the structural similarities and differences online.

Binary Form

To this point, we have used the word *form* in two distinct ways: conceptually, to refer to the idea of organizing musical elements in time; and concretely, to refer to those aspects of each of the themes that give them structure and coherence. The similarity in the themes' outlines points to a third meaning of *form*: a well-established plan or sequence of events.

The form used for both themes is rounded binary form. As its name implies, **binary form** is a two-part form in which both the first and the second parts are typically repeated. That is the case with both themes.

Binary form is a two-part form.

In a **rounded binary form**, the second part ends with a substantial or complete restatement of the first part. In both themes, the restatement of the first part is complete.

Conventional formal plans such as rounded binary form are valuable because they are specific enough to enable listeners to anticipate major structural events yet flexible enough to allow for differences in specific realizations of the form. We notice that the Gluck theme has more variety (contrast instead of variation; varied repetition instead of literal restatement), but that does not begin to obscure the underlying similarity in formal outline between the two themes. If we were to listen to yet another similar theme, we would almost certainly have little difficulty navigating our way through it: it would be like following a familiar route home from work.

Binary form can serve as the form for a complete work, as it does in so much dance music from the seventeenth and eighteenth centuries. Or it can serve as the building block for a more extended work, as it does here.

VARIATION FORM

We sense the larger form of the themes mainly through a time-tested strategy: change followed by the return of earlier material. Throughout the centuries, musicians have relied on return after change as the most direct way to convey formal organization. That is the case in the rounded binary form of our themes and with the variation sets as a whole. To appreciate the organizing power of return after change, we will consider the idea of repetition with no intervening change and the relationship between the theme and the variations.

Take a moment to imagine in your head the first section of the melody of "Twinkle, Twinkle" (from "Twinkle" to "are") repeated over and over, without interruption. Your experience would, in effect, be a replay—in very slow motion—of your experience listening to shamanic drumming: each repetition of the section would correspond to a beat of the drum. In both cases, there is

no measure of time beyond the repetition of the event. Simple repetition does not convey any larger organization. Only when the repetition stops can we sense a larger unit: the entire work, which consists of X number of repetitions.

In his variation sets, Mozart used the theme as a formal template for the variations. Although there is certainly variety in melody, texture, rhythm, and—to a lesser extent—harmony, the basic formal outline remains consistent from theme to first variation and then for several more variations.

As we listen to each variation set unfold, we may sense a kind of modular design. It is as if the theme and each of the variations are musical Legos, building blocks of different colors and designs but identical size, which are used to assemble a larger work. In both cases, we hear a long string of variations that retain the form, tempo, and tonic of the theme. There are no obvious cues to suggest a larger grouping; it is as if the variations could go on forever—or at least until Mozart's ideas or the endurance of the audience is exhausted. Certainly there is change from variation to variation. But from a formal perspective, the changes are cosmetic; the template doesn't change.

> **binary form** Two-part form in which both the first and the second parts are typically repeated
>
> **rounded binary form** Two-part form in which the second part ends with a substantial or complete restatement of the first part

It is as if the theme and each of the variations are musical Legos.

To bring each of the variation sets to a close, Mozart shifts to a much slower tempo in the next-to-last variation. This interrupts the periodic rhythm created by the string of variations: each slow variation lasts about four times as long as the theme or any earlier variation. The final variation returns to a fast tempo but in a different meter. Because the contrast in tempos is so dramatic, and because there is only one such contrast, they convey change, then return; the fast/slow/fast pattern created by the changes in tempo is a strong signal that the set is coming to an end.

Each of the variation sets is in (not surprisingly) variation form. **Variation form** (also known as **theme and variations**) typically begins with a theme; the rest of the work is an indeterminate number of variations based on the melody, harmony, and/or other musical elements of the theme. Unlike rounded binary form, which has a predictable structure and a clear beginning and end, variation form is modular and open-ended. Mozart's strategy for conveying large-scale structure through dramatic tempo change is optional and personal; it is not an essential component of the form.

Strophic Form: Variation for Words but Not Music

Here's one version of the original lyrics for "Twinkle, Twinkle," written by Jane Taylor in 1806:

> Twinkle, twinkle, little star,
> How I wonder what you are.
> Up above the world so high,
> Like a diamond in the sky.
> Twinkle, twinkle, little star,
> How I wonder what you are!

> When the blazing sun is gone,
> When he nothing shines upon,
> Then you show your little light,
> Twinkle, twinkle, all the night.
> Twinkle, twinkle, little star,
> How I wonder what you are!

> Then the traveler in the dark
> Thanks you for your tiny spark;
> He could not see which way to go,
> If you did not twinkle so.
> Twinkle, twinkle, little star,
> How I wonder what you are!

We would sing the now mostly forgotten second and third stanzas to the same melody as the first stanza. The melody will remain unchanged, but the words vary with each repetition. We call a vocal form in which different lyrics are sung to each repetition of the same melody *strophic form*. Another example of **strophic form** is the standard church hymn.

Why Bother Understanding Form?

Most of the music that we will encounter will have recognizable forms. What does this mean for us as listeners? If we are aware of the structure of a particular musical work, then we can process the same information at different levels, all of which unfold more slowly than the actual events in the music. For example, we hear the third (or fourth, or second) variation on a local level as a musical unit in rounded binary form and on a more global level as the next module in the sequence of variations (the large-scale structure). In real time, music can whiz by us, like a subway car going in the opposite direction, so that we may find it hard to hold on to the music that we hear. Understanding form enables us to anticipate what might happen, or at least when it will happen; it enables us to put the sounds we hear into a coherent framework. Then the music slows down for us—psychologically, if not in reality. When we sense form, it's like looking out a train window at the slowly passing countryside rather than at the quickly passing surroundings of a subway car. In essence, it helps to simplify or make more understandable longer, more complicated works.

CHAPTER 7

Style

"Punk, soul, and grunge are style labels."

In the 2003 film *School of Rock*, Dewey Finn (Jack Black), an unemployed rock-guitarist-turned-teacher at an exclusive private school, gives his class a crash course in rock appreciation. Filling the blackboard with little boxes containing words like *punk, soul,* and *grunge* as well as a host of band names and lines connecting the various boxes, he takes his students on a whirlwind tour of fifty years of rock.

As he points to the boxes, Finn relies on his students to make connections between the boxed words and the music that they have heard. This pedagogical approach is a frenetic version of one strategy for introducing students to music: play examples of different kinds of music and link them to words that represent the style of each example.

Punk, soul, and *grunge* are style labels. In a single word, a style label evokes the common features of similar musical works. For instance, we expect a punk song to be loud and fast and have an insistent rhythm, distorted guitar sounds, screamed vocals, and confrontational lyrics. In its ability to convey information succinctly, a style label functions much like *house* or *car*, labels that identify an object and lead us to expect that object to have certain features.

Style labels in music work only to the extent that they call to mind a set of choices in one or more musical elements. Whether it is Baroque or blues, hip-hop or bebop, Romantic or rock, a label is meaningful only if it evokes sound images that are representative of the style.

If you've ever used a style label, you know intuitively how it works. Our work together should help you understand it conceptually as well. Accordingly, our objectives in this chapter are to define what we mean by musical style, to show the relationship between the elements discussed in the previous chapters and listening for style, and to discuss briefly the connection between style and meaning.

LO7 Musical Style

We define **style** in music as a consistent and comprehensive set of choices that define a body of music from a time, place, culture, or creative entity (a composer, performer, or group). The choices need not be universal, but they must be probable: rock songs probably have a rock beat; before the 1950s, no songs had a rock beat. A style description is a composite, a generic portrait in words of what we might expect to hear in a body of music

> **Did You Know?**
>
> Style provides the common ground between creator and audience, no matter how distant they may be, which makes meaningful communication between them possible.

> **style** A consistent and comprehensive set of choices that define a body of music from a time, place, culture, or creative entity (a composer, performer, or group)

© Photos 12 / Alamy

connected by time, place, circumstance, and, sometimes, composer. It accumulates from hundreds, even thousands, of instances. It describes likely features, not requirements.

STYLE AND THE ELEMENTS OF MUSIC

Style emerges from consistent ways of handling all of the musical elements. For example, based on our recent experience, we might say that we expect a Mozart theme-and-variations form to begin with a tuneful melody in rounded binary form supported by a simple accompaniment. Such a statement does not describe in great detail the Mozart themes that we've heard, but it does underscore what they have in common.

Style descriptions are useful to the extent that they faithfully and comprehensively represent a particular body of music. To that end, we might add other observations about Mozart's variations:

- *Instrumentation and texture:* Piano is the only instrument.
- *Rhythm:* The theme has a steady beat at a moderate tempo.
- *Harmony:* The theme begins and ends on the tonic chord.
- *Form:* Clear punctuations or cadences separate one section of the theme from the next.

These additional observations begin to flesh out a sound portrait of this musical style. The more elements we add, and the more precisely we describe their characteristic realizations, the more closely our observations describe the style.

In some cases, certain elements may be more prominent, or more indicative of the style, by either their presence or their absence. For example, extreme distortion is the sound signature of heavy metal: its absence is so uncharacteristic that we would be challenged to associate any song without distortion with heavy metal. Still, no single element defines style. It is the cumulative impression gathered from all of the elements.

Listening for Style

For us, perhaps the most important question about style is this: *Why* listen for style? After all, isn't it enough simply to let the music wash over us? Here's an answer. We study style because style is the gateway to understanding a work, its creator, and the culture from which it comes. Listening for style is valuable for all the music that you encounter, in and outside class. Keep in mind that it is something that you already do. Our hope is that by listening comprehensively and systematically for style and meaning, your awareness of style will become sharper—the aural equivalent of moving from conventional to high-definition TV.

LISTENING GUIDES

To assist you in listening for style, we provide, in CourseMate and the eBook, an Active Listening Guide for each example. Each Active Listening Guide has several components:

- *Background information* on the musical example and the musicians responsible for it
- An Active Listening *timeline* that highlights noteworthy events in the recording, as it plays
- A *Profile* that describes the characteristic handling of each element
- Several *Key Points* about style, meaning, and the connection between the music and the culture that nurtured it
- A *quiz* to test your familiarity with the example
- A button allowing you to print out a Listening Guide for reference (see next page)

The text includes a Listen Up! cue telling you that an Active Listening Guide is available online and summarizing the piece's takeaway point, style, form, genre, instruments, and cultural context. The cue for that first selection in Chapter 9 appears below. Clicking on the blue arrow icon in the eBook will open the full Active Listening Guide. Clicking on the ear icon will play the music streaming while you read the eBook.

LISTEN UP!

CD I:I
Hildegard of Bingen, "Nunc aperuit nobis"

Takeaway point: Long, flowing melodic lines without a steady beat

Style: Chant

Form: Through-composed

Genre: Antiphon

Instruments: Female voices

Context: Song for worship in a monastery

STYLE, STYLE LABELS, AND MEANING

To return to Dewey Finn's crash course: most of the music that you'll hear in this course is much further removed in time, place, and culture than the rock styles Finn so quickly surveyed. The sounds, style labels (Renaissance, Baroque, Classical), and terms associated with these styles (madrigal, ritornello, sonata) are less likely to be familiar to you. However, you will have weeks, rather than minutes, to connect the sounds with the words that summarize and identify them. And you'll have many more resources than Finn's students apparently had.

Here's the key point about this chapter, about this book, and about this course: We all agree that music has meaning. Style provides the common ground between creator and audience, no matter how distant they may be, which makes meaningful communication between them possible. Every musical example was meaningful to its original audience, and it can also be meaningful to listeners like us who aren't from that particular time, place, and culture. Much of the music that we'll hear has been valued by music lovers in every generation since it appeared: Handel's *Messiah*, Mozart's *Don Giovanni*, and Beethoven's Fifth

Music Concept Check

Check out a sample Listening Guide for the first selection in Chapter 9, online.

Symphony are true classics. All of the music has something to tell us about the culture from which it came, which is both inherently interesting and can provide a valuable perspective on our own music and culture.

Collectively, the musical examples show the many ways music has been used, from connecting with the divine and elevating the spirit through putting into sound the full range of human emotions and just having fun. The examples also convey some sense of the extraordinary evolution of music over the centuries, from the chant of Catholic nuns and the ritual music of Africans and Native Americans to the cornucopia of sounds in our contemporary world.

The elements chapters have given you a foundation for style-based listening. The Active Listening Guides will help you identify salient characteristics of each style. As you progress through the course, you should find that listening comprehensively for style becomes a matter of habit, not only in the musical examples discussed in this book but also in the music you encounter outside class. That is one of the lasting benefits of a music appreciation course, whether the music comes from the rock era or from over a thousand years and five continents.

UNIT 3
MUSICAL LIFE, 1000–1700

Learning Outcomes

After reading this unit, you will be able to do the following:

LO1 Understand the significance of the growth of secular music.

LO2 Describe and understand the importance of the development of polyphony and common practice harmony.

LO3 Understand the use of instruments during the Middle Ages, Renaissance, and early Baroque.

LO4 Explain the evolution of music as a profession.

LO5 Grasp how technology came to shape musical life.

© Angels playing musical instruments, detail from a predella panel of an altarpiece, Florentine (panel) (detail of 79968), Italian School, (14th century) / Museo Nazionale del Bargello, Florence, Italy / The Bridgeman Art Library International

CHAPTER 8

Medieval, Renaissance, and Early Baroque Music

"Between 1000 and 1700, European music went from ancient to modern."

A thousand years from now, historians with access to today's artifacts will be able to reconstruct musical life in our time with considerable precision and in excruciating detail. They will hear music exactly as its creators intended, and they will be able to disassemble recordings to better understand the creative and production processes. They will experience music in performance, via video recordings. They will read writings about music, from fan magazines and blogs to scholarly commentary. They will sift through data concerning sales, distribution, audience share, artist compensation, profits and losses, and other matters related to the music business. Their biggest problem may be simply managing the enormous amount of information available to them.

Those who study musical life at the beginning of the last millennium have the opposite problem. There is almost no documentary evidence of the music being made in Europe around the year 1000. Moreover, what has come down to us is in a form impossible to decode with certainty, and what it does convey provides us with only the sketchiest information about the sound of the music. We do know that music manuscripts came from monasteries scattered throughout Europe and that monks created this music for use in daily worship. And we believe that it was a monophonic vocal music with free rhythm.

Just over 500 years separate the first and last European musical examples discussed in the following part.

Did You Know?

Henry VIII of England owned seventy-four flutes.

The first is an antiphon (a type of chant) composed by Hildegard von Bingen in the middle of the twelfth century (ca. 1150). The last is an operatic aria composed by Henry Purcell toward the end of the seventeenth century. An antiphon is a musical commentary on a psalm. Hildegard, the abbess of a convent, composed her antiphon for performance by nuns during worship. Its sole purpose was to glorify God. Opera, on the other hand, is a fusion of music and drama whose purpose is to delight and edify its audience. By the time Purcell composed his opera *Dido and Aeneas*, opera had become the most lavish court entertainment in western Europe and the first open to the paying public.

As these examples suggest, during the five centuries that separate the two works, music evolved from compositions almost exclusively for church use to a broad array of styles and genres, both sacred (of the church) and secular (of the world, nonreligious). Music making became a profession with careers in composing, performing, and teaching that enabled a select few to transcend class boundaries. By the end of the 1600s, the concept of music as a form of paid entertainment furthered the growth of the music business throughout western Europe. New technologies made it possible for skilled craftsmen to create an array of musical instruments and publishers to facilitate the dissemination and preservation of musical compositions.

The seven centuries between 1000 and 1700 span the greater part of three major eras in Western culture: medieval, Renaissance, and the early Baroque. Using these eras as a loose framework, we trace the evolution of music itself, the musicians who created and performed it, the activities that supported it, and the audiences who heard it.

THE LANGUAGE OF MUSIC

EVOLUTION OF MUSICAL NOTATION

In previous chapters we introduced the notational system used to preserve and disseminate most of the music we will hear. Between 1000 and 1700, this system evolved gradually from a system of vague reminders to performers who knew the music to a system for rendering instrumentation, pitch, rhythm, and dynamics with considerable accuracy. The following images highlight important stages in the evolution of this system.

Very early (ca. 900 CE) example of musical notation

What's New: The fact of it, the notation itself. But note the absence of lines: staff lines to indicate pitch, bar lines to indicate measures, stems and beams to indicate the duration of individual notes. We are unable to say with any certainty what the notational symbols mean.

Chant notation, thirteenth century

What's New: (1) Four-line staff. (2) Clef sign. The staff and the clef sign enabled composers to specify exact pitches. (3) Rectangular noteheads to indicate specific pitches. Groups of notes linked together are sung to a single syllable.

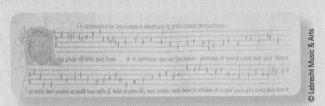

Work by Guillaume de Machaut, fourteenth century: early mensural notation (system for notating complex rhythmic values)

What's New: Early attempt at notating rhythm. Note the different notehead shapes and the use of stems. Still there is no meter signature, and there are no barlines.

Passage from Monteverdi's opera *Orfeo*, early seventeenth century

What's New: The notation of rhythm is much closer to modern notation: there are barlines, a time signature, and a wider range of durations, including notes with flags and dots. In addition, in Monteverdi's early orchestral scores (not shown here), all parts lined up, and all instruments were specified, showing, for instance, five trumpet parts.

What's New: This is essentially a modern score. The notation of rhythm and pitch is identical to that in current practice. New features include a tempo indication at the top left, articulation indications (the slurs—long curved lines covering several notes that instruct the performer to play as connectedly as possible), and dynamic markings (the *f* at the end).

First edition of Chopin's Funeral March (mid-nineteenth century)

Musical Trends and Developments, 1000–1700

Early music tells us something about economics and education in the first part of the second millennium. Virtually all of the music that has come down to us from the eleventh and twelfth centuries is sacred music because the church was the sole repository of learning, and it was the only institution with the wealth necessary to support the tedious task of copying music. Texts were in Latin, and the music usually accompanied the Mass or the Divine Office, the prayers said or sung by monks at different times of day.

LO1 The Growth of Secular Music

For scribes, copying books and music was both an art and a tedious task.

Toward the end of the thirteenth century, **secular music** (nonsacred music), especially polyphonic secular music, began to appear more frequently in manuscripts, an indication that the nonclerical aristocracy was cultured enough to appreciate it and wealthy enough to support it. A distinct secular style emerged in the fourteenth century, especially in France and Italy. It was simpler and more accessible than the sacred music of the same period, even when composed by the same musician. With this more accessible style came the use, in vocal music, of **vernacular** (everyday language of a particular region) rather than Latin, the universal language of the Catholic Church and of the educated.

As Renaissance values took hold in western Europe during the fifteenth and sixteenth centuries, the influence of secular culture on musical life grew significantly. The most obvious evidence was a dramatic increase in the ratio of secular to sacred compositions. A clear sign of the times: *Harmonice Musices Odhecaton*, the first sheet music printed with movable type, is a book of **chansons** (French secular songs) published by Ottaviano Petrucci in 1501. Secular vocal music intended for amateur performance flourished during the sixteenth century. This vocal music ranged from solo songs and simple homophonic settings of songs for several voices to Italian and English madrigals, which often featured contrapuntal textures and expressive text settings of highly regarded poetry.

More subtle was the integration of secular material into sacred compositions and the blurring of the stylistic boundary between sacred and secular. Secular songs, especially those by masterful composers, became more contrapuntal (like sacred compositions), and sacred compositions began to include more homophonic passages (like secular songs).

The Protestant Reformation of the sixteenth and early seventeenth centuries brought music making to ordinary churchgoers in worship services. Martin Luther reintroduced congregational singing into services, a practice in the early church that had previously disappeared. And he composed several well-known hymns, many of which were inspired or even borrowed from the secular songs of the day. Congregational singing would become common practice in virtually all Protestant denominations, in sharp contrast to the complex polyphonic masses and motets (polyphonic vocal works) that trained choirs sang at Catholic churches and cathedrals.

Among the most far-reaching developments in seventeenth-century music were the invention of opera and the increased focus on composition for instruments. Opera productions required the first orchestras for accompaniment, and dancing became an integral component of opera, especially in France. In Venice, Italy, opera became the first important commercial music, as theaters competed for patrons; they opened their doors to anyone who could afford a ticket.

LO2 Polyphony and Tonality

Development of Polyphony. The musical foundation for the proliferation of polyphonic music was the evolving system of pitch organization. Although polyphony, both written and improvised, seems to have been part of musical practice prior to 1000, most of the repertoire that has survived from the earliest sources is **chant**, a monophonic liturgical music. Polyphonic composition began in the late 1100s, in the hands of churchmen-composers Leonin and Perotin at Notre Dame Cathedral in Paris, as a simple secondary part

secular music Nonsacred music

vernacular Everyday language of a particular region

chanson Secular French song of the fifteenth and sixteenth centuries

chant Monophonic liturgical music

to a chant melody: either a dronelike sustained tone or a tone moving in parallel with the chant melody (same rhythm, same contour, but lower or higher in pitch). This early polyphonic music is called **organum**.

Over time, composers added more parts and gave them greater independence. In some instances, a work would use a dramatically slower chant melody as a foundation; the other parts would weave around it. This basic melodic part was called the **tenor**, from the Latin word *tenere*, meaning "to hold," to indicate that each note in the melody was held far longer than usual. By the fifteenth century, composers were writing magnificent sacred works in which four or more melodic parts were woven together contrapuntally into a seamless fabric of sound. Many also used familiar secular melodies rather than chants as a point of departure. Other, less contrapuntal approaches also surfaced, especially in secular music. Songs with more than one part often had voices moving in similar or even identical rhythm, creating a more homophonic texture. We speculate that dance music may have featured **heterophony**, musical texture in which two or more instruments simultaneously play different versions of the melody. Heterophony is a common practice in many folk traditions. Western audiences often hear it in country blues and Celtic music.

The sixteenth century was a glorious period for unaccompanied polyphonic vocal music. The most treasured works include masses and sacred motets as well as madrigals.

Common Practice Harmony. As is evident even in early chant, tonality gave musicians the power to regulate musical time and create points of arrival. The most basic form of doing so was establishing a tonic—a focal pitch—and using it as a point of departure and return. The addition of other melodically independent parts enabled composers not only to heighten the sense of closure at the end by supporting it with certain intervals (such as the octave) but also to articulate intermediate points in the work by other conventional interval choices.

The relationship between melody and harmony tilted from melody toward harmony during the late Renaissance. Prior to 1500, composers typically viewed cadences, the points of closure, as the purposeful coincidence of several independent parts. After that time, composers began to treat simultaneous groups of pitches as chords. This is evident in homophonic vocal works (and homophonic passages in largely contrapuntal works) and even more in the chordal accompaniments used in the first operas.

During the seventeenth century, chords were increasingly arranged in predictable progressions, particularly at cadences. By 1700, the major/minor system of harmonic organization that is still in use today had become common practice, allowing musicians to shape musical events into coherent overall musical structures. Common practice harmony gave composers the structural foundation for more extended compositions: operas, cantatas, concertos, and sonatas. It is no coincidence that instrumental composition took off as common practice harmony took shape in the seventeenth century: harmony came to replace or support text as the key structural element in music.

LO3 Instrumental Music

Although the first instrumental compositions date from the thirteenth century and the first instances of music composed for a specific instrument—the organ—appeared about a century later, composers and publishers continued to favor vocal music through the Renaissance. About ten times more vocal music than instrumental music was published during the course of the sixteenth century. Still, instruments were widely used, most often to replace singers in both sacred and secular multipart vocal works.

Three significant trends—increased compositional output, idiomatic instrumental writing, and the formation of large ensembles—signaled the growing importance of instruments and instrumental music in seventeenth-century musical life. The amount of instrumental music increased in quantity and variety: it included both sacred and secular music, with secular music far more common.

The practice of composing works that exploit the capabilities and distinctive sounds of a particular instrument dates back well before 1600. Works for keyboard instruments such as organ and harpsichord, as well as fretted instruments, most notably the lute, appeared with increasing frequency with the advent of printing around 1450. Many made technical demands

organum Early polyphonic music with a simple secondary part added to a chant melody

tenor Basic melodic part in chant, in which each note was held far longer than usual

heterophony Musical texture in which two or more instruments simultaneously play different versions of the melody

and achieved effects that were impossible to duplicate vocally. By the sixteenth century, theatrical productions in Italy often included instrumental ensembles, with particular instruments matched to certain characters and situations, such as the use of woodwinds to evoke pastoral settings. However, not until the seventeenth century did writing idiomatically for melody instruments, such as violins and brass, also become common practice.

Large ensembles date from the sixteenth century; so do string bands playing dances at the European courts. However, the ensemble that would soon evolve into the modern orchestra did not take shape until the seventeenth century, first in opera, then as an independent entity. Opera composers who scored for orchestras wrote mainly for multiple string players and chord instruments (both keyboard and fretted); the orchestras accompanied singers and provided instrumental music for dance numbers and music before and between acts of the opera.

Instrumental music for large ensembles became increasingly popular in the latter half of the seventeenth century, in large part because of the dazzling impression that the string orchestra at the French court—the "twenty-four violins of the king"—made on visiting royalty. Repertoire for these ensembles included both dance music and independent works strictly for listening. The most important new genre was the concerto, a multi-movement work composed for an orchestra comprising mainly or exclusively strings and a keyboard instrument. Concertos began to appear mainly in Italy during the last two decades of the century.

LO4 Music as a Profession

Music became a profession during the late Middle Ages, mainly because of the rise of a middle class and with it a demand for secular music. The earliest composers known to us were clergy; their musical activities were simply part of their work. Among the first professional musicians were minstrels, all-around entertainers often attached to a court. Troubadours were in effect the first

The "twenty-four violins of the king": a string orchestra playing for dancers at the court of Louis XIII of France

singer-songwriters: they wrote sophisticated poems, usually about love, which they often set to music. Troubadours and their counterparts throughout western Europe were active from the twelfth through the fourteenth centuries. Many were of aristocratic birth, and virtually all enjoyed a higher social station than minstrels.

Musicians began to form **guilds**, associations of professionals with common interests and concerns, in Vienna and Paris about 1300. Other guilds soon appeared throughout Europe, for both church and secular musicians. Among the most important functions of musicians' guilds were the creation of monopolies on official performance occasions, such as holidays, weddings, and church services; the establishment of professional standards for members and a training program for apprentices; and the support of sick and invalid members. All of this raised the social status of guild musicians considerably.

During the same time, churches and courts retained singers and composers to provide music for religious services and other functions. Singers received training at cathedral schools; composers relied on treatises, study of available music, and apprenticeships with other composers to learn their craft. In short, the music profession grew in stature during the

Troubadours were the first singer-songwriters.

fourteenth and fifteenth centuries, even though the professional musician attached to church or court was a servant, often with menial nonmusical duties. Documentary evidence suggests that the singer-composer Josquin des Prez (joss-CAN duh PRAY; 1445?–1521), perhaps the most esteemed musician in Europe during his lifetime, also performed tasks such as delivering hunting dogs for his employer.

Formal music making—composition and performance for church and court—was still an exclusive affair at the beginning of the sixteenth century. Most music had to be copied by hand. The church continued to be the primary musical patron, and even those musicians in the service of a court often performed for religious services as part of their duties. There were few stars, and by contemporary standards, they did not shine brightly: a composer like

guild Association of professionals with common interests and concerns

Singer-composer Josquin des Prez performed tasks such as delivering hunting dogs for his employer.

Josquin would be well known mainly to other church musicians and patrons; performers typically enjoyed only local fame, as they were in the service of a particular court.

However, by the end of the seventeenth century, musical life had begun to resemble that of our modern musical world. Music printing made music much more accessible. Opera had emerged as the first, most prominent, and most prestigious form of public musical entertainment. The top singers were stars. Composers, especially those with strong patronage, also enjoyed high social status. Among them were Claudio Monteverdi (1567–1643), the first great composer of opera; Jean Baptiste Lully (1632–1687), the musical director for Louis XIV; and Arcangelo Corelli (1653–1713), an esteemed violinist and composer. In the wake of the Reformation, the rise of secular culture, and economic growth, more jobs were available for musicians and for those connected to the music industry, for example, instrument makers, publishers, and theater administrators. Yet formal music making was mainly an elite activity: both composers and performers relied heavily on patronage from church and court.

LO5 Music and Technology

The technological expertise that produced such diverse artifacts as full-body armor, pocket watches, telescopes, and sailing ships sturdy enough to cross the Atlantic found widespread application in two music-related areas: instrument making and music printing and publishing.

MUSICAL INSTRUMENTS, TECHNOLOGY, AND CRAFTSMANSHIP

The first instrument to benefit from emerging technology was the organ. The pipes, keyboards, and mechanisms used to connect everything and drive air through the pipes were among the technological marvels of the fourteenth century. The harpsichord, the other major keyboard instrument of the era, first appeared with some frequency in the sixteenth century and by the seventeenth century had become central to secular music making as a solo, chamber, and orchestral instrument.

Many modern orchestral instruments were first developed during the sixteenth and seventeenth centuries. Early versions of the flute were popular during the sixteenth century—Henry VIII of England owned seventy-four of them! The first oboes and bassoons appeared in the seventeenth century. As instruments came into widespread use, professional instrument makers standardized and refined the instruments so that musicians could use them in large and small ensembles. The most notable examples of this craft are the violins, violas, and cellos made by the Amati, Stradivari, and Guarneri families. They were among several generations of luthiers (stringed-instrument makers) who worked in Cremona, Italy, from the sixteenth through the eighteenth centuries. Andrea Amati, the first in the line, established the form of the modern violin; instruments by Antonio Stradivari and Guarneri del Jesu remain the exemplars of the craft and the most valuable instruments extant: a Guarneri violin recently sold for over $3.5 million.

MUSIC PRINTING AND PUBLISHING

The other technological breakthrough that reshaped musical life was the invention of movable-type printing. Printing aided the dissemination of music and writings about music and quickly spread throughout western Europe, as publishers opened shops in other major musical centers, such as London, Paris, and Rome. Music printing made music much more accessible; publishers printed a much greater variety of music, from polyphonic choral works, cantatas, and concertos to hymnals, songs, dance tunes, and ballads. Most publishers targeted religious organizations or aristocrats, but seventeenth-century English publisher John Playford was the first to target a middle-class audience and become enormously successful.

Printing also facilitated the dissemination of books about music—most notably, theoretical treatises, practical guides to composition and performance, and encyclopedic works like Michael Praetorius's three-volume *Syntagma Musicum* (1614–1620), which remains an important resource about musical life in the early seventeenth century.

Musical Communication

The striking contrast between Hildegard's antiphon and Purcell's aria—one an unaccompanied liturgical song composed by an abbess for cloistered, in-convent use; the other a secular work with orchestral accompaniment, composed by a professional composer for public performance—highlights the enormous expansion and diversification of the audience for composed music deemed worthy of preservation.

Composers responded to these larger, more diverse audiences not only by composing works in a greater variety of genres but also by developing compositional approaches that enabled them to express more specifically the emotional message that they wished to convey. In the early sacred music that we encounter, the message is mainly in the style. In Catholic liturgical music, texts are often unintelligible (whether from great prolongation of the notes or from multiple simultaneous lines obscuring one another), which makes text expression general at best; in Lutheran hymns, the text is intelligible, but the style is deliberately simplified to facilitate congregational singing. Secular songs from the earliest surviving sources merged music with poetry of substance, and the texts were more intelligible than in sacred music.

Toward the end of the sixteenth and into the seventeenth centuries, composers became much more responsive to text. It is evident first in madrigals, polyphonic secular songs in which composers highlighted words or phrases with evocative musical figures. Opera went even further, using expressive melodic gestures to amplify the meaning of the text. Expressive impact was often more powerful in opera than in madrigals because of the dramatic setting and the focus on solo voices.

Concurrently, some composers attempted to depict events and emotions in purely instrumental music: among the works collected in early seventeenth-century British keyboard anthologies is William Byrd's *The Battell*, which contains nine sections, each purportedly describing a scene in battle. It is one of several fancifully titled works in the anthologies. By the end of the century, music theorists asserted that instrumental music could convey quite specific emotional states, or "affects," and associated particular scales, dance rhythms, instruments, and forms with such moods.

Cumulatively, these changes transformed the sound of church and court music from the ethereal sounds of Renaissance polyphony, madrigals, and relatively simple songs and dances into the Baroque arias, concertos, sonatas, and suites that are part of today's classical musical world. The music of Purcell may be over 300 years old, but its musical vocabulary is familiar in a way that the music of the madrigalists or Renaissance composers is not. We hear this transformation through many of the examples in the next unit.

Looking Ahead

Between 1000 and 1700, European music went from ancient to modern.

There is little about musical life in 1000 that would seem familiar to contemporary audiences. The music of the late Middle Ages and Renaissance that has come down to us is different from our music, in its venues, resources, musical language, and expressive intent. The sounds that we will hear—of chant, early song and dance, Josquin's mass, and even Monteverdi's opera—as beautiful as they are, belong to a distant past. Even Luther's hymn, which is still familiar, sounds different in its original version.

However, by 1700, the foundation of modern musical life was in place. Opera was a public entertainment, in Italy and elsewhere. Most of the modern orchestral instruments, including the string section, the core of the modern orchestra, were in place. The musical language of composers like Purcell and Corelli is still very much in use at the beginning of the twenty-first century. We hear music from around this time not only in the concert hall but also in restaurants, stores, and television commercials. These sounds are far more familiar than those of the previous eras. The first part of our survey highlights these changes.

There is a large body of music that we do not know nearly so much about: the music of the middle and lower classes, the music of aboriginal cultures, music from outside Europe. What this music might have sounded like is an educated guess. None of it was preserved in notation as it was performed; we have only anecdotal evidence about how it might have sounded. However, we introduce, later in this part, music that might well have been heard in the Americas during the seventeenth century: Native American drumming, African-inspired music from Cuba, and folk songs and dances from the British Isles via Canada and the United States. Folk music, especially by displaced Africans and those who emigrated from the British Isles, would influence more commercially oriented music in the centuries that follow.

UNIT 4
THE MIDDLE AGES

© Réunion des Musées Nationaux / Art Resource, NY

Learning Outcomes

After reading this unit, you will be able to do the following:

LO1 Describe monastic life in the Middle Ages.

LO2 Define chant and its three forms of text setting.

LO3 Recognize the style of an antiphon through Hildegard of Bingen's "Nunc aperuit nobis."

LO4 Become more familiar with the emergence of secular culture during the late Middle Ages.

LO5 Understand more about minstrels and troubadours, the most important secular musicians of the time.

LO6 Describe the life, poetry, and music of Guillaume de Machaut, an important fourteenth-century composer.

LO7 Analyze an example of the earliest dance music that has come down to us.

LO8 Recognize "L'homme armé," a popular song from the fifteenth century.

AMONG THE DEVELOPMENTS with the greatest impact on musical life in the Middle Ages—the roughly 500 years after the turn of the millennium (1000–1500 CE)—was the primacy of the Catholic Church, which dominated both the spiritual and the intellectual life of its members. The church preserved classical learning, first in monasteries, then in universities, and amassed great wealth that it spent lavishly on magnificent cathedrals found throughout western Europe and on music for its services. A large body of work without religious or classical themes also sprang up in the new millennium, especially in music: secular song and dance music first appeared in the thirteenth century.

CHAPTER 9

Chant and Hildegard of Bingen

"The overriding purpose of chant is to connect the human with the divine."

P erhaps the most surprising Top Five hit album of the 1990s was *Chant*, a recording of Gregorian chant by the Benedictine monks of Santo Domingo de Silos. The recording, which eventually sold over 2 million units, brought an ageless music to the attention of the modern world. In this chapter we explore chant and the world in

Did You Know?

You can hear vocal flourishes on a single syllable (melisma) not only in the songs of Mariah Carey and Beyoncé but also in ancient Gregorian chant.

which it was created, with particular focus on the life and music of Hildegard of Bingen, and consider why chant still resonates with so many listeners today.

LO1 Monastic Life in the Middle Ages

Monasteries, convents, and abbeys are places where monks and nuns live, work, and pray. In our secular, fast-paced society, the prospect of retreating from the world to devote one's life to prayer and work has not been a popular one. Although almost 68 million Catholics live in the United States, there are only about 135 monasteries and convents, and most of these religious communities are small.

Monastic life was much more popular in the Middle Ages, for both spiritual and secular reasons. For those living in medieval Europe, the central fact of life was the afterlife. Life on earth was the prelude to eternity; how you lived it determined whether you would spend that eternity in heaven or hell. For many, the best route to heaven was to live apart from the world in a community devoted in principle to poverty, chastity, and obedience. Members of a monastic community followed a particular *rule*, a stringent set of guidelines drawn up by the founder of the order; the monks of Santo Domingo de Silos still follow the rule of St. Benedict of Nursia (ca. 480–543), established 1,500 years ago. Strict adherence to the rule not only made earthly life more fulfilling but also virtually guaranteed entrance into God's heavenly kingdom.

There were also more mundane reasons for joining a monastery, which date from the fall of the Roman Empire. After the collapse of the empire, the Catholic Church gradually became the dominant institution in Europe. It was the universal religion and the

© iStockphoto.com/Tomas Navratil

© Kevin Mazur/WireImage/Getty Images

main—almost exclusive—repository of learning. Until the fourteenth century, cathedral schools, monasteries, and convents were the only places where a young person could receive an education.

It was an institution whose wealth grew through such revenue sources as landholdings, donations, dowries, and fees for joining the clergy or a religious order. And it also became a political force to be reckoned with, through its links with rulers throughout Europe and through the moral authority that it wielded, often for nonspiritual reasons.

If there was one moment that symbolized the rise in power of the church, it came on Christmas Day in 800. On that day, Pope Leo III crowned Charlemagne (742–814), who had conquered, then reunited, much of the old Roman Empire, as Holy Roman Emperor. For the rest of his reign, Charlemagne was the secular counterpart to the pope; his empire was a single political entity with a single religion. Although it did not remain united under one ruler after his death, the Holy Roman Empire would last for a millennium. The pope's coronation of Charlemagne highlights the near-indivisible bond between church and state at that time, and the rarely questioned authority of the church.

Members of the clergy enjoyed a social standing comparable to that of nobility; both were well above peasant, artisan, or tradesman status. For many, entering the clergy meant maintaining or elevating one's social status, getting an education, and living within a relatively stable, well-protected community. For noble families, a religious vocation often helped resolve inheritance issues: there was one fewer heir to share the estate. And there were few career options during the Middle Ages. As a result, many joined the clergy, though not all were fully committed to the religious life.

Still, in those monasteries where the rule was carefully observed, life centered on God. The daily routine alternated between prayer—eight times a day, in addition to Mass—and work. The periods of daily prayer, called the **Divine Office**, occurred at regular intervals of the day, from sunrise to after sunset. Following the maxim of St. Augustine "to sing is to pray twice," prayers were sung as well as spoken. Among the sung prayers were parts of the Mass, psalms, and prayers that commented on the psalms, such as the antiphon discussed later.

Among the most important work of the religious orders was copying books and music; for scribes, this was both an art and a tedious task. Monasteries typically included a library and a *scriptorium*, a room where monks or nuns would copy documents for the library. Monastery libraries have been our main source of chant and other medieval sacred music.

LO2 Chant

The music used in both the Mass and the Divine Office was **plainchant**, or simply **chant**. Several distinct chant practices developed in both western and eastern Europe during the early Christian era. However, after Charlemagne's father, King Pippen, ordered that liturgical practice follow the Roman model—an initiative that Charlemagne continued—**Gregorian chant** became the most widely used chant in western Europe. There is still debate about whether the Gregory of Gregorian chant

There is still debate about whether the Gregory of Gregorian chant is Pope Gregory I, shown here hard at work, but the name remains in common use.

Divine Office Periods of daily prayer in monasteries, which occurred at regular intervals in the day, from sunrise to after sunset

plainchant (chant) Music used in both the Mass and the Divine Office

Gregorian chant The most widely used chant in western Europe

is Pope Gregory I (Gregory the Great, 590–604) or Gregory II (715–731); despite the confusion, the name remains in common use.

Most Gregorian chant was created between the eighth and eleventh centuries. It survived only in oral tradition until the ninth century, when scribes began to notate it. We surmise that the first efforts at notation were simply reminders for those who were still learning the chants by ear. By the eleventh century, however, the notation of chant had become precise enough for modern-day scholars to reconstruct its pitches, if not its rhythms, with some accuracy, and by this time, the basic chant repertory was in place. Later chants, such as those of Hildegard, serve as fresh commentary on the established texts and chants.

Chant is pure melody. It is a single stream of pitches, sung by an individual singer or group. Most often, it is sung without accompaniment; if there is any other part, it will be a single pitch sustained by singers or instruments. Its rhythm is free; the notes of the melody do not line up with a steady beat. Because it is a single, rhythmically free melodic line, we can sense in it the close connection between speech and song.

The setting of the text generally takes one of three forms. The simplest is **syllabic**, or one note per syllable of text. A **neumatic** text setting generally has two to four notes per syllable. The most elaborate form of text setting is **melismatic**, in which a single syllable may be sustained for many notes—sometimes as many as fifty or seventy-five notes. Our example of chant features several melismatic passages.

LO3 Hildegard of Bingen

Hildegard of Bingen (1098–1179) was one of the most extraordinary women of the Middle Ages. When she was eight, her parents promised her to the church, and she entered a Benedictine abbey when she was fourteen. Eventually, she became the prioress, the nun in charge of a priory or ranking next below the abbess of an abbey, then left to found her own convent around 1150. She had an extraordinary range of talents. Her work includes volumes on science, lives of the saints, poetry, artwork, and songs. Toward the end of her life, she corresponded with both popes and princes.

Ecstatic visions, which she had experienced since the age of five, informed much of her work. She captured their essence in her poetry and music, as we hear in "Nunc aperuit nobis," an **antiphon** (a chant with

prose, not poetic, text, sung before and sometimes after a psalm) and one of seventy-seven works collected in a volume entitled *Symphonia Harmonie Celestium Revelationum (Symphony of Harmony of Heavenly Revelations).*

MELODY IN CHANT

The chant melody soars above a **drone**, a note continuously sounding throughout the piece or a large section of the piece, similar to the sound you would hear listening to music played on bagpipes. Although the chant melody occasionally dips below the drone, it never stays there for long. The melodic movement is mostly by step, with few skips to high notes. In effect, this mostly stepwise movement is speech inflection, magnified so enormously that it has taken on an identity of its own. One can almost imagine Hildegard needing to set her words to music because the words as spoken cannot project the power of her vision. Especially if we take into account the use of symbolism in medieval art, we might suggest that the drone is earthly reality and that the chant

syllabic Used to describe chant text setting having one note per syllable of text

neumatic Used to describe chant text setting that generally has two to four notes per syllable

melismatic Used to describe the most elaborate form of text setting, in which a single syllable may be sustained for many notes

antiphon Chant with prose (not poetic) text, sung before and sometimes after a psalm

drone Note continuously sounding throughout a piece or a large section of a piece

melody represents Hildegard's ecstatic state during her vision, which the text reflects.

It is the text that determines the pacing of the chant; the melody comes to rest at the ends of words and, more decisively, at the ends of phrases. The absence of a steady pulse directs our attention to the pacing of the text, where we frequently hear key syllables extended by melismas. The melismas magnify the rhythm of the text as spoken, much as the melodic flourishes magnify its inflection. Together, they project the ecstasy of Hildegard's mystical experiences.

Hildegard's antiphon, and chant in general, underscores both the close connection between speech and "pure" melody, and the notion that chant, as song, transcends speech. In this context, it is intended to open the door to the divine.

KEY, SCALE, AND MODE

As we listen to Hildegard's antiphon, we notice that the sustained tone acts as a home base for pitch. It is the starting note of the melody and of several phrases, and it is always the ending note of a phrase. The melody soars above it and swoops below it but always comes to rest on it. Because this sustained tone serves as a point of orientation for every other note in the melody—a point of departure and, even more, a point of return—we can say that in the broadest, most modern sense, this music is tonal. In this general way, *tonal* means that the other notes of the melody are understood in terms of a single referential pitch. This sense of a home tone is explicit in "Nunc aperuit nobis" because of the sustained tone; in chant with only one line, it is also present but not as persistent.

However, the chant is not tonal in the more specific modern sense of being constructed from the major or minor scale or using the chord progressions associated with it. It does use a seven-note scale identical to the major scale at the outset. However, at cadences, such as the one on the word "nobis," Hildegard makes use of a different arrangement of the seven scale tones. We refer to such alternate arrangements of seven-note (diatonic) scales as *modal scales*. At the time Hildegard composed this chant, eight modes were in use: two variants each of four basic modes. These modes gradually gave way

Hildegard of Bingen

Fast Facts

- *Dates*: 1098–1179
- *Place*: Today's western Germany
- *Reasons to remember*: Most famous female composer of chants; a gifted "woman of letters"; works include volumes on science, lives of the saints, poetry, artwork, and songs, much of it informed by ecstatic visions

© Erich Lessing / Art Resource, NY

Hildegard of Bingen receives one of her visions as the monk Voldmar peers in at her, in awe.

to the major/minor system of tonality during the late sixteenth and early seventeenth centuries. Over time, only two of the original eight modes survived in common use. The Ionian and Aeolian modes, also known as our modern major and minor scales, are still the basis for the vast majority of musical works in both Western art music and popular music.

Summary

Hildegard's antiphon has introduced us to chant, the monophonic vocal music used in the Catholic liturgy. We have encountered its salient features: free rhythm, melismatic passages, absence of harmony, and text-dictated form. We have also explored the ideas that these features are a way of using melody to transcend speech and that the function of chant is to bridge the gap between human and divine: on one level we can understand Hildegard's chant as ecstatic communion with the divine. Moreover, the fact that chant and chant-derived music were virtually the only music preserved during Hildegard's lifetime strongly suggests the central place of religion in daily life through the twelfth century. That would change in the next century, as we learn in the next chapter.

CHAPTER 10

Secular Song and Dance in France

"A vast gulf separated the sacred and the secular in the Middle Ages."

A whirlwind history of rock's early years: A bold new dance music thrills some and horrifies others. The opponents of the new music are aghast, claiming that this new dance music is a corrupting influence. Within a few years, young folksingers, inspired by an itinerant balladeer (Woody Guthrie), revive old songs and write new ones, accompanying themselves simply on a guitar. Within a few years, the new dance music has become respectable enough that everyone from the president on down is doing dances like the twist. Soon after, the simple folk songs and the new dance music come together (as Bob Dylan goes electric) to form one branch of a new, more complex, and more influential music. Among the stars of this new kind of music are singer-songwriters: those who write both words and music to their songs, then perform and record them.

If we travel back to France in the late Middle Ages, we find a similar sequence of developments, although they unfold over centuries rather than decades. We learn of troubadours, who first sang their own poems about love during the eleventh century. We find the first notated dances appearing in the thirteenth century, indicating that dance music had become sufficiently upscale to warrant preservation in notation. And in the fourteenth century we meet Guillaume de Machaut, arguably the first great singer-songwriter whose music has come down to us. All of this indicates an emergence of secular culture in France. In this chapter we consider the circumstances of this cultural secularization, then sample some of the music it produced.

Did You Know?

The practice of constructing dance music from similar-sounding modules of equal length is as old as the earliest notated dance pieces and as new as the latest techno.

LO4 Secular Culture in France

Secular culture in what is now France emerged gradually within the rigid constraints of feudalism in the first four centuries of the new millennium. Feudalism organized society around land and war. The feudal arrangement—land from a lord in exchange for loyalty from a vassal—began as a response to the devastating invasions of the Vikings and Goths after the fall of the Roman Empire. Over time, the invasions stopped, but the wars didn't. The most drawn out was the Hundred Years' War (1337–1453), an on-again, off-again series of battles involving squabbles over property rights between nobles in England and France that dated from the twelfth century.

Feudal society atrophied as those who had power worked hard to hold on to it. The nobility closed ranks; it was rare for a commoner to attain noble status. Members of the nobility preserved their power and wealth through inheritance, which presented complex, even insoluble, problems for noble fathers. It was customary for land and the wealth associated with it to pass from father to firstborn son. For daughters and remaining sons, the options were often less appealing. Some entered the clergy or joined a religious order. Noble families arranged marriages; the package included not only a bride but also a dowry. All of this complicated landholdings, as did the hierarchical structure of feudal allegiances.

Feudalism created a privileged class with time and money and made possible a new culture distinct from both the church and peasant life. One dimension of this culture was **chivalry**, the code of behavior expected of the noble class.

> **chivalry** Code of behavior expected of the medieval noble class

Although certainly shaped by church teachings, chivalry represented a set of values independent of church authority. As such, it is a sign of the gradual emergence of secular culture. Its cultural corollary was courtly love, discussed in the next section.

The other major factor in the secularization of European culture was a series of Crusades to the Holy Land, which began in the eleventh century and would continue through the end of the thirteenth century. Their intended goal was to reclaim Jerusalem for Christianity; in this respect, they were a failure. However, they dramatically increased trade, which brought wealth back home and opened new perspectives on the world for those who ventured abroad. Ironically, the Crusades, although undertaken at the urging of the pope, helped undermine church authority by making people more aware of the material world.

LOVE AND MARRIAGE IN THE MIDDLE AGES

It seems obvious to us that a couple decides to marry because they believe they are in love. So it may be surprising to discover that marrying for love is a relatively recent development, especially among the upper classes. Keep in mind that Cinderella is a fairy tale; for royalty, the reality has been closer to the sad tale of Edward VIII of England, who reigned for less than a year in 1936 before abdicating the throne so that he could marry Wallis Warfield Simpson, a divorced American commoner. The class boundaries that prohibited Edward from marrying Mrs. Simpson and retaining his throne date from the late Middle Ages. In medieval times, a relationship based on love, especially among the nobility, was more often a happy accident than a likely outcome. Political and social constraints, most prominently the use of marriage for political gain and stringent class division, presented almost insurmountable obstacles to love and its expression.

In medieval times, a relationship based on love, especially among the nobility, was more often a happy accident than a likely outcome.

courtly love Rigid medieval social protocol in which a man could think of having an adulterous relationship with a woman but could not consummate it

do with family and power than it did with love. In a society where land was the basis of wealth, marriages were used to consolidate landholdings.

The poster woman for this kind of arrangement was Eleanor of Aquitaine (1122–1204), the daughter of Duke William X of Aquitaine, whose domain was larger than that of the king of France. At fifteen, she inherited his duchy and immediately married the heir to the throne of France; two years later he became Louis VII. Their relationship was one-sided: he apparently adored her, and she apparently considered him a wimp. In 1152, she traded him in for a stronger man, Henry Plantagenet, who became Henry II of England two years later. She bore him eight children (five sons and three daughters); she had had two daughters with Louis. One of the sons became known as Richard the Lion Hearted. Other children married into families that controlled parts of modern-day Germany, Italy, and Spain. Eleanor spent much of her later years taking sides in disputes between her husband and her sons, for which she was imprisoned, and between various children and grandchildren.

Eleanor was, by all accounts, both beautiful and promiscuous. For her, love and marriage did not go hand in hand. Marriage was instead about preserving and augmenting power and influence. Bernart de Ventadorn, a troubadour employed at Eleanor's court and allegedly her lover, reputedly wrote a poem that obliquely expressed his disappointment after, while hiding in a closet, he had witnessed Eleanor's amorous encounter with another man.

The tale of Eleanor and Bernart is a perfect example of a peculiar social protocol that evolved during the Middle Ages. **Courtly love** was a rigid convention in which a man could think of having an adulterous relationship with a woman but could not consummate it. He could only imagine every aspect of an amorous relationship because circumstances—far more men than women, rigid class barriers, and arranged marriages—prevented him from ever experiencing it. A relationship based on love was usually out of the question, except in the poet's mind.

Social Barriers. Bernart's plight points up the disadvantageous position of commoners. A few might, through some special talent—in arms, music, verse,

Arranged Marriages. During the Middle Ages, marriage among the nobility typically had much more to

dancing—come to the attention of a noblewoman. They might even gain her favor and occasionally enjoy the pleasures of her intimate company, if she were so inclined. But troubadours like Bernart, even those of noble birth, were forced to conduct their affairs in secret, or only in their head, because an open relationship was not possible. The almost unbearable conflict between passion and decorum gave rise to a new set of attitudes regarding the relationship between men and women and a new way of expressing it—the poetry of the troubadours. The poems were not in Latin but in the vernacular—that is, the everyday language of a particular region.

Vernacular Language and Secular Culture

The writing of poetry in vernacular was a clear indication of the reemergence of secular culture. For centuries Latin had been the official language of the church. (It would remain so until Vatican II, which opened in 1962.) There were symbolic and practical reasons for this. The use of Latin in church affairs fostered the connection with the past, which was a central component of the church's authority. Because it was not an everyday language, it helped preserve an elite status for those who used it, both in and outside religious orders. Moreover, it was a crucial unifying element for the church. Mass would sound much the same in any part of western and central Europe, and it provided a common language for conducting church affairs. Having a "universal" language was especially appropriate because so many more languages and dialects existed in Europe than do now. In France alone, three language families were used during the Middle Ages: the Romance languages (Parisian French, Occitan/Provencal), Germanic (Burgundian), and Celtic (Breton). These subdivided into numerous local dialects, most of which have been lost.

Because of the influence of the church in secular civil affairs, Latin was also the language of scholarship, law, and politics. It was used in universities, monastery schools, and cathedral schools and in serious discourse: a relevant example is that music treatises of the Middle Ages were written in Latin. In both sacred and secular domains, Latin was a church-imposed element of control.

In this context, we can see the use of the vernacular to express intimate and personal feelings as a bold if inevitable step in the emancipation of secular culture. It would lead to a flowering of literature in the fourteenth century: notably Dante's *Divine Comedy*, Chaucer's *Canterbury Tales*, and Boccaccio's *Decameron*.

LO5 Minstrels and Troubadours

The music of the emerging secular culture included song and dance. The musicians most responsible for this new secular music were minstrels and troubadours. When we think of minstrels, we may recollect—with a cringe—the blackface entertainers so popular in America (and Europe) during the latter part of the nineteenth century. And when we conjure up the image of a troubadour, we may call to mind a happy-go-lucky songster: a fellow who travels around singing his own poetry to music. For the forerunners of these more contemporary entertainers, life and work were quite different.

The Minstrel

Minstrels were multifaceted entertainers.

During much of the Middle Ages, **minstrels** were multifaceted entertainers. They might sing or play an instrument, recite poems and tell stories, dance, juggle, do acrobatic routines, and more; many were skilled in more than one area. However, by the thirteenth century, "minstrel" had acquired a more specific connotation: it typically referred to an instrumentalist, usually attached to a court. Among their numerous duties, minstrels played for dancing and often accompanied singers.

Early in their recorded history, minstrels lived on the fringes of society. Unlike serfs and vassals, clergy and the religious, they were not bound to a higher authority. They were often itinerant—the legendary "wandering minstrels." They moved from place to place in response to the demand for their services. Church authorities routinely condemned them and the music that they produced.

> **minstrel** Multifaceted entertainer who, by the thirteenth century, was typically an instrumentalist usually attached to a court

Over time, however, many minstrels found steady employment as part of the court retinue; they essentially became the house band for a particular noble. Like the cooks and grooms, they were servants, usually paid accordingly, but some enjoyed the favor of their masters. Their more elevated status parallels the greater value placed on secular music.

THE TROUBADOUR

The original **troubadours**, poets who wrote and sang about courtly love, lived throughout France—especially Provence, in southern France—and came from the upper and lower classes. The man generally regarded as the first troubadour was William IX of Aquitaine, a duke and the grandfather of Eleanor. By contrast, Bernart de Ventadorn, generally regarded as the finest of the troubadour poets, was reputedly the son of a castle baker. Regardless of their station, troubadours needed to cultivate refinement, courtesy, and skill to obtain success.

The troubadours put women on a pedestal, an unaccustomed height for them prior to this time. It went beyond the idealized portraits of them in the poems; troubadour poetry gave expression to the atmosphere of cultivation and grace that became an essential aspect of courtly life during the latter part of the Middle Ages. This newfound attention to women, especially those of noble birth, emerged as the invasions from the north, east, and south tapered off. With survival no longer such a pressing issue, court members had leisure time; the dynamics of courtly love helped regulate social interactions.

Troubadour poems typically portray the agonies and ecstasies of an idealized love. They are concerned above all with the sensations of romantic love—infatuation, despair, sublimation—and absolute fidelity, regardless of the circumstances. The affair that the poet describes and longs for may never take place; the entire relationship may take place at a distance. Indeed, one famous if fictional account of the life and sweet death of the troubadour Jaufre Rudel tells how Rudel fell in love with a countess after hearing of her from pilgrims. He journeyed to her, became mortally ill on the trip, and died in her arms.

We can see troubadour poetry as a response to the influence of the church and the realities of the social world of the nobility. In its emphasis on romantic,

troubadours Poet-musician who wrote and sang about courtly love

even erotic, love, it seems at odds with the emphasis on chastity and the denial of the body that was central to official church doctrine. Yet, in content and tone, troubadour poems run parallel to the love of the Virgin Mary portrayed in devotional writings around the same time. Troubadour poetry also affords those who wrote it and those who read it a way to come to terms with the fact that a real relationship with a desirable woman was often not possible.

Troubadour poetry would influence lyric poetry and the music that accompanied it for generations. Among those it strongly influenced was the fourteenth-century poet-composer Guillaume de Machaut.

LO6 Guillaume de Machaut and Secular Song

For the last half of the twentieth century or so, it has been almost an article of faith that musicians deliver a complete package: they write the words and the song, then perform it, either individually or as part of a group. However, only a very few of these singer-songwriters have enjoyed comparable acclaim as poet and musician: Leonard Cohen, Joni Mitchell, and, above all, Bob Dylan stand out in this regard. In classical music, it is the rare composer who sets his own words; most successful song composers use preexisting poems rather than their own words as inspiration. It is with this frame of reference that we view the unique career of Guillaume de Machaut.

LIFE

We know little of the early life of Guillaume de Machaut (ca. 1300–1377). We do know that he became a priest and spent his life in service, first to King John of Luxembourg through 1340, then to the cathedral at Reims. Although attached to the cathedral, he was largely free of everyday priestly responsibilities, so he was able to write and compose. By this time, he had acquired an extensive list of patrons.

Machaut stands apart from every other musician of the time, for several reasons. He was equally renowned as a poet and a composer; indeed, much of his work consists of poems without music. He was the first musician identified as the composer of a complete mass, the *Mass of Notre Dame*. Machaut is among the very first composers for whom we have a substantial record

Guillaume de Machaut

Fast Facts

- *Dates:* ca. 1300–1377
- *Place:* France
- *Reasons to remember:* Equally renowned as a poet and a composer; one of the first singer-songwriters and the most esteemed composer in France during the fourteenth century; the first musician identified as the composer of a complete mass, the *Mass of Notre Dame*

of composition; he spent much of his later years preparing definitive versions of his music. And we know him better than other composers of the time because his writings contain personal commentary. He worked primarily in service to John of Luxembourg and, after John's death in battle in 1346, other patrons.

Although the age of the troubadours had passed by the time Machaut was born, the idea of courtly love was still very much in the air. The majority of his poems and compositions, including the rondeau we hear next, express the refined sensibility that we associate with courtly love.

THE RONDEAU

The rondeau was the oldest of the song forms popular in fourteenth-century France. Its roots date from dance songs from the twelfth and thirteenth centuries. Machaut revised the **rondeau** to become a multipart song with a recurrent refrain. These songs had vernacular

LISTEN UP!

CD 1:2

Guillaume de Machaut, "Puis qu'en oubli" (mid-fourteenth century)

Takeaway point: Melody made up of several short phrases, with homophonic accompaniment

Style: Late medieval

Form: Modified strophic form

Genre: Rondeau

Instruments: Voice and viols

Context: Song for the court expressing courtly love

texts that described some aspect of love. In the rondeau presented here, the poet-admirer bemoans his fate, maintaining his fidelity to a woman who is so indifferent to him that she does not remember who he is.

rondeau Multipart song with a recurrent refrain

mensural notation Notation developed in the mid-thirteenth century that, for the first time, indicated specific rhythmic relationships as well as pitch

LO7 The Emergence of Instrumental Music

Dancing seems to be about as ancient as singing. Both the Bible and the writings of Homer make reference to it. In ancient Greece and Rome, it became not only an elegant art but also an elaborate, often erotic entertainment for all social classes. We know that such dances typically had instrumental accompaniment, but we know virtually nothing about either the dance or the music for it. The same holds true for dance in the Middle Ages. Folk dancing almost certainly remained a part of life for serfs. Eventually, it also became part of court life; the most compelling evidence is the recording of dances in manuscript, beginning around 1250. The first preserved instrumental music is music for dancing.

DANCE MUSIC

Although we are glad to have these earliest examples of dance music, we have only a sketchy picture of what the dances looked like and at best an imperfect understanding of the way the music for them sounded. The first treatises on dance did not appear until the fifteenth century, and the notated music typically has only a single line. There are no clues to instrumentation, tempo, dynamics, texture, and other features; there is just the melody.

Mensural Notation. Almost all of the early dance pieces make use of **mensural notation**; that is, notation that indicates specific rhythmic relationships as well as pitch. Mensural notation was a thirteenth-century innovation, used to write down dances and more complex polyphonic sacred music. In the case of dance music, it was absolutely necessary because the dances have a strong, definite rhythm.

Reconstructing Dance Music. In the absence of notated instructions for performance beyond the melody, performers of this music must try to infer its sound from extramusical sources. These sources are as diverse as paintings and illustrations, poetry and literature, treatises, and court records, which tell us, for instance, how many musicians were engaged for a particular social function. The musicians on the recording used here surrounded the melody with other compatible and appropriate sounds.

The Estampie. The **estampie** was a dance popular in France and Italy from the twelfth through the fourteenth centuries. In aristocratic circles, it was probably a couples dance. We can only speculate about the steps and the origin of the name; scholars offer several possibilities. We do know that it is the first dance identified by name in musical sources.

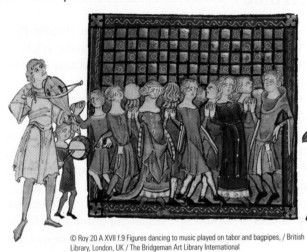

© Roy 20 A XVII f.9 Figures dancing to music played on tabor and bagpipes, / British Library, London, UK / The Bridgeman Art Library International

Like other medieval dances, the estampie appeared first as a sung poem; the earliest examples have words but not music. There are two possible interpretations of this circumstance: the poems were set to preexisting estampies known only in oral tradition, or the sung estampies eventually became dance tunes. Both were likely, since at least one troubadour song was set to an existing estampie, and documentary evidence suggests that the songs of Machaut and others were also performed as instrumental pieces.

The earliest estampies were lively dances in a fast, simple triple meter. Their melodies comprised several groups of short phrases. Typically, each phrase group is heard twice, and each group ends with a refrain, a device related to both sacred and secular song. We hear the last of a set of eight estampies included in a late thirteenth-century manuscript, whose title (*Manuscrit du roi*, or *The King's Manuscript*) denotes its noble origins.

This medieval dance

estampie Dance for couples, popular in France and Italy from the twelfth through the fourteenth centuries

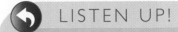

LISTEN UP!

CD 1:3
Anonymous, "La uitime estampie real"

Takeaway point: Sprightly dance with simple rhythms in triple meter

Style: Medieval

Form: Multisectional, with instrumental refrain

Genre: Estampie

Instruments: Flutes, shawm, bagpipes, dulcimer, drums

Context: Dance music for French court

sounds both strange and familiar at the same time. The sounds of authentic instruments date the style to the Middle Ages; so does the style of the melody—fairly quick notes moving mainly by step in a narrow range. However, the practice of building dance music from short segments and linking them with a refrain is still a common practice in contemporary dance music. And we can view the tabor (drum) accompaniment as an early ancestor of the contemporary rhythm section.

Although it is one of only a few examples, this estampie conveys in notation what was almost certainly the case in oral tradition: the presence of vigorous dance music in the courts of the twelfth and thirteenth centuries. The fact that it was notated underscores the growing independence of secular culture from church control.

Summary

When we compare the two examples in this chapter with Hildegard's chant, we can sense how vast a gulf separated the sacred and the secular in the Middle Ages. Hildegard's chant—streams of melody spinning out over a drone—seems to want to escape the world. The estampie, with its strong, definite rhythms, is very much of this world; we can imagine nobles of both sexes spinning around the dance floor. We can hear the influence of dance music in the subtler but still definite rhythms of Machaut's rondeau. We are aware from the lyric that the song is about love, the most compelling of earthly experiences, and we find the lyric set to a tuneful melody with a simple, clearly outlined form. The contrasts with Hildegard's chant could hardly be more fundamental: no instruments versus instruments; free rhythm versus steady beat; soaring melodic lines versus short phrases repeated frequently; virtually formless versus clear sectional form.

These three examples must represent for us about four hundred years of music. Necessarily, our picture of musical life in the Middle Ages is incomplete. Yet we can begin to understand the difference between sacred and secular music and the cultural separation that the music implies.

cantus firmus
Preexisting melody that serves as the starting point for a polyphonic composition

PEOPLE'S MUSIC 1

"L'homme armé"

"'L'homme armé' became a musical symbol of the Christian man-at-arms, familiar and potent enough to be meaningful even when stripped of its lyrics and placed in a radically new context."

In our world of instant classics, the average stay on the top of the pop charts is less than a month; the majority of pop hits last only a week or two at number one. Only a small percentage of hit songs survive a generation; for every song like Nirvana's "Smells Like Teen Spirit" that remains popular today, there are dozens of songs like Timmy T's "One More Try," also a 1991 platinum hit, that no longer enjoy a similar popularity. So, it may be hard to imagine a song staying current for almost two centuries. However, that was the case with the late medieval French song "L'homme armé."

Did You Know?

"Take Me Out to the Ball Game" has remained one of the most popular songs from the turn of the twentieth century because of its use at baseball games.

LO8 "L'homme armé"

As its title and opening words suggest, "L'homme armé" is a French song about an armed man. We don't know who composed it, and we aren't sure of the date of its earliest use in a composed work. We do know

that sometime after 1450 it began to appear as a **cantus firmus**—a preexisting melody serving as the starting point for polyphonic compositions—in masses by numerous composers. It is likely that the song predates its earliest use by at least a few decades, because its popularity was one of the key reasons for quoting it, and in that era, it would have taken some time for a song to become popular. It appeared around 1475 as an independent work in a collection of secular songs. Composers continued to use it for more than a century; it appeared in over thirty-five masses composed in the fifteenth and sixteenth centuries. The fact that composers used secular melodies in sacred music was not in itself unusual; early Renaissance composers occasionally wove popular melodies into their masses. However, "L'homme armé" occurs almost ten times more frequently than any other popular tune of the time. Its popularity had less to do with its inherent musical interest than with its significance as a musical symbol.

"L'HOMME ARMÉ": WORDS AND MUSIC

"L'homme armé" has come down to us in several forms: woven into extensive and elaborate polyphonic settings, highlighted in the three-voice setting found in the first existing secular version of the song, and as a monophonic song, the way people would have most often heard it during the fifteenth and sixteenth centuries.

The lyric of "L'homme armé" consists of a single stanza:

The man, the man, the armed man:
the armed man is to be feared.

Everywhere the cry has gone out.
Everyone should arm himself with
a breastplate of iron.

The man, the man, the armed man:
the armed man is to be feared.

The words simply make a statement; there is no time to tell a long, drawn-out story. The vigorous, tuneful melody supports the song's martial theme, one familiar to people in a society where war was a constant. The style of the melody would also have been familiar to fifteenth-century folk; one can imagine men belting it out in a tavern or singing it while going off to battle.

Why does a song about battle find its way into so many sacred compositions? *In The Maze and the Warrior*, a fascinating study of symbols in medieval and Renaissance Europe, music scholar Craig Wright offers a compelling explanation: the song became a symbol of the Christian warrior.

Melody as Symbol

Melody is typically the most distinctive feature of a musical work. For this reason, memorable melodic material can acquire extramusical associations: we experience this in advertising jingles and television theme music, church hymns and national anthems. The melody may be appropriate to its symbolic purpose, as is the case of "God Save the King," the British national anthem. Or it may not: the tune for the American national anthem, "The Star-Spangled Banner," was originally a drinking song. In either case, the symbolic meaning comes from its function, not from its inherent musical qualities.

Holy Wars and a Holy Warrior

In a country that has insisted on the strict separation of church and state, the notion of a holy war often seems to be literally a foreign concept, seen from a distance in the constant turmoil between Muslims and Jews in the Middle East and the ongoing clashes between Protestants and Catholics in Ireland. But none of this is comparable to the holy wars of the eight crusades undertaken between 1095 and 1272.

The Crusades. In 1095, the pope proclaimed a holy war—a crusade—to reclaim Jerusalem from the Muslims. Christians recaptured Jerusalem in 1099 but could not maintain control. Seven subsequent crusades over the next two centuries also ended in failure, as Muslims reclaimed Christian territories. The fall of Constantinople, the center of eastern Christendom, to the Turks in 1453 added insult to injury. Although the Crusades failed to achieve their goal, they nourished the idea of the righteous warrior.

Chivalry. The word *chivalry* derives from the French word *cheval*, meaning "horse." Originally it identified knights—that is, mounted men-of-arms—as opposed to the foot soldiers recruited from the peasantry. By the twelfth century, the term referred not only to the knight but also to the honorable and courteous conduct expected of a knight of the noble class. At least in ideal circumstances, nobility referred to both a social class and a set of values. The chivalrous code of conduct helped the nobility justify endless wars, either against the Muslims or against each other. Those who followed the code could place themselves above those who raped and pillaged the conquered.

The Armed Man. Given the active role of the church in both the Crusades and numerous territorial

In the religious art of the period—paintings, stained glass, altars, illuminations, even musical manuscripts— we find St. Michael, the personification of the Christian warrior, protected by a breastplate of iron, or Christ offering bread and wine to a fully armed man.

disputes, it is not surprising that the noble knight would gain a spiritual analogue: the Christian warrior. The spiritual counterpart to the holy wars— indeed, their spiritual dimension—was the war between good and evil. Good Christians might enlist the aid of the archangel St. Michael, the leader of the heavenly hosts and protector of both Jews and Christians, or even of Christ himself, in their battles against Satan.

In the Middle Ages, the most powerful symbol of the warrior was his armor. It covered him from head to toe—the breastplate of iron mentioned in the lyric was just one of his many pieces of equipment. As the militant and the spiritual merged during the Middle Ages, armor identified both the knight and the Christian soldier.

"L'homme armé" became a musical symbol of the Christian man-at-arms, familiar and potent enough to be meaningful even when stripped of its lyrics and placed in a radically new context. In the next chapter we will hear such an occurrence in a movement from a mass by the early Renaissance composer Josquin des Prez.

ABA form Three-part form featuring an opening section, a contrasting middle section, and the repetition of the opening section

LISTEN UP!

CD 1:4

Anonymous, "L'homme armé" (early fifteenth century?)

Takeaway point: Vigorous melody supporting martial lyric

Style: Late medieval

Form: **ABA form** (three-part form featuring an opening section, a contrasting middle section, and the repetition of the opening section)

Genre: Chanson

Instruments: Male voices

Context: Aural symbol of the Christian warrior

KEYS TO MEDIEVAL MUSIC

Key Concepts

1. **Multiple styles.** Medieval music is not one style but several. Sacred music, secular vocal music, and secular instrumental music are decidedly different from each other. Medieval sacred and instrumental music are opposites in some respects: free-flowing melody versus short phrases with a definite, repetitive rhythm. These differences diminish by the end of the era, but the divisions between sacred and secular, and vocal and instrumental, are still evident.

2. **Multiple centuries.** Our overview of medieval music effectively covers over three centuries, from the 1100s to the 1400s. During this time, both sacred and secular music evolved considerably, from monophonic chant and secular song through sophisticated counterpoint and harmony.

3. **Multiple performance possibilities.** The medieval musical scores that have come down to us offer only the sketchiest clues to such details of performance as instrumentation, dynamics, tempo and rhythmic nuance, and performing style. As a result, performers of early music try to reconstruct performance traditions from a variety of indirect sources, such as paintings, documents, and instruments. Their interpretations may lead to widely divergent versions of the same material.

Key Features

1. **Ad hoc instrumentation.** About the closest thing to a constant in medieval instrumentation is vocalists singing the most prominent part in vocal music. Other parts could be sung or played by any instrument. Instruments could be added to provide a drone or rhythmic support.

2. **Modal music.** Sacred and secular music use modes, seven-note scales in which the order of half- and whole steps differs from that heard in major and minor scales.

3. **Every part for itself.** Polyphonic medieval music followed several paths: elaborate parts in free or measured rhythm over a slow-moving tenor; parts moving in the same rhythm; one active part, with the rest in simpler rhythms. In all options, there is often the sense that the parts were conceived layer by layer. The parts are generally consonant on the beats and follow predictable cadences, but there is little exchange between parts until the end of the era.

4. **Restricted rhythmic options.** The most common rhythmic options are either the largely undifferentiated but unmeasured flow of chant or measured rhythm typically formed by simple, repetitive rhythmic patterns.

5. **"Empty" harmonies.** The chords formed by the alignment of multiple parts often sound "empty" because they lack the middle note of a typical triad. Three-note chords become increasingly common by the end of the era.

 **Music Concept Check**

To assist you in recognizing its distinctive features, we present an interactive demo of medieval music in CourseMate and the eBook.

Key Terms

1. **chant.** A monophonic vocal music in a free rhythm, used for the Catholic liturgy and divine office.

"Having the music integrated with the eBook . . . awesome!"
Samantha Williams, student, Metropolitan State College

"I like the idea [of the eBook]. People nowadays have their laptops everywhere and having access to the book is great."
Shaan Duggal, student, Boston University

We know that no two students read in quite the same way. Some of you do a lot of your reading online.

To help you take your reading **outside the covers** of **MUSIC,** each new text comes with access to the exciting learning environment of an interactive eBook containing **live links to:**

- **Active Listening Guides**
- **Streaming music**
- **Demos of musical concepts**
- **iTunes, Rhapsody, and YouTube playlists**

To access the eBook and many other resources, visit CourseMate at **www.cengagebrain.com**

UNIT 5
THE
RENAISSANCE

© A Choir of Angels, 1459 (oil on oak), Marmion, Simon (fl. 1450-89) / National Gallery, London, UK / The Bridgeman Art Library International

Learning Outcomes

After reading this unit, you will be able to do the following:

LO1 Recognize the main features of Renaissance polyphony.

LO2 Understand the function of sacred music, in particular polyphonic music, in the late Middle Ages and early Renaissance.

LO3 List the parts of the Catholic Mass that are typically set to music, and hear a mass movement set by Josquin des Prez.

LO4 Understand how, during the Protestant Reformation, Martin Luther connected to Christian believers by adapting secular song for religious purposes.

LO5 Describe the madrigal, its history in Italy and England, its sound, and its social function.

LO6 Understand Elizabethan solo song, the instrument that typically accompanied it, and the use of song in theatrical productions.

LO7 Identify the sounds of Renaissance instruments and their roles within a chamber ensemble.

THE SIXTEENTH CENTURY was a glorious century for singing. A wealth of great vocal music came from all over western Europe. Polyphonic motets and settings of the Catholic Mass stand out as a high point in contrapuntal composition, and hymns for congregational singing spawned a new tradition of religious song. The madrigal, which flourished in the latter part of the century, represented a new kind of secular polyphonic vocal music, one in which the music often responded specifically to poetry of high quality. Simpler but appealing songs with lute accompaniment also appeared toward the end of the century, as well as instrumental settings of them. Music printing, begun in 1501, made all of this music much more accessible.

CHAPTER 11

Josquin des Prez and Renaissance Polyphony

"The effect is of voices weaving together to produce a rich tapestry of sound."

Meet Josquin des Prez (1445?–1521), the most famous composer that you've probably never heard of. But music scholars, students of sacred music, and fans of early music certainly know of Josquin, perhaps the most respected composer of the fifteenth and sixteenth centuries. Although born somewhere in Burgundy (now northeastern France), Josquin—who, like Elvis and unlike almost every other composer of distinction, is familiarly known by his first name rather than his family name—was an international figure who held positions in France and Italy, including an extended stay at the papal chapel (ca. 1489–1495). He enjoyed the admiration of his peers. His music was well known and highly regarded by musicians and commentators, both during his lifetime and for more than a century after.

Did You Know?

The brief quotation of "L'homme armé" in Josquin's mass is similar to hip-hop sampling. Both involve putting familiar fragments from existing material in a drastically different context.

LO1 Renaissance Polyphony

Josquin's music epitomizes Renaissance polyphony, a style of composition that flourished throughout most of the fifteenth and sixteenth centuries. Renaissance polyphony represents a high point in the evolution of contrapuntal writing, which had begun at least 500 years earlier with simple drones set against a chant melody. The majority of Renaissance polyphonic music was composed for liturgical use, in the Mass and other religious celebrations. In this chapter, we briefly trace the early evolution of polyphony, speculate about why it developed only in Catholic Europe, and consider the Kyrie from a mass by Josquin that incorporates the "L'homme armé" tune.

POLYPHONY AND COUNTERPOINT

The word *polyphony*, which you first read about in Chapter 5, comes from two Greek roots: *poly*, "many" (as in *polygon*, a many-sided geometric shape); and *phonos*, "sound" or "voice" (as in *phonograph*). The word *counterpoint* comes from two Latin words: *contra*, "against" (as in *contrary*); and *punctus*, "point," a word used in medieval times to identify musical notes. Counterpoint thus means literally "note against note."

"Polyphonic" can denote any texture with more than one voice—as opposed to the monophonic (single-voiced) texture of music like "L'homme armé." However, as it is most widely used now, "polyphonic" identifies textures in which two or more parts have comparable melodic independence and interest. By this definition, none of the four previous examples qualifies as polyphonic, even though all but "L'homme armé"

Josquin des Prez

Fast Facts

- *Dates:* 1445?–1521

- *Place:* Burgundy (now northeastern France)

- *Reasons to remember:* The most esteemed composer of the early sixteenth century and a master of Renaissance polyphony

IOSQVINVS PRATENSIS.

imitation Polyphonic technique in which other parts restate—imitate—a melodic idea soon after its first presentation

have more than one part, because the supporting parts are not particularly interesting or independent: mainly drones (Hildegard's antiphon and the estampie) or slow-moving harmonies (Machaut's rondeau).

Counterpoint is the compositional procedure; polyphony is the result.

Counterpoint is the practice of combining melodically interesting parts. This is often done according to well-established practice; aspiring composers often study sixteenth- and eighteenth-century counterpoint. We might describe the relationship between counterpoint and polyphony this way: Counterpoint is the compositional procedure; polyphony is the result.

Early Counterpoint

The making of music in parts began simply. The first notated efforts at combining voices, which date from the ninth century, generally took one of two forms: a drone added to a chant melody, as we heard in Hildegard's chant, or voices moving in parallel motion, as we hear today in rock guitar riffs harmonized with power chords. In either case, the subordinate voices have no rhythmic interest or independence. The first steps toward true independent voices took two forms: parts with different melodic contours but identical rhythms;

The making of music in parts began simply.

or an embellished, often melismatic, part against a slower-moving one. In either case, the rhythm was unmeasured, that is, without a steady and predictable beat, as in chant.

By the twelfth century, composers had begun to notate measured rhythms. Multipart music included not only works like Machaut's rondeau, in which one part is dominant, but also two-, three-, and four-voice works in which each voice had a different melodic shape and a different—occasionally *quite* different—rhythm. Often, one voice—the tenor (which derives from the Latin word *tenere*, "to hold")—would move in slow values while the other voices danced around it at a much quicker pace. In the music of the thirteenth and fourteenth centuries, rhythm distinguished one part from its neighbors, either because it moved at a much different pace or because different parts used different rhythmic patterns. Although the harmonies created when the parts lined up rhythmically were almost always consonant, there was often little sense that the parts blended together. Indeed, in numerous instances not only did each part have its own text but the texts were also in different languages! That would change in the fifteenth century.

LO2 The Innovations of Renaissance Polyphony

The use of two distinctly different approaches in early polyphonic composition underscores the challenge faced by composers of sacred music: how to translate the flow of monophonic chant into music for two or more parts while maintaining the rhythmic and harmonic coordination necessary for effective performance. The decorative elaborations of a slow-moving chant melody maintained the rhythmic flexibility of chant but made more than the most rudimentary coordination between parts almost impossible. More measured rhythms make possible more intricate coordination among the parts but sacrifice the rhythmic suppleness of chant. Not until the early Renaissance did composers find ways to merge these contrasting approaches.

The major innovation in Renaissance polyphony was the distribution of rhythmically and melodically distinctive material among all of the parts. This is most obvious in the use of **imitation**, where other parts restate—imitate—a melodic idea soon after its first presentation. (If you've ever sung a round, like "Frère Jacques" or "Row, Row, Row Your Boat," you've experienced a very specific kind of imitation.) However, even when imitation is not used, there is a consistency in the melodic material among the parts. The effect is of voices weaving together to produce a rich tapestry of sound. They mesh into beautiful harmonies yet flow seamlessly, without the obvious marking of time in at least one part. It was as if Renaissance composers had created the earthly counterpart to the celestial harmonies of choirs of angels, which figured so prominently in medieval Christian theology. We hear these sounds in a movement from a mass setting by Josquin that quotes "L'homme armé."

© An illuminated missal, from Bressanone, in the Tyrol, 15th century (vellum) Private Collection/ The Bridgeman Art Library

The medieval practice of manuscript illumination parallels early counterpoint, in that both involved the elaborate decoration of an enormously distended sacred text. In music, the sacred text was the chant found in the tenor part; each note of the tenor was prolonged, while one or more parts wove decoratively around it. In art, the sacred text was scripture: the first letter of the passage was drawn much larger than the subsequent letters, and it was colored and typically surrounded with images and other decoration.

LO3 Music for the Catholic Mass

The listening example for this chapter is the Kyrie from Josquin's mass *Missa l'homme armé sexti toni* (*Mass of the Armed Man in the Sixth Tone*). The mass is one of two in which Josquin quotes the famous "L'homme armé" tune. The Kyrie is one of five movements included in a complete setting of the mass.

THE MASS

The heart of the Catholic liturgy is the Mass (the word *mass* comes from *missa*, the Latin word for "dismissal"; the celebrant said or sang the phrase "Ite, missa est" to mark the end of the service). The Mass consists of two parts: the liturgy of the word, which consists mainly of readings from scripture; and the liturgy of the Eucharist, in which the celebrant and the congregation symbolically relive Christ's death and resurrection. In both the liturgy of the word and the liturgy of the Eucharist, there are parts that change daily (Mass is said every day in most parishes) and parts that do not change. The **proper** comprises the changing parts of the Mass; the **ordinary** comprises the unchanging parts.

> **proper** Parts of the Mass that change from day to day
>
> **ordinary** Unchanging parts of the Mass

THE FIVE MASS MOVEMENTS

The five parts of the Mass used in musical settings are the Kyrie, Gloria, Credo, Sanctus, and Agnus Dei. All come from the ordinary; each takes its name from the first words of the text used in the Mass: "Kyrie eleison" (Greek for "Lord have mercy"); "Gloria in excelsis Deo" (Glory to God in the highest); "Credo in unum deum" (I believe in one God); "Sanctus, Sanctus, Sanctus" (Holy, Holy, Holy); and "Agnus Dei" (Lamb of God). The Kyrie and Gloria belong to the liturgy of the word. The Credo is the bridge between the liturgy of the word and the liturgy of the Eucharist, and the Sanctus and Agnus Dei occur shortly before communion, the part of the Mass when celebrant and congregation partake of the bread and wine.

The texts vary widely in length and content. The Kyrie is the shortest: three 2-word phrases. The Credo, which is a profession of the central tenets of Catholicism, is the longest—over 160 words in Latin. The Gloria, a hymn of praise, is the next longest. The Agnus Dei also contains just three phrases—each begins with the phrase "Lamb of God, who takes away the sins of the world." The Sanctus is also a hymn of praise but not as lengthy as the Gloria.

SYMBOLISM IN MUSIC FOR THE MASS

The heart of the Mass is the transubstantiation. Shortly before communion, the celebrant performs a highly ritualized ceremony, transubstantiation, in which Catholics believe the bread and wine are literally transformed into the body and blood of Christ. That the

The heart of the mass is the transubstantiation.

transubstantiation occurs is a central article of faith for Catholics. It must be an act of faith because the outward appearance of the bread (the host) and wine does not change.

The challenge for composers like Josquin was to create music that conveyed a comparable message. As in the Mass, they could begin with everyday materials, in this case a popular tune of the day. And they could, through divinely inspired art, transubstantiate it into heavenly music. The tune they used most frequently was "L'homme armé."

"L'homme armé" fused into a single symbol the two most pervasive facts of life in the Middle Ages: religion and war. Recall that both were constants, and both often came together, most notably in the Crusades. The image of the Christian warrior was among the most powerful symbols of the era, especially because the constant wars on earth mirrored the more important and even more constant war between good and evil, heaven and hell.

Setting this song within a polyphonic mass movement, a sound and style that strives to connect with celestial music, in effect transubstantiates the song into a spiritual symbol. We hear this in the Kyrie from Josquin's *Mass in the Sixth Tone* next.

Summary

Josquin's mass movement exemplifies the culmination of five centuries of musical evolution: from the simplest of beginnings—drones and parallel motion—polyphonic composition evolved into the richly woven tapestries
of sound characteristic of Renaissance polyphony. In the compositions of Josquin and his contemporaries, music for the Catholic liturgy reaches a pinnacle: arguably, no music before or since better expresses the Catholic understanding of the divine.

Josquin began his Kyrie by quoting the familiar "L'homme armé" melody, which served simultaneously as a melodic hook (because his listeners would recognize the melody) and as a symbol (because the words of the melody would call to mind the Christian warrior). By transforming it so drastically, Josquin essentially converted mundane musical material into sacred sounds.

That sacred compositions such as Josquin's *Mass in the Sixth Tone* would quote familiar melodies hints at a key feature of sacred polyphony: the *style is also a symbol*. The overall sound is quite consistent from work to work; the tunes that composers quoted helped distinguish one from the next. Imparting an individual character to a particular work is, at best, a secondary concern. The overriding objective is to present the text of the Mass ordinary in elevated musical language. In this respect, Renaissance polyphony is the multivoice analogue to chant. Both use singing to transcend the limitations of speech; in polyphony, it assumes a far richer and more complex form.

ABC Form A three-part form in which each section is different

Lutheran Chorale

"What began five hundred years ago as the musical branch of the Reformation movement in Germany has been standard practice in Christian churches ever since."

"Da Preachin Puerto Rican," eD-Die [*sic*] Velez, an ordained minister who hosts the nationally syndicated Holy Hip Hop Radio show, describes the goal of Holy Hip Hop: "We're trying to get like a . . . not a new message, but a new flavor of the same message." Velez's message resonates better on the street than it does in mainline churches, which prefer congregational hymns, some of them dating back half a millennium. But despite their obvious differences, holy hip-hop and congregational hymn singing sprang from the same impulse: to connect to Christian believers by adapting secular song for religious purposes. This practice took root almost 500 years ago as part of the Protestant Reformation.

LO4 Luther and the Hymn

Martin Luther (1483–1546) was the father of both the Reformation—the Protestant reform movement that swept sixteenth-century northern Europe—and Protestant congregational singing. Luther, like almost everyone in western Europe at the time, was raised Catholic. He would have grown up hearing the Mass said or sung in Latin, not in the language of the congregation. Especially in the major churches, singing would be the work of a choir, not a creation of the people. Luther sought to close the distance between those who said or sang the Mass and those who heard it. He did so by encouraging hymn singing in the vernacular and by composing

Did You Know?

English carols like "Greensleeves," which appeared around 1580, are still-familiar examples of tuneful songs with religious themes.

hymns and hymn tunes himself. Several, including "Ein' feste Burg ist unser Gott" ("A Mighty Fortress Is Our God"), are still familiar.

Even as the Protestant Reformation gathered momentum, Catholic liturgical music was reaching its artistic peak. The music of Josquin des Prez, at the end of the fifteenth century, and that of Palestrina, William Byrd, and others, at the end of the sixteenth century, frame the glory years of Renaissance sacred music. The masses and motets of these and other composers remain among the finest examples of their kind.

However, theirs was music for an elite. Churches subsidized both composers and the choirs that sang their music. The music itself was richly contrapuntal, often with five or six lines—or more—woven together. The text wasn't really intelligible to the people, not only because of its counterpoint but also because of its extensive use of melisma. Some motets and masses were based on familiar tunes, but the tunes were typically difficult to pick out from the contrapuntal lines in which they were nested.

Luther was especially well qualified to bring a new kind of music into his liturgical reforms. As a boy, he sang well enough to earn free room and board at school. He was apparently a skilled performer on both the flute and the lute, and had some knowledge of music theory. During his formative years, he heard and admired the music of Renaissance polyphonists, including Josquin des Prez, whose music he described as "as free as the song of the finch." However, in composing music for his newly reformed liturgy, he turned to secular song for inspiration, and perhaps more.

MUSIC FROM THE PEOPLE

Carol-like religious songs and secular folk songs were among Luther's sources and models. So, too, were the poems and songs of the *Meistersingers*, German lyric poets of the fourteenth through sixteenth centuries, most notably Hans Sachs, Luther's contemporary. We presume that Luther composed many of his hymn tunes, including "Ein' feste Burg," often using existing songs as models (some scholars think that Luther's hymn was inspired by one of Sachs's most famous melodies). In addition, he adapted preexisting songs and chants, altering the melody as necessary to suit his new text. Luther's insistence on integrating congregational singing may have been new, but his musical models were familiar and well established.

Martin Luther took advantage of the invention of the printing press to advocate that scripture be read in local vernacular languages like German and English rather than Latin.

MUSIC FOR THE PEOPLE: CONGREGATIONAL HYMNS

Luther wasn't the first reformer to encourage vernacular hymn singing by the congregation—that honor belongs to the followers of the fifteenth-century Czech reformer Jan Hus. But Luther's central role in the Reformation and his activity as a composer of hymns make him the key figure in bringing music making to the congregation.

Hymn singing had theological and practical benefits for Luther. At the heart of his reforms was the idea that the most direct way to know God was through scripture rather than through church teaching. Hymns, many of which served as commentary on scripture, gave him a powerful way to get the important

Meistersinger German lyric poet of the fourteenth through sixteenth centuries

chorale Lutheran hymn designed for congregational singing

strophic form Musical form in which multiple stanzas of text are set to the same melody

points in the scripture reading across to the congregation in an accessible way: "Ein' feste Burg" is based on Psalm 46. Moreover, singing in the vernacular made worship services more appealing.

In the wake of Luther's Reformation movement, virtually all the new Protestant denominations adopted congregational singing. There were varying practices: some admitted no instruments; some sang only psalms; Lutherans and others encouraged more elaborate settings of the hymns—such as the sophisticated settings of Walter and Bach. Around the time that Bach was harmonizing hymns, the English reformer John Wesley (1703–1791) was updating hymnody (the composition of hymns) as part of his Methodist movement. Like Luther, Wesley borrowed from the music around him: he set new texts to music by English composers such as Henry Purcell and William Boyce as well as popular songs and other fashionable music. In addition, he encouraged the enthusiastic and heartfelt singing of hymns. The success of the Wesley family helped stimulate an interest in hymn singing in English-speaking countries; for example, the Anglican hymnal *Hymns Ancient and Modern*, first published in 1861, has sold over 160 million copies. What began 500 years ago as the musical branch of the Reformation movement in Germany has been standard practice in Christian churches ever since.

"EIN' FESTE BURG IST UNSER GOTT"

Luther's "Ein' feste Burg" is a **chorale**, a Lutheran hymn designed for congregational singing. Luther's first version was monophonic—just the melody (as you can see in the photo of the first edition below). In this form, the distinctive features of a hymn are evident: a melody that moves in mostly even values, with gently changing contours; syllabic setting of the text; frequent pauses after each line of text; and strophic form (in

Luther's hymn "Ein' feste Burg ist unser Gott," as printed in 1529. For centuries, hymnals and psalters remained among the most popular music publications in Europe and North America.

strophic form, two or more stanzas of text are set to the same melody). Almost immediately, it appeared in

LISTEN UP!

CD 1:6

Luther/Walter, "Ein' feste Burg ist unser Gott" (ca. 1525)

Takeaway point: Singable melody with short phrases and even rhythm setting text syllabically

Style: Renaissance—Baroque

Form: Strophic

Genre: Chorale (monophonic/polyphonic/homophonic)

Instruments: Mixed voices (plus instruments in Bach)

Context: Liturgical music based on tuneful secular song to encourage congregational singing; a key component of the Protestant Reformation

a four-voice setting by Johann Walter (1496–1570), Luther's frequent collaborator and the other key figure in the rise of Lutheran hymns. We hear one stanza of each setting, although a complete performance would include four stanzas. Both melody and setting changed with the times: Johann Sebastian Bach's famous setting of the chorale is more homophonic and rhythmically regular than Walter's version.

Hymns like "Ein' feste Burg" are a kind of popular music. There was a business aspect to their production: the printing of hymnals, the hiring of musicians, the training of singers to lead the congregation. But commercial success was, of course, not the goal. Accessibility was. The qualities that made Lutheran chorales accessible to the people—syllabic setting of a vernacular text, mostly regular rhythm, smoothly flowing melodies, and frequent pauses—were as radical a departure from the polyphony of Catholic sacred music as Luther's theology was from Catholic orthodoxy.

CHAPTER 12

Music in Elizabethan England

"The most glorious era in English music prior to the rock era occurred around four centuries ago."

One can convincingly argue that the most memorable era in British music has been the last half century. From The Beatles to Radiohead, it's been an incredible run. Never in its history has British music enjoyed greater popularity, prestige, or influence. One can also argue that the most glorious era in English music prior to the rock era occurred around four centuries ago, during the reign of Elizabeth I, the first Queen Elizabeth. **Ayres**—solo songs with lute accompaniment—were popular, and so were sacred music for Anglican and

Did You Know?

In 2006, British rocker Sting recorded a collection of songs for lute and voice by Elizabethan composer John Dowland.

Catholic worship, imported and domestic madrigals, a wealth of keyboard music, and songs and instrumental music for music making at home.

Traveling back in time to Elizabethan England, we might find ourselves in the audience at William Shakespeare's Globe Theatre. Early in the second act of Shakespeare's comedy *Twelfth Night*, Sir Toby Belch and Sir Andrew Aguecheek ask Feste, the clown, to sing a love song. Feste obliges them with "O Mistresse Mine," a song often attributed to Thomas Morley (1557/8?–1602). Robert Armin, a member of Shakespeare's troupe who often played clown roles and was apparently a fine singer, performed

ayre Elizabethan solo song with lute accompaniment

Dutch painter Frans Hals's famous portrait of a clown (1638) reminds us that playing the lute was one of the skills expected of court jesters.

the song in the first productions of the play, probably accompanying himself on the lute.

We don't know for certain whether Morley composed the song; his strongest connection to the song is a setting for instruments that appeared in 1599, three years before Shakespeare borrowed it for *Twelfth Night*. (We will hear this setting later.) It seems more likely that "O Mistresse Mine" was an already-familiar song that *both* Shakespeare and Morley adapted for their own purposes. It is far more certain that accompanied solo song was a well-established and popular genre by the beginning of the seventeenth century, when Shakespeare's play had its premiere.

In this chapter, we sample three short pieces from the outpouring of music in the Elizabethan era: a madrigal by John Wilbye, a setting of "O Mistresse Mine," and a set of variations on this popular melody by Thomas Morley. All three evidence important changes in musical life in Europe around 1600.

LO5 The Madrigal

In 1588, Nicholas Yonge, an enthusiastic English singer, published *Musica Transalpina* (*Music across the Alps*), a collection of fifty-seven Italian madrigals with texts translated into English. Yonge's volume must certainly have been a labor of love as well as a good business

proposition: in the preface to the volume, Yonge mentions that a "great number of gentlemen and merchants of good account" gather daily at his house to sing madrigals, which were "yearly sent me out of Italy and other places."

Yonge's anthology whetted England's already-healthy appetite for Italian madrigals and helped inspire English composers to compose their own. It soon bore fruit. In 1601, Thomas Morley, an enthusiastic admirer of Italian music in general and of the madrigal in particular, published a volume of twenty-five madrigals by twenty-three different English composers. Entitled *The Triumphes of Oriana*, it was Morley's tribute to Queen Elizabeth I, who had supported his work by giving him a monopoly on printing music. ("Oriana" referred to Queen Elizabeth I; all of the madrigals ended with the refrain "Long live fair Oriana.")

The **madrigals** composed in the sixteenth and early seventeenth centuries were polyphonic settings of secular poems. The settings generally contain four to six parts, and they were typically performed **a cappella** (without instrumental accompaniment), with each singer reading his or her part from a "partbook." The

madrigal
Polyphonic setting of a secular poem, composed in the sixteenth and early seventeenth centuries

a cappella
Without instrumental accompaniment

Five madrigal singers sitting around a table, reading from their respective partbooks (1568)

poems were generally of high quality: the first published collection (1530) to use the word *madrigal* for such settings included several texts by Francesco Petrarch, whose poetry was very fashionable during the early sixteenth century.

The impulse to set the text polyphonically reflects composers' newfound awareness of the quality of secular texts. They seemed to think that good poetry demanded a more substantial approach than the simple homophonic settings used in lighter song genres. The polyphony of the madrigal trickled down from the imitative polyphony used in sacred music, such as the Josquin mass movement; it is a similar approach but not as complex. The influence of sacred polyphony on the madrigal is not surprising, because many of the first composers of madrigals were, like Josquin, northern European composers working in Italy.

The Madrigal in Italy

The madrigal emerged in Italy during the 1520s and flourished in many of the major Italian cities—Rome, Venice, and Florence, the home of the Medicis. Madrigals provided entertainment for aristocrats—either at court or in academies formed to perform this music. Many madrigals, especially those written in the middle of the century, were intended for amateur performance. However, others were composed for more elaborate entertainments—for example, as intermission pieces between acts of a play, which sometimes upstaged the main attraction, and for festive occasions.

During the second half of the sixteenth century, the madrigal became the most popular form of aristocratic musical entertainment in Italy and ultimately throughout most of Europe. Among the most popular and prolific madrigalists was Luca Marenzio (1553–1599), who had ten volumes of madrigals published during his lifetime.

The madrigal flourished during a century-long gap between the advent of music printing and the widespread adoption of keyboards and stringed instruments. Printing had made music much more widely available, much less expensive, and much more quickly disseminated. Recall that the first volumes of printed music came off the press in the early sixteenth century, shortly before the emergence of the madrigal. By contrast, the core instruments of the seventeenth century—the violin family and the harpsichord—were still in the early stages of their evolution during the sixteenth century. And during the sixteenth century, the lute was far more popular than the harpsichord, with idiomatic composition for strings and keyboard not even evident

until after 1600. The musical environment was ideal for madrigals to blossom.

The Madrigal in England

The madrigal was the first Italian genre to enjoy popularity throughout Europe. (Opera and the concerto would follow in the seventeenth century.) Among the most enthusiastic admirers of the Italian madrigal were the English "gentlemen . . . of good account" mentioned in Yonge's preface. Madrigal singing enjoyed great popularity in England during the reign of Elizabeth I (r. 1558–1603), who was herself a skilled musician. Inspired by the availability of the madrigals in translation and the emergence of major English poets such as Edmund Spenser and Sir Philip Sidney, composers created an English madrigal school. Some composers, such as John Wilbye, are known mainly for their madrigals. Others, such as Thomas Morley and Thomas Weelkes, composed madrigals as well as music in many other genres.

By the time English composers began composing madrigals, it was a well-established genre. Its social functions were well defined, and its musical conventions were in place. For English composers, it was mainly a matter of language: composing to English texts rather than Italian texts. In either language, the challenge for madrigal composers was to integrate words and music—to have the music enhance the message of the words.

The Madrigal: Words and Music

The madrigal featured two major innovations: musical settings that responded to the text, and the use of imitative polyphony in a secular style. At first glance, these innovations might seem to be working at cross purposes. It would seem that the first requirement for expressing a text is to present it intelligibly—it is more challenging for listeners to sense the connection between words and music if they can't understand the words. Imitative polyphony complicates that because all parts share text as well as melodic material. This isn't so much a problem in sacred polyphony, at least in those settings where the text is familiar. Josquin could assume that everyone who heard one of his masses would have the text firmly in mind. (For other genres, it was so much a problem that members of the Catholic hierarchy tried to ban polyphonic music during the Counter-Reformation.) Rendering the text intelligible was an issue in madrigal composition, even in those works where the text was familiar—as it was in the writings of Petrarch. Madrigal composers found solutions to this problem, as we'll discover shortly.

> *The challenge for madrigal composers was to integrate words and music—to have the music enhance the message of the words.*

In addition, composers sought to find ways to amplify the meaning of the text in music. Typically, they used two strategies, one general and one specific. The general strategy was to establish a musical mood consonant with the overall sense of the text: a somber mood for a sad poem or a bright mood for more lighthearted verse. The specific strategy, which came to be called **text painting** or **word painting**, was to highlight meaning in the text—even a single word—with striking musical gestures, such as a melodic inflection, a bold harmony, or a quick change of rhythmic pace. For instance, sadness came to be conveyed by descending tones. We hear examples of many of these text/music relationships in John Wilbye's "Adew, Sweet Amarillis" (Adieu, Sweet Amaryllis).

JOHN WILBYE, MADRIGALIST

John Wilbye (1574–1638) remains one of the most highly regarded English madrigal composers active around 1600. Wilbye grew up in Suffolk, in the eastern part of England, and spent most of his career in the service of a local landowner who valued his services. Wilbye was not a prolific composer. He composed mostly madrigals, and only sixty-six have survived. Almost all appeared in two volumes, published in 1598 and 1609. Wilbye set poems by Sydney and Spenser; he also wrote his own, including "Adew, Sweet Amarillis."

Wilbye's poem is a lover's brief but heartfelt lament on the end of his relationship: "breaking up is hard to do" circa 1600. Amarillis (now usually spelled Amaryllis) was a beautiful shepherdess mentioned by the Roman poet Virgil in his *Eclogues*; given the time and place—Renaissance Europe—the classical allusion should not surprise us. Here is the text of the poem:

> Adew, sweet Amarillis:
> For since to part your will is,
> O heavy tyding,
> Here is for mee no biding:
> Yet once againe ere that I part with you,
> Amarillis, sweet Adew.

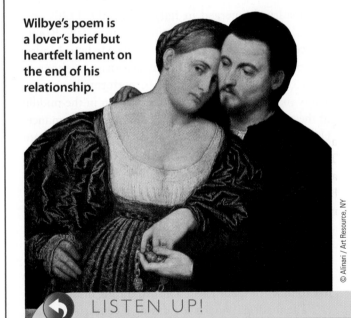

Wilbye's poem is a lover's brief but heartfelt lament on the end of his relationship.

© Alinari / Art Resource, NY

LISTEN UP!

CD 1:7

Wilbye, "Adew, Sweet Amarillis" (1609)

Takeaway point: Conversational exchanges among four singers

Style: Late Renaissance

Form: Through-composed

Genre: Madrigal

Instruments: Four mixed voices

Context: Song for recreational singing among skilled men and women of "good account"

John Wilbye

Fast Facts

- *Dates:* ca. 1574–1638

- *Place:* England

- *Reasons to remember:* One of England's most important composers of madrigals

© Tamsin Lewis

The overriding theme is resignation leading to acceptance, a quality that Wilbye emphasizes in the music. The poet has been rejected by Amaryllis. Her decision is bad news for him ("O heavy tyding"), and they will not meet again ("here is for mee no biding") before going their separate ways.

Wilbye enhances the dark mood of the poem by opting for minor mode throughout most of the madrigal; the shift to major toward the end, combined with the good-bye ("adew") in the text, suggests a kind of resignation and acceptance. Wilbye presents the text clearly. The setting of the title phrase, which we hear several times, has the most imitative texture. The other lines of the poem have a more chordal setting.

THE MADRIGAL AND MUSICAL MEANING

In the madrigal, more than any other Renaissance genre, we begin to hear a transformation in how music becomes an active interpretive partner in realizing the meaning of the words. Machaut's rondeau is pleasing to the ear, but we are hard pressed to connect its words and music, to find in the music features that enhance the meaning of the text.

By contrast, Wilbye's madrigal seems much more specifically connected to the text, in its general character and in the shift in mood from section to section. There are numerous instances of text painting. For example, the phrase "O heavy tyding" is set to sustained harmonies, as if a heavy weight makes it impossible to move quickly. The phrase "yet once againe" is set to a melodic figure that descends slowly after reaching a peak, to help convey sadness leading to acceptance. And the switch of the opening material from minor to major completely changes the expressive message, from despair to acceptance. Here, it is the music, not the words (which are the same), that tells us of the protagonist's change of heart. In these musical gestures, we hear composers trying to resonate with life experience: for example, slowing down or speeding up the rhythm, or shaping melodic contour to amplify the rise and fall of speech.

The idea that music can convey a specific mood—that it can communicate meaning through the interaction of several elements—was an enormous change in attitude. Indeed, some music historians have argued that it is the most significant change in the history of Western art music. We will hear such changes even more clearly in opera, and by the eighteenth century, in instrumental music as well. The beginning of this shift is most clearly evident in the madrigal.

LO6 Solo Song in Elizabethan England

The madrigal and the accompanied solo song are siblings. Both surfaced around the same time, in the second quarter of the sixteenth century. Both were concerned with presenting the text clearly and in a way that approaches the rhythm and pacing of the words as they might be spoken. Both typically featured texts about love—as is true of "O Mistresse Mine," Wilbye's madrigal, and hundreds of other works. The most significant differences between madrigal and song have to do with the tone of the texts—more serious in the madrigal versus lighter in the song; the complexity of the texture—imitative counterpoint in madrigal versus melody plus chordal accompaniment in song; and a setting for several voices in madrigal versus one voice and instrument in song. But even here, the rules are not hard and fast. Many sixteenth-century madrigals and songs were published in two versions: for voices alone and for solo voice with instrumental accompaniment.

The sound of the accompanied solo song should resonate well with contemporary listeners: it is the Renaissance forerunner of songs by rock-era folksingers and singer-songwriters. It typically features a singer whose theme is the ups and downs of love, supported by a plucked string instrument—in our time, the guitar; in Elizabethan England, the lute.

THE LUTE

The lute's closest cousin in the guitar family might well be the twelve-string guitar, because lutes, like twelve-string guitars, typically had two strings per pitch. (Pairs of strings tuned to the same pitch are called **courses**.) Like the modern guitar, the Renaissance lute typically had strings tuned to six different pitches, although lutes with seven courses were also common, especially toward the end of the sixteenth century.

The most obvious differences between the modern guitar and the lute are the shape of the body and the shape of the neck. The

Lute

© iStockphoto.com/cenap refik ONGAN

body of the lute is flat on the front (the side next to the strings) and rounded in the back—much the same shape as half a pear cut lengthwise. The neck, upon which the strings are stretched, has a pronounced bend at the end of the fingerboard.

The lute evolved from an ancient Middle Eastern instrument called the *oud*, which was brought to Spain by the Moors and known in Europe by the ninth century. Evidence of the lute—especially from paintings and illustrations, treatises, and other writings—dates from the fifteenth century. During the sixteenth century, the lute became the dominant household instrument for well-to-do families and the most popular solo instrument among professional musicians. The quantity of music composed for lute far exceeded that composed for harpsichord or any other instrument.

The Strophic Song

A **strophic song** is one in which the same melody sets two or more stanzas of text. "O Mistresse Mine," the song to be discussed next, uses a single five-phrase melody to set four stanzas. Declamation of the text—matching the inflection of the text with the music—is more difficult because the same music must serve multiple texts. In this situation, the composer responds most directly to the rhythm of the words. Specific responses to particular words or phrases of the text, such as those we heard in Wilbye's madrigal, are simply not possible in a strophic song.

Chordal Harmony

In songs like "O Mistresse Mine," the distinction between melody and harmony is about as clear as it can be: the singer sings the melody while the lutenist plucks chords that follow the rhythm of the melody. Only occasionally does the lutenist play a melody-like **obbligato**, a second melody playing under the main melody. The idea of chordal accompaniment of a melody wasn't new with the solo song. Recall that we heard this texture at times in the Machaut rondeau and in parts of Josquin's Kyrie and Wilbye's madrigal. However, here it is consistent throughout.

Precisely for this reason, we can hear even more clearly than in the Wilbye madrigal how harmony had evolved into chord sequences that closely resemble common practice harmony. What makes this development significant is the fact that harmony already plays such a key role in organizing musical thought. Chord progressions help define musical phrases and sentences; chord choice at cadences determines the decisiveness of the musical punctuation—a period versus a comma. In this instance, the most decisive punctuation in the melody is the last one, in large part because it is supported by a chord progression that signals a strong close. This song is our first encounter with purposeful harmony—a preview of what we will hear in the next century.

"O Mistresse Mine"

For generations, it was generally assumed that William Shakespeare wrote the lyrics to "O Mistresse Mine" and Thomas Morley composed the melody. Recent scholarship has cast doubt on both assumptions. Authorship of both words and music is now an open question. We know that music was an important component of Elizabethan drama—and indeed, Renaissance drama in general. Music was performed before plays began, between acts, and oftentimes within the act, as part of the drama, as was the case in *Twelfth Night*. We also know that Shakespeare drew on sources and resources from all strata of society. "O Mistresse Mine" was almost certainly a popular song known only in oral tradition before Morley's arrangement of it. It's all but certain that Shakespeare kept the tune and the title but added his own words to make the lyric connect to the plot: it contains lines that allude to characters and events in *Twelfth Night*. For example, the first stanza identifies a "true love" that "can sing both high and low." Many commentators view this as a

LISTEN UP!

CD 1:8
Morley (attributed), "O Mistresse Mine" (ca. 1599)

Takeaway point: A sweet, simple melody with chordal accompaniment

Style: Late Renaissance

Form: Strophic

Genre: Accompanied song

Instruments: Voice and lute

Context: Song arranged for a theatrical production

reference to Viola, a woman who presents herself throughout much of the play as a man.

Songs like "O Mistresse Mine" blur the boundary between popular and art music. As we hear it, it is an elegant lament. But its uncertain lineage suggests that it began as a popular song; so do its accessible melody and simple form. As other British songwriters would show about 360 years later, it *is* possible to create artful music in a popular style.

LO7 Composing for Instruments

The most direct connection between Thomas Morley and "O Mistresse Mine" comes from his 1599 publication *The First Booke of Consort Lessons*, which contained settings of songs and dances by "divers exquisite Authors," including Morley himself. (Keep in mind that Morley was a one-man music industry: composer, performer, publisher, teacher, promoter. He was involved in just about every aspect of musical life in Elizabethan England.) The pieces in the collection were arranged for "6 Instruments to play together, the Treble Lute, the

Thomas Morley

Fast Facts

- *Dates:* 1557/8?–1602
- *Place:* England
- *Reasons to remember:* A true "Renaissance man"— composer, performer, publisher, teacher, promoter—in Renaissance England

Pandora, the Cittern, the Base-Violl, the Flute & Treble Violl." It wasn't the first such publication, but it did signal an important new trend in music: composition specifically for instrumental ensembles.

Thomas Morley was a one-man music industry: composer, performer, publisher, teacher, promoter.

THE INSTRUMENTATION OF THE CONSORT

Consort is a term used in England during the sixteenth and seventeenth centuries to identify a small group of diverse instruments. The term is related to *concert*, in the sense of playing together; it came into use toward the end of sixteenth century, during the Elizabethan era, and remained in use for much of the next century.

Although the instrumentation of a consort could vary in number and type, it was generally agreed that certain combinations of instruments sounded better together. The six instruments mentioned by Morley formed an ideal consort. At its heart was the viol. Its most compatible partners were what Morley called the flute (we now call them recorders) and lutelike instruments.

These instruments, all mentioned in Morley's consort book, were especially popular in Elizabethan England. They represent three families of instruments. Viols are bowed stringed instruments; the flute/recorder is a gentle wind instrument; and the lute, pandora, and cittern are similar plucked instruments. As is typical of the era, all three instrument types came in several sizes, to correspond roughly to the ranges of the human voice. Thus, Morley recommends a treble (high range) and bass (low range) viol; plus three lutelike instruments in high, middle, and low ranges; and a flute, which also comes in several ranges (in this version of "O Mistresse Mine" the recorder is in a soprano range).

If you crossed a cello or violin with a guitar, you'd get a viol. Like the cello, the viol has a curved front, and the performer produces sound by bowing it. Like the guitar, it has a flat back, six strings, and frets. When played well, it produces a sweet, somewhat nasal sound—stronger than that of an acoustic guitar but not as powerful as that of a violin or cello. The viol is also called a viola da gamba (viol of the knee), because it rests on the lap or between the legs of the performer rather than under the chin. It was an especially popular instrument among music amateurs from the sixteenth through the early eighteenth centuries.

Elizabethan consort music was published with wealthy amateur performers in mind, and it is thought that Bach composed the viola da gamba part in his sixth Bran-

consort Small group of diverse instruments in Elizabethan England

denburg Concerto for Prince Leopold, his employer at the time. Then as now, instruments had differing social status. Viols, because of their delicate sound and relatively comfortable playing technique, were high on the list. By contrast, wind instruments like the shawm, a predecessor of the oboe, were usually left to professionals or lower-class amateurs because they had an abrasive sound and required that the player disfigure his face when playing it. (It may be for this reason that women seldom played the shawm.)

You will notice that on this recording, viols play the two most prominent parts, the melody and the bass line; both are considerably simpler than the lute part. This is consistent with the place of the viol in the consort, and in society: amateurs of modest skill could play the prominent parts, while a more skilled lutenist, perhaps a musician in the service of an aristocrat, would play the more intricate running figures in the background.

COMPOSING FOR INSTRUMENTS

Morley's First Booke of Consort Lessons specifies the instruments to be used, as we have noted. In indicating the instrumentation, at least in general terms, Morley was following the practice of the time: such indications were common in mixed consort music. As such, they represent an important innovation in instrumental music.

Most medieval and Renaissance music that made use of instruments did not indicate specific instruments—in many cases even whether instruments were

 LISTEN UP!

CD 1:9
Morley (attributed), "O Mistresse Mine" (ca. 1599)

Takeaway point: Gently elaborated version of the melody, with other lines swirling around it

Style: Late Renaissance

Form: Variation (one statement of the melody, with varied repeats)

Genre: Consort music

Instruments: Viol, lute, recorder

Context: Instrumental music for amateur music making

to be used at all. These were decisions left to the performers. As a result, we must infer an appropriate instrumentation from such features as the notation (such as the special notation used for the lute) or the context in which the composition might be heard (a church versus a court setting).

By contrast, Morley narrows the choices considerably. By specifying the instruments to be used, he virtually guarantees that they will blend well together. This narrowing of instrument choice can be understood as an important intermediate step between the almost complete freedom of earlier practice and the more contemporary practice of specifying instrumentation precisely.

STYLE AND FORM IN INSTRUMENTAL COMPOSITION

Our inclusion of both a vocal and an instrumental version of "O Mistresse Mine" enables us to explore two questions about composing for instruments. The first has to do with the difference between writing for voice and writing for instruments. The second has to do with the form of instrumental compositions.

Idiomatic composition for an instrument—that is, composing in a way that makes use of its distinctive sounds and capabilities—goes hand in hand with designating a particular instrument for a specific part. In this recording, the viols play the melody and the bass, the two parts that require a sustained sound. The recorder plays a subordinate role. The lute, which can be played with speed and delicacy, has a running line in the background.

Both of the viol parts are singable. There are a few embellishments of the melody that would require some vocal agility. Otherwise, the melody is much as it is in the vocal version. By contrast, the lute part is constantly active, running up and down scales for the most part. In this context, this kind of part works best on the lute—although any of the instruments could play it—because it enriches the texture without covering the melody.

In effect, this version is a variation on "O Mistresse Mine," for instruments. As we mentioned in the discussion of Mozart's variations, variation is one of the easiest ways to create an instrumental composition: simply take a familiar tune and play it several times, each time changing some aspect of it. The form is essentially a strophic form for instruments: melodic

and textural embellishment substitute for variety in the text. In this version we hear only one statement of the melody, but the setting as a whole is richer and more elaborate than the setting for voice and lute heard previously.

Although this version of "O Mistresse Mine" is brief, it is rich in information. We hear some of the most characteristic instrumental sounds of the late Renaissance. We also get strong hints of three important developments during the years around 1600. One is writing specifically and idiomatically for instruments. Another is the gradual shift from the more balanced imitative polyphony of the Renaissance (Josquin, Wilbye) to a texture in which melody and bass are most prominent and are connected by chords. The third is the use of variation procedures to convert a song into an instrumental piece. This practice became fashionable in both solo and consort music around this time.

Summary

In our small sample of Elizabethan music, we encountered three developments that marked major new directions in music. In the madrigal, we heard the text painting and other effects designed to make music specifically expressive: to convey in music the emotions behind a word or line of text. In the vocal setting of "O Mistresse Mine," we heard a version of a popular song, or at least a song in popular style, presented in a version suitable for upper-class consumption. And in the instrumental setting, we encounter our first example of idiomatic instrumental composition.

All would become a significant part of musical life in the seventeenth century. Opera would play a crucial role in developing and popularizing expressive musical gesture and instrumental composition, as we discover in the next two chapters.

Although composing for instruments dates from the thirteenth century, not until about 1600 did composing specifically and idiomatically for instruments really take hold. We gauge this primarily from three kinds of evidence: the quantity of music composed and published, the increased variety of instrumental resources, and the appearance of compositions that exploit the

idiomatic composition
Composing in a way that makes use of an instrument's distinctive sounds and capabilities

capabilities of specific instruments. In the first quarter of the seventeenth century we find intricate keyboard and lute pieces, compositions for brass choirs (to be heard in St. Mark's Basilica in Venice), music requiring a proto-orchestra, sonatas for violin and continuo, and music for various small ensembles. Compared to what had come before, it was an explosion of instrumental composition.

KEYS TO RENAISSANCE MUSIC

Key Concepts

Integration. If there is an all-encompassing trend whose multiple realizations distinguish Renaissance from medieval music, it might well be integration. Integration is evident in several important parameters: voices and instruments, sacred and secular, and the relationship between parts.

Key Features

1. **Imitation.** In Renaissance polyphonic music, the sharing of melodic material among two or more parts became commonplace, in both sacred and secular music. Typically, one voice would present a melodic idea, and other voices would enter soon after with the same melodic material.

2. **Full harmonies.** Typically, the harmonies in both polyphonic and homophonic passages are complete triads rather than the emptier-sounding harmonies of medieval music. They flow smoothly in sequences that anticipate, but do not consistently follow, the progressions of common practice harmony.

3. **Instruments on their own.** During the Renaissance, composers began to write more specifically for instruments: solo music for keyboard instruments and lute, music for instrumental groups, and instrumental accompaniments and obbligato parts for vocal music. Instruments also continued to substitute for voices in polyphonic works.

4. **Rhythmic flexibility.** In both sacred and secular music, there is greater rhythmic variety and contrast: for example, slow-moving parts in some voices versus faster-moving lines in polyphonic music; rhythms that declaim the text in homophonic music; fast-moving instrumental lines versus slower vocal lines. The resulting rhythms may flow with a subtly measured pulse or move along with a sharply defined beat.

5. **Textural contrasts.** Contrasts between imitative counterpoint and more homophonic textures are common in both sacred and secular vocal music. Also common are numerous gradations between these extremes, such as a pair of faster-moving voices against more sustained sounds.

Key Terms

1. **Madrigal.** A polyphonic setting of a secular poem. Madrigals were popular in Italy and England during the latter part of the sixteenth century. Their popularity waned in the early years of the seventeenth century

2. **Renaissance polyphony.** A polyphonic compositional approach characterized by frequent use of imitation among the various parts. Imitative counterpoint was standard practice in music composed for the Catholic liturgy.

3. **Consort.** A term that came into use toward the end of the Renaissance to describe a small instrumental ensemble. An ensemble made up of varied instruments—such as viol, lute, and recorder—is often referred to as a *broken consort*.

 **Music Concept Check**

To assist you in recognizing their distinctive features, we present an interactive comparison of medieval, Renaissance, and Baroque style in CourseMate and the eBook.

UNIT 6
EARLY AND MIDDLE BAROQUE OPERA

© Erich Lessing/Art Resource, NY

Learning Outcomes

After reading this unit, you will be able to do the following:

LO1 Understand what opera is, the particular challenge of setting drama to music, and the usefulness of developing musical gestures that can depict feelings and moods.

LO2 Understand the revolutionary impact of the first operas in Europe.

LO3 Recognize the importance of Claudio Monteverdi and the sound and vocal style of his opera *Orfeo*.

LO4 Recognize a large ensemble, as well as new ways of composing for instruments.

LO5 Understand the growth of opera, including musical and dramatic changes, during the seventeenth century.

LO6 Recognize an early example of the use of recitative and aria, as well as the expressive capabilities of common practice harmony, in Henry Purcell's "Dido's Lament."

OPERA WAS THE most spectacular musical achievement of the seventeenth century. Because it was *dramma per musica* ("drama through music"), opera demanded a new kind of musical communication to portray the moods and actions of the characters and sustain the narrative.

In this unit, we highlight important developments in early Baroque music, as manifested in opera: expressive vocal writing that responded to mood; composing for specific groups of instruments, often in ways that took advantage of their distinctive capabilities; vocal and instrumental virtuosity; and, toward the end of the century, widespread use of common practice harmony as a means of organization. Although there are sixteenth-century precedents for most of these developments, they occurred far more extensively and with more sophistication in seventeenth-century music. They highlight key distinctions between Renaissance and early Baroque style.

CHAPTER 13

Monteverdi and Early Opera

"No form of live entertainment has enjoyed greater prestige, from the time it was conceived to the present, than opera."

For the better part of four centuries, opera has been the most spectacular and lavish form of stage entertainment in Western culture. It can offer timeless stories, powerful drama, memorable music, expressive dance, evocative scenery, and marvelous stage effects. Although it began as an intellectual exercise within a small circle of Italian aristocrats, it soon attracted a large following that included not only aristocrats but also urban audiences of all classes. By the mid-seventeenth century, kings and other royalty emptied their state treasuries to underwrite opera productions. During the same time, opera became the first commercial music: by the 1640s, opera houses in Venice, then in other Italian cities, offered public performances, which anyone who could afford or cadge a ticket could attend.

Opera's prestige and popularity continue into our own time, as an art and a benchmark for those who aspire to artistic status. When The Who wanted to make an artistic statement, they called their concept album *Tommy* (1969) a rock *opera*. Recordings by the Three Tenors—Luciano Pavarotti, Plácido Domingo, and José Carreras, all major opera stars—have gone platinum, outselling those of many rock bands. No form of live entertainment has enjoyed greater prestige, from the time it was conceived to the present, than opera. In this chapter, we consider the defining characteristics of opera and explore the beginnings of this all-encompassing art.

Did You Know?

Recordings by the Three Tenors—all major opera stars—have gone platinum, outselling those of many rock bands.

LO1 Opera Is...

Opera is drama in which all dialogue is sung. This distinguishes it from other kinds of sung stage entertainment, such as musicals, in which much of the dialogue is spoken. The music to be sung may be a kind of sung speech (**recitative**, a section of an opera that generally contains dialogue to further the action and features syllabic setting of the text, delivered in a rhythm approximating speech); a fully developed melody (performed in a chorus, duet, trio, other combinations, or as an **aria**—accompanied solo operatic melody); or something in between. Typically, however, *all* of the text is sung. From the start, this has been the closest thing to a constant in opera.

There is usually much more to opera than constant singing, especially as we might experience it in the early twenty-first century. If we were to attend an opera performance at New York's Metropolitan Opera House, we would expect a production on a grand scale. The opera would have a serious subject, perhaps drawn from mythology or history or adapted from a literary work of distinction (there have been many operas based on Shakespeare); it might treat

opera Drama, either tragic or comic, in which all dialogue is sung

recitative Section of an opera that generally contains dialogue to further the action; features syllabic setting of the text, delivered in a rhythm approximating speech, often with strings of repeated notes

aria Accompanied solo operatic melody

a comic subject with sophistication. It would require tremendous resources: for example, elaborate sets, star singers dressed in appropriate costumes, a chorus, a full orchestra, and a setting that can accommodate all of this. It is entertainment at its most lavish. Opera didn't begin this way, but it quickly evolved into a grand spectacle.

One can understand the enthusiasm for a genre that integrates drama and music (and often dance and much more). Still, there is a contradiction inherent in the full integration of drama and music. It lies at the heart of opera, and it has challenged composers from Monteverdi to the present.

THE PARADOX OF OPERA

Opera is an art form based on a fascinating paradox: it is a form of drama that is, on the surface, not dramatically credible. If we attend a theater production or view a film, we are aware that what we're seeing and hearing is not "real." At the same time, however, it is often only a small step to imagine that what we're seeing and hearing is, in fact, real—we could say the lines spoken by the members of the cast and connect to the emotions that they project as if it were our own experience.

It is a much bigger step to project ourselves into characters' roles when all of the dialogue is sung. It isn't just that we don't regularly converse in song. Nor is it only a question of intelligibility: today's opera houses often provide supertitles (the text being sung is projected on a display placed above the stage), even when the opera is in English. It also grows out of the fact that we process music more slowly than we process words; music usually unfolds more slowly and requires more repetition before it sinks in. As a result, during many of the most musically memorable moments of an opera, the dramatic action slows down, or even grinds to a halt. Despite this, opera *can* work dramatically, but only if the music enables us to engage with the plot. We suspend our disbelief and allow ourselves to let both words and music tell us the story.

OPERA AND MUSICAL EXPRESSION

Musicians are accustomed to giving, and we are accustomed to listening for, musical gestures that imply or evoke a specific emotion or image. We find such musical clues in film soundtracks, television commercials, or orchestral works such as those of Hector Berlioz (as we will discover in Chapter 32). However, what is commonplace today was still a novel idea four hundred years ago. Composers were just coming to grips with the evocative capabilities of music. Opera would accelerate that process.

In order for music to work dramatically, it had to become a more specifically expressive art. Composers had to be able to compose music tailored to particular dramatic situations (danger, duplicity, jealousy) or expressive of particular emotions (joy, sorrow, serenity). We noted in the discussion of Wilbye's madrigal that expression of emotions was an innovation heard in much of the modern music of the late sixteenth century. In opera, however, it occurred on a much grander scale and often involved the music given both to singers and to the orchestra. In writing opera, composers developed or adapted musical devices that both musicians and audiences found evocative.

© Beatriz Schiller/Time Life Pictures/Getty Images

...music tailored to particular dramatic situations (danger, duplicity, jealousy)

LO2 The Beginnings of Opera

Opera began as the last and ultimately the grandest effort to revive classical Greek drama during the Renaissance. Girolamo Mei, an Italian Renaissance historian who produced the first serious study of Greek music, proposed that all Greek drama was sung, not spoken. His work strongly influenced the Camerata, a circle of cultured aristocrats and musicians supported by Giovanni de' Bardi, a Florentine nobleman who was also a skilled musician. From this group and other like-minded Florentine musicians would come works generally regarded as the first operas. The earliest opera to come down to us in complete form was Jacopo Peri's *Eurydice*, produced in 1600 for the wedding of Marie de' Medici and Henri IV, the king of France.

Especially when compared to what would soon develop, these first operas were musically simple in the extreme: they consisted of dramatic text sung in a speech-like rhythm with sparse accompaniment from bass and chord-producing instruments. At the same time, composers sought to exploit the expressive potential of the human voice. Giulio Caccini (1558–1618), an important member of the Camerata and a contributor to the production of *Eurydice*, published a volume of songs in 1601, which he called *Le nuove musiche* (*The New Music*). The preface to the songs was part manifesto and part method; Caccini supplied a detailed description of melodic ornamentation within a discussion of both aesthetics and practice. In part because of these vocal techniques, opera soon became a much more elaborate entertainment. These and other developments, including the extensive use of instruments, set the stage for a thorough transformation of musical life in Europe.

OPERA AND A MUSICAL REVOLUTION

Opera was at the heart of a seventeenth-century musical revolution—the kind that comes along once every couple of centuries. It profoundly affected every aspect of musical life: who made the music, how it sounded, who listened to it, who organized it. It was warmly embraced by some and denigrated by others.

The revolution occurred in northern Italy four hundred years ago. At our distance from it in time and space, and with limited contact with the music and the culture that produced it, we may have difficulty appreciating how radical a revolution it was. However, by relating to the most recent musical revolution of comparable impact—the one that produced rock in the 1950s and 1960s—we can understand the extent to which this seventeenth-century revolution transformed musical life, first in Italy, then throughout Europe. Here are some interesting comparisons:

1. *A change in attitude, toward a more deeply felt music.* Rock proclaimed that it was "real," that it confronted life as it really is right now. Caccini claimed that the "new music" composed by him and other like-minded composers should "move the affect [i.e., emotion] of the soul" and "delight the senses." It, too, represented a much stronger appeal to feelings.

2. *Star power.* Rock icons like Elvis and The Beatles

were music stars, and they enjoyed an unprecedented degree of adulation. Opera quickly developed a similar star system; the top singers were perhaps music's first real celebrities. (Orpheus, the subject of Monteverdi's opera, was the mythological musical star.)

3. *A generation gap.* Frank Sinatra, arguably the biggest pop singer of the 1950s and early 1960s, called rock and roll "the most brutal, ugly, desperate, vicious form of expression it has been my misfortune to hear." The old guard of composers and critics prior to the seventeenth-century musical revolution similarly attacked those who created and promoted the new music.

> *The old guard attacks those who create and promote new music.*

4. *Radical musical change.* Rock gave popular music a new beat and new vocal and instrumental sounds; it also emphasized an integrated, interdependent group conception over a solo-oriented approach, which influenced both melody and texture. The new music of the seventeenth century put the spotlight on the soloist instead of diffusing interest throughout the ensemble; it presented new textures, a more flexible approach to rhythm, and new ways of integrating voices and instruments.

5. *New kinds of virtuosity.* In the 1960s and early 1970s, rock's guitar gods and R&B's inventive bass players went beyond technical mastery to add an astonishing variety of sounds. Their seventeenth-century counterparts were the solo singers, who introduced a dazzling array of new vocal sounds seemingly overnight; there is no account of such techniques prior to the end of the sixteenth century, nor are there musical styles that would seem to demand them.

These parallels give us some perspective on the far-reaching musical changes that emerged with early opera. There are, of course, obvious differences. One important difference is that opera began as an exercise for cultivated aristocrats and the musicians in their employ; rock is a grass-roots music, although some of its top acts quickly developed artistic aspirations. Still, the many similarities between the two may help give us a clearer sense of the revolutionary impact of Monteverdi's opera.

LO3 Monteverdi's *Orfeo*

A significant percentage of the most celebrated and influential musicians in Western culture belong to one of three groups. One group includes innovators, such as Franz Joseph Haydn, Claude Debussy, Louis Armstrong, and The Beatles. These musicians appear at the beginning of an era; they help shape the new style and introduce a new aesthetic. Another group is their complement: those who come at the end of an era and who summarize it in a highly personal way. We will meet several of them: J. S. Bach, George Frideric Handel, and Johannes Brahms. The most exclusive group includes those musicians whose music simultaneously summarizes the prevailing style and decisively influences the music of the next generation. One such musician is a household name: Ludwig van Beethoven. Another member of this group is the Italian composer Claudio Monteverdi.

CLAUDIO MONTEVERDI

Claudio Monteverdi came of age at the end of the Renaissance. He spent the first part of his life in Cremona, where he began composing at an early age: his first works were published when he was only fifteen. Like most musicians of his time, Monteverdi was a composer and a performer. He was apparently a skilled vocalist (subsequently, he taught voice) and violinist (not surprising, since he grew up in Cremona, then center of fine violin making). Such versatility was expected of professional musicians of this time—and for the next two centuries. It would profoundly affect his compositions.

In 1590, Monteverdi took a position as a court musician for the duke of Mantua. There he came in contact with some of the most forward-thinking musicians of the era. Building on their work, he transformed the madrigal into an even more expressive genre and composed the first significant operas. Both earned him an international reputation. In 1613, frustrated at what he considered inferior pay and difficult working conditions, he took a position as the director of music at St. Mark's Basilica in Venice, where he spent the rest of his career.

Monteverdi composed mainly according to the requirements of his position, or for those situations that promised the possibility of remuneration or recognition. He composed madrigals, then operas and other large-scale entertainments, as part of his duties in Mantua, then a good deal of church music for his position at St. Mark's. When opera houses opened in Venice in 1637, he revived his career as an opera composer, turning out three works for Venetian audiences that were quite different from his earlier operas.

By the time he composed *Orfeo* in 1607, Monteverdi was already a highly esteemed composer. He had published five books of madrigals, some of which had been published outside Italy. The modern elements in his madrigals made him the target of Giovanni Artusi, a conservative musical theorist. Monteverdi responded to Artusi's attacks by pointing out that there were two "practices," by which he meant ways of composing, and that the second practice, which he used, allowed for more expressive responses to text. Still, Monteverdi's innovations were occurring in a genre that was on the wane; his eight books of madrigals represent the final significant contribution to the genre. His significance as a composer rests more substantially in his operas, the genre that he helped bring to life.

ORFEO

It was all but inevitable that the first operas, the first dramas in music, would take a classic Greek story about the power of music as their subject. Their composers chose the most famous musical story of all, the legend of Orpheus and Eurydice. Here is the most familiar version: Orpheus is the son of a king and one of the Muses. He has supernormal musical abilities. His singing and playing of the lyre, a harplike instrument, are of such surpassing beauty that he can charm anything that he encounters: gods, people, animals—even plants and rocks. After returning from a voyage, Orpheus marries Eurydice, a beautiful mortal, who dies from snakebite shortly after they marry. What happens next is the crux of the story, at least for Monteverdi: Orpheus, although distraught at the death of Eurydice, resolves to go to the

Claudio Monteverdi

Fast Facts

- *Dates:* 1567–1643
- *Place:* Italy
- *Reason to remember:* The first important composer of opera and a key figure in the transition between Renaissance and Baroque music

When Orpheus sees the sun again, he looks back to Eurydice, who then vanishes.

score Notated musical document that contains every part to be performed

"POSSENTE SPIRTO"

For Monteverdi, it seems, the demand for "supernatural" music—spectacular music suitable for a demigod—offered an opportunity to showcase a new and blatantly virtuosic kind of solo singing. We surmise that the virtuosic element was vitally important to Monteverdi because he supplied two versions of the melody of "Possente spirto," the aria discussed here, in the published **score** (a notated musical document that contains every part to be performed) of the opera. One is an absolutely bare-bones version of the melody; the other is the lavishly ornamented version we hear. This second version guides those performers not prepared to provide their own ornamentation; it is an insurance policy of sorts, guaranteeing that no performance will lack the impact that such ornamentation provides.

Orpheus's singing is the most dramatically potent new element in Monteverdi's opera, but there is another novel feature of this aria: the interplay between voice and instruments. To this point in our survey of early music, we've heard voices alone, instruments alone, and—in the lute song—instruments in a subordinate role. This aria offers yet another kind of relationship: one in which voice and melody instruments alternate, each performing in a manner idiomatic to the instrument: vocal acrobatics versus darting scales from the violins, fanfare-like figures from the trumpets, high and low scales from the harps.

This way of combining instruments and voice was an important innovation. While the practice was already in existence in 1607, the particular form it took in *Orfeo*—a sort of vocal-instrumental interplay—was without significant precedent. In this respect, Monteverdi's way of combining voice and instruments points toward the future, not only to his later operas but also to all of opera as a genre. The use of instruments, both in the supportive role heard during the vocal sections and as alternative melody instruments, certainly expands the composer's sound palette. But there's more to it than just the inherent musical interest in this kind of variety. We can understand Monteverdi's vocal-instrumental interplay in the service of the most fundamental goal of opera: to convey drama through music. Subsequently, opera composers would take the lead in expanding the expressive possibilities of instruments as well as voices as a means to achieve this goal.

underworld to rescue her. He lulls Charon, who ferries souls across the River Styx, and his dog, Cerberus, to sleep by singing and then playing the lyre; when they are asleep, he steals the ferry to enter the underworld. Orpheus serenades Hades, the king of the underworld; his music so moves Hades that he agrees to let Eurydice return from the dead, on the condition that neither Orpheus nor Eurydice looks back. When Orpheus sees the sun again, he looks back to Eurydice, who then vanishes. There are several different endings to the legend; the most powerful has Orpheus being killed by women belonging to the cult of Dionysus, the rival of Apollo.

It is easy to understand the appeal of the Orpheus legend to Peri (recall that his setting of the legend in 1600 is the first complete opera that has come down to us), to Monteverdi, and to their audience. It is a timeless story with a direct connection to classical Greek culture, and it virtually demands that music play both a symbolic and a dramatic role. Indeed, music makes the main dramatic events of the story possible. Without music, the decisive events of the story—Orpheus's entry into the underworld and his rescue of Eurydice—cannot happen. Monteverdi underscores this by placing the first of these encounters at the midpoint of the opera. It is as if the fate of Eurydice depends on the musical skills of Orpheus, as indeed it does. Orpheus's encounter with Charon comes

© Look and Learn/The Bridgeman Art Library International

THE LANGUAGE OF MUSIC

One of the major innovations of Baroque music and a defining feature of Baroque style is **basso continuo**, or continuous bass. As the term implies, basso continuo is a continuous bass line, as well as harmony built on the bass, in support of the melody. Because the continuo roles were generally played by some combination of bass and chord-producing instruments, **continuo** also refers to the group of instruments that supports the melody with bass line and chords. Continuo instruments used in "Possente spirto" include organ and a low-pitched strummed instrument.

DRAMMA PER MUSICA

"Possente spirto" gives us the opportunity to explore the question, How can music work dramatically? As the aria begins, the stage is set. We (and Monteverdi's audience, who knew the story well) are aware that we've reached a crucial point in the plot: if Orfeo can't convince Charon to let him cross the river, then the story ends. We know that Orfeo will use music to try to persuade Charon to help him. But we don't know *how* Orfeo will charm Charon. Monteverdi conveys the dramatic urgency of the situation through two complementary strategies: he composes an extraordinarily virtuosic vocal line (remember that the score contains the outline and Monteverdi's elaboration), and he builds toward the end, reaching a climax on the last line of the third stanza.

In our discussion of chant, we made the point that song derives much of its power by transcending speech; it begins where speech ends. Imagine, then, Orfeo's impact during this aria: the vocal techniques that Monteverdi requires go so far beyond everyday singing that they must have dazzled his audience. At the time of the premiere of *Orfeo*, these striking effects were still brandnew; it's likely that many of those who attended the premiere hadn't heard anything like them before. Most were accustomed to the more conventional singing heard in solo songs and madrigals, so this kind of singing might well have come as a delightful shock.

This is functional virtuosity, virtuosity with a purpose beyond showing off. Here, Orfeo *must* sound extraordinary, because he is Orfeo and because the dramatic situation requires that he use all his powers. And it is the sheer brilliance of Orfeo's singing that makes the scene dramatically credible. It helps us immerse ourselves in the drama and connect with Orfeo emotionally as he tells his sad tale to Charon. It is only through music that this scene works dramatically. The text certainly lays out the situation for Charon, but it does nothing special to persuade him to let Orfeo cross the river. You or I could do the same. The dazzling elaborations of the aria and the phrases that build to the climax on "tanta bellezza" make Orfeo's plea extraordinarily compelling. The fact that the plea is ultimately unsuccessful does not detract from its dramatic impact, on Monteverdi's audience and on us.

LO4 The Orchestra

In the course of *Orfeo*, Monteverdi requires forty-two instruments, including five trumpets and five trombones (more than in a modern orchestra!), plus recorders, violins, and other strings, as well as a large array of continuo instruments. Performances almost certainly did not require forty-two musicians, because there is no one section within the opera where all of the instruments are playing at the same time. More typical is the arrangement

basso continuo
Continuous bass line, as well as harmony built on the bass, in support of the melody

continuo An innovation of Baroque music, a group of both bass and chord-producing instruments, providing a strong bass line and continuous harmonic support

LISTEN UP!

CD 1:10
Monteverdi, "Possente spirto," *Orfeo* (1607)

Takeaway point: Dazzling vocal display with orchestral accompaniment and interplay

Style: Early Baroque

Form: Strophic, with variation

Genre: Opera aria

Instruments: Voice, continuo, violins, trumpets, harp

Context: Brilliant vocal writing charms Charon so that Orpheus can enter the underworld heard in "Possente spirto," where we hear continuo plus a few other instruments in support of the voice. Moreover, most musicians of Monteverdi's era, including Monteverdi himself, played more than one instrument. Still, by early seventeenth-century standards, it is a massive ensemble; in its size and variety, we can see the beginnings of the modern symphony orchestra. The ensemble is not an orchestra in the modern sense, but it is an orchestra in concept and spirit.

With size comes the matter of managing it. In this respect, Monteverdi's score is unusually detailed: in many (but not all) of the numbers, Monteverdi specifies particular combinations of instruments. (This was the case in "Possente spirto"; there is an organ continuo as well as the three sets of melody instruments.) Monteverdi was an innovator here as well, specifying the instrumentation of a composition was still a relatively new practice in 1607.

Summary

Orfeo is the first significant opera. As such, it was the catalyst for a revolution in music. Its impact reverberated throughout the musical world of the upper and middle classes, especially those living in cities. Many of the revolutionary changes were already in the air, but *Orfeo* helped bring them together, harness them, and provide a springboard for further change—more than any other single development of the period. These are among the most influential and far-reaching consequences of *Orfeo*:

1. The integration of drama and music
2. A major step in the transformation of opera from a small-scale private entertainment into a grand spectacle
3. The formation of an orchestra, along with the use of orchestral effects and some attention to idiomatic instrumental writing
4. The creation of textures that focus attention on the star
5. Flamboyant vocal devices that gave audiences a reason to focus on the star
6. The integration of song and dance within a musical drama
7. Above all, the development of a language that can convey expressive meaning through musical gesture

We will hear these reverberate throughout the music of the next several centuries.

Ironically, despite its long-lasting impact, *Orfeo* was also the last important opera to subscribe to the Camerata's vision of a *dramma per musica*. The free rhythm of the vocal lines and spare setting in "Possente spirto" soon gave way to more tuneful melodies with a steadier pulse and richer accompaniment. We will hear mature examples of this in opera arias by Purcell and Handel.

CHAPTER 14

Henry Purcell and Middle Baroque Opera

"'Dido's Lament' is one of the most moving scenes in all opera."

Recitative and rap would seem to be strange bedfellows. Recitative, or speechlike song within an opera, came from the salons of Florence, Italy, at the end of the sixteenth century, while rap came from the street corners of the South Bronx, New York, toward the end of the twentieth century. Still, despite obvious differences in time, place, and circumstances, they both inhabit the middle ground between speech and song in a musical setting. Both typically deliver a lot of words quickly, and more intensely than in everyday speech. In recitative, speech is more intense because it is sung; in rap, speech is more intense because it is resonant and rhythmic. In this way they are complementary: recitative has definite pitch but indefinite rhythm; rap has definite rhythm but indefinite pitch.

But opera composers soon developed a tuneful complement to recitative—the aria. Arias quickly became the expressive focal points of operas and played a key role in opera's emergence as the first commercially successful musical genre.

LO5 The Growth of Opera

During the middle of the seventeenth century, opera became a business. By the early 1640s four theaters sponsored by the leading Venetian families were competing for the patronage of a ticket-buying audience. The season was short: just the six-week Carnival season that preceded Lent. Opera soon became a major cultural export from Venice as troupes toured throughout Italy and into France and German-speaking Europe. Characteristically, the culturally and politically independent and powerful French court of Louis XIV developed its own operatic tradition in reaction to the Italian model, although an Italian-born musician, Jean-Baptiste Lully, played the principal role in formulating it. English audiences warmed up to opera slowly. Because there was relatively little demand for opera in England, Henry Purcell (1658/9?–1695), the leading English composer of his day, composed only one, *Dido and Aeneas* (uh-NEE-us), and none of his important contemporaries were active in the genre.

MUSICAL AND DRAMATIC DEVELOPMENTS: ARIA AND RECITATIVE

Throughout the seventeenth century, opera continued to be identified as *dramma per musica*; this inscription appeared frequently on the front page of **librettos** (the texts to be sung in operas). The plots, adapted mainly from mythology, epics, and ancient history, quickly assumed a conventional structure featuring noble lovers, with comic servants providing intermittent relief from the tragedy that almost invariably ensued. Operatic plots typically revealed themselves over three acts.

Then as now, singers were the star attraction, and their showcase was the aria. Composers quickly abandoned the aria style used in "Possente spirto" for more tuneful melodies with an underlying pulse. For each opera, they wrote a lot of them, to give all of

libretto Text to be sung in an opera

Did You Know?

Purcell's aria "When I Am Laid in Earth" is a lot like a blues: a slow, sad song over a repetitive chord progression.

the leading singers opportunities to display their vocal prowess. Many were lullabies, mad scenes, or laments.

As the aria developed away from the heightened recitative of "Possente spirto" into tuneful, rhythmic music, aria and recitative assumed different functions, which corresponded to their musical features. Recitative told the story; the focus was on the words. By contrast, arias offered characters moments of reflection, where they could express their feelings. Operas typically proceeded in recitative/aria (or recitative/duet) pairs: their alternation gave the drama a start/stop rhythm.

By the late seventeenth century, musical differences between recitative and aria were clear:

	Recitative	**Aria**
Function	Move the plot along	Express intense emotion through music
Text/Setting	Large amounts of text, set syllabically, and with no repetition	Not much text, with both syllabic and melismatic settings, and frequent repetition of phrases
Melody	Irregular phrases and contours, often with several repetitions of a single pitch	Regular phrases that coalesce into sections
Rhythm	Intermittent, unmeasured rhythm approximating the rhythm of speech	A steady if sometimes subtle pulse, with occasional slowing down for expressive purposes
Instrumentation	Just continuo instruments: chordal instrument; bass instrument	Full orchestra: at least strings, and sometimes winds and brass, plus continuo
Form	Through-composed	Da capo aria or other well-defined formal stereotype

To illustrate the emergence of the aria and to exemplify the differences between aria and recitative, we consider "Dido's Lament" from Henry Purcell's opera *Dido and Aeneas*.

LO6 Henry Purcell's *Dido and Aeneas*

For Henry Purcell, *Dido and Aeneas* was an anomaly. The work was his only opera, and he apparently composed it in the mid-1680s, well before he began to compose extensively for the stage. Interestingly, the only known performance of *Dido and Aeneas* took place at a girls' boarding school, probably in 1689. Scholars speculate that it had previously been staged at court, but there is no record of that.

HENRY PURCELL

Purcell was the most eminent composer of his time and one of the most distinguished British composers of any era. For most of his career, Purcell was a court musician, the "composer-in-ordinary" to a succession of kings, and the organist at Westminster Abbey and the Chapel Royal. The majority of his important works were composed as part of his duties; they include anthems and odes to celebrate important occasions. His most substantial output for the stage was a series of **semi-operas**, works in which the main characters speak and minor characters sing and dance. This genre flourished in England during the latter stages of Purcell's career.

Henry Purcell

Fast Facts

- *Dates:* 1658/9?–1695
- *Place:* England
- *Reason to remember:* The most important English-born composer of the Baroque era

DIDO AND AENEAS

Although it became the quintessential musical product of the Baroque era, opera was a product of Renaissance culture. This is clearly evident in the plots, which were almost always drawn from antiquity. Our three examples of Baroque opera feature librettos based on a Greek myth (Orpheus and Eurydice), a Roman epic poem (the *Aeneid*), and history—the complicated romance of Caesar and Cleopatra (in Chapter 18).

There were compelling reasons for basing plots on the classics. The stories would be familiar, because classical learning was part of every cultured person's education. There was honor by association: entertainment suitable for an aristocratic audience should feature principal characters of even more esteemed social status: noble heroes and heroines, gods and demigods. And the enduring stories from classical civilization often contained moral conflicts with tragic consequences, whose resolution was supposed to edify the audience. In the case of *Dido and Aeneas*, the conflict is between duty and love for both Dido and Aeneas.

Purcell's opera is based on the tragic meeting of Dido and Aeneas, which occurs in the first part of Virgil's *Aeneid*. Aeneas is a Trojan hero, the son of a prince and the goddess Venus, and one of the few survivors of the fall of Troy. His ultimate destiny is to found the city of Rome; the *Aeneid* recounts his roundabout route there from Asia Minor to Italy. In Purcell's opera, Aeneas meets, woos, and then abandons Dido, the recently widowed queen of Carthage.

semi-opera Work in which the main characters speak and minor characters sing and dance

The Death of Dido, depicted in characteristically overwrought Baroque style by French artist Simon Vouet

The opera begins with Dido entertaining Aeneas and his fellow travelers. Through the intercession of Cupid, Dido submits to Aeneas, much to the delight of her courtiers. In a famous scene that happens offstage, the couple goes off to a cave, where they presumably consummate their relationship. Meanwhile, a sorceress and her cronies plot Dido's death. Dido is expecting that their night of love has persuaded Aeneas to marry her. However, one of the witches impersonates Mercury, the messenger god, who commands that Aeneas instead sail away. (In Virgil's version, Aeneas is simply reminded of his destiny and departs.) When Dido discovers that Aeneas is leaving, she confronts him, and they have a bitter exchange, but nothing changes; Aeneas still plans to leave. Distraught, Dido decides that she must die. It is at this point that she sings the famous lament, one of the most moving scenes in all opera.

The plot machinations, shaped by gods, demigods, witches, and other supernatural creatures, must have strained the credulity of its audience, just as it does ours. But Dido's distress rings true, and it is this deep emotion that Purcell captures so poignantly in the lament.

COMMON PRACTICE HARMONY AND MUSICAL EXPRESSION

"When I Am Laid in Earth" is the emotional high point of *Dido and Aeneas*; it is the most tragic moment in this tragic opera. To convey Dido's grief, Purcell shapes several musical elements to resonate with painful life experience: a slow tempo, labored rhythms, and the interplay between the relentlessly descending bass line and a melody that fights against it. In addition, he uses the structural and expressive capabilities of common practice harmony, a relatively recent musical development, in a way that adds power and nuance to his poignant melody.

The melody is laid over a *ground*. **Ground** (or **ground bass**) is the English term for **basso ostinato** (obstinate bass). Both terms identify a bass line that is recycled without interruption through the entire composition. The practice of composing extended works over a basso ostinato developed in the early seventeenth century and remained popular through the end of the Baroque era. Composers would establish the bass pattern, then create varied melodic (and sometimes harmonic) material over it. The pattern used in "Dido's Lament" was a cliché in Venetian opera, but Purcell found new magic in this well-worn device.

© David Farrell/Lebrecht Music & Arts

Dido cannot escape her fate, no matter how much she tries.

Purcell's ground sends musical messages at two different levels. The most direct is the slow but inexorable descent through each iteration; every statement of the ground starts high and ends an octave lower. Its persistent measured descent exerts a gravitational pull on Dido's melody. Its implicit, impersonal message is that Dido cannot escape her fate, no matter how much she tries. Its specific design animates her struggle.

There is also an expressive message in the pitches of the ground. It contains ten notes that span an octave, divided into two segments. The first six notes descend by half-step; the last four progress conventionally to a cadence. The first segment is harmonic free fall; it *could* end anywhere, although it always ends in the same place. And because the harmonic destination is momentarily in doubt, Dido's fate—at least in her mind—is also momentarily in doubt. By contrast, the second segment is almost predictable. Because it is so conventional, it reinforces the sense of inevitability.

Purcell uses the oscillation between harmonic instability and harmonic inevitability to dramatize Dido's conflicting emotions as she prepares to die, and he magnifies and personalizes them in the melody. In those passages set over the first segment, we hear Dido fight against her fate: her melody resists the gravitational pull of the ground. Conversely, we sense her resignation most clearly in the second segments, when the melody line descends or she doesn't sing at all. When she is silent during the last statement of the ground, we know musically that the end has come. Dido knows that she is going to die, and so do we. Purcell's music enables us to feel her anguish.

Looking Back, Looking Ahead

The outstanding achievement of early seventeenth-century opera was the personalizing of musical expression.

When Orfeo sings, we know that it can be only him singing—no one else is capable of such virtuosic display, and we know that he is using all of his powers to try to persuade Charon to let him enter Hades and rescue Eurydice.

The development of the aria, the harnessing of common practice harmony, and the outstanding achievements of late seventeenth-century opera made operatic singing even more expressive. The aria brought melody, harmony, and rhythm into balance. It showcased the expressive power of a single voice, the most personal of all instruments, and supported the voice with an accompaniment of unprecedented richness. Although rigid dramatic and formal conventions limited the overall dramatic effectiveness of the aria in Baroque opera, individual arias such as "When I Am Laid in Earth" offer moments of transcendent beauty and emotional depth.

Purcell's aria is our first encounter with common practice harmony in our historical survey. Although early seventeenth-century music—Morley, Monteverdi—certainly anticipates many of its features, common practice harmony became common practice only during the latter part of the century. For the next two centuries, it would provide the structural foundation for operas and oratorios, symphonies and concertos, songs and sonatas, and much more music. It would give coherence to large-scale compositions, even those lasting an hour or more, and provide a common language for music that is still familiar today.

© iStockphoto.com/Tyler Stalman

...a slow but inexorable descent...

UNIT 7
MUSIC IN THE AMERICAS

Learning Outcomes
After reading this unit, you will be able to do the following:

LO1 Know the sound and cultural function of authentic Native American music.

LO2 Hear the sound of an African musical style from the Americas and understand its use in a religious practice that integrates elements of the Catholic and Yoruba religions.

LO3 Know Anglo-Celtic folk song and its influence on other kinds of music.

LO4 Hear authentic Anglo-Celtic dance music and understand its dissemination in Europe and North America.

© Erich Lessing/Art Resource, NY

IF YOU HAD accompanied the missionaries proselytizing among native peoples in the Americas or Africa four centuries ago, what music would you have heard? If you were with the first British colonists in North America, what would the music that you brought from home have sounded like? It is impossible to know for certain. But we can surmise, because folk styles in isolated communities changed slowly, that the sound would have been reasonably close to that of twentieth-century folk recordings. Accordingly, in this unit we correlate the accounts of missionaries in North America with a recording of Native Americans, and those of missionaries in Africa with a recording of Cubans of African descent. We hear a woman from Tennessee sing a song mentioned three centuries earlier by Samuel Pepys (pronounced "peeps"), and we compare the jigs found in a seventeenth-century collection of dances with a jig by a Canadian fiddler.

Native American Ceremonial Music

"The traditional music of Native Americans is essentially timeless."

The sorcerer, who, hour after hour, sang and drummed without mercy—sometimes yelling at the top of his throat, then hissing like a serpent, then striking his drum on the ground as if in a frenzy, then leaping up, raving about the wigwam, and calling on the women and children to join him in singing. Now ensued a hideous din; for every throat was strained to the utmost, and all were beating with sticks or fists on the bark of the hut to increase the noise.

Did You Know?

Native American ceremonial music is closely akin to shamanic drumming: both use continuous, throbbing percussive sounds to help induce an altered state.

This account by the nineteenth-century American historian Francis Parkman describes the efforts of a Huron medicine man to cure Paul LeJeune, a Jesuit missionary, in 1634. LeJeune survived and lived another thirty years; he would spend eight more years in New France (France's colonies in today's Canada).

During the middle decades of the seventeenth century, LeJeune and other French Jesuit missionaries explored much of the Great Lakes region, helping to extend the boundaries of New France and attempting to convert

© iStockphoto.com/Eric Isselée

Plains Indians used buffalo as a source of food, clothing, and housing.

those Native Americans with whom they came in contact. They recorded their experiences in great detail in a series of volumes called *Jesuit Relations*.

The missionaries' comments about Native American music-making were generally far from complimentary. Writing about the singing at a feast with the Hurons, LeJeune wrote, "I believe that if the demons and the damned were to sing in hell, it would be about after this fashion. I never heard anything more lugubrious and more frightful." Others describe the singing similarly, comparing the singing of a medicine man to that of a "damned soul" or the singing of the Abenakis to "the cries and howling of wolves."

LO1 Ceremonial Music of the Plains Indians

The Plains Indians include those tribes that inhabited the vast area between what is now central Canada and New Mexico, and between the Mississippi River and the Rocky Mountains. Among the important Plains tribes were Sioux, Blackfoot, Cheyenne, Crow, and Pawnee. Some of the tribes were nomadic, following the migration of the buffalo. Others tended to build more stable communities, particularly near rivers, where the land was more fertile.

PLAINS INDIANS WAR DANCE, 1958

For Native Americans, dancing and music making were a community activity. There were leaders among the members of the group, but no specialists. The dancing and accompanying music served multiple purposes:

to seek help from the spirit world for such matters as the health of the community (the annual Sun Dance), rainfall, and victory in battle (the War Dance); to tell a story, such as the battle between good and evil (the Devil's Dance); or simply as a social activity. The War Dance discussed here was a spritual preparation for battle.

Native American music and dance were simple compared to the professional and skilled amateur music making in Europe at the same time. The dance steps required only the most basic kind of footwork and body movement, so that the dancers could instead express their feelings with vigorous shouts and yells. The most common musical support consisted only of long phrases sung on **vocables**—sung wordlike sounds that have no meaning—accompanied by drums and rattles.

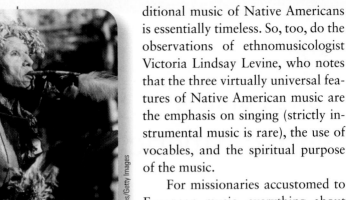

© Michael Ochs Archives/Getty Images

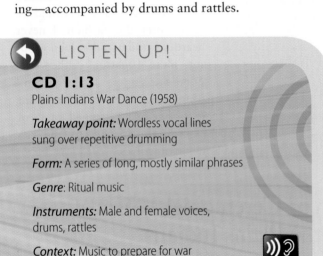

LISTEN UP!

CD 1:13

Plains Indians War Dance (1958)

Takeaway point: Wordless vocal lines sung over repetitive drumming

Form: A series of long, mostly similar phrases

Genre: Ritual music

Instruments: Male and female voices, drums, rattles

Context: Music to prepare for war

CONNECTIONS AND CONTINUATIONS

There seems to be a correlation in function between seventeenth-century missionary accounts and this contemporary performance, in that both invoke the spirit world for assistance. What the missionaries described as the "howling of wolves" could be similar to the high, wordless vocals; the repetitive drumming and percussive sounds echo their comments about drums and "beating with sticks." Both function and features suggest that the tra-

vocable Sung wordlike sounds that have no meaning

ditional music of Native Americans is essentially timeless. So, too, do the observations of ethnomusicologist Victoria Lindsay Levine, who notes that the three virtually universal features of Native American music are the emphasis on singing (strictly instrumental music is rare), the use of vocables, and the spiritual purpose of the music.

For missionaries accustomed to European music, everything about the music of Native Americans would have seemed strange. The use of drums to lay down a steady beat, melodies without words, the absence of harmony, the strange vocal style, and the seemingly irregular flow of the melody: all of these were mostly outside the missionaries' experience. Accordingly, they described it pejoratively, mainly in terms of what it wasn't—the music that they were familiar with.

It's also unlikely that they would have understood the *function* of the music. In their homeland, music was performed as part of a carefully orchestrated religious service or for entertainment. What amounted to medicinal use of music was almost certainly beyond their grasp.

Indeed, the War Dance has a much stronger connection to our very first examples than it does to the music from Europe that we have heard. The drumbeat of the War Dance is similar in its simplicity to shamanic drumming; the wordless, repetitive melody might be viewed as an elaborated *om*. We might also note the parallel between Native American singing and melismatic chant. In chants such as "Nunc aperuit nobis," there is a text, but so many of the syllables are spun out that the effect is much the same as vocables.

There is, of course, also a similarity in intent; the War Dance becomes a conduit to the supernatural. As we listen to it, we may gain a clearer sense of its purpose and power by imagining ourselves carried away as participants in the dance.

Until very recently, Native American music has remained apart from mainstream culture. One reason is the social isolation that Native Americans have endured through American history: devastated by disease, decimated by military combat, driven westward and then onto reservations. But another must be the pronounced difference in style and intent between Native American music and the music brought by European settlers. It has been largely misunderstood by mainstream culture. It has been parodied in films, on television, in cartoons—and in piano pieces for children. A few composers of concert music have tried to integrate Native American elements into their compositions, but Native American music has not been the wellspring from which distinctively American art music has developed. Only recently have Native American musicians begun to merge their traditional music with music from other traditions.

Afro-Cuban Music

"A santería ceremony without music would be almost inconceivable."

[Drums were] commonly made use of at unlawful Feasts and Merry-makings, and [were] beaten upon with the Hands, which nevertheless makes a noise to be heard at a great distance.

Did You Know?

Call and response between a solo singer and a group are key to both the song in this chapter and black gospel music.

Written by the missionary Girolamo Merolla in 1682, this is among the earliest accounts of African music. Merolla and two other missionaries kept detailed journals about their experiences on the African continent. Merolla noted, and other writers confirmed, that the Africans they observed used drums in religious ceremonies, including sending the dead to the next world, and for long-distance communication, especially in wartime.

Merolla's work took him to the Congo and to southwest Africa—what is now Angola. However, percussion instruments were apparently used extensively all along the west coast of sub-Saharan Africa at that time. Drawings by Giovanni Cavazzi, another missionary, as well as written accounts by other Europeans, show Africans from Senegal to the Congo playing drums, rattles, marimba-like instruments, and other percussion.

LO2 Middle Passage: Music from Africa to the Americas

The first slaves arrived only a decade after Columbus first landed in the Americas; they were brought to Hispaniola from Spain. The slave trade grew quickly as the demand for labor increased, and it became clear that the native population was not capable of surviving the rigors of such oppressive conditions. The first African slaves landed in Cuba in 1513, in Brazil about 1550, and in Virginia in 1619, just twelve years after the first permanent colony in what would become the United States had been established. The slave trade continued through the early nineteenth century, bringing Africans to most of the eastern half of the hemisphere.

AFRICANS IN THE COLONIES

Treatment of African slaves varied according to the colonial power. In the British colonies, such as America and Jamaica, slave owners tried to sever all ties with their slaves' homeland. They banned native languages, religious practices, and tribal and personal items, such as drums. For a variety of reasons, the colonies under

French, Portuguese, and Spanish rule allowed slaves to retain African customs and practices. As a result, many elements of African culture took on a new life, especially in Cuba, Haiti, and Brazil. We will examine the musical and cultural connection between Africa and Africans in Cuba in this chapter's example, a short excerpt of *santería* music.

FROM AFRICA TO CUBA

Over 600,000 African slaves were taken to Cuba in the nineteenth century to work on sugar plantations and in the mills. Many of them came from Nigeria and were members of Yoruba-speaking tribes. They retained much of their culture, although slaves were separated indiscriminately. There were several reasons for the retention of Yoruba culture. One was the sheer number of slaves, with so many coming from the same general region. Another was the generally lax supervision of their personal lives by the overseers of the plantations and mills. Most important, perhaps, was the formation of *cabildos*. These were mutual aid societies, formed under the auspices of the Catholic Church, which included both slaves and free blacks. *Cabildos* enabled Africans to group along ethnic lines and revive key elements of their heritage, including language and religion. As a result, many African ethnic groups created syncretic religions that merged their traditional practices with Catholicism, especially the adoration of saints. The most prominent of these religions has been *santería*.

SANTERÍA

Santería is an adaptation of Yoruba religious practices by African slaves, mainly from what is now Nigeria. In the traditional religions of the Yoruba people, initiates seek to establish a personal relationship with a patron spirit, called an *orisha*, a minor deity who serves as an intermediary between the person on earth and God. In this respect, the function of an *orisha* is much the same as that of saints in the Catholic Church; many devout Catholics pray to particular saints, asking them to intercede with God on their behalf. In *santería*, the two merged: for example, Saint Peter, who holds the keys to heaven, was linked with Eleguá, the gatekeeper of the gods. (In the following example, Odudua, the god of the earth and the underworld, is linked with San [Saint] Manuel.) Because of the close as-

santería Adaptation of Yoruba religious practices by African slaves, mainly from what is now Nigeria

sociation of *orishas* and saints, this adaptation of Yoruba religious practice in Cuba has become known as *santería*, or "the way of the saints." Music and dance are integral components of *santería* ceremony; it is through music and dance that initiates communicate with their personal orisha.

If you wander through Hispanic sections in any major city in the United States, you are likely to find, sprinkled among the storefronts, *botánicas*, shops that sell herbs and other items needed for *santería* ceremonies. Because *santería* is not an organized religion, it is difficult to determine the number of people who practice it. However, it is estimated that there are tens of thousands of priests and hundreds of thousands of practitioners in the United States alone.

Despite its strong association with Catholicism, *santería* remains essentially African. Indeed, it is as pure an expression of this particular branch of West African culture as one is likely to find in the Americas.

Music is integral to *santería* rituals; a *santería* ceremony without music would be almost inconceivable. Indeed, practitioners believe that the batá drums, the drums used in *santería* rituals, must be consecrated before they can be used in ceremonies involving initiates.

CD 1:14

Anonymous, Song for Odudua

Takeaway point: Complex rhythms support pentatonic melody with repetitive refrain

Form: From free form to refrain-based repetition

Instruments: Mixed voices with male soloist; *batá* drums

Context: Song to invoke the presence of a Yoruba deity

Cuban Yoruba community performing a *santería* healing ceremony today

The reason? When consecrated, the drums contain *aña*, the *orisha* associated with drumming; they become the place where God's power resides and the voice through which God and the *orisha* communicate with devotees.

Like shamanic and Native American drumming, Odudua's song reminds us of the power of the beat; as in other instances, its function is to induce an altered state that encourages communication with the divine. In this case, however, the drumming features complex, repetitive rhythms in a ritually prescribed sequence, with two of the drummers repeating the patterns over and over while the master drummer follows a more improvisatory path. As a result, the rhythms are far more complex, with several distinct layers of activity and syncopation, and with the beat implied by the rhythmic interaction and the vocal line rather than consistently marked with a drum.

CONNECTIONS AND CONTINUATIONS

There are clear correspondences between the accounts of what seventeenth-century missionaries heard and what we hear in our Afro-Cuban example, in particular, the extensive use of percussion instruments as accompaniment for singing and dancing, and the use of the hands to play them. Both the musical features and the singer's use of an old dialect of Yoruba underscore the close affinity between an African culture and its re-creation in Cuba.

Like Native American music, *santería* music contrasts sharply with the European music that we have heard: prominent percussion, rhythm over melody, extensive repetition, and no harmony. Unlike Native

American music, however, musical exchanges between European and African musical cultures date from colonial times. By the early nineteenth century, we read accounts of slaves singing religious songs in a different way at camp meetings, encounter the *contradanza habanera* (contradance from Havana), imported to Cuba from Haiti and then exported to Spain, and hear the plucking of the banjo in "blackface" entertainment. We encounter early fruits of their interactions in the nineteenth century, in the music of the minstrel show and in the *habanera* from Georges Bizet's opera *Carmen*.

If we compare this example with the music of the next several chapters, we will become aware of the oppositional relationship between African music and the European music that would have traveled to the Americas during the years of the slave trade—the seventeenth through early nineteenth centuries. Both urban music (opera and opera parodies, hymns and other liturgical music, sonatas, symphonies, and songs) and folk music (the Anglo-Celtic folk song and folk dance heard next) present sharply contrasting musical values. Among the most outstanding are these: emphasis on melody versus emphasis on rhythm; keyboards, strings, and winds versus percussion instruments; and clear division between performer and audience versus call-and-response interaction between leaders and group. And in the case of urban music versus African music, we can note these additional differences: harmony versus no harmony, and major/minor scales versus pentatonic scales.

Anglo-American Folk Song

"Ballads were often morbid, even grisly, and usually had a moral."

In his entry for January 2, 1666, English diarist Samuel Pepys wrote, "But, above all, my dear Mrs. Knipp, with whom I sang, and in perfect pleasure I was to hear her sing, and especially her little Scotch song of 'Barbary Allen.'" Pepys (1633–1703), a British naval administrator, kept his diary between 1660 and 1669. Published in 1825, the diary gives us an inside look at daily life in upper-class England during the middle of the seventeenth century. More to our point, it mentions a folk song already well known in London over 350 years ago.

"Barbara Allen" must surely have come to the United States with the earliest English and Scottish immigrants, well before the American Revolution. Many of the immigrants settled in the southern Appalachians, where their descendants remained isolated until well into the twentieth century. As a result, there are hundreds of extant versions of the song from the region: one early twentieth-century researcher tracked down ninety-eight versions of it in Virginia alone.

The lyric differs widely in amount of detail; only the basic story line remains the same. The melodies to which various versions are set resemble each other only in the most general way. It would seem that such widely divergent variants would accumulate only over several generations. The findings of Cecil Sharp, an English folklorist, support this view. Sharp traveled throughout England to catalog an almost forgotten repertoire of songs. He also visited the southern Appalachians in the 1910s, where he discovered songs that existed in England only in memory.

By the 1930s, folklorists reclaimed this musical heritage more directly by recording performances of folk songs and dances. Among the pioneers in this new direction were John and Alan

ballad Song with a simple, tuneful melody and a lyric that tells a story

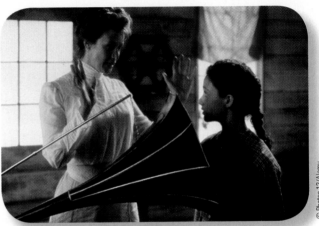

The movie *Songcatcher* (2000) documents the story of a turn-of-the-century musicologist who for the first time transcribes and records a treasure trove of Scots-Irish ballads surviving in the Appalachians.

© Photos 12/Alamy

LISTEN FURTHER

You can hear a clip of "Barbara Allen" from *Songcatcher* in the YouTube playlist.

Did You Know?

By the early twentieth century, ninety-eight different versions of the seventeenth-century ballad "Barbara Allen" survived—in Virginia alone.

Lomax. Working under the auspices of the Library of Congress, the Lomaxes ventured into remote rural districts throughout the United States, visited prisons and work camps, and in the process, discovered Leadbelly and other talented performers, black and white. The Lomaxes also brought folk performers to Washington, D.C. Among their guests was Rebecca Tarwater, a native of Tennessee, who recorded "Barbara Allen," a song she had learned from her mother, in 1936 for the Library of Congress archives.

LO3 The Anglo-Celtic Folk Ballad

"Barbara Allen" is a folk ballad, one of the most common types of folk songs. **Ballads** are songs with a simple, tuneful melody and a lyric that tells a story. These stories were often morbid, even grisly, and usually had a moral. In this respect, "Barbara Allen" is typical. It intertwines love and death—two of the most enduring themes in art and life—in a most understated and succinct way, as we can see in the lyric:

> 'Twas in the lovely month of May, The flowers all were bloomin'.
> Sweet William on his death-bed lay, For the love of Barbry Allen.
> He sent his servant to her door, He sent him to her dwellin'.
> My master's sick and he calls for you, If your name be Barbry Allen.
> Then slowlye, slowlye, she got up, And to his bedside goin':
> No better, no better, you will ever be. For you can't have Barbry Allen.
> He turned his pale face to the wall, And burst out a-cryin'.
> Adieu, adieu to all below, And adieu to Barbry Allen!
> Sweet William died on a Saturday night, And Barbry died on Sunday.
> Their parents died for the love of the two, They was buried on Easter Monday.
> A white rose grew on William's grave, A red rose grew on Barbry's.
> They twined and they twined in a true-lover's knot, A-warnin' young people to marry.

The version presented here is an especially brief account of the story of Barbara Allen and Sweet William. Most other versions of the song give more details, which—not surprisingly—differ from one to the next. For instance, several versions have William slighting Barbry so that she has a reason for rejecting his plea. Others give more detail about William's death and her remorse: in some, as she is leaving, Barbry hears the church bells peal, announcing William's death. It is only then that she regrets her coldness and asks her mother to prepare her deathbed.

However, even in the most elaborate versions, the tale unfolds quickly, and each act has grave consequences: there are six deaths in three days in our account. The laconic, almost impersonal, recounting of the tale also invests it with power and poignancy. It's almost as if the narrator is numb with shock, although the emotional reserve in both text and presentation is part of the style. Indeed, the tale is more myth than account; it is a familiar story line.

The musical setting is emotionally divorced from the lyric. A sweet, gracefully arched melody, formed from four short phrases, conveys no sense of the string of tragedies recounted in the several stanzas of the lyric.

CONNECTIONS AND CONTINUATIONS

Ballads have been popular in the British Isles since before Pepys's time and in North America for almost as long. Although their roots are in the countryside, ballads traveled to the cities, as we learn from Londoner Pepys.

For well over two centuries, Anglo-Celtic folk songs have inspired music at virtually all levels of discourse, both in the British Isles and in North America. Traditional performance of folk songs remained a customary part of life in isolated regions through the early twentieth century. Electricity, then clear-channel radio, interstate highways, and cable television eventually connected these pockets of traditional culture to the outside world. However, even as "authentic" performances of these folk songs became rarer, a wave of folk revivals brought new versions of songs like "Barbara Allen" to new audiences. The Celtic music movement has gone beyond merely reviving this music. Celtic bands recreate traditional material, often with as much authenticity as research can provide, and create new music on this solid traditional base, typically by blending traditional and contemporary musical elements.

LISTEN UP!

CD 1:15
Anonymous, "Barbara Allen"

Takeaway point: Simple melody made up of four short phrases that form a graceful arch

Style: Anglo-Celtic folk song

Form: Strophic

Genre: Ballad

Instruments: Solo voice

Context: Song sung recreationally by rural folk

These songs have also shaped popular music in the British Isles and in North America for over two centuries. Thomas Moore's sanitized settings of Irish melodies in the early nineteenth century and Robert Burns's Scottish song settings (including "Auld Lang Syne") were among the most popular English-language songs of the nineteenth century. Their influence is evident in the middle-class songs of Stephen Foster and others. In the second quarter of the twentieth century, folk songs were a point of departure for both country music and the urban folk music of Woody Guthrie and others.

Both fed into rock-era music, most notably the music of Bob Dylan and other singer-songwriters. Folk song also touched rock more directly, in the music of The Beatles and others.

Folk song from the British Isles has been used in concert music in several ways: in elegant settings, such as those of Haydn and Beethoven, and as a source and model for music on stage, from the early eighteenth-century production *The Beggar's Opera* (Chapter 18) to Stephen Sondheim's grisly musical *Sweeney Todd: The Demon Barber of Fleet Street*.

PEOPLE'S MUSIC 6

Anglo-American Folk Dance

"The English Dancing Master is evidence of the extent to which lower-class, rural music penetrated into middle- and upper-class culture."

With the publication of *The English Dancing Master* in 1651, John Playford (1623–1686/7?) launched a career that would soon make him the dominant music publisher in England. His company would publish six more editions before his death, and eleven more after that, the last appearing in 1728.

What was new about Playford's anthology wasn't the dances but the publication of them. Country dances were already popular in Elizabethan times. It's likely that many dated back decades, if not centuries. *The English Dancing Master* for the first time gathered together and issued such dances in a single volume.

Most of the dances consist of a single strain, usually between eight and sixteen measures in length; some have two slightly contrasting strains. Playford's

Did You Know?

The fiddle would become one of two signature instrumental sounds in country music. The other was the steel guitar, which entered country music by way of Hawaii in the 1930s.

anthology shows only the melody, to be played by a treble instrument, preferably the violin (as Playford noted on the title page of the second edition). We can infer that accompaniment was optional and typically improvised. The dances are short; they last less than a minute. Fiddlers extended these dance tunes into longer numbers by repeating the strain or combining two or more similar melodies.

LO4 The Jig

About two-thirds of the dances in Playford's anthology are in compound duple meter (two beats to the measure, with each beat typically divided into three

What was new about Playford's anthology wasn't the dances but the publication of them.

equal parts). In our time, we associate this meter most often with the **jig**, a sprightly dance popular throughout the British Isles. The jig dates from the fifteenth century; Ireland is, to the best of our knowledge, its home. Few of these dances in compound duple meter are actually called jigs; some instead have fanciful names like "An old man is a bed full of Bones." However, the meter and the rhythm of the melody often match the rhythm we associate with the jig in other contexts. These musical features and the occasional title tell us that the jig was very much a part of musical life in seventeenth-century England, in both the country and the city.

Newfoundland, Canada, 1982

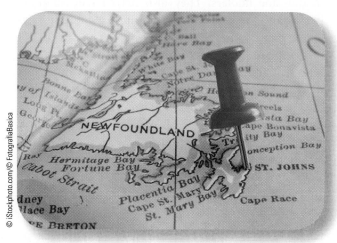

Even as Playford presented to upper-class audiences the country dances that he had gathered, many of the English, Scottish, and Irish working class were immigrating to North America. Some flocked to cities like Boston and New York. Others settled in remote rural areas, such as Newfoundland, where they would remain isolated for generations.

Newfoundland is the fifteenth-largest island in the world. It is northeast of Maine and east of the Canadian mainland. On the outskirts of St. John's, the capital city, is Cape Spear, the easternmost point in North America, just south of the pushpin in our map. New-

foundland has the longest documented connection with Europe of any region in the Americas. Viking explorers landed on the island five centuries before Columbus. John Cabot founded St. John's in 1497; the city is the site of the oldest European settlement in North America. Fishermen, first from Portugal and England and then from Ireland, fished the waters off the Newfoundland coast. Eventually, emigrants from the southeastern part of Ireland and the southwestern part of England established permanent settlements on the island. From the mid-seventeenth century through much of the eighteenth century, England and France fought over Newfoundland and its fishing grounds. Eventually the English prevailed, but not before the French devastated English settlements. Today, most Newfoundlanders are of Irish and English heritage; however, there is a small pocket of French-speaking citizens in the southwestern corner of the island. England discouraged colonization because it was to its advantage to retain the fishing rights rather than to cede them to a colony.

Climate and geography have also kept Newfoundland isolated from the rest of Canada. For much of the year, the waters around the island are frozen; ice creates a barrier between Newfoundland and the rest of Canada. As a result, the settlers

jig Sprightly dance popular throughout the British Isles

Climate and geography have kept Newfoundland isolated.

retained much of their culture—especially so outside St. John's. The similarity between the accents of Irish living in southeastern counties like Kilkenny and the accent of Newfoundlanders is evidence of this. Musically, the connections seem just as strong, as we will hear in "Boston Laddie," a jig performed by Rufus Guinchard (1899–1990).

"Boston Laddie": A Jig from Newfoundland

Especially during the latter part of his life, Rufus Guinchard was one of the most popular fiddlers in Newfoundland. At the time of this recording he was eighty-three. "Boston Laddie" is Guinchard's tune, but it is also very much in the style of a traditional jig. Newfoundland is heavily Irish, so he would have heard dance tunes in this style growing up. Guinchard's style of playing seems deeply rooted in the past; it's similar to the fiddle playing one hears on the earliest recordings of American old-time music, which date from the 1920s.

"Boston Laddie" consists of two short strains. Each strain is constructed from short phrases of fast-moving notes; the melody typically contains rhythmic patterns of three equal notes to a beat, or two notes per beat in a long/short pattern. The complete jig consists of the two strains played in alternation four times; the first strain comes back at the end for a fifth time. We can diagram the sequence of tunes by using A and B to identify the two tunes: A = the first tune, or its repetition; B = the second tune.

Connections and Continuations

The dances in *The English Dancing Master* are in effect seventeenth- and eighteenth-century country music, in the sense that they convert folk music into commercial music while preserving something of the original character. We have no way of knowing how these dances sounded in London ballrooms, but we can assume that they would have gained some polish and lost some vitality.

We do know that by the time Playford published his first edition, the jig had been a staple in English stage entertainment for about a century—it was a dance commonly used in a jigg, an often bawdy burlesque, with acting, singing, and dancing, and elsewhere. It had also become a more aristocratic and somewhat more sedate dance in France, Italy, and Germany. In France, it was the *gigue*; in Italy, the *giga*. There it became part of a suite made up of several dances—as we will discover in Chapter 16.

In Canada, especially in Newfoundland, the musical heritage exemplified by Guinchard's jig led to a late twentieth-century revival of Celtic music—the Celtic music scene was one branch of a movement on both sides of the Atlantic to reclaim this centuries-old music and bring it into the present. In the southern Appalachians, as in Newfoundland, jigs were in the repertoire of old-time fiddlers. They also played reels (another lively dance, from Scotland), hornpipes, and other up-tempo dance tunes.

Playford's editions of *The English Dancing Master* represent an important step in the urbanization of folk music because they presented the dances in as authentic a form as possible at the time. It is further evidence of the extent to which this lower-class, rural music had penetrated middle- and upper-class culture. We will encounter further evidence of the influence of Anglo-Celtic folk dance in a gigue by Bach, a sung jig from John Gay's *The Beggar's Opera*, and a minstrel-show song by Stephen Foster.

LISTEN UP!

CD 1:16
Guinchard, "Boston Laddie" (1982)

Takeaway point: Vigorous, fast-moving rhythm at a brisk tempo

Style: Anglo-Celtic folk dance

Form: Two melodies in alternation

Genre: Jig

Instruments: Fiddle and boots (for timekeeping)

Context: Good-time music: tunes for vigorous folk dancing

UNIT 8
MUSICAL LIFE IN THE EIGHTEENTH CENTURY

Learning Outcomes

After reading this unit, you will be able to do the following:

LO1 Understand the growth of the music business in the eighteenth century.

LO2 List the major developments in eighteenth-century music.

LO3 Contrast the two main styles of eighteenth-century music, Baroque and Classical.

© The Minuet (oil on canvas), Le Clerc, Jacques Sebastien (c. 1734-85) / Musee de la Ville de Paris, Musee du Petit-Palais, France / Giraudon / The Bridgeman Art Library International

CHAPTER **15**

From Baroque to Classical

"The eighteenth century saw the end of one musical era and the emergence of another."

Go from town to town in the United States around Christmas, and chances are you'll hear an excerpt from Handel's *Messiah* at a school or church in each town. Walk through the stores in a mall or have a meal at an elegant restaurant, and you might hear a movement from Vivaldi's Four Seasons, one of Bach's Brandenburg Concertos, a Mozart piano concerto, or a symphony or string quartet by Haydn. If you don't want to venture out, just call the IRS for fun, and listen to the recorded music while you're on hold. And if you've taken piano lessons for any significant length of time, chances are you learned pieces that Bach wrote for his children and students, or minuets that Mozart composed when he was six and seven years old, and sonatas that he composed somewhat later.

For us, perhaps the most meaningful aspect of the music of the eighteenth century is that so much of it is still with us. Music by Bach, Handel, Vivaldi, Haydn, Mozart, and others is still very much in the air. That's not true of the music before 1700; we aren't likely to casually encounter music by Josquin des Prez or Claudio Monteverdi, despite its quality. Why is this so? One answer is simply that the eighteenth century offers great music that deserves to be heard. But there's more to it than that. The music of these great composers was the product of two major developments: the growth of music as a business and the almost universal adoption of common practice harmony by European composers.

Did You Know?

Among the biggest fans of Baroque music were heavy-metal guitarists Ritchie Blackmore of Deep Purple and Eddie Van Halen. Blackmore acknowledged borrowing from Bach for his classic solo "Highway Star."

It is mainly because of these developments that this music is still familiar and accessible to twenty-first-century listeners.

LO1 The Growth of the Music Business

It is only in the eighteenth century that we can begin to see music as a commercial enterprise—a multidimensional business that provided employment for not only musicians but also those working in music-related fields. Certainly, many of the components of the industry were already in place by 1700: public performance for profit, instrument making, music publishing, and private musical instruction had been viable enterprises for decades, even centuries. However, all of these grew significantly during the eighteenth century, and more were added—most notably, writing about music.

PUBLIC PERFORMANCE

In 1700, opera—serious opera—was arguably the most prestigious form of public, musical stage entertainment. By the end of the century, music available in public performance included not only serious opera but also opera parodies, such as John Gay's *The Beggar's Opera* (Chapter 18), German light stage entertainments such as Gluck's *Die Pilgrime von Mekka* (the source of "Unser dummer Pöbel meint"), comic operas such as *Don Giovanni* (Chapter 22), and oratorios like Handel's *Messiah* (Chapter 19). Moreover, by the end of the century, concerts of orchestral music were common in larger musical centers. Mozart premiered several of his piano concertos, including the one we will hear in Chapter 23, in public concerts. Haydn traveled to England twice in the 1790s at the invitation of the violinist and impresario J. P. Salomon, each time bringing six symphonies with him to be premiered in London (among the first set of six was the "Surprise" symphony discussed in Chapter 21).

Concerts of popular music were common enough to be depicted—albeit somewhat fancifully—by eighteenth-century painters.

PRODUCTION OF MUSICAL INSTRUMENTS

The production of musical instruments increased substantially in response to greater demand for them. The early eighteenth century also saw the peak of the golden age of violin making: the shops of the Amati, Stradivari, and Guarneri families were still producing the most valued instruments of all time well into the century, and there were other fine violin makers throughout western Europe during the entire century.

The century began with Bartolomeo Cristofori's invention of a new kind of keyboard instrument, the **pianoforte**, so called because performers could play both soft (*piano*) and loud (*forte*) by changing their touch. However, not until the 1780s did it replace the harpsichord as the keyboard instrument of choice in public performance. Keyboard instruments, first the harpsichord, then the piano, became fixtures in upper-class households and in the households of those who aspired to upper-class status. Learning to play the piano became a customary part of the education of young women, and of young men with evident musical ability.

pianoforte Eighteenth-century keyboard instrument, so called because performers could play both soft (*piano*) and loud (*forte*) by changing their touch

Learning to play the piano became a customary part of the education of young women.

THE GROWTH OF MUSIC MAKING

Music making in the home, both vocal and instrumental, and by both professionals and amateurs, grew throughout the century. An increasingly literate musical public demanded those goods and services that supported it. Professional musicians from Bach to Beethoven supplemented their income through teaching. Music publishers brought out a wide range of music—from simple airs (songs) to sonatas that still challenge professionals. Booksellers offered instructional methods and guides to performance: among the several important eighteenth-century treatises are those by J. S. Bach's son Carl Philipp Emanuel on keyboard playing and by Wolfgang Amadeus Mozart's father, Leopold, on violin playing.

As late as 1700, virtually all of those professional musicians who produced the music that has come down to us had relied almost exclusively on the patronage of church and court. Music that was popular then also existed, as we have heard, but virtually no commercial popular music—because there was no industry to disseminate it. That began to change early in the eighteenth century. Public performance, publishing royalties, and private instruction supplemented—and in some cases, replaced—patronage as sources of income for musicians. For example, George Frideric Handel, whom we will meet soon, was an entrepreneur as well as a composer. During his time in London, he was involved with two opera companies; both enjoyed public support, though they eventually failed. After the second failure, he began to compose oratorios, such as *Messiah*. Mozart made a good living, mainly from performances, teaching, composition, and publishing royalties. He died penniless in part because he spent his money as fast as it came in.

The career of Joseph Haydn epitomizes the transition from patronage to independence. Haydn spent much of his career in the service of Miklós (Nicolas) Esterházy, a Hungarian nobleman who was among the richest men in Europe. Haydn was a servant. Early on, he slept in the stable while composing symphonies and string quartets that we still hear today. When Esterházy died in 1790, Haydn received a pension and release from his duties. In the interim, he had become one of the most esteemed composers in Europe, due in large part to the publication of his music—in both authorized and unauthorized editions. A century earlier, he might well have served a patron, but he would have enjoyed neither the esteem nor the income that came his way after he left Esterházy.

Musical Centers

Most of the eighteenth-century music still familiar to us originated in western Europe: Italy, France, Germany, Austria, and the British Isles were the main centers of activity. At the beginning of the century, Italian music was the most influential. Opera was the most popular vocal music, and sonatas and concertos were the cutting-edge instrumental music. Early in the century, the influence of Italian music, the one truly international music of the era, was pervasive. Nevertheless, the music of France and Germany had a distinctly national character. The British Isles had a rich folk music tradition, and there had been English composers of distinction in the late sixteenth and seventeenth centuries, including William Byrd, John Dowland, and Henry Purcell. But the most important classical musicians in London during the early eighteenth century came from abroad. Moreover, Italian musicians found employment throughout Europe, where they spread their influence, and composers from other countries went to Italy to receive advanced training.

However, by the end of the century, Vienna had become the main center of musical activity and influence. Haydn, Mozart, and Beethoven all settled there—Haydn after his lengthy service to the Esterházy family; Mozart after growing up in Salzburg (and throughout Europe; he spent much of his youth visiting European cities as a child prodigy); and Beethoven, who left Bonn, Germany, in 1792 to seek fame, fortune, and instruction from Haydn.

LO2 Major Developments in Eighteenth-Century Music

The two major developments of the 1700s were the widespread acceptance of common practice harmony and the explosion of instrumental music. The term **common practice harmony** identifies a system of harmonic organization that was all but universal from the end of the seventeenth century through the first half of the nineteenth century—William Billings's defiantly different harmony (People's Music 8) is an exception that proves the rule—and has continued to be a widely used and understood harmonic practice in Western music up to our own time. Common practice harmony is unique in that its conventions, particularly cadences and standard progressions, were so widely understood that composers could use them to shape form.

This capability was a major reason for the explosion of instrumental music. Before the eighteenth century, large-scale compositions were almost exclusively vocal; the text helped shape the work, as we discovered in the Josquin mass movement and Monteverdi's opera aria. Now, there was no need for texts to hold compositions together; harmony provided the structure. Composers' skill with this still-new practice increased throughout the century. An opening movement in a typical Baroque concerto is about three or four minutes long. The first movement of a Mozart piano concerto is typically at least three times as long.

Common Practice Harmony

Common practice harmony came into widespread use just before 1700, as we heard in the Purcell aria. In the first decades of the century, composers like Bach and Handel used common practice harmony to create musical statements that typically expressed a single emotional state—joy, anger, serenity. However, by the last two decades of the century, composers had developed another approach. In their works, musical events followed one another like a rational

> **common practice harmony** System of harmonic organization that was all but universal from the end of the seventeenth century through the first half of the nineteenth and continues to be widely used and understood in Western music; its conventions, particularly cadences and standard progressions, were so widely understood that composers could use them to shape form

argument that presented, then reconciled, contrasting musical materials. Indeed, music theorists of the time frequently compared music and rhetoric. The development of a clear, coherent, and comprehensive musical style based on common practice harmony can be understood as the quintessential musical expression of the **Enlightenment**—that eighteenth-century period in Western culture when reason came to be embraced as the main source of legitimacy for authority.

INDEPENDENT INSTRUMENTAL MUSIC

Another major development was the exponential growth of independent instrumental music. Much of the instrumental music before 1700 was functional: either for a church service (for example, organ preludes) or for dancing, onstage or for social occasions. There are sonatas, concertos, suites, and other music just for listening that date from the early 1600s, but it took almost a century for these forms to become well established. Once that happened, the stream of instrumental works became a flood. Tens of thousands of concertos, sonatas, and suites, genres that we will soon experience, were composed in the first part of the eighteenth century. The latter part of the century saw the emergence of the symphony, the grandest of all instrumental forms, along with new kinds of sonatas; chamber music for numerous instrumental combinations, most notably the string quartet; and concertos for one or more instruments and orchestra, reconceived as more of a dialogue between soloists and orchestra.

With quantity of instrumental music were both quality—as we will discover in subsequent chapters—and the *perception* of quality. Through the seventeenth century, vocal music, especially opera, had reigned supreme in the secular world; instrumental music was considered inferior. That perception began to change in the eighteenth century. By the beginning of the 1800s, the roles were reversed: many commentators regarded abstract instrumental music, such as Beethoven's symphonies, as the most sublime form of musical expression. So, we can trace our more balanced view of the relative worth of vocal and instrumental music—opera and symphony, song recital and chamber concert, musical theater and jazz—back to the beginning of the eighteenth century.

LO3 Music and Musical Styles: From Baroque to Classical

The eighteenth century saw the end of one musical era and the emergence of another. As the century began, Baroque music, which had begun to take shape around the time of Monteverdi, was approaching its artistic peak. It would flourish in the first half of the century before giving way to several transitional styles, few of which have remained popular. However, during the last quarter of the century, Haydn, Mozart, and their contemporaries synthesized the Classical style from these diverse trends. Their music has remained popular; indeed, one might well assert that it is more widely known now than during their lifetime.

Most of the music discussed in this unit exemplifies either late Baroque style or Classical style. These are the styles used in the more complex music performed by professionals and skilled amateurs and heard in opera houses and concert halls, as well as churches that retained capable musicians on staff. In addition, there were other developments with a more populist orientation. Among the examples considered in this part of the text are Gay's opera parody, national anthems (a musical response to the diminishing authority of monarchies during the Enlightenment), and music to fan the flames of revolution in the American colonies.

An eighteenth-century altarpiece in the Church of the Miracle, Catalonia, Spain, captures the excess that characterized Baroque aesthetics.

BAROQUE AND CLASSICAL

We call the music of the seventeenth and early eighteenth century **Baroque**. The term originally referred to an irregularly shaped pearl or a convoluted thought process. It came into use to describe the new art and architecture that emerged in the late sixteenth century and continued through the early eighteenth century, which some critics found bizarre, even grotesque. The term gradually lost its pejorative connotation among art historians and came to designate simply the art of the period. However, not until the middle of the twentieth century did music historians apply the term to the music of this era. As used in music, it describes the style of the era; there is no real connection between the term and the aesthetic of the period, as there is with Classicism or Romanticism. The music that we will consider here from the first part of the eighteenth century is typically designated as late Baroque.

We refer to the music of the latter part of the eighteenth century as Classical. The **Classical style** in music took shape in tandem with a neoclassical movement in architecture and the visual arts, and shared many of the same values. However, the term *Classical*, as applied to music, has more to do with the growing historical consciousness of nineteenth-century musicians and commentators. As they preserved, published, and performed the music of the past, they referred to the music of Haydn, Mozart, and Beethoven as "classical" in its more general sense, to designate exemplary artifacts of a particular genre, or simply work of supremely high quality.

Thomas Jefferson's mansion in Virginia—Monticello (completed 1772)—epitomized the clean, balanced Classical lines of the new eighteenth-century style.

Over time, the meaning of the term *Classical* has expanded to refer to the prevailing concert music of the late eighteenth century, not just the music of Haydn, Mozart, and Beethoven (the Classical *style*); and more generally to refer to the large body of concert music of the last millennium (classical *music*).

They shared the same century and musical language, but late Baroque music and Classical music grew out of distinctly different aesthetics. Baroque composers sought to express a single mood in a composition or a major section. Classical composers sought to create musical tension through contrasts, then to resolve the tension. The most outstanding difference between the music of these two eras is the greater frequency and degree of contrast in Classical music.

> **Baroque** In music, a term that identifies much of the concert music of the seventeenth and early eighteenth centuries; late Baroque music seeks to project a single mood in a composition or a major section
>
> **Classical style** In music, a term that identifies the concert music of the late eighteenth century; Classical composers sought to create musical tension, typically through contrasts, then to resolve the tension

THE BEGINNINGS OF POPULAR MUSIC

To this point we have encountered music that was popular, such as the "L'homme armé" tune. But not until the eighteenth century do we begin to encounter music created by specific individuals that conveys the attitude and addresses the audience that we associate with popular music. We offer just a small sample in this part: an opera parody by John Gay and Christopher Pepusch, and a revolutionary song by William Billings. The Billings song was exceedingly popular during the American Revolution, but only the Gay opera was specifically popular entertainment. Still, we will find in both Gay's parody and Billings's defiance the anti-establishment attitude that we associate with the freshest popular music. We will also find European monarchs reaching down and revolutionaries reaching out to the masses by adopting or commissioning national anthems. We begin our survey of eighteenth-century music in 1700 with the music of Arcangelo Corelli.

UNIT 9
LATE BAROQUE INSTRUMENTAL MUSIC

Learning Outcomes

After reading this unit, you will be able to do the following:

LO1 Understand Baroque instruments and ensembles, as well as idiomatic use of instruments.

LO2 Recognize the sound of the Baroque sonata through the music of Arcangelo Corelli.

LO3 Become familiar with the Baroque suite through the music of J. S. Bach.

LO4 Review the prevailing Baroque musical aesthetic and style.

LO5 Understand how the orchestra evolved during the Baroque era.

LO6 Become acquainted with the Baroque concerto through Vivaldi's *The Four Seasons*, a famous early example of program music.

LO7 Gain insight into Bach's fascination with instruments by listening to his Brandenburg Concertos.

INSTRUMENTAL MUSIC IN the late seventeenth and early eighteenth centuries had a decidedly national cast. Italy was home to the sonata, for small ensembles, and the concerto, for orchestra. From France came the suite, a collection of dances. There were suites for solo instruments, chamber groups, and orchestras. The most distinctively German music came from the Lutheran north. These were works for organ or harpsichord—typically, free-form compositions such as the prelude, fantasia, or toccata, followed by a fugue, which was a consistently contrapuntal composition.

The three instrumental genres that gained an international presence were the sonata, the suite, and the concerto. They became popular in England and Germany as well as their home countries. Each served mainly an elite audience, with most composed for the amusement of patrons and their retinue. We consider the sonata and suite in this chapter and the concerto in the next.

© View of the Organ in the church at Rotha (photo). / St. George's Church, Roetha, Germany / The Bridgeman Art Library International

CHAPTER 16

Sonata and Suite

"Purely instrumental music was now a suitable vehicle for expressive musical communication."

What does a Baroque chamber music ensemble have in common with a jazz combo or a classic rock band? Quite a bit—despite the obvious differences in time, place, genre, and audience. The similarity begins with instrumental roles. All three groups typically have these features.

Did You Know?

The late Baroque composers Corelli and Bach were fluent improvisers, much like today's rock and jazz musicians.

ticular combination of instruments was novel—indeed, the electric bass was just over a decade old when the first British rock bands invaded America. And in each case musicians developed new sounds and new ways of playing, which often exploited the capabilities of the instruments. Our first encounter with the distinctive texture of Baroque instrumental music will be in a violin sonata by the Italian composer Arcangelo Corelli.

LO1 Baroque Instruments

The core instruments of Baroque music are the harpsichord and members of the string family, especially the violin and cello. We will hear several examples of Baroque music in Part 3. All feature strings, most notably violins and cellos, and a keyboard instrument, most often a harpsichord. Instrumental works that did not include strings or even a harpsichord were far less common.

Harpsichords and violin-family stringed instruments were not new even in 1600. What changed during the course of the seventeenth century were the quality of the instruments, the ways in which composers and performers exploited the capabilities of these instruments, and the roles played by the various instruments within an ensemble.

THE VIOLIN FAMILY

By the time Corelli composed his violin sonatas at the end of the seventeenth century, the violin family had for the most part assumed its modern form. The bows of the modern violin family have a different shape and are held differently than earlier ones. The necks of the

	Baroque chamber ensemble	Jazz combo	Rock band
One or two melody instruments	Violin, flute	Saxophone, trumpet	Lead guitar(s)
A chord-producing instrument	Harpsichord or organ	Piano or guitar	Rhythm guitar
A bass instrument	Cello or bassoon	String bass	Electric bass
One or more percussion instruments	Harpsichord (see later discussion on the harpsichord)	Drum kit	Drum kit

In addition, all the textures are similar, featuring a prominent melody supported by a strong, active bass line, and with chord-producing instruments supplying harmony between melody and bass.

But the kinship among genres goes beyond the similarities in roles and texture. In each case, the par-

By the early eighteenth century, the violin family had assumed its modern form.

Harpsichord with two manuals (1634)

instruments are a little longer, and the strings are made of metal or gut wound with metal, rather than just gut. But the instruments are substantially the same now as they were three hundred or more years ago.

The violin was the most widely used melody instrument of the Baroque era, and the cello was the preferred bass instrument. String instruments were equally at home in small groups and large ensembles and were suitable for use in church and chamber settings, as well as in orchestra pits and outdoors.

THE HARPSICHORD

The **harpsichord** is a keyboard instrument in which depressing a key causes a **plectrum**, a plucking device made of quill (the hard shaft of a bird feather), to pluck one or more strings. The sound produced by this plucking has a sharp attack followed by a ringing tone that decays quickly. Although the harpsichord is a pitched instrument, the overall effect is quite percussive: in an ensemble, one often hears the rhythm of the harpsichord part much more clearly than its pitches (hence the identification of the harpsichord as a percussion instrument in a Baroque "rhythm section").

Unlike the piano, the harpsichord is not a touch-sensitive instrument. There is virtually no correlation between the force with which the player pushes down the key and the amount of sound produced. To introduce sound variety, harpsichord makers created several sets of strings for each key. These could be coupled together: that is, depressing a key would cause two or more strings to be plucked; they might be the same pitch or an octave apart. More elaborate harpsichords typically had two keyboards, or manuals, one low and toward the performer, the other higher and farther away. This en-

abled performers to use different sets of strings for each manual.

In the Baroque era, the harpsichord was a popular solo instrument; it was also the preferred chord-producing instrument in chamber ensembles and orchestras performing secular music. Many surviving harpsichords from this era have beautifully crafted and decorated cases. They are seldom used in performance, however; most reside in museums or private instrument collections. Contemporary harpsichordists typically perform on modern reproductions of earlier instruments.

BASSO CONTINUO: THE BAROQUE RHYTHM SECTION

Basso continuo, or continuous bass, is a bass line that typically continues steadily throughout a musical work or extended section within the work. The bass line and the chords that complement it can be sustained, slowly changing, or active. But it is almost always there in Baroque music: in ensemble music—vocal and instrumental—the characteristic Baroque texture is one or more melodic parts at the top, a steady basso continuo on the bottom, and keyboard chords filling in the space between top and bottom.

Continuo also refers to the instrumental combination playing the bass line and enriching it with harmony: typically a bass instrument, such as the cello, and a chord-producing instrument, such as the harpsichord. We can think of the continuo instruments as a Baroque-era rhythm section: like the modern rhythm section of

harpsichord Keyboard instrument in which depressing a key causes a plectrum to pluck one or more strings

plectrum Harpsichord plucking device made of quill (the hard shaft of a bird feather)

drum kit and rhythm guitar, for instance, they supply a bass line, harmony, and steady underlying rhythm.

The unique texture and sound of the continuo are among the defining features of Baroque music. It was not used in Renaissance music, and both the harpsichord and the consistent, steady movement of the bass disappeared from the sound world of concert music in the latter part of the eighteenth century. Indeed, the sound of an active, continuous bass does not return until the 1930s in the music of the swing era.

LO2 The Baroque Sonata

Sonata is the Italian word for "sounded." It came into use toward the end of the sixteenth century to identify an instrumental composition not derived from dance. The style of the sonata derived most directly from the **canzona**, an Italian instrumental genre itself derived from polyphonic vocal music. By the middle of the seventeenth century, **sonata** was the term of choice in Italy for solo and small-group instrumental compositions. By the early eighteenth century, the sonata had taken on the shape it would assume for the next several decades: an instrumental work in three or four separate movements. A **movement** is a self-contained section of a larger work, typically separated from adjacent movements by silence and distinguished from them by tempo, meter, and occasionally key.

CORELLI AND THE BAROQUE SONATA

If there was one musician working in 1700 who could be considered a legend in his own time, it would have been the violinist and composer Arcangelo Corelli, one of the finest violinists of his era and the most influential teacher. He worked in Rome under a series of patrons: Queen Christina of Sweden and two cardinals. Because

Arcangelo Corelli

Fast Facts

- *Dates:* 1653–1713
- *Place:* Rome, Italy
- *Reasons to remember:* One of the finest violinists and most influential composers of his era

© Lebrecht/ColouriserAL

this support put him in a relatively comfortable financial situation—almost uniquely so for composers of his era—Corelli could afford to be particular about the music he made available to the public.

During his lifetime, Corelli published only six sets of works: four sets of what were termed trio sonatas, a set of solo sonatas, and a set of concertos, for strings and continuo. These works were, by the standards of the time, exceedingly popular throughout western Europe. They were reprinted many times during Corelli's lifetime and after his death and were the most widely circulated models of all three genres. The six sets of works helped to solidify Corelli's reputation; he was the first composer to make a name for himself strictly as a composer of instrumental music.

SOLO AND TRIO SONATAS

Corelli's sonata sets played a key role in establishing the function, form, and instrumentation of the sonata. The **church sonata** (*sonata da chiesa*), a four-movement sonata, often served as music for the mass; the **chamber sonata** (*sonata da camera*), a secular sonata in three or more movements, entertained the aristocratic audiences that supported his music.

Baroque composers like Corelli were somewhat inconsistent in their terminology but not as mathematically challenged as it might seem at first glance. **Solo sonatas** typically require three players: one playing a featured melodic instrument, such as

continuo Instrumental combination playing chords and a bass line: typically a bass instrument, such as the cello, and a chord-producing instrument, such as the harpsichord

canzona Italian instrumental genre derived from polyphonic vocal music

sonata By the middle of the seventeenth century, the term of choice in Italy for solo and small-group instrumental compositions; by the early eighteenth century, a three- or four-movement work whose movements have alternately slow and fast tempos

movement A self-contained section of a larger work, typically separated from adjacent movements by silence and distinguished by tempo, meter, and occasionally key

church sonata (*sonata da chiesa*) Four-movement sonata, which often served as music for the Mass

chamber sonata (*sonta da camera*) Secular sonata in three or more movements

solo sonata Instrumental composition that typically requires three players: one playing a melodic featured instrument, such as a violin, plus continuo (chord-producing and bass instruments)

trio sonata Instrumental composition that typically calls for four performers: two playing melodic instruments and two others playing the continuo

ritornello Melodic idea that is introduced at the beginning of a movement and returns periodically, often in different keys, as a kind of musical milestone; form that uses this device

opus In the eighteenth century, a term usually followed by a number, used to identify a musical composition or (more often) a group of compositions in a particular genre deemed worthy of publication

as a violin, and two playing chord-producing and bass instruments (the continuo). Here "solo" refers simply to the spotlighted instrument. A **trio sonata** typically calls for four performers: two playing melodic instruments and two others playing the continuo. In this case, "trio" refers to the three independent lines: two treble and one bass.

Solo or trio, the sonata was a multimovement work. Typically, there were four movements, in a slow-fast-slow-fast sequence, although this could vary. Church sonatas followed this pattern more consistently than chamber sonatas.

THE RITORNELLO

The typically fast second movement introduces us to a distinctively Baroque formal device: the ritornello. **Ritornello** (Italian for "little return") refers to a melodic idea that is introduced at the beginning of a movement and returns periodically, often in different keys, as a kind of musical milestone. "Ritornello" also refers to a form that uses this device.

THE SOUND OF THE BAROQUE VIOLIN SONATA

Corelli's sonata exemplifies several characteristic features of late Baroque music for instrumental ensembles. Running throughout both movements is the melody/continuo texture played on the core instruments: violin (melody), harpsichord (chords, obbligato lines, bass line), and cello (bass). Rhythmically, there is consistency in approach within each movement: the first features alternating sustained and rapid rhythms over a steady bass; the second has mostly fast-moving patterns at a brisk tempo. There is little melodic repetition in the first movement but a consistency in melodic style. In

 LISTEN UP!

CD 1:17–18
Corelli, Sonata in C major, Op. 5, No. 3, first and second movements (1700)

Takeaway point: Characteristically Baroque sound and texture: melody + continuo

Style: Baroque

Form: Through-composed (without repetitions) first movement; ritornello-like form in second movement

Genre: Solo chamber sonata

Instruments: Violin, harpsichord, cello

Context: Instrumental music for the entertainment of elite audiences

THE LANGUAGE OF MUSIC

You'll notice in the Listen Up! feature that the title of the work contains the following information: the genre (sonata), its key (C major), and the abbreviation "Op. 5, No. 3." This abbreviation reads as "Opus 5, Number 3." *Opus* is the Latin word for "work." In music, **opus** refers to a musical composition or, in this case, a set of musical compositions; here, "No. 3" identifies the third sonata in the set. Composers began to use the word *opus* around this time to identify a set of pieces, usually in the same genre, of sufficiently high quality to merit publication. This designation enabled those who bought the music to distinguish one set of works from another. In the Baroque era, opus numbers provide some sense of chronology, because we generally have publication dates. However, a set of works, such as Corelli's sonatas, may have been composed over a period of several years prior to publication; the numbering within a set is not a reliable guide to the date of composition. Beginning with Beethoven's works, opus numbers begin to provide a fairly reliable guide to the date of composition.

the second movement, Corelli periodically brings back the opening melodic idea—the ritornello. All of these features are in the service of the dominant Baroque aesthetic, which called for one mood, or "affect," per movement (see discussion on page 122).

Composing for Orchestral Instruments: A Baroque Innovation.

The demands of the solo line, most notably the elaborate figuration in the first movement and the arpeggiated chords in the second, evidence Corelli's expertise as a violinist. These melodic figures are not only distinctively instrumental but also especially suited to the violin.

By 1700, the practice of composing idiomatically for the string and wind instruments used in Baroque orchestras and chamber music was so well established that the relationship between vocal and instrumental composition had been reversed: now vocal lines often featured instrumental-style figuration. Because we have grown up hearing instruments played in idiomatic ways, it may be difficult to appreciate how radical a development this was.

To get some idea of the impact of idiomatic composition and performance, imagine that Jimi Hendrix and Eddie Van Halen had limited their guitar lines to what they could do vocally. Their solos would have had none of the brilliant virtuosity or special effects for which their playing is famous. But that was how almost all composers wrote for these instruments prior to 1600.

Composition and Improvisation.

If you've taken music lessons or played in a band or orchestra, you're used to playing what someone else wrote. By contrast, if you're part of a rock band or jazz combo, you may well be playing your own material, which may be partially written down or worked out without notated music.

Corelli's original version of the sonata—especially the first movement—falls somewhere between these two extremes, especially for the harpsichordist and the violinist. The harpsichordist uses the bass line and a series of numerical symbols (called **figured bass**) as a shorthand system for indicating the notes and chords to be played. This is the Baroque equivalent of the chord changes used in jazz and some rock. In the first movement, the violinist starts with a bare-bones outline and is then expected to add lavish ornamentation to it.

All of this was done in the moment (improvised). The keyboardist and the violinist created music on the spot, much like an improvising jazz or rock musician would today. This ability was a skill expected of any accomplished musician. In this respect, skilled musicians in Corelli's time were more like today's rock and jazz musicians than like many of today's classically trained musicians. They were well-rounded musicians who composed, improvised, and performed their own compositions and occasionally those of others. They also had big hair, although it was store bought.

> **figured bass** Bass line and series of numerical symbols used by Baroque musicians as an abbreviated system that indicates specific notes and chords to be played by a keyboard player
>
> **suite** Collection of dances linked by key and sometimes by melodic material

Skilled musicians in Corelli's time were more like today's rock and jazz musicians than like many of today's classically trained musicians.

LO3 The Baroque Suite

A **suite** is a collection of dances linked by key and sometimes by melodic material. The practice of grouping dances in this way dates from the fourteenth century but didn't become widespread until the late sixteenth century. The first common groupings were pairs of dances, such as the courtly pavane and galliard. By the middle of the seventeenth century, dance pairs had grown into a suite of several dances, first in France, then elsewhere in Europe.

THE "CLASSIC" BAROQUE SUITE

Within a Baroque suite, the number and sequence of dances were infinitely variable. However, for about a century—circa 1640 to 1740—the heart of the suite consisted of four dances. In typical order of appearance, they were the allemande, courante, sarabande, and gigue. Suites typically included other popular dances, such as the minuet and the gavotte, and larger-scale suites often began with a prelude, overture, or other grand movement.

The suite is the most important French contribution to Baroque music, so it is curious that its four central dances have such an international flavor. **Allemande** is the French word for "German"; in this case, it means a German dance. Typically, it was in quadruple meter and had a moderate tempo. The **courante** (the French word for "running") is a French dance, but it has an Italian counterpart, the *corrente* (the Italian word for "running"). Both are in triple meter; the Italian version typically has a faster tempo. The first sarabandes were hot-blooded dances brought to Spain from the New World and so racy that they were banned in certain quarters. However, by the time it surfaced in the suite, the **sarabande** had become a slow, stately dance in triple meter, with a characteristic short-long rhythm in the melody. **Gigue** is a cognate for the English *jig*. Like the jig, the gigue is typically in compound duple meter (two beats per measure; beats divided into three equal parts). The main dances come from four different points of the compass—a pleasing symmetry.

Baroque composers composed suites for solo instruments, chamber ensembles, and orchestras. In the first part of the seventeenth century, the lute was by far the most common solo instrument. However, by the end of the century, the harpsichord had supplanted the lute as the favored solo instrument and would remain dominant during the rest of the Baroque era.

In France, enthusiasm for dance started at the top. Louis XIV (the "Sun King"), firmly ensconced on the French throne, is outfitted here as Apollo for a court ballet performance.

allemande German dance, typically in quadruple meter with a moderate tempo

courante French dance with an Italian counterpart, the *corrente*; both in triple meter, but the Italian version typically has a faster tempo

sarabande Slow, stately dance of Spanish origin, in triple meter, with a characteristic short-long rhythm in the melody

gigue Dance, typically in compound duple meter, inspired by the jig; customarily the last movement of a suite

The suite for solo instrument was far more common than any other kind. Suites for small ensembles were much less common, although individual dance movements appeared frequently in sonatas. Orchestral suites often required large ensembles, with strings, winds, brass, and percussion. The use of winds, brass, and percussion instruments suggests that such works were often performed outdoors, where the sound of these instruments carried well.

JOHANN SEBASTIAN BACH

On March 11, 1829, Felix Mendelssohn (1809–1847), already an acclaimed composer, conducted a performance of J. S. Bach's *St. Matthew Passion* at the Berlin Singakademie. The performance, a milestone in the revival of Bach's music, brought his music to the attention of scholars and audiences and helped raise him from relative obscurity to his current stature as one of the greatest composers of any era.

Today, Johann Sebastian Bach is a household name. Along with Beethoven and Brahms, he is one of the "three B's" and among that handful of composers whose name recognition extends well beyond the classical music world. We hear his music everywhere—not only in the concert hall but also on radio and TV, in stores, even on the telephone as we wait on hold. Keyboard students encounter his music early in their training; a steady diet of Bach is essential for their development.

It wasn't always so. Bach was born in Eisenach, a town in what is now Germany. At ten, he was orphaned

and went to live with his older brother. Bach never left Germany. He spent most of his professional life as a music minister for Lutheran churches in out-of-the-way cities in the heart of Germany: Arnstadt, Mühlhausen, Weimar, and Leipzig. His one secular post, in the service of Prince Leopold of Cöthen, spanned the six years between 1717 and 1723. Despite this isolation, Bach was able to familiarize himself with the main musical trends of the eighteenth century, which he integrated into the Lutheran musical world in which he worked for most of his life.

Johann Sebastian Bach

Fast Facts

- *Dates*: 1685–1750

- *Place*: Germany

- *Reasons to remember*: The bridge between Baroque and Classical music; the last of the significant Lutheran composers and the last of the great contrapuntal composers of sacred music

© Fotosearch Stock Photography

Bach was remarkable for his thoroughness. Despite time-consuming duties at his several posts and a large family (twenty children, of whom only ten survived to maturity), Bach produced an astonishing amount of music. He had a passion for taking on—and completing—enormous projects: for example, a five-year cycle of cantatas for church services—about three hundred in all—composed during his first years in Leipzig; and two sets of preludes and fugues for keyboard, in all twenty-four keys, entitled *The Well-Tempered Clavier*. And that's the tip of the iceberg: Bach wrote extensively in every major genre except opera.

In the history of classical music, Bach is the bridge between old and new. He was the last of the significant Lutheran composers and—more important—the last of the great contrapuntal composers of sacred music, a tradition that extended back centuries. He was a profoundly spiritual man, living at a time when secular values were in the ascendancy.

Although his music brings a centuries-old tradition to a close, Bach also influenced important music of every subsequent generation. For the first seventy-five years after his death, Bach and his music were little known to anyone but musicians; Haydn, Mozart, and

Beethoven learned from his music. After Mendelssohn's performance of Bach's *St. Matthew Passion*, those influenced by his music included not only such distinguished composers as Chopin, Brahms, Debussy, and Stravinsky but also leading jazz and rock musicians. He was even indirectly responsible for the first big electronic music hit: Walter/Wendy Carlos's *Switched-on Bach*.

BACH AND THE SUITE

Bach's numerous, diverse suites provide a unique perspective on his compositional personality. In them, we can hear Bach summarize one of the important genres of the Baroque era and use it as a springboard for his imagination and a means to apply his personal stamp.

Bach composed more than thirty suites. Over half of them are for keyboard, including three sets of six suites, but there are also suites for solo violin, cello, flute, and lute, and four suites for orchestra. Like most composers of his time, Bach wrote most of his music for specific purposes and occasions. Not surprisingly, he composed the majority of his suites during his six-year tenure at Cöthen. However, the genre continued to interest him after he moved to Leipzig: he composed the six partitas (his last set of suites), the four orchestral suites, and his last and largest keyboard suite, the Overture in the French Style, there.

As the title of his last suite suggests, Bach regarded the suite as a distinctively French genre. He drew inspiration from the French composers Jean-Baptiste Lully and François Couperin as well as German composers from previous generations, most notably Johann Froberger and Dietrich Buxtehude. By way of example, the opening movements of several larger suites, including

LISTEN UP!

CD 1:19

J. S. Bach, Gigue, from Orchestral Suite No. 3 in D major (1731)

Takeaway point: From jig to gigue: a rich, contrapuntal setting of this lively dance

Style: Baroque

Form: Binary

Genre: Suite

Instruments: Strings, harpsichord, trumpets, timpani, oboes, bassoon

Context: Dance-inspired music for the enjoyment of those in Bach's circle in Leipzig

the four orchestral suites, use Lully's overtures as a model. At the same time, Bach freely mixed and matched French-inspired music with other national styles. The opening movements of an earlier set of suites (the so-called English Suites) resemble concerto movements, and the famous air from the third orchestral suite evokes an Italian aria. Here we hear Bach's connection with French tradition and key features of his musical personality in a gigue, the final movement of his third orchestral suite (see Listen Up! on page 121).

BACH'S GIGUE AND THE SUITE

Bach's gigue has introduced us to one of the most popular genres of the Baroque era, the suite. While it is only one movement of several—Bach's suites typically have five or more—it does show key features of the genre: the connection with dance, the use of binary form, and the consistency of rhythm and melody throughout.

We get a taste of Bach's art in the gigue. It is evident in such features as the counterpoint, which enriches, rather than impedes, the bright mood projected in the theme—it's as if everyone joins in the music making—and in his ability to introduce variety into the basic melodic material, even as he sustains rhythmic momentum throughout each section.

LO4 Baroque Aesthetics and Style in Instrumental Music

The sonata and the suite signaled both the increased popularity of instrumental composition and its rise in status. The sonata (and the concerto) *began* as an elite music, serving church and court. Of the dances that merged into the Baroque suite, almost all had humble origins but *became* an elite music. Instrumental music was not as esteemed as opera and other vocal music during the early eighteenth century, but it was far more important in musical life than it had been at the beginning of the seventeenth century.

In our discussion of "Possente spirto" in Chapter 13, we highlighted the profound shift in musical values that took place around 1600: for Monteverdi and like-minded composers, musical gestures could now convey expressive meaning. In vocal music where the composer tries to convey specific emotions and moods, the text typically served as a moment-to-moment guide to the meaning. That was not the case in instrumental music, although composers may have given their works descriptive titles or even indicated in the score what a passage depicted (we hear this in Vivaldi's "Spring" in the next chapter).

Nevertheless, by the early eighteenth century, composers felt that their music—even instrumental music—could communicate quite specific emotional states, such as joy, languor, or melancholy. Some writers went so far as to link moods with particular dances. Writers on music described such moods as "affects" or "affections." This aesthetic principle thus became known as the **Doctrine of Affections**.

To communicate a particular affect or emotion, a composer would establish the mood at the outset of a movement, then sustain it throughout. Interest came mainly from varying the material; new musical ideas generally amplified or elaborated upon the original idea. The effect is akin to seeing an object from different perspectives: the object remains the same, but the view is constantly changing.

The three movements considered here approach, in different ways, the "one movement = one affect" idea that is so central to Baroque music. In the first movement of his sonata, Corelli sustains the mood by spinning out the melody and keeping the texture consistent. In the second, he reuses the opening idea throughout the movement. Bach establishes and maintains a relentless rhythmic flow, interrupted only by the cadence at the midpoint. Variety comes from the addition and subtraction of parts and the many permutations of the musical material.

The rise of instrumental music exemplified by Corelli's sonata movements and Bach's gigue—an infinitesimally small sample of the prodigious output of Baroque composers—represents the second and final stage of the musical revolution begun a century earlier. Purely instrumental music was now a suitable vehicle for expressive musical communication. Composers and performers believed this to be true—to the extent that they occasionally noted the affect in the title. This in turn depended on two key developments of the seventeenth and early eighteenth centuries: idiomatic composition for instruments and common practice harmony. Both were securely in place by 1700. We hear further examples of their realization in the next chapter.

The Baroque Concerto

"The concerto added a potent new expressive dimension to Baroque music."

You hear them in restaurants, in upscale stores, on hold on the telephone, on the radio, and in commercials. Even if you don't know these works by name, chances are you'll recognize the movements from them that we will discuss in this chapter. What are they? Vivaldi's *The Four Seasons* and Bach's Brandenburg Concertos. These are among the most familiar examples of the Baroque concerto, the most popular orchestral genre of the early eighteenth century.

LO5 The Orchestra during the Baroque Era

During the seventeenth century, the orchestra evolved from a large but somewhat random collection of instruments into a more standardized ensemble, which closely resembles the heart of the modern orchestra. Among the most significant developments were these:

- Building the orchestra around bowed stringed instruments and standardizing the string section
- Scoring for specific instruments, with each instrument or instrument section typically having its own part
- Composing independent orchestral works as well as orchestral accompaniments to operas, ballets, and sacred music

The man most responsible for the development of the seventeenth-century orchestra was the Italian-born French composer Jean-Baptiste Lully (1632–1687),

Did You Know?

Baroque composer Antonio Vivaldi bragged that he could compose a concerto faster than the copyists could copy the parts.

who until his untimely death presided over musical life at the court of Louis XIV. Lully would conduct his ensembles by stomping a cane on the floor while sitting at his keyboard instrument. During a performance of his *Te Deum* in January 1687, he injured his foot with the point of a cane he was using. Gangrene set in, and within three months of the injury, Lully died. Who would have thought that conducting an orchestra could be a life-threatening activity?

In addition to his duties as the primary court composer, Lully directed two string orchestras, one containing twenty-four players, the other about eighteen. For important events, he would combine the two orchestras and add wind and percussion instruments as needed. The size of his orchestras and the precision of the musicians' playing impressed visiting royalty, to the extent that many of the sovereigns who visited France and heard Lully's orchestras formed their own, more modest ensembles on returning home.

LO6 The Concerto

In the late Baroque era, the concerto was the dominant orchestral genre. It was especially popular in Italy, its home, and spread throughout much of western Europe, although France resisted it until the 1730s. In this and other respects, the concerto was the large-scale instrumental counterpart to the sonata.

The most distinctive feature of the **concerto** was the contrast between large and small: an orchestra made up of strings along with one or more spotlighted instruments. The number of spotlighted instruments determined the type of concerto. A concerto that features a single solo instrument, such as a violin or flute, is called, appropriately enough, a **solo concerto**. A concerto that

concerto Dominant orchestral genre of the late Baroque, featuring contrast between large and small; orchestra made up of strings along with one or more spotlighted instruments

solo concerto Concerto that features a single solo instrument, such as a violin or flute

concertino Small group of soloists featured in a concerto grosso

concerto grosso Concerto that features a small group of soloists (the concertino)

tutti Referring to passages in which everyone plays

ritornello Section of a concerto that returns, in fragments or in complete statements

features a small group of soloists (the **concertino**) is called a **concerto grosso**. The classic concertino is two violins and cello—in effect, the instrumentation of a trio sonata embedded in an orchestral setting. Other concertinos were possible; they could be formed from virtually any combination of instruments.

The relationship between orchestra and soloists was both collegial and competitive. Sometimes they worked together; at other times, they were in opposition. The presence of larger and smaller groups made it possible for composers to create contrasting sound masses. **Tutti** passages, in which everyone played (*tutti* means "all" in Italian), alternated with passages in which just the soloists and the continuo played, or at least were prominently featured.

This relationship between orchestra and soloists was still relatively new in 1700. However, the term *concerto* had already been in use for almost two centuries. It first surfaced in the sixteenth century as an all-purpose term for a composition with voices and instruments. Not until the end of the seventeenth century did it acquire the more specific meaning that it has today: an orchestral work that features one or more soloists.

THE DESIGN OF THE BAROQUE CONCERTO

Late Baroque concertos, especially those modeled after Vivaldi's concertos, typically have three movements: the first is fast, the middle is slow, and the third is again fast, although not necessarily in the same tempo (or meter) as the first movement.

The outer movements typically begin with an emphatic statement that sets the character of the movement. Composers used two approaches to give weight to the opening statement. One way was to have the parts enter one by one, playing the main melodic idea. In that way, listeners would hear the melody three or four times, each time with the support of an additional voice. (After a part played the melody, it would slip into more of a background role.) This is the approach Corelli used in the second movement of the sonata heard in the previous chapter, but on a much grander scale.

The other approach was to have all the instruments play at the same time. Some would play the main melodic idea; the others would support this melody with harmony or other lines. The opening tutti statement is called the **ritornello**, because it returns, sometimes in fragments (the little return), or in complete statements.

The movement grows out of the opening ritornello. The role of the soloists is to elaborate on the basic character of the movement. Periodically, the orchestra interjects a fragment of the ritornello to reaffirm the affect presented at the outset and mark an intermediate destination on the harmonic round-trip from tonic to tonic. Often the movement ends with another complete—or nearly complete—statement of the ritornello.

The two approaches achieved much the same result by different means: in either case, the listener would know the basic character of the movement from the outset. As the movement progressed, there would be contrast in sound (more instruments/fewer instruments) and activity (the solo sections were often busier), but the character remained relatively consistent throughout the movement.

VIVALDI'S *THE FOUR SEASONS*

Google "Italian Baroque concertos" and you'll get dozens of composers whose names end in *i*—from Albinoni and Corelli to Locatelli and Torelli. However, the name that appears most often is that of the Venetian composer Antonio Vivaldi.

Vivaldi was a prolific composer. He published thirteen sets of sonatas and concertos during his lifetime and composed hundreds more, including over five hundred concertos. Many feature instruments other than strings: he composed concertos for oboe, bassoon, and even mandolin. Some were composed in great haste to fulfill an immediate need. As a result, the quality is uneven, but the best of them rank with the finest and most influential examples of the genre.

Music Concept Check

The tonic, or home key, is the focal pitch of a scale, to which the other pitches are related and to which a piece of music tends to return.

Vivaldi's practice was to give his sets of concertos distinctive titles. He called his first set of twelve concertos, published in 1711 as Opus 3, *L'estro armonico*, which translates loosely as *Harmonic Fancy*. However, in his Opus 8, which he entitled *Il Cimento dell'armonia e dell'inventione* (*The Contest of Harmony and Invention*), he went a step further. He designated the first four concertos of the set *The Four Seasons*; each depicts a season of the year, beginning with spring. They are the most famous early example of program music.

Antonio Vivaldi

Fast Facts

- *Dates*: ca. 1685–1741
- *Place*: Venice, Italy
- *Reason to remember*: A prolific and influential Baroque composer best known for his numerous concertos

PROGRAM MUSIC

Program music is instrumental music in which a composer depicts an extramusical inspiration, such as a scene, a story, or an idea, or the experience or feeling that the inspiration arouses. As explained by Franz Liszt, the famous nineteenth-century composer and pianist who brought the term into use, the program—a poem or perhaps just a few words of description—serves as a preface to the composition in order to "direct [the listener's] attention to the poetical idea." The idea of composing programmatic music was fashionable throughout the nineteenth century, from Beethoven's "Pastoral" symphony through the tone poems of Liszt,

Richard Strauss, and others. Liszt's description summarized prevailing practice even as it guided both future composers and listeners.

The first programmatic works date from the sixteenth century—we noted previously William Byrd's "Battell" music—and by 1700, there were numerous works with clear programs, most notably a set of six biblical sonatas by Johann Kuhnau, Bach's predecessor in Leipzig. Opera, particularly French opera with its extensive dance scenes, also required descriptive music. But no work composed before 1800 has matched the fame of Vivaldi's *The Four Seasons*, and few match Vivaldi's skill in depicting the program.

"SPRING"

"Spring" is a solo concerto: the featured instrument is the violin. In the first movement, Vivaldi harnesses the tutti/solo dynamic of concerto form to express and elaborate on the affect of the movement. The ritornello suggests the joy of spring, at the outset and every time it returns. The solo episodes amplify and clarify the spring-like mood by translating sounds of spring—bird calls, a babbling brook, and a thunderstorm—into music.

Vivaldi's interpretations of nature sounds do not replicate the actual sounds. But they approximate them closely enough that listeners can make the association with written descriptions, which Vivaldi provided in the score and to which concertgoers might have access.

"Spring" introduces us to the Baroque orchestra, the Baroque concerto, and program music. Because there's such a clear delineation between solo and tutti, we can hear not only the composition of the orchestra—strings plus keyboard—but also the specific roles assigned to each instrument. The frequent contrasts between orchestra and soloist present the prevailing mood from different perspectives. And in this movement, idiomatic composition is harnessed to the program: the dazzling effects—effectively playable only on the violin—serve the expressive goal of portraying springtime in sound.

Vivaldi's music was a significant influence on J. S. Bach, who went so far as to arrange several of Vivaldi's concertos for other instruments. In the previous chapter, we considered how Bach borrowed from the French. In this next example, we explore how he transformed the Italian concerto.

CD 1:20

Vivaldi, Violin Concerto in E major, Op. 8, No. 1 ("Spring" from *The Four Seasons*), first movement (1723)

Takeaway point: Baroque-era program music at its finest

Style: Baroque

Form: Ritornello

Genre: Solo concerto

Instruments: Solo violin; orchestral strings (violin, viola, cello, bass) and keyboard

Context: Music appropriate for public or private, and sacred or secular, performance in multiple venues: church, theater, large rooms

LO7 Bach's Brandenburg Concertos

A Pepsi commercial for the 2004 Super Bowl featured a young Jimi Hendrix trying to decide whether to buy a Pepsi or a Coke. Both soda machines stand in front of music stores: the Pepsi machine in front of a pawnshop selling an electric guitar, the Coke machine in front of Bob's Accordion World. As the eleven-year-old Hendrix opts for Pepsi, we hear strains of "Purple Haze." As the camera pans over to Bob's Accordions and the Coke machine, we hear the opening guitar riff of the song played on an accordion, as the commercial announces, "Whew . . . that was a close one"—disaster barely averted by choosing the right soda.

What does this commercial have to do with Bach's Brandenburg Concertos? Both are demonstrations of the significance of instrument choice. The commercial is a warning about the dire consequences of choosing the wrong instrument. Bach's concertos are the flip side: they show the enormous appeal of instrumental variety.

Instrumental sounds were as important to Bach as they would become to Hendrix. Bach had a fascination with instruments and instrumental sounds throughout his life. He was the leading consultant on organ construction in Germany during his lifetime. His cantatas require instruments that were obscure in his own time and obsolete now. His estate contained, among other items, eight keyboard instruments and ten stringed instruments.

With the Brandenburg Concertos, Bach took ad-

vantage of the musicians available to him to create the most diverse set of concertos produced by him or any of his contemporaries. Each concerto has a decidedly different instrumentation: a large orchestra in one; a high trumpet in another; all strings in a third; recorders in a fourth; a solo group of harpsichord, violin, and flute in the fifth; and no violins in the sixth. Moreover, each concerto has a unique relationship between solo and tutti. This diverse instrumentation sets these works apart from not only Bach's other concertos but also the concertos of his contemporaries. There's no other set quite like it.

BACH'S DIFFERENT PATH

How can we account for the uniqueness of the Brandenburg Concertos? We can perhaps understand them as a response to the varied instrumental resources available to the composer. But Bach's mixing of instruments goes well beyond what other composers of the time did, and there are other aspects of the concertos that set them apart, as we will discover. It may be presumptuous to try to establish a causal connection between character and composition—especially in Bach's case, because we have so little firsthand information about him. Still, we can perhaps infer, from the study of his career as a musician and the amount and kinds of music that he composed, something of his character.

Whether he undertook a project in fulfillment of his professional duties; to meet an immediate need for, say, teaching pieces for his children and other pupils; or simply for its own sake, Bach seemed to compose from an overpowering inner need. He composed prodigiously, often far beyond what was needed to satisfy the demands of a particular responsibility. There was little financial incentive to compose: he received no royalties from his works and obtained few commissions. For Bach, it seems, the quality and nature of his work were far more important than recognition or financial gain.

Both his music and certain incidents in his life suggest a strongly independent character. We can sense it

from the time that he spent in prison, the result of a conflict between him and the duke who employed him in Weimar, and his occasionally contentious relationship with the town councilors in Leipzig. We can also infer it from certain aspects of his compositions, such as the choice of projects—the Goldberg Variations and the Mass in B minor, both monumental works with virtually no prospects for performance in major venues—and his adherence to a contrapuntal style, even as it grew increasingly out of fashion. Indeed, he wanted to leave the last word on counterpoint before he died—his final work was *The Art of the Fugue*, which he did not finish—even as the most fashionable music of the day moved toward a lighter, more accessible style.

These observations and inferences may help us understand the uniqueness of the Brandenburg Concertos as a set and so many of the distinctive features of the individual works. Bach would place on them the unmistakable stamp of his personality.

BACH'S THIRD BRANDENBURG CONCERTO

In terms of instrument choice, it would seem the third concerto is the most conventional of the six: the orchestra is just strings, as it was for Vivaldi. What makes it different is the number of strings: three violins, three violas, three cellos, and continuo of double bass and harpsichord. By specifying precisely the number of string players and assigning each performer a distinct part, Bach created a chamber music work that verges on being orchestral. In some sections, such as the opening ritornello, each group of three strings plays the same part, as in an orchestra. In other passages, each group of strings breaks into close harmony, as in the first episode. And there are passages where a single instrument is in the spotlight, with other instruments in an accompanying role, as in a solo concerto. Indeed, Bach presents so many instrument combinations that it is as if he has upgraded from the stark black and white of the solo/tutti format to gray scale.

As in the Vivaldi concerto, the entire movement grows out of the opening ritornello. But whereas Vivaldi begins with short, clearly articulated phrases, which he repeats, Bach begins at a more molecular level. The concerto opens with a three-note motive, a simple, generic musical idea. The opening ritornello spins out from this very basic idea in three interlocked installments, each of which presents a new perspective on the motive.

BACH AND BAROQUE STYLE

We've heard four Baroque instrumental works to this point: two by Italian composers and two by Bach. If we compare the Italian sonata and concerto to the two pieces by Bach, we can surmise that Bach's music is distinguished in part by these characteristics:

1. It tends to be denser and more contrapuntal.
2. It is more consistent in its rhythmic flow.
3. Melody is generated by permutations of an opening idea; multiple different melodic ideas are less likely.
4. Bach's instrumentation is more inventive.
5. Bach's music is likely to be more expansive: the first movement of his concerto is almost twice as long as the first movement of Vivaldi's "Spring."

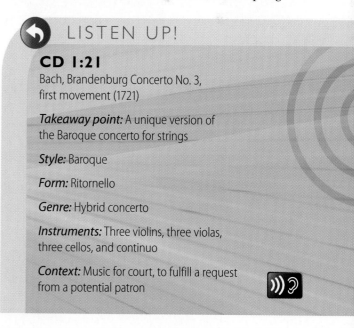

🔊 LISTEN UP!

CD 1:21
Bach, Brandenburg Concerto No. 3, first movement (1721)

Takeaway point: A unique version of the Baroque concerto for strings

Style: Baroque

Form: Ritornello

Genre: Hybrid concerto

Instruments: Three violins, three violas, three cellos, and continuo

Context: Music for court, to fulfill a request from a potential patron

UNIT 10
LATE BAROQUE VOCAL MUSIC

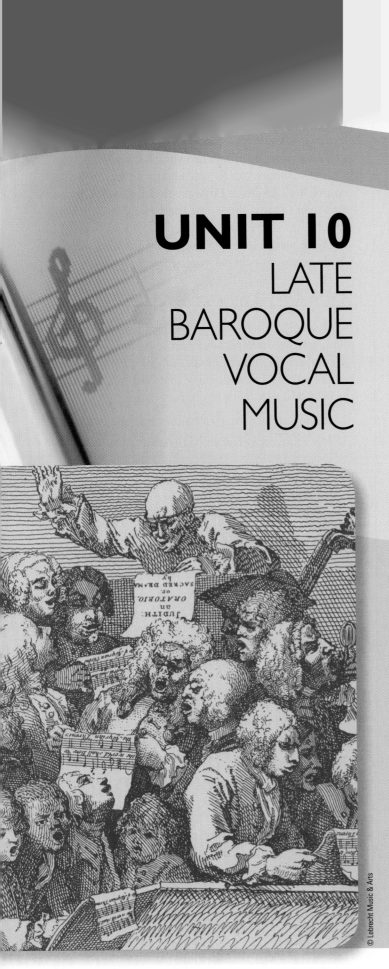

© Lebrecht Music & Arts

Learning Outcomes

After reading this unit, you will be able to do the following:

LO1 Understand the changes in Baroque opera from Monteverdi to Handel.

LO2 Become familiar with recitative and aria in Baroque opera through Handel's *Giulio Cesare*.

LO3 Encounter excerpts of a famous early example of truly popular music in John Gay's *The Beggar's Opera* and understand why it can be considered popular music.

LO4 Understand how Bach integrated familiar hymns into his music for the Lutheran liturgy.

LO5 Get acquainted with the Baroque oratorio, its importance to Handel's career, and Handel's most successful oratorio, *Messiah*.

LO6 Experience the coming together of sacred and secular music in the late Baroque.

THE FIRST HALF of the eighteenth century was a grand era for vocal music. During this period, Baroque opera reached its height. Italian opera was a popular public entertainment throughout western Europe, with the exception of France, which had its own tradition of grand opera. Lighter forms of musical stage entertainment also emerged; John Gay's *The Beggar's Opera* sparked a new genre even as it lampooned high culture, even grand opera itself. Sacred vocal music blurred the boundary between sacred and secular. Handel's oratorios were musical settings of biblical texts, often presented in secular venues. Although Bach's cantatas were liturgical music, he did not differentiate musically between sacred and secular. For both grand opera and sacred vocal music, the late Baroque era represented a high point and an end point. Neither would figure as prominently in musical life after 1750.

CHAPTER 18

Late Baroque Opera . . . and "Opera" in England

"If we compare Handel's operas to the Star Wars series, then John Gay's The Beggar's Opera is Spaceballs."

Prima donna is Italian for "first lady." The *Oxford American Dictionary* gives two definitions of the term: (1) the chief female singer in an opera or opera company and (2) a very temperamental person with an inflated view of his or her own talent or importance. The two meanings often coexist in one individual, as George Frideric Handel knew all too well.

In 1719, a group of English noblemen formed an opera company, the Royal Academy of Music, and engaged Handel as music director. Four years later, the Academy engaged Francesca Cuzzoni, one of the leading sopranos of the day. During the rehearsal of her first

Did You Know?

Before Madonna there was Faustina. Faustina Bordoni, "the new siren" of late Baroque opera, was famous enough to be identified by her first name only.

role for the Academy, Cuzzoni refused to sing an aria because she believed that it was intended for another soprano. According to a contemporary historian, Handel confronted her, saying, "Oh! Madame, I know well that you are a real she-devil, but I hereby give you notice, me, that I am Beelzebub, the Chief of Devils." He then threatened to pick her up and throw her out of the window if she persisted in her refusal. She sang the aria, with great success, and soon became a favorite of London audiences. She would create many of the leading female roles in Handel's operas, among them Cleopatra in *Giulio Cesare in Egitto* (*Julius Caesar in Egypt*).

Not long after, the Academy engaged Faustina Bordoni, the most celebrated singer on the Continent. After protracted negotiations, Faustina made her debut in January 1726. A fierce rivalry quickly developed among the supporters of the two *prime donne*. In May 1726, it spilled onto the stage. During a performance of the Italian opera *Astinatte*, hissing, catcalling, and fighting in the audience apparently led to a spat onstage, where, according to the *British Journal*, "coiffures were clawed, [and] vulgar words escaped those lips which moments before had ravished the ears with trills and divisions." The ensuing scandal brought the season to a premature close, although both singers would continue to perform for the Academy until 1728.

In spite (or because) of diversions like the fight between the rival *prime donne*, opera in London was a grand spectacle during the early eighteenth century. It was also an easy target for parody, as we discover in our overview of music on the London stage during the 1720s.

"Oh! Madame, I know well that you are a real she-devil, but I hereby give you notice, me, that I am Beelzebub, the Chief of Devils."
—George Frideric Handel, to Francesca Cuzzoni

LO1 Late Baroque Opera

When Handel arrived in England for the first time in 1711, he brought with him a newly revamped form of opera from Italy, where he had been working, and it would soon be called *opera seria*.

OPERA SERIA

About a century after the Camerata first formulated the idea of opera, the Arcadian Academy, another group of Italian aristocrats, took it upon themselves to reform opera. Their primary goal was to elevate its dramatic content, in both subject and style. Plots became more coherent and slightly more credible, and comic episodes disappeared—at least from this new, nobler form of opera. Replacing them were skillfully constructed libretti, based mainly on classical mythology, historical figures, and classic literature. This new kind of opera was known as **opera seria**. For most of the eighteenth century, it was the most prestigious form of musical expression, although its popularity and prestige declined toward the end.

THE DA CAPO ARIA

During the early eighteenth century, the most common aria type was the **da capo aria**. *Capo* means "head" in Italian, and *da capo* means literally "from the head," or "return to the beginning." A da capo aria has three sections: an opening section (A), a contrasting section (B), and a reprise of the opening section (A). This generally involved an adjustment of the Baroque aesthetic of one emotion per movement, in that the singer would express one emotion in the first A section, perhaps change emotions in the middle, then return to the initial emotion in the reprise of the A section.

In practice, da capo aria form was a vehicle for vocal display. Singers would sing the first A section and the B section much as the composer notated them. However, in the reprise of the A section, singers were expected to embellish the melody; the taste and virtuosity with which they did this was one measure of their art. Unlike today, this was considered an essential part of the singer's art and was the aspect of opera that most thrilled audiences: it wasn't just that the melody was elaborated; there was also an element of surprise, because singers improvised their embellishments, or at least prepared them in secret.

opera seria Form of more serious dramatic opera, based mainly on classical mythology, historical figures, and classic literature, that thrived during most of the eighteenth century

da capo aria Aria with three sections: an opening section (A), a contrasting section (B), and a reprise of the opening section (A) in which singers were expected to embellish the opening melody

LO2 Handel and Baroque Opera

George Frideric Handel's compositional gifts were ideally suited to opera; he could spin out gorgeous melodies and compose powerfully dramatic and evocative music. He composed more than forty operas, the most successful of which was *Giulio Cesare in Egitto*.

GEORGE FRIDERIC HANDEL

Handel was the most cosmopolitan composer of the early eighteenth century. He was born in Halle, a city in what is now east-central Germany. After training in Hamburg, he went to Italy for three years to gain more experience composing opera. Encouraged by the warm reception given his opera *Rinaldo* in 1711, he made several trips to England during the decade, finally settling there in 1717. For the greater part of two decades, he devoted most of his energy to composing and producing opera. Between 1718 and 1734, he was the major composer for, and musical director of, two opera companies. Both enjoyed some success but ultimately failed after several years. After the failure of the second company, he turned his attention to writing oratorios. The most successful of these was *Messiah*, but there were many others, including *Israel in Egypt* and *Judas Maccabeus*.

Handel composed in almost every current genre. His output included operas, oratorios, and other smaller-scale vocal works, including concertos and suites for orchestra, solo and trio sonatas for several different instruments, and keyboard works.

Handel's legacy is full of ironies. He was a German composer strongly influenced by Italian music who is remembered mainly for vocal music in English, a language he apparently spoke with a thick accent. He was the most versatile composer of his time, yet his enduring fame is linked securely to a single work. He was the greatest opera composer of the era, an era when opera was the most prestigious musical genre, yet his operas remain obscure, not because of their inferior quality (they contain some splendid music) but because of flaws inherent in the genre. At the time of his death, he was widely acknowledged as the finest composer of his era; through his oratorios, he would become the first "classical" composer.

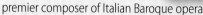

George Frideric Handel

Fast Facts

- *Dates*: 1685–1759

- *Place*: Germany/Italy/England

- *Reasons to remember*: One of the great composers of the late Baroque era and the premier composer of Italian Baroque opera

GIULIO CESARE IN EGITTO

Giulio Cesare in Egitto was first staged in 1724, revived again and again over the next eight years, and performed in Europe during that same time.

The opera has all the ingredients of effective drama—it featured a scenario worthy of soap opera on the grandest scale. The plot begins with one of the great love affairs in history, that of Caesar and Cleopatra. It includes physical lust and lust for power, betrayal, murder, intrigue, and despair, counterbalanced by honor, fidelity, love, and ultimately a happy ending. Handel and his librettists exercised dramatic license with history, keeping only the basic outline of Caesar's time in Egypt and fictionalizing it as necessary to make the story more sensational.

The plot is complex. The main characters include Cleopatra and her brother Ptolemy, engaged in a power struggle for the throne of Egypt; Pompey and Caesar, Roman generals engaged in a civil war that is resolved in Egypt in the most drastic manner possible, when Ptolemy brings the head of Pompey to Caesar at the beginning of the opera; and other subordinate characters, including Cornelia and Sextus, the wife and son of Pompey.

The recitative and aria presented here come from Act III. Cleopatra has been imprisoned by Ptolemy. As the scene begins, she stands alone with the guards. In the recitative, she despairs that Caesar is dead (he isn't, but she doesn't know that) and bemoans the fact that Cornelia and Sextus cannot come to her aid. She

fears that all is lost. In the aria, she expresses her grief in the A section, swears to "torment the tyrant" in the B section, then returns to her state of grief in the reprise of the A section. Handel's aria vividly projects her shifts in mood.

Handel's audiences must have been extremely gullible or attending the opera simply to hear his glorious music. It's hard to imagine Cleopatra the beautiful seductress and Caesar the noble, ardent lover played by two more unlikely principals. Francesca Cuzzoni may have sung beautifully, but she was no beauty. Charles Burney, a reliable commentator on eighteenth-century musical life, described her as "short and squat, with a doughy cross face, but fine complexion." Burney went on to note that she was not a good actress, dressed poorly, and "was silly and fantastical." Caesar was played by Senesino, one of the most famous **castrati** singers in Europe. Castration prior to

LISTEN UP!

CD 1:22–23

Handel, "E pur così" and "Piangeró," from *Giulio Cesare in Egitto* (1724)

Takeaway point: Stellar example of the Baroque da capo aria

Style: Late Baroque

Form: Ternary: ABA

Genre: Opera aria

Instruments: Voice and small orchestra

Context: Solo vocal number in a dramatic setting, designed to move the story along and express the character's feelings

It's hard to imagine Cleopatra and Caesar played by the unlikely couple: Senesino (left) and Cuzzoni (right)

puberty preserved the castrato singer's voice in the female range. Needless to say, manliness was not one of Senesino's attributes.

LISTEN FURTHER

Hear the voice of Alessandro Moreschi, "the last castrato," in the YouTube playlist.

LO3 *The Beggar's Opera* and the Beginnings of Popular Music

In 1728, as the Royal Academy of Music was closing down, John Gay produced *The Beggar's Opera*. With a run of sixty-one performances, it was enormously successful by the standards of the time. If we compare Handel's operas to the *Star Wars* series, then John Gay's *The Beggar's Opera* is *Spaceballs*, Mel Brooks's spoof of *Star Wars*. *The Beggar's Opera* depends on opera for much of its meaning, yet it is an anti-opera, as well as the first notable musical comedy.

John Gay was an English poet and dramatist, not a composer. His play *The Beggar's Opera* presents a slice of life in London's underworld. The plot centers around the romantic misadventures of a highwayman (robber) named Macheath, who is married to at least two women, Polly Peachum and Lucy Lockit. Polly is the daughter of a professional thief and a prostitute, and at the beginning of the opera her parents bemoan the fact that she has married for love rather than for money or social advancement. Lucy is the daughter of the jailer at Newgate Prison; when we meet her in the opera, she is several months' pregnant. And at the end of the opera we learn that Macheath probably had several other wives here and there.

The plot is scaffolding for a wickedly funny look at London's seamy underbelly. At the same time, it takes aim at almost all of English society, from the prime minister on down. Gay's in-joke reference to Robert Walpole, then prime minister of England, was obvious enough to get *Polly*, Gay's sequel to *The Beggar's Opera*, banned. Handel's Royal Academy of Music was another of Gay's choice targets, although that didn't stop him from filching one of Handel's marches.

Peachum

To liven up the play, Gay included sixty-nine songs, which the characters sing at dramatically significant moments. Gay did not compose the songs. Instead, he simply chose songs that were already in the air, set new words to them, and had the composer John Christopher Pepusch (1667–1752)—like Handel, a German who spent most of his career in England—compose simple accompaniments.

Because so much of its dialogue is spoken rather than sung, *The Beggar's Opera* isn't really an opera at all, by either the standards of Handel's time or those of our own. Rather, the title of the play is the first clue that the play is, among other things, a satire of opera—more particularly, Handel's operas as produced in London. The main characters are criminals with dubious morals rather than famous mythological or historical figures guided by reason and full of virtue. Instead of telling his tale in lavish pastoral metaphors, Gay uses eighteenth-century London-style street talk. Instead of unrequited love, we have twice-requited love.

John Gay

Fast Facts

- *Dates:* 1685–1732
- *Place:* England
- *Reasons to remember:* The co-creator of one of the earliest works of popular music

Even the happy ending of *The Beggar's Opera*, which seems to follow that most important of operatic conventions, is in fact a parody of it. With its uncommonly common (as opposed to noble) characters and its grisly plot, *The Beggar's Opera* has more in common with a ballad like "Barbara Allen" than it does with a Baroque opera. And ballads, as Gay's audience well knew, are supposed to contain a moral. Up until the final scene, we are primed to see Macheath hang for his countless misdeeds. But just before the executioner is

Macheath

about to slip Macheath's neck into the noose, the Beggar and the Player, the emcees who introduce the play, return to stop the action.

THE MUSIC OF *THE BEGGAR'S OPERA*

There are two unique aspects to Gay's use of songs: the sheer number of them and their varied sources. The songs come from all levels of English society, from Handel operas to sea chanteys. Then as now, it was common practice to fit new lyrics to existing melodies, and Gay and Pepusch did so on a grand scale. We hear their efforts in a group of three short airs.

The first song is "I'm Bubbled," an Irish jig. Gay and Pepusch set it as a duet between Polly and Lucy, the two women who think they are married to Macheath. The brisk tempo of the dance is the ideal expression of the two women's distress described in the lyrics. And the rapid-fire exchange adds to the fun.

The next air, "Cease Your Funning," simply adds fuel to the fire, which bursts into flames in the third song of the group: "How Now, Madam Flirt." Here Polly and Lucy are at their cattiest, trading tart insults. To kick the music up a notch, Gay and Pepusch spice up the song (a popular tune entitled "Good Morrow, Gossip") with operatic melismas. With this sudden musical reference to operatic style, Gay and Pepusch mock the onstage spat between Faustina and Francesca Cuzzoni, which had scandalized London less than two years previously.

THE SUCCESS OF *THE BEGGAR'S OPERA* AND THE BEGINNINGS OF POPULAR MUSIC

The Beggar's Opera was enormously popular when it was first produced. Indeed, in the opinion of several commentators its success contributed to the demise of Handel's first Academy. And it has remained popular since that time. It has

Polly Peachum

been revived numerous times, from the mid-1700s to the present. A production mounted during the 1920s ran for over one thousand performances. Gay would have been delighted.

Gay and Pepusch's "opera" is different in two important ways from the popular songs we've discussed previously. First, it is a work created by specific people; we know who assembled the work, even though much of the music for it was well-known music of the day. Second, it was public entertainment that was intended to be popular. To this end, Gay chose music that would cut across social boundaries and have wide appeal. Gay targeted a broader audience than did Handel; his musical choices reflect that. His purposeful use of accessible music introduces the commercial element into popular music: it is no longer simply music that is popular but also music designed to be popular. That Gay could mount a successful production shows that disposable income had begun to trickle down to the middle and lower classes.

Like so many innovations in popular music, *The Beggar's Opera* grew out of new ways of combining old materials and ideas. The practice of supplying new words to well-known songs had been around for centuries. **Broadside ballads**, topical lyrics sung to old, familiar songs, had been part of English life since the

broadside ballad
Topical lyrics sung to an old, familiar song

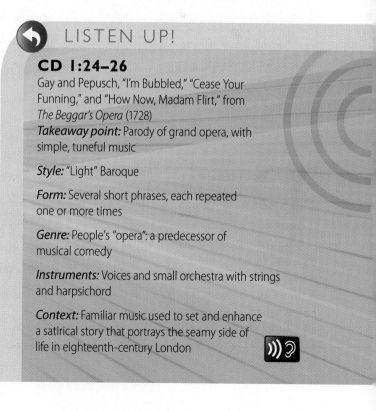

↩ LISTEN UP!

CD 1:24–26

Gay and Pepusch, "I'm Bubbled," "Cease Your Funning," and "How Now, Madam Flirt," from *The Beggar's Opera* (1728)

Takeaway point: Parody of grand opera, with simple, tuneful music

Style: "Light" Baroque

Form: Several short phrases, each repeated one or more times

Genre: People's "opera": a predecessor of musical comedy

Instruments: Voices and small orchestra with strings and harpsichord

Context: Familiar music used to set and enhance a satirical story that portrays the seamy side of life in eighteenth-century London

fifteenth century. (Broadside ballads were the urban counterpart to folk ballads like "Barbara Allen.") And the idea of interpolating songs into drama was not a new idea; Shakespeare and Marlowe had done it well before Gay. However, in Gay's "opera," the music is more central.

Eighteenth-century broadside ballad, including notation. These "musical newspapers" distributed by street singers may have used music from ballads like "Barbara Allen" and "Greensleeves." Through publication, they became popular songs of the time, quite separate from folk tradition.

(Sheet Music) © Lebrecht Music & Arts
(Paper) © iStockphoto.com/Duncan Walker

CHAPTER 19

Sacred Vocal Music: Cantata and Oratorio

"Both cantata and oratorio represent in different ways the culmination of a long period of musical evolution and new syntheses of sacred and secular traditions."

Did You Know?

Have you ever wondered why people always stand at the beginning of the Hallelujah Chorus? Legend has it that King George II was so moved by it that he rose to his feet. Of course, when the king stands, everybody stands.

Productive contemporary artists typically put out an album every year or two. They may spend months in the studio to produce about an hour of music. For example, Radiohead, among the most acclaimed bands of the last two decades, released seven studio albums over a fifteen-year span, from *Pablo Honey* (1993) to *In Rainbows* (2007), the famous pay-what-you-want album.

By contrast, George Frideric Handel composed nineteen oratorios, large musical compositions including *Messiah*, between 1739 and 1749. Recorded performances of these works consume about forty CDs. But Handel's impressive accomplishment pales next to J. S. Bach's prodigious output in his first years at Leipzig. Upon assuming his duties as cantor of Thomaskirche (St. Thomas Church), Bach began composing cantatas, vocal music for the Lutheran church year: all fifty-two Sundays, plus numerous holy days. Between 1723 and 1729—five calendar years—Bach produced five such cycles, plus at least two settings of the Passion of Christ—easily sixty CDs of music. While composing his massive five-year cantata cycle, Bach also taught school, directed a boys' choir, rehearsed his music, raised a large family (and mourned the deaths of the three children who died at birth or in infancy during this time), taught his own children and others, composed other music, played organ for services, weddings, funerals, and other occasions—to make some extra money—and pursued assorted other activities. Bach's industry was mind-boggling.

Handel and Bach undertook these tasks for different reasons. After making and losing a fortune with his two opera academies, Handel turned to oratorio, which involved less risk and greater reward. For Bach, the new position in Leipzig enabled him to fulfill his grandest professional ambition: to create a "well regulated church music."

Their genres of choice, the church cantata and the sacred oratorio, flourished during the Baroque era and reached an artistic pinnacle in their compositions. Both cantata and oratorio represent in different ways the culmination of a long period of musical evolution and new syntheses of sacred and secular traditions.

LO4 Bach and the Church Cantata

Bach's cantatas were "occasional" music. They were an integral component of Sunday services at St. Thomas's, as crucial to worship as the pastor's sermon, and they delivered parallel messages. The overall design of the most common type of **church cantata** included three kinds of music: one or more choruses, a series of recitative/aria pairs, and a setting of a chorale for congregational singing. Cantatas were not, however, always intended for church use; there were also secular **cantatas**, such as Bach's "Coffee Cantata," which also included recitative/aria pairs and choruses. **Choruses** were large-scale works for chorus and orchestra that were built around the **chorale** for the service, a religious song for the congregation that is directly related to scripture readings. Although a bit confusing, the term *chorus* in this context is different from the same term that is used synonymously with a choir (group of singers). The recitative/aria pairs set contemporary commentaries on the scripture readings. A simple harmonization of the chorale for the day allowed the congregation to participate musically in the service; we heard Bach's setting of the chorale "Ein' feste Burg" in People's Music 2.

THE CHORUS FROM CANTATA NO. 80

Bach composed Cantata No. 80, which is based on the chorale "Ein' feste Burg," for a festival celebrating the Protestant Reformation. This cantata contains eight movements: two choruses, an aria with chorale, two recitatives, a solo aria and a duet, and a setting of Luther's chorale for congregational singing. The five stanzas of Luther's chorale are dispersed among the movements; the opening chorus features the first stanza. The second movement, the aria with chorale, features an instrumental-style vocal line woven around the second verse of the chorale. The fifth movement, also a chorus, embeds the third stanza of the chorale in a rich instrumental accompaniment. The final two stanzas are the simple four-part chorale harmonization, to be sung by musicians and the congregation.

In setting the third stanza of Luther's chorale "Und wenn die Welt voll Teufel wär" ("And Though This World Was Filled with Devils"), Bach turned to the time-honored strategy of adapting it to his particular circumstances. Among the earliest kinds of polyphonic music was organum, which featured a slow-moving chant part and one or more other parts weaving actively around it. The chant melody is an instance of a cantus firmus (see People's Music 1), a preexisting melody used as the basis for a musical composition.

In adapting this practice to the Lutheran service, Bach often used the chorale as the cantus firmus. Because both words and melody were so familiar to the congregations in Leipzig, they in effect served as the Bible passages on which Bach would sermonize. The use of familiar chorales gave Bach's congregation a head start in understanding the message in his music. By surrounding the chorale melody with much richer music that has a clear affect, Bach could convey his interpretation of the message expressed in the lyrics of the chorale. It is as if he were giving a homily in music even

church cantata Cantata written for church use

cantata Church or secular music including one or more choruses, a series of recitative/aria pairs, and a setting of a chorale

chorus Large-scale work for chorus (choir) and orchestra that is built around the chorale for a church service

chorale Religious song for the congregation that is directly related to scripture readings

as the scriptures were being read. He effectively fused the expressive power of Baroque style with the familiar message of the chorale.

To present his message in large movements like the chorus, Bach adapted ritornello form by inverting the relationship between solo and tutti. Recall that in a Baroque concerto, the ritornello contained the main musical message, and the solo episodes elaborated on it. Here the main message is in the chorale tune; the ritornello is essentially a musical commentary on the chorale text. Compositionally, however, nothing has changed. The instrumental statements are like bearing walls: they support the form, even as they reinforce Bach's musical message.

Compositionally, nothing has changed. The instrumental statements are like bearing walls: they support the form, even as they reinforce Bach's musical message.

↩ LISTEN UP!

CD 1:27

Bach, "Und wenn die Welt voll Teufel wär," from Cantata No. 80, *Ein' feste Burg ist unser Gott* (1724)

Takeaway point: Bach's chorus as a musical sermon on Luther's chorale

Style: Baroque

Form: Ritornello

Genre: Church cantata

Instruments: Choir plus orchestra consisting of oboes, strings, and continuo

Context: Music for a Lutheran church service

BACH: THE END AND THE BEGINNING

Johann Christian Bach, the youngest son of J. S. Bach, considered his father old-fashioned. While composers such as Vivaldi and Handel were moving toward a more transparent and melodic style, the older Bach continued to compose music rich with counterpoint. By contrast, J. C. Bach's music was simpler and more decorative—high-class aural wallpaper for aristocrats. It was, for the eighteenth century, an up-to-date sound and a major influence on Mozart.

J. S. Bach and his music effectively ended several musical eras—in particular the glory years of Lutheran church music. In not only his cantatas and passions but also his organ music, no Lutheran church composer after him came close to his achievements.

Bach, seemingly behind the times in his own lifetime, has spoken to every subsequent generation of musicians.

Because Bach came at the end of the Baroque era, his music summarizes his understanding of Baroque style. There is in much of it a sense of wrapping things up, of having the final say. That is certainly the case with the cantatas and the Catholic mass that he composed; with works like *The Well-Tempered Clavier* and the four volumes of keyboard music that he published himself; and with contrapuntal works composed at the end of his life, including *The Musical Offering* and *The Art of the Fugue*.

Yet Bach's music has influenced major composers from Mozart and Beethoven through Romantics such as Schumann and Chopin to twentieth-century masters such as Debussy, Stravinsky, and Bartók, and generations of jazz and rock musicians. There is a poetic justice in all of this: Bach, seemingly behind the times in his own lifetime, has spoken to every generation of musicians that followed him, while those who dismissed his work as old-fashioned—we have record of one particularly malicious attack on Bach by a young man named Scheibe, an important critic in his time—are now footnotes to history.

LO5 Handel and the Baroque Oratorio

"Haaaaaaaaal-le-luu-jaah!" The four-note motive that sets this word rivals the opening of Beethoven's Symphony No. 5 as the most popular four notes in history. We hear it at Christmas, in television commercials, on cell phones, and in a host of other places. People may not know about Handel, but there's a good chance they know this motive. But there's more to the Hallelujah Chorus than the opening motive, more to *Messiah* than the Hallelujah Chorus, and more to Handel's music than *Messiah*.

© iStockphoto.com/Sondra Paulson

HANDEL AND ORATORIO

In Handel's time, opera and **oratorio** were cousins. Both told a story through music, using various forms of recitative, arias, and ensemble numbers (duets, choruses, and the like). In Handel's vocal music, there are two major differences: the subject and its presentation. His operas took their plots from history, particularly ancient history, as was the case with *Giulio Cesare*. By contrast, almost all of Handel's oratorios are based on religious subjects. Many are from the Old Testament, although *Messiah*, the most famous, draws from both Old and New Testaments. Moreover, unlike opera, oratorio is not staged; it is simply presented in concert. There is no action or scenery; words and music carry the story along without visual aids.

Oratorio, and especially *Messiah*, turned out to be a much better proposition for Handel than opera, although it didn't seem that way at first. The Bishop of London prohibited the 1732 performance of Handel's oratorio *Esther* in a theater. He felt that presenting religious material in a secular setting was inappropriate. His position was soon reversed, and by the 1740s, Handel's oratorios had become not only an extremely popular genre in England but also a force for morality and religious feeling.

Handel's oratorios were even more successful than his operas, for several reasons. One was the cost factor: it was far less expensive to present an oratorio than to mount an opera production. No scenery had to be built, no costumes had to be sewn, and far fewer stagehands were needed. (One happy result of these savings seems to have been the expansion of the orchestra. *Messiah* is more richly scored than many of Handel's operas; the orchestra contains strings, organ, harpsichord, oboes, bassoons, trumpets, horns, and timpani.)

Another was the change in subject: although a good eighteenth-century education included classical languages, literature, and history, scripture was even more familiar, at least to churchgoers. Even more important was the use of English instead of Italian. Audiences knew the text immediately; they no longer had to wonder what the characters were saying. In the case of *Messiah*, following the narrative presented no problem; no biblical account was more familiar to audiences than the life of Christ. It was like a favorite movie that they had seen fifty or a hundred times. They knew how the story would end, as well as all the lines. Its familiarity was certainly one component of its success.

MESSIAH

Handel composed *Messiah* at a critical point in his career. Although he was the most famous and respected composer in England, he felt uncertain enough about his future to travel to Germany, to tour as an organist, and perhaps to entertain an offer of employment from Frederick the Great, king of Prussia and himself a serious musician. Whatever his plans, we do know that he gave a "farewell concert" in London in the spring of 1741. At about this time, he received an invitation to provide a work for Dublin charities. The project, which became *Messiah*, reinvigorated him and kept him in England. He finished the massive work in approximately three weeks.

Messiah is the best known of Handel's several collaborations with Charles Jennens, a rich landowner, literate man, and devout Christian. He greatly admired Handel's music and had previously supplied him with English texts to set to music.

After its London premiere in 1742, *Messiah* was performed annually, just as it is in our time. Among the most significant of these annual performances were those mounted to support the Foundling Hospital, from 1750 through 1754.

THE HALLELUJAH CHORUS AND HANDEL'S STYLE

In the context of Baroque style, the most striking feature of the Hallelujah Chorus is the contrast

oratorio Like opera, genre that tells a story through music, using various forms of recitative, arias, and ensemble numbers but, unlike opera, presented in concert rather than staged

CD 1:28

Handel, Hallelujah Chorus, from *Messiah* (1742)

Takeaway point: A triumphant musical statement, and one of the most famous compositions of all time

Style: Late Baroque

Form: Through-composed

Genre: Oratorio

Instruments: Choir plus orchestra of strings, winds, brass (especially trumpet), and timpani

Context: A sacred subject in a secular concert setting

from phrase to phrase. In the course of the movement, we hear the bouncy rhythm of the opening phrase; a declamatory "for the Lord God"; a second statement of the text and melody, now enhanced by "Hallelujahs" coming from chorus and orchestra; a suddenly serene "The Kingdom of this World" followed by an emphatic restatement of the same phrase; an abrupt contrast in both melody (the jagged rise and fall) and texture (contrapuntal instead of hymnlike) in the setting of "and He shall reign"; another declamatory phrase "King of Kings"; followed by glorious combinations of many of the earlier motives; and, after a dramatic pause, the final, "amen" "Hallelujah."

Still, Handel sustains a single affect even as he creates bold contrasts on several different levels. How? The text helps, of course. So do the quick "Hallelujahs," which are in effect a more insistent and penetrating ritornello. There is the triumphant character of the chorus, underscored orchestrally by the trumpets, horns, and timpani. And there is tremendous momentum, as each phrase spills into the next, spurred on by the repetitions of the refrainlike "Hallelujah." All of these qualities combine to project an integrated whole, despite dramatic changes between and even within sections.

Contrast and continuity are opposites. One requires difference; the other requires similarity. In the music of Handel's time, their use was most often an either/or proposition. What Handel did better than any other composer of his time was to integrate contrast into continuity. He was able to maintain a consistent affect even as he incorporated bold contrasts in detail. This is one of the hallmarks of his musical style, and an important source of its power, as the Hallelujah Chorus shows in such a spectacular way.

THE ENDURING APPEAL OF HANDEL'S MUSIC

From his time to ours, Handel's music has retained its appeal because it is both accessible and artful. That it is both makes it unusual. Artistry and accessibility have been opposing tendencies in music, as in all art. One promises sophistication; the other, simplicity.

Handel's music contains elements that draw us in: the melodic hooks ("Hallelujah"), the trumpet flourishes, the strong melodic and textural contrasts all stand out. And there are other features that sustain our interest even through repeated hearings, such as inventive accompaniments and busy counterpoint. Handel's ability to combine immediate appeal and continuing interest demonstrates his ability to embrace and integrate opposing tendencies. Here it happens at the highest level. It is a quality evident in so much of the great music of every era—from Mozart to Motown, from Beethoven to The Beatles. And it is a useful lesson for all aspiring musicians: find something to bring your audience in, and find something else to keep them coming back.

Handel's oratorios occupy a special place in the history of music. They were the first "classical music": music from an earlier generation that never went out of fashion and that was acknowledged as "classic"—that is, the epitome of a particular genre—by the music world of the late eighteenth century and beyond.

For Handel and his audience, the libretto of Messiah *was like a favorite movie that they had seen fifty or a hundred times.*

© iStockphoto.com/james steidl

LO6 Sacred and Secular in Baroque Sacred Music

Bach's cantatas and Handel's oratorios highlight two significant and seemingly irreversible changes in the relationship between sacred and secular music: the extensive use of instruments and the blurring of the boundary between sacred and secular styles. In addition, Handel's oratorios demonstrate the divorce of sacred music from liturgical function.

Sacred music remained almost exclusively vocal music through the end of the sixteenth century, in Catholic and even in some Protestant churches. That began to change in the early Baroque era, and by the early eighteenth century, large-scale sacred works, such as Bach's cantatas and Handel's oratorios, featured full orchestral accompaniment.

Hand in hand with the use of instruments came the blurring of the stylistic boundary between sacred and secular. Flash back to Josquin and Wilbye, and consider how different their works are, even though both are Renaissance-era polyphonic works for voices, without accompaniment. By contrast, Bach's instrumental commentary on Luther's chorale speaks the same musical language as his gigue and concerto movement, and in much the same dialect. His "spiritual jig" retains the character of its secular model.

Like Bach, Handel makes little fundamental distinction between sacred and secular style: we hear tuneful melodies supported by strong bass lines in both the opera aria and the chorus, and more fundamentally, the sustaining of a single affect through entire sections of music. The most obvious differences are solo voice versus chorus, the expansion of the orchestra, and the form—ABA form in the aria versus the largely through-composed form of the chorus. In both works, Handel vividly paints the message of the text in sound. However, in the Hallelujah Chorus it seems that he is liberated from the formal restraints of the da capo aria; he can respond to the text line by line, without having to tailor the design to a rigid formal model. As with Bach, the musical tone is elevated, but there is no sharp musical distinction between sacred and secular.

Handel's oratorios go even further in blurring the boundary between sacred and secular by bringing the secular into the sacred world and by bringing the sacred into the secular world. Performances of Messiah and other oratorios in concert venues in effect deinstitutionalized the sacred: one could experience the word of God via scripture directly—apart from an official worship service of an organized religion.

In different ways, Bach and Handel set the tone for the relationship between sacred and secular music for subsequent generations. Handel's oratorios have remained popular since their composition, equally at home in church and concert venues, and the Bach revival of the early nineteenth century effectively divorced his sacred music from its original context. We are now much more likely to hear a Bach cantata in a concert hall than at a Lutheran church service. Partly because of these developments, composers since Bach and Handel have almost always scored large-scale sacred compositions, such as masses, requiems, and oratorios, for voices and orchestra. The boundaries between the two worlds that seemed so firm in the sixteenth century had dissolved by the end of the eighteenth century and have remained so into our time.

KEYS TO BAROQUE STYLE

Key Concepts

One mood per movement (or other complete musical statement). Accomplished musically by creating the mood at the outset and sustaining it throughout the work. Melodic and rhythmic consistency help maintain the mood throughout the movement. Contrasting material generally comments upon or amplifies the basic mood.

Key Features

1. **Basso continuo.** Basso continuo, or simply continuo, is the instrumental, harmonic, and rhythmic foundation of Baroque ensemble music. It comprises a bass instrument (usually cello) and a chord-producing instrument (harpsichord or organ).

2. **Blocks of sound.** Sections within a movement typically maintain a consistent dynamic level, texture, and instrumentation. Changes between sections typically involve sudden changes in all three elements.

3. **Steady rhythms.** Particularly in medium- and fast-paced movements, Baroque rhythms generally maintain a consistent level of activity. Often, composers use a particular rhythmic pattern as a unifying device.

4. **Melodic consistency.** The opening material establishes the mood. Subsequent melodic material helps sustain the mood by spinning the melody out from the opening idea or periodically returning to the opening idea (or a variant of it) after contrasting material.

5. **Melody instrument.** The characteristic sound of the Baroque is the steady support for a mid- or high-range melody instrument: voice, violin, flute, oboe.

Key Terms

1. **Concerto.** A composition for orchestra and one or more soloists. In the Baroque era, the orchestra typically featured only strings and continuo. Almost any instrument can be a solo instrument; the most common was the violin.

2. **Da capo aria.** The most widely used form in Baroque compositions for a solo singer, such as opera, oratorio, and cantata. A da capo contains a self-sufficient opening section, a contrasting middle section, and a restatement of the opening section (*da capo* means "from the head," or "return to the beginning"). Singers typically embellished the restatement, often lavishly.

3. **Ritornello.** *Ritornello* means "little return." It identifies the opening melodic idea in a movement and any fragmentary or complete restatement of the idea.

4. **Sonata.** An instrumental work for a small group of musicians. A solo sonata features a melody instrument, such as a violin, plus continuo. A trio sonata features two melody instruments and continuo.

5. **Suite.** An extended work for solo instrument or ensemble composed of several dances. The dances are often preceded by a prelude, overture, or other introductory movement.

Music Concept Check

To assist you in recognizing their distinctive features, we present an interactive comparison of Renaissance and Baroque style in CourseMate and the eBook.

UNIT II
MUSIC AND POLITICS

Learning Outcomes

After reading this unit, you will be able to do the following:

LO1 Identify two well-known anthems and learn about the historical context in which they emerged.

LO2 Know about America's first memorable composer and become familiar with his most famous song.

© iStockphoto.com/jim plumb

MOST AMERICANS KNOW the words and melody of "The Star-Spangled Banner." You've heard it in various forms: played by military bands or by a superb rock guitarist; sung by opera stars, R&B greats, even sitcom stars. You probably learned in grammar school that Francis Scott Key wrote the words to the anthem during the War of 1812, but you may not know that Key fitted the lyrics to a popular English drinking song, "O Anacreon," or even that "The Star-Spangled Banner" didn't officially become the national anthem of the United States until 1931. Because we grow up with them, anthems and other patriotic songs acquire an almost timeless quality for us. We may know something about the circumstances of their creation—as in the case of Key and "The Star-Spangled Banner"—but we may not see them as a product of a particular time and a particular set of circumstances. Nevertheless, they were. The first patriotic songs appeared in the latter part of the eighteenth century. Why not before? Because until then there was apparently no need for them. Kings and other royalty ruled autocratically and absolutely, so it was not necessary to arouse patriotic sentiment. Not until the will of the people began to matter—either to defend a regime or to overthrow it—did patriotic music emerge.

National Anthems

"The adoption of hymnlike anthems became a tool to affirm monarchical authority."

I n 1745, Bonnie Prince Charlie, the "Young Pretender" to the throne of England, mounted what would be the last significant attempt by the Jacobites to restore the Stuart line to the British monarchy. His initial success in Scotland spread alarm farther south. Among the responses in London was the fitting of new words to an old familiar song— "God Save the King"—which had been published for the first time only a year before. (Imagine the tune for "My Country 'Tis of Thee" while you read the lyrics.)

Did You Know?

Jimi Hendrix performed a soaring improvisation on the U.S. national anthem, "The Star-Spangled Banner," at the historic Woodstock music festival in 1969.

Lord grant that Marshal Wade
Shall by thy mighty aid
Victory bring.
May he sedition hush,
And like a torrent rush
Rebellious Scots to crush—
God save the King.

King George II triumphant over Bonnie Prince Charlie

© iStockphoto.com/Mike Bentley

© George II, from 'Kings and Queens' by Eleanor and Herbert Farjeon, pub. 1932 (colour block print, Thornycroft, Rosalind (1891-1973) / Private Collection / The Stapleton Collection / The Bridgeman Art Library

LO1 The First National Anthems

During the campaign against Bonnie Prince Charlie, the song was performed several times at two London theaters, Drury Lane and Covent Garden, in an arrange-ment by Thomas Arne, one of the leading English composers of the day. The British army suppressed the Jacobite uprising within a year, but the melody, minus the topical lyric, remained popular. It soon became the custom to perform the anthem as a greeting to King George II whenever he attended a public event. Over time, it became—as if by acclamation—the first **national anthem** (a hymn, march, or other song used as a patriotic symbol) and was recognized as such not only in Great Britain and the colonies but also in western Europe.

ANTHEMS: SOUND AND SYMBOL

The British got it right the first time. Their anthem has a simple message, at least in the first verse, and a memorable melody. It was certainly regarded in this light, since many other countries have used it as their anthem at one time or another.

The melody is ideally suited to its purpose because it is, in effect, a secular hymn. It moves mostly by step; the phrases are short and clearly punctuated; the rhythm of the melody moves mainly at beat speed, with little contrast; and the form is strophic. These features closely parallel hymn melodies such as that for "Ein' feste Burg." And like most hymns, it is easy to sing.

ANTHEMS ACROSS BOUNDARIES

Two more anthems with sharply contrasting character appeared in the 1790s. "La Marseillaise" (lah mah-say-EZZ), the French national anthem, was composed during a single night in April 1792 by Claude Rouget de Lisle,

national anthem
Hymn, march, or other song used as a patriotic symbol

© Bildarchiv Preussischer Kulturbesitz / Art Resource, NY

**Franz II, emperor of Austria and the last
Holy Roman Emperor**

an army officer and amateur musician. Five years later, Franz Joseph Haydn, the most celebrated composer in Europe at the time, composed "Gott erhalte Franz den Kaiser" ("God Save Franz the Emperor" [Franz II, the last Holy Roman Emperor]) at the request of an Austrian nobleman, at a time when the Holy Roman Empire had no anthem. The tune for "Gott erhalte" later be-

came a Protestant hymn, "Glorious Things of Thee Are Spoken," as well as the national anthems of Austria, then Germany.

These anthems emerged during a century of tumultuous change in Europe and North America. The absolute authority of rulers, which they claimed as a divine right, came under attack, first in the writings of Enlightenment philosophers such as Voltaire and Rousseau in France, John Locke in England, and Thomas Jefferson in the United States, then through revolutions in colonial America and France.

The adoption of hymnlike anthems—a happy accident in England, a commissioned work in Austria—became in effect a rear-guard action: a tool to affirm monarchical authority. The lyrics express this message overtly; the melodies, sedate and hymnlike, send an even more powerful message subliminally. By contrast, "La Marseillaise" and "The Star-Spangled Banner," which Key retrofitted with new lyrics at a time when the freedom of the new republic was under attack, are much more vigorous melodies.

Taken together, the four anthems suggest a connection between melodic style and political stance: sedate, hymnlike melodies for the establishment, martial melodies for the revolutionaries. All suggest that politically oriented music—either to defend a regime or to overthrow it—became part of life in the late eighteenth century because the attitudes of the people began to matter.

Revolutionary Song

"The American Revolution had a sound track."

If you go to the Songwriters Hall of Fame website and navigate to Inductee Exhibits, you'll find them arranged in three groups: early American song, Tin Pan Alley, and rock 'n' roll. The earliest of the early American songwriters was a leather tanner and singing teacher named William Billings.

Did You Know?

A descendant of revolutionary songs—confrontational protest music—made a comeback in the early 1960s, thanks to Bob Dylan, Phil Ochs, and other politically oriented members of the folk revival.

acquired new words after relocation. Other songs were homegrown. Among the best, best-known, and most incendiary songs were those of America's first important songwriter, William Billings. His most popular song would become the unofficial anthem of the American Revolution.

WILLIAM BILLINGS'S "CHESTER"

A key ingredient in the push for independence was an attitude of self-reliance. In New England, this seemed to be a defining characteristic of the Yankee spirit. Few exemplified this spirit more thoroughly than William Billings, who was born in Boston and died there.

As a young man, Billings had to overcome the lack of vision in one eye and legs of unequal length. As a musician, he had to overcome the lack of traditional training. Although he received some musical instruction in his youth, he was largely self-taught as a composer. Billings used his lack of formal training as a license for independence. As he wrote, "For my own part, . . . I don't think myself confined to any rules of composition, laid down by any that went before me."

EXPLORE ONLINE >

Check out the Songwriters Hall of Fame.

LO2 Songs of the American Revolution

The American Revolution had a sound track. Some of the music—like "Yankee Doodle"—came from England; as was customary at the time, the songs typically

© iStockphoto.com/M. Eric Honeycutt

William Billings

Fast Facts

- *Dates*: 1746–1800

- *Place*: United States (Boston)

- *Reasons to remember*: Self-taught composer who published the first collection of music by an American composer

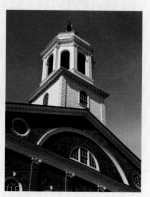

© iStockphoto.com/Kenneth Wiedemann

Billings published the first of his six volumes of music in 1770. Entitled *The New-England Psalm-Singer* and engraved by Paul Revere, it contained 120 of his compositions and was the first collection of music by an American composer. As the title suggests, the volume contained mainly psalms and hymn tunes. Billings would later develop his own original approach to counterpoint, in what are called "fuguing tunes." These appeared in later volumes.

Billings was a strong voice in the fight for independence; he counted among his friends such leading patriots as Paul Revere and Samuel Adams. To provide music for the militias, he set new words to "Chester," one of his hymns from the 1770 collection. He wasn't one to mince words, as the first stanza shows:

Let tyrants Shake their Iron rod
And slav'ry Clank her galling Chains
we fear them not we trust in God
New England's God forever reigns.

LISTEN UP!

CD 1:31
Billings, "Chester" (1770)

Takeaway point: Brisk, easily remembered melody, with short phrases and clear rhythm

Style: Yankee choral music

Form: Strophic

Genre: Political song

Instruments: Mixed voices

Context: Incendiary song, intended to inflame the spirits of the colonists

In the stanzas that follow, he names names—of British generals—and continues his impassioned plea to overthrow British rule. The song would become the unofficial anthem of the revolution—at least in New England. The words leave no doubt as to where Billings stands, and the simple tune makes the lyrics easily accessible.

It's easy to imagine patriots singing "Chester" in a tavern.

A People's Music

Billings's "Chester" was a song by the people—specifically, an ordinary citizen with a lot of energy—and for the people. During the revolution, fewer than twenty thousand people lived in Boston. The cultural life that would flourish there during the nineteenth century was still far into the future. And what little there was—by contemporary standards—was another world to someone like Billings, who was born into a poor family, worked at a trade, and died penniless.

"Chester" lacks the sophistication and craft of European music, in large part because Billings had almost no access to the centuries-old European musical tradition. In a characteristic display of Yankee ingenuity, he figured out his own path. Certainly his song is rough around the edges, which is apparent when it is compared to Haydn's anthem. Still, what it may lack in art, it makes up for in gusto. It's easy to imagine the militia singing the song while marching or patriots singing it in a tavern.

UNIT 12
THE CLASSICAL STYLE

Learning Outcomes

After reading this unit, you will be able to do the following:

LO1 Recognize Classical style and sonata form through exploring a movement from a Mozart piano sonata.

LO2 Discover the sound of the string quartet, the main chamber ensemble of the Classical era, through a string quartet by Franz Joseph Haydn.

LO3 Be familiar with the Classical symphony, as exemplified by Haydn's Symphony No. 94.

LO4 Describe the changes in opera during the late eighteenth century, as evidenced in two excerpts from Mozart's *Don Giovanni*.

LO5 Understand the form and style of the Classical concerto.

© The Temple Bridge, from Ackermann's 'Repository of Arts', 1822 (colour litho), Papworth, John Buonarotti (1775-1847) / Private Collection / The Stapleton Collection / The Bridgeman Art Library International

IN THE LAST quarter of the eighteenth century, several diverse trends would coalesce into what came to be called the Classical style. Its home was Vienna, and its two leading proponents were Haydn and Mozart. The music of these composers and their contemporaries included new genres, most notably the symphony and the string quartet, and radically new approaches to existing genres, including opera, the concerto, and the sonata. The composers employed new resources: orchestras expanded to include winds, brass, and percussion on a consistent basis, and the piano replaced the harpsichord as the keyboard instrument of choice during the 1770s. Their music was performed in public concerts for paying audiences as well as in the salons of the aristocracy. The Classical style introduced a new aesthetic—one based on conflict, contrast, and resolution rather than consistency of mood. We explore it in excerpts from five works by Mozart and Haydn.

CHAPTER 20

Classical Sonata and String Quartet

"Among the salient characteristics of Classical style are contrast, marked by decisive punctuation, and a strong sense of moving toward goals."

Did You Know?

In The Beatles'"Eleanor Rigby," two string quartets replaced the usual guitars, bass, and drums.

In music, as in other aspects of life, timing can be crucial. Half a century after the rock revolution, the seminal rock acts of the 1950s and 1960s—Elvis, Chuck Berry, The Beatles, Bob Dylan, Aretha Franklin, James Brown, and many others—are still household names, and their music is still heard today. By contrast, the R&B acts of the late 1940s and early 1950s that helped lay the groundwork for the rock revolution—Louis Jordan, T-Bone Walker, the numerous doo-wop groups, and others—are much less familiar.

A similar fate befell composers active during the middle of the eighteenth century.

The Emergence of the Classical Style

Like the post–World War II years, the middle of the eighteenth century was a time of transition between musical eras. The household names of Classical music come before and after: Vivaldi, J. S. Bach, and Handel earlier in the century, and Haydn, Mozart, and Beethoven toward the end.

BETWEEN BAROQUE AND CLASSICAL

Certainly, distinguished and influential musicians were active in the middle of the century. Christoph Willibald Gluck (1714–1787) led a reform of opera, and Johann Stamitz (1717–1757), based in Mannheim, Germany, played a key role in the development of the orchestra. Two sons of J. S. Bach were trendsetters. Carl Philipp Emanuel Bach (1714–1788) cultivated a style with heightened expression (the German word is *Empfindsamkeit*), while his younger brother Johann Christian Bach (1735–1782) developed a style that sought to be pleasant and elegant (*galant*). Both Bach sons were among the most famous musicians of their name; they were far better known during their lifetime than their father was during his. Today, however, almost all the music by these composers is mainly known only to specialists and devotees of eighteenth-century music.

These and other composers in the latter half of the eighteenth century created new stylistic directions in a rapidly changing musical scene. Increasingly, they catered to a broadening audience that offered new sources of income: sales from publications, teaching opportunities, and public performances. Their music needed to be both sophisticated and accessible. C. P. E. Bach was certainly aware of this: during his long career, he published a series of keyboard sonatas "for connoisseurs and amateurs."

THE CLASSICAL STYLE

By the 1770s, a new style—what we now call the Classical style—had taken shape. If listeners from the time of Corelli, Vivaldi, and Handel could have been transported to concert venues in late eighteenth-century London or Vienna, they would have been surprised to hear a full symphony orchestra performing Haydn's "Surprise" symphony or accompanying Mozart as he performed one of his piano concertos. By the 1780s, the size and instrumentation of the orchestra had grown considerably, with winds, brass, and percussion becoming regular members and additional strings balancing these instruments. Moreover, orchestras performed in public concerts for paying customers as well as in the homes of aristocrats.

The music that audiences would have heard featured stronger and more frequent contrasts within movements, and greater length. The contrasts touched every element: for example, dramatic shifts between loud and soft, varied melodic material, homophonic versus contrapuntal textures, and slow versus fast rhythms. The consistent, comfortable rhythm of the continuo was now an anachronism. Moreover, the contrasts almost demanded greater breadth, to present and ultimately reconcile more diverse material. As a result, movements in genres inherited from the Baroque era, such as the concerto, were up to four times longer.

LO1 Sonata Form and Classical Style

To shape varied materials into more expansive and coherent statements, Classical composers gradually developed a set of procedures that were consistent in principle yet remarkably varied in their realizations. Typically, these procedures were used most extensively and expansively in the first movements of instrumental compositions: sonatas, quartets, symphonies, concertos, and the like.

"Sonata Form"

If you had asked Mozart (in German) about his approach to sonata form in one of his string quartets, he probably wouldn't have understood what you were asking, because he wouldn't have recognized the term. For Mozart, Haydn, and their contemporaries, the sequence of events in what we now call sonata form was simply the way it was done; they didn't give the resulting form a specific name, such as "minuet and trio" or "rondo." Not until 1793, two years after Mozart's death, did the composer/theorist H. C. Koch publish a comprehensive and accurate description of the form—as an expansion of the minuet! The term *sonata form* and the terminology to describe it didn't come into use until the 1840s, when theorists coined them in an effort to describe the first movements in Beethoven sonatas.

The sonata and "sonata form" are two entirely different entities. In the Classical era, the sonata is a multimovement work for one or two instruments. **Sonata form** is an enormous and comprehensive expansion of the rounded binary form used in minuets and variation forms. Not surprisingly, there is considerable variance between compositions in the way sonata form is realized. To provide a frame of reference for sonata-form movements, let's review a basic template of the form.

Movements written in sonata form contain at least three large sections: exposition, development, and recapitulation. An **introduction** in a slow tempo occasionally precedes the exposition, to convey a greater sense of importance. Introductions are relatively common in late Classical symphonies but rare in other genres. And a concluding coda may follow the recapitulation, to bring the movement to an even more emphatic close.

Within these broad, large-scale guidelines, there is virtually unlimited flexibility, in thematic content, connections and contrasts, and proportions. The following detailed descriptions of each section highlight typical features.

Exposition

The **exposition** serves two main purposes: to establish the basic character of the movement and to present the musical ideas that are to be worked out in the rest of the movement. It does so through a predictable sequence of musical gestures, each of which has a different function.

First Theme. The purpose of the first theme is to set the basic parameters of the movement. Accordingly, the movement typically begins with a complete musical statement that establishes or implies six features:

Establishes	Implies
Key	Length
Meter	Mood
Tempo	
Melodic material	

Key, meter, and tempo are relatively generic. The Mozart piano sonata discussed later is in F major, has a 3/4 meter, and proceeds at a fast tempo; so do many others, including another by Mozart. The other features are more specific. Although it may resemble other melodies, the opening theme is unique to the movement and is its most distinctive feature. The length of the first theme generally previews the overall length of the movement. Melody and accompaniment set the mood, which usually reverberates throughout the rest of the movement. In the sonata that we will hear shortly, Mozart creates a pastoral feeling from the outset.

Transition. The **transition** section has two functions: to move to a new key and to make that move seem like a big deal. Moving from the tonic to a new key is strictly a harmonic procedure. In most sonata-form movements, it can be accomplished with only three chords and can sound bland when presented simply. However, the opposition of the tonic and the new key is the structural basis of the musical tension characteristic of the form. Accordingly, the other function of the transition is to dramatize the move to the new key. Typically, composers draw on tension-increasing strategies in several elements to highlight the change of key. These may include more active and syncopated rhythms, more contrapuntal textures, irregular phrases, an overall rise in register, and predominantly rising melodic lines. The transition typically concludes with a decisive cadence that prepares the new key.

Second Theme. To highlight arrival in the new key, composers typically present memorable, accessible melodic material. Among the most common options are a new melody that is tuneful, even singable, or a literal or modified restatement of the first theme in the new key. Because the music before and after the second theme is typically more active, the second theme stands out as a moment of relative calm as well as a milestone in the progress of the form.

The first theme and the second theme are the two places in the exposition that confirm a key: the tonic and the contrasting key. The use of memorable melodies at these two points in the movement puts a distinctive face on the otherwise generic opposition of the two keys.

Closing Section.
The main function of the music that concludes the exposition is to reinforce the new key. This material can be brief or extensive; it is generally far more active than the second theme, and it ends with a decisive cadence.

Taken as a whole, the exposition sets up an enormous imbalance. Only the very opening—usually less than one-quarter of the exposition—is in the home, or tonic, key. The remainder is either moving to a different key or confirming the new key. As a result, the decisive cadence at the end of the exposition doesn't sound like the end of the movement. Instead, the exposition ends with considerable unresolved tension, despite the strong cadence.

It is customary to repeat the exposition in performance. This has the dual function of reinforcing the sense of imbalance within the exposition and making the events in the subsequent development section even more surprising.

DEVELOPMENT

The function of the **development** section is to further increase the musical tension created in the exposition. It fulfills this function through the extensive use of developmental procedures and the presentation of unstable new material.

To "develop" musical material is to modify it in ways that change important features: for example, compressing the rhythm, fragmenting the melody, changing the harmony, making the texture richer and more complex. Such modifications make the music less predictable and more unsettled. In a sonata-form movement, development of musical material can occur in any section, particularly in transition sections. It unfailingly occurs in the development section, however.

Not surprisingly, the sequence of events in a development section is for the most part unpredictable. Unlike the exposition and recapitulation, there is no established sequence of events. The development may

transition Portion of the exposition in sonata form that moves decisively to a new key and highlights the move

development Section of sonata form where material from the exposition (and occasionally new material) is developed, or manipulated through fragmentation and alteration, to project great instability

modulation Musical process whereby a piece moves away from the home key

recapitulation Mostly literal restatement of sonata form's exposition, but with all the material in the contrasting key restated in the home key

coda Optional section of sonata form that comes after the end of the recapitulation

feature reworked versions of previously presented material and—less commonly—brand-new material. About the only constant feature is preparation for a return to the home key at the very end.

In most sonata-form movements in the Classical era, the return to the home key from the contrasting key can be as simple as a two-chord progression. The development section resists this simple return; instead, it purposely **modulates** away from the tonic, so that when the music ultimately returns to the home key in the recapitulation that follows, it is a much more striking event. It is as if you return home from your next-door neighbor's by first heading off in the opposite direction, then wandering around for a while before finally arriving back at your doorstep.

© iStockphoto.com/Russell Tate

It is as if you return home from your next-door neighbor's by first heading off in the opposite direction, then wandering around for a while before finally arriving back at your doorstep.

RECAPITULATION

Capo is the Italian word for "head"; to *recapitulate* means "to go to the beginning"—in this case, the beginning of the exposition. The return of the opening theme in the tonic key is the most important point of arrival within the movement. The arrival at the tonic after the circuitous harmonic path through exposition and development releases the harmonic tension accumulated since the beginning of the transition; the return of the opening theme highlights the return in the most emphatic possible way.

The **recapitulation** is a mostly literal restatement of the exposition, with one major difference: the second theme and other material that was stated in the new key in the exposition are now restated in the *home* key. The restatement of previously presented material in the home key stabilizes and balances the movement harmonically and structurally. Only the transition section is likely to be substantially different, as the composer must reroute the harmony so that it cadences in the home key rather than the new one. Mozart and Haydn delighted in presenting surprising twists and turns in the transition section of the recapitulation to inject excitement into a passage that begins and ends in the same place harmonically.

CODA

A movement in sonata form can conclude at the end of the recapitulation, when the material that ended the exposition in the contrasting key is heard in the home key. However, to counterbalance the tension created in the exposition and development, and make the ending even more emphatic, composers may extend the movement beyond this obvious ending point. The term **coda** identifies the section of music that comes after the end of the recapitulation. It is optional but not uncommon.

See below for a typical movement in sonata form. This description of sonata form is abstract at this point, and necessarily so. Sonata form is the most complex and most variable form that we will encounter. We can generally predict the broad outline of a sonata-form movement, and we can identify the milestones and the activity in between that makes them significant. We cannot be more prescriptive than that. We hear both the consistent elements of and variable paths through

Introduction	Exposition (may repeat)				Development	Recapitulation				Coda
	1st theme	Transition	2nd theme	Closing Section	Working over of musical ideas; moves away from new key *and* tonic key	1st theme	Transition	2nd theme	Transition	
Optional	In tonic key	Moves to new key	In new key			Return to tonic key				Optional; in tonic key

Sonata form

sonata form in movements from a piano sonata by Mozart and a string quartet by Haydn.

Mozart and the Piano Sonata

The sonata at the end of the eighteenth century was a radically different genre from the early eighteenth-century sonata. Only the name remained the same. The differences began with the number of instruments: Baroque sonatas typically required three or four musicians. By contrast, during the latter half of the century, "sonata" almost always referred to an independent, multimovement composition, either for keyboard alone or for keyboard and a melody instrument, usually violin. One finds keyboard sonatas and sonatas for violin (or flute or oboe or any number of popular instruments of the time) and piano listed in publishers' announcements beginning in the 1760s.

Differences between Baroque and Classical sonatas are also evident in other large-scale features, such as the number and sequence of movements and the characteristic forms of these movements. During the late eighteenth century, sonatas usually had three movements. Typically, the first movement had a lively tempo, the second was slower, and the final movement was again fast. The forms of the individual movements were more variable than the tempo sequence.

At the center of this new kind of sonata was the piano, an instrument still in the mind of its inventor, Bartolomeo Cristofori, when Corelli composed his solo and trio sonatas in the Baroque style.

THE PIANO

The full name of the instrument we call the piano is "pianoforte." Its name comes from two Italian words, *piano* and *forte*, the terms for "soft" and "loud." The name of the instrument celebrates the feature that most distinguishes it from the harpsichord, the instrument it would replace: the ability to control dynamic level through touch. On the harpsichord, depressing a key causes a plectrum to pluck a string (or several strings). The action is like an on/off switch: the same amount of sound comes out whether you depress the key gently or firmly. By contrast, the action of the piano is more like a volume control. Depressing a key causes a hammer to strike strings. The speed of the key's descent determines the speed at which the hammer strikes the strings: the faster the descent, the louder the sound.

Bartolomeo Cristofori, the instrument keeper for

Bartolomeo Cristofori and his invention

the Medici family, invented the piano. He began work on it about 1700; by 1726, he had resolved many of the mechanical issues. Over the next several decades, other manufacturers, especially in England and German-speaking Europe, made improvements to Cristofori's instrument. By 1780, the piano had almost completely supplanted the harpsichord as the keyboard instrument of choice.

Because of its more sustained tone and capability of note-to-note nuance, the piano assumed a more varied and prominent role in music making, especially in ensemble music. In Baroque ensembles, the harpsichordist generally filled the gap between melody and bass, much like a good rhythm guitarist does in a rock band. By contrast, the pianist could balance other instruments or support them. As a result, it became the preferred

Wolfgang Amadeus Mozart

Fast Facts

- *Dates*: 1756–1791
- *Place*: Salzburg/ Vienna, Austria
- *Reason to remember*: One of the two greatest composers in the Classical style

solo instrument in concertos, an equal partner in chamber music, and the only accompanying instrument in solo song, a genre that emerged in the late eighteenth century in large part because of the piano. Composers such as Mozart also exploited the distinctive capabilities of the piano in solo literature, most notably in the piano sonata.

Mozart's Sonata in F Major

Mozart composed his Sonata in F major, K. 332, sometime in the early 1780s, around the time he also composed his variations on "Ah, vous dirai-je Maman." (**K.** in the titles of Mozart compositions stands for **Köchel**, the man who attempted to arrange all of Mozart's known works in chronological order.) This sonata and the Haydn string quartet discussed later are among the first works to display those features we associate with the mature Classical style.

The sonata has three movements, in the customary fast-slow-fast sequence. All three make use of the procedures that characterize sonata form; the first movement is the most characteristic realization of the form. In it we hear Mozart evoking a clearly pastoral mood.

The salient features of sonata form, particularly the instability of the transition and development sections, the arrival at the new key with the second theme, and the return to the home key at the beginning of the

recapitulation, are clearly evident in this movement. The online Listening Guide describes these features in greater detail.

This opening movement of Mozart's piano sonata is about as close to a textbook example of sonata form as one is likely to find. The next example, the first movement of Haydn's String Quartet in C major, resembles the Mozart in its overall design. In other respects, such as the character of the musical material, the proportions between and within sections, there are discernible differences. Comparing them gives us insight into both the fundamental impulses behind sonata form and the variety in its realization.

LO2 The String Quartet

The **string quartet** is a chamber ensemble consisting of two violinists, a violist, and a cellist. It is also a work composed for this ensemble. The string quartet was a product of the new sensibility that ultimately shaped the Classical style. It has no direct ancestors of any note. The first quartets date from around 1760, around the time the Classical style began to take shape.

Timbre and Texture in the String Quartet

The sound of the string quartet is different from that of any other small-ensemble instrumental music that we have heard because all the instruments share the same basic timbre. For example, in Corelli's solo sonata, the sound of the harpsichord contrasts with the sounds of the violin and cello. Before 1760, this mixing of sounds was virtually universal. There are isolated instances of small-ensemble compositions with instruments whose timbres match, but the norm was an ensemble with mixed timbres. What separated the string quartet (and

Composers could conceive of the string quartet as a single instrument capable of playing four (or more) pitches simultaneously, much like the piano.

© iStockphoto.com/Jarek Szymanski

other all-string chamber groups) from even these isolated examples of matched sound was the fact that composers like Haydn and Mozart composed specifically for the ensemble; string quartets sound best when played by stringed instruments, rather than by winds, brass, or keyboards.

The matched timbres of the string quartet opened up a significantly new way of thinking for composers. They could conceive of the string quartet as a single instrument capable of playing four (or more) pitches simultaneously, much like the piano. And as with the piano, it is possible to fine-tune dynamics within the string quartet, not only in shaping a melodic line but also in balancing notes sounding at the same time. So, in a homophonic texture, the melody could be loud while the accompanying parts were soft. By contrast, in a more contrapuntal texture, all the parts could operate at about the same dynamic level. The possibility of four musicians playing as if they were a single instrument also gave composers unprecedented flexibility in shaping textures: one could add or subtract instruments, distribute the melody among the various instruments, give each instrument a distinct role, or . . . the possibilities seemed limitless.

Franz Joseph Haydn

Franz Joseph Haydn is remembered as the father of the symphony and the string quartet. He composed prolifically in both genres: 104 symphonies and sixty-eight quartets.

Haydn was born in Rohrau, a small village about twenty-five miles east of Vienna. As a boy, he sang in the choir at St. Stephen's Cathedral. He left the choir school shortly after his voice broke, then worked as a freelance musician in Vienna until accepting positions with nobility. The first position lasted only a short while. The second, with the Esterházy family, lasted almost thirty years. At first, Haydn lived and worked in Eisenstadt, near Vienna, where the Esterházy family had their winter home. Beginning in 1766, he spent most of his time at Esterháza, on the Esterházy family's sumptuous estate in Hungary, halfway between Vienna and Budapest.

The distance between Vienna and Esterháza is about seventy miles, but for all intents and purposes, it could have been seven hundred or seven thousand. Haydn stayed busy with his numerous commitments, and during his time there he composed an enormous amount of music, even by eighteenth-century standards. Between his duties and the relative isolation of Esterháza, Haydn had relatively little contact with musicians in Vienna and other cultural centers. Prince Nicolas, Haydn's em-

Esterháza—often called the Hungarian Versailles—is a magnificent palace containing 126 rooms, including a 400-seat theater.

ployer, was wealthy enough to have an orchestra that eventually numbered around twenty musicians. Most of them had other responsibilities, but one of their main duties was to serve as the court orchestra, either to play concerts or to accompany the operas staged in the palace theater.

The combination of a supportive patron and an in-house orchestra created a laboratory-type environment for Haydn. He was free to experiment, and did so, even as other composers throughout Europe were also composing thousands of orchestral works. Although during his tenure, Haydn seldom left Esterháza, his music did. Haydn's reputation grew during the decades he spent there. By the time the prince died in 1790, Haydn had transformed the symphony and string quartet from light entertainment into substantial instrumental genres and elevated his reputation to one of the most distinguished composers in Europe. Upon the death of the prince, Haydn moved to Vienna, where he remained for the rest of his life, except for two visits to London.

Haydn is remembered mainly for his symphonies and quartets. However, he also composed oratorios,

Franz Joseph Haydn

Fast Facts

- *Dates*: 1732–1809
- *Place*: Vienna, Austria
- *Reasons to remember*: One of the two greatest composers in the Classical style; father of the symphony and the string quartet

masses, operas, concertos, piano sonatas and trios, and many other works. With Mozart, he is considered an exemplar of the Classical style. Although Haydn was old enough to be Mozart's father and they were in quite different professional circumstances—Haydn ensconced at Esterháza, Mozart all over the continent—both seemed to find a new level of mastery around 1780, in much the same way.

HAYDN AND THE STRING QUARTET

Haydn's compositions seem to fall into two groups: those he composed because he had to, and those he composed because he wanted to. In the first group are works such as his operas and baryton trios (the baryton is a complicated bowed string instrument; Prince Nicolas played it recreationally), both composed to please his patron. In the latter group are the symphonies and string quartets; these he composed throughout his career.

The musician most responsible for establishing the string quartet as an important genre was Joseph Haydn. He virtually invented the genre; a set of six quartets was his first work and among the very first quartets of which we have record. He returned to the genre on a regular basis throughout most of his career; his last two quartets date from 1799. The quartet that we hear comes from a set of six published as Opus 33 in 1782, around the midpoint of Haydn's career. Haydn saw the quartets as a turning point: he claimed that he had composed them "in a quite new, special manner." He did not specify what was so new or special about them, but a comparison with his earlier quartets suggests that they are simultaneously more sophisticated and more accessible.

HAYDN'S HUMOR

Haydn's compositions seem to attract nicknames, in part because of the vivid sound images that he created and in part because he cracked musical jokes. This third quartet of the set is nicknamed the "Bird"; the second is called the "Joke"; the symphony that we hear in the next chapter is the "Surprise."

Haydn is the funniest "serious composer" in the history of Classical music. No composer was more consistently funny, and no composer found more ways to be funny. Haydn's comic repertoire ranged from musical sleight of hand that would bring a knowing smile to the face of a connoisseur to slapstick effects and barnyard humor.

Comedy depends a great deal on surprise and timing. Both depend on expectation. The clarity of Classical

Haydn is the funniest "serious composer" in the history of Classical music.

© John Minnion/Lebrecht Music & Arts

style, the product of such features as frequent, decisive punctuation, well-articulated melodies, and predictable harmony, made it possible for listeners to track musical events in a composition and anticipate what might come next. This in turn enabled composers to play with these expectations, often as a matter of course. Sometimes the comic elements are obvious, such as the bird chirps extracted from the first theme. Other times, they are more like inside jokes for musicians.

This isn't to say that the style is only comic. Haydn's music could also be serious, sublime, simple, or spiritual, when his mood or the situation warranted. Rather, it is that the comic has been added to the range of moods and character available to composers such as Haydn and Mozart. There are dark moments in the movement discussed here; part of the magic is that Haydn is able to shift through so many moods in such a short time and that the shifts are not governed by formal conventions. The capability of shifting moods at will is one of the hallmarks of Classical style; it is one of the qualities that makes it so thoroughly human. It isn't surprising that Haydn, by all accounts a man of good humor and very much down to earth even though he had become the most distinguished composer in Europe by the 1790s, would play a key role in shaping the style.

In the "Bird" quartet, Haydn's humor is evident from the outset. The movement begins tentatively, with neither melody nor bass, and as soon as the key is established, the musicians stop, then resume with the same material but on a different chord. They stop again, only to resume yet again on a harmony that is even farther removed from the key of the movement. In this third try, Haydn finally cadences in the home key and simultaneously sets off on the transition.

Later in the movement, Haydn turns this comic molehill into a mountain: After getting completely lost harmonically during the development—and highlighting it with music that sounds even more indecisive—he begins the recapitulation on a harmony other than the tonic. Only when the cello enters does he present the home chord.

Why would eighteenth-century audiences have found this humorous? There are five structural milestones in a sonata-form movement: establishing the tonic at the outset, establishing the new key later in the exposition, returning to the home key at the beginning of the recapitulation, repeating the second theme in the tonic, and closing the movement with a decisive cadence. Of these, the most dramatic is the coincidence of opening theme and opening harmony at the beginning of the recapitulation.

Return after contrast or development occurs in any movement or movement section in rounded binary form: variation themes, minuets and trios, and the like. Eighteenth-century audiences would have heard this pattern thousands of times. "Sonatafying" this familiar pattern—by expanding the form, adding contrasting material, and making the route back to the home key more tortuous—typically makes the reprise a grander event.

By beginning tentatively and returning even more tentatively, Haydn undermines listeners' expectations for this pattern. It is not slapstick humor, although Haydn's music has some of that. But it probably would have brought a smile to the faces of attentive members of the audience. The larger point is that humor is possible in the Classical style to a far greater degree than in any previous style because the sense of expectation is so strong, so composers such as Haydn and Mozart could subvert these expectations for comic effect.

Classical Music: Form and Style

Our encounter with sonata form and Classical style in two different settings—piano sonata and string quartet—has given us a three-dimensional perspective on both. By comparing the two movements, we can get a workable first impression of both form and style. Two things are evident about sonata form. First, it is not genre-dependent; that is, its essential qualities are not dependent on particular combinations of voices and instruments. Second, its basic architecture and the procedures used to animate it remain consistent from work to work, but they can be realized in infinitely varied ways.

Among the salient characteristics of Classical style that emerge from the two musical examples are frequent contrast, typically articulated by decisive punctuation, and a strong sense of moving toward goals. This is apparent on the smallest and largest scales. Sections generally contain multiple melodic ideas, varied rhythms, frequent changes in texture, dynamic contrast, and gradual change, and activity generally increases as the music approaches a cadence. The two strongest gestures in a sonata-form movement are the transition, which signals the move to the new key, and the development, which leads the music back to the home key via a circuitous route.

We next add a new dimension to our understanding of both sonata form and Classical style through another new genre, the symphony.

LISTEN UP!

CD 2:4–6

Haydn, String Quartet in C major, Op. 33, No. 3 ("Bird"), first movement (1782)

Takeaway point: A good-humored sonata-form movement in a new genre

Style: Classical

Form: Sonata form

Genre: String quartet

Instruments: Two violins, viola, and cello

Context: A new kind of music for the salon, for professionals or skilled amateurs

CHAPTER 21

The Classical Symphony

"Haydn is widely regarded as the 'father of the symphony.'"

S hortly after Haydn re-located to Vienna in 1790, Johann Peter Salomon, a com-poser, violinist, and impresario—a sort of eighteenth-century concert promoter—came to Vienna to personally invite Haydn to England, where he already enjoyed an enthusiastic following. Haydn accepted Salomon's invitation, which included lucrative guarantees for several works, including six symphonies. Haydn arrived in England for the first time on January 2, 1791, and stayed through the following year. The visit was successful enough that he returned in 1794 for another visit, once again producing six new symphonies.

The Orchestra in the Late Eighteenth Century

London, then as now, was a great place to hear orches-tral music. The orchestra that Salomon made available to Haydn for his first visit included about forty musi-cians. By the time of his second visit, it had grown to about sixty. Salomon's London orchestras suggest the extent to which the orchestra grew in size during the eighteenth century. Much of the growth was due to the addition of string players. However, the most signifi-cant change in the orchestra was the permanent addi-tion of woodwind, brass, and percussion instruments.

THE INSTRUMENTS OF THE LATE EIGHTEENTH-CENTURY ORCHESTRA

The six symphonies that Haydn composed for his first

Did You Know?

London's King's Theatre, venue for the premiere of Haydn's symphonies, has since hosted Andrew Lloyd Webber's *Phantom of the Opera*, which has run for more than ten thousand performances.

visit to London require not only a good-sized string section but also pairs of flutes, oboes, bassoons, trumpets, horns, and timpani—all of which had been in use throughout the eighteenth cen-tury. Those he composed for his second visit included all of the above instruments plus a pair of clarinets.

The major difference be-tween early and late eighteenth-century orchestras was that these new instruments were no longer op-tional. In the latter half of the century, compositions that required an orches-tra—symphonies, concertos, operas, and sa-cred choral works—were scored for strings and most or all of these woodwind, brass, and percussion instruments, and occasionally even more. The perma-nent addition of woodwinds and brass came gradually through the late eighteenth century. Trumpets and tim-pani were used intermittently during the last quarter of the century but did not become fixtures in the sym-phonic orchestra until the 1790s.

The woodwinds of the late eighteenth century are fundamentally similar to their modern counterparts. They lack the keys found on contemporary instruments but were capable of playing all the notes in all keys throughout the range of the instrument. By contrast, the brass instruments of the late eighteenth century did not have the valves or pistons that enabled performers to easily play all the notes of the scale. Hornists devel-oped techniques that enabled them to play most notes of a scale, but late-eighteenth-century trumpets could play in only a limited register. Timpani of the era were limited to one note per drum, because they could not be tuned easily once a work was under way; the mechani-cal device that allows rapid tuning of the drum had not been invented. Typically, therefore, a timpanist had two or three timpani at his disposal.

Salomon's orchestra is the core of the modern sym-phony orchestra. Other wind, brass, and percussion instruments would be added in subsequent generations, but the main instruments within each section of the orchestra were already present. This is one important reason why contemporary symphony orchestras perform Mozart and Haydn far more frequently than they do Bach and Handel.

ORCHESTRATING THE CLASSICAL SYMPHONY

The addition of winds, brass, and percussion added a wealth of tone color and greatly expanded the opportunity for timbral, dynamic, and textural contrast. Winds, brass, even percussion could share the solo spotlight with strings, and the dynamic range grew significantly—from one or two instruments alone to the massed orchestra. Even more striking are the new textures made possible by the choir of winds plus trumpets, horns, and timpani.

Frequent and vivid contrasts in timbre, dynamics, and texture are one quality that distinguishes the Classical symphony from earlier orchestral music. We consider other distinguishing features in a brief introduction to the *symphony*, that long, multimovement work for symphony orchestra.

LO3 The Classical Symphony

Haydn arrived in London as a celebrity. He was received by royalty, granted an honorary doctorate at Oxford, and attended numerous events, including concerts at Westminster Abbey (where he heard Handel's oratorios performed). Although his contract with Salomon included the six symphonies as well as an opera and twenty other compositions, the symphonies were clearly the centerpiece of the contract. They were the highlight of the concerts in which they were presented; unlike contemporary orchestra concerts, these also included a fair amount of non-orchestral music. Critics couldn't find enough good things to say about Haydn's music.

These circumstances—Haydn's visit, the active concert scene in London, Salomon's administrative and musical skill, the receptiveness of the London audience and critics—all point to a dramatic shift in urban musical life. Vocal music—opera and oratorio—was no longer preeminent in public performance. Instrumental music, and the symphony in particular, had grown in prestige during the eighteenth century; by the end of the century, some even considered it equal or superior to vocal music as a form of musical expression.

HAYDN'S LATE SYMPHONIES

By the time Haydn arrived in London, the main features of the symphony—not only the instrumentation but also such features as the number and forms of the movements—were well established.

Like the string quartet, the **symphony** had four movements, in a predictable sequence; fast-slow-fast-fast. The first movement might begin at a fast tempo, or it might have a slow introduction. In either event, the fast part would be cast in sonata form.

The slow introduction to a symphony originated at the French court. As the opening part of the overture, it helped get Louis XIV to the royal box. Throughout the eighteenth century, it signaled the serious intent of the music that followed.

The second movement was slow. It could take almost any form, from a trimmed-down sonata form to simple variations. The third movement was either a minuet, a popular eighteenth-century dance in triple meter, or a **scherzo**, a playful, more high-spirited alternative. Although derived from

> **symphony** An extended work for orchestra that typically contains four movements in fast-slow-fast-fast tempos: a first movement in sonata form, a slow movement, a minuet or scherzo, and a finale
>
> **scherzo** Playful, high-spirited third movement of a symphony

dance music, neither was music for dancing. The last movement was typically a **rondo**, a form in which a tuneful and simple opening theme returns again and again, but only after alternating with one or more contrasting themes.

This sequence of movements was front-weighted. That is, the forms that required more attention occur earlier; those that were easier to follow come later. This seems to be a response both to the relative complexity of sonata form and to the increased length of the movements. For example, a performance of all three movements of Vivaldi's "Spring" will take less time than a performance of the first movement of the "Surprise" symphony.

"He claimed that his intention was to surprise the public."

HAYDN'S SYMPHONY NO. 94

Haydn's Symphony No. 94 owes its nickname—the "Surprise" symphony—to the loud chords that periodically disrupt the soft statement of the simple melody that opens the second movement. In the wake of the premiere of Haydn's "Surprise" symphony, a story apparently began making the rounds among Haydn's English audience that Haydn had interjected his "surprise" into the second movement to wake up those members of the audience who had dozed off. Within a few years, it had become legend, one that is still heard today. Some years later, Georg Griesinger, a confidant of Haydn, asked him in jest whether there was any truth to the story. Haydn denied that it was so; instead, he claimed that his "intention was to surprise the public with something new, and to debut in a brilliant manner, in order to prevent my rank from being usurped by Pleyel, my pupil." In fact, there was a competing concert series in London during Haydn's first visit. It featured works by Pleyel, which were causing quite a

sensation, so Haydn certainly had sufficient motivation to provide something novel. Whether Haydn's official version of the surprise was the truth or simply a discreet way of covering his tracks, we will never know. What we do know is that the famous surprise in the second movement is only the most unmistakably obvious of many surprises in the entire work. They do give some credence to Haydn's claim that he wanted to provide something novel, and they offer further proof of his sense of humor.

In the first movement, Haydn's surprises have to do with the expectations for sonata form. By the time of the work's premiere in 1792, he had composed hundreds of works in which he employed sonata form, and he evidently assumed that his London audiences were familiar with the form, through listening and performance.

For listeners, it is the outlining features—decisive punctuations and memorable themes marking the main structural goals—that most clearly mark the progress through a movement in sonata form, while the ebb and flow of activity that leads to and continues from major landmarks give shape to the form. In this movement, Haydn deliberately subverts these expectations: the most decisive and memorable melodic material is displaced; it does not line up with the important structural goals. He uses the introduction to set up these surprises.

In general, the primary function of the introduction is to convey a sense of solemnity and importance—to let the audience know that something significant is under way. The clearest clue is the stately tempo, but the character of the melodic material typically contributes as well. As a rule, introductions simply precede the main

© iStockphoto.com/Joshua Blake

LISTEN UP!

CD 2:7–10

Haydn, Symphony No. 94 in G, first movement (1792)

Takeaway point: The sound of the Classical orchestra in a high-spirited symphonic movement

Style: Classical

Form: Sonata form

Genre: Symphony

Instruments: Symphony orchestra: full string section, plus flutes, oboes, bassoons, horns, trumpets, and timpani

Context: A work composed for Haydn's first visit to London

part of the movement; it is rare that musical material from the introduction returns later in the movement in its original form. That is the case here.

However, the introduction in this symphony seems to set off a chain reaction. Because it begins with a simple tuneful melody that immediately locks in the home key, the introduction seems to absolve Haydn of the need to use the first and second themes to orient the listener. As a result, the first theme is just a wisp of a melody that begins far away from the home key; it lasts only a few seconds before being overrun by a vigorous new section. The remainder of the movement takes its cue from the first theme: the other most surprising moments occur at those points in the form where we expect the greatest clarity: the entrance of the second theme, the end of the exposition, the beginning of the recapitulation. In each case we expect a decisive punctuation and a memorable melody. But in this symphony, these junctures seem to whiz by; we discover only after the fact that we have passed a major point of arrival in the form. It is the material that comes later that seems to best fit our expectations for first- and second-theme material. These are the most apparent of numerous surprises throughout the movement, from the "mystery" section in the introduction to the pseudo-development and the restatement of the opening theme by the lower strings in the recapitulation. Haydn's London audience certainly would have heard it as "something new."

There's something for everyone

© iStockphoto.com/Aiija

Haydn, the Symphony, and Classical Style: Something for Everyone

Haydn's "Surprise" symphony has been a favorite of audiences for over two hundred years. Audiences loved this symphony in 1792, and they love it now. What's the "wow factor" for audiences in this Haydn symphony? There's something for everyone. The musical events cross class boundaries; they range from folklike materials to passages of great sophistication. His audience may have been dazzled by the first movement, but after the first performance they probably left the theater humming the tune of the second movement.

The mix of art and accessibility isn't specific to Haydn; it was the norm during the latter half of the eighteenth century. But Haydn's music is both more accessible and more artful than that of any other composer of his time, with the exception of Mozart. Next we hear a special mix of art and accessibility in two excerpts from Mozart's grandest opera, *Don Giovanni.*

CHAPTER 22

Mozart and Opera

> "Imagine a production with an absolutely unscrupulous, sex-crazed leading man; a string of scorned women; murder; spectacular special effects; and a spine-chilling ending."

Imagine a production with an absolutely unscrupulous, sex-crazed leading man; a string of scorned women; murder; spectacular special effects; and a spine-chilling ending. The latest Hollywood blockbuster? Perhaps. But a surer candidate is Mozart's magnificent opera *Don Giovanni*.

More than any other opera of the eighteenth century, *Don Giovanni*, an operatic setting of the legend of Don Juan, not only shows the changes in operatic style during the era but also reflects—more than any other single musical work of the era—the significant changes in European society. We outline the story and sample the music as we explore why *Don Giovanni* has been held in such high regard since its premiere.

LO4 The Development of Opera during the Eighteenth Century

There's about a sixty-year gap between the productions of Handel's *Julius Caesar* (1724) and Gay's *The Beggar's Opera* (1728) and the premiere of Mozart's *Don Giovanni* in 1787. One can view *Don Giovanni* as a synthesis of the traditions represented by the two earlier works. But at the same time, the opera would have shocked early eighteenth-century audiences, especially the aristocracy; they probably wouldn't have known what to make of it and almost certainly would have tried to get it banned.

OPERA AND SOCIETY

One can use opera as a barometer of social change in eighteenth-century Europe. At the beginning of the century, *opera seria* reigned supreme; so did the absolute monarchs, like Louis XIV, who supported it. The connection between court and plot went deeper: although it wasn't made explicit, there was a presumption that the ruler who sponsored a particular opera identified with the noble mythical or historical hero. By contrast, *The Beggar's Opera* lampooned both opera seria and aristocratic society alike.

The Beggar's Opera anticipated an important trend: "lighter" forms of music and theatrical entertainment

The flourishing art of caricature during the eighteenth century reflected the fact that the aristocracy was no longer being viewed through rose-colored glasses.

that often contained social commentary, sometimes overt, other times thinly disguised. Their rise in popularity coincided with drastic changes in the social order. The premiere of *Don Giovanni* came about a decade after the American Revolution and two years before the start of the French Revolution. In *Don Giovanni*, it is quite clear that the aristocracy is no longer being viewed through rose-colored glasses. *Don Giovanni* is the notorious Don Juan, a Spanish nobleman who is anything but noble. In Mozart's opera he is an antihero.

OPERA: FROM REFORM TO RECONCEPTION

The radical transformation of opera during the latter part of the eighteenth century grew out of three interrelated developments: the growing popularity and sophistication of new, lighter forms of stage entertainment; the reform of serious opera; and the dramatic change in musical style. Collectively, they reshaped opera into a more flexible and more dramatically credible genre.

New Forms of Musical Stage Entertainment.
The Beggar's Opera was a singular success in England, but it was far from an isolated instance of new, less formal kinds of musical stage entertainment. By midcentury, one could hear French **opéra comique** and Italian **opera buffa** (both terms translate as "comic opera") not only in their home countries but also all over Europe. The **Singspiel** was the German-speaking counterpart to opéra comique; both featured spoken dialogue instead of recitative. Gluck's *Die Pilgrime von Mekka*, the *Singspiel* from which Mozart took "Unser dummer Pöbel meint," was originally produced as an opéra comique: *La Rencontre imprévue*. (Opéra comique had a substantial following in Vienna.) The version in German appeared somewhat later.

Like *The Beggar's Opera*, these lighter operatic forms were less bound by convention. They were often comic in spirit (as opposed to *opera seria*) and topical in subject matter, with an undertone of social commentary.

However, unlike Gay's "opera," much of this music was composed rather than borrowed. Over time, both drama and music became more sophisticated: *Don Giovanni* was identified as an *opera buffa*, although it ends about as seriously as one can imagine. This contributed to the blurring of boundaries among the several types of musical stage entertainment.

The Reform of *Opera Seria*.
Throughout almost the entire history of opera there has been a tension between drama and music. Recall that opera was originally conceived of as "drama through music." The pendulum quickly swung the other way: the plot became scaffolding for a series of arias—an excuse to enjoy singing and singers. The reform movement of the Arcadian Academy led to the more noble operas of Handel and other Baroque-era composers. But infighting among singers helped undermine efforts of librettists and composers to create dramatically cogent opera. The two most flagrant musical abuses were the demands for equal time in the spotlight—if singer X gets three arias, then so should singer Y—and the retention of the da capo aria, in order to allow singers to display their virtuosity and inventiveness. Add backstage bickering, which often reached scandalous proportions, and plots that were literally incredible, and one finds that opera had strayed far from the high-minded ideals of its founders and was in serious need of yet another reform. That would come in midcentury.

The musician most responsible for the reform of serious opera was the German composer Christoph Willibald Gluck. Gluck composed mainly for the theater: not only lighter entertainment such as *Die Pilgrime von Mekka* but also ballets and *opera seria*, including another famous version of the Orpheus legend, entitled *Orfeo ed Euridice*, the first of Gluck's three reform operas. In his preface to *Alceste*, the second of the reform operas, Gluck issued a reform manifesto. In bold language, he outlines the abuses that cripple *opera seria*. He targeted singers, whose "mistaken vanity" causes them to stifle dramatic action with a "useless superfluity of ornaments." He asserted that his goal was simply "to restrict music to its true office of serving poetry by means of expression and by following the situations of the story." To do this, Gluck put aside many of the rigid conventions that had hamstrung Baroque opera.

Despite these reforms, *opera seria* lost its dominant position in the operatic world. There was still an audience for it during Mozart's lifetime—*La Clemenza di Tito*, an *opera seria*, was Mozart's last opera—but *opera buffa* and *Singspiel* by Mozart and his contemporaries were more popular.

opéra comique
Humorous French stage entertainment that blends spoken dialogue with song

opera buffa In the 1700s, Italian comic opera, often with contemporary everyday characters instead of gods and historical heroes

Singspiel Literally "song/play"; lighthearted stage entertainment in German that, like *opéra comique*, combines spoken dialogue with song

A Flexible Musical Language. Another reason for the ascendancy of *opera buffa* was that it grew up with the new Classical style. This style allowed for frequent and dramatic contrast, which enabled composers to respond more flexibly to dramatic demands. We will hear Mozart's skill in this regard in the two selections from *Don Giovanni* discussed later.

Mozart, Opera, and *Don Giovanni*

Although Mozart composed masterfully in every genre, he is perhaps most esteemed for his operas. Virtually since their composition, Mozart's best operas have been regarded by many as not only his supreme achievements—if only because of their magnitude and complexity—but also the most successful operas of any era.

Mozart began composing for the stage at age ten and produced works in practically every fashionable genre, from *opera seria* to *Singspiel*. However, the works for which he is best remembered are four late comic operas—*The Marriage of Figaro*, *Don Giovanni*, *Cosi fan tutte*, and *The Magic Flute*. Critics have praised them for the beauty of the music and their dramatic power.

Don Giovanni

Mozart composed *Don Giovanni* in 1787 for a performance in Prague. *The Marriage of Figaro*, which premiered the previous year, had been exceptionally well received and resulted in a commission for the new opera.

Don Giovanni, with a libretto by Lorenzo da Ponte, tells the tale of Don Giovanni, a Spanish nobleman and the most notorious womanizer in Europe. (Even today, the Spanish version of the name, "Don Juan," is a term for a man who lives to seduce women; he woos one, then quickly drops her to pursue a new conquest.) Although Leporello, his manservant, reminds us periodically that his conquests number in the thousands, the plot concerns mainly his amorous relations with three women: Donna Anna, Donna Elvira, and Zerlina. Don Giovanni tries to seduce Donna Anna early in the opera. He fails, is discovered, and then is challenged to a duel by her elderly father, the Commandant, whom he kills. Donna Anna swears revenge. Donna Elvira is an earlier conquest who, with exquisitely bad timing, has resurfaced in Seville. She is the archetypal jilted lover. Zerlina is a peasant girl who is about to be married; Don Giovanni spies her as he escapes from an encounter

Leporello (left), Don Giovanni's faithful if timid sidekick, offers comic relief in an often deadly serious story.

with Elvira and tries to seduce her right under the nose of her soon-to-be husband.

The plot grows out of the complications ensuing from Don Giovanni's pursuit of these women. By the second act, Giovanni has men and women alike after him—the men trying to kill him and Donna Elvira trying to reform him.

The plot sends a host of conflicting signals about Don Giovanni. He is, by Leporello's account, an incorrigible rake. But not only does he fail to bed any of the women during the course of the opera but also bungles every attempt to do so. He runs away from each of the women at different points in the opera but stands up to the statue of the dead Commandant that comes to life at the end, despite the threat of damnation. Does his lack of repentance express the courage of his convictions or arrogance so overwhelming that he is blind to its consequences?

In its grand scheme, *Don Giovanni* is a comic opera with a tragic ending. There are laughs throughout, but the end is a graphic reminder that immorality leads to damnation. Don Giovanni is the hero or, more properly, the antihero. He and Leporello are the focus of the plot; it is their antics that entertain the audience. Yet the subtitle of the opera is *Il dissoluto punito* (*The Rake*

Punished), and after Don Giovanni goes up in flames on his way down to hell, the rest of the cast comes onstage to wag their collective finger and warn the audience that evildoers will always be punished.

The composition and production of *Don Giovanni* clearly signaled that aristocratic control of culture and society had weakened significantly. The heart of the plot of *Don Giovanni*—a murdered man returns as a statue, invites his murderer to dinner, and casts him into hell—is a legend that dates from the Middle Ages. Da Ponte, the librettist, drew on *Dom Juan*, a setting of the story by the seventeenth-century French playwright Molière that scandalized French authorities and was effectively banned during Molière's lifetime. Da Ponte and Mozart present Don Giovanni as an ignoble nobleman, a complex and substantially evil character, a rake, a buffoon, yet a man unafraid of death. This more realistic and far less flattering portrait of a member of the nobility would have been at odds with the honorable heroes presented in opera seria and a far cry from the image that the nobility sought to project to the masses.

Mozart's Music for Don Giovanni

Without question, the legend of Don Juan was a terrific point of departure for an opera, but it was Mozart who transformed it into one of the great operas of all time. We get some sense of the range and dramatic power of his music through a comparison of two scenes. The first is a duet, "Là ci darem la mano" (Give Me Your Hand); the second is Don Giovanni's final scene, "A cenar teco" (To Dine with You).

© ArenaPal/Topham/The Image Works

We can hear how Mozart characterizes Don Giovanni's wooing and Zerlina's reluctance (Tom Erik Lie as Don Giovanni and Michelle Walton as Zerlina).

LISTEN UP!

CD 2:11
Mozart, "Là ci darem la mano," *Don Giovanni* (1787)

Takeaway point: Simple, spellbinding music for a seduction in song

Style: Classical

Form: AA′BA″ with extensions and a coda

Genre: Opera

Instruments: Voices with orchestral accompaniment

Context: A simple, irresistible melody for a simple peasant girl

"LÀ CI DAREM LA MANO"

The duet occurs early in the opera, but Don Giovanni has already tried to seduce Donna Anna, killed her father, and encountered Donna Elvira, a former conquest who refuses to take no for an answer. After he eludes Donna Elvira, Don Giovanni goes on the hunt again and comes upon a wedding of two peasants, Zerlina and Masetto. He is attracted to the bride-to-be, so he invites Masetto and the rest of the wedding party to his estate so that he can make his move on Zerlina. In the course of the duet, he converts her from a girl who can say no to another potential notch on his belt by promising to marry her, even though her wedding to Masetto is imminent.

How does Mozart help Don Giovanni seduce Zerlina? The melody that Don Giovanni sings sends two strong signals: it is simple, and it is irresistible. In the context of the opera, the duet requires simple music because Zerlina is a peasant, albeit a beautiful one. So Mozart simplifies his musical language (compared to that in the rest of the opera) so that it reaches Zerlina (and everyone else) directly. Then the pure loveliness of the melody takes over. Could anyone singing a melody so sweet be a bad guy? The answer is yes, of course, but Zerlina doesn't know that; she is momentarily spellbound.

Mozart's setting of the melody certainly heightens the mood. Among the details are the simple accompaniment at the beginning, underscoring the simplicity of the melody, and the quickening rhythm of exchange—he sings, she sings at increasingly shorter intervals, until they go off together. And there are parts of the melody where Mozart guides the action. In the contrasting section ("Vieni, mio bel diletto!"), we can hear how Mozart characterizes Don Giovanni's increasingly ardent wooing and Zerlina's steadily decreasing reluctance.

Nevertheless, at the heart of it all is Mozart's simple and charming melody. It draws us in, it makes sense apart from the words, and it also makes dramatic sense. It is an invitation to love, specifically for Don Giovanni's seduction of a peasant girl.

"Là ci darem la mano" shows one aspect of Mozart's art, the ability to compose captivating melodies that function flawlessly in a dramatic context. Such a beautiful melody would be horribly out of place in the next scene, in which Don Giovanni literally goes down in flames. Instead, we hear what may well be the most terrifying music of the eighteenth century.

"A CENAR TECO"

"A cenar teco" takes place in the scene in which Don Giovanni meets his fate. Shortly before, Don Giovanni and Leporello are trading their cloaks, which they had exchanged earlier so that Don Giovanni could pass himself off as a servant. They are in a cemetery, near a statue of the Commandant. As Don Giovanni brags about his flirtation with Elvira's maid, they hear a sepulchral voice telling them that Don Giovanni will stop laughing before morning. The voice comes from the statue. Leporello is appropriately terrified, but Don Giovanni impudently invites the voice to supper.

Later, as Don Giovanni is eating, the Commandant—in statue form—arrives at his castle. As Leporello cowers under the dining table, Don Giovanni invites the statue to join him for dinner. The Commandant declines, instead inviting Don Giovanni to dine with *him*. He takes Don Giovanni's hand and asks him to repent. As the Commandant does so, Don Giovanni discovers that the hand is very cold and begins to realize that something is gravely amiss. When Don Giovanni refuses the Commandant's invitation, he is engulfed in flames. Voices from below direct him to the hell where he will spend eternity.

If taken literally, the plot is simply not believable: a statue comes alive to become the agent of Don Giovanni's immolation. It is Mozart's music that can get us beneath the story: it enables us to experience this final scene emotionally, as if it were true. The orchestral accompaniment, from the first terrifying chord to the final push to the end, lets us know that Don Giovanni's end is near. There are clues everywhere: swirling violins, voice-of-doom trombones, relentless rhythms. The vocal lines of the three characters match their personalities. The wide intervals and downward thrust of

The Commandant presides over Don Giovanni's demise.

the Commandant's melodic material depict the voice of doom; Leporello's chattering underscores his cowardice; Don Giovanni's answers resonate with defiance.

The scene's music gains power precisely because it is so different from that in "Là ci darem la mano." The contrasts between the two scenes highlight many facets of Don Giovanni's character: charmer, arrogant but gracious host, courageous if foolhardy libertine. The music helps us to identify with him, even as we are repelled by his obsessive need for seduction, which he pursues without regard for the hurt he causes, and to be horrified at his fate.

LISTEN UP!

CD 2:12–13

Mozart, "A cenar teco," *Don Giovanni* (1787)
Takeaway point: Terrifying music for a terrible moment

Style: Classical

Form: Through-composed

Genre: Opera

Instruments: Voices with orchestral accompaniment

Context: Don Giovanni being damned to hell: just deserts for an immoral life

Mozart, Classical Music, and Opera as Drama

Numerous commentators have observed that Classical music, both instrumental and vocal, was inherently dramatic because of the underlying patterns of tension and release and the frequent contrast and directional thrust used to animate both tension and its resolution. However, in instrumental music, the dramatic events are often a matter of interpretation. In these two excerpts from *Don Giovanni*, we know from the libretto exactly what the music is supposed to convey. Here we seek to discover how the music works dramatically.

If we compare either of these scenes to Cleopatra's aria in Handel's *Julius Caesar*, we immediately sense a fundamental difference. The Baroque da capo aria is dramatically static, whereas these two scenes are dynamic. In "Piangeró," the plot is essentially in the same place at the end of the aria as it was at the beginning. Cleopatra lets us know that she is distressed, that she will make life a living hell for Ptolemy if she dies, then reminds us that she is, indeed, distressed. The music is gorgeous and evocative, but there is no *action*. By contrast, Mozart not only helps Don Giovanni seduce Zerlina but also gives us the details: his gentle first step in the simple melody, Zerlina's initial reluctance in the

extension of her answer, the Don's more impassioned plea, Zerlina's quick reply, her gradual weakening, then her acquiescence at the shift in tempo. The music not only helps advance the plot but also tells us about both characters. We learn—from the music as well as the libretto—that Don Giovanni is a relentless, unprincipled charmer and that Zerlina is gullible, dazzled by riches and power, and not particularly principled herself.

The final scene is the most dramatic moment in the opera. Mozart invests it with foreboding in the spine-tingling chords that open the scene. He crafts all three vocal lines to match the characters: bold skips in the Commandant's music, Leporello chattering away, and the Don absolutely defiant, especially in the jagged rhythms just before he gives his hand to the Commandant. Underneath, the orchestra is turbulent, violent, agitated, leaving no doubt that Don Giovanni is doomed. Again, the story moves relentlessly toward its denouement: Don Giovanni's bizarre dinner guest (when was the last time you invited a statue to dinner?) sends him to hell.

It is in music like this that we can feel most powerfully the dramatic potential of opera. In both scenes, the music does the dramatic work. The text—and the acting onstage—lets us know what is happening, but it is the music that compels us to feel the drama, in a way that is impossible with words alone.

CHAPTER 23

The Classical Concerto

"Mozart's late concertos, especially those he composed for his own use, were instrumental dramas in which he was not only the star but also the only main character."

Did You Know?

Like the explosive solos of heavy-metal guitarists, cadenzas in concertos are an opportunity for virtuosic solo display within a group context.

Y ou are at a symphony orchestra concert. The program includes an overture to Verdi's opera *La forza del destino*,

Mozart's Piano Concerto No. 24 (the work discussed later), and Tchaikovsky's Fourth Symphony. The members of the orchestra gradually take their places. The concertmaster comes onstage; the oboist plays an A, the note to which the rest of the orchestra will tune. The musicians tune, then become quiet. So does the audience, in anticipation of the conductor's entrance. The conductor walks onstage, acknowledges the audience with a generous bow, then takes his place at the podium. He raises his baton and with a bold gesture commands the brass players to intone their solemn call. Although this is an overture for an opera, there are no sets, nor are there singers. This is an in-concert performance of part of an opera that is strictly orchestral. The overture concludes with a flourish, led by brass and timpani. The conductor turns to the audience, thanks them with a bow, steps down from the podium, and walks offstage.

The musicians stand up as stagehands move their chairs to clear a space at the front of the stage. Some of the musicians leave, because they will not be needed in the next work. In a few minutes, a grand piano—nine feet in length—is situated in front of the podium, the stage is rearranged, and the musicians have returned to their seats. The concertmaster stands up, walks over to the piano, and plays the tuning note. The orchestra tunes to the A from the piano, then grows quiet once again; so does the audience. The conductor comes onstage once again, but this time he is preceded by a young Asian woman, the soloist in the Mozart concerto. She is elegantly dressed in a long sleeveless gown that allows complete freedom of movement in her arms. She and the conductor acknowledge the applause of the audience; she takes her seat at the piano while the conductor steps up on the podium. Once in place, he turns to the soloist, as if to ask, "Are you ready?" She answers with an affirmative nod. Again he raises his baton, but this time he begins with a subtle gesture, to express the soft, suspenseful beginning of the concerto. The young pianist sits quietly at the piano for over two minutes, while the orchestra plays the first part of the concerto. They conclude, and she begins to play a mournful melody. For almost half a minute, there is no orchestral accompaniment; it is as if Mozart is shining a spotlight on the piano. Then the orchestra enters again, and the interplay between soloist and orchestra begins.

The concert that you're attending is an orchestral concert, not an opera. But the influence of opera pervades the first half of the program. It is explicit in the Verdi overture and implicit in Mozart's concerto. Indeed, Mozart's late piano concertos are the closest that instrumental music has come to opera-like drama. The only thing that could make the drama more evident would be to have the soloist walk on after the orchestra has begun to play, arriving at the piano just in time to play—much like a leading character in an opera making a grand entrance.

The Concerto in Eighteenth-Century Cultural Life

Quick question: What are the names of the four Beatles? It's a good bet that you know, and if you don't, it's an even better bet that your parents—and grandparents—do. It seems to be a basic urge, at least in our culture, to relate to individuals, to single them out even when they're part of a group. This impulse helps explain the transformation of the Baroque concerto, a genre in which the soloist emerges from the orchestra, into the Classical concerto, in which the soloist is set off against the orchestra.

This transformation was a consequence of several major changes in musical life during the latter part of the eighteenth century: the continued growth of instrumental music, major improvements in the piano, the emergence of instrumental stars, and the increasing frequency of public concerts. These circumstances created an ideal breeding ground for a new kind of concerto. Hundreds of composers began turning out thousands of concertos, for keyboard and most orchestral instruments. The most familiar concertos of the Classical era are those of Mozart, who understood the dramatic potential of the genre far better than any of his contemporaries.

Mozart frequently performed his concertos in public concerts. These public concerts were far different from contemporary orchestral concerts. The music was new—in Mozart's case, so new at times that the ink was barely dry—and the programs were far more diverse. They were showcases for a particular composer rather than the revival of traditional repertoire. And they were usually ad hoc affairs; resident orchestras, concert series, and other institutions found in contemporary musical life did not exist.

Public concerts did not replace private engagements

before royalty and in the homes of the aristocracy. But they did add an important new outlet and source of income for musicians, especially those with an entrepreneurial bent.

LO5 Mozart and the Classical Concerto

The concertos of Mozart, especially the keyboard concertos, are the only eighteenth-century concertos that routinely appear on the concert programs of contemporary symphony orchestras. There are practical reasons for this: the late keyboard concertos typically have full wind sections (that is the case here), so more of the orchestra is used. There are aesthetic reasons as well: Mozart's concertos are marvelous works. They strike an ideal balance between solo and orchestra. Still another reason is that they are the first concertos that truly embody our contemporary understanding of the concerto and concerto performance: the soloist is a star; the orchestra can be a partner, an adversary, a support system, or occasionally just a bystander.

MOZART, STAR SOLOIST

In the 1760s and early 1770s, a talented child musician was thrilling royalty throughout Europe. At the age of seven, Mozart and his family left Salzburg, Austria, and began a three-year tour of Europe, which took them to England, France, Belgium, and Germany. At each stop, young Wolfgang played for heads of state and their courts, and in many locations gave public concerts. Audiences were amazed at the extraordinary ability of the child, whose hands were barely able to span five keys, to play his own difficult music and improvise everything from a set of variations to an opera aria. Six years after the first tour, the Mozart family toured Italy for two years, where the boy made an even more powerful impression. By the time he left Salzburg for Vienna in 1780, Mozart enjoyed an international reputation not only as a superb composer but also as one of the finest keyboard players in Europe.

In the 1760s and early 1770s, Mozart was a talented child musician who was thrilling royalty throughout Europe.

Mozart continued to perform, mainly in Vienna, throughout his career: many of his concertos, including the one discussed later, received their first performances at concerts of his music, which might also include a symphony, vocal music, and improvisations.

THE CONCERTO, FROM BAROQUE TO CLASSICAL

Mozart's concertos introduce a new relationship between soloist and orchestra, one that is significantly different from that heard in Baroque concertos. Recall that the concerto movements by Vivaldi and Bach open with an orchestral ritornello. Solo passages, no matter how brilliant, expanded upon the character of the ritornello. In the sense that the music played by the orchestra determined the fundamental character of the movement, the orchestra was in charge.

By contrast, in the Classical **concerto**, the soloist is heard in opposition to the orchestra rather than as an extension of it. The idea of opposition and its harmonious resolution is inherent in the Classical style. In instrumental music, this dialectic is realized most powerfully in the concerto, because composers can put a face on it: soloist versus orchestra, more than soloist with orchestra, or orchestra with soloists. This is apparent visually and aurally—in performance one hears and sees the contrast between solo and orchestra, when that is the intent of the composer.

THE KEYBOARD CONCERTO

Piano concertos are different in kind from all other solo concertos because the piano is a self-sufficient solo instrument. That is, pianists can play both melody and harmony, with as many parts as necessary to create a complete texture, as we heard in Mozart's piano sonata. It was—and is—customary to compose for piano alone, in ways that are not possible on the violin, bassoon, horn, or any other orchestral instrument.

The harpsichord has the same capability, but it does not have the capacity for the expressive nuance that was so important to post-Baroque composers. For this reason, composers wrote far more flute and violin concertos than keyboard concertos in the 1750s and 1760s. However, as the piano

> **concerto** In the Classical era, a work for solo instrument and orchestra in which the soloist counterbalances the greater numbers of the orchestra through virtuosity, harmonic ingenuity, and lyricism

replaced the harpsichord as the keyboard instrument of choice in the 1770s, piano concertos appeared on concert programs far more frequently. Mozart's piano concertos, most of which were composed after 1780, far outnumber his concertos for all other instruments combined.

A piano concerto is—or can be—an unequal contest among equals. Piano and orchestra are equal in the sense that both can provide complete textures: melody, accompaniment, even countermelody. The pianist can play alone for extended stretches or exchange musical ideas back and forth with the orchestra without the feeling that something is missing. However, in terms of forces, it's David versus Goliath: one modestly loud instrument versus an orchestra of thirty or more musicians. No one understood the dramatic potential of this dynamic better than Mozart, and no one surpassed his strategy for bringing this inequality into balance.

MOZART AND THE CONCERTO

Of the twenty-seven concertos typically attributed to Mozart, only the last eighteen are customarily played. These eighteen concertos (seventeen for one piano, and one for two pianos) fall into two groups: those he composed for others, most notably his student Barbara Ployer, and those he composed for his own use. Many of those he composed for himself are identifiable by what they lack: notes in the solo part. (Mozart knew in general what he wanted to play, so at times he left just enough information to reconstruct his part in performance or outline a passage that he would improvise.)

We know that Mozart had an unsurpassed affinity for drama through music. So it is only a small step to understand Mozart's late concertos, especially those he composed for his own use, as instrumental dramas, dramas in which he was not only the star but also the only character. It is from this perspective that we consider the first movement of his Concerto in C minor.

Mozart's Concerto in C Minor and the Classical Concerto

A sense of balance is integral to the Classical style, and especially to the music of Mozart. It is a balance created by complementary energies, like purposely holding one's breath, then giving in to the urge to exhale.

It is evident in its most characteristic form: in sonata form, the recapitulation releases the tension built up in the exposition and development. And it is often evident in smaller entities such as an aria: in "Là ci darem la mano" we hear it in the question/answer pattern of the first two phrases and in the exchanges between Don Giovanni and Zerlina.

We mention this point because the defining feature of a piano concerto is the apparent imbalance between orchestra and soloist. It is evident at the beginning, both visually (many against one) and aurally (the orchestra throws down the gauntlet, with a long opening statement). Mozart's self-imposed challenge was to bring them into some kind of parity by the end of the movement.

Mozart's strategy was to counterbalance the power of the orchestra with solo-only features and opportunities. To portray the conflict and resolution of these opposing forces on the grandest scale, Mozart expanded and modified the sonata-form model found in sonatas, chamber music, and symphonies. First movements in the later Mozart piano concertos typically follow this sequence of events:

The Orchestral Exposition. The concerto opens with a long orchestral statement. It presents melodic material that returns later in the movement, and it features frequent contrasts in activity, dynamics, texture, and instrumentation. In these respects, it sounds like an exposition. But it is harmonically static; it remains in the same key throughout. The structural tension between contrasting keys that underpins all of the events in the movement has been postponed.

Solo Exposition. The key events in this second and different exposition are designed to empower the soloist:

- The soloist's entrance, with little or no accompaniment, playing tuneful music—either the orchestral first theme, if it is lyrical, or new material that precedes the restatement of the first theme if it is not

- A transition to the new key, usually highlighted by brilliant figuration

- A *new* second theme to spotlight the arrival in the new key, which confirms that only the soloist has the power to initiate harmonic change

- More brilliant figuration leading to a decisive cadence that closes the solo exposition.

Development Section. The typical sequence of events within the development section includes the central tutti, an extended statement by the orchestra; rapid, often argumentative dialogue between soloist and orchestra that wanders far afield harmonically; and a long preparation for the return of the opening theme.

Recapitulation. The recapitulation merges the orchestral and solo exposition, as if to signal that the soloist and orchestra are now on an equal footing. Mozart does not include all the material from both expositions; themes not used almost always appear in the development or coda.

Coda. The coda, like the development, begins with a big orchestral statement and then pauses at a point of great harmonic tension. At this point, the soloist plays a **cadenza**, a rhapsodic and virtuosic improvisation of variable length. This final moment or two in the spotlight cements the soloist's status as an equal partner. It ends with the soloist leading the orchestra back to the tonic key. The orchestra brings the movement to a close; the pianist may join in but seldom does.

LISTEN UP!

CD 2:14–18

Mozart, Concerto No. 24 in C minor, K. 491, first movement (1786)

Takeaway point: Instrumental music as tragic drama

Style: Classical

Form: Classical concerto form (expansion of sonata form)

Genre: Concerto

Instruments: Piano and symphony orchestra with strings, winds, brass, and timpani

Context: Mozart showcases himself in public performance as a composer, pianist, and improviser

Mozart's Music as Drama and a Preview of Romanticism?

In the previous chapter, we noted that opera was the most specifically dramatic genre of the Classical era, because the role of the music is to bring the libretto to life. Mozart's mature piano concertos, especially those

Could this concerto be Mozart's way of expressing his struggle with authority?

composed for his own use, are the most *personally* dramatic music of the Classical era, as this movement amply demonstrates.

Concerto movements like this are the most first-person music of the era. In performance—the only way Mozart's audience would have encountered it—we can hear and see the interaction of one against many. But the concerto is far more than soloist versus orchestra. The drama is in the dynamic relationship between soloist and orchestra: it changes during the course of the movement, much as the drama moved forward during Don Giovanni's duet with Zerlina or his fateful encounter with the statue of the Commandant. Mozart's gifts to the soloist—harmonic ingenuity, lyrical lines, brilliant figuration, and the cadenza where they all come together—bring the soloist and orchestra into balance by the end of the movement.

The ease with which we can link the solo part to the composer historically and the inherently dramatic nature of the concerto and Mozart's music may prompt us to consider to what extent the concerto is autobiographical. This is a provocative inquiry, because the movement (and the concerto as a whole) is an uncharacteristically dark piece. The vast majority of Classical-era compositions, by Mozart and his contemporaries, are brighter in mood: they are in major mode and generally more optimistic in tone. This movement is gloomy from the foreboding opening theme to the enigmatic ending, in which soloist and orchestra fade away rather than finish triumphantly. We know that Mozart was by late eighteenth-century standards a free spirit—not to the extent

cadenza Virtuosic and rhapsodic improvisation of variable length that typically occurs close to the end of each of the outer movements of a concerto

that he is portrayed in *Amadeus* perhaps, but certainly not the solid citizen that Haydn was. Could this concerto be Mozart's way of expressing his struggle with authority?

Autobiographical or not (and we will never know), this concerto certainly explains why Mozart's contemporaries considered him a Romantic. It is a highly personal work, and it is emotionally charged. The Romantic generation, inspired by Beethoven—who himself was deeply inspired by Mozart and this particular concerto, which served as a model for his third piano concerto—would focus on the personal feeling to a far greater degree than eighteenth-century composers did. We get a foretaste of it in this concerto.

KEYS TO CLASSICAL STYLE

Key Concepts

Drama with or without words. In its most sophisticated and characteristic expressions, the Classical style is inherently dramatic, because composers can create, regulate, and resolve musical tension within a movement or work.

Key Features

In the Classical style, contrast is comprehensive and frequent. It is often evident in these ways:

1. **Melody plus simple, frequently changing accompaniments.** Accompaniment patterns tend to be simple. They include occasional chords filling out the harmony, repeated chords, and various arpeggiated chord patterns. More contrapuntal textures occur mainly in developmental sections. Frequent change of texture is typical.

2. **Terraced and tapered dynamics.** Dynamic change is frequent. The two most common options are abrupt shifts between loud and soft and crescendos, such as gradual change from soft to loud. Diminuendos (gradual change from loud to soft) are less common.

3. **Varied rhythms.** Rhythmic contrast occurs on both a local and a global scale. It can occur within a melody, typically between phrases, and it almost always occurs between sections. Moreover, rhythms usually accelerate in the approach to structural goals, such as the end of a major section or the end of the movement.

4. **Melodic contrast.** The most pronounced contrasts are those between tuneful melody and figuration or other faster-moving lines. These typically occur between sections but can also occur within a theme. Contrast between different kinds of melodic material within a theme or section, such as a statement and response, also occurs regularly.

5. **Well-articulated forms.** Classical compositions generally feature frequent articulation through decisive cadences and/or sudden shifts in multiple elements.

Key Terms

1. **Sonata form.** The most common form in first movements of Classical instrumental compositions. Such movements contain an exposition, development, and recapitulation. Some sonata-form movements also feature an introduction and a coda.

2. **String quartet.** Ensemble featuring two violinists, a violist, and a cellist. Also the term used for compositions written for this ensemble.

3. **Cadenza.** Rhapsodic and virtuosic passage for the solo instrument in a concerto, characterized by rhythmic freedom and an improvisatory succession of events.

Music Concept Check

To assist you in recognizing their distinctive features, we present an interactive comparison of Baroque and Classical style in CourseMate and the eBook.

UNIT 13
MUSICAL LIFE IN THE NINETEENTH CENTURY

Learning Outcomes
After reading this unit, you will be able to do the following:

LO1 Chart the development of diverse trends in nineteenth-century musical life: music publishing, music education, musical instruments and technologies, and entertainment.

LO2 Describe the characteristics of Romanticism.

LO3 Discuss the increasing stratification of musical life, particularly in the latter part of the nineteenth century.

CHAPTER 24

The Romantic Era

"If the Enlightenment was Western civilization's left brain at work, Romanticism was its right brain.."

In a three-year span during the late 1820s, the musical world witnessed a birth, a death, and a resurrection that would profoundly influence musical life in Europe and the Americas.

On July 4, 1826, Stephen Foster was born in Lawrenceville, Pennsylvania. During his brief career, he became the most important and well-known American songwriter. By the end of the nineteenth century, publishers had sold 20 million copies of his plantation song "Old Folks at Home."

On March 26, 1827, Ludwig van Beethoven passed away. Three days later, twenty thousand people lined the streets of Vienna to observe his funeral procession. By the time of his death, Beethoven had become a celebrated figure throughout Europe and especially in Vienna, although his deafness had kept him from performing publicly for almost two decades. Contemporary reports suggest that the size of the crowd—over 5 percent of Vienna's population—surpassed that for any previous funeral.

On March 11, 1829, Felix Mendelssohn conducted a performance of J. S. Bach's St. Matthew Passion at the Berlin Singakademie. It was the first public performance of the work since Bach's death, although Mendelssohn's teacher Carl Zelter had rehearsed it privately as early as 1815. The concert, so successful that it was repeated twice within a few weeks, was the catalyst for the resurrection of Bach's music.

Taken together, these three events highlight profound changes in musical life during the nineteenth century. The widespread and enduring popularity of

Did You Know?

Long before Van Halen, Italian violinist Niccolò Paganini was rumored to be "runnin' with the devil" because of his cadaverous appearance and otherworldly virtuosity.

Foster's music heralded the emergence of a new kind of popular music: commercial music directed at a mass audience. Beethoven's lionization by the Viennese signaled the ascension of the artist: the musician was no longer a servant; greatness was now measured by achievement, not birth. The Bach revival both stimulated and confirmed interest in music of the past; "classical music"—that is, music from the past worth preserving or reviving—became a significant and regular part of musical life. The corollary to heightened awareness of the past was a vision of the future; indeed, one of the important new directions in the latter part of the century was "music of the future." Further, the posthumous veneration of Beethoven and Bach gave nineteenth-century composers hope that future generations would value their music, even if contemporary audiences did not.

Moreover, the institutionalization of classical music and the emergence of a distinct popular music tradition played a key role in expanding the music profession by creating new opportunities in performance, research, publishing, and teaching.

LO1 The Expanding Musical Life

In the nineteenth century, the erosion of monarchical authority, the decline of the influence of organized religion, economic growth, new technologies, better transportation, and an expanding middle class transformed the music professions from a system that relied heavily on church and court patronage to one that derived much more of its revenue from the marketplace. Music publishing grew exponentially to cater to increased demand. Writing about music became a profession. Public performance, from operas and orchestral concerts to minstrel shows and band concerts, grew at a comparable rate, and institutions and industries grew up around them. Newly founded conservatories trained professional and amateur performers and composers. Instrument makers applied newly developed manufacturing processes to invent new and to improve existing instruments.

MUSIC PUBLISHING

Music publishing flourished in the 1800s for several reasons. Most significant was the growth of the middle class; their numbers, added to those of the upper class, greatly expanded the market for secular musical compositions, especially songs and piano music. Both came at several levels of sophistication, from art songs by Schubert and Schumann to minstrel show ditties, from virtuoso pieces to simple dance tunes for one or two players. The market grew for these genres as pianos became less expensive and more readily available.

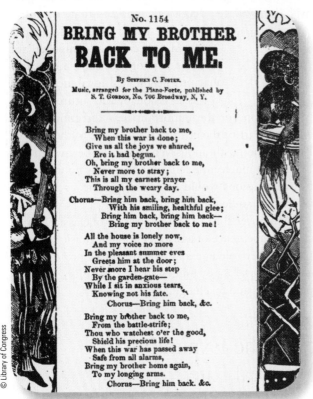

For most of the nineteenth century, Americans could learn lyrics to the latest songs from published song sheets. These were new songs being sung in music halls or new lyrics to familiar songs, like "Yankee Doodle" or "The Last Rose of Summer." Some of America's most beloved tunes were printed as song sheets, including "The Star-Spangled Banner" and the "Battle Hymn of the Republic."

The growing interest in classical music also contributed to the growth of music publishing. This included both new editions of established repertoire and publication of earlier music previously available only in manuscript. The most notable instance of the latter came about with the formation of the Bach Gesellschaft in 1850 (the centenary of J. S. Bach's death), which had as its main goal the publication of all of Bach's extant music. For much of the century, music publishers' catalogs contained all kinds of music. However, in the last quarter of the century, a few music publishers in New York began issuing only popular songs. This was a crucial step in the formation of a distinct popular-music tradition.

MUSIC AND WORDS

Words and music came together in a multitude of new ways during the nineteenth century. The most prominent was an outpouring of song: sophisticated art songs for sophisticated audiences; simpler songs, many of which were settings of old folk melodies, created mainly for home use; and songs for various kinds of mass public entertainment. There was also music inspired by words: instrumental compositions that used literary works, such as Lenau's *Don Juan*, as a program, as well as programs written by the composer.

MUSIC EDUCATION

With the growth in music publishing and writing came a drive for music education at all levels, from music literacy for everyone to the highest-level training for aspiring professionals. For the general public, vocal-music education became a component of public school instruction in Europe and North America over the course of the nineteenth century.

More specialized musical training had been mainly the province of church schools from medieval times through the eighteenth century. As they closed, conservatories were formed to take their place. Among the first was the Paris Conservatoire, founded in 1795. Other conservatories were founded in major European musical centers, such as Vienna and London, throughout the nineteenth century. The first American conservatory was the Peabody Conservatory in Baltimore, founded in 1857 and now part of Johns Hopkins University. Many of these conservatories were formed to train orchestral musicians, who required more rigorous training to meet the demands of increasingly difficult orchestral music in the concert hall and the opera orchestra pit. Conserva-

"Home Sweet Home" by Walter Dendy Sadler. In a time before recordings, radio, and television, many middle-class families made their own music.

tories also catered to amateurs; their fees helped make ends meet. Their popularity was one sign of a growing middle class, many of whom had upper-class aspirations. Conservatories also trained singers, for opera and oratorio, keyboard performers, and composers.

Academic study of music as an independent scholarly discipline gradually took shape during the nineteenth century, especially in France and German-speaking Europe. The work of pioneering **musicologists** (scholars who research the history of music) provided essential support for the rediscovery of music of the past—not only Bach and his contemporaries but also medieval and Renaissance composers.

Collectively, these developments put in place the structure of the contemporary classical music world. Many of the major institutions in contemporary musical life have been in place since the latter part of the nineteenth century.

MUSICAL INSTRUMENTS AND TECHNOLOGY

The technological advances introduced during the nineteenth century had a substantial impact on almost every aspect of musical life, including the size and makeup of audiences, the venues where they heard music, transportation, publishing and dissemination of music, and—toward the end of the century—sound recording. However, the most significant impact was the introduction of manufacturing into the production of musical instruments.

Manufacturing made working with metal easier, more efficient, and more consistent. Accordingly, most of the major innovations in instrument making involved metal. Instrument makers invented dozens of new instruments; most were metal wind instruments. The most famous maker was the Belgian Adolphe Sax, who gave his name to full lines of saxophones and saxhorns.

Of the instruments invented during the nineteenth century, only one, the tuba, has become an integral part of the symphony orchestra. Others, such as the saxhorns and euphonium, found a home in bands. The saxophone eventually became a part-time member of the orchestra, a full-time member of the military band, and since the 1920s, the dominant wind instrument in popular music.

More far reaching were the modifications of existing instruments, most significantly the piano and the wind, brass, and percussion instruments of the orchestra.

The Piano. Around 1800, the piano was a delicate wood-framed instrument with a range of five octaves. By 1900, it had grown into the concert instrument that we know today. The most significant improvement was the development of a one-piece metal frame by the American piano builder Alpheus Babcock in 1825. This allowed piano makers to string the piano much more tightly, which in turn dramatically increased the amount of sound the instrument could produce. By the 1850s, the metal-frame piano was the norm in the United States and Europe. There were other improvements: a faster, more reliable action and expansion of the range to more than seven octaves. In the latter part of the century, piano manufacturers converted to a factory system, which enabled them to make more instruments less expensively. The piano became the household instrument of choice for middle- and upper-class households, as well as the most popular concert instrument.

Orchestral Instruments. Among woodwinds, the flute underwent the most dramatic change; it became a metal instrument, although it remained part of the woodwind section. All of the woodwinds acquired extra keys for greater fluency. Brass instruments benefited even more from new technology; trumpets and horns acquired valves or pistons, which enabled musicians to play any note in any scale within the range of the instrument. These advances allowed brass instruments to play a more active role in orchestras. Timpani received a similar upgrade through devices that enabled the performer to rapidly change the pitch of the drum.

Improvements to existing woodwind and brass instruments and the invention of new wind instruments led

musicologist
Scholar who researches the history of music

to the expansion of the military band and its entry into civilian life. Civic bands, both professional and amateur, became increasingly popular in both Europe and North America during the nineteenth century. Some were brass bands (no woodwinds), while others were mixed wind and percussion instruments. They became a popular alternative to the symphony orchestra, and by the turn of the century, concert bands such as the one led by John Philip Sousa were the most popular musical ensembles in the United States.

By the turn of the century, concert bands such as the one led by John Philip Sousa were the most popular musical ensembles in the United States.

Sound Recording. In 1877, the great American inventor Thomas Edison successfully captured his voice on a device he called a "phonograph"; the recording medium was a cylinder covered with tinfoil. Eleven years later, he produced and marketed an improved version; so did a company that included Alexander Graham Bell, the inventor of the telephone. By 1890, the record business was up and running. Among the first groups to be recorded was the Sousa band. In 1894, Emile Berliner, who would eventually found Victor records, began issuing recordings on discs rather than cylinders. His technology would eventually win out and remain in place for the better part of the twentieth century. The most significant fact about these early sound recordings is that they happened. Early acoustic recordings are virtually unlistenable because the fidelity is so poor and the surface noise so disruptive. Still, it was the beginning of a technology that would transform the music industry and transform the listening experience in subsequent generations.

Descendant of Edison's "phonograph"

THE GROWTH OF MUSICAL ENTERTAINMENT

In the nineteenth century, music went public. Musical entertainment—and entertainment in which music is an integral part—grew rapidly in the first half of the century, then mushroomed during the second half. A major reason for this accelerated growth was the rapid increase in mass entertainment. By the end of the century, professional musical entertainment included several well-established genres directed toward a mass audience. In the United States, these ranged from musical comedy, minstrel shows, and vaudeville to concerts by touring concert bands.

The growth of what gradually became classical music was comparably dramatic. Among the most important trends was the institutionalization of classical music: resident opera companies and orchestras in major cities; public concerts by solo performers, especially singers and pianists; and formation of societies for the preservation and exploration of earlier music, like the Berlin Singakademie, where Mendelssohn conducted Bach's *St. Matthew Passion*, and Boston's Handel and Haydn Society, one of America's most venerable musical institutions. Other important developments include the emergence of new music-dependent art forms, most notably ballet.

Opera flourished during the nineteenth century, musically and commercially. Four generations of Italian composers, including the well-known Gioachino Rossini, Giuseppe Verdi, and, at the end of the century, Giacomo Puccini, composed the works that quickly became opera's core repertory. Rossini and Verdi were among the most popular composers of the century; much of their music trickled down into popular culture. Opera further diversified culturally and geographically. Among the most significant developments were Richard Wagner's music dramas, which were based on Teutonic myths; nationalistic operas from Bohemia, Russia, and elsewhere; grand and comic opera in France; and Gilbert and Sullivan's operettas in England. Opera singers were among the most celebrated artists in Europe and North America; they enjoyed rockstar–like celebrity.

During the nineteenth century, orchestras joined opera companies as major cultural institutions. At the beginning of the century, resident civic orchestras did not exist: the orchestra that Salomon assembled for Haydn's visits was an ad hoc ensemble. By the end of the nineteenth century there were resident symphony orchestras in London, Paris, Vienna, Berlin, Amsterdam, and other major European cities, as well as New York, Boston, Chicago, and several other American cities. Most were formed in the latter part of the century; the New York Philharmonic, formed in 1842, was one of the first. Orchestra programs included a mix of well-known standard repertoire and contemporary works.

Among the stars of nineteenth-century musical life were touring soloists and conductors. Audiences flocked to hear singers such as Jenny Lind and instrumentalists such as the violinist Niccolò Paganini and the pianist Franz Liszt. Conductors were the quintessential nineteenth-century musical figures: an individual in charge of a big ensemble. With Felix Mendelssohn in the 1830s, and Berlioz and Wagner in the 1850s, conductors literally grew in stature from first violinists occasionally beating time with their bows to dictatorial figures standing on a podium waving a baton as they led orchestras in their personal interpretation of Beethoven's or—in many cases—their own music.

Ballet went solo during the nineteenth century. For the better part of two centuries, it had been an integral part of opera, especially in France. After 1830, it emerged as an independent expressive art. By the last quarter of the century, it was well established in France and in Russia, where French high culture was dominant. The most important nineteenth-century composer of ballet was Russian Pyotr Ilyich Tchaikovsky.

More popular and commercially oriented analogs to these classical genres also took shape during the nineteenth century, especially after 1850. Musical stage entertainment included operettas, popular both in England and North America and in German-speaking Europe; musical comedy; and the minstrel show, an American entertainment that also became popular in Europe, especially England and France. Bands were the popular counterpart to orchestras; in America, professional concert bands, most notably the one led by John Philip Sousa, were among the top attractions.

Social dancing became a more commercial enterprise that appealed to all classes. Venues ranged from elegant ballrooms to working-class dance halls. Musical accompaniment was similarly varied, from the sophisticated Viennese dance orchestras, most notably those of the Strauss family, to a fiddler or piano player. The waltz, a dance of humble origins, became the most popular social dance of the nineteenth century. Folk dances, especially from exotic locales or subcultures, became popular music for dancing or performing at home. They ranged from "Hungarian" and Slavonic dances to jigs, reels, and cakewalks.

By the end of the century, audiences had many more choices for musical entertainment. Some types—from ballet and traveling

Conductors grew in stature to become dictatorial figures.

opera stars and virtuosi to concert bands and minstrel troupes—were almost unimaginable at the beginning of the century. At the dawn of the twentieth century, musical entertainment was truly a business, and a thriving one.

LO2 Romanticism and Nineteenth-Century Music

The 1800s were the Romantic century. They were also a century of industrialization and urbanization, exploration and colonization. Romantic values both resonated with and reacted against tumultuous changes in Western society. Even as they continued the secularization and democratization of society brought about by the Enlightenment and the two major revolutions of the late eighteenth century, they rejected Enlightenment values.

If the Enlightenment was Western civilization's left brain at work, **Romanticism** was its right brain. The Enlightenment valued rationality and the human's role in society. Romanticism valued subjectivity, feeling, and inspiration and venerated individuals whose work expressed those values. A Romantic sensibility underpinned many of the significant musical trends during the century. Among them were a focus on individuality, an obsession with size, and a fascination with the exotic. Each found multiple forms of expression during the course of the nineteenth century.

Romanticism
Cultural movement of the nineteenth century that valued subjectivity, feeling, and inspiration and venerated individuals whose work expressed those values; a Romantic sensibility that had a focus on individuality, an obsession with size, and a fascination with the exotic

virtuosity
Performance skills far beyond the norm; extraordinary technical abilities

etude
Musical work designed to develop a particular technical skill

INDIVIDUALITY

The Romantic emphasis on subjectivity and feeling focused the spotlight on the individual. Among the most significant musical expressions of this tendency were the quest for individuality, the rise of the virtuoso performer, and the growing division between composition and performance.

Personal Styles.

The most esteemed Romantic composers cultivated a personal style to a much greater degree than their eighteenth-century predecessors. The differences between Berlioz, Liszt, and Schumann, or Wagner, Brahms, and Tchaikovsky are more pronounced than those between Haydn and Mozart, or Bach and Handel. The cultivation of a personal style was a product of several cultural forces. Most generally, it involved the elevation in status of the musician, especially the composer, from servant to artistic genius. This dynamic new environment encouraged composers to follow their own path, regardless of where it took them. Another factor was a heightened awareness of the past, particularly of Beethoven, whose music is notable for its individuality, both in general style and from work to work. It is no coincidence that the stylistic contrast from composer to composer increased as the idea of classical music became more entrenched.

Virtuosity.

Through Paganini and Liszt, the musical world fell in love with **virtuosity**, performance skills well beyond the norm. Their breathtakingly brilliant playing mesmerized audiences, who found their seemingly superhuman abilities incredible—it was widely rumored, and apparently often believed, that Paganini had made a pact with the devil in order to achieve his supreme mastery of the violin.

The most obvious compositional evidence of the heightened appreciation for virtuosic performance was the elevation of the etude. An **etude**—*étude* is the French word for "study"—is a musical work designed to develop a particular technical skill. In Beethoven's time, these were pieces used to prepare performers for real repertoire. With Liszt, Chopin, and their contemporaries, the etude became concert music. Virtuosity was not confined to the etude; much of the important solo and orchestral literature demanded greater fluency and new techniques. The piano music of, for example, Chopin, Liszt, and Schumann; the concertos of Brahms and Tchaikovsky; and the orchestral music of Wagner and Strauss still challenge today's best musicians.

At its worst, virtuosity is a stunt—an excuse to show off a particular skill. However, for many Romantic composers, virtuosity dramatically extended the range of possibility: more elaborate figuration; richer, more florid accompaniments; stunning sounds; and more powerful gestures. Liszt, the king of piano virtuosos, claimed that "virtuosity is not an outgrowth, but an indispensable element of music." For him and many other Romantic composers, it was.

"Virtuosity is not an outgrowth, but an indispensable element of music." —Franz Liszt

Composers and Performers.

In the 1830s and for most of the 1840s, Franz Liszt, perhaps the most celebrated pianist of any era, toured Europe—from Russia to Ireland. He dazzled audiences, broke hearts, composed fiendishly difficult works, arranged the works of other composers for the piano, and generally caused a sensation wherever he played. In 1847, at the urging of his new mistress, Carolyn Sayn-Wittgenstein, he abruptly stopped performing. He settled in Weimar, a small duchy in Germany with a long and rich artistic heritage, where he concentrated on composing, teaching, and conducting the orchestra.

It is almost as if Liszt flipped a switch in 1847. Several major composers from the first half of the century—Beethoven, Mendelssohn, Chopin, Liszt—were also outstanding performers; most of the major composers from the latter half—Wagner, Tchaikovsky, Richard Strauss, Dvořák—were not well known as performers, although Brahms toured occasionally as a pianist. Moreover, those composers who focused on opera, most notably, Rossini, Verdi, Wagner, and Puccini, are remembered exclusively for their composing.

The division of musical labor that occurred in the nineteenth century resulted from numerous factors. Among the most significant were the increasing demands of composition and performance—the twin pressures of size and originality made composition a more arduous task, and the increasing difficulty of the music that composers produced compelled performers to devote more time to preparing music for performance.

In the wake of the success of Paganini and Liszt, virtuosi rivaled opera stars as celebrity musicians. Women swooned; men sat in amazement at their skill. They became the object of admiration, especially when they married technical brilliance with expressive artistry. Their popularity, and the popularity of conductors in the latter part of the century, was due not only to musical changes but also to changes within society: the increase in the number of public concerts, the Romantic appreciation of artistic genius, focus on the individual, and sensitivity to feeling. Instrumentalists and conductors personified the music that audiences heard. It is through them that audiences connected to the music. Then as now, they received the lion's share of the attention.

It was still possible to be a successful composer *and* a successful performer at the end of the nineteenth century. What was seemingly not possible was the pursuit of both activities simultaneously. Mozart's practice of performing a concerto completed the night before was all but inconceivable a century later; the music had become too difficult, and standards in solo and orchestral playing had risen considerably. Those musicians who pursued both careers typically did so in alternation: Gustav Mahler conducted during the concert season, which paralleled the school year, and composed in the summer; the Russian composer/pianist/conductor Sergei Rachmaninoff admitted that he was most comfortable when he could devote his time and energy to only one activity at a time. In general, fewer musicians elected to follow multiple paths.

Size

The nineteenth century was obsessed with size—from colonial empires, most notably the British, on which the sun never set; to the territorial expansion of the United States and the railroad that spanned it; to rapidly growing cities, many with skyscrapers by the end of the century; to enormous fortunes acquired by captains of industry and the palatial estates on which they spent them; to international expositions in London (1851), Paris (1889), and Chicago (1893). All this and more earned public admiration.

The obsession with bigness carried over into almost every aspect of musical life. Festivals drew huge crowds who heard mammoth ensembles. Among the most spectacular was the World's Peace Jubilee and International Musical Festival, organized by American bandmaster Patrick Gilmore and presented in Boston in 1872; it featured a twenty thousand–voice chorus and a two thousand–member orchestra playing in a newly erected pavilion that held one hundred thousand people.

Stage performances could feature enormous casts and last for hours, or even days. However, the grandest staged music event of the century was Richard Wagner's *Der Ring des Nibelungen*, a cycle of four music dramas that last about fifteen hours. After 1876, one could hear the Ring cycle at the Bayreuth Festspielhaus, the theater constructed specifically for performances of Wagner's works.

Orchestras more than doubled in size during the course of the century, in response to increased demands from composers. Many required much larger brass, wind, and percussion sections, with string sections also expanded to balance the rest of the orchestra. Inspired by Beethoven, who increased the size of the orchestra and lengthened symphonic works, composers such as Berlioz, Bruckner, and Mahler wrote expansive symphonies often lasting more than an hour.

Bigness was even evident in miniatures such as Chopin's preludes, which expanded what would be a short section within a larger work into a stand-alone composition.

BEYOND THE NORM

At the beginning of the century, the music business catered mainly to urban upper- and middle-class audiences. From this center, nineteenth-century musicians reached out in every direction to expand the musical world that they had inherited. They looked to the past and projected into the future. They looked and listened in the countryside to find inspiration and national identity. They were stimulated by the exotic: faraway places and people. They bypassed established religion to explore the spiritual directly or delve into the diabolical. They sought inspiration from and communion with the other arts: literature, the visual arts, and dance. Their open-mindedness was comprehensive and unprecedented.

Past and Future. In 1860, Richard Wagner published "Zukunftsmusik" ("Music of the Future"). Wagner claimed that the future direction of music was the synthesis of the arts that he championed in his later operas. It wasn't, but Wagner still became the most influential composer of the late nineteenth century.

atonality
System of tonal organization in which pitches do not focus around a tonic

> **The Black Crook (1866), generally regarded as the first American musical comedy, featured one hundred ballerinas and reportedly lasted for almost five hours.**

Wagner's main partner in this musical vanguard was Franz Liszt; each influenced the other significantly. Liszt was not a polemicist, but his later works anticipate important developments in twentieth-century music, including more rigorous adaptations of folk materials, musical impressionism, and **atonality** (a system of tonal organization in which pitches do not focus around a tonic).

Wagner's pronouncement was the corollary to nineteenth-century musicians' greater awareness of the past (if there's a past, there must also be a future) and, more specifically, the sense, especially among German and German-based musicians, that their music was a continuation of Beethoven's legacy.

More pervasively, the music of previous generations, especially the music of Beethoven, both inspired and intimidated nineteenth-century composers, who typically followed one of three paths: emulate the classics, outdo the classics, or find a completely novel path.

Major instrumental genres—the sonata, the concerto, and especially the symphony—gained in prestige during the course of the century. Most of the important instrumental composers of the century composed some of each, even though the presence of Beethoven loomed over them (just as it does in the painting at the beginning of this unit). No major nineteenth-century composer completed more than nine symphonies, and only a very few of those works were as monumental as Beethoven's own Ninth Symphony. Still, a few composers took established genres beyond what Beethoven and the eighteenth century had done: Chopin's set of twenty-four preludes, Liszt's piano sonata, Brahms's second piano concerto, and Berlioz's *Symphonie fantastique* stand out in this regard. The more common paths toward originality were the creation of new forms and genres, such as the tone poem, and the reinvigoration and expansion of small forms, many of them from dances.

Opera maintained its elite status while embracing a far wider range of subject matter; not surprisingly, the music dramas of Wagner were the most forward looking, even as they reached back into a distant Teutonic past. The most important and innovative vocal genre of the century was the *Lied* (German for "song"; see Chapter 27), which embedded melody in individual, often complex accompaniments and elevated song into a higher artistic statement.

Folk Music, Nature, and National Identity.

One consequence of rapid urbanization was a nostalgia for and idealization of the countryside and those who lived there. Nature was a recurrent theme in both vocal and instrumental music; it inspired composers to create evocative effects, especially in orchestral music and music for solo piano. Folk song settings, such as Thomas Moore's ten volumes of *Irish Melodies*, were among the most popular music of the century. Folk dances, especially those with a clear cultural identity, were the instrumental analog to folk song settings: Brahms's *Hungarian Dances* (actually inspired by gypsy music rather than Hungarian peasant music) were among his best-selling compositions. Folk dances also provided a clear musical signal of national identity for expatriates like Chopin and for those on the periphery of Germany. The geographic identity of the waltz, Europe's most popular dance, was even more specific; its most characteristic version came from Vienna, the capital of the Austrian Empire, the most diffuse and diverse political entity in Europe.

The folk songs and dances presented in middle- and upper-class musical settings were thoroughly cleansed of many of the defining features of authentic folk style. We know this from comparisons of nineteenth-century folk settings with twentieth-century field recordings of folk performers. Still, the best settings captured much of the vitality of the original and merged it with the craft and richness of classical music. Folk music found a more direct route to the stage in the early minstrel show, whose performers portrayed blacks but sounded more like Irish and Scottish folk musicians.

Exoticism.

For Europeans, minstrelsy was an exotic entertainment. The continued expansion of colonial empires took Europeans to distant lands; international expositions brought the world to Europe, and eventually the United States. Foreign lands—the Orient (Asia), the Near East, Africa, the Americas, even the Iberian Peninsula—inspired nineteenth-century composers as locales for opera and images and sounds for instrumental compositions. The musical settings, which typically filtered any foreign elements through nineteenth-century musical practice, reflected the cultural imperialism of the age. The exploration of the exotic, like the use of folk traditions, represented a far greater willingness to embrace nondominant cultures.

Death and the Dark Side.

The Romantic fascination with death and the dark side expressed itself in numerous ways. The most impressive sacred choral works of the century were requiems, musical settings of the Catholic funeral Mass. Those by Berlioz and Verdi were spectacular and decidedly secular; Brahms's was nondenominational. The *Dies irae* (Day of Wrath), the dire plainchant from the Catholic requiem Mass, became the sound symbol of damnation and witches, demons, and devils. It inspired numerous instrumental compositions.

Marriage of the Arts.

A dominant theme in innovative Romantic music was a marriage of the arts. It is most evident and pervasive in the coming together of music and literature. Poetry and music merged in the art songs of Schubert, Schumann, Brahms, and others. Classic and contemporary literature—such as poetry, drama, and novels—inspired instrumental music. Programmatic works appeared far more frequently, and the programs, often drawn from literature, were usually more detailed.

The visual arts also inspired Romantic-era composers: the composer Robert Schumann claimed that "the educated musician will be able to derive as much usefulness from the study of a Madonna by Raphael as will a painter from a Mozart symphony"; six years later, Liszt composed a piano piece about a Raphael painting. Perhaps the best-known visually inspired work of the century was Modest Mussorgsky's piano tableaus *Pictures at an Exhibition*.

Characteristically, Wagner proposed the grandest artistic synthesis of all. In his theoretical writings, he asserted that music, poetry, and dance must be reunited, as they were in ancient Greece; further, artists and architects would contribute to the production of works that brought together the three classical arts. He called such fusions *Gesamtkunstwerke*, total works of art, or works that synthesize all of the arts.

> **Gesamtkunstwerk**
> Total work of art, or work that synthesizes all the arts; associated with Richard Wagner

LO3 The Stratification of Music and Musical Life

The cumulative effect of these wide-ranging musical developments was the stratification of music and musical life. At one extreme was the idea of "art for art's sake," which led to musical styles far removed from everyday musical language and the formation of an artistic elite around the composers of this music. At the other was popular—and often populist—"lowbrow" music, particularly in the United States.

Around the time Wagner was formulating his ideas of an integrated artistic experience, performers in blackface were living it. These performers, the members of a minstrel show troupe, sang; played fiddles, banjos, tambourines, and bones; danced; told jokes; acted out skits; parodied Shakespeare; and did just about anything else that would entertain their audience. The minstrel show, an overnight sensation in 1843, became the most popular form of entertainment in America through the rest of the century and the first American entertainment to develop a substantial audience in Europe. The minstrel show was lowbrow mass entertainment from America; it stood in sharp contrast to highbrow culture in both Europe and the United States. However, despite its lowly social status, it opened the door for African American performers. By the end of the century, ragtime was in the air, which in turn laid the foundation for new kinds of popular music.

In between were multiple levels of musical discourse. There were art songs for sophisticated salons and sentimental songs for middle-class parlors. There were piano pieces for earnest amateurs and sonatas, fantasies, and etudes for skilled professionals. There were operas, operettas, and musical comedy; music for and about dancing; symphonic music that drew inspiration from widely different sources, including folk songs and dances of national and ethnic groups; and music for chamber ensembles of varying sizes.

As a result, musical life in the latter part of the century was different from that in previous generations: the musical languages of the past, present, and future were all part of musical life; moreover, they were heard at varying levels of sophistication, from the most basic common practice harmony found in popular song and dance music to the complex chromatic harmony of elite classical composers. It is from this time that the idea of "heavy" and "light" music—classical versus popular, heavy classics versus light classics—takes shape, in practice, if not in theory.

We touch on all of these trends in the rest of Part 4.

UNIT 14
BEETHOVEN

Learning Outcomes

After reading this unit, you will be able to do the following:

LO1 Understand the revolutionary qualities in Beethoven's music that set it apart from the music of other composers.

LO2 Describe Beethoven's radically different approach to the piano and the piano sonata.

LO3 Understand Beethoven's conception of a four-movement symphony as an integrated musical statement.

LO4 Grasp the impact of Beethoven and his music on nineteenth-century culture, and gauge his influence on other composers.

IN OCTOBER 1802, Beethoven wrote to his brothers Carl and Johann a famous letter known as the Heiligenstadt Testament (after the town where he wrote it), in which he reveals his loss of hearing, which had plagued him since 1796. It is impossible to overestimate how cursed Beethoven must have felt—imagine a sculptor who is almost blind. Beethoven would live almost twenty-five more years, and his hearing would deteriorate even further. Yet he would rise from the depths of despair to triumph over his affliction again and again. Remarkably, he composed many of his greatest works after penning this letter. Beethoven's achievements and influence are unmatched by any other composer. He played the leading role in the transformation from Classical to Romantic and in elevating instrumental music to a status higher than that of vocal music. That he was able to compose with his hearing increasingly impaired only makes his achievements more astounding. In this unit we consider Beethoven's unique place in the history of music and examine two compositions that reveal the qualities that make his music so exceptional.

CHAPTER 25

Beethoven and the Piano Sonata

"Beethoven was 'more of a Romantic than any composer who has existed.'"
—E. T. A. Hoffmann

Long before there were battles of the bands, there were piano playoffs. One of the favorite amusements of Viennese aristocrats during the late eighteenth century was a duel between rival pianists, usually featuring a local favorite versus a touring virtuoso. A noteworthy piano duel, one that was closer to a clash between heavyweight boxers than a contest of keyboard artists, was the "Scene in Wien," a rematch between Daniel Steibelt and Ludwig van Beethoven.

When Steibelt arrived in Vienna in 1800, fresh from successes in Paris and Prague, a duel between him and Beethoven was arranged at the home of Count Fries. Beethoven, by now a fixture in Viennese salons, performed a movement from a recently composed trio: a set of variations on a popular tune. Steibelt then played one of his own compositions, which apparently dazzled the audience. Beethoven refused to play after Steibelt.

Steibelt was easy to dislike. Numerous accounts portray him as extraordinarily egocentric and self-promoting. He was without scruples, often leaving town with a pile of unpaid debts, selling the same music to competing publishers, and claiming others' music as his own. His playing and composing offered more flash than substance. Still, he enjoyed a successful career as both a composer and a pianist, although he often outstayed his welcome and left town before being apprehended by the authorities.

A few weeks later, Count Fries hosted another duel between Steibelt and Beethoven. This time Steibelt went first. To show his disdain, Steibelt and a local string quartet performed his freshly composed quintet for piano and strings on the same theme that Beethoven had used in his trio, much to the delight of the audience. Beethoven responded in kind by walking to the piano, grabbing the cello part from the cellist's music stand on his way, putting it on the piano rack upside down, poking out a theme, then proceeding to improvise on it rhapsodically. The audience was overwhelmed. It would have been a knockout for Beethoven, except that a humiliated Steibelt sneaked out before Beethoven finished. Later, Steibelt told people never to invite him if Beethoven was also going to be present.

Contemporary accounts of Beethoven's improvising repeatedly mention the magic in his playing. They suggest that the piano gave Beethoven his most direct way of communicating through music. We cannot reconstruct his improvisations, but we can get some sense of their boldness through his piano sonatas, the genre in which Beethoven gave his imagination the freest rein.

LO1 Beethoven the Revolutionary

Ludwig van Beethoven was born in Bonn, in what is now west-central Germany. His father, a musician of moderate skill and terrible temper, recognized his son's talent and tried to promote him as Leopold Mozart had done with his son. Beethoven was not a prodigy but became a superb pianist and one of the great innovators in keyboard music.

In the late eighteenth century, Vienna was the musical capital of Europe. Beethoven went there twice—

> ## Did You Know?
>
> Charles Schulz sometimes showed actual excerpts from Beethoven's music whenever he featured Schroeder at the piano in the comic strip *Peanuts.*

Ludwig van Beethoven

Fast Facts

- *Dates:* 1770–1827

- *Place:* Germany/Vienna

- *Reasons to remember:* Composer whose achievements and influence are unmatched by any other; played the leading role in the transformation from Classical to Romantic and in elevating instrumental music to a status higher than that of vocal music

briefly in 1787 and for the rest of his life in 1792. When he returned to Vienna in 1792, it was to study composition with Haydn and make a name for himself as a pianist and composer. His relationship with the great composer was both cordial and complicated. He maintained his respect for Haydn as a composer and was grateful for his support, but he apparently told several acquaintances that he felt he learned next to nothing from Haydn during his period of study.

Beethoven made a profound impression as a pianist and gained a reputation as an *enfant terrible* because of his disdain for social conventions, his bad temper, and his relentless assaults on delicate Viennese instru-

Beethoven gained a reputation as an *enfant terrible* because of his disdain for social conventions, his bad temper, and his relentless assaults on delicate Viennese instruments.

ments; he reportedly broke more strings than any other pianist in Vienna. The most sensational parts of his performances were his improvisations. His pupil Carl Czerny noted that they often moved audiences to tears, an observation confirmed by other accounts.

Why did the Viennese lionize Beethoven so? The overriding reason was, of course, Beethoven's inherent genius. In his own time, Beethoven was recognized in Vienna and throughout Europe as not only the greatest living composer but also as a man who was almost single-handedly transforming musical life. The popular novelist and critic E. T. A. Hoffmann, himself a first-generation Romantic, wrote in 1813 that Beethoven was "more of a Romantic than any composer who has existed." However, he also benefited from living in a time when the stature of the artist rose dramatically. This in turn was a product of significant changes in European society.

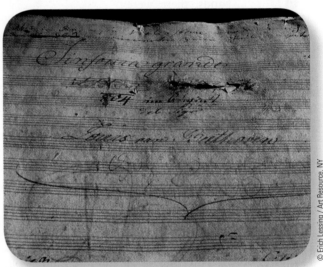

The title page to Beethoven's Third Symphony, with a dedication to Napoleon scratched out

POLITICAL, ECONOMIC, AND SOCIAL REVOLUTIONS

Beethoven's musical revolution echoed the revolutionary changes in European life in the years around 1800. The American and French revolutions took place during Beethoven's youth. Napoleon's rise and fall came during his early maturity; Beethoven initially dedicated his Third Symphony to Napoleon but later retracted the dedication when Napoleon declared himself emperor of France. In the original manuscript, it can be seen that Beethoven violently scratched out the name "Bonaparte" in a moment of disdain over Napoleon's decision to declare himself emperor. After the retraction he renamed the work "Sinfonia eroica, composta per festeggiare il sovvenire d'un grand'uomo" (Heroic symphony composed to celebrate the memory of a great man), now known simply as the "Eroica" Symphony. The realignment of Europe after the Congress of Vienna, for which Beethoven composed an overture, occurred toward the end of his career.

During this same time the first stage of the Industrial Revolution was under way, first in England, then on the continent and in North America. James Watt patented the first steam engine in 1769, the year before Beethoven's birth; steam power would become a core technology in the development of industry, revolutionizing production and transportation.

These political and economic revolutions helped reshape the structure of European society, tilting political power and social status away from the landed aristocracy and organized religion and toward industrialists, merchants, and the bourgeoisie, whose wealth was usually earned, not inherited. With this shift in ideology and power came the idea that social standing should be based on achievement, not birth. The transformation of cultural life was gradual; the aristocracy fought to preserve their privileges. However, the two revolutions opened the door to a more egalitarian society, and there was no way for the nobility to close it.

BEETHOVEN'S REVOLUTIONARY SPIRIT

Then as now, the Viennese valued greatness in the arts. This cultural climate, when coupled with the political and social changes that occurred during Beethoven's lifetime, made it possible for Beethoven to earn unprecedented recognition for his achievements. What made this recognition even more remarkable was Beethoven's disregard for courtly protocol; on several occasions, he was more than willing to bite the hand that fed him. His deafness, which began early in his career and worsened incrementally until he was totally deaf for the last decade of his life, only exacerbated his social difficulties. Despite his awkward manners, which at times descended into boorishness, Beethoven gained a loyal following among aristocrats, including three who supported him with an annual stipend that enabled him to concentrate on composing.

Vienna embraced Beethoven as a performer before they enjoyed him as a composer. His Opus 1, a set of three piano trios, was not published until 1795, three years after his arrival; Opus 2, a set of three piano sonatas, did not appear in print until the following year.

LO2 Beethoven and the Piano Sonata

We can sense in his sonatas Beethoven's almost symbiotic relationship with the piano in several ways. First, he composed far more piano sonatas than symphonies, string quartets, or any other major genre. Second, he single-handedly elevated its status from a part of the education of young women to serious music for public performance. Third, his piano sonatas document his unparalleled growth as a composer more fully than any other single genre in which he worked. And most compellingly, the sonatas were his laboratory—the place where he experimented with bold new approaches and ideas, which he often used subsequently in other genres.

TRANSFORMING THE PIANO SONATA

In the eighteenth century, the piano was, for the most part, a woman's instrument. Like learning to dance the minuet elegantly, learning to play the piano was part of a well-bred young woman's education. Publishers issued thousands of sonatas, variation sets, and dances for the piano to cater to the demand for new piano music. Most of Haydn's piano sonatas, including his last three, are dedicated to women. Men composed most of this music, and those composers who were fluent pianists,

Like learning to dance the minuet elegantly, learning to play the piano was part of a well-bred young woman's education.

such as Mozart, Clementi, and C. P. E. Bach, certainly performed their own music. But in their dimensions and impact, their sonatas were, with few exceptions, far more modest than their symphonies (which were intended for public performance) or their string quartets (string players were usually men).

With his first set of three sonatas, which he designated Opus 2, Beethoven took the sonata out of the parlor. All three have four movements, like symphonies and string quartets, but unlike earlier piano sonatas. In addition, they are bigger in scale and gesture; in all three sonatas, Beethoven uses the entire range of the piano, rather than the middle and upper registers, to a much greater extent than Mozart, Haydn, and their contemporaries. In the process, he raised the piano sonata's stature to a level comparable to that of the string quartet, concerto, and symphony.

In Beethoven's lifetime, the piano sonata was not a genre performed in public concerts nearly to the extent that the symphony or concerto was. Still, one can easily imagine Beethoven playing his sonatas in the salons of the Viennese aristocracy, demanding more of the pianos than they were able to give. In his person and in his playing, power and passion figured much more prominently than refinement and elegance. In that setting, their impact would have been comparable to a symphony heard in a theater.

Beethoven composed thirty-two piano sonatas with opus numbers over a twenty-five–year period, from about 1795 to 1821. He composed the majority of them before 1807 but returned periodically to the genre at key points in his career. It is not surprising that he composed more sonatas early in his career, because he was active as a pianist at that time. What is more surprising is that he continued to compose boldly experimental sonatas after he stopped performing publicly because of his deafness.

One of the most remarkable aspects of Beethoven's music is its tremendous growth over the course of his career. The changes in his music were so dramatic that commentators, beginning the year after his death, began grouping his works into three periods: early, middle, and late. In the early-period works, Beethoven built on the Classical style as defined by the music of Mozart

Piano sonatas were Beethoven's laboratory.

and Haydn, even as he sought to go beyond its conventions. In the middle-period works, Beethoven clearly straddled the boundary between Classical and Romantic: works such as his Fifth Symphony feature bold contrasts, expansive gestures, and distinctive character that foreshadow Romantic music's emphasis on feeling and individuality. In his late works, Beethoven follows two distinct paths. In his more public music, most notably the Ninth Symphony, he continues his expansion of Classical style: this monumental work would both inspire and intimidate a century of symphonic composers. In music composed for more intimate settings, most notably the string quartets and late piano sonatas, Beethoven drew inspiration from the music of Bach and Handel to chart a future path that only he took. These works are among the most sublime music ever created.

The idea that Beethoven's music falls into three periods has enjoyed broad acceptance since it was proposed. More recently, music scholars have suggested also grouping Beethoven's piano sonatas into five periods, to account for several more experimental sonatas, including the famous "Moonlight" sonata, as well as the distinct differences between the last five sonatas and the four that preceded them.

It is in his piano sonatas that the stages in Beethoven's growth as a composer are most fully documented, for two reasons. First, there are many more of them than there are symphonies, or even string quartets, so there is more evidence. Second, Beethoven often worked out compositional problems in the piano sonatas before working through the same problem in other genres. The two works in C minor discussed in this unit evidence this. Beethoven composed six piano sonatas in minor mode, including the "Pathétique," as he worked out how to compose a work that was both intense and concentrated yet constructed on a large scale. Only after completing the "Appassionata" sonata did he complete his first symphony in minor mode.

Beethoven's piano sonatas are more consistently daring than his compositions in any other genre, as we'll soon discover. We can easily imagine how works like the "Pathétique" sonata, which begins with a loud chord in a low register that is allowed to reverberate for several seconds, or the "Moonlight" sonata, whose opening movement sustains an ethereal mood throughout, must have surprised listeners accustomed to snappy themes in brisk tempos. The experimental quality of so many sonatas is evident in virtually every important aspect of the works: they range from the form and sequence of movements and key relationships to character and mood and the use of the instrument.

BEETHOVEN'S "PATHÉTIQUE" SONATA

Imagine that you are a mature Viennese aristocrat—perhaps between forty and fifty years old. Perhaps you have some ability at the piano and have mastered some of the easier sonatas and sonatinas composed by Mozart and his contemporaries. You've heard Mozart perform his sonatas and concertos, and you've heard Beethoven perform several times in the salons of your peers. You have been invited once again to hear Beethoven perform; he will introduce his new sonata in C minor, which he will call the "Pathétique."

You've heard Beethoven play some of his earlier sonatas and are perceptive enough to realize that he has been exploring new directions in his piano music. Still, years of listening to and playing sonatas have accustomed you to expect the sonata to begin with a melody in the high midrange of the piano, with a discreet accompaniment, and performed at a brisk tempo. Beethoven sits down to play, and the first sound that you hear is a thick chord in the low register of the instrument that seems to last forever—about three or four seconds. As it dies away, other, softer chords follow. Another explosion, this time a little higher, then more chords, then still another explosive chord, followed by more urgent chords, which lead to a single note and a whoosh down the keyboard. You're stunned . . . you've never heard a sonata begin like this.

You're stunned . . . you've never heard a sonata begin like this.

One problem with listening to music from earlier generations is that it is hard to be surprised by it. In our own time, Elvis sounds tame; to those who grew up in the 1950s listening to pop crooners and musical theater stars, he was radical indeed. Even acts as deliberately confrontational as the Sex Pistols or Public Enemy lose their shock value when the music becomes familiar. So it is difficult to put ourselves in the place of those who encountered this sonata soon after Beethoven composed it. However, only by trying to do so can we gain a sense of how radically innovative Beethoven's music was.

The differences between a more conventional sonata, such as the Mozart sonata discussed in Chapter 20, and Beethoven's radical departure give us insight into Beethoven's genius and appeal and also highlight his role in the transition from Classical to Romantic.

The slow introduction is the most distinctive feature of the sonata, first because of its presence, then because of its recurrence. Slow introductions were relatively common in grand orchestral music, such as opera overtures and symphonies. They also occurred occasionally in chamber music: quartets and quintets for strings, and various combinations of instruments with piano. However, there is no significant precedent for Beethoven's use of it in a piano sonata; not surprisingly, perhaps, Beethoven's more traditional contemporaries considered it eccentric. What made the appearance of a slow introduction even more striking was its reappearance; this was far rarer in instrumental music of any genre. Its return on two occasions demonstrates its crucial role in the expressive message of the movement.

The introduction is the first truly bold example of two qualities that would characterize so much of Beethoven's music throughout his career: individuality and expansion. The slow introduction and its recurrence immediately and obviously set the sonata apart from any other piano sonata composed up to that time, by Beethoven or any other composer. Within the framework of late eighteenth-century music, Beethoven could not have found a more powerful way to assert his individuality.

What makes Beethoven's expansion of Classical forms so dramatic is that it is comprehensive: works are longer, the contrasts are deeper, and the expressive range is greater. The impact of the introduction on the overall length of the movement is significant; it accounts for more than one-third the length of the movement. Without it, the movement would be less than four minutes long (without repeating the exposition)—below average length for a late eighteenth-century sonata and much too short for the big sonatas that Beethoven was motivated to compose.

The contrast between slow and fast is the most pronounced of the contrasts that Beethoven creates in this movement. Through this and other strong contrasts—loud versus soft, high versus low—Beethoven paints musical oppositions in broad, bold strokes. Their impact is immediate and unmistakable. Collectively, these contrasts establish and maintain the expressive message of the movement: conflict without resolution. We hear it unfold next.

BEETHOVEN'S PIANO SONATAS: POWERFUL IDEAS, POWERFUL MUSIC

This is the fourth example of sonata form that we have explored: the first three were the opening movements of the Mozart piano sonata, the Haydn quartet, and Haydn's "Surprise" symphony. As we compare it to the other three movements, especially Mozart's sonata, we can easily hear how innovative it is. It is most

We can hear Beethoven literally ripping apart the conventions of Classical style.

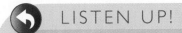

obvious in the introduction, and its recurrence at the end of the exposition and recapitulation. But there are other features, such as the use of minor mode and remote keys even in normally restful places, such as the second theme, that also deviate from convention.

These innovations are the product of expressive necessity rather than simply a desire for novelty. As is evident from start to finish, the sonata movement is about conflict created by strong oppositions. The most innovative features are in the service of making the oppositions stronger and more obvious to all listeners and sustaining the sense of conflict throughout the movement. We can hear Beethoven literally ripping apart the conventions of Classical style.

Beethoven's "Pathétique" sonata also gives us a hint of the "piano sonata as laboratory." Although the first movement of the Fifth Symphony (Beethoven's only work in C minor that is better known than the "Pathétique") is quite different—from the opening motive to the final chord—they are closely related in mood. Not surprisingly, there are procedures that carry over from this early work to the symphony, written almost a decade later. We consider them next.

CHAPTER 26

Beethoven and the Symphony

"Thus Fate knocks at the door!"

On the evening of December 22, 1808, Ludwig van Beethoven presented a benefit concert at the Theater an der Wien. It featured works that were, as an advertisement in the *Wiener Zeitung* stated, "entirely new, and not yet heard in public." The concert was a marathon event that lasted about four hours. The program included the fourth piano concerto; a choral fantasy for piano, orchestra, and chorus; an aria with orchestral accompaniment; three movements from a mass; an improvisation by Beethoven; and the Fifth and Sixth Symphonies. The vast theater was not adequately heated, so patrons sat in bitter cold. A visiting composer made the uncharitable comment that he "experienced the truth that one can easily have too much of a good thing—and still more of a loud."

For the Sixth Symphony, Beethoven provided programmatic descriptions, which he called "recollections of country life," for each of the five movements. For the

Did You Know?

Compact discs (CDs) originally contained about seventy minutes of music because those who established the standard wanted to get Beethoven's Ninth Symphony onto one disc.

Fifth Symphony, he provided nothing other than tempo markings. However, Anton Schindler, a close associate of Beethoven during the composer's later years, recalled in the third edition of his biography *Beethoven As I Knew Him* (1860) that the composer allegedly "pointed to the beginning of the first movement [of the Fifth Symphony] and expressed in these words the fundamental idea of his work: 'Thus Fate knocks at the door!'"

Unfortunately, scholars have discovered that Schindler's testimony about his interactions with Beethoven is so unreliable that nothing he wrote can be assumed to be true unless corroborated by other evidence. However, Beethoven scholar Owen Jander, using Schindler's remark as a point of departure, makes a compelling case that the symphony represents Beethoven's struggle with deafness and his eventual triumph, and that Beethoven goes so far as to embed in the music clues of the symptoms of his deafness. Although Jander's argument must remain speculation, there is little argument that the Fifth Symphony depicts struggle and triumph with unprecedented boldness and originality.

LO3 Beethoven and the Symphony

With the exception of opera, Beethoven transformed every important genre of the Classical era: the piano sonata; chamber music, including duo sonatas for violin or cello and piano, the piano trio, and the string quartet; the concerto; and the overture. But the nine symphonies are the peak of his many achievements. If we listen to them in order, we come away with a sense of Beethoven's enormous growth as a composer: from the first two symphonies, impressive but clearly derived from Classical models, through the next several symphonies—each a

The vast theater was not adequately heated.

© iStockphoto.com/Laura Neal

© Lebrecht Authors

powerful statement—and culminating in the Ninth Symphony, this was work of enormous originality and scale. Indeed, with Beethoven, the symphony replaced opera as the most esteemed genre of art music.

Subsequent generations of composers have found Beethoven's symphonies to be inspiring because of their originality, expansion of Classical style, and expressive impact. They also found them intimidating precisely because of these qualities and because they knew that Beethoven's symphonies would be the yardstick by which their own symphonies would be measured. How to account for the unparalleled prestige of Beethoven's symphonies? We can gain some insight into the special qualities of Beethoven's symphonic music through an exploration of his Fifth Symphony.

Beethoven's hearing aid, an ear trumpet

Beethoven's Fifth Symphony

The writer E. T. A. Hoffmann, a contemporary of Beethoven and a leading figure in the Romantic movement, claimed that Beethoven's Fifth Symphony not only symbolized the ascendancy of instrumental music but also signaled the full emergence of Romanticism in music. Hoffmann's perceptive observation highlights a unique quality of Beethoven's famous work: its uncanny ability to portray the past, present, and future of music simultaneously. Its link to the Classical past is evident in its overall design and use of formal plans and procedures derived directly from Haydn, Mozart, and their contemporaries. Like the Classical symphonies of

Haydn, Mozart, and others, the work has four movements in the typical sequence—sonata-form first movement, slow second movement, scherzo and trio (updated from minuet and trio) third movement, and brisk final movement. However, Beethoven expands, integrates, and individualizes these procedures in ways that stamp the work as a product of the nineteenth century. His innovations would in turn have a decisive influence on most of the important composers of the 1800s. To gain some sense of the symphony's distinctive place in the orchestral literature, and in the history of music, we focus on three qualities that typify Beethoven's style: his comprehensive expansion of Classical models, his ability to impart a distinctive identity to a musical work, and the power with which he expresses feelings through sound.

BEETHOVEN'S EXPANSION OF CLASSICAL STYLE

In his Fifth Symphony, Beethoven's expansion of Classical style is evident in the length of the work and the resources required to perform it. A sense of increased size comes not only from the overall length of the work but also from the internal proportions and the distribution of length among the movements. The sense of bigness comes in large part from the addition of instruments, especially in the fourth movement, which increases the dynamic range of the orchestra.

Length of the Work. A typical contemporary performance of the symphony lasts about thirty-five minutes—almost ten minutes longer than the average length of one of Haydn's London symphonies. But even this increase is deceptively small because of the distribution of length among the four movements. In eighteenth-century symphonies, the length typically decreased progressively from movement to movement: the first was generally the longest; and the last, the shortest. In historically accurate performances of Beethoven's Fifth Symphony, however, the order is often reversed. In performance, the first is typically the shortest. By contrast, the last is the longest and seems even longer because the third movement leads directly into it without interruption.

More Instruments, More Sounds. The expansion of Classical style extends to the instrumental resources and range. For the last movement, Beethoven adds piccolo and contrabassoon, which extend the range of the woodwind section higher and lower, and three trombones, which reinforce the lower range of the brass section.

More instruments, more sounds

Beethoven maximizes the contrast in volume available from these additional resources by calling for dynamic extremes: fortissimo, pianissimo, even pianississimo (almost imperceptibly quiet), occasionally in rapid alternation or succession. These changes give the symphony presence and impact well beyond those of the typical late eighteenth-century symphony.

INTEGRATION AND INDIVIDUALIZATION

The Fifth Symphony is remarkable for its integration and distinct identity—even for Beethoven. Not only the first movement but the entire work reverberates out of the famous opening motive; it is as if the motive is a stone tossed in a pond and the symphony forms the ripples when the stone hits the water.

Beethoven integrates and individualizes the symphony through a multidimensional strategy. Some aspects are obvious: the unbroken connection between the third and fourth movements, the brief flashback to the third movement midway through the fourth movement, and numerous versions of the four-note motive employed in every movement of the symphony. Others, such as the dramatic reworking of Classical approaches to form and character to serve the immediate expressive needs of the symphony, are more subtle. All work together to create a unified four-movement symphony that progresses from almost unbearable tension to triumph.

First Movement. The beginning of the symphony is one of the extraordinary moments in music history. It encapsulates not only one of the most memorable musical ideas of all time but also the transition from the Classical to Romantic era and the impulses that motivated that transition.

The boldness and originality of the opening stem from what it does and what it does not do. What it does is announce in the most emphatic terms, "This is what

Fate knocking at the door?

this piece is about!" Whether this is Schindler's fate knocking at the door or something else known only to Beethoven, it stays in our ear because it is short, distinctive, powerful, and pure—there is no accompaniment.

What it does not do is provide the immediate orientation that opening statements typically provide. It doesn't establish key (it could as easily be in the secondary key as the home key), meter (the short-short-short-long rhythm works as well, if not better, in a compound meter, or in a fast triple meter), or tempo (the long unmeasured pauses after each statement of the motive undermine any sense of beat). As a result, the opening projects enormous instability and uneasiness, which resonate through the entire first movement as well as the remaining three movements.

In this opening gesture, Beethoven makes clear that the conventions he inherited from Haydn, Mozart, and their contemporaries are subordinate to the musical message that he intends to communicate. If the message is conveyed more powerfully by deliberately flouting them, then he does so without hesitation. Indeed, much of the expressive power of the opening, both in the moment and retrospectively, derives from its defiance of the normal way of doing things. For Beethoven, conventional practice was a resource and a frame of reference, not a straitjacket.

Beethoven opens the symphony with a motive, not a melody. Because it is short, distinctive, and memorable, Beethoven can and does use it as a building block for other thematic material. Varied versions of

the motive permeate and unify the first movement: sections based on this famous motive include the entire first theme, the transition material, the first part of the second theme, and the final closing material. In addition, it occurs throughout developmental passages and as periodic counterpoint to other melodic material. Indeed, one reason the movement sounds so distinctive is that so much of the melodic and accompanying material develop from the famous opening motive rather than more generic material, such as scales, arpeggios, and arpeggiated accompaniment figures.

The movement ends with a dramatic change. The end of the recapitulation, which could easily be the end of the movement, is in major; it seems to be bringing the movement to a close. But Beethoven cuts it off and moves abruptly into a turbulent coda, which seems to give up just before the end when the first theme returns softly before a series of powerful chords. The silence after the final chord vibrates with unresolved tension; there is clearly unfinished business that must be addressed in the following movements.

Second Movement. The second movement responds to the unreleased tension of the first movement with a more serene and positive mood. To convey this sense of relative repose, Beethoven uses variation form, in many ways the most predictable of all Classical forms. Although the second movement sounds a more optimistic tone, with prominent rising melodic gestures in both the main and contrasting sections, it does not completely dissipate the tension. Indeed, the movement—at the center of the symphony—looks to the past and the future, most clearly in

LISTEN UP!

CD 2:24–27

Beethoven, Symphony No. 5 in C minor, first movement (1808)

Takeaway point: The opening movement of perhaps the most famous instrumental composition in the history of music

Style: Late Classical/early Romantic

Form: Sonata form with extended coda

Genre: Symphony

Instruments: Full orchestra

Context: Beethoven straining against the conventions of Classical style

LISTEN UP!

CD 2:28–29

Beethoven, Symphony No. 5 in C minor, second movement (1808)

Takeaway point: A moment of relative repose between the tension-filled first and third movements

Style: Late Classical/early Romantic

Form: Variation form, with contrasting material and development

Genre: Symphony

Instruments: Full orchestra

Context: A movement with a distinct identity and range of moods but with strong connections to the other three movements

the contrasting theme. It connects to the first movement through the use of the rhythm of the opening motive, and it anticipates the final movement because the reshaped motive rises and is played loudly by brass and other instruments.

Third Movement. As in the previous movements, Beethoven uses a conventional form as a point of departure: in this case, the scherzo and trio. Typically, **scherzo and trio** (and its predecessor, minuet and trio) movements are relatively light and lighthearted: *scherzo* is the Italian word for "joke." Beethoven's movement is an "anti-scherzo"; it is somber, with low strings playing a prominent role and an altered version of the "fate" motive—the most obvious reference to the first-movement motive in the last three movements—casting a cloud over the movement. The music fades as if dying away at the end of the movement: pizzicato strings, then the timpanist tapping out the rhythm of the "fate" motive over suspenseful strings.

Beethoven extends the movement from within by repeating the trio, then developing the obligatory restatement of the scherzo. Then, after a long, suspenseful transition, he effectively continues to extend the movement by connecting it directly to the finale; there is no break between movements.

LISTEN UP!

CD 3:1–3

Beethoven, Symphony No. 5 in C minor, third movement (1808)

Takeaway point: Beethoven's "anti-scherzo": a dark, foreboding movement that leads directly to the finale

Style: Late Classical/early Romantic

Form: Scherzo and trio, expanded and developed

Genre: Symphony

Instruments: Full orchestra

Context: A return to the mood of the opening, which sets up the triumph of the last movement

Fourth Movement. In the fourth movement, Beethoven again turns Classical convention on its head. Typically, the finale of a symphony or sonata is a short, lighthearted movement, with a form to match—the most common fourth-movement form is the rondo, a form in which a tuneful opening theme returns several times after contrasting material. By contrast, Beethoven's

LISTEN UP!

CD 3:4–8

Beethoven, Symphony No. 5 in C minor, fourth movement (1808)

Takeaway point: Triumphal conclusion to a remarkable, and remarkably integrated, symphony

Style: Late Classical/early Romantic

Form: Sonata form

Genre: Symphony

Instruments: Full orchestra, with extra high and low winds added

Context: An emphatically positive ending to a symphony that began with great foreboding

finale is the longest of the four movements. In it, he uses sonata form, the most substantial and serious form in the Classical style.

The sun breaks through at the beginning of the fourth movement, as the brass-led orchestra blasts out an affirmative melody. The mood remains upbeat through most of the movement. The most extended agitation comes in the development section, which ends with a great "wait a minute" moment: first, the orchestra gets stuck on the chord that should lead back to the recapitulation, then dissolves into a brief recollection of the third movement. This passage suggests a momentary setback on the inevitable road to triumph.

The fourth movement sprints to the end with a sudden shift to a faster tempo, then concludes with a long string of tonic chords. The ending is the final evidence of Beethoven's conception of the symphony as a multimovement narrative: the chords are much too emphatic for the close of a movement—even a long movement. But as the conclusion of a symphony that began with such a struggle, it serves as a final affirmation of the triumph of will over fate.

SOUND AND FEELING

Beethoven's Fifth Symphony is a powerful statement with a clear emotional message; no discerning listener would likely hear the first movement as happy and serene or the last movement as agitated and somber. Beethoven achieves this expressive power through an approach that is simultaneously direct and subliminal. The directness comes from elemental oppositions—loud/soft, fast/slow, up/down, thick/thin, measured/unmeasured—that are sound-painted in broad strokes and from the opening motive, the musical seed from which the entire symphony grows. The subliminal impact comes from the complex network of associations spawned from the opening motive and Beethoven's forceful bending of customary practice in the search for greater expression.

A large part of Beethoven's genius in this symphony is his ability to put ordinary material in extraordinary settings, to heighten or oppose the unsettled mood of the opening. Beethoven crafts the opening motive from generic materials: two notes of a chord, a simple rhythm. But because he invests it with such significance by presenting it initially out of time, out of key, and without accompaniment, it immediately becomes specific to the symphony and emotionally charged. And because so much of the remaining thematic material is either an outgrowth of it or a response to it, Beethoven can intensify, shift, or contrast moods while still retaining a sense of identity.

LO4 Beethoven and the Nineteenth Century

Beethoven cast a long shadow over the nineteenth century, musically and culturally. All felt his presence, and most claimed him as an influence; those few who didn't, such as Chopin, felt compelled to assert that he did not influence their work.

Beethoven elevated the status of the composer from servant to artist.

Moreover, Beethoven elevated the status of the composer from servant to artist. Haydn worked for the Esterházy family. Beethoven demanded a pension from his aristocratic patrons so that he would not have to concern himself with such mundane matters as money. Our modern conception of the musician as artist derives most directly from him.

Beethoven was indirectly responsible for the idea of classical music as we now understand it. It was only after Beethoven's death that the practice of offering concerts of music by deceased composers really took root.

One important reason was to keep alive Beethoven's musical legacy. Franz Liszt, the great nineteenth-century piano virtuoso (and "grand-pupil" of Beethoven, having studied with Carl Czerny, one of Beethoven's piano students), began programming piano recitals that included Beethoven sonatas (and his own piano transcriptions of the symphonies). Newly emerging resident orchestras made his symphonies the cornerstone of their repertoire—as they are now.

BEETHOVEN'S MUSIC: FROM CLASSICAL TO ROMANTIC

In his ability to project strong emotions and moods through his music, and invest compositions with decidedly individual character, Beethoven was in tune with two main currents of Romanticism: the emphasis on feeling and the focus on the individual. The symphony discussed in this chapter stands apart from earlier works in the boldness of its conception and the way it expresses a range of moods so comprehensively and cogently. Add to that the power of Beethoven's personality and his role in elevating the stature of the artist, and we can readily understand why Hoffmann considered Beethoven the ultimate Romantic.

At the same time, Beethoven's music retains the logic and coherence that characterize the best music of the Classical style. The slow introduction to the "Pathétique" and the pure opening motive of the Fifth Symphony are dramatic departures from convention that communicate a sense of breaking free of the constraints imposed by the expectations of Classical style. However, as the movements unfold, we discover that each is a necessary first step in projecting the expressive intent of the movement, and that there is an indivisible connection between opening gesture and large-scale conception. In retrospect, we are left with the distinct impression that the movements had to begin as they did; anything less bold would have diluted their expressive message.

Beethoven challenged himself again and again to stretch the boundaries of Classical style without forsaking its integrity. That he succeeded so often is even more shocking than the musical features that so often shocked his audiences. His willingness to challenge himself and his ability to meet, even exceed, these self-imposed challenges are key measures of his greatness.

BEETHOVEN'S LEGACY

Beethoven's position in the history of classical music is unique. He and his music were revered during his

Beethoven's hair gives us some insight into the changing times and his place in them. From the seventeenth through the early nineteenth centuries, men's wigs were an external symbol of high rank. During the eighteenth century, members of the upper class and those who moved in upper-class circles—such as Bach, Handel, Haydn, and Mozart—routinely wore wigs. By contrast, even the earliest authentic portraits of Beethoven show his hair. These images suggest the power of his personality—his determination to be his own person, his disdain for class standing based on birth rather than achievement.

Then there is Beethoven the man, the man who lived for his art, who overcame a devastating affliction, and who struggled to transcend the limitations imposed by society and his musical contemporaries. And he also had the good fortune to be born in the right place at the right time. He lived during an era when the centuries-old monarchical tradition was disintegrating, when what you achieved and what you stood for began to matter more than who your parents were. Beethoven's life and work became a symbol of this new order, not only for his time but also for subsequent generations. He came at a time of musical transition; almost single-handedly, he engineered the shift from Classicism to Romanticism, and the wholesale change of values that went with it. Beethoven was clearly a man for his times.

Beethoven is the quintessential composer. In his music and his life, he epitomizes the composer as artist—as one hyperenthusiastic biographer put it: Beethoven, the Man Who Freed Music. Virtually since his arrival in Vienna, people have responded to the power and boldness of his music and his personal magnetism, and in particular, his struggle with the musician's ultimate adversity: deafness.

We sense in Beethoven's music that he is almost compelled to follow his own path rather than write on demand. No other composer has gone through such a dramatic evolution in style. That he continued to develop as a composer despite the seemingly insurmountable obstacle his deafness imposed makes his achievement even more compelling. No single person has had a greater impact on musical life in Western civilization than Beethoven.

lifetime and have never gone out of favor. His music—the symphonies and sonatas, concertos and chamber music—has been consistently performed, analyzed, and emulated since its composition. The music that we have heard is over two hundred years old, but it is more familiar to us than it was to people in Beethoven's own time, and far more familiar than any contemporary orchestral or piano music.

Why this unique status? It begins, of course, with the music. Beethoven's important music is big and bold. It has personality: major works sound like Beethoven and no one else, yet each work has a highly individual character. His music evolved over several decades; until his death, Beethoven was searching for new directions. Much of Beethoven's music is at once accessible and sophisticated—it can go straight to the heart and challenge the mind. It is optimistic: even works that begin darkly, like the Fifth and Ninth Symphonies, end in triumph.

UNIT 15
VOCAL MUSIC IN THE NINETEENTH CENTURY

© Leemage/Lebrecht Music & Arts

Learning Outcomes
After reading this unit, you will be able to do the following:

LO1 Describe the flowering of song in the nineteenth century.

LO2 Recognize the art song, through the *Lieder* of Franz Schubert.

LO3 Describe the emergence of popular music in America, its audience, and its relationship to the art song, using songs by Stephen Foster

LO4 Reexamine the musical and social boundaries between sacred and secular, and religious and spiritual, through an exploration of Brahms's *Requiem*.

LO5 Relate developments in European spiritual music to Protestant music for worship in nineteenth-century America.

LO6 Recognize the implications of the development of operetta in the nineteenth century.

LO7 Differentiate *opéra comique* from other types of nineteenth-century opera.

LO8 Describe how Giuseppe Verdi reformed Italian opera.

LO9 Recognize how Richard Wagner changed music and opera.

NINETEENTH-CENTURY vocal music clearly shows the stratification of music and culture, which grew more pronounced as the century progressed. There was music for the most sophisticated tastes and music directed toward the masses. Still, vocal music and its performance also crossed the seemingly unbridgeable gulf between high and low class, from singing societies that drew their membership from all levels of society to the co-opting of opera by popular songwriters and minstrel show troupes. We hear a broad cross-section of this music in the next several chapters.

CHAPTER 27

Schubert and the Art Song

"Friends described Schubert's composing style as virtually unconscious—as if he were a medium channeling inspiration from a higher power."

LO1 Song and Singing in the Nineteenth Century

The hottest tickets in Boston and New York in the fall of 1850 were those to concerts by Jenny Lind, the "Swedish nightingale." Lind was one of the leading operatic sopranos in Europe during the 1830s and 1840s; wherever she appeared, impresarios raised ticket prices and still sold out theaters. P. T. Barnum, the man who both raised promotion to an art and also gave it a bad name, sent an agent to London to persuade Lind to come to America for a series of up to 150 concerts. Barnum's agent was persuasive; so was a deposit of $187,500 in a London bank (worth about $4.5 million today). With the contract signed and Lind on the way to the United States, Barnum, who had made his reputation promoting midgets, Siamese twins, mermaids, elephants, and other real and fake "oddities," promoted her visit so well that a crowd estimated to be over thirty thousand people was waiting dockside when she arrived in New York. Barnum auctioned off tickets for her opening concerts: the first one sold for $225 (over $5,000 today). The entire nation was gripped in "Jennymania"; her one-person Swedish invasion was even more far reaching than the British rock invasion a century or so later. Barnum sold out theaters wherever

Did You Know?

Before Gen X, hippies, and beatniks, there were "bohemians," arty types who lived on the fringes of society without putting down roots.

she sang and memorabilia as fast as he could produce it. People named children, towns, schools—even clipper ships—after her. Jenny Lind was America's first imported celebrity.

Lind had made her reputation as an opera diva. Toward the end of the 1840s, she also began to sing in oratorio performances, collaborating when possible with Felix Mendelssohn; she would eventually marry Otto Goldschmidt, one of Mendelssohn's piano pupils. However, on her American tours, she sang an eclectic mix of vocal music that included not only arias from contemporary operas and an aria from Handel's *Messiah* but also songs popular in the United States at the time. These included "Home Sweet Home," the most popular song in America for much of the century, genteel arrangements of folk songs from the British Isles like the Scottish song "Comin' through the Rye," and even "plantation songs" by Stephen Foster. In so doing, she met her audience halfway. Her programs cut across class boundaries: they included acknowledged classics, such as arias from operas and oratorios; popular songs intended for a mainly middle-class audience; and even the most respectable kind of song from the minstrel show, a decidedly lowbrow form of entertainment.

The overwhelming success of Lind's American tour highlights the central place of singing and song in nineteenth-century musical life. Seemingly everyone sang, from opera stars like Lind to laborers learning the current favorites or participating in singing clubs. Song with piano accompaniment, a relatively new genre in 1800, flourished as it hadn't before and hasn't since, in all strata of society. Music for stage entertainment, from music dramas to minstrel shows, was often disseminated via sheet music in arrangements for voice(s) and piano. Music was available for every taste and almost every occasion.

Among the most significant reasons for the enormous popularity of singing, both amateur and professional, were the following:

- *Publishers*. Music publishing took off in the nineteenth century, with products aimed at all classes: classical choral works and art songs; popular songs published as sheet music and in "songsters," which contain only words; hymnals, including shape-note hymnals that simplified music reading.

- *Pianos*. Pianos became the accompanying instrument of choice, and piano manufacturing made them affordable for middle-class families and small businesses.

- *Public performances*. Vocal music in performance grew in multiple ways. Music onstage diversified, from music dramas to minstrel shows. Choral societies in Europe and North America, made up of singers from all classes, performed new and classic choral works. Professional singers performed songs—*Lieder*, popular songs of the day, arias, and more—in concert, in theaters, and in salons.

- *Parlors*. A rapidly growing middle class sang at home in their parlors, the middle-class counterpart to the salons of the upper class, and at church; joined choral societies to sing classical choral masterworks; and attended concerts to hear singers like Jenny Lind.

LO2 The *Lied*, a Romantic Genre

In October 1814, at the age of seventeen, Franz Schubert composed the song *Gretchen am Spinnrade (Gretchen at the Spinning Wheel)*. The following year, he composed *Erlkönig (The Elf King)*. The songs were among Schubert's first successes; he would publish them as Op. 2 and Op. 1, respectively, some years later.

Lied (plural, Lieder) Song for voice and piano in which both melody and accompaniment amplify dominant themes and images in the text

art song Nineteenth- and early twentieth-century song that set poetry to music of comparable quality

Both songs used texts by the renowned German Romantic poet Johann Wolfgang von Goethe. The first sets a heartbreaking scene from Goethe's drama *Faust*; the second is a setting of Goethe's poem *Erlkönig*. During Schubert's brief lifetime, Goethe was the most important literary figure in German-speaking Europe and one of the most influential thinkers of the era.

By contrast, Schubert was virtually unknown when he composed these songs. During his brief career, he lived precariously on the fringes of Viennese society, although he had well-to-do friends who championed his music. He periodically received royalties from the sale of his music, but he spent the money as fast as it came in. He was the stereotypical starving artist to whom widespread recognition comes only posthumously.

Schubert desperately wanted to meet Goethe, so his well-connected friends sent Goethe copies of Schubert's songs that used the poet's texts. Apparently, Goethe wasn't impressed because he never made an effort to arrange a meeting. He was far more enthusiastic about the songs of his good friend Carl Friedrich Zelter, who set Goethe's poems much more simply. Ironically, Goethe's poems are far better known in Schubert's settings than they are as poetry—at least outside German-speaking Europe.

Schubert's two early songs are harbingers of Romanticism. Both the genre and Schubert's realizations of it help usher in a new era and turn the page on the Classical style.

Lied (plural, *Lieder*) is German for "song." Although the term can refer to any song in German, it has also acquired a more specific connotation: nineteenth- and early twentieth-century song for voice and piano in which both melody and accompaniment amplify dominant themes and images in the text. Romantic *Lieder* were among the first instances of the art song. The goal of the **art song** was to set poetry with music of comparable quality. This practice took shape first in German-speaking Europe, most decisively and importantly in the *Lieder* of Schubert.

Lieder exemplified many of the qualities and characteristics associated with the early Romantic movement. The *Lied* was, first of all, a marriage of the arts: fine poetry set to beautiful music that brought added depth to the feelings expressed in the text. German *Lieder* form the most substantial and important musical repertoire in service of this goal. The extent to which words and music merged was sometimes evident in the form of a song: the music typically took its formal cue from the poem rather than employing a conventional musical form, such as the da capo aria, that required adaptation of the text. At the simplest level, this might involve the use of strophic form. However, both songs discussed later offer more complex narrative forms.

The use of German also fostered national sentiment on at least three levels. First, it favored the local language over Italian, the de facto international language in secular vocal music through much of the eighteenth century. In this respect, it was the art counterpart to the folk song settings that were especially popular in the British Isles and elsewhere in the first years of the nineteenth century. Second, it affirmed the importance of the writers whose poetry was set to the music. Among Schubert's most esteemed songs are those using the texts of Goethe, Müller, Schiller, and other leading poets of the era.

Most important, the musical settings in well-composed songs were able to bring out the idiomatic qualities of the language because the composers were responsive to the inflection and rhythm of the text. German is a heavily inflected language, with considerable difference in accentuation between strong and weak syllables. Schubert's settings of Goethe's poems amplify the inflection and rhythm of the text as spoken. The text remains intact and intelligible, even as the melody goes beyond the expressive capabilities of speech.

This sensitivity to the nuances of language is evident in art songs in many languages throughout the nineteenth century and into the twentieth. Some of the musical differences between the *Lieder* of Schubert, Schumann, and Hugo Wolf, and the *chansons* (the French counterparts of the *Lied*) of Fauré and Duparc, are attributable to the differences in inflection between German and French.

Franz Schubert

Franz Schubert was born near Vienna into a musical family. He received his musical education at home, then at a school in Vienna where he studied under Mozart's rival, Salieri. After leaving the school, he tried teaching for a while but didn't take to it. Instead, he became the first noteworthy musical bohemian. He developed a loyal circle of friends and professional acquaintances who supported him when he lacked funds or even a place to stay. The group included writers, painters, and others who led a bohemian lifestyle: work in the morning (or not at all), then spend the afternoon and evening talking, drinking, and generally having a good time in a café. Bohemians were the first counterculture, the un-

Puccini's opera *La bohème*—the story of a young poet falling in love with a seamstress afflicted with tuberculosis—romanticized the "Bohemian" life.

Bohemians were the first counterculture, the underbelly of a new cultural elite.

derbelly of a new cultural elite. They rejected the values of the bourgeois, who aspired to respectability. They became poets, painters, and musicians rather than bankers, merchants, or civil servants, and they often lived off an inheritance or their friends.

Schubert composed at a feverish pace. Friends described his composing style as virtually unconscious—as if he were a medium channeling inspiration from a higher power. Accurate or not, there's no question that Schubert was extraordinarily prolific. It is hard to imagine anyone creating more music of value in a shorter time. In a career that lasted barely more than a decade, he created an enormous amount of music, despite suffering horribly from syphilis over the last six years of his life. In addition to the songs, he composed several symphonies (although two were left unfinished), a great deal of important chamber music, and music for solo piano and piano duet. Although connected to the Viennese Classical traditions, Schubert's music is Romantic in its emphasis on deep personal feeling expressed in lyric melody, distinctive settings, and adventurous harmonies.

SCHUBERT AND THE *LIED*

Schubert's legacy begins with his songs. He composed more than 660 of them, many of which exemplify the very best of the genre. Beginning with *Gretchen am*

Franz Schubert

Fast Facts

Franz Schubert

- *Dates:* 1797–1828
- *Place:* Vienna, Austria
- *Reasons to remember:* Composer who almost single-handedly established the art song as a significant and distinctly Romantic musical genre

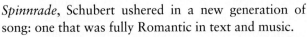

Spinnrade, Schubert ushered in a new generation of song: one that was fully Romantic in text and music.

Schubert's genius as a composer of songs begins with a sensitivity to the text—its inflection, its rhythms, its meaning. It is expressed most directly through an extraordinary melodic gift: Schubert's melodies are not only intrinsically beautiful but often specifically responsive to the text that they set.

However, Schubert's most significant innovation in song composition was expanding the role of the accompaniment. Compared to earlier songs and contemporaneous folk song settings, Schubert's accompaniments are typically richer, more individual, and more demanding for the pianist (the accompaniment to Schubert's *Erlkönig* is extraordinarily fatiguing). Moreover, they now not only provide support for the melody but also bring to life a key aspect of the text. In the case of *Gretchen am Spinnrade*, the piano evokes the spinning wheel where Gretchen sits waiting for her lover. In *Erlkönig*, the accompaniment depicts the frantic galloping of the horse as father and son try to elude the evil Elf King.

Schubert's *Lieder* manifest the Romantic ascendancy of feeling over thought. The two songs presented here express some of our deepest emotions: love given and abandoned, and the intrusion of death into life. In *Gretchen am Spinnrade*, Gretchen, pregnant and alone, recalls her lover with desire and anguish. In *Erlkönig*, father and son lose a race with death, personified by the Elf King. In both, the accompaniment evokes a vivid image so that changes in it can signal moments of intense emotion.

Lieder are the most intimately personal first-person music of the Romantic era. Through both words and music, the singer assumes the persona—or personae— depicted in the poem. In convincing performances of *Gretchen am Spinnrade*, we can feel Gretchen's lust and pain as if the singer herself were experiencing it. *Erlkönig* presents a more formidable challenge: the singer must portray not one persona but four: the narrator, the father, the son, and the Elf King. Whether singers project a character or simply narrate, they sing in the first person.

The circumstances of performance made *Lieder* particularly personal. The venues were intimate. Early performances typically took place in the salons of private homes; audiences seldom exceeded one hundred. There were no props, no costumes, and only the support of a pianist. *Gretchen am Spinnrade* is exceptional in its reference to a longer narrative; in most cases, the poem is self-contained. The vocal artifice associated with opera and oratorio is largely absent: texts are set syllabically, and melodic elaboration is rare. The focus is on the words, the melody, and the person singing them.

Schubert's songs were warmly received in Viennese salons, grand rooms in the mansions of the wealthy, whose diverse audiences were a mix of the aristocratic, the wealthy, the cultured (university professors, professional musicians) and those members of the middle class drawn to the world of high culture, and the artistic, bohemian and otherwise. The salon remained an important venue for the art song throughout the nineteenth century.

GRETCHEN AM SPINNRADE, ERLKÖNIG, AND NARRATIVE

In both songs discussed here, Schubert crafts the form to the story. In *Erlkönig*, he uses **through-composed form**, which means that there is no large-scale formal repetition. The glue that holds the song together musically is not the melody but the accompaniment, which hammers away relentlessly—except when the Elf King sings and, devastatingly, when the father discovers that his child has died in his arms. Schubert uses fluctuations

In 1821, Franz von Schober, one of Franz Schubert's circle of friends, organized at his lodgings the first **Schubertiade**, an evening of music written and sometimes performed by Schubert.

in dynamics, dramatic harmonic shifts, differing melodic contours, and occasionally changes in accompaniment to portray the characters and move the action forward, until it stops abruptly just before the end.

In *Gretchen am Spinnrade*, Schubert must shift between reality and remembrance. To do so, he adapts a familiar musical device, the refrain. In this song, the refrain depicts Gretchen in the present, with no peace and a heavy heart. As the music wanders away from the refrain, we can almost visualize Gretchen retreating from a dismal present into the erotic memories of her time with Faust. Each time the refrain returns, it brings her abruptly back to reality.

The two songs signal a shift in the expressive intent of form. The Classical conflict and resolution outlined by the opposition of two main keys and filled in by frequently contrasting musical materials now belong to the previous generation. In Schubert's songs, harmony is more responsive to the sense of the text. Like the poems, the music tells a story, shifting mood along with the text. The songs evidence how the emphasis on narrative replaced the dramatic tension of Classical music. Narrative, and forms that conveyed it, would become a key feature of Romantic music, both vocal and instrumental.

LISTEN UP!

CD 3:10
Schubert, *Gretchen am Spinnrade* (1814)

Takeaway point: Sensitive, evocative musical setting of a poignant scene from Goethe's *Faust*

Style: Early Romantic

Form: Episodic, with refrain

Genre: Lied

Instruments: Voice and piano

Context: Song for a Schubertiade

The Art Song after Schubert

Schubert wasn't the first composer of *Lieder*. Mozart, Haydn, and especially Beethoven composed memorable songs; so did several others, including Goethe's friend Zelter and Johann Zumsteeg, a composer whose songs Schubert especially admired.

However, with *Gretchen am Spinnrade*, *Erlkönig*, and the hundreds of songs that followed, Schubert almost single-handedly established the art song as a significant and distinctly Romantic musical genre. Schubert would go on to compose two major **song cycles** (which set a series of related poems within a larger work): *Die Schöne Müllerin (The Beautiful Miller's Maid)* in 1823 and *Die Winterreise (The Winter Journey)* in 1828. *Die Winterreise* contains twenty-four songs; it is a full evening of music. *Die Schöne Müllerin* wasn't

Schubertiade
An evening of music composed by Franz Schubert, often with Schubert as accompanist

through-composed form Form in which there is no large-scale formal repetition

song cycles A series of related poems set as songs within a larger work

LISTEN UP!

CD 3:9
Schubert, *Erlkönig* (1815)

Takeaway point: Dramatic song with vivid piano accompaniment; a tour de force for the skilled vocalist who can portray all four characters

Style: Early Romantic

Form: Through-composed

Genre: Lied

Instruments: Voice and piano

Context: Song for a Schubertiade

the first important song cycle; Beethoven's *An die Ferne Geliebte (To a Distant Beloved),* composed in 1816, holds that distinction. However, Schubert's two cycles quickly became the standard for composers in subsequent generations.

More generally, important features of his style—most notably text declamation, distinctive and expressive accompaniments, interplay between voice and piano, expressive melody that amplifies the inflection and emotions of the text—became both inspiration and model for nineteenth-century song composers in German-speaking Europe and elsewhere. Moreover, those songs published during his lifetime and the first few years after his death became the core repertoire for nineteenth-century art song.

German-speaking composers, most notably Robert Schumann, Johannes Brahms, and Hugo Wolf, would enrich this repertoire. Composers in other countries followed the lead of German *Lieder* composers. Among their most notable works are songs in Russian by Modest Mussorgsky and Pyotr Ilyich Tchaikovsky, songs in Polish by Frédéric Chopin, and songs in French by Gabriel Fauré and Henri Duparc. However, none surpassed Schubert's achievements as a composer of song.

Stephen Foster and Popular Song

"John Sullivan Dwight likened Foster's 'Old Folks at Home' to a 'morbid irritation of the skin.'"

As I once intimated to you, I had the intention of omitting my name from my Ethiopian songs, owing to the prejudice against them by some, which might injure my reputation as a writer of another style of music, but I find that by my efforts I have done a great deal to build up a taste for the Ethiopian songs among refined people by making the words suitable to their taste.

Did You Know?

Blacks in nineteenth-century minstrel shows also wore blackface to look the way white audiences expected them to.

In this letter to his publisher E. P. Christy, Stephen Foster voiced his "class versus cash" dilemma. Foster had begun his career as a songwriter addressing two distinct audiences: highbrows and lowbrows. Highbrows viewed themselves as the cultured members of American society. They looked to Europe for their music and looked down their noses at the rough-and-tumble world of the minstrel show. For musical entertainment, they generally preferred sentimental parlor songs and the European classics, both in their original form and in watered-down versions. They abhorred, or pretended to abhor, less refined music. John Sullivan Dwight, whose *Journal of Music* served as the semi-official arbiter of good taste among the cultivated, likened Foster's "Old Folks at Home" to a "morbid irritation of the skin."

Lowbrows, who came mainly from the country and the urban working class, flocked to the theaters and dance halls where minstrels performed. They enjoyed the clacking of the "bones" (animal bones played as percussion instruments) and the scraping of the fiddler's bow across the strings, and the bouncy, tuneful melodies that they played. They guffawed as minstrels crudely caricatured black speech and manners and lampooned high culture.

In 1852, the year that Foster wrote to Christy, a cultural abyss separated highbrows (and those in the middle class who aligned with them) from lowbrows. Foster felt this division keenly enough that he originally allowed his "Ethiopian songs"—that is, songs for the minstrel show—to be published under Christy's name.

However, with the success of songs like "Old Folks at Home," which had been published the previous year and whose overwhelming success probably prompted him to write Christy, Foster belatedly changed his tune.

In "Old Folks at Home," Foster tried to straddle the abyss by creating a new song style: the plantation song. Plantation songs were Foster's innovative synthesis of the two dominant popular song styles in America at midcentury: the parlor song and the minstrel show song. He was more successful musically than commercially. "Old Folks at Home" became the best-known song in nineteenth-century America; estimates of sheet music sales of the song reach as high as 20 million, and the song remains familiar to this day. However, Foster saw almost none of the profits. His terrible business sense and struggles with alcoholism led him into a series of disastrous deals with his publishers. He would die penniless at thirty-seven.

Foster began his career as a songwriter addressing two distinct audiences: highbrows and lowbrows.

Foster's minstrel show songs were in the vanguard of America's first cultural revolution; they would help popularize the first distinctively American popular music. In them, we hear features that point the way to ragtime, rock, and rap. By contrast, he directed his parlor songs toward the rear guard, the "respectable" middle- and upper-class members of American society. In these songs, Foster used European music from earlier in the century as inspiration. Still, they are among the first fruits of a more conservative tradition within American popular music, which would be manifested in the twentieth century most prominently in musical theater. We consider an example of each later.

LO3 The Parlor Song

The most popular musical genre in America during the nineteenth century was the **parlor song**. As the name implies, parlor songs were songs for amateur musicians. They fostered an intimate and social kind of music making. Families and perhaps a few friends would gather in the parlor to hear the more talented among them sing and play old chestnuts and current favorites. Parlor songs resembled the art songs of classical music in much the same way that parlors resembled the salons of the upper class: they were similar in style and resources but more modest in their expressive range and musical requirements. Parlor songs told sentimental stories, set to simple melodies with an unobtrusive accompaniment.

Parlor songs composed in America followed English middle-class taste, which favored Italian opera and folk songs from the British Isles. In the early nineteenth century, the most popular folk-song settings were those of Thomas Moore (1779–1852), an Irish poet and musician who lived in England most of his career and set his own poems to traditional Irish folk melodies. A skilled singer and pianist, he made these adaptations himself and published them in ten volumes between 1808 and 1834. Moore's settings were genteel and "correct" according to the musical standards of the day. In this form, they appealed to and circulated among musically literate members of the middle and upper classes. Among those familiar with Moore's *Irish Melodies* was Stephen Foster.

For "Jeanie with the Light Brown Hair," Foster used Moore's song settings as a point of departure. Its connection with folk songs like "Barbara Allen" is evident in the reliance on a pentatonic scale, a graceful melody made up of short phrases, and the strophic setting of the text. But Foster's lyric is a sweet, sentimental portrait of a young lady rather than a grisly morality tale. His melody is more elaborately constructed, with four interlocked sections and a brief but striking vocal flourish just before the reprise of the opening. And of course, there is also a part for the piano, which provides a soft cushion for the vocal melody and instrumental interludes between verses.

parlor song
Nineteenth-century song for amateur musicians that resembled the art songs of classical music, told a sentimental story, and was set to a simple melody with an unobtrusive accompaniment

LISTEN UP!

CD 3:11
Foster, "Jeanie with the Light Brown Hair" (1854)

Takeaway point: A sweet, sentimental song suitable for amateur performance

Style: Nineteenth-century popular song

Form: Strophic

Genre: Parlor song

Instruments: Voice and piano

Context: Music suitable for amateur performance in respectable households

If he had never written a single song for the minstrel show, Stephen Foster would still rank as America's best songwriter during the nineteenth century. But today he is remembered more for his songs for the minstrel show, among them the perennial favorite "De Camptown Races."

Minstrelsy

Blackface **minstrelsy** was a form of lowbrow entertainment that mixed music, dancing, humor, storytelling, skits, and just about anything else the performers thought would please their often-rowdy audiences. Early minstrel troupes typically featured a core group of four performers, each of whom played an in-

minstrelsy
A form of lowbrow nineteenth-century American entertainment that mixed music, dancing, humor, storytelling, and skits, performed by blacks or whites in blackface

strument: fiddle, banjo, tambourine, and bones. The latter three instruments were widely used by slaves; scholars have suggested that they are re-creations of African instruments.

Three of the four performers also filled the key roles in the nonmusical part of the show. One person was an interlocutor, a pompous asker of questions who sat in the middle of a semicircle. Answering him were two endmen made up in blackface: one played the tambourine; the other played the bones.

Blackface entertainment dates from the eighteenth century in England. Solo blackface performers were hugely popular in both England and America during the late 1820s and 1830s, so it was just a matter of time before several banded together to form a troupe. By most accounts, the Virginia Minstrels, a four-man group, put on the first minstrel show in 1843. They were a sensation; almost overnight, minstrel troupes sprang up across the country. Within a few years, minstrelsy had become the most popular form of entertainment in America, much to the chagrin of the cultivated members of society.

> *It was as if blackface minstrels were both ventriloquist and dummy.*

Minstrelsy seemed to embody the best and worst of nineteenth-century American culture. The worst was, of course, the racial stereotyping of a totally disadvantaged minority. Minstrelsy took off at a time when most blacks were slaves and even freed blacks faced relentless discrimination in both North and South. At the same time, minstrelsy brought energy, fun, and the beginnings of a more democratic attitude into popular entertainment. Minstrels took aim at both those below them socially and those above them. They mocked high culture and people in high places—politicians, captains of industry, and others of their ilk. Parodies of Shakespeare and opera were staples in the minstrel show.

Blackface was important not only for what people saw—a gross distortion of the appearance of African Americans (replicated on the sheet music covers of thousands of songs)—but also for what they didn't see. Blackface in effect served as a mask that the performers could hide behind; it enabled them to say and do things that they wouldn't have said and done without the mask. It was as if they were both ventriloquist and dummy.

Few white minstrel performers based their portrayals on firsthand encounters with blacks. However, after the Civil War, black minstrels (in blackface) began to appear in minstrel shows. They quickly replaced white minstrels because they were, after all, much better at portraying themselves or—more precisely—the parodies of themselves that white audiences expected.

The music for the early minstrel show captured the good and the bad. The music had energy and appeal. However, song lyrics helped create and perpetuate the stereotypes that are still part of our culture. They were especially cruel because audiences had virtually no realistic images or sounds of blacks to balance it against.

MUSIC FOR THE MINSTREL SHOW

Early minstrels tried to look black, but they almost certainly sounded white. Despite the use of three instruments typically used by slaves, the most important influence on minstrel show music was Anglo-American folk-dance music, mainly jigs and reels from the British Isles. The sound and style of folk fiddlers like Newfoundland's Rufus Guinchard became a foundational element in minstrel show music, and dance rhythms underpin most of the characteristic songs from the era. Typically, the melodies are short, made up of short phrases based on a pentatonic scale, and usually include a refrain. Syncopation is rare, but the rhythms are upbeat.

Foster's "De Camptown Races," published in 1850, is a classic example of the style, a simple and appealing tune that one could remember after only a couple of hearings. The lyrics are typical of the style: a patchwork of images built around the account of a horse race, described in pseudo-black dialect.

Our hybrid recording of "De Camptown Races" hints at the two ways in which songs like this were dis-

LISTEN UP!

CD 3:12

Foster, "De Camptown Races" (1850)
Takeaway point: High-spirited silliness set to a lively tune

Style: Nineteenth-century popular song

Form: Strophic, with refrain

Genre: Minstrel show song

Instruments: Variable—up to the performers

Context: Song intended for the minstrel show stage and for home use by people of all classes

seminated. The first part is a performance based on the sheet-music version of the song; the second part is a contemporary, more spontaneous performance built around the song as it has come down in oral tradition. In 1850, publishers made money on songs by selling sheet music, so even as the song went onstage, it also went into stores and shops. However, because the melody is simple, self-contained, and repetitive—even at first hearing, everyone would know the refrain by the final statement—it also passed from singer to singer in oral tradition, much like "Barbara Allen." To support this more viral mode of dissemination, publishers put out **songsters**, which contained only the lyrics of the song. As a result, the song existed apart from any particular performance tradition, as these two quite different but effective performances demonstrate.

The Birth of American Popular Music

American popular music—that is, music that is distinctively and recognizably American and widely popular—began with minstrelsy. There had been music that was popular in America before minstrelsy, but no popular music that *sounded* American until minstrel show songs.

Even in its published form, the minstrel show song introduced two innovations that would become a permanent part of popular song: the

songster Handout containing only the lyrics of a song

American popular music Music that is distinctively and recognizably American and widely popular

use of a recurrent refrain and dance rhythms. As performed onstage, it introduced the mixed-timbre accompaniment, complete with percussion—tambourine and bones. Just as important, minstrelsy brought a fresh, unpretentious, sometimes defiant attitude into American culture—T-shirts and blue jeans instead of white tie and tails. This attitude continues to resonate in the twenty-first century.

The tension between high and low culture that Foster articulated in his letter to Christy would become a source of creative friction in the popular tradition, particularly in the twentieth century. It would generate numerous important syntheses, including the classic rags of Scott Joplin, the "symphonic jazz" of George Gershwin, the musicals of Jerome Kern and Leonard Bernstein, the bebop of Charlie Parker, and the all-embracing songs of The Beatles.

CHAPTER 28

Spiritual Music: The Requiem

"Brahms eventually became the third B, after Bach and Beethoven."

On February 2, 1865, Johannes Brahms lost his mother, Christiane. Born in 1789, she had married a much younger man just after turning forty and had given birth to three children in short order. Johannes was her second child and first son, with whom she remained close until her death. After she passed away, Brahms composed a large-scale work for chorus, vocal soloists, and orchestra that he would call *Ein deutsches Requiem (A German Requiem)*.

The very title of the work underscores the extent to which spirituality and religion had grown apart by the middle of the nineteenth century. The composition is not in Latin, and it is not a liturgical work. Instead, it is both a personal and a universal affirmation of the spirit. We consider the work in the context of this growing separation.

deism
A belief originating in the seventeenth century that asserted that the divine could be understood through reason alone

LO4 Religion, Deism, and Spirituality

In the wake of the Renaissance and the Protestant Reformation came a challenge not only to the Catholic Church but also to the very idea of organized religion. Among European intellectuals, the idea of **deism**, the belief that the divine could be understood through reason alone, took root. Deists proposed that God created the world, then set it in motion and left it alone, and that the existence of God could be discerned by reason alone. Consequently, there was no need for organized religion to serve as an intermediary.

The movement took shape in England in the seventeenth century and spread to the continent and the colonies during the eighteenth century. But deism did not—could not—attract mass support. The most notorious attempt to impose it on a people came during the French Revolution, when Hébertists, the most radical revolutionaries in France, briefly renamed Notre Dame cathedral "The Temple of Reason" and attempted to transform Catholicism into the "Cult of the Supreme Being." This ended in failure.

Deism's indirect impact on the framers of the Constitution and the Bill of Rights would prove far more influential: many of the founders—among them George Washington, Benjamin Franklin, Thomas Jefferson, John Adams, and Thomas Paine—expressed deistic views in their writing. Their philosophical position fundamentally altered the relationship between religion and politics in the newly formed United States, which in turn served as a model for change in Europe. As a result, societies in France and in Protestant Europe and North America were more open to and tolerant of differing expressions of the relationship between God and humanity at the beginning of the nineteenth century than they had been at the beginning of the eighteenth century.

The separation of religion and spirituality deepened during the nineteenth century, particularly among intellectuals. Among the key factors were extensive contact with the scriptures of Eastern religions, Darwin's theory of evolution, and philosophical writings by Immanuel Kant, George Hegel, Herbert Spencer, and others, which offered historical views of religion, in some cases as an artifact of humanity rather than a divinely ordained phenomenon.

Ein deutsches Requiem is a musical work in step with these progressive developments. It is a requiem only in the broadest sense of the term. It is not a work composed for use in a religious service; its most common venue is the concert hall, not the church. In numerous ways, it reflects the more free-thinking attitudes of many nineteenth-century intellectuals, as we will discover.

The Requiem in the Nineteenth Century

In Catholic liturgy, a **requiem** is a Mass offered to honor the dead. The dead may be an individual, or it may be a small or large group; many parishes offer Requiem Masses on All Souls' Day, the day in the liturgical year set aside to honor those who passed away during the previous year. The text for a Requiem Mass differs from that for an Ordinary Mass; the term *requiem* comes from the most common form of the opening prayer, which begins "Requiem aeternam dona eis, Domine" (Eternal rest grant unto them, O Lord).

Musical settings of the Requiem Mass are far more variable than musical settings of the Ordinary Mass. Both the Gloria and the Credo are omitted. Instead, composers choose to set some or all of the customary texts, which include the Kyrie, Sanctus, and Agnus Dei

© iStockphoto.com/Pierluigi D'Eramo

from the Ordinary Mass as well as prayers specific to the requiem service, such as the opening "Requiem," the sequence "**Dies irae**" (day of wrath), and the communion prayer "Lux aeterna" (eternal light).

Nineteenth-century composers were drawn to the requiem; there are many more settings of the requiem by important composers than there are of the mass. Among the most admired requiems that set the Catholic liturgy are those by Berlioz, Verdi, Bruckner, Dvořák, and Fauré. This would seem to be one manifestation of the Romantic fascination with death (see Chapter 24). (We encounter others in upcoming chapters: Verdi's *La traviata* and Bizet's *Carmen* end with the deaths of the leading characters; Berlioz quotes the plainchant setting of "Dies irae" in his *Symphonie fantastique*.)

Although these requiems use liturgical texts, most are not suitable for use in the Mass. In particular, those by Berlioz and Verdi are far too theatrical for liturgical use; they are closer to sacred oratorio than to music for a church service. The premiere of Verdi's *Requiem*

requiem
A Mass offered to honor the dead
Dies irae
A section of the Requiem Mass that deals with the day of judgment

took place in the church of San Marco in Milan but was not part of a church service; it was repeated three days later at La Scala, the famous opera house in Milan. Subsequently, it received numerous performances in traditional concert venues rather than churches.

In composing works that use liturgical texts but are not intended for liturgical use, composers such as Berlioz and Verdi were elevating these texts to much the same status as biblical readings. Brahms went well beyond this. For his German requiem, he chose readings from Luther's translation of the Bible from both Old and New Testaments, instead of using liturgical texts. Significantly, none mentioned Christ.

Johannes Brahms

Fast Facts

- *Dates:* 1833–1897

- *Place:* Germany

- *Reasons to remember:* One of the most important and highly regarded German composers of the latter half of the nineteenth century

Johannes Brahms and His Requiem

Brahms seemed destined to compose a large-scale choral work. His first important position included among its responsibilities direction of a choir, and his first position in Vienna was directing the Vienna Singakademie, a concert choir formed in 1858 to perform classic choral literature. And in an enthusiastic article about Brahms, his mentor Robert Schumann had written that he should "direct his magic wand where the massed forces of chorus and orchestra may lend him their power."

Brahms was born and raised in Hamburg, Germany. His mother was a seamstress, his father a versatile musician who played several instruments as a member of symphony orchestras, bands, and popular orchestras. Brahms's first training came as a pianist. His major teacher inculated a love of Bach, Mozart, and Beethoven—an approach customary in our time but still novel in the 1840s. Brahms regularly gave concerts during the first part of his career and premiered both

His major teacher inculated a love of Bach, Mozart, and Beethoven—evidenced by their images adorning the walls of his apartment.

of his piano concertos himself. However, his early professional experiences were almost as varied as his father's: accompanying theatrical performances, teaching, and playing in working-class but respectable taverns. His first important professional experience came with a Hungarian violinist named Remenyi, who introduced him to gypsy music.

These early experiences shaped two complementary sides of his musical personality. The side influenced by popular and folk music is revealed in tuneful, expressive melodies and accessible, invigorating rhythms, such as those heard in his famous *Hungarian Dances*. On the other side, Brahms's formative piano study fueled a deep interest in and reverence for the music of the past. As a choral conductor, he performed music by Renaissance and Baroque masters, and as a music scholar helped prepare modern editions of early music. The more learned passages in his works reflect this passion.

After establishing himself in Germany as an important pianist and composer, Brahms moved to Vienna in 1863, following a successful visit the previous year. He would call the city home for the rest of his life, although he would travel extensively, for business and pleasure. There was a practical reason for Brahms's choice of Vienna. The city remained the most vital musical center in German-speaking Europe. Institutions in that city, including the university, a newly formed conservatory, and the *Gesellschaft der Musikfreunde* (Society of Friends of Music), supported his interest in the music of the past. In turn, Vienna's musical world recognized and appreciated his connection to Vienna's musical heritage. Many leading musicians and commentators view him as the most important successor to Mozart and Beethoven.

It is this sense of continuation of a valued legacy that makes Brahms's choice of Vienna seem symbolic as well as practical. Like Beethoven, Brahms came to Vienna from a part of Germany at some distance from the Austrian capital. Clearly, Beethoven was the dominant musical influence on Brahms; his music both inspired and intimidated Brahms. Brahms's first piano sonata is modeled on Beethoven's biggest piano sonata; like Beethoven, Brahms composed a great deal of chamber music and music for piano; he did not complete his first symphony until 1876, after working on it for fourteen years. Brahms eventually became the third B, after Bach and Beethoven. Their common bonds included not only their German heritage and the initial of their last name but also their predilection for instrumental music and avoidance of opera; like Bach, Brahms never composed an opera, although he composed extensively for voice.

EIN DEUTSCHES REQUIEM

It is this context that we can understand *Ein deutsches Requiem* as a fiercely independent work, for Brahms, for Germans, and for humanity. It is Brahms's biggest work—a typical performance requires about seventy minutes. It is his most distinctive work, unique not only in Brahms's body of work but also in important nineteenth-century music; there is no other piece quite like it.

It is a nationalistic work, although not overtly so. The title *A German Requiem* was Brahms's own: Brahms identified the work in this way in an 1865 letter to Clara Schumann. The "German" apparently refers to the choice of language (German, not Latin) rather than a musical statement representative of the German people. Still, it appeared at a time when nationalistic fervor was on the rise in Germany. Otto von Bismarck became minister-president of Prussia, the largest German state, in 1862; he would lead the push toward German unification and autonomy from the Austro-Hungarian Empire in 1871. The fact that Brahms chose to compose a "German" requiem is certainly in step with the mood in what is now Germany. The German character of the requiem, evident not only in the title but also in the use of texts from Luther's translation of the Bible, suggests Beethoven's influence: it was Beethoven who popularized the use of German instead of Italian in musical scores to indicate tempo, character, and other musical information. Other composers, most notably Schumann and Brahms himself, followed his lead.

"WIE LIEBLICH SIND DEINE WOHNUNGEN"

Brahms composed *Ein deutsches Requiem* in stages. Within months of his mother's passing, he had completed the first, second, and fourth movements. By August 1866, he had completed the third, sixth, and seventh movements. He added the fifth movement in 1868; the premiere performance of the complete work took place in February 1869, four years after the death of his mother. "Wie lieblich sind deine Wohnungen" ("How Lovely Is Thy Dwelling Place"), which sets verses from Psalm 84, is the fourth movement of the work.

Brahms's familiarity with the rich sacred choral music tradition is evident throughout the movement. The rich counterpoint and sweeping phrases reach back to the Renaissance and Baroque choral music that Brahms knew so well and evoke them in a contemporary musical language. His consummate craft is evident throughout the movement. It is particularly evident in the expressive setting of the text. The work requires substantial resources: a large, well-trained choir plus a full symphony orchestra (and two soloists in a few of the other movements).

In the fourth movement, Brahms lets the psalm verses guide both form and content. Each verse has a distinct musical identity. The opening verse, which states the overriding theme of the movement, returns periodically as an affirmation of this central message. The verses that Brahms selected use all three persons: *you*, *me*, and *they*. The musical settings of those directed to the Lord Almighty are serene, with seemingly endless melody flowing from the choir over a rich orchestral accompaniment. The shift to the first person—those still on earth—prompts more agitated musical settings, with more active rhythms and a more contrapuntal texture. And when Brahms composes in the third person by depicting those who have already gone to the other side, he pays tribute to J. S. Bach, who composed to praise God, by briefly evoking the rich polyphonic texture so often heard in the choral movements of his cantatas. Throughout, the largely homophonic choral writing emphasizes that the "my" in the psalms is not an individual but all of humanity "cry[ing] out for the living God."

BRAHMS'S "ANTI-REQUIEM"

Ein deutsches Requiem is a musical work that is a spiritual response to death; for Brahms it was solace for the loss of his beloved mother. In that sense, his titling the work *Requiem* is accurate. But in virtually every other way, it is the opposite of a traditional requiem. By using the vernacular language instead of Latin and by selecting texts that scrupulously avoided not only affiliation with a particular denomination but—even more—mention of Christ, Brahms created a musical document whose message transcends any particular religion and even Christianity. Indeed, Brahms wrote to a colleague that he felt that the work was a "human requiem."

In disassociating his requiem both from its Catholic context and from a specifically Christian orientation, Brahms effectively divorced the spiritual from the religious. What little we can infer from available sources about Brahms's religious beliefs suggests that he followed his own path within Lutheran tradition and that he, like other nineteenth-century German liberals, associated Lutheranism with national identity. The *Requiem* conveys much the same impression; so does its customary venue—the concert hall rather than a church. Moreover, the texts for the seven movements reorient the traditional focus of a Requiem Mass. Their function is to comfort those left behind rather than pray for the soul of the deceased.

Thus, in every respect, *Ein deutsches Requiem* blurs boundaries—between religious and spiritual, sacred and secular, personal and universal. It is a monumental work in which we can hear Brahms, speaking for humanity, address the divine directly. In this respect, it stands as a powerful symbol of the new spirituality of the nineteenth century.

PEOPLE'S MUSIC 10

Protestant Hymn

"Those who sought to praise God through song did so by opening their hearts and lifting their voices."

In 1801, William Little and William Smith published *The Easy Instructor,* which they subtitled "A New Method of Teaching Sacred Harmony." As they made clear in their preface, their goal was to make "a choice collection of Psalm tunes and anthems" available to "those who have not the advantage of an instructor." To this end, they relied on a simplified system of pitch notation, which they had patented in 1798. It involved replacing the tilted-oval notehead of conventional musical notation with one of four shapes: square, oval, triangle, or diamond. The square represented the first or fourth (fa) note of the scale. The oval represented the second or fifth (sol) note. The triangle represented the third or sixth note (la), and a diamond represented the seventh note, which Little and Smith called "mi." The four symbols reduced the pitch choices from seven to one or two widely separated choices.

Did You Know?

The story that "Nearer, My God, to Thee" was played as the Titanic sank is probably apocryphal. The woman who reported it had left on a lifeboat more than an hour beforehand.

The opening of "Amazing Grace," as published in William Walker's *The Southern Harmony and Musical Companion*. Note the three different shapes: square, oval, and triangle. The seventh note of the scale is not used in this excerpt, so there is no diamond.

This process greatly simplified pitch reading for those who were familiar with the system but did not know how to read conventional notation.

The Easy Instructor got off to a slow start in Philadelphia, where it was published. It caught on only after being printed in Albany, New York, in 1805, and sold briskly in less settled parts of the United States. It would go through several printings, the last in 1831. More important, the system of notation that Little and Smith patented, called **shape-note (fasola) notation**, quickly caught on. Other hymnals using shape note notation soon appeared.

LO5 A Conflict in Spiritual Styles

The popularity of shape note tune books provoked a harsh reaction from more musically literate New Englanders. Critics mocked them as music books for the simpleminded and illiterate. They preferred hymns composed or harmonized according to the principles manifested in the music of such eighteenth-century masters as Handel and Haydn, music that they deemed "scientific." They took it upon themselves to "reform" the sacred music of Billings (see People's Music 8) and others, purging it of those qualities that deviated from the common practice of the late eighteenth and early nineteenth centuries. (Ironically, this reform movement deepened America's cultural dependence on Europe even as the nation's political independence grew.)

In 1822, Boston's Handel and Haydn Society published a hymnal assembled by Lowell Mason, a businessman turned hymn composer and music educator. Mason went on to publish numerous volumes of hymns under the auspices of the society, of which he became president in 1827. They were remarkably popular: one sold more than five hundred thousand copies in less than twenty years. The extraordinarily industrious Mason would become America's first influential music educator, introducing music instruction into public school education in Boston and providing teacher training through institutes.

Mason and the society positioned themselves as purveyors of "good taste." Good taste meant appreciation of the European classics and the production of simpler music, such as Mason's hymns and hymn settings, which spoke the same musical language. Both had a profound influence on musical life in Boston and, less directly, throughout the United States.

By contrast, the shape-note tune books and hymnals typically used harmonies that were more reminiscent of Billings's music than that of the European masters. They became most popular in the South, as some of their titles suggest: *Kentucky Harmony*, *Southern Harmony*, and the most widely known, *Sacred Harp*.

The contrast between notational styles—shape note versus conventional notation—was a visible symbol of a pronounced difference in music for congregational worship and its function.

> **shape-note (fasola) notation**
> Simplified system of pitch notation, which involved replacing the tilted-oval notehead of conventional musical notation with one of four shapes: square, oval, triangle, or diamond

The Protestant Hymn in Nineteenth-Century America

The highbrow/lowbrow division in nineteenth-century American musical life surfaced in the pew before it breached the parlor. Throughout the nineteenth century, American Protestant sacred music existed in two largely exclusive worlds: the cultivated urban middle and upper class, located mainly in the Northeast, as opposed to the unsophisticated rural working class in the South and on the frontier. Musically, the differences between highbrow and lowbrow were similar to those heard in popular song: highbrow was a simplified version of established European practice; lowbrow was a rough-edged, homegrown sound that had its deepest roots in the folk music from the British Isles.

The musical differences between the two approaches resulted in part from the differences in the perceived function of music within the worship service. According to the eminent American music historian Richard Crawford, churchgoers who sang the hymns of Mason and his peers felt that the function of music in worship was to edify the congregation. By contrast, those living outside urban areas, especially in the South, used music to praise God.

Those who favored edification approached God through the head. They believed that worship music, like homilies, should inspire moral and intellectual improvement. Good form was important, even paramount; after all, there was a right way to do things. They were able to marshal compelling arguments in support of their positions, and they did so with vigor.

Those who favored edification believed that worship music, like homilies, should inspire moral and intellectual improvement.

Those who sought to praise God through song did so by opening their hearts and lifting their voices. Shape-note singers in Massachusetts do the same today, with the help of their leader.

By contrast, those who sought to praise God through song did so by opening their hearts and lifting their voices. They were not concerned with decorum, refinement, or "correctness." Feeling was more important than form.

EDIFICATION: "NEARER, MY GOD, TO THEE"

This sense of worship music as an edifying experience is evident in "Nearer, My God, to Thee," one of most popular hymns of the century. Sarah Adams, a British poet, wrote the verses; in the United States, they were set to Lowell Mason's melody "Bethany," which he composed in 1856. This is the first stanza:

> Nearer, my God, to thee, nearer to thee!
> E'en though it be a cross that raiseth me,
> Still all my song shall be,
> Nearer, my God, to thee;
> Nearer, my God, to thee, nearer to thee!

The opening stanza is an affirmation of Christ's role in salvation. The sentiment is noble, its expression elevated and impersonal (note the archaic "raiseth"). There is no sense of human fallibility, or even human emotion. That those who sing this hymn are leading upright lives seems taken for granted.

Mason's hymn is very much in step with Adams's verse. It is simple, using only the three basic chords of common practice harmony. It is correct—or, as Mason would have it, "scientific"—with no jarring progressions, no melodic surprises, and a gentle crest in the middle. Each statement of the melody has four short sections, which are further articulated into two short phrases. It seems to exemplify moral as well musical rectitude: Mason is doing the right thing.

 LISTEN UP!

CD 3:16
Adams/Mason, "Nearer, My God, to Thee" (1856)

Takeaway point: Edifying hymn for untroubled souls

Style: Protestant hymn

Form: Strophic

Genre: Nineteenth-century American hymn

Instruments: Generally congregation or church choir with keyboard accompaniment

Context: Music for Protestant worship

This is comfortable music for worshippers who are seemingly comfortable with their station in life and the state of their souls. By contrast, those who praised God through music followed a distinctly different musical path, as we hear in a melded performance of "Amazing Grace."

PRAISE MUSIC: "AMAZING GRACE"

In 1748, John Newton survived a storm at sea while traveling to England on a slave ship. The experience sparked his conversion to Christianity. Although he renounced his libertine lifestyle, he would captain three more slave ships before changing his professional course to become an Anglican priest. Later in life, he became active in the movement to abolish slavery throughout the British Empire. Working with the poet William Cowper, Newton published a book of religious verse in 1779 entitled *Olney Hymns*. Included in the volume were the familiar words of the hymn "Amazing Grace."

The first stanza of "Amazing Grace" sends a quite different message from "Nearer, My God, to Thee."

> *Amazing Grace, how sweet the sound*
> *That saved a wretch like me.*
> *I once was lost but now am found,*
> *Was blind, but now, I see.*

In four short lines, we meet a sinner whose soul has been saved through the intercession of the spirit. The language is direct; the before/after contrasts are powerful. The sense of gratitude for the gift of grace is palpable. It is an intensely personal lyric; for believers, there can be no more powerful message. And it is deeply felt.

Fifty years later, "Amazing Grace" surfaced in hymnals throughout the American South, set to a melody called "New Britain." The source of the melody is unknown. However, musical evidence suggests that it is probably an Anglo-Celtic folk song. The similarities between "Barbara Allen" and "Amazing Grace" are significant. Both make use of the Anglo-American pentatonic scale, contain four phrases of moderate length that create a gentle rise and fall, and move in a gentle rhythm in triple meter.

As published in numerous hymnals during the nineteenth century, including the *Columbian Harmony*, the *Virginia Harmony*, as well as the even more popular *Southern Harmony* (1835) and *The Sacred Harp* (1844), "Amazing Grace" is harmonized. However, the harmony is derived not from the European hymn style heard in the Bach chorale and Haydn's anthem but the brusquer sound of Billings's "Chester." A bass line and a **descant** (a vocal line above the melody) sandwich the melody. The harmonies formed by the three parts are often similar to conventional chords, but the "incorrect" voicings and progressions would have horrified Mason.

In practice, the hymn would have been sung in countless versions, some based on the shape note setting found in the various hymnals and some simply created spontaneously by the congregation. We hear two versions of "Amazing Grace" that exemplify this: a performance of the published setting and an ad hoc version recorded by folk artist Doc Watson around 1960.

descant
a vocal line above the melody

LISTEN UP!

CD 3:17
Newton, "Amazing Grace" (1779)

Takeaway point: Heartfelt hymn and a perennial favorite

Style: Protestant hymn

Form: Strophic

Genre: Sacred Harp–style folk hymn

Instruments: Voices

Context: A popular hymn for praise worship

The battle lines that seemed so sharply drawn in 1822, when Mason first published his hymnal, are considerably more blurred in our time. The emergence of African American worship music—both songs and style—and the incursions of popular culture into sacred music have resulted in widespread exchange among traditions. "Amazing Grace" is typically harmonized more conventionally, and "Nearer, My God, to Thee" is sung by diverse congregations in diverse ways. Indeed, among those who have recorded both hymns are famed gospel singer Mahalia Jackson and Elvis Presley.

CHAPTER 29

Operetta and *Opéra comique*

"New operas in the late nineteenth century had to be not only good but also novel."

In May 1855, the Paris World's Fair (Exposition Universelle) opened on the Champs-Élysées, then as now one of the most famous streets in the world. At the center of the exposition area was the spectacular Palais d'Industrie. Newly anointed Emperor Napoleon III, a champion of industrial progress, was determined to outdo the English: the structure, which is no longer standing, was France's answer to London's Crystal Palace, which dazzled those who attended the enormously successful Great Exhibition of 1851.

On the periphery of the exposition grounds was a small wooden theater, the Folies-Marigny. To capitalize on the huge crowds attending the exposition, Jacques Offenbach (1819–1880) rented the theater and renamed it Théâtre des Bouffes-Parisiens. Offenbach, a German-born virtuoso cellist, conductor at the Comédie-Française, and aspiring composer, had tried without success for several years to get his witty stage works produced at Parisian theaters. With the opening of the fair, he took matters into his own hands. Although the modest dimensions of the theater limited him to one-act works featuring a handful of performers and a small orchestra, his endeavor was successful enough that he resigned his position with the Comédie-Française and continued his productions through the winter at the Salle Choiseul, which became their permanent home the following year.

In 1856, to recruit other composers for his new enterprise, Offenbach announced a composers' competition. As part of the competition guidelines, he supplied a historical guide to *opéra comique*, which he felt had moved far away from its roots. Among the

operetta
Light (not too serious), opera-like form of stage entertainment

winners of the competition was a young composer named Georges Bizet (bee-ZAY). Offenbach's efforts did little to reshape *opéra comique*, as we will discover presently, but it did spawn a new genre, *opéra bouffe*, which took its name from the theater that Offenbach used during the exposition.

Opera lovers are confronted with an array of labels that don't always mean what they seem to mean. *Opéra bouffe* is a cognate of the Italian *opera buffa*, but they are distinct genres; the differences go beyond the language. Similarly, *opéra comique* is a cognate of "comic opera," but there are important *opéras comiques* that lack even a trace of comedy. Distinctions between genres change over time, and they often have more to do with conventions, cultural differences, composers' agendas, and even venue than they do with content. We explore this point in a discussion of *The Pirates of Penzance*, an operetta by Gilbert and Sullivan, and Bizet's *Carmen*, the most famous of all *opéras comiques*.

LO6 Operetta: Gilbert and Sullivan's *The Pirates of Penzance*

As the term implies, **operetta** is a light (not too serious), opera-like form of stage entertainment. Characters in an operetta often escape to a make-believe world—an imaginary kingdom, an exotic locale, a land inhabited by fairies or other supernatural creatures. Operettas may spin out impossibly romantic stories or use the faraway locale as a mask for topical humor. Spoken dialogue replaces recitative, and tuneful melodies and danceable music are common.

Operetta grew out of Offenbach's *opéras bouffes*. They began as one-act productions but were expanded

Characters in an operetta often escape to a make-believe world.

into a full evening's entertainment. Offenbach's music soon gained ardent followings beyond Paris, and composers began adapting the genre to their locale. During the latter part of the nineteenth century, the most notable new operettas came from Vienna, where Johann Strauss, the "Waltz King," moved his music from the dance floor to the stage, and from England, where Gilbert and Sullivan teamed up for a series of surpassingly popular operettas.

GILBERT AND SULLIVAN

Synergy is the coming together of two or more forces to produce an effect greater than the sum of the individual forces. Perhaps the most glorious example of synergy in British musical life was The Beatles, in particular the partnership of John Lennon and Paul McCartney. Not far behind, and certainly far above any other team in nineteenth-century British music, was the collaboration of playwright-librettist W. S. Gilbert (1836–1911) and composer-conductor Arthur Sullivan (1842–1900).

Although they were active in their respective fields before and after their work together, their reputation rests almost entirely on the eleven operettas they produced between 1875 and 1889, among them *H.M.S. Pinafore* (1878), *The Pirates of Penzance* (1879), and *The Mikado* (1885). As with Lennon and McCartney, their success was a creative fusion of quite different temperaments. Gilbert was mercurial, hot-tempered,

devastatingly funny, and far from dazzled by the upper classes. Sullivan was staid, solid, and chummy with those whom Gilbert so often skewered. Not surprisingly, their relationship was, at times, tense; they dissolved their partnership in 1890, although they would reunite later in the decade for two less-than-successful works. Nevertheless, their partnership brought them enormous success and acclaim: Sullivan was knighted for his work in 1883; Gilbert, in 1907.

Operettas typically provided escapist entertainment: frothy plots with the inevitable happy ending; tuneful melodies, some of which the audience hummed as they left the theater; entertaining—even titillating—dance numbers; and high and low comedy. The objective was to entertain, not edify. However, for Gilbert and Sullivan, the lighthearted surface of the story and the accessibility of the music served as a veneer that frequently covered stinging satire of British customs, institutions, and the upper class. In this respect, Gilbert and Sullivan tapped into a long tradition of lampooning the foibles of British society, especially the upper class. We encountered an early instance of it in *The Beggar's Opera;* Gilbert and Sullivan's is far more elaborate, as we hear later.

The plot of *The Pirates of Penzance; or, The Slave of Duty* (Gilbert and Sullivan operettas customarily sported double titles) revolves around two misunderstandings. The first occurs when Frederic is apprenticed by his nursemaid Ruth to a band of pirates; Frederic's father had wanted to apprentice him to a "pilot," not a "pirate," but she misunderstood him. Frederic seemingly comes of age, at which point he resolves to do his duty and capture the very pirates to whom he was apprenticed. Upon leaving them, he has his first encounter with women other than Ruth: a group of young ladies, all the daughters of Major-General Stanley. He quickly becomes enamored of Mabel, one of the daughters.

The second misunderstanding concerns Frederic's age: his plan to arrest the pirates is derailed when Ruth and the Pirate King inform him that he was born on February 29 and has only had five birthdays rather than the twenty-one required in his apprentice contract. Always a slave to duty, Frederic rejoins the pirates, who are, for a second time in the story, ready to kill the major-general and his daughters, until he appeals to their loyalty to Queen Victoria. Then it is discovered that the pirates are in fact noblemen who have gone astray; the pirates and the daughters marry, and all presumably live happily ever after.

In Gilbert and Sullivan operettas, words are preeminent, because they embed social commentary into storytelling. Sullivan's challenge was to create a musical setting that both supported and showcased the words. He was not an innovator; his personal style is based on the musical language from the first part of the nineteenth century, as heard in such music as the comic operas of Rossini, the instrumental music of the early Romantic composer Felix Mendelssohn, military music, Victorian choral music, and parlor songs. However, precisely because this music was familiar, Sullivan was able to parody all of it for dramatic effect. The music sounded original yet evoked the associations of the style or genre that Sullivan parodied.

"I AM THE VERY MODEL OF A MODERN MAJOR-GENERAL"

"I Am the Very Model of a Modern Major-General" occurs early in the operetta and introduces Major-General Stanley. It is a **patter song**, a type of song in which the words pour out in a stream much faster than in conventional song or everyday speech. Patter songs had been injecting humor into comic operas and other musical stage entertainment since the late eighteenth century. Here Gilbert and Sullivan give the patter song a decidedly British spin, through Gilbert's words and Sullivan's blending in overtones of the British military band. It is evident in the marchlike rhythm, the instrumental-style melody, and the prominence of wind instruments in the orchestration. The touch of military music is, of course, dramatically appropriate as well.

I am the very model of a modern Major-General
I've information vegetable, animal, and mineral
I know the kings of England, and I quote the fights historical
From Marathon to Waterloo, in order categorical.

The major-general's song is funny on several levels. The most obvious is the patter: the unnaturally fast delivery of the lyrics is both amusing because it's so unusual and admirable because it's so hard to do. Another level is the use of a patter song to characterize a major-general. Instead of heroic-sounding music, we hear a musical style generally reserved for low comedy: the choice of style brands Major-General Stanley as ineffectual even before we hear the words. The lyrics are similarly funny on at least two levels. The more obvious is the clever wordplay (such as rhyming "a lot o' news" with "hypotenuse"). Beneath that is the implicit message of Stanley's self-aggrandizing portrait: his extensive book knowledge, acquired through a traditional upper-class education, is of virtually no use to him on the battlefield. Gilbert is taking dead aim at the members of the British upper class who bought their military commissions and served as officers without any real military qualifications. It was a perversion of privilege seemingly built into the British class system, which Gilbert was only too eager to lampoon. (A century later, the Sex Pistols would replace Gilbert's scalpel with a sledgehammer: on the occasion of the silver anniversary of the coronation of Queen Elizabeth II, Johnny Rotten would scream "God Save the Queen, the fascist regime" while floating down the Thames on a barge.)

 LISTEN UP!

CD 3:18

Gilbert and Sullivan, "I Am the Very Model of a Modern Major-General," *The Pirates of Penzance* (1879)

Takeaway point: A funny song set up by fast words and pseudo-military music

Style: Light Romantic

Form: Strophic

Genre: Operetta

Instruments: Voices and orchestra

Context: A satirical portrait of an ineffectual military leader, as part of a thinly disguised lampooning of the British upper class

The Gilbert and Sullivan operettas haven't traveled well outside the English-speaking world. Only *The Mikado* has received frequent performances in non-English-speaking countries. The most probable reason for their lack of popularity is the primacy of the

words. The role of the musical setting is to showcase and project the words; in our example, the musical dimension of the humor lies mainly in the effort that the major-general expends delivering the words. Lines like "About binomial theorem I'm teeming with a lot o' news / With many cheerful facts about the square of the hypotenuse" lose much of their humor if one has to ponder them too much.

Sullivan's music may not transcend the words, but it suits them perfectly. The Gilbert and Sullivan operettas have maintained a large, enthusiastic following in the English-speaking world since their premieres in the late nineteenth century.

LO7 *Opéra comique:* Bizet's *Carmen*

Few operas have sparked more controversy than Georges Bizet's *Carmen*. The rumblings started before the premiere, as several morning papers printed letters denouncing the work. Reviews were generally unfavorable, with critics finding fault on grounds both musical and moral. One provided some historical perspective:

> The stage [in general] is given over more and more to women of dubious morals. It is from this class that people like to recruit the heroines of our dramas, our comedies, and now even our comic operas. But once they have sunk to the sewers of society they have to do so again and again; it is from down there that they have to choose their models.

Others found the opera too "Wagnerian" or too "Chinese." Despite the unfavorable press—or perhaps because of it—the opera ran for forty-eight performances at the Opéra Comique, and then was a sensation throughout Europe and in New York.

OPÉRA COMIQUE

One reason that audiences found *Carmen* so scandalous was its venue. The Opéra Comique, the company that presented *opéras comiques*, appealed mainly to a middle-class audience—much like the audience for Broadway musicals a century later. And like the Broadway musical of the 1940s and 1950s, *opéra comique* was a genre that featured spoken dialogue alternating with musical numbers.

Opéra comique is a genre that dates from the early eighteenth century, as we learned in Chapter 22.

Originally, it mixed humorous spoken dialogue with preexisting melodies. In this respect, it was the French counterpart to the British ballad opera: imagine *The Beggar's Opera* in French. By the beginning of the nineteenth century, the dialogue remained, but the music was composed specifically for the opera. Plots traded satire for sentimentality; they embodied middle-class virtues. By midcentury, *opéra comique* was wholesome family entertainment, much like the musicals of Rodgers and Hammerstein.

In composing an opera that was neither funny nor sentimental, Bizet hoped to reform and invigorate *opéra comique*. *Carmen* had the opposite effect; it all but obliterated the genre.

EXOTICISM

While central Europe sought to unify, the major western European powers sought to colonize. In particular, both England and France expanded their colonial empires. With this expansion came an interest in other cultures, which was brought home to many through the numerous exhibitions and expositions that were part of late nineteenth-century life. Partly through this contact, exotic settings appeared in opera with increasing frequency toward the end of the nineteenth century and into the twentieth; Bizet's *Carmen*, which premiered in 1875, was among the first.

The Great Exhibition of London's Crystal Palace amazed attendees with, among other exotic wonders, a replica of a Tunisian bazaar.

Bizet based *Carmen* on a novella of the same name by the French author Prosper Mérimée. Mérimée tapped into the nineteenth-century fascination with the exotic. In both novella and opera, the exotic embraced both person and locale. Carmen is a gypsy, an occasional "next-door stranger" for many Europeans. The story takes place in southern Spain: during the nineteenth century and into the twentieth, the Iberian Peninsula and its cultures were a world apart from the rest of Europe, so they counted as "exotic" realms.

Gypsies. Gypsies, now most often called Roma, have been a largely migratory people. Although today the largest concentration of Roma is found in the Balkan region of Eastern Europe, there are Romany populations all over Europe, the Americas, and Africa. The origins of the Roma people are unknown. Linguistic and genetic evidence suggests that they originally migrated from northern India as early as the eleventh century; the cause of their migration remains a mystery. They made their way to Europe by the fourteenth century, and to western Europe, including Spain, by the fifteenth century.

Throughout their history, Roma have been a closed society. They have migrated without regard to national borders, have a culture with distinctly different values from virtually all the settled peoples with whom they share space, and seem to have little regard for non-Roma. They have worked gainfully in nontraditional fields, such as the circus. As a result, the dominant societies have regarded them as outsiders: they have been blamed for numerous evils, banished, persecuted, and murdered.

Men saw gypsy women as forbidden fruit.

© iStockphoto.com/pidjoe

In the nineteenth century, mainstream European society regarded Roma with a mix of fascination and contempt. It considered them immoral, dishonest, and depraved and positioned them lower than the lowest class, despite their obvious skills in certain areas. At the same time, people were drawn to what they felt was their hot-blooded, licentious nature. Men saw gypsy women as forbidden fruit: in *Carmen*, the wanton

gypsy Carmen seduces Don José, not only severing his relationship with Micaëla, the "girl next door," but also leading him to ruin. For Bizet's audience, the fact that Carmen was a gypsy would have made this course of events all but inevitable.

Spain, an Exotic Part of Europe. For centuries, Spain has been both a part of western Europe and separate from it. In politics and religion, it was a major player for hundreds of years, as evidenced by its vast colonial empire; its marriages with other royal families and dominion over other parts of Europe, such as southern Italy and Sicily; and its staunch support of the Catholic Church—Spain was, after all, home to the Inquisition. However, the prominent place of minority cultures, including Moors, Jews, and Roma, helped produce a culture quite different from that of the rest of Europe. Flamenco music, the most distinctively Spanish musical tradition, has strong roots in gypsy music. Moreover, Spain's relative isolation—the range of mountains known as the Pyrenees forms a natural boundary between France and the Iberian Peninsula that made land travel between the two difficult and treacherous—only increased the perception that Spain was an exotic locale. For Bizet and his audience, the exoticism of the gypsy and of Spain was part of the appeal of *Carmen*.

Georges Bizet

Fast Facts

- *Dates:* 1838–1875
- *Place:* France
- *Reason to remember:* Composer of *Carmen*

© Portrait of Georges Bizet (1838-1875), French composer (litho), Eichhorn Albert (1811-1851) / Private Collection / Roger-Viollet, Paris / The Bridgeman Art Library International

CARMEN

Bizet's masterwork was *Carmen* (1875), his last complete composition and the work that has brought him enduring fame. It was the last of six operas that have survived; none of the others has attracted a fraction of the attention given to *Carmen*. Sadly, Bizet did not live to enjoy the success of Carmen or to compose an even more successful sequel; he died of a heart attack directly after the conclusion of the thirty-third performance in Paris.

This ultra-short plot summary of *Carmen* comes from the writer Jean Henri Dupin. In a remark to

Meilhac, one of the librettists, the morning after the premiere, Dupin disparagingly summarized the plot like this: "A man meets a woman. He finds her pretty. That's the first act. He loves her, she loves him. That's the second act. She doesn't love him anymore. That's the third act. He kills her. That's the fourth!"

The story, which takes place in Seville, a town in the southern part of Spain, revolves around two triangles. One includes Don José, a corporal in the guard; Micaëla, a peasant girl and his hometown sweetheart; and Carmen, a gypsy working in a cigarette factory. Carmen attracts Don José, who soon falls in love with her. Because of her, he does things that turn him from a soldier into an outlaw. In the meantime, Carmen has attracted the interest of Escamillo, a famous toreador. He and Don José compete for Carmen's attention. Carmen ultimately rejects Don José, who murders her in a fit of jealous rage.

Opéra comique, like operetta, alternates spoken dialogue with musical numbers. However, Bizet's decision to compose an *opéra comique* almost certainly had more to do with business than with musical taste: the commission for *Carmen* came from the Opéra Comique (the institution). Throughout the opera, we can hear Bizet straining at the conventions of the genre. The orchestra plays a far more important role than in *The Pirates of Penzance*, and the orchestral writing is more varied. (Indeed, the importance and independence of the orchestra are demonstrated by two orchestral suites extracted from the opera after the composer's death.) In the same vein, Bizet goes well beyond dialogue that is periodically interrupted by tuneful melody. Although there are set numbers, such as the habanera discussed later, there are more extended numbers with recitative, accompanied dialogue, aria, and numerous gradations in between. Bizet also makes use of a bold and prominent "reminiscence" motive, a musical idea introduced early in the opera that returns with telling effect. Bizet introduces the motive that signals Carmen's ultimate fate in the orchestral prelude to the opera. It occurs right after the high-spirited opening; its message

© 'Carmen' by Georges Bizet (1838-75) cover for issue number 81 of 'La Musique pour Tous', 1911 (colour litho), Clerice Brothers, (fl.1908-14) / Private Collection / Archives Charmet / The Bridgeman Art Library International

is unmistakable. The motive returns in the final scene between Carmen and Don José. It brutally interrupts the music associated with the bullfight, which is going on in the background, to signal that Don José has lost control and will kill Carmen.

Bizet's decision to use more complex strategies and make the orchestra more important made dramatic sense: it would have been difficult to convey the intense passions of the leading characters in conventional forms. It is in these qualities that we sense the musical dimensions of Bizet's attempt to reform *opéra comique*.

Carmen is a story of passions, in this case uncontrollable ones. Both Don José and Carmen are doomed: Carmen by choice, and Don José because he cannot help himself. The skillful, often transparent orchestral writing, with a prominent role for woodwind instruments (an approach common in French music); the glorious, memorable melodies and motives; and the occasional touches of musical exoticism—all of these qualities musically support this compelling story. Bizet's miracle is music that is evocative, imaginative, dramatically responsive, and—above all—accessible.

THE HABANERA

There is a karmic completeness to the fact that a Frenchman composed the most famous habanera, because although the **habanera** is most fundamentally an Afro-Cuban dance genre, the French were the catalysts for its creation.

Habanera means "of or related to Havana," the capital city of Cuba. The dance, and the songs built on its distinctive rhythm, acquired its name only after it left Cuba. In Havana, it was known as the contradanza. The **contradanza** (English "country dance", French *contredanse*) came to Cuba with the French colonists who fled Haiti in the wake of the slave insurrection of 1791. By the early nineteenth century, it was among the most popular dances in Cuba.

habanera An Afro-Cuban dance genre

contradanza English "country dance"; French *contredanse*

The orchestras that accompanied the contradanza were typically made up of Afro-Cuban musicians. As they did in other parts of the New World, African-diaspora musicians interpreted this European dance in terms of their musical heritage. As the dance traveled back to Spain, it acquired a name—the habanera—and a distinctive rhythm, which was a European reinterpretation of the rhythm of the contradanza, as performed by black musicians. From Spain it spread throughout Europe. Bizet borrowed the melody for his habanera from a popular song by the Spanish composer Sebastian Iradier, which Bizet mistakenly assumed was a folk song. (When he learned of his error, he acknowledged Iradier in his vocal score.) Iradier had been to Cuba, where he heard and was intrigued by what was called Creole music, and what we now more precisely term Afro-Cuban music.

The pulsating rhythm of the habanera injected a vitality into European concert music via Spanish popular songs, such as the one Bizet inadvertently borrowed from Iradier. In particular, French composers found it irresistible: Bizet, Debussy, and Ravel were among those who used the rhythm to give their music a Spanish tinge. The habanera also spread throughout the Americas. It went to Argentina, where it eventually merged with local music to become the tango, and to Mexico, from where it would enter the United States via New Orleans, and strongly influence both ragtime and early jazz.

"L'amour est un oiseau rebelle"

Carmen's famous habanera, also identified by the first line of the lyric, "L'amour est un oiseau rebelle" ("Love Is a Rebel Bird"), is Carmen's first big number. It comes early in the opera, as she returns from lunch with a group of girls who work with her at the cigarette factory across from the guardroom. She uses the song to solicit admiration from the soldiers, especially Don José, who ignores her.

The habanera is one of a small number of Spanish-flavored numbers in the opera, and arguably the most evocative. By introducing Carmen with what he believed to be a familiar Spanish folk song, Bizet immediately establishes place and social class. And by placing her in Spain as a member of an outsider group, Bizet turns the "Latin lover" legend that we encountered in *Don Giovanni* on its head: the sexual aggressor now is not the male but the female. Carmen's provocative song would have been wildly inappropriate for a noblewoman, or for Micaëla, the innocent peasant girl whom Don

José tosses aside for Carmen, but it matches perfectly the nineteenth-century stereotype of the promiscuous gypsy whose sensuality knows no limits.

Bizet turns the "Latin lover" legend that we encountered in *Don Giovanni* on its head: the sexual aggressor now is not the male but the female.

LISTEN UP!

CD 3:19
Bizet, "L'amour est un oiseau rebelle," *Carmen* (1875)

Takeaway point: Exotic, erotic music for an exotic, erotic leading lady

Style: Romantic

Form: Expanded verse/refrain form

Genre: Opéra comique

Instruments: Soprano and orchestra

Context: Introduction of Carmen through the habanera, giving a strong first impression of her character

The Best of Times, the Worst of Times: The Diversity of Late Nineteenth-Century Opera

As *Carmen* quickly gained a following, it ascended the operatic social ladder. For a Viennese production in 1875—the year of the French premiere—Bizet's friend and fellow composer Ernest Guiraud· converted the spoken dialogue into recitative. It was performed in this manner until the mid-twentieth century, when Bizet's original version was restored.

The sudden upgrade of *Carmen* from *opéra comique* to opera hints at the increasing diversity of opera during the latter part of the nineteenth century. Among the important sources of this diversity were genre and geography. Traditional opera, as exemplified in the music of Verdi, gained company above and below. In the hands of Gilbert and Sullivan, Johann Strauss the Younger, and others, operetta acquired musical sophistication and a sophisticated audience.

Bizet's *Carmen* both popularized *opéra comique* and expanded its range; opera bouffe, best exemplified by the work of Jacques Offenbach, replaced opéra comique as the operetta-like family entertainment. Richard Wagner would take a more high-minded approach; his revolutionary reform of opera would produce a new synthesis of words and music, as we discover in the next chapter.

CHAPTER 30

Opera and Music Drama

"As a group, composers are hard people to like, and the two discussed in this chapter are no exception."

During its 2006–2007 season, the Metropolitan Opera, the most prestigious opera company in North America, devoted half of its twenty-four productions to four operas by Giuseppe Verdi, five by Giacomo Puccini, and four by their Italian contemporaries. There were five other operas in Italian: three by eighteenth-century German-speaking composers (Handel, Gluck, and Mozart) and two by early nineteenth-century Italian composers (Rossini and Bellini). The remaining operas were in other languages: German, French, Czech, Russian, and English. Of the operas in German, only one was by Richard Wagner. The Met's season underscores the fact that virtually since the time of their composition, the Italian operas of Verdi, Puccini, and their contemporaries have formed the heart of the operatic repertoire.

However, the most influential composer of the latter half of the nineteenth century was the German opera composer Richard Wagner. Compared to Verdi, Wagner has had a more modest impact on the operatic world.

Did You Know?

The best-selling classical album of all time is the first Three Tenors recording: *Carreras—Domingo—Pavarotti: The Three Tenors in Concert*, recorded live in Rome in 1990.

German opera after Wagner was not as popular as Italian opera and did not fully reflect Wagner's high-minded vision. Yet no other late nineteenth-century composer exerted more influence on the direction of classical music during his lifetime or played a greater role in shaping the dominant musical directions of the first half of the twentieth century.

We explore this paradoxical state of affairs in this brief introduction to late nineteenth-century opera.

LO8 Giuseppe Verdi and the Resurgence of Italian Opera

Opera is an Italian art. It began in Italy, and Italian has been its dominant language from the outset. During the seventeenth and eighteenth centuries, Italian composers produced a prodigious number of operas, and some of these composers, such as Alessandro Scarlatti, Leonardo Vinci, and Giovanni Pergolesi, were particularly influential. But you probably haven't heard of them because very little of their music is performed today, and almost none of it is standard operatic repertoire. Only in the early nineteenth century did Italian composers begin to compose operas that became standard fare.

The first such composer was Gioachino Rossini (1792–1868), who remains well known for his comic operas, most notably *Il barbiere di Siviglia (The Barber of Seville)*, a cousin of Mozart's *The Marriage of Figaro*. (Both operas were based on plays by the French playwright Beaumarchais.) The next generation of Italian opera composers included Vincenzo Bellini and Gaetano Donizetti. All three composers wrote arias in *bel canto* style. *Bel canto*, which means "beautiful singing" in Italian, prizes evenness of sound, vocal agility, and sweetness. These operas have remained in the repertoire mainly because they are vehicles for glorious singing and, in the case of Rossini's, their wit. It was Giuseppe Verdi who would inject opera with a dose of reality.

GIUSEPPE VERDI

Just as it is possible to imagine young, small-town guitarists who dream of playing to adoring fans in overflowing arenas, so is it possible to imagine a young Giuseppe Verdi dreaming of succeeding Rossini as Italy's greatest composer. In nineteenth-century Italy, being a great composer meant composing great opera: all of the important composers in this time and place focused on and are remembered for opera. Verdi succeeded, perhaps beyond his wildest dreams. By the end of his career, he was a national hero, more honored than Rossini or any other composer had been.

For Americans, the name Giuseppe Verdi rolls off the tongue impressively. Translated into English, however, it sounds far more humble: Joseph Green. Verdi's early circumstances were comparably humble; he was the son of a village innkeeper. It was a point of pride for

him. In 1863, when he was an internationally known celebrity and a national hero, he wrote, "I was, am and always will be a peasant from Roncole."

After early training in Busetto, a nearby town, and an apprenticeship with a Milanese opera composer, Verdi got his first opera performed at the famed opera house La Scala in 1839. It led to three more commissions, one of which (*Nabucco*, 1842) established him as Italy's most important composer. For the next three decades, he would be the preeminent opera composer in Europe. The most important phase of his career began with the composition of *Rigoletto* in 1851, followed by *Il trovatore* (produced early in 1853) and *La traviata*. These and the operas that he composed after them are his most frequently performed works. Verdi's final operas, *Otello* (1887) and *Falstaff* (1893), are adapted from plays by Shakespeare; many consider them to be his masterworks.

© Rob Moore/Lebrecht Music & Arts

VERDI AND REALISM

In his mature operas, Verdi transformed Italian grand opera from a vehicle for gorgeous singing into true musical drama by making it more real. Verdi's reforms addressed four crucial aspects of opera: the stories, the musical flow, the use of the orchestra, and the singers.

More Realistic Plots. More than any other composer, Verdi brought opera into the present. In several of his mature operas, including *La traviata*, plots are drawn from contemporary fiction rather than Classical myths and history, and all of them portray characters with real personality and passion. Through them,

Giuseppe Verdi

Fast Facts

- *Dates:* 1813–1901
- *Place:* Italy
- *Reasons to remember:* Transformed opera in Europe, Italian opera in particular, with a new focus on realistic characters with real, deep feelings

© Portrait of Giuseppe Verdi (1813-1901) (crayon on paper), Boldini, Giovanni (1842-1931) / Private Collection / The Bridgeman Art Library International

audiences encountered love and lust, life and death, hate and revenge, honor and dishonor. They empathized with characters such as Violetta, Alfredo, and Giorgio (the principals in *La traviata*) partly because both the characters and their situations were believable and part of the audience's immediate experience.

Flow and Form. However, it is the music that makes opera work, and it is in the music that Verdi's genius comes to the fore. Verdi's operas overflow with gorgeous melodies that begin simply enough for an audience to leave singing snippets of them yet flower into grand gestures that convey deep emotions and enable great singers to showcase their voices.

> *Verdi's operas overflow with gorgeous melodies that begin simply enough for an audience to leave singing snippets of them yet flower into grand gestures that convey deep emotions.*

But Verdi's achievement went well beyond melody. One magical aspect of Verdi's art was his ability to paint emotions and moods with bold musical strokes and to dovetail one musical moment into the next, to highlight the events and emotions taking place onstage. A key element in Verdi's ability to shift emotions so dramatically without losing continuity was his blurring of formal boundaries. He achieved this mainly by making the distinction between recitative and aria less pronounced and by reshaping the formal conventions of the aria to accommodate the dramatic requirements of the scene.

Verdi all but abandoned the rigid alternation between recitative and aria. Arias and duets are discrete enough to stand alone, yet, almost imperceptibly, they emerge from and merge into the music that surrounds them. Verdi's beautiful melodies become moments of emotional expansion and intensification, but they do not disrupt the dramatic momentum of the scene. With Verdi, the stop-and-start rhythm of eighteenth-century opera becomes an ebb and flow.

Verdi and the Orchestra. For Verdi, the orchestra is the ideal complement to the voice: the voices are the emotional focus of the opera; the orchestra is both supporter (behind the singers) and commentator (when they are not singing). Verdi had the ability to change the atmosphere quickly and decisively. As we listen to Verdi's music, we may have to consult the synopsis or the supertitles to learn what events caused the shift in mood, but we have no trouble recognizing that the mood has shifted, and we usually have a pretty good idea what the new mood is. The orchestra is most responsible for these shifts; they take place in the interludes between vocal statements and in the character of the accompaniments. Verdi masterfully exploited the capabilities of the orchestra to enhance and extend the message conveyed in words and melody.

Verdi and His Singers. In writing for the voice, Verdi traded grace for drama. He forsook the flowery, light-voiced style demanded in *bel canto* arias. His vocal writing demanded power and expressive range rather than agility, for both men and women.

In particular, both Verdi and Wagner spearheaded a movement to inject masculinity into male vocal roles. In the first part of the eighteenth century, castrati played many of the lead male roles: in the original productions of Handel's *Giulio Cesare*, Julius Caesar was a castrato. The practice died out toward the end of the century; Mozart's Don Giovanni is a baritone. Most glamorous roles in early nineteenth-century opera belonged to sopranos, who had the vocal agility to sing elaborately ornamented arias. Wagner deemed similar vocal display by men as "unmanly, weak, and lackluster." He and Verdi helped give the leading male roles a more masculine character by requiring more sound and stamina and less ornamentation in tenor roles—Wagner's *Heldentenor* (heroic tenor) and Verdi's *tenore robusto* (robust tenor). Others achieved a similar result by giving lead roles to baritones: Boris Godunov, the central figure in Mussorgsky's opera of the same name, *Boris Godunov* (1874), is a baritone.

Thus, in the course of a century and a half, the customary range of the leading male operatic roles dropped from unnaturally high (castration left the castrato's voice in the vocal range of a woman's), to high through the use of falsetto, to a midrange much closer to that of the normal male voice. As a result, the main male characters were more believable vocally as well as dramatically.

Taken together, these changes resulted in opera that was dramatically more compelling because it was more musically powerful. We hear and see them in an extended scene from Verdi's *La traviata* (which translates roughly as "the fallen woman").

LA TRAVIATA

It is a safe bet that Verdi never put himself under greater pressure than he did during the composition of *La traviata*. The premiere of the opera took place on March 6, 1853. Although he had agreed to compose an opera for the Venetian Carnival season (the period immediately preceding Lent) the previous April, he didn't settle on a subject for the opera until November. He and his librettist decided to base the opera on *La Dame aux camélias (The Lady of the Camellias),* a novel by French author Alexandre Dumas the Younger, which he had adapted into a play early in 1852. Apparently, Verdi did not begin composing in earnest until early in 1853. The premiere went on as scheduled but was not successful. Verdi subsequently revised it and engaged different singers; a production mounted the following year was an unqualified success.

The heroine of *La traviata*, Violetta Valery, is a courtesan, an upper-class call girl, dying of tuberculosis. At the beginning of the opera she flits about, living for the moment, perhaps because she is aware that she has little time to live, then dies within a year. At a party

For Dumas, art mirrored life in *The Lady of the Camellias*. Dumas's fictional character Marguerite was based on his real-life lover, Marie Duplessis, a courtesan who died at twenty-three from tuberculosis.

to celebrate her release from the hospital, she encounters Alfredo Germont, who has admired her from afar. Moved by his declaration of love, she falls in love with him and resolves to abandon her former loose lifestyle. They set up house in her country villa. However, their scandalous affair has jeopardized the wedding of Alfredo's sister, so Alfredo's father, Giorgio, visits Violetta while Alfredo is away, to plead with her to renounce Alfredo and preserve the family's honor. She reluctantly but honorably agrees, out of love for Alfredo, and promises Giorgio that she will not reveal the reason for severing their relationship. She pretends to love another, which sends Alfredo into a jealous rage. Later, he discovers the truth and comes to her, only to find her on her deathbed. They declare their love for each other. This momentarily invigorates her, but almost immediately she relapses and dies.

"DITE ALLA GIOVINE"

"Dite alla giovine" (roughly, "Say to this child of thine") is the latter half of the pivotal scene in the opera, the moment when Giorgio Germont comes to Violetta's country estate while Alfredo is absent, to ask her to terminate her relationship with Alfredo for the sake of his family's honor. At first their confrontation is testy, because Giorgio presumes that Violetta is a gold digger as well as a courtesan. But he quickly forms a much more positive impression of her after she responds to his rather brusque introduction and shows him papers that establish that she is selling off her possessions to support Alfredo. He tells her that she must give up Alfredo. After some discussion, she agrees.

This extended excerpt includes three discrete movements, which flow seamlessly from one to the next. In it, we can hear how Verdi modified existing operatic conventions to improve musical flow and dramatic credibility. "Dite alla giovine" is a cleverly disguised da capo aria, with Violetta singing the A section, Giorgio singing the B section, and the two of them singing the reprise of the A section, which Verdi extends by recalling fragments of Giorgio's B section. Through these changes, the aria is no longer dramatically static; instead, we see and hear Violetta and Germont grow closer. Accompanied recitative follows smoothly as the two continue their planning, momentarily retreating from the emotional peak of the aria. The orchestra takes over by abruptly creating a suspenseful mood. This leads to the final movement in the scene, a more active aria that contrasts with the more lyrical "Dite alla giovine." The slow/fast aria sequence was another convention of

Italian opera. As before, Verdi modifies it to match the dramatic events—underscoring the growing accord between Violetta and Giorgio and the enormous sacrifice required of her to achieve it. At the beginning of the scene, Giorgio considers her contemptible because of her profession and what he believes her character to be. By the end of it, he has nothing but admiration for her. Through his skillful and innovative handling of form and vivid use of the orchestra, Verdi makes the transformation a continuous process.

LISTEN UP!

CD 3:20–24
Verdi ,"Dite alla giovine" and "Morrò! Morrò!" *La traviata* (1853)

Takeaway point: Glorious music that softens an old man's hard heart

Style: Romantic

Form: Modified da capo aria; recitative; through-composed

Genre: Italian opera

Instruments: Solo voices and orchestra

Context: Giorgio Germont begins the scene with nothing but contempt for Violetta; by the end, he has nothing but admiration for her.

VERDI'S LEGACY

Verdi's considerable compositional art helped underscore deep feeling by credible characters. Violetta may not have been most audience members' next-door neighbor, but she and her story were believable in a way that the stories of Orfeo and Dido (who never lived), Cleopatra (who lived long ago and far away), and Don Juan (who is damned through the intervention of the supernatural) are not. *La traviata* is powerful in part because it is so personal: Violetta's transformation through love from a capricious courtesan into a woman of honor has resonated with audiences from Verdi's time to ours because it is a timeless story. That she dies from tuberculosis, a leading cause of death in the nineteenth century, only makes the story more poignant.

Verdi worked within a musical tradition—Romanticism—that encouraged grand gestures and sumptuous sounds; within this tradition, Verdi became a master of conveying even the most emotionally charged moments.

The salient features of his style—glorious melodies, evocative orchestral writing, dramatic pacing, and flexibility of form—serve to project deep feelings on a grand scale.

Verdi's mature works from the 1850s and 1860s transformed opera in Europe, Italian opera in particular. It became the new standard against which other operas would be measured, and its focus on realistic characters with real feelings inspired the next generation of Italian opera composers to follow the same path. Some of them adapted *verismo* (realism), an Italian literary movement, to opera: the libretti often portrayed sordid, violent stories. Verdi's most important successor was Giacomo Puccini (1858–1924), who, like Verdi, reshaped the conventions of his time into a personal idiom. Puccini's death brought to an end an era spanning over a century in which Verdi and his countrymen created the heart of the standard operatic repertory.

Verdi worked within opera conventions, modifying them to make them more dramatically effective. Richard Wagner, his German counterpart, followed a far more radical path, which ultimately led him to music that was not really opera in the conventional sense but something much grander.

verismo (realism)
Nineteenth-century Italian literary movement adapted to opera; sordid, violent stories often portrayed in the libretti

LO9 Richard Wagner and Music Drama

The 1800s were a century-long quest for bigness. In both North America and Europe, a striving for and fascination with size played out in every arena. Napoleon set the tone for the century as he sought to dominate all of Europe. After his defeat, those countries that were capable vigorously expanded their colonial empires: the British boasted that the sun never set on the British Empire. In the United States, a transcontinental railway was completed in 1869; it linked a country that had spent the preceding decades expanding westward to the Pacific. The first skyscrapers appeared in the 1880s in the United States and then Europe. Around the same time, the Rockefellers, the Vanderbilts, and other enormously wealthy capitalists began building grand mansions in Newport, Rhode Island, and along New York's Fifth Avenue during the Gilded Age, a period that extended from the end of the Civil War to the turn of the twentieth century.

With his expansion of the symphony and the symphony orchestra required to play it, Beethoven had set the same tone in the musical world. But the man who perhaps best exemplified nineteenth-century bigness in thought, word, and deed was Richard Wagner. Wagner had one of the truly colossal egos in recorded history: no other musician thought so highly of his own music that he spent much of his career working to get a theater built in an out-of-the-way town so that audiences could travel, with some difficulty, to experience his music exactly as he wanted it presented. In his theoretical writings, he set out to change opera—the grandest of all genres—so radically that it would become something completely new, even as it echoed the Germanic mythical past. And his fourteen-hour operatic *Ring* cycle, *Der Ring des Nibelungen (The Ring of the Nibelungen),* extended Beethoven's expansion of musical form and resources on the grandest possible scale.

Richard Wagner

Fast Facts

- *Dates:* 1813-1883

- *Place:* Germany

- *Reasons to remember:*
  The creator of music dramas and the most influential musician of the latter half of the nineteenth century

RICHARD WAGNER

For those curious about the connection between formative experiences and works of art, the life of Richard Wagner offers a treasure trove of material ripe for speculation. Wagner was born into a humble family in Leipzig; his presumed father was a clerk, who died within a year of Wagner's birth. Even before his death, however, Wagner's mother had moved in with an artist/playwright/actor named Ludwig Geyer, who was probably Wagner's biological father. Young Richard received relatively little formal musical training, and in his reminiscences he downplayed even that, seeking to portray himself as an untutored genius.

He was a true intellectual. He read widely, wrote extensively, and was well acquainted with many of the important ideas of his time. In his writings, he espoused the most high-minded and idealistic values: the nobility of art uncorrupted by commerce and the purity of the soul of the German people. But if you were a man with an attractive wife, you were better off admiring him from afar. He had numerous affairs, including at least two with partners of his supporters and benefactors. The most egregious was that he had two children with his second wife, Cosima, while she was still married to Hans von Bülow, the man who had conducted the premieres of two of his operas. And you wouldn't want to lend him money if you expected to get paid back; he repeatedly accumulated debts that he was unable to repay.

Wagner's almost obsessive preoccupation with being German—he considered himself to be the most German of men and propounded the notion of a German Volk, or people—might be linked to his own uncertain roots, as well as the ideas of radical thinkers like Karl Marx and the nationalistic fervor that would soon lead to German unification. His numerous extramarital affairs could also be attributed to his uncertain paternity. His grand lifestyle, often without the means to support it, may have grown out of his humble circumstances growing up.

As a group, composers are hard people to like. Handel reportedly had a devastatingly sharp tongue; Beethoven was, on occasion, boorish; Brahms was often irascible and brusque; Verdi was stubborn and difficult to deal with. Much of this arises from an almost obligatory need to focus on their art. But Wagner would seem to be in a league of his own, not only because of the sordid episodes in his personal life but also because of his persistent and especially virulent anti-Semitism, which surfaced after he had sought and received aid from the Jewish opera composer Giacomo Meyerbeer during his time in Paris. His anti-Semitic writings and calls for racial purity have tarnished his reputation, particularly since the rise and fall of the Third Reich.

There is no major composer with a more conflicted legacy than Wagner. This is especially unfortunate, because he was unquestionably the most influential musician of the latter part of the nineteenth century. His innovations set German/Viennese music on its future path—indeed, classical music is still grappling with his legacy—and his musical achievements were monumental.

MUSIC DRAMA

In keeping with his strong literary inclinations—he wrote the librettos for his works—Wagner identified his later works variously as "drama," "dramas of the future," and "stage festival play," as well as opera. Commentators typically refer to the late works, and especially the *Ring* cycle, as **music dramas**, to distinguish them from more conventional operas. Among the musical features that distinguish his later works from conventional opera are what might be called "endless melody," the use of leitmotifs, and the expansion of the orchestra and its role.

Endless Melody. In Wagner's particular marriage of verse, voice, and orchestra, endless melody replaces the start/stop rhythm of recitative and aria, or even the ebb and flow heard in Verdi. It was important to him that the text be comprehensible, so he set his texts syllabically. The vocal line amplifies the accentuation and inflection of the text; the elaborate melismatic writing heard in more conventional opera is absent.

What makes the melody truly endless is the absence of typical melodic punctuation. In opera, as in so much other vocal music, we are accustomed to hearing regular phrases punctuated by cadences. Wagner's alternative was to string together a series of melodic ideas, some sung and some played, which respond directly to the text. Their function is to amplify the message of the text; as the music unfolds, there is a constant shifting from one idea to the next, without the sense of articulation or conclusion that cadences provide.

This was a truly radical departure from conventional practice. There are no stand-alone arias in the *Ring* cycle, or even larger self-contained sections that can be easily extracted. Instead of letting musical conventions—regular phrases, cadences, melodic repetition, and simple variation—dictate the flow of the text, Wagner allows the text to shape the music. His approach presented a challenge both for the audience, because the familiar musical signals are absent, and for Wagner, to find a means of holding these sprawling music dramas together and shaping them into a coherent whole. His solution was the leitmotif.

The Leitmotif. In opera, the idea of using a theme to recall a character, mood, or event dates back to the late eighteenth century; such themes are called **reminiscence motives**. Typically, a reminiscence motive was a literal repetition of a melodic idea heard earlier in an opera. Wagner transformed this procedure, usually an isolated event, into a key, recurring element of his compositional approach. He saturated his operas with motives, which were assigned to a character, object, emotion, event, or anything else that needed signifying. They were subsequently altered or developed according to the dramatic demands of the passage. Contemporaries

who studied his music called these motives **leitmotifs**. The German word is *Leitmotiv(en)*; its usual English translation is "leading motive."

Leitmotifs occur in both vocal and orchestral lines; indeed, they appear more frequently in the orchestral parts. They often appear in the spotlight, at the beginnings of new sections, where the singers have dropped out and the orchestra takes over, when a singer reenters, and at climactic moments. They range in length from a few notes to a short phrase. Typically, Wagner tries to invest leitmotifs with something of the character of whatever they symbolize. In this sense, the term *leitmotif*, with its strictly melodic implications, is somewhat misleading, especially in reference to instrumental statements, because the choice of instrument or register (high or low) often does more to convey the expressive message than the melodic shape of the motive.

> *Leitmotifs are the glue that holds Wagner's music dramas together.*

Leitmotifs are the glue that holds Wagner's music dramas together. Collectively, they form a dense network of connections that replace conventional methods of outlining and unifying a piece. In effect, they were Wagner's effective method for reconciling the conflicting demands of words and music. Repetition is not common in literature; it is customary in music. Bringing them into balance has challenged even the greatest composers. Opera initially privileged words, as we heard in the excerpt from Monteverdi's *Orfeo*. By contrast, the da capo aria swings the pendulum to the other extreme, in which music is dominant. With leitmotifs, Wagner can allow the narrative to move forward while still supplying the repetition that helps embed the music in the ear of the audience.

music drama
Term for Wagner's later works that distinguishes them from more conventional operas, encompassing such traits as "endless melody," the use of leitmotifs, and expansion of the orchestra and its role

reminiscence motive
Theme used to recall a character, mood, or event

leitmotif Motive or theme assigned to a character, object, emotion, or event in a Wagnerian music drama

Symphonic Opera. The high concentration of leitmotifs in the orchestra highlights another distinctive feature of Wagner's music dramas: the orchestra plays a much more significant role than in other operatic genres. We might summarize the difference this way: In the works of composers like Verdi, the orchestra supports the voices through accompaniment, changing moods, or commentary. In Wagner, voices and orchestra blend together into a unified whole. Singers are first among equals, but there is not the clear separation between melody and accompaniment that is the rule in other genres. Indeed, Wagner's orchestral writing is often more memorable than his vocal writing. We can sense that the merging of voice and instruments was Wagner's intent from the design of the Festspielhaus, the theater in Bayreuth that he had built to his specifications for the production of his works: the orchestra pit has a hood that directs the sound back to the stage, where it can merge with the voices before going out to the audience.

DIE WALKÜRE

We hear all of these features of Wagner's music in an excerpt from Act 1 of *Die Walküre (The Valkyrie)*, the second of the four "stage-festival plays" that make up Wagner's *Der Ring des Nibelungen*. As such, it is an episode in a much longer story, culled from medieval Norse, German, and Icelandic sagas. The story develops a timeless theme: the conflict between power and greed, which corrupt, and love, which redeems.

The Valkyries of the title are nine of the chief god Wotan's immortal daughters, who bring slain heroes to Valhalla, the palatial home of the gods, where they are returned to life in order to guard the castle. Wotan's two mortal children, Siegmund and Sieglinde, twins separated shortly after birth and the central characters in *Die Walküre*, appear in this excerpt. As *Die Walküre* begins, Siegmund and Sieglinde have come of age. At the end of the first act, they discover their kinship, which only

intensifies their desire for each other. As the act ends, they come together to conceive Siegfried, the hero of the third episode in the *Ring*.

> *No other musician thought so highly of his own music that he spent much of his career working to get a theater built in an out-of-the-way town so that audiences could travel, with some difficulty, to experience his music exactly as he wanted it presented.*

In our excerpt, the vocal lines are an intensified means of expressing the text. They cannot stand alone as independent musical statements. There are striking musical gestures, but these are not developed into phrases punctuated by cadences. Instead, the vocal line responds directly to the narrative.

Wagner surrounds the voices with a lavish orchestral setting that plays a far more prominent role than is customary in opera. The orchestra commands much of the melodic material and the majority of the leitmotifs. Some of the melodic material is shared with the singers, and some of it weaves around the vocal line, sustaining the emotion while the singer reveals more of the narrative. The frequent and sudden shifts in the musical flow and the periodic appearance of the leitmotifs dramatize and give depth to the text.

🔊 LISTEN UP!

CD 3:25–29
Wagner, Act 1 conclusion, *Die Walküre* (1870)

Takeaway point: Rich, sensuous music for a sensual couple

Style: Late Romantic

Form: Through-composed

Genre: Wagnerian music drama

Instruments: Solo voices and large orchestra with expanded brass section

Context: A climactic scene in a long saga

The "Music of the Future" and the Future of Music

In 1849, Wagner published an extended essay entitled *Das Kunstwerk der Zukunft (The Artwork of the Future)*. It was the first of several writings on this topic. Although music did not evolve as he had projected, his music would chart the dominant evolutionary path for the late nineteenth century, one that would continue well into the twentieth.

Wagner challenged basic assumptions not only about opera but also about music in general. It was an attack on two fronts: the elements of music and the underlying structure. In Wagner's music, the familiar points of orientation—sound, melody, and rhythm—are less obvious than in most of the music that we have encountered to this point. There are striking sounds and melodic ideas (the leitmotifs), but they repeat only as demanded by the text rather than recur regularly. Moreover, timekeeping is more supple and less obvious; the orchestra typically avoids marking the beat with a simple, easily discernible pattern.

Wagner also avoids the conventional harmonic and rhythmic procedures that outline the structure of a composition at all levels, from the phrase to the work as a whole. Regular phrases and cadences to separate them are exceptional. There are in our excerpt no repetition of sections and none of the other cues that normally help listeners grasp the structure of the work. The only decisive cadence comes at the very end of the act.

Wagner's approach represents an attack on the very foundations of musical discourse as it was practiced in the latter half of the nineteenth century. For the better part of two centuries, common practice harmony had provided the structural foundation of musical composition. Wagner uses many familiar chords, but they are often arranged in patterns that deliberately avoid the cadential progressions that articulate the form of a work. This loosening of the rules in the service of the grandest possible gestures would eventually lead to the abandonment of tonality altogether in some works of the twentieth century.

Verdi and Wagner

The two excerpts in this chapter clarify important differences between Verdi and Wagner. Both overhauled the operatic traditions that they inherited. However,

Siegmund and Sieglinde rediscover each other.

Verdi worked within these traditions. He adapted the prevailing conventions, giving the orchestra a more substantial role, composing vocal lines that emphasized expression over display, blurring the boundaries between numbers to improve the dramatic flow, and delineating character and mood much more sharply as a result. Verdi's changes were akin to a thorough and modernizing remodeling of an existing structure.

By contrast, Wagner essentially tore down the structure and built something quite different in its place. His integration of drama and music was a thorough reconception of how the two should be merged. In hindsight, it would appear that successful works of this type required Wagner's singular genius. Wagner's strategy of responding in music to the narrative on a moment-to-moment basis would find a more substantial following among film composers, where both words and image tell the story, and musical continuity and coherence are not as much an issue.

The Stratification of Musical Life

The music of Wagner and the rapid growth of popular music for home use and onstage led to the stratification of musical life in the latter part of the nineteenth century. In effect, "mainstream" classical music, as represented by such music as the operas of Verdi and Puccini and the orchestral works of Brahms, Tchaikovsky, and Dvořák, became a middle layer in the professional musical world. Wagner's music and the culture that supported it formed the topmost layer; church hymns, band and dance music, the sea of popular songs, and musical entertainment that made use of these genres formed the lower layers.

Even at midcentury, there was a continuum between "classical" and socially acceptable "popular" music. For example, many of Schubert's songs were popular in Europe and North America; simplified versions and piano arrangements of opera arias sold well; Mason's hymns were based on "scientific" principles; dances like the waltz appeared both as music for dancing and as more sophisticated music for listening. Moreover, most of these genres used the same musical language—certainly in widely varying degrees of sophistication, but still with the same foundation.

Musically the stratification occurred because much of the popular music retained a simplified version of the musical language of the early nineteenth century, whereas classical music continued to evolve away from this comfortable common language, and Wagner outright filed for divorce from it. As a result, there emerged a discontinuity between the most elite music and the more mundane middle-class music: Wagner is difficult to dumb down—and trim down—so his music reached larger audiences mainly through short excerpts, such as the famous "Ride of the Valkyries" (from the third act of *Die Walküre)* and performances of the overtures and preludes to the operas. And around the time of Wagner's death, music publishers in the United States began focusing their offerings on songs with (hoped for) popular appeal. This was the beginning of what came to be known as Tin Pan Alley.

These musical changes precipitated realignment within the cultural world. In the eighteenth and early nineteenth centuries, economic (rich versus modest) and social (aristocracy versus commoners) standing influenced musical choices more than strictly musical considerations. However, during the latter part of the nineteenth century, an artistic elite of intellectuals emerged. They were a select group—a minority within a minority—and a prestigious, if not always a financially comfortable one.

By imagining, then creating, a futuristic music, Wagner played a pivotal role in creating this artistic elite. In making explicit in his writings what was implicit in Beethoven's music, he liberated high-minded composers from catering to the marketplace or to the patrons who supported the institutions that provided performance opportunities. Composers could follow their muse wherever it led them, even if it meant (at least in their minds) that their music would be understood fully only by subsequent generations. For some of them, "art for art's sake" was more important than a full stomach.

Moreover, Wagner's music makes musical communication a two-way commitment between musicians and audience. To fully appreciate his operas, listeners needed to know not only the German language and the plot but also the significance of the numerous leitmotifs, which become apparent only with study and repeated hearing—a formidable challenge in the days before recordings. Beginning around the turn of the twentieth century, the most avant-garde composers would transfer the difficult burden of understanding their music from themselves to their audience.

As a result of these developments—the further evolution of classical music, the emergence of a forward-looking mentality and an artistic elite to nurture it, and the growth of a branch of the music industry that catered to mass taste—the musical world in Europe and North America was far more stratified in 1900 than it was in 1850. This trend would continue through much of the twentieth century, as we discover in subsequent chapters.

{ Speak Up! }

"I think the way subject matter is presented really straightens out the brain and it was come a part of... Compared to other books I have used in the past, this book is more helpful and it makes reading more fun and interesting."

Daniel Cespedes, student, Queensborough Community College

MUSIC was built on a simple principle: to create a new teaching and learning solution that reflects the way today's faculty teach and the way you learn.

Through conversations, focus groups, surveys, and interviews, we collected data that drove the creation of the version of MUSIC that you are using today. But it doesn't stop there—in order to make MUSIC an even better learning experience, we'd like you to SPEAK UP and tell us how it worked for you. What did you like about it? What would you change? Are there additional ideas you have that would help us build better tools for next semester's music appreciation students?

Speak Up! Go to
www.cengagebrain.com

UNIT 16
ROMANTIC INSTRUMENTAL MUSIC

Learning Outcomes

After reading this unit, you will be able to do the following:

LO1 Explain how the piano became the most common vehicle for the first generation of star soloists during the nineteenth century.

LO2 Describe the conservative approach of early Romantic piano composers Robert and Clara Schumann, and Felix and Fanny Mendelssohn.

LO3 Contrast the conservative approach with the more progressive approach of Paris-based piano composers Frédéric Chopin and Franz Liszt.

LO4 Understand Hector Berlioz's transformation of the orchestra through an exploration of his *Symphonie fantastique*.

LO5 Through an examination of one of Brahms's symphonies, describe how the Romantic symphony expanded on the tradition of Haydn, Mozart, and Beethoven.

LO6 Encounter the more technically difficult, soloist-dominated concerto of the nineteenth century through a movement from Tchaikovsky's violin concerto.

LO7 Grasp the changing role of dance and dance music in the nineteenth century.

LO8 Recognize the conscious nationalism exemplified by Dvořák's music as an important trend in European cultural life during the latter half of the nineteenth century.

IN THIS UNIT, we consider Romantic instrumental music for piano and for orchestra. The piano music underscores the instrument's central role in musical life; the orchestral music provides samples of repertoire for that most prestigious instrumental ensemble. Collectively the works exemplify key themes of the era: newfound reverence for the past, fascination with bigness, the quest for individuality, and a new aesthetic.

CHAPTER 31

Early Romantic Piano Music

"In the 1830s, the piano became the most common vehicle for the first generation of star soloists."

Clara and Robert Schumann, classical music's most famous married couple, had a complex relationship that bore much fruit but ended much too soon—about two months before their sixteenth wedding anniversary. They enjoyed an artistic communion unique in the history of Western music: shared diaries and musical explorations, compositions undertaken together and inspired by each other, and seemingly unreserved support for each other's work. But throughout their relationship, from the beginning of their courtship through Robert's difficult last years, they faced enormous obstacles, from without and within.

Robert Schumann was almost ten years older than Clara. The son of a publisher and bookseller, he grew up with twin passions in literature and music. In 1828, he went to the university in Leipzig, ostensibly to study law, a discipline that had no appeal for him and to which he devoted almost no effort. Instead, he spent much of his time either reading or at the piano and began study with Friedrich Wieck, one of Leipzig's most highly regarded piano teachers and, more important, Clara's father. Wieck recognized Robert's potential and took him on as a student. However, Robert permanently injured two fingers on his right hand, which cut short his career as a pianist. He quickly turned to journalism, first writing for an established journal, then in 1834 founding his own, the *Neue Zeitschrift für Musik* (*New Magazine for Music*), with a group of like-

Did You Know?

The switch from wood-frame to iron-frame construction for pianos was like the switch from acoustic to amplified electric guitar: both innovations gave the instruments greater power and resonance.

minded friends. Schumann soon became one of the most respected music critics in Europe. His first published compositions appeared during this time, although by the end of the decade he was still better known as a critic than as a composer.

Meanwhile, Clara Wieck was becoming the darling of the European concert world. She made successful debuts in Leipzig at the age of eleven, Paris at twelve, and Vienna at eighteen. Her programs included not only popular works by other composers but also her own compositions and improvisations. Among her fans were Goethe, Paganini, Mendelssohn, and, of course, Robert, who had watched her mature as a pianist, composer, and woman. They began their courtship around 1835, when she was only fifteen.

Musically, Clara and Robert were a mutual admiration society. Several of Robert's early piano works include references to and even musical quotations from Clara. Clara's early compositions are clearly influenced by Robert and other first-generation Romantic composers, and a few quote themes from Robert's works. Throughout their time together, before and during their marriage, they studied music together and supported each other's work. Among the fruits of their combined efforts was the publication of a joint collection of songs in 1840, the Schumanns' "year of song."

It took Clara and Robert more than five years and a trip to court before they were able to marry. Their adversary was Clara's father, who had apparently hoped that his daughter would find a wealthy husband and had a better opinion of Robert as a musical talent than as a prospective son-in-law. He respected Robert's gifts but also had firsthand knowledge of Robert's lack of discipline and fondness for drink, and he was skeptical

Clara and Robert Schumann

Fast Facts

- *Dates:* Clara, 1819–1896; Robert, 1810–1856
- *Place:* Germany (Leipzig)
- *Reasons to remember:* Premier nineteenth-century piano composers and performers in the Classical style

about Robert's financial prospects. After a two-year struggle in and out of court, Robert and Clara married the day before her twenty-first birthday.

At the time of their marriage, Clara had a much bigger reputation than her husband's. She was known and admired throughout Europe, while her husband was struggling to establish himself as a composer. She had accepted and applied her father's discipline, which served her well. Although she was almost ten years younger than her husband, she seems to have been the one who held the household together. During their relatively brief marriage—effectively about fourteen years, because Robert spent the last two years of his life in a sanatorium after a failed suicide attempt—she gave birth to eight children; provided the bulk of the family income through teaching and concert tours, which she booked herself; and dealt with the fearsome mood swings of her husband, who suffered from what seems to have been bipolar disorder throughout his adult life. She continued to compose while Robert was still alive but shut down after his death. In her forty years of widowhood, she promoted his music through performances and publications but silenced her own muse.

Robert's reputation as a composer grew during their marriage, to the point that there was some reconciliation with his father-in-law. Clara's compositions, well received when she was active as a composer, were largely ignored after Robert's death until the latter part of the twentieth century.

During her widowhood, Clara remained one of the most esteemed pianists in Europe. However, she stood apart from most of her peers because she was a woman and took such a high-minded approach to programming, disdaining flashy showpieces for the music of her husband and the classics. Far more common were flamboyant virtuosos, most notably Franz Liszt.

LO1 Pianists and Pianos in the Nineteenth Century

The Romantic piano virtuosi were the guitar gods of the nineteenth century. They dazzled audiences with their virtuosity and showmanship. And at least a few of them enjoyed celebrity-style perks as some compensation for their rigorous travel schedules and hours of practice. Franz Liszt, the greatest of the virtuoso pianists, allegedly fathered several children out of wedlock, not only with one of his mistresses but also presumably with the many women who threw themselves at his feet after—or even during—his concerts.

© iStockphoto.com/Gerad Coles

Romantic piano virtuosi were the guitar gods of the nineteenth century.

THE VIRTUOSO PIANIST

In the 1830s, the piano became the vehicle for the first generation of star soloists. Five necessary components were in place: the instruments, the music, the performers, the venues, and the appeal. For the next quarter century, a new generation of pianist-composers, including, above all, Liszt, Frédéric Chopin, Robert and Clara Schumann, and many others, composed piano music that capitalized on the new capabilities of the piano. Some of their music was flamboyant and virtuosic; other works were more intimate.

Pianists dazzled their audiences with their technical prowess and their artistry. Increasingly, their concerts included not only their own music and that of their contemporaries but also music of earlier generations, especially the sonatas of Beethoven. Liszt reputedly gave the first solo piano recital, toward the end of the 1830s. Prior to this, public concerts typically involved several musicians—singers, pianists, and other instrumentalists. The program was typically a musical potpourri. The solo piano recital included only piano music, of course, but there was already plenty to choose from.

There were numerous advantages to the solo recital. It cost less to put on, because there was only a single performer. It allowed audiences to focus on the performer to an unprecedented degree, and many did. Women swooned and fainted at Liszt's concerts and fought over locks of his hair. There was more to this reaction than Liszt's unsurpassed mastery of the piano. He looked the part: in the portraits we have of him as a young man, he is the match of any matinee idol. However, the reaction was also a sign of the times: the growing stature of the artist and the opportunity to see him display his art in performance, and more generally, the Romantic era's glorification of the individual.

Most of the virtuoso pianists were also composers. Much of their work represented new genres and was intended for audiences ranging from talented amateurs to the most accomplished pianists of the era.

Liszt looked every bit the part of a matinee idol.

© Scala / Art Resource, NY

ROMANTIC PIANO MUSIC

Romantic pianist-composers poured out a profusion of piano pieces beginning in the 1830s. They brought a Romantic sensibility to eighteenth-century forms, such as the prelude, sonata, and variation set, and to old and new dances. They invented a host of new forms, some with literary allusions (including ballade, romance, and song without words) and some more visual (nocturne and barcarolle—an evocation of Venetian gondoliers). And in free-form fantasies and rhapsodies, they abandoned conventional forms altogether. At times, they would infuse their music with patriotic sentiment (the Polish mazurkas and polonaises of Chopin) or explore the exotic (Brahms's Hungarian, or gypsy, dances for piano duet). Some of this piano music was overtly programmatic: Liszt's depictions of his years in Italy and Switzerland, Robert Schumann's descriptively titled piano works. A few works focused on virtuosity: the etude graduated from boring practice-room fare to dazzling concert music. Most of these pieces were short—less than five minutes, as a rule—yet they were usually big in conception.

Small Forms, Big Gestures. Romantic piano music presents an apparent paradox. Most Romantic piano pieces aren't very long, but they often feature big gestures. This represents a digression from Beethoven's expansion of Classical style, where both size and gesture were grand.

One reason that Romantic piano works often sound "bigger" than their Classical antecedents even when brief is that they start from small forms and expand them. For many shorter Romantic piano works, the comparable Classical formal unit is at most a small movement, such as a minuet and trio—indeed, it may be only a section of a movement or even a simple two-phrase theme. Romantic composers, however, expanded these smaller formal units from within by making phrases and sections longer, and from without by increasing the number of sections. In our survey of Romantic piano music, we hear several different approaches to making a small formal unit sound big.

There were sound commercial reasons as well for composing extensively in smaller forms. Piano works were typically published as parts of larger sets rather than as stand-alone compositions. A set of piano pieces was in some ways the nineteenth-century counterpart to the CD album: in effect, multiple tracks issued in a single package. (In fact, several composers, including Robert Schumann, referred to sets as *Albumblätter*, "album leaves"). Often, one or more pieces were within the capabilities of an amateur pianist with some training: the E minor prelude by Chopin discussed later is a good example. The inclusion of an attractive and pianistically accessible work or two, like the hit single a century or so later, would give the set commercial appeal.

All of the works discussed in this chapter come from sets, as do most of the shorter piano pieces published during the middle of the nineteenth century. Robert Schumann composed several sets, often with fanciful names—*Fantasy Pieces, Scenes from Childhood, Forest Scenes*. Chopin titled his works by genre—prelude, etude, waltz, mazurka—but all of the shorter works appeared in sets. Among the most popular piano works of the era, especially in Germany and England, were Mendelssohn's *Songs without Words*, published in sets of six pieces.

Musical Approaches in Romantic Piano Music. The first generation of Romantic composer-pianists, most notably the two Schumanns, Felix Mendelssohn and his sister Fanny, Chopin, and Liszt, brought to the public new kinds of piano music that took advantage of a rapidly evolving instrument. As the instrument became sturdier and more powerful, composers created more sonorous music: soaring, sustained melodies; richer textures; wider registral spans; and more extreme dynamics.

Within this general trend were conservative and progressive tendencies. The more conservative early Romantics were German, most notably Robert and Clara Schumann and the Mendelssohns. Their conservatism is evident in their approach to the piano, which exploited the full range and sonority of the instrument less frequently and less dramatically, closer adherence to established forms, steadier and less contrasting rhythms, thicker textures, and more predictable harmony.

The most important of the more progressive Romantics were two Paris-based expatriates: Chopin came to Paris from Poland; Liszt left Hungary for Paris as an adolescent and used the city as his home base throughout the first part of his career. Their piano music featured more elaborate and wide-ranging figuration and accompaniment patterns; more open textures; greater dynamic range, from thundering octave passages to delicate filigree; more flexibility in tempo; and more adventurous forms and harmonies.

© Concert Grand Piano, case made by Marsh & Jones, Leeds, action made by Erard, London, 1885 (satinwood inlaid with other woods). Bevan, Charles (fl.1865-83) / © Leeds Museums and Galleries (Lotherton Hall) U.K. / The Bridgeman Art Library International

The contrasting approaches to piano sonority between the German and Paris-based composers seem closely aligned with the differences between pianos manufactured in each region. Paris was home to the Erard and Pleyel piano builders. Both firms produced some of the most advanced and powerful instruments of the era. Liszt preferred an Erard piano like this seven-octave instrument from the mid-1830s; Chopin, the Pleyel. By comparison, the Viennese pianos, which were popular throughout German-speaking Europe during the 1830s and 1840s, were underpowered.

LO2 German Romantic Piano Music: The Schumanns

Robert Schumann composed his eight *Fantasy Pieces*, Op. 12, during the 1830s, relatively early in his career; they were published in 1838 during his courtship of Clara. Clara completed the *Three Romances*, Op. 21, in 1855, after Robert's failed suicide attempt and move to a sanatorium. They would be her last piano works to receive an opus number. These two works offer complementary views of German Romanticism and the Schumanns as composers.

CLARA SCHUMANN'S ROMANCE

For Romantics, **romance** was a generic title with a literary allusion but no specific program. It typically referred to a short, lyrical piano piece. The third of Clara Schumann's late *Three Romances* heard here is exceptional in that regard, in that it is expansive and agitated in the outer sections; it is a big, bold example of the German Romantic piano piece.

More generally, however, Clara Schumann's romance provides a helpful introduction to significant features of Romantic piano music. The work is in a large-scale ternary form, a common choice in Romantic piano music. The most direct Classical antecedent is the minuet and trio, and more particularly the third movements of Beethoven's early four-movement sonatas. Compared to these Beethoven movements, the dimensions of Clara Schumann's romance are bigger, the boundaries between and within major sections are less sharply drawn, and the contrast between sections is deeper.

LISTEN UP!

CD 3:30

Clara Schumann, Romance in G minor, Op. 21, No. 3 (1855)

Takeaway point: A mature, expansive example of German Romantic piano music

Style: Romantic

Form: Ternary

Genre: Romance

Instruments: Piano

Context: Music composed for the advanced amateur or professional pianist

The intricate figuration in the outer sections is characteristic of Romantic style in two important respects. First, the figuration is distinctive and unique to this work. It avoids more generic patterns, such as simple scales or arpeggios, often found in Classical figuration. Second, the figuration/accompaniment texture is maintained for extended stretches rather than quickly moving on to contrasting material. The middle section is comparably expansive and full of harmonic twists and turns.

The tradition of German Romantic piano music exemplified by Clara Schumann's romance began with the late piano pieces of Beethoven and the shorter piano works of Schubert and effectively ended with the late piano pieces of Brahms, composed at the end of the century. By contrast, Robert Schumann cultivated a highly personal, even idiosyncratic style, almost from the outset of his career.

ROBERT SCHUMANN'S FANTASY WORLD

In a diary entry on his twenty-first birthday, Robert Schumann described the split between his inner and outer worlds: "as if my objective self wanted to separate itself completely from my subjective self, or as if I stood between my appearance and my actual being, between form and shadow." Jean Paul and E. T. A. Hoffmann, two contemporary novelists whose writings captivated Schumann, undoubtedly influenced his self-reflection. The idea of a doppelgänger, a shadow self, was a recurrent theme in their work.

Schumann's notion of a shadow self would soon take a more personal form. Around the same time, he

Schumann's notion of a shadow self would take a more personal form.

began giving the members of his circle fanciful names. He himself became first "Florestan the improviser," a projection of his aspirations for a career as a virtuoso pianist. Later, he would add another persona, Eusebius, which he connected to Saint Eusebius, who was a pope for only sixteen months in 309 and 310. Florestan and Eusebius would come to represent the manic and depressive sides of Schumann's seemingly bipolar condition. He introduced them publicly in several early works, most notably in *Carnaval*, where he identifies them by name and characterizes them musically. Florestan is all energy and passion; Eusebius is dreamy.

Literature fueled Schumann's fantasy world and found expression in his music in numerous ways. Writings of Paul and Hoffmann inspired two important early piano works: *Papillons* and *Kreisleriana*. It helped shape the Davidsbund (League of David), Schumann's partly fictional, partly real group whose purpose was to preserve art from the uncultured. Many of his works have titles that represent characters or moods associated with particular states or situations. Among these works are the eight *Fantasiestücke* (*Fantasy Pieces*), Op. 12.

In "Aufschwung," the second of the eight fantasy pieces, Florestan is dominant, although there are moments of relative repose. In it, Schumann portrays a dimension of his fantasy world, using devices inspired by his reading. These include an *in medias res*, "start-in-the-middle," beginning and an equally abrupt ending, and a series of contrasting sections that are in various ways fragmentary or at least incomplete.

Unlike eighteenth-century works, which almost always begin by establishing the home key, Schumann's fantasy jumps right in with a chord reverberating with tension, and the first short section ends away from the tonic. This immediate immersion into the work is analogous to the novelist's strategy of beginning the story in the middle of the action.

The overall design of the piece is ternary on several levels. There are three big sections: energetic outer sections frame a less agitated middle section. But the outer sections also have a ternary design, with a strongly contrasting subsection sandwiched between the opening statement and its reprise. By contrast, the several segments that compose the middle section seem to flow almost imperceptibly from one to the next. With the exception of the final restatement of the opening material, none of the major sections or subsections is a complete musical statement. This fragmentary sectional structure also seems to take its cue from the novel; it is as if the story has several threads and the author/composer moves from one to the next as if shifting scenes.

Schumann delineates the sectional structure with textures that embed or support melody with distinctive, often thickly textured accompaniments in different registers. As in Clara Schumann's romance, there is nothing generic about the musical material.

The piano pieces by the two Schumanns differ fundamentally: one is programmatic; the other is not. Still, both highlight characteristic features of German Romantic piano music—relatively thick texture concentrated in the middle and lower range of the instrument, consistent rhythmic patterns in melody and accompaniment, flexible interpretations of large-scale ternary form. The piano music of Chopin, admired very much by both Schumanns, evidences a different approach to the piano and piano music.

LO3 Chopin's Piano Music

Frédéric Chopin was the poet of the piano. Although highly regarded as a pianist by those who knew his playing, Chopin did not pursue a concert career. He had neither the inclination nor the stamina to commit himself to the rigors of touring. However, he was committed to the instrument in a way that no other major composer was. All of his music involves the piano. He composed two concertos and other shorter works for piano and orchestra, some chamber music for piano and strings, and a few songs, but the bulk of his work is for solo piano.

His compositions opened up new sound possibilities: rich figuration, singing melodies, chords and patterns that tapped into the piano's idiomatic resonance. Some works seemed to tell stories without words or paint images in sound—although, unlike many of his contemporaries, Chopin never attached programmatic titles to his pieces.

More significantly, he opened up a completely new, piano-based sound world. In his compositions, he showed how to take advantage of the increased range and power of his rapidly changing instrument (although it should be emphasized that the pianos Chopin played and composed on were still some distance from the modern piano). His music features room-filling cascades of sound and delicate shadings; rich chords and elaborate figuration that take advantage of the damper pedal, which allows pianists to sustain notes after they have finished playing them; melodies that seem to sing yet go beyond what the voice can do. It demands new kinds of skills to produce these new sounds. Quite simply, no composer, before or since, has ever made the piano sound better.

Frédéric Chopin

Fast Facts

- *Dates:* 1810–1849
- *Place:* Poland
- *Reasons to remember:* The poet of the piano; wrote more idiomatically and beautifully for the instrument than any other composer

© Frédéric Chopin (1810-49) (oil on canvas), Scheffer, Ary (1795-1858) (after) / Chateau de Versailles, France / Lauros / Giraudon / The Bridgeman Art Library International

THE ETUDE

No group of Chopin's early works better shows the interconnection between composer, performer, and instrument than Chopin's Op. 10 etudes. *Étude* is the French word for "study." Before Chopin's etudes, the etude was a teaching piece designed to develop technical facility. Each etude typically focused on a particular difficulty: scales, chords, jumps, and so on. They were usually dry, relatively uninteresting pieces not intended for public performance.

Chopin elevated the status and stature of the etude from practice piece to concert music—an especially challenging concert music. In his etudes, the technical problem is no longer just an end in itself—a difficulty to be mastered—but also the main source of its musical impact. This is virtuosity put to expressive use, as we hear in Chopin's "Revolutionary" etude.

Chopin's etudes were directed toward serious pianists. They represented a small but significant part of Chopin's music for the piano. Among his other works are larger-scale pieces like the sonatas and ballades; various dance-inspired works—including two Polish dances, the mazurka and the polonaise; melodious, slow-paced works that he called nocturnes; and the twenty-four preludes, a set of miniatures in all keys. Some of these works were accessible to less advanced pianists, including many of his students. We consider two of the preludes next.

CHOPIN'S PRELUDES

Among the most familiar sets of short pieces are Chopin's twenty-four preludes. Chopin took his cue from Bach, who had composed two sets of twenty-four preludes and fugues, in each of the twelve major and twelve minor keys. The preludes pay homage to Bach, but Chopin's style is very much up to date.

Regarding the preludes, two qualities stand out, their brevity and their variety. Most of the **preludes** are very short; several require less than a minute to play. In the two preludes considered here, Chopin expands a small-format unit—the two-phrase parallel period—into a complete piece. A **two-phrase parallel period** consists of two phrases that begin the same way and end differently. Typically, the first phrase ends with a comma-style cadence, while the second ends with a period-style cadence.

We can gauge Chopin's expansion and transformation of this modestly sized formal unit by comparing the two preludes to an earlier instance of the form. "Là ci darem la mano," Don Giovanni's duet with Zerlina,

opens with a simple two-phrase parallel period; it takes about twenty seconds to perform. It is only one segment in the overall form of the duet. In the whirlwind G major prelude, Chopin lengthens the gestures, adds a short introduction and coda, and more than doubles the overall length. Partly for this reason, this two-phrase period is no longer a segment of a larger formal unit but a complete, if short, musical statement. The doleful E minor prelude unfolds much more slowly. Even more impressively, it is a complete statement; there is nothing ephemeral about it.

The two preludes also showcase the extraordinary variety in Chopin's music. The E minor prelude has a drawn-out melody supported by what seem to be simple repeated chords. But the unpredictable changes of harmony make the accompaniment distinctive, not generic. A more fragmentary melody rides on the wavelike accompaniment of the G major prelude. The contrast between one prelude and the next is striking, because both melody and accompaniment are distinctive and expressive and because the two complement each other in defining the character of the prelude. The distinctive character of both melody and accompaniment is one of the features that most clearly distinguishes Romantic music from Classical.

The piano music by the Schumanns and Chopin offer comparisons with the past and with each other. In these five Romantic works, we can hear the continued

evolution of piano music in the direction charted by Beethoven and made possible by improvements in the instrument: expanded musical gestures, more individuality in musical materials, wider range, more challenging execution. The five works also exemplify different approaches in Romantic piano music—the rich sounds and regular rhythms of German Romanticism versus Chopin's more sonorous and flexible style. In all of the works, there is evidence of a new aesthetic, one that emphasizes narrative over drama. Explicitly or implicitly, the five works seem to be more about telling a story or painting a scene than conducting a musical argument of the kind heard in Mozart's sonata movement discussed in Chapter 20.

Chopin's miniatures represent one extreme in musical Romanticism. Next we encounter its opposite: an extremely large five-movement work for a massive orchestra, composed about the same time as Chopin's preludes.

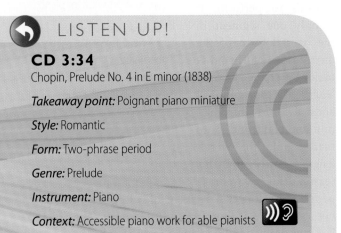

LISTEN UP!

CD 3:34

Chopin, Prelude No. 4 in E minor (1838)

Takeaway point: Poignant piano miniature

Style: Romantic

Form: Two-phrase period

Genre: Prelude

Instrument: Piano

Context: Accessible piano work for able pianists

CHAPTER 32

The Romantic Orchestra and Program Music

"Berlioz played the guitar expertly, but his real instrument was the orchestra."

If you were asked to name a phenomenal guitarist who wrote music depicting an artist on a drug-induced trip being hounded by demons, you'd probably volunteer the names of several prominent rock stars. However, first in line— at least chronologically—would be the French composer Hector Berlioz. The musical evidence? Numerous anecdotal accounts of his guitar playing and the last two movements of his *Symphonie fantastique* (1830), one of the most astoundingly original works in a century that prized originality.

Did You Know?

Berlioz gave the saxophone its name in 1842. Adolphe Sax, its inventor, had originally described it as a "new ophicleide" (a low-pitched brass instrument).

LO4   Berlioz and the Orchestra

Hector Berlioz was a key figure in early Romantic music. He achieved distinction not only as a highly original (and misunderstood) composer but also as a conductor, writer, and critic.

From contemporary accounts, we learn that Berlioz played the guitar expertly, but his real instrument was the orchestra. This is evident in three important ways. First, Berlioz studied the orchestra more systematically than anyone before him. Second, his performing "instrument" was the orchestra; he was the first widely known orchestral conductor. Third, his music typically requires a large and varied orchestra—sometimes even with newly invented instruments—and makes unprecedented demands on the musicians, to create effects never before imagined.

BERLIOZ ON THE ORCHESTRA

In the middle of the eighteenth century, several eminent musicians wrote major treatises on playing a particular instrument: for example, C. P. E. Bach wrote one for keyboard, and Mozart's father, Leopold, wrote one for violinists. These were intended for performers.

Berlioz's *Grand traité d'instrumentation et d'orchestration modernes* (*A Treatise on Modern Instrumentation and Orchestration*) was a tool for composers. In it, he described the instruments of the orchestra and assessed their character and how they might best be used in a composition. He drew examples from his own music, as well as the music of other composers of his and earlier times, most notably Beethoven and Gluck. He also included chapters on the ideal disposition of the orchestra and conducting.

The work was a product of intense study and vivid imagination. Berlioz spent hours in the library of the Paris Conservatory studying scores, from which he drew some of his conclusions about the effective use of instruments. Other suggestions came from his own novel ideas about instruments, their character, and their possibilities. The treatise was published first in 1843 and again in 1855 in an expanded second edition.

Berlioz began this work during his student years, so that by the time he set out to compose his grand work, the *Symphonie fantastique*, he was ready to demand unusual combinations, timbres, and sounds from the orchestra. His score study was the compositional counterpart to the rigorous practice regimen that a serious performer undertakes to achieve mastery of an instrument.

BERLIOZ THE CONDUCTOR

Berlioz became Europe's most visible symbol of a new kind of virtuoso: the conductor. Instead of performing on an instrument, he directed an instrument made of performers—a hundred or more, if he had his way. It was a demanding task, more so in those days because both orchestras and much orchestral music—including Berlioz's own works—were new, and Berlioz's works asked for many new and difficult musical effects. (By contrast, the top orchestras of today have performed works such as the Beethoven symphonies and Berlioz's *Symphonie fantastique* dozens, even hundreds of times.)

Berlioz became a conductor out of necessity. After too many disastrous performances of his own works conducted by others, he wanted to make sure that his music was presented as he had imagined it. And he needed the money, often to help defray the debts he had incurred producing performances of his works. Fortunately, there was demand for his services. By the early 1840s, Berlioz's fame had spread throughout Europe. Among his many tours were several trips to London, several to Germany, where Liszt also conducted his music on occasion, and two to Russia; the rigors of a second trip to Russia in 1867–1868 hastened his death. In an age of stellar virtuosi—Paganini, Liszt, and others—Berlioz was in this respect also a virtuoso, of a large and often unwieldy instrument, the orchestra.

Berlioz's orchestra-related activities—composing exclusively for the orchestra (no piano music, no chamber music), studying orchestration, and establishing a conducting career—were firsts. So was the oversized orchestra that he required for the *Symphonie fantastique*.

© Leemage/Lebrecht Music & Arts

The often-caricatured Berlioz conducting the artist's nightmarish vision of the expanded "new orchestra"

EXPANDING THE ORCHESTRA

Fewer than two generations—from 1791 to 1830—separate Haydn's "Surprise" symphony from Berlioz's *Symphonie fantastique*. However, the orchestra required for Berlioz's mammoth symphony is more than double the size of Haydn's, and it features an array of new sounds. He utilized additional members of the woodwind and brass families—including the piccolo, English horn, E♭ clarinet, cornets, and the ophicleide, a newly invented instrument that added a bass voice to the brass section (it would be superseded by the tuba); plus additional percussion instruments and the harp, all of which were in use during Haydn's lifetime but were not part of the orchestras for which he composed. The following table details this expansion.

	Haydn, Symphony No. 94	Beethoven, Symphony No. 5	Berlioz, *Symphonie fantastique*
Woodwinds			
Flutes	2	2 + piccolo	2 + piccolo
Oboes	2	2	2 + English horn
Clarinets	0	2	2 + E♭ clarinet (high register)
Bassoons	2	2 + contra-bassoon	4
Brass			
Trumpets	2	2	2 + 2 cornets
Horns	2	2	4
Trombones	0	3	3
Ophicleides	0	0	2
Percussion and harp			
Timpani	2	2	4
Drums	0	0	Snare drum, bass drum, cymbals, bells
Harps	0	0	2

Berlioz's enormous orchestral requirements are not just about power but also about sound color. His expanded sound palette, which includes new instruments like the ophicleide and new uses for existing but seldom used instruments like the E♭ clarinet, English horn, and bells, is tangible evidence of his aural sound imagination, as we hear in the last movement of the *Symphonie fantastique*.

Symphonie fantastique

Although Berlioz had been successful enough as a student composer to win the Prix de Rome, the top award for composers at the Paris Conservatory, the work that announced his arrival as an important composer was the *Symphonie fantastique*, first performed in December 1830. It is hard to imagine a grander entrance. The work is quintessentially Romantic. It is intensely subjective, cast on a massive scale, and strikingly original in conception and detail—a thorough embodiment of the new Romantic sensibility.

The seed from which the symphony grew was Berlioz's all-consuming infatuation with Harriet Smithson, an English actress whom he had seen as Ophelia in Shakespeare's *Hamlet*. He fell in love with her on the spot and pursued her so ardently that she spurned him. Rejected, he vowed to immortalize her in his first symphony.

Although Harriet Smithson rejected him at first, Berlioz eventually wooed and won her; they married in 1833. Within a decade, the marriage was on the rocks, in part because of his philandering.

We can gauge the autobiographical impulse that characterizes this symphony by its working title: *Episode in the Life of an Artist*. The artist, of course, was Berlioz, and the episode is his failed pursuit of Harriet Smithson. He made her the focal point of the work by portraying her in melody. He identified this as an **idée fixe**, a "fixed idea" or melodic representation of the object of the artist's obsession. The melody appears early in the first movement and returns in various forms throughout the work.

And to make sure nobody missed the connection, Berlioz wrote out a program for the symphony that described the events and feelings depicted in each movement. This program was much more detailed—and much more personal—than the brief notes that Beethoven had provided for his Symphony No. 6, the "Pastoral" symphony. It turned Berlioz's symphony into a new genre: the **program symphony**, a symphony whose movements depict a series of scenes relating to the work's overall program, or theme.

Both the idée fixe and the program dramatize the stunning paradigm shift in cultural life in the early nineteenth century. To be so boldly and baldly personal would have been unimaginable fifty years earlier. It's almost inconceivable that Haydn would compose a "fantastic" symphony at Esterháza in 1780. And even if he had, it's doubtful that his patron would have received it warmly. By Beethoven's time, the shift had certainly begun, in large measure because of him. But Berlioz openly portrays himself as an artist who is pouring out his feelings in music. Composers had, in the space of two generations, moved up the social ladder from servants to citizens with significant social status. The composer may starve, or scuffle to pay the rent, but he is an admired member of society, at least in principle.

Berlioz's extensive and highly personal program is just one of the many original features of the *Symphonie fantastique*. Indeed, there is hardly anything significant about it that is *not* original, or at least a significant departure from convention. Most obvious, perhaps, are the size and sequence of movements. The symphony is a huge piece; it takes almost an hour to perform. Of all the orchestral works from this time and earlier that are still performed regularly, only the ninth symphonies of Beethoven and Schubert are noticeably longer.

There are five movements, not the conventional four. The first is comparable in size and tempo to a standard symphonic first movement. However, the second movement is a scene from a carnival. We hear a lovely waltz, not the slow movement we expect. The third movement is slow—it places the artist out in the country, where time seems to stand still. Only the tempo suggests a connection to a more conventional slow movement. The fourth movement is a march, not the usual minuet and trio: in it, the artist, drugged by opium, sees himself taken to the gallows to be executed rather than to the ballroom to dance a minuet.

All of this is novel enough; still, Berlioz saved the best for last. The opium-induced nightmare continues for the artist in the fifth movement. Here, Berlioz paints in sound the artist's funeral. It features demons and sorcerers swirling around him; his dearly beloved, whom he killed earlier in the dream, returning as a witch; and the booming voice of doom.

> He [the artist] sees himself at the witches' Sabbath, in the midst of a ghastly crowd of spirits, sorcerers and monsters of every kind, assembled for his funeral. There are strange noises, groans, bursts of laughter, far-off shouts to which other shouts seem to reply. The beloved tune appears once more but it has lost its character of refinement and diffidence; it has become nothing but a common dance tune, trivial and grotesque; it is she who has come to the Sabbath. . . . A roar of joy greets her arrival. . . . She mingles with the devilish orgy. . . . Funeral knell, ludicrous parody of the *Dies irae*, Sabbath dance. The Sabbath dance and the Dies irae in combination.

Romantic-era depiction of a witches' sabbath: Gustav Adolph Spangenberg's *Walpurghis Night* (1862)

"DREAM OF A WITCHES' SABBATH"

The title of the last movement, "Songe d'une nuit de sabbat" ("Dream of a Witches' Sabbath"), tells us at once that it's going to be different. Some historical perspective can help us hear

idée fixe "Fixed idea"; melodic representation of the object of the artist's obsession

program symphony Symphony whose movements depict a series of scenes relating to the work's overall program, or theme

exactly how different. Consider the orchestral pieces that we have encountered to this point: in each case, the opening melodic material of a movement has told us what the movement is about. The music that follows has been a coherent argument developed from that opening idea. Moreover, the character of the piece has grown out of this initial melodic material; its pitches, rhythm, and harmonic and textural setting resonate throughout the movement. The opening material is in effect what the movement is about.

Berlioz follows a radically different path, one that has more to do with opera than with symphonic music. The character of the movement comes not so much from the melodies that Berlioz invents as from the sound choices that he makes: what instruments he uses, the special effects that he asks for, the registers in which they operate, the dynamic levels and patterns of dynamic change. In this respect, Berlioz has an aesthetic like that of a rock band. The musical message is as much in the quality of the sound—how much distortion, what special effects—as it is in the riffs.

There is, of course, melodic material, but it serves different functions. Some of it, like the low string growls and the delicate descent in the high strings that follows, is deliberately neutral. This directs attention away from melody to the striking sound qualities the composer requests. Another strategy is to use melody symbolically; it isn't the inherent quality of the melody itself that is paramount but what it stands for. This happens two different times. The first is the parody of the *idée fixe*; the second is the quotation of the *Dies irae* (Day of Wrath), from the Catholic Mass for the dead. Both would have been familiar to Berlioz's audiences: the first from earlier in the symphony, the second from their prior experience. Both help depict the events in the program by association rather than through their inherent musical qualities. There is original and distinctive melodic material in the movement, but it is a motive that never becomes a full-fledged theme. A conventional melody, with a beginning, clear midpoints, and an end, is not part of the fabric of this movement.

The form is just as innovative. There is a section that Berlioz called "Ronde [rondo] du sabbat," but it is miles away from a typical rondo. Instead, the movement proceeds as a series of episodes or scenes. The musical events are a series of gestures that make sense not so much through a process of internal relationships as through their connection to Berlioz's program. Many would be equally at home in an opera highlighting action onstage. The music starts and stops, and the ideas and sounds tumble over one another until they finally reach the massive climax at the end.

With this approach, Berlioz seems to be asking himself not "How can I put a new spin on existing symphonic forms?" but "How can I tell a story using only instruments as dramatically and vividly as possible?" It is a different point of departure, and it leads to a very different result.

Berlioz's Legacy

Berlioz's *Symphonie fantastique* is a true original; its novel features are significant and fundamental. They include a design dictated more by a narrative than by formal conventions, a new expressive balance between sound and melody that often leans toward sound, the symbolic use of familiar materials and melodies, and the exploration of new sound possibilities and effects.

Some of these—such as the expansion of the orchestra—continue trends set in motion by Beethoven, whom Berlioz admired, learned from, and championed. Others are adaptations of operatic orchestral devices and effects for a purely instrumental context. In either case, Berlioz puts his own stamp on them. His idée fixe certainly derives from the idea of a motive that returns throughout a multimovement work, like the opening motive of Beethoven's Fifth Symphony, but it begins with a far different impulse—the portrayal of the artist's beloved—and it returns for programmatic reasons. As such, it unifies the work in a quite different way.

Berlioz's music embodies several of the most compelling features of early Romanticism: an emphasis on performing skill, often to virtuosic levels; acceptance of large musical gestures, whether in miniatures or in grand works; inspired and imaginative settings that open up a new sound world; greater focus on the individual, whether the performer or the subject of a musical program; and a quest for innovation.

His vision was too singular and forward-looking to lend itself to imitation by his contemporaries. Berlioz's greatest impact on orchestral music came in the latter half of the nineteenth century. It is most evident in the expansion of the orchestra and the emphasis on tone color, and in new literary-based forms. Musical futurists such as Wagner and Russian composers such as Tchaikovsky and Rimsky-Korsakov followed his lead in expanding the orchestra and cultivating a distinctive palette of sounds. (Recall from Chapter 2 how Tchaikovsky's orchestration made Mozart's pitches and rhythms sound Romantic.) Berlioz's music was also a major influence on the **tone poem**, a programmatic orchestral genre consisting of one movement that emerged

during the latter half of the century. Liszt, the inventor of that genre, acknowledged Berlioz's influence; it is also evident in the music of Richard Strauss, the master of

the literature-inspired tone poem. Particularly in these areas, Berlioz's influence was substantial if indirect.

Berlioz was one of the original Romantics. In true Romantic fashion, Berlioz conceived his works on a grand scale and with a highly individual character. He seldom repeated genres, preferring instead to invent them, or at least transform them drastically. He demanded large resources, not only for bombastic effects but also for passages of extreme delicacy. Like his major works, he was one of a kind. He has no counterpart in the nineteenth century.

> **tone poem**
> Programmatic, one-movement, Romantic orchestral genre

CHAPTER 33

The Symphony and Concerto in the Romantic Era

"The Romantic-era orchestra concert was seen as the most high-minded musical experience available to the general public."

Did You Know?

On Yes's 1972 album *Fragile*, keyboardist Rick Wakeman "covered" the third movement of Brahms's Fourth Symphony using only synthesizers.

The most oddly named of the major European symphony orchestras is the Gewandhaus Orchestra of Leipzig, Germany. Most orchestras take their name from their host city: the Vienna Philharmonic, the London Symphony, the Orchestre de Paris, and so on. The Gewandhaus Orchestra took its name from the building that housed its first dedicated performance space. In 1781, the mayor of Leipzig ordered the construction of a five-hundred–seat concert hall within a building that housed the clothier's exchange (*gewand*, meaning "clothing" or "garb" in German) to serve as

the home for a music society that had been formed in 1775.

In 1835, the composer Felix Mendelssohn (1809–1847) became the conductor of the Gewandhaus Orchestra, a position that he would retain for the rest of his life. Under his direction, the Gewandhaus became one of the finest orchestras in Europe. Among his important contributions were conducting from the podium and using a baton (before Mendelssohn, the concertmaster directed the orchestra from his chair at the front of the first violin section); resurrecting Schubert's last symphony,

A watercolor of the Gewandhaus painted by Felix Mendelssohn

which had never been performed; reviving the music of Bach in a series of "historical concerts"; and organizing several fund-raising events to secure a firmer financial footing for the orchestra.

Orchestras and Their Audiences

The rise of the Gewandhaus Orchestra under Mendelssohn and its continued growth after his death reflected the emergence of the symphony orchestra as a major cultural institution in the larger cities of Europe and the Americas during the nineteenth century. At the beginning of the century, most concert orchestras were ad hoc ensembles put together for a particular occasion, such as an evening of music by Beethoven. (Theater orchestras offered more frequent and more reliable employment for orchestral musicians.) By the end of the century, however, cities from Chicago to St. Petersburg, Russia, had resident professional orchestras.

ORCHESTRAS AS CULTURAL INSTITUTIONS

Many of the major orchestras in Europe and the United States began as concert societies. The London Philharmonic, formed in 1813 by a society of professional musicians, was ahead of its time. A few more formed around midcentury: the Vienna Philharmonic in 1841 and the New York Philharmonic in 1842 are notable instances. Many more in Europe and the United States came together toward the end of the century.

These orchestras became an integral part of the cultural life in their cities, joining opera companies as the most prestigious resident musical institutions. Over time, a natural evolution of supporting enterprises developed around them: performing venues (Amsterdam's symphony also takes its name from its concert hall, the famous Concertgebouw), conservatories to train musicians for orchestral positions (Mendelssohn founded the Leipzig Conservatory in 1843), as well as administrative support and governmental and private patronage.

As with opera, audiences for symphony orchestras became more diverse. Some orchestras, especially in England and Paris, offered concerts in larger spaces for relatively low prices; others maintained high prices in order to limit the audience to the upper class. Outdoor festivals and concerts, at times with enormous orchestras, attracted large audiences—as many as five thousand

listeners. (These were the predecessors of today's pop concerts.) During the course of the century, the prevailing trend was toward larger venues, with ticket prices at several levels, and seating to match—from the most exclusive boxes to the nosebleed section in the back.

Franz Liszt conducting a concert

The Romantic-era orchestra concert was seen by many musicians, critics, and audience members as the most high-minded musical experience available to the general public. They considered such events an aesthetically satisfying and morally uplifting experience, not mere entertainment.

NINETEENTH-CENTURY ORCHESTRAL INSTRUMENTS AND REPERTOIRE

As we've seen, orchestras grew in size and instrumental variety during the course of the century. A key reason was the dramatic improvement in conventional instruments—woodwinds, brass, and percussion—and the

Ophicleide

Tuba

New instruments, most notably the tuba, which replaced the less dynamic ophicleide, greatly contributed to the nineteenth-century orchestra.

invention of new instruments, most notably the tuba. Composers such as Berlioz were quick to capitalize on these new and improved resources.

Accordingly woodwind, brass, and percussion sections expanded, and string sections also grew in size, to balance the increased size of the other sections. As a result, the underlying structure of the orchestra did not change. Strings were still the dominant section, although nineteenth-century composers made far more use of the other sections than did their eighteenth-century counterparts. Despite the proliferation of new instruments, orchestras added no new sections during the nineteenth century; both the tuba and the additional woodwinds were larger or smaller cousins of existing instruments.

One reason for the consistency in instrumentation was the gradual accumulation of standard repertoire—those works that continued to be performed widely in the years and generations after their composition. From the start, the symphonies of Beethoven were at the heart of this standard repertoire. The size of the repertoire continued to grow because it went back in time, to the orchestral works of Haydn, Mozart, and (because of Mendelssohn's popularization) Bach, and other eighteenth- and early nineteenth century-composers, and then began to add contemporary works with staying power. Although Mendelssohn's "Italian" and "Scottish" symphonies, concert overtures, and violin concerto were obviously new works during Mendelssohn's lifetime, they had become standard repertoire by the time Brahms completed his first symphony in 1876. As a result, the ratio of classics to new works grew during the latter two-thirds of the century. Works went in and out of fashion, as they have in our own time. However, much of the newly standard repertoire remains central to orchestral programs in our time: the symphonies and concertos of Beethoven, Brahms, Tchaikovsky, and Dvořák.

Among the most popular and prestigious genres in nineteenth-century orchestral music were the symphony and the concerto. Both were inherited from the eighteenth century, and both reflect Beethoven's continuing influence on nineteenth-century orchestral music—especially on the symphony, whose prestige stemmed directly from the awe that Beethoven's symphonies inspired. Composers knew full well that their symphonies would be measured against Beethoven's. All the important symphonies composed during the course of the nineteenth century thus borrowed something from Beethoven's—size, programmatic reference, individuality, developmental procedures. Even the *number* of Beethoven's symphonies was intimidating; no important composer produced more than nine.

Gustav Mahler, the last of the great Romantic symphonists, died with his tenth symphony incomplete.

> *Even the number of Beethoven's symphonies was intimidating: no important composer produced more than nine.*

Beethoven's influence on the concerto was almost as pronounced. His concertos form a bridge between the Classical concertos of Mozart, with their dialectical give and take between soloist and orchestra, and the more expansive, virtuosic, and formally adventurous Romantic concertos.

LO5 Brahms and the Romantic Symphony

As the reputation of Johannes Brahms as German-speaking Europe's greatest living composer took shape, he found himself being compared favorably to Beethoven and Bach—together, they had become "the three B's." But for Brahms, acclaim brought pressure as well as prestige. Indeed, a bust of Beethoven glowered down at Brahms from the wall of his apartment. Nowhere was this more evident than in the painfully slow gestation of his first symphony.

Brahms began working on his first symphony in 1862. It would take him fourteen years to complete; in that interval, he composed eight major chamber works, dozens of songs, and numerous other works, in addition to *Ein deutsches Requiem*. The publication of the symphony seemed to lift the burden of composing "Beethoven's tenth symphony" from his shoulders. In the following eleven years, Brahms would compose

> *A bust of Beethoven glowered down at Brahms from the wall of his apartment.*

most of his important orchestral music: three more symphonies; three major concertos for violin, piano, and a double concerto for violin and cello; and two concert overtures.

THE ROMANTIC SYMPHONY

For Romantic composers, a symphony was a statement. Composers like Brahms and Dvořák may have made much of their money from the sale of songs and dances, but they made their reputation with their symphonies. They intended each work to be a major contribution to the orchestral repertoire; it would have been the product of months—even years—of effort. The numbers tell the story: Haydn composed more symphonies for his two visits to London (six for each visit) than many composers (Brahms, Mendelssohn, Schumann, Franck, Saint-Saëns) composed during their entire career.

The Romantic symphony expanded upon the symphonic tradition of Haydn, Mozart, and Beethoven, whose dominant influence is evident in three of its most distinguishing features: size, originality, and individuality. In general, Romantic symphonies were longer than their late eighteenth-century counterparts. Lengths ranged from around thirty minutes to over an hour, with thirty-eight to forty minutes as a midrange length. In particular, the symphonies of the late nineteenth-century Austrian composers Anton Bruckner and Gustav Mahler are sprawling works; most of them last at least sixty minutes. The expansion of the Classical symphony was most evident in the final movements. In many nineteenth-century symphonies, the last movement is about as long as or even longer than the opening movement; in Classical symphonies, it is often the shortest.

Symphonies that were obviously original—evident in such features as the title of the work and its inspiration, as well as the number, sequence, and tempo of movements—were the rare exception, not the rule. Hector Berlioz stands out in this regard. His programmatic symphonies include not only the five-movement *Symphonie fantastique* but also his even grander "symphonie dramatique" on Shakespeare's *Romeo and Juliet*, which requires voices and orchestra and lasts over an hour and a half. In the latter half of the century, composers wishing to depart from the conventional symphonic model typically composed symphonic poems, which were inherently programmatic, rather than program symphonies like those of Berlioz. Those who pursued a more traditional approach (Mendelssohn, Schumann, Brahms, Dvořák, Tchaikovsky) adhered almost religiously to the standard four-movement sequence established in the Classical symphony. Typically, they expressed their originality within this well-established plan by modifying such features as the form and sequences of keys.

We have observed the Romantic predilection for melody in the flowering of art song and the diversification of opera as well as in piano music and music for dance. So it should not surprise us that the approach to melody was among the most significant differences between the Classical and the Romantic symphony. Romantic composers understood symphonic forms in melodic terms. Typically, they crafted movements around expressive, tuneful melodies rather than around the more instrumentally conceived themes of Classical symphonies; scherzo movements were an occasional exception to this practice. Behind this emphasis on melody was the idea that melody embodied the character of the work. Composers expressed this understanding through the repetition and transformation of earlier melodic ideas, which helps to unify the work and show the development of the character embodied in the original idea.

Brahms's symphonies typify the more traditional form of the Romantic symphony. All have four movements, in the typical sequence. They range in length from around thirty-five minutes (the Third Symphony) to over forty-five minutes (the First Symphony). Brahms's creativity finds expression within this traditional framework. There are no programs, explicit or implicit, although each has a distinct character, and there are no dramatic departures from the norm. Rather, Brahms used conventional forms and materials as a point of departure and transformed them in distinctive, often radical ways. As we listen to his symphonies, we hear both their connection to the rich symphonic tradition of the late eighteenth and nineteenth centuries and the highly individual aspects of his compositional approach.

BRAHMS, THE PROGRESSIVE TRADITIONALIST

Following the Vienna premiere of Brahms's First Symphony, the critic (and champion of Brahms's music) Eduard Hanslick compared the work to the symphonies of Beethoven. The conductor Hans von Bülow went a step further, dubbing it Beethoven's tenth. Brahms's more astute contemporaries acknowledged Brahms's strong connection with the past.

Because his innovations use established forms and genres as a familiar point of departure, they do not seem as radical as those of Berlioz, Liszt, and Wagner. Nevertheless, Brahms's thoroughgoing and highly personal transformations of these familiar forms make clear that Brahms viewed his musical heritage as a source of inspiration rather than a model to be imitated.

To illustrate this quality of Brahms's music, we study his Second Symphony, with particular focus on the third movement. Brahms composed the symphony in 1877, just a year after completing the First. The symphony is in four movements: an opening movement in an expansive sonata form, a slow movement, a moderately paced third movement, and a brisk finale. The symphony begins innocuously with a simple four-note motive in the lower strings. The horn enters on the fourth note, stating the first theme of the movement; both the instrument and the melody convey the essentially pastoral character of the symphony. However, it is the seemingly generic three-note pattern heard at the outset, not the opening theme, that is the seed from which the symphony grows. The motive returns throughout the first movement, and different versions of it return in the third and fourth movements, in which they submit to further transformation.

A brief refresher course in the form of the minuet and trio: both minuet and trio are typically in rounded binary form, with both sections repeated. The minuet and the trio have different melodies and usually contrast in key or mode, as we heard in the third movement of Beethoven's Fifth Symphony.

Brahms uses the minuet and trio as a point of departure; the opening melody evokes the rhythm and grace of a minuet. The innovative aspects of the movement include these interrelated features:

- Altering the proportions of the form and blurring the formal boundaries so that contrasting sections merge into one another

- Creating contrast between sections through changes in tempo and meter rather than melody

- Deriving virtually all the melodic material from the inversion of the three-note pattern heard at the very beginning of the symphony

- Replacing literal repetition with developmental variation

All of these features extend Beethoven's own modification of the form. They are progressive because they go beyond Beethoven rather than because they chart a new path.

BRAHMS, WAGNER, AND BEETHOVEN

In the German-dominated musical world of the late nineteenth century, Brahms and Wagner were the towering presences and the opposing parties in one of the most vigorously contested musical battles of the nineteenth century. Both were regarded as the heirs apparent to Beethoven, the most prestigious honor that German-speaking culture could bestow on a musician—Wagner by his own reckoning and Brahms by influential critics. Brahms apparently had a high regard for Wagner's music; Wagner apparently resented Brahms's "coronation" as the next Beethoven.

Even the small sampling of music by the two composers that we have encountered highlights key differences. Wagner composed only opera; Brahms never composed an opera. Wagner reconceived form and wedded it to words; Brahms adapted well-established forms, often in innovative and individual ways. Wagner's music is the ultimate program music; the musical events amplify the story told in the libretto almost moment by moment. Brahms's music represented what was called **absolute music**, a term that came into vogue in Germany during the nineteenth century to describe music whose aesthetic value is self-contained; it does not require any extramusical reference, such as lyrics, drama, dance, or a program. Wagner foretold the future of music; Brahms was firmly rooted in the past, in the minds of his contemporaries and subsequent generations.

> **absolute music** Music whose aesthetic value is self-contained and does not require any extramusical reference, such as lyrics, drama, dance, or a program

These pronounced differences may obscure striking similarities in their musical approach. Both are extraordinarily high-minded—Wagner overtly so and Brahms implicitly so in the imagination and craft of his major compositions. More specifically, both unified their compositions by creating complex thematic networks from memorable motives, which in turn enabled them to introduce considerable variety in the setting of the motives and to manipulate form in inventive, even radical ways. That Wagner abandoned traditional forms while Brahms reworked them does not alter this underlying affinity. In this respect, both extend Beethoven's practice of unifying a piece by permeating it with material derived from a single melodic kernel.

Brahms and Wagner have retained the stature that they earned during their lifetime: they remain the most important and highly regarded German composers in the latter half of the nineteenth century. One measure of their achievement was their individual and quite different responses to Beethoven's legacy.

LO6 Tchaikovsky and the Romantic Concerto

In the last third of the nineteenth century, the Hungarian-born Leopold Auer was among the most distinguished violinists in Russia. In 1868, Auer accepted an invitation to become the concertmaster of the orchestra of the St. Petersburg Imperial Theatres, where he would remain for almost half a century. Tchaikovsky was enamored of his playing and dedicated his *Serenade melancolique* (1875) to him. Three years later, he dedicated his newly composed violin concerto to Auer, who refused to play it because he found it too difficult. In 1881, three years after Auer rejected it, Adolph Brodsky, another Russian violinist, championed the work, performing it with great success in Vienna. It quickly became part of the violin repertoire.

The circumstances of their creation and first performance highlight two major changes in the concerto during the nineteenth century. One was that the composer wasn't necessarily creating the concerto for his own use. Although the concerto remained an important outlet for composer-performers from Paganini to Rachmaninoff, many of the most widely performed concertos were composed by musicians such as Robert Schumann and Dvořák, who were not active concert performers, or by composers writing for an instrument they did not play at a concert level, such as the violin concertos of Mendelssohn and Brahms. The other was that concertos became far more challenging technically. Tchaikovsky's concerto is difficult—far more demanding in certain respects than the concertos of Bach, Vivaldi, and Mozart.

THE ROMANTIC CONCERTO

Romantics glorified the individual, so it should come as no surprise that Romantic composers transformed the concerto into a vehicle for individual brilliance. Baroque solo concertos like Vivaldi's *Four Seasons* afforded the soloist opportunities to step into the spotlight. In the fast outer movements, the technical demands of the solo part were greater than those of the orchestral parts, and the slow movement often gave the soloist a chance to display the expressive side of his musical personality. In Mozart's concertos, especially those for piano and orchestra, expressiveness and virtuosity served a dramatic purpose. Technical and musical demands increased, particularly in the cadenzas at the ends of the outer movements, which were typically improvised. By the early nineteenth century, virtuosic display had become, for many composers, the raison d'être (reason for being) of the concerto. The orchestra is an almost silent partner in Chopin's concertos when the pianist is playing. Even in those concertos with a more balanced relationship between soloist and orchestra, the soloist tends to be the focal point of the work.

The standard Romantic concerto retained the most general features of the Classical concerto. It was an extended work in three movements, in a fast/slow/fast sequence. The solo part included lyric moments and brilliant passagework, and there was at least one cadenza. The orchestral episodes provided a foil for the soloist. Both the lyric and virtuosic sections offered the opportunity for dialogue and other interactions; the contrast between soloist and orchestra typically highlighted the superior skill of the soloist.

A concise survey of the history of the concerto: in the Baroque era, the soloist came from within the orchestra; in the Classical era, the soloist competed with the orchestra; in the Romantic era, the soloist dominated the orchestra.

One obvious difference between the Classical concerto and the typical Romantic concerto was the disappearance of an extended orchestral tutti at the beginning of the work. It was as if neither soloist nor audience could wait the two or three minutes required to perform it. This undermined the drama inherent in the opening movement of a Classical concerto: the progress of the soloist toward equality. In effect, by entering quickly—and usually with a splash—the soloist asserted his dominant position from the outset.

Within the basic three-movement structure, the Romantic concerto was more flexible in design than either the Classical concerto or the Romantic symphony. More often than not, the second movement continued into the third without interruption; cadenzas could appear anywhere in a movement, beginning, middle, or end; dramatic shifts in tempo and character within a movement were more common. We hear many of these features in the last movement of Tchaikovsky's violin concerto.

PYOTR ILYICH TCHAIKOVSKY

There was a good reason why Pyotr Ilyich Tchaikovsky initially planned to become a civil servant: it was exceedingly difficult to obtain adequate musical training in Russia during the first half of the nineteenth century. Indeed, Tchaikovsky, at age twenty-one, was a member of the first class admitted to the newly formed St. Petersburg Conservatory.

> *"Tchaikovsky drew unconsciously from the true, popular sources of our race."* —Igor Stravinsky

Then as now, Russia had been both a part of Europe and apart from Europe. It lies on the eastern periphery of the European continent (Europe and Asia are the only continents without an obvious boundary) and for centuries was on the outside culturally as well as geographically. From the time of Peter the Great through the Russian Revolution, Russia looked to the West for culture: French was the preferred language among the aristocracy.

Tchaikovsky's music symbolizes the westward-looking aspect of Russian culture. By birth (his mother was born in Germany), training, and inclination, Tchaikovsky looked to the West more than his peers did. His dominant musical influences were Italian opera and Mozart. His music is not overtly nationalistic, as is the music of many of his important contemporaries, such as Modest Mussorgsky and Nikolai Rimsky-Korsakov. Yet Igor Stravinsky, also Russian and his only peer as a composer for ballet, noted that "Tchaikovsky drew unconsciously from the true, popular sources of our race."

Tchaikovsky was the first Russian composer to attract a substantial following outside Russia. His orchestral music brought him fame and, toward the end of his life, invitations to conduct in Europe and the United States (he attended the inauguration of Carnegie Hall in 1891), and the awarding of an honorary doctorate from Cambridge University in 1893.

Tchaikovsky stands apart from virtually every other Romantic composer in his versatility. He composed significant music in essentially every important genre: symphony, concerto, and other orchestral music; opera; chamber music and song; and especially ballet. Among his most enduring works is his only violin concerto.

Pyotr Ilyich Tchaikovsky

Fast Facts

- *Dates:* 1840–1893
- *Place:* Russia
- *Reasons to remember:* The most popular and versatile composer of the Romantic era

© Piotr Ilyich Tchaikovsky (1840-93) 1860, Panov, M. (19th Century) / Tchaikovsky Museum, Klin, Russia / The Bridgeman Art Library International

TCHAIKOVSKY'S VIOLIN CONCERTO

The premiere of Tchaikovsky's violin concerto reminds us how creativity may be damaging to the ego. In his review of its December 1881 premiere, Eduard Hanslick wrote that the concerto "brought us face to face with the revolting thought that music can exist which stinks to the ear." Perhaps Hanslick, one of the most influential critics in Europe and one of Brahms's staunchest supporters, was trying to protect Brahms's reputation; Brahms's violin concerto had received mixed reviews from musicians and critics upon its introduction almost three years previously. Or perhaps the work was not performed well (a constant danger at premieres, especially with a difficult work). Despite Hanslick's scathing review, the concerto quickly caught on; its success vindicated Tchaikovsky while he was still active.

Although he was not a violinist—he relied on the advice of a violin-playing student of his during the composition of the concerto—Tchaikovsky understood the idiomatic qualities and distinctive attributes of the instrument. As a result, the concerto showcases the violin's potential for brilliance and lyricism.

In the hands of a skilled performer, the violin is unmatched in the variety of timbres that can be produced. As a lyric instrument, it can come closer than any other to matching the nuance and expressiveness of a beautiful voice. As a brilliant instrument, it can generate tremendous energy not only because it allows extraordinarily fleet playing but also because performers can give each tone in a fast passage a percussive bite. Moreover, it has a wide range, from the lower notes of a woman's vocal range to the upper threshold of human hearing. The violin can sing, it can dance, and it can soar over the orchestra.

The violin can sing, it can dance, and it can soar over the orchestra.

© iStockphoto.com/Vetta Collection

In the last movement of his Violin Concerto in D major, Tchaikovsky exploits all of these qualities in a movement that epitomizes characteristic features of the Romantic concerto. Tchaikovsky uses the Classical *rondo* (a form in which a bright and tuneful opening section returns in alternation with contrasting material) as his point of depature and paints the form in bold strokes. Right from the start, the solo violin is in the spotlight, beginning with the brief but bravura cadenza that bridges the second and third movements. The vigorous opening theme gives violinists an opportunity to display their agility. The two themes in the contrasting section show the passionate and lyric possibilities of the instrument. Throughout the movement, the soloist dominates; even when the orchestra takes over, as in the lyric part of the contrasting sections, it's just a matter of time before the soloist "one-ups" the wind instruments.

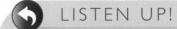
The dominance of the soloist is one dimension of the Romantic interpretation of the concerto. Others that stand out are the richness of the orchestral accompaniment, the extended sections that maintain and manipulate the same melodic material and texture, and the dramatic contrast in thematic material and tempo. For Tchaikovsky and the audience, it was a winning formula: a brilliant, musically compelling solo part; lavish accompaniment; boldly delineated contrasts between energetic and lyric sections in an easily tracked form; and—as is so often the case with Tchaikovsky—memorable melodic material.

Tchaikovsky, German Greatness, and a Question of Value

In one of his rock-and-roll–defining songs, Chuck Berry asks Beethoven to roll over and tell Tchaikovsky the news. In Berry's catchy lyric is the implication that, in popular culture, Beethoven and Tchaikovsky are comparably important: both are (in the vernacular of Berry's era) "longhair" composers. Within the world of classical music that was not the case.

Wagner and Brahms may be the most-esteemed composers of the latter part of the nineteenth century, but Tchaikovsky's music is arguably the most popular. His ballets, concertos, and symphonies have remained audience favorites for over a century, and their appeal shows no signs of diminishing.

By contrast, critical reception of Tchaikovsky's music has been far more mixed. During his lifetime, he received criticism from his fellow Russian composers because his music wasn't fiercely nationalistic enough, while central European critics (and those in other parts of the world who followed their lead) felt that his music didn't belong in the exalted company of Beethoven and the other great German-speaking composers because it deviated too much from their compositional approach.

In part because of the dominant presence of German thought in all aspects of musical education—scholarship, performance, composition (in the nineteenth century, aspiring American composers went to Germany for advanced training), German values have held sway over musical aesthetics from the middle of the nineteenth century through much of the twentieth. Indeed, they are still strong. As a result, the aesthetic hierarchy that they propounded has until relatively recently enjoyed almost unquestioned acceptance.

The issue is less the greatness of Bach and Beethoven than it is that the worth of other composers' music should be evaluated according to a set of values derived from the music of Bach and Beethoven. The particular nature of Tchaikovsky's genius, especially his remarkable gift for expansive melody and orchestral color, was not suited to this aesthetic. If Tchaikovsky had adhered to a Beethoven-like approach to melodic and formal development—an approach similar to Brahms's—it would have placed a compromising constraint on his music.

We will encounter this notion of relative worth with increasing frequency in the upcoming chapters. Highly original composers such as Debussy and Gershwin found their music relegated to second-class status because it expressed a markedly different aesthetic. Only recently—especially since the rock revolution of the 1960s—have musicians and commentators begun to take a broader view of musical worth, using criteria such as the appropriateness of musical choices to the intended result, instead of an attractive but ultimately arbitrary absolute.

CHAPTER 34

Music and Dance: The Waltz

"We remarked with pain that the indecent foreign dance called the Waltz was introduced . . . at the English court on Friday last."
—*London Times*, July 1816

During the finale of the first act of Mozart's *Don Giovanni*, Don Giovanni invites Zerlina, Masetto, and the villagers to a festive affair at his residence, an event also attended by Donna Anna, Donna Elvira, and Don Ottavio. There is dancing, with orchestras onstage (as well as in the pit). After Don Giovanni welcomes the villagers, one of the orchestras begins playing a minuet to which Anna, Elvira, and Ottavio dance. Shortly after the dance begins, two other orchestras begin playing distinctly dif-

Did You Know?

"Wow, this guy, what a cat; he can really move in his own way."—Ballet star Mikhail Baryshnikov, talking about Michael Jackson

ferent dances, a *contredanse* in simple duple meter and a *deutscher*, a peasant dance, in a fast compound meter. Mozart's compositional tour de force draws class distinctions through dance music. The minuet retained its strong association with the aristocracy throughout the eighteenth century. The *contredanse* (a French version of the English "country dance") had replaced the minuet as the most popular dance in France among the aristocracy and the bourgeoisie. (Recall also that it spread to the French colonies; it was the starting point for the habanera.) Because of its less elite association, Mozart uses it to accompany Don Giovanni as he tries once more to seduce the peasant girl Zerlina on her wedding day; the dance tells us that they have found a social middle ground. The *deutscher* accompanies Leporello as he tries to distract Masetto by dancing with him.

LO7 Dance in Nineteenth-Century Life

By incorporating dances from three social classes in his opera, Mozart anticipates the most salient aspect of dance in nineteenth-century life: it was the most upwardly mobile of the expressive arts. Ballet, a part of opera since the seventeenth century, would become an independent art form in the 1830s. Social dancing would flourish among all levels of society as more and more people moved into the city. Folk dances scaled the social ladder, offering rhythmic support to popular music and a sense of national identity in art music. Reams of dances were published, from simple pieces for one or two pianists and fiddle tunes to complex, dance-inspired compositions.

THE GROWTH OF DANCE IN INDUSTRIALIZED NATIONS

The rapid growth of the middle class and the Industrial Revolution, which brought working-class people into the cities, triggered an explosion of dance in the nineteenth century. During the course of the century, both wages and working conditions improved, providing people with more money to spend and more time to spend it. Improved transportation made it easier to move around, and—toward the end of the century—electric lights made it safer to go out in the evening.

© Ball in a Paris Suburb, c.1892 [pencil on paper] [see also 193271], Steinlen, Theophile Alexandre (1859-1923) / Hermitage, St. Petersburg, Russia / The Bridgeman Art Library International

There was an explosion of dance in the nineteenth century.

Ballrooms and dance halls sprang up in major cities throughout Europe, none more so than Vienna. Two large dance halls were opened in consecutive years, in 1807 and 1808; the larger held over six thousand people. These popular venues provided steady employment for musicians. The most popular were two generations of Strausses, who periodically left their Viennese home base to tour throughout Europe.

Dance also became an increasingly important part of theatrical entertainment, either as part of a varied entertainment or, in the case of ballet, as an evening built around dance. The use of dance in musical entertainment cut across class boundaries. Ballet was an important component of opera, especially in Paris; operettas featured dance numbers—Jacques Offenbach's famous "Can-Can," from his 1858 light opera *Orpheus in the Underworld* brought this working-class dance into a "respectable" venue; dance was also an integral part of more lowbrow entertainment, which included musical comedies and minstrel shows.

© Tristram Kenton/Lebrecht Music & Arts

The can-can

Dance-inspired music also entered the home via the thousands of dances composed for pianists. Some were for solo piano; others were for piano duet—duet playing was a popular pastime in the nineteenth century. Franz Schubert was the first important composer to produce a large quantity of dance music for piano, both solo and duet: hundreds of waltzes, galops, *ecossaises*, *deutscher*, polonaises, and *ländler*; only some of it—mostly the pieces for piano duet—was published during his lifetime. And Schubert wasn't alone. Virtually every important composer of piano music composed music derived from popular dances.

The rise of dance and social dancing in the nineteenth century parallels the rise of song and amateur singing in several respects. Both had been part of musical life since prehistory among all classes. But not until the nineteenth century did those in the business of music discover how to make substantial amounts of money from them. The profusion of dance pieces, from challenging works suitable for concert performance to simple duets for amateurs, was comparable to the outpouring of song, from the most sophisticated art songs to simple ditties. The more widespread use of dance in theatrical productions, either integrated into some kind of staged vocal work or as a complete entertainment in itself, was one dimension of the explosion in stage entertainment for all classes of society. The sudden popularity of social dancing was analogous to the enthusiasm for amateur choral singing; both were, in essence, group activities that attracted people from all walks of life.

Social Dancing: The Waltz

In a scathing editorial published in July 1816, a writer for the *London Times* expressed his outrage over the introduction of the waltz at a ball given by the Prince Regent a few nights earlier:

> We remarked with pain that the indecent foreign dance called the Waltz was introduced (we believe for the first time) at the English court on Friday last. . . . It is quite sufficient to cast one's eyes on the voluptuous intertwining of the limbs and close compressure on the bodies in their dance, to see that it is indeed far removed from the modest reserve which has hitherto been considered distinctive of English females. So long as this obscene display was confined to prostitutes and adulteresses, we did not think it deserving of notice; but now that it is attempted to be forced on the respectable classes of society by the civil examples of their superiors, we feel it a duty to warn every parent against exposing his daughter to so fatal a contagion.

Partners typically held each other so closely that there was "compressure" up and down the torso.

The editor of the *Times* was not alone in voicing his disapproval of this new dance that was taking Europe by storm. Religious leaders were virtually unanimous in their condemnation of the waltz, and so were the more priggish members of society. What scandalized them was "the voluptuous intertwining of the limbs and close compressure on the bodies": in dancing the waltz, particularly at the brisk pace so often used in the nineteenth century, partners typically held each other so closely that there was "compressure" up and down the torso.

Despite (and perhaps also because of) these objections, the waltz became the most popular ballroom dance by far—during the nineteenth century, among all classes. Queen Victoria, the quintessential English female during her sixty-three–year reign, loved to waltz. So apparently did Franz Josef I, the ruler of the Austro-Hungarian Empire; he was the dedicatee of Johann Strauss's *Emperor Waltz*.

The **waltz** is a social dance in a fast triple meter. Beyond the triple meter and the tempo, the most pervasive rhythmic characteristic of the waltz is a pronounced difference in the strength of the beats within the measure. Typically, the first beat (often called the **downbeat**) receives more emphasis—by far—than the second; the third is more emphasized than the second, but lighter than the first beat. A visual representation of the difference in emphasis.

$$\mathbf{1} \text{-} 2 \text{-} 3 \,/\!/\, \mathbf{1} \text{-} 2 \text{-} 3 \,/\!/\, \mathbf{1} \text{-} 2 \text{-} 3 \,/\!/\, \mathbf{1} \text{-} 2 \text{-} 3 \,/\!/$$

The movements of the dancers reflect this pattern of emphasis: they typically consist of a strong step combined with a lift of the bodies on the downbeat, followed by two small steps in alternation:

$$\mathbf{L} \text{-} R \text{-} L \,/\!/\, \mathbf{R} \text{-} L \text{-} R \,/\!/\, \mathbf{L} \text{-} R \text{-} L \,/\!/\, \mathbf{R} \text{-} L \text{-} R \,/\!/$$

Dancers repeat this pattern of steps endlessly as they twirl around the dance floor, bobbing from one downbeat to the next.

The waltz takes its name from the characteristic movement of the dancers. In German, *wälzen* means "to roll or turn"; in the waltz, the dancers twirl around as they glide across the dance floor. The waltz began as a humble peasant dance in the more rural parts of southern Germany, Austria, and Bohemia (now part of

waltz Social dance in a fast triple meter

downbeat First, emphasized beat in a measure

the Czech Republic); it was one of many such "German dances." It began to spread into the cities toward the end of the eighteenth century, and the name appears in dance collections with increasing frequency during the 1780s and 1790s. For many, it was a simpler and more appealing dance than the minuet, a more complex dance that had retained its favored place among aristocrats through much of the eighteenth century.

In the 1820s, the waltz enjoyed a surge in popularity, first in Vienna, then throughout Europe. The catalysts were the Viennese composers Joseph Lanner and Johann Strauss the Elder, who delighted Viennese audiences as a team, then as leaders of their own dance orchestras. Strauss soon toured relentlessly throughout Europe, bringing the Viennese waltz to a much wider audience. Strauss's son (and rival) Johann Strauss the Younger would enjoy even greater success, in Vienna and ultimately throughout Europe and the United States. As the waltz grew in popularity, composers increased their production of waltzes for home use, for dancing, and as concert music.

Johann Strauss the Younger and the Viennese Waltz

Three of the elder Strauss's sons became professional dance musicians; Johann the Younger was the eldest of them. From the bare facts of their careers, it would seem as though the father prepared his sons for careers, much as J. S. Bach did for his sons. In fact, the opposite is true; the father actively discouraged them from pursuing musical careers, although they received instruction in piano and heard music constantly at home. All received good educations in preparation for "respectable" careers: Johann the Younger was to be a banker. Johann received his advanced musical training without his father's knowledge. Indeed, if the father had not been distracted by his longtime relationship with his mistress and frequently absent while on tour, it is possible that none of the sons would have pursued careers in music.

Although he made a successful professional debut at nineteen, Johann's career did not take off until his father's death in 1849, after which he merged his and his father's orchestras. For the next half century, he and his brothers dominated the ballrooms of Vienna. Johann's music was both exceedingly popular and well received critically. He was a revered and respected figure in Vienna virtually his entire career, despite fallout from siding with revolutionaries during the 1848 uprising.

Johann Strauss the Younger (center in the caricature of him and his brothers) became the "Waltz King," the composer whose music virtually defined the Viennese waltz as a genre and whose name is all but synonymous with the waltz. Although he published around five hundred dances of various types (waltzes, polkas, marches, and quadrilles) and several operettas, the heart of his musical legacy is the series of memorable waltzes composed at the height of his career. Among the best known are *The Beautiful Blue Danube* (1867); *Wine, Women, and Song* (1869); and *The Emperor Waltz* (1889).

These waltzes are extended works, effectively a medley of several—as many as five or six—waltz tunes, and are generally framed by an introduction and a coda. They typically include features borrowed from concert music, such as development of previously presented material, multiple changes of key, and interruption of the periodic rhythm of the dances with interludes and compression and expansion of sections.

The most distinctive and engaging feature of Strauss's waltzes are his melodies. Two qualities above all distinguish his melodies. First, they are tuneful, even singable; by contrast, many earlier waltzes have melodies more appropriate for instruments. Second (and more distinctively), they capture the lilt inherent in the dance itself: the musical counterpart to the movements of the dancers is the interplay of buoyant melody and the

Joseph Strauss the Younger

Fast Facts

- *Dates:* 1825–1899

- *Place:* Austria

- *Reasons to remember:* The "Waltz King," whose music defined the Viennese waltz as a genre

© Lebrecht Music & Arts

LISTEN UP!

CD 4:10

Strauss, *The Emperor Waltz*, excerpt (1889)

Takeaway point: A quintessential example of the Viennese waltz

Style: Romantic

Form: Multisection

Genre: Waltz

Instruments: Orchestra

Context: Music for the ballroom, and occasionally the concert hall

steady rhythm of the accompaniment rhythm. We hear these features in an excerpt from *The Emperor Waltz*.

Strauss's waltzes are functional music—music intended for social dancing—although they are also performed as concert music. The next dance is also a waltz but for a quite different purpose.

Tchaikovsky and the Ballet

Dance is to the French much as singing is to Italians: not only a basic human activity but also part of their cultural identity. Not surprisingly then, France is the home of ballet, just as Italy is the home of opera. However, ballet would find a second home in Russia.

BALLET

The word *ballet* is French, a cognate of the Italian word *balletto*, meaning "little dance." For many of us, "ballet" conjures up the sounds and images of *The Nutcracker*, Tchaikovsky's Christmastime favorite: dancers, including ballerinas on their toes, dressed in elaborate costumes, telling a story through elaborately choreographed movement, with the musical support of a full orchestra.

Tchaikovsky's ballets, most notably *The Nutcracker*, *Swan Lake*, and *The Sleeping Beauty* (which we sample later) are the most famous examples of what is most often called "classical ballet" or "Romantic ballet," which flourished from about 1830 to the end of the nineteenth century. The emergence of Romantic ballet marked the beginning of dance as an independent art in contemporary culture. In turn, it was the direct product of an evolutionary development that began in the middle of the seventeenth century.

Dance before Classical Ballet. The godfather of ballet was Louis XIV, an enthusiastic dancer and dance enthusiast himself. During the early years of his reign (b. 1638, r. 1643–1715), he sponsored or supported several important institutions and developments, including the formation of the Académie Royale de Danse, which brought together the leading dancing masters in France; the formation of a professional dance troupe within the Académie Royale de Musique,

Marie Taglioni *en pointe*

© Marie Taglioni (1804-84) in 'Flore et Zephire' by Cesare Bossi, c.1830 (litho), Chalon, Alfred-Edward (1780-1860) (after) / Victoria & Albert Museum, London, UK / The Bridgeman Art Library International

a training ground for the opera; and the publication of numerous dance treatises.

These developments supported the growth of dance as a virtuosic and expressive art. The formalization of training and the formation of a professional dance troupe expanded the ever-widening gap between skilled amateur and professional dancing; indeed, Louis XIV gave up dancing in public in 1670. In late seventeenth-century French opera, dance became an integral part of the expressive message rather than a diversion, as it had been during the Renaissance. Hybrid genres, such as Lully's opera-ballets, in which dance both animated and complemented vocal numbers, evidence the emergence of professional dancing. Collectively, these developments provided a foundation for ballet as a discipline and a starting point for its evolution into an independent art form.

During the eighteenth century, dance continued to be an important part of opera, in Italy as well as France, and in European centers, such as Stockholm and St. Petersburg, where French cultural influence was prominent. This is reflected in the growth of dance troupes connected with opera companies and the steady employment of choreographers and dancing masters. The use of dance in Italian opera differed from the French approach: typically, it served as an interlude between acts of an *opera seria*. Still, ballet and the music for it played a significant role in opera. Gluck, whose works initiated a thorough reform of opera, was praised for the way in which his music supported the pantomime of the action.

The Ballerina and the Emergence of Classical Ballet. Although the practice of composing and producing ballet as an independent stage work dates from the late eighteenth century, dance historians cite an 1832 production of *La sylphide*, a work choreographed by Filippo Taglioni, as the beginning of classical, or Romantic, ballet. The star of the production was Marie Taglioni, Filippo's daughter and star pupil, and the first of the great prima ballerinas. The most spectacular feature of her performance was dancing almost exclusively *en pointe* (on the toes). Marie Taglioni's use of pointe was a startling innovation; other dancers had experimented with it, but none before Taglioni had integrated it so fully into her dancing.

ballet An independent, expressive dance genre in which movement and music tell the story

Filippo Taglioni's ballet broke new ground in several respects. First, it established the narrative **ballet** as an independent genre. Movement and music suffice to tell the story. Second, Marie Taglioni's use of pointe made this practice the norm: it became the defining feature of classical ballet. Third, it completed the gradual shift in dance from masculine to feminine. In seventeenth-century France, the first dance stars were male; men continued to dominate dance through the eighteenth century, although women were more prominent. However, with the emergence of Marie Taglioni and other prima ballerinas, the spotlight shifted to women. The central character in *La sylphide* is a sylph, a female fairy who falls in love with a mortal. In Tchaikovsky's *Sleeping Beauty*, the characters who move the story forward are fairies; Sleeping Beauty is a princess.

Ballet: Expression and Virtuosity. Dance is the most obviously athletic of the arts. Ballet audiences cheered Mikhail Baryshnikov after a series of leaps featuring two complete turns—a 720 done in time to the music!—as enthusiastically as Chicago Bulls fans cheered Michael Jordan after one of his spectacular dunks. Even the proverbial person on the street is aware of the particular challenge of dancing lightly on one's toes—in classical ballet, only women have traditionally danced en pointe, although that has begun to change.

Ballet audiences cheered Mikhail Baryshnikov after a series of leaps featuring two complete turns—a 720 done in time to the music!

However, ballet and the dancing tradition from which it evolved have also been an expressive art. As early as 1668, a French dance theorist described ballet (as his culture understood it) as "a mute representation, in which the gestures and movements signify what could be expressed through words." The very fact that ballet evolved into an art in which music and dance merge to tell a story demonstrates that the expressive dimension of ballet is central.

The interplay between virtuosity and expression is as central a tension in ballet as the tension between vocal virtuosity and expression is in opera. In both, the ideal has been virtuosity in the service of expression. The challenge for composers and choreographers is to create works in which this is possible. In the nineteenth century, the composer who met this challenge most successfully was Tchaikovsky.

THE SLEEPING BEAUTY

It is ironic that Handel and Tchaikovsky, the most versatile composers of their respective eras, owe their place in the popular imagination to a single work. Just as many know Handel most familiarly from *Messiah*, so do many know Tchaikovsky's music mainly, or even exclusively, through *The Nutcracker*, his most famous ballet. Tchaikovsky composed successfully in more genres than any other important nineteenth-century composer, as we noted previously. However, his three ballets, *Swan Lake*, *The Nutcracker*, and *The Sleeping Beauty*, set him apart from every other major nineteenth-century composer.

He composed *The Sleeping Beauty* (1889) and *The Nutcracker* (1892) during his later years, despite the poor reception of his first major ballet, *Swan Lake*, more than a decade earlier. In the thirteen-year interim between *Swan Lake* and *The Sleeping Beauty*, Tchaikovsky's star had risen. During that same period, Ivan Vsevolozhsky, a creative mind with considerable administrative skill and a passion for excellence, had assumed control of the Imperial Theatres in St. Petersburg in 1881. In 1889, he instructed Marius Petipa to choreograph the fairy tale of the sleeping beauty and commissioned Tchaikovsky to compose the music; Vsevolozhsky designed the costumes and set himself. As was the custom, Petipa provided Tchaikovsky with detailed guidelines; Tchaikovsky collaborated with Petipa in preparing the score. The result was what many commentators regard as the quintessential classical ballet.

Petipa and Tchaikovsky based *The Sleeping Beauty* on a fairy tale first recounted by Charles Perrault in 1697 and later adapted by the Brothers Grimm, whose version the team used as a point of departure. The story is an allegory of good and evil, set in an imaginary kingdom in an unreal world. King Florestan and his queen invite six fairies, who will serve as godmothers, to the christening of their daughter, Aurora. All but one have bestowed their gifts on the infant when Caraboose, an evil fairy who is outraged because she was not invited, puts a curse on Aurora: on her sixteenth birthday, she will prick her finger and die. The Lilac Fairy, who had not presented her gift, mitigates Caraboose's curse by modifying its terms: Aurora and the kingdom will sleep

LISTEN UP!

CD 4:11

Tchaikovsky, Waltz, from *The Sleeping Beauty* (1889)

Takeaway point: A concert waltz for professional dancers

Style: Romantic

Form: Multisectional

Genre: Ballet

Instruments: Orchestra

Context: The use of a waltz within a ballet as an exuberant sound symbol of celebration

The beginning of the waltz was enough to communicate the message; this in turn liberated both composer and choreographer from the necessity to adhere strictly to the conventions of the dance. As a result, Tchaikovsky's waltz is not music for social dancing. The most fundamental reasons are rhythmic: the intermittent timekeeping in the accompaniment and the frequent syncopations that regroup beats into pairs. Strict timekeeping is not necessary in ballet, and Petipa's original choreography features elaborate dancing that bears no resemblance to the waltz as danced socially. The dancers make clear what is implicit in the music: Tchaikovsky's waltz is music about waltzing and the occasions at which waltzing takes place rather than music for waltzing.

Rhythm, Dance, and Art

The two waltzes here, one for social dancing and the other for ballet, offer an unusually explicit case study of rhythmic differences between music for amateur dancers and music for professionals. In both cases, the defining rhythm of the waltz serves as a kind of aural graph paper onto which the composers map their musical designs. In *The Emperor Waltz*, Strauss had to maintain the OOM-pah-pah rhythm to keep dancers on the beat. The rhythmic play must come mainly in the melody—and also in the performing tradition, in which the anticipation of the second beat undermines the regularity of the accompaniment rhythm. By contrast, Tchaikovsky was liberated from the regular marking of time, because the elaborate choreography does not require the relentless waltz rhythm. He needed to suggest only periodically the rhythmic feel of the waltz to maintain it as a symbol. As a result, there are extended passages where the characteristic waltz accompaniment is absent and also occasional syncopations.

Both works are functional, in the sense that they accompany dancing. However, there is a clear difference in function: social dancing versus dance as art. More generally, Tchaikovsky's rhythmic liberties are characteristic of the rhythmic relationships between dance-inspired art music and the dances that inspired it; the ratio of rhythmic variety and rhythmic play to timekeeping increases when composers are not constrained by the need to mark time for dancers. We will encounter similar circumstances in the next chapter and in later discussions of jazz and rock.

for one hundred years, when a prince will discover Aurora and wake her—and the kingdom—with a kiss. The prince finds the castle, overgrown after the hundred years, overcomes Caraboose, and awakens Aurora. The remainder of the ballet is a celebration of the wedding, in which not only fairies but also a parade of fairy-tale creatures join in the festivities.

The waltz occurs early in Act I, as part of the celebration for Princess Aurora's birthday, the occasion where she pricks her finger and puts herself and the kingdom to sleep. The scene provides an opportunity for the dance corps to shine.

In *The Sleeping Beauty*, the waltz is an evocative symbol because it was an especially direct way to convey a festive celebration through music and dance.

The Rise of Dance

Those who attended late nineteenth-century performances of *Don Giovanni* would have understood the dance scene described at the beginning of the chapter as a true period piece. It did not reflect the contemporary relationship between dance and class, because gentrified country dances—polka, galop, and above all, the waltz—blurred class boundaries, which were drawn so sharply in the opera. Everyone danced the waltz, from royalty to the working classes. In this way, the waltz and the institutions that sprang up around it—dance halls and ballrooms, publishing of dance music for concert and domestic use, touring orchestras—reflected the reluctant but relentless movement toward a more egalitarian society in both Europe and North America.

Ballet represented a different kind of ascendancy: the emergence of dance as an independent expressive art. At the beginning of the nineteenth century, ballet was still largely tied to opera. By the end of the century, ballet as a distinct and self-sufficient art form flourished in France and Russia and was gaining a presence in Europe and the United States. The innovations of Marie Taglioni and others raised the bar, establishing classical ballet in the process. Tchaikovsky's ballets introduced music of comparable quality to the dance.

These and other trends, such as the use of dance rhythms in popular song and the composition of elaborate dance-inspired instrumental works, evidenced the increasing importance of dance in cultural life during the course of the nineteenth century. We consider yet another role of dance, the affirmation of cultural identity, in the next chapter.

CHAPTER 35

Nationalism

"The Americans expect great things of me. I am to show them the way into the Promised Land, the realm of a new, independent art, in short a national style of music!" —Antonín Dvořák, September 1892

Did You Know?

Calypso (Trinidad), samba (Brazil), and reggae (Jamaica) are Afrocentric, dance-based musical styles that are firmly rooted in their home countries.

In June 1891, the Czech composer Antonín Dvořák received a telegram from Jeannette Thurber with the following message: "would you accept position director national conservatory of music New York October 1892 also lead six concerts of your works."

Jeannette Thurber was the daughter of a violinist, the wife of a wealthy businessman, and a musician who had studied at the Paris Conservatory. With the support of fellow philanthropists, she founded the National Conservatory of Music of America in New York in 1885. Her ultimate goal was to create a uniquely American national conservatory along the lines of the Paris Conservatory. She would attract numerous eminent musicians to the faculty. During its first years, the conservatory was open to students of all races, and tuition was free.

One of the most important components of Jeannette Thurber's vision for the conservatory was fostering a national school of classical composition. To increase its prestige and further her vision, she recruited Antonín Dvořák as director. Dvořák was her ideal candidate because he was an ardent nationalist and one of the most highly regarded composers in Europe. He was initially reluctant to leave Prague, but a visit by a National Conservatory faculty member and the offer of an annual salary of $15,000 (over $350,000 today) convinced him to come.

His charge was to guide American composers in the formation of a national school of composition. He accepted enthusiastically, as he indicated in numerous public statements and private correspondence. Shortly after arriving in the United States in late September, he wrote to a friend: "The Americans expect great things of me. I am to show them the way into the Promised Land, the realm of a new, independent art, in short a national style of music!"

The conscious nationalism exemplified by Dvořák's music was an important trend in European cultural life during the latter half of the nineteenth century. In music, it was the second wave of nationalism, a continuation of and a response to the dominant international style that emanated from German-speaking Europe.

LO8 Nationalism in Nineteenth-Century Music

The idea of national styles in music dates from the early sixteenth century, with the publication of vernacular songs, such as the Italian *frottola* and the French *chanson*. Dances with a regional identity quickly followed songs in print, but the association with their roots tended to dissolve as they moved up the social ladder and from one land to the next. Through the early eighteenth century, composers were more concerned with pleasing patrons and employers than consciously attempting to portray the identity of a people. During the Baroque era, the most identifiably French music was the overture, which was the entrance music of the king.

In the first part of the nineteenth century, the most prominent nationalistic movement involved not a country but a language. German-speaking Europe after the fall of Napoleon included the Austrian part of the Holy Roman Empire and the thirty-nine states of the German Confederation. With the cultural ascendancy of instrumental music, the widespread veneration of Beethoven, the classicizing of Haydn and Mozart, and the resurrection of Bach's music, German/Viennese music challenged the prestige and influence of Italian opera. The *Lied* added another more specific dimension to the shared culture of German-speaking people. Karl Maria von Weber's *Der Freischütz* (*The Freeshooter*), advertised as a "Romantic opera" and first staged in 1821, tapped into the German fascination with *Volk* (peasants), nature, and the supernatural—themes also evident in *Erlkönig*. It was immediately recognized as a German national opera, in Germany and elsewhere, and exerted a powerful influence on Wagner. Weber's opera would anticipate the unification of Germany by fifty years: the German Empire was formed only in 1871.

German musical nationalism soon became German musical imperialism. By midcentury, the music of German composers dominated the symphonic repertoire, much as the music of Italian composers dominated opera, and German music became the de facto international style in instrumental music. As a result, in the latter part of the century some composers outside German-speaking Europe, particularly in Slavic countries, Scandinavia, and Spain, began to cultivate a national style, to declare cultural independence—at least to some degree—from German and Italian music. To do so, they focused on the folk traditions and history of their cultures.

For nineteenth-century composers, **nationalism** in music was a means of asserting national identity—a sense of the distinctive cultural characteristics of a nation. Nationalistic composers found three important ways to invest their music with a national identity. They based works on the legends, myths, history, and literature of the people, particularly in opera and in programmatic instrumental music. They created vocal music in their own language and provided folk melodies within sophisticated musical settings, in opera and song. And they composed instrumental works based on the folk dances of their cultures.

Nationalistic dance music is in some ways the most accessible, because listeners do not have to know the language to discern its message and because its characteristic rhythms are often immediately recognizable.

nationalism In music, a nineteenth-century movement that sought to portray a uniquely national identity by drawing on the legends, myths, history, and literature of the people; creating vocal music in their own language; and drawing on folk song and dance

National Dances and Nationalism

Dance music has typically been associated with place, as we noted in our discussion of the Baroque dance suite. However, dances intended as expressions of national identity represent a shift in attitude, in that part of their purpose is to convey not only a particular locale but also the character and spirit of the folk who inhabit it. The emergence of concert and domestic music inspired by national and regional dances can be seen

Dances intended as expressions of national identity conveyed not only a particular locale but also the character and spirit of the folk who inhabit it.

as a reflection of the changing political and social landscape in the nineteenth century. The history of the polonaise is instructive in that regard.

Polonaise is the French name for the *polonez*, a dance from Poland. Like many European dances, the *polonez* first came to light as a folk dance. In the seventeenth century, the Polish aristocracy adapted it for their use; in this setting, it became slower and statelier. Beginning in the late seventeenth century, it began to spread throughout Europe where it was popular in courts and appeared occasionally in instrumental suites. During this time, the French name for the dance gained currency; it was known even in Poland as a polonaise.

For the polonaise/*polonez* and other folk-derived dances, the seventeenth and eighteenth centuries might be understood as an era of colonization, in the sense that the process of assimilating folk dances into upper-class society stripped away the sense of place and class—in the case of the polonaise, even to the name! That process was reversed to some extent in the nineteenth century. Chopin, a Polish expatriate in the wake of the 1830 uprising and its suppression by Russia, apparently used the dances of his homeland as an expression of solidarity with the Polish people. His later polonaises are grand pieces: many commentators feel that they not only connect to Chopin's homeland but also capture the revolutionary spirit that was suppressed so violently. Similarly, his numerous mazurkas are sophisticated concert pieces and implicit expressions of national identity and pride.

For others, like Robert Schumann and Liszt, the polonaise was simply a characteristic rhythm, without nationalistic overtones. As a result, Polish dances such as the polonaise and mazurka appeared both as social dances or dance-inspired concert music and, for Chopin, as works conveying the spirit of the Polish people.

What was relatively rare in the first half of the century became fashionable toward the end. Increasingly, composers from Spain, Scandinavia, and Slavic regions published collections of piano pieces based on regional folk dances. There were practical as well as political reasons for greater interest in national and regional dance music. In 1869, Brahms's publisher Simrock released the first set of his *Hungarian Dances*. These immensely popular pieces made Simrock and Brahms large sums of money. Much of their appeal came from their distinct regional character. For nineteenth-century Europeans, exoticism was the other side of the nationalism coin, and what was national in Prague, Barcelona, or Oslo was exotic elsewhere—a visit to a foreign land without leaving town.

Among the most popular sets of dances were the *Slavonic Dances* of Antonín Dvořák, a little-known Czech composer at the time of their publication.

Dvořák's *Slavonic Dances*: From Village Square to Concert Hall

In July 1874, Antonín Dvořák, newly married and struggling to put food on the table for himself and his bride, applied for a grant from the Austrian government, submitting fifteen of his compositions in support of his application. He received the grant and similar grants during the next four years. The second year, when Brahms was a member of the panel, he learned of Dvořák's music and was particularly drawn to his *Moravian Duets* for two sopranos and piano.

Perhaps Brahms felt kinship on several levels: a common interest in folk music, similar experiences during their formative years (both played extensively in orchestras that performed the popular music of the time and place), a firsthand knowledge of economic hard times. Certainly, he found value in Dvořák's music and offered him musical advice, which Dvořák gratefully accepted. They would establish a close friendship, which lasted until Brahms's death.

Brahms also wrote to his publisher Simrock on Dvořák's behalf, encouraging him to publish some of Dvořák's music. Simrock soon asked Dvořák to compose a set of folk dances for piano duet, in the hope that Dvořák's dances would replicate the success of Brahms's *Hungarian Dances*. He got his wish: the publication of the *Slavonic Dances* in the fall of 1878 brought Simrock healthy sales and brought Dvořák international recognition almost overnight. The choice of title—"Slavonic," rather than "Bohemian"—reflected Dvořák's responsiveness to the Pan-Slavic movement of the late nineteenth century.

ANTONÍN DVOŘÁK

Antonín Dvořák grew up in a village north of Prague in Bohemia, which is now the western and middle third of the Czech Republic. His childhood music-making experiences included playing violin in the village band, which often accompanied local dances. He moved to Prague in 1857, where he received much of his training (at an organ school) while supporting himself giving piano lessons and playing in theater orchestras, in which he performed under Bedrich Smetana, the ardently nationalistic Czech composer and conductor.

Antonín Dvořák

Fast Facts

- *Dates:* 1841–1904

- *Place:* Austrian Empire; now Czech Republic (Bohemia)

- *Reasons to remember:* Leading nineteenth-century nationalistic composer, best known for his instrumental music

© Postcard depicting Antonín Dvořák (1841–1904) before 1914 (colour litho), Austrian School, (20th century) / Private Collection / Archives Charmet / The Bridgeman Art Library International

With the success of the *Slavonic Dances*, Dvořák gained the support of leading German musicians and critics. His international renown made him a hero at home and the composer of choice for state occasions. Ten years later he would serve briefly as professor of composition at Prague Conservatory, before leaving for the United States in 1892. In between came several trips to London, which were gratifying to his spirit and his wallet. His time in the United States was productive for him and the conservatory: he composed his famous "Symphony from the New World" and cello concerto in America. Upon his return to Europe, he devoted himself almost exclusively to opera. However, his reputation as a leading nineteenth-century composer is based mainly on his instrumental music—symphonies, concertos, and other orchestral music, and chamber music for various combinations of strings.

SLAVIC IDENTITY

"Slavonic" is an alternate form of "Slavic," a term that identifies a family of languages spoken in Eastern Europe, from Poland to Macedonia and from the contemporary Czech Republic to Russia, and those who speak these languages. The underlying connection among these diverse languages has provided a common bond, despite differences in alphabet (some languages, such as Czech and Polish, use the Roman alphabet; others, like Russian and Serbian, use the Cyrillic alphabet) and religion (some, such as Poles, Czechs, and Slovenes are predominantly Catholic; others, such as Russians, Serbians, and Ukrainians, are predominantly Orthodox).

Prodaná nevěsta.

Tak tvr-do-šij : hva, di u-ka-jai, že mácho-rá pra. vdu   svě. dát.

Czech folk costumes

© Lebrecht Music & Arts

The Austrian (and later, Austro-Hungarian) Empire was the nineteenth-century incarnation of the Habsburg dynasty, which had ruled central Europe since the fifteenth century. The empire was a loose confederation of diverse peoples that stretched from Bohemia (the western two-thirds of the modern Czech Republic) in the northwest and what is now northern Italy in the southwest, to Montenegro in the south and Transylvania in the east. The empire was a checkerboard of peoples, whose languages belonged to four different language groups: German, Slavic, Romance (Italian), and Finno-Ugric (Hungarian). German was the official language throughout the empire, much as Russian was the official language of the Soviet Union during its seventy-year history.

In the nineteenth century, a group of Slavic intellectuals and artists who lived in territories governed by the Habsburgs founded a Pan-Slavic movement. Their initial aim was to cultivate an awareness of their common heritage through the study of folk traditions and vernaculars, and promote a sense of Slavic unity despite the geographical separation of the Slavic groups. This quickly led to a drive for the political autonomy of Slavic peoples under Habsburg rule, which did not succeed. However, the movement spread to Russia and other Slavic regions.

As their title implies, Dvořák's *Slavonic Dances* are both a fruit and an expression of this Pan-Slavic movement, which was centered in Prague. The first set of eight dances, published in 1878, features two each of three dances from Bohemia: the *sousedska*, a slow couples dance in triple meter; the *skocná*, a fast duple-meter dance in which the male dancer leaps about; and the *furiant*, a triple-meter dance at a moderate to fast tempo; plus a polka, another Bohemian dance that had already spread through Europe and the Americas, and a *dumka*, a slow song of lament popular throughout the Slavic world, which Dvořák underpinned with a steady dance rhythm. We consider the last of the eight dances, a vigorous *furiant*. Following Brahms's example, Dvořák orchestrated the dances; we discuss the orchestral version here.

THE *FURIANT*

In Czech, *furiant* means "a proud, swaggering, conceited man." The *furiant* is a couples dance in a moderate to fast triple meter characterized by a specific rhythm in the melody, which Dvořák uses throughout the dance. In his version, each short phrase of the melody in the main section of the work consists of two long notes, each lasting two beats, plus additional shorter values, in a strict rhythm. A common form of this melodic rhythm is shown in the chart. The long notes conflict with the underlying triple meter and are the principal source of the rhythmic excitement that pervades the piece.

Melody rhythm	**1**	**2**	**1**	**2**	**1**	**2**	1	2	&	3	1	2	&	3
Meter	1	2	3	1	2	3	1	2		3	1	2		3

LISTEN UP!

CD 4:12

Dvořák, Slavonic Dance in G minor (1878)

Takeaway point: Czech folk dance as brilliant and evocative classical music

Style: Romantic

Form: ABA with coda

Genre: Nationalistic dance

Instruments: Orchestra

Context: Sophisticated, folk-inspired dance music for concert performance rather than social dancing

In a typical performance of the work, this rhythmic pattern takes about three seconds to perform. It serves as the building block from which melodies, then complete sections grow: the two large sections in the dance consist mostly of this rhythm set to several different melodic shapes and in several different keys. Through Dvořák's skillful manipulation of contour, key, and orchestral setting, this three-second rhythmic pattern spawns a four-minute composition.

In most respects, Dvořák's musical language is very much in the mainstream. However, the distinctive and persistent melodic rhythm, which conflicts with the underlying triple meter, immediately distinguishes the dance from the waltz, polonaise, and other triple-meter dances of the era; the vitality of Dvořák's setting projects the spirit and energy of folk dance music.

It may be difficult for us to understand the mind-set of the late nineteenth-century American commentator who remarked disparagingly about Dvořák's "Slav naïveté . . . that degenerates into sheer brainlessness." Dvořák's espousal of nationalism in music was, for him, a double-edged sword. It was his gateway to fame and fortune, but it also relegated his music to second-class status in the musical world of the time, at least in the minds of some critics. Nevertheless, the quest for an identifiably national music was central to his musical identity.

The intriguing question for us is the relationship between folk and art: What is the role of the folk element in concert music? At least in this particular instance, Dvořák's use of the characteristic *furiant* rhythm is far more than a cosmetic overlay. It is the rhythmic seed from which the entire dance springs, and it is the source of the rhythmic vitality that is its essence. It is all but impossible to reconstruct what the *furiant* lost in its journey from village square to concert hall. However, we do know that Dvořák grew up playing this music in its original environment (the village band) and that this kind of rhythmic energy is an organic component of his music. The symphonic setting may give it a gloss that it didn't have in its original home, but it does not enervate the rhythm.

Thirty-five years later, another Slavic composer would turn the world upside down with even more energetic rhythms. We hear excerpts from Igor Stravinsky's *The Rite of Spring* in Chapter 39.

KEYS TO ROMANTIC STYLE

Key Concepts

Telling stories or painting scenes. In much Romantic music, composers tell a story through a series of episodes or scenes. Unlike Baroque music, which developed a single affect, or Classical music, which created, then resolved dramatic tension through well-defined harmonic paths, Romantic music is episodic. It often presents a series of colorful but loosely connected scenes that are more often linked by melodic material than by well-defined formal structures. These features are most evident in many new genres, including art song, ballet, program music, and Wagner's music dramas.

Key Features

1. **Endless melody.** Much Romantic music, both vocal and instrumental, features long, flowing melodies that develop over the course of a long section, or even an entire work.

2. **Distinctive figuration and accompaniment.** Romantic music replaces Classical music's generic scales and arpeggios with distinctive and evocative figuration and accompaniment.

3. **Expanded sound resources.** In instrumental composition and accompaniments for vocal compositions, composers take advantage of increased ensemble size, increased instrumental capabilities, and greater performer virtuosity to expand the range and variety of timbral choices.

4. **Dynamic contrasts.** Because of the increased size of ensembles and increased power of many instruments, dynamic contrasts can be more pronounced. Dynamic change can be gradual as well as abrupt, with long crescendos and diminuendos helping to define waves of sound.

5. **Blurred boundaries.** Partly because of the expansion of size and gesture in Romantic music, the boundaries between sections often feature gradual transitions extending over several measures rather than the decisive cadences of Classical style, which sharply outline sectional divisions.

Key Terms

1. **Nationalism.** Nineteenth-century movement that sought to portray a uniquely national identity by drawing on the legends, myths, history, and literature of the people; creating vocal music in their own language; and drawing on folk song and dance

2. **Absolute music.** Music whose aesthetic value is self-contained and does not require any extramusical reference, such as lyrics, drama, dance, or a program

3. **Through-composed form.** Form in which there is no large-scale formal repetition

4. **Romanticism.** Cultural movement valuing subjectivity, feeling, and inspiration; focus on individuality, obsession with size, fascination with the exotic

5. **Virtuosity** Performance skills far beyond the norm

 Music Concept Check

To assist you in recognizing their distinctive features, we present an interactive comparison of Classical and Romantic style in CourseMate and the eBook.

UNIT 17
MUSICAL LIFE IN THE TWENTIETH CENTURY AND BEYOND

Learning Outcomes
After reading this unit, you will be able to do the following:

LO1 Recognize the widespread impact of technology on every aspect of music in the twentieth century.

LO2 Describe the major musical developments during the twentieth century.

LO3 Paint a picture of the fragmented sound world of the twentieth century in terms of changes in the musical elements.

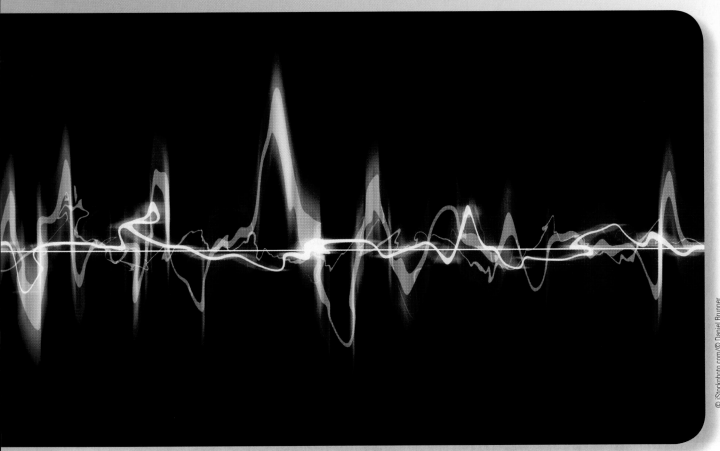

© iStockphoto.com/© Daniel Brunner

The Twentieth Century and Beyond

"The most remarkable fact about musical life in the twentieth century was that the assault on 'music' began at the beginning of the century and never let up."

The lexicographer who prepared the entry for the first *Oxford English Dictionary*, published between 1884 and 1928, began his definition of music this way:

> That one of the fine arts which is concerned with the combination of sounds with a view to beauty of form and the expression of emotion; also, the science of the laws or principles (of melody, harmony, rhythm, etc.) by which this art is regulated.

Microsoft's *Encarta World English Dictionary*, available online and in a print version published in 1999, first defined music this way:

> Sounds, usually produced by instruments or voices, that are arranged or played in order to create a pleasing or stimulating effect.

The second definition includes no mention of a "fine art," or "beauty of form," or the "science" of music. Instead, music can now be simply "pleasing" or "stimulating." These differences reflect the far broader understanding of what music is at the beginning of the twenty-first century.

The most remarkable fact about musical life in the twentieth century was that the assault on traditional "music" began at the beginning of the century and never let up. Music that was brand-new to twentieth-cen-

Did You Know?

Jimmy Page of Led Zeppelin used an updated version of the first electronic instrument, the theremin, in the middle section of "Whole Lotta Love."

tury audiences covered a wide spectrum, from avant-garde experiments to centuries-old folk styles suddenly preserved on recordings, and it came from every corner of the globe. It received unprecedented support from rapidly evolving technologies, which affected music making, performing, and dissemination in every conceivable way.

LO1 Music and Technology

A century of technological innovation, from sound recording to the Internet, had an impact on every aspect of music: its sounds, creation, performance, dissemination, and the ways people listen to and learn it. For the first time in history, it became possible to preserve musical events exactly—from Appalachian folk songs and African drumming to jazz improvisations, compositions for electronic synthesizer, and The Beatles' *Sgt. Pepper's Lonely Hearts Club Band*—as they were first conceived or performed. Each new generation produced technology so novel that previous generations could barely have imagined it. What we all took for granted at the beginning of the twenty-first century would have been beyond even the most futuristic thinkers' comprehension a century earlier.

SOUND RECORDING

Sound recording became a commercial enterprise in the late nineteenth century and grew rapidly after the turn of the century due to improvements in production techniques and playback equipment. At the outset, there were two competing technologies: Thomas Edison's cylinder and Emile Berliner's disc. The two-sided disc eventually won out by the 1910s, because it was easier to produce and stock and because it included recordings on both sides.

The first recordings were primitive: performers sang, spoke, or played their instruments into a megaphone, which transferred the vibrations to the recording medium. This acoustic process didn't work particularly well, and certain instruments were almost impossible to record. A new, much-improved recording process would supplant it almost overnight in 1925.

THE ELECTRICAL REVOLUTION
OF THE 1920S

New electronic technology developed in the first part of the twentieth century sparked a revolution in the production and dissemination of music. Between 1920 and 1927, inventors refined equipment that made possible the conversion of sound into an electrical signal, the transmission of that signal, its conversion back into sound, and its amplification. They applied these new technologies to radio broadcasting, electric recording, amplification of live performance, and talking films. Radio came first.

The first commercial broadcast in the United States took place on November 2, 1920, when KDKA, a Pittsburgh radio station, began broadcasting. By 1925, electrical technology—microphones, amplifiers, and

On November 2, 1920, KDKA, a Pittsburgh radio station, began broadcasting.

speakers—had replaced the more primitive acoustic technology of early radio. The Radio Corporation of America (RCA) formed the National Broadcasting Corporation (NBC), the first important U.S. radio network the following year. It was the first audio-based mass medium and made real-time transcontinental communication possible. The technology developed for radio was soon adapted to recording: electrical recordings offered a dramatic improvement in quality over the acoustic recordings from the first part of the century. Microphones and amplifiers also became standard equipment on the bandstand and in larger venues, and the "talking film" became a reality in 1927 with the release of *The Jazz Singer,* starring Al Jolson, one of the top popular singers of the era.

Within only a few years, the sound world of the twentieth century had changed dramatically. Electrical recording offered much-improved fidelity for all kinds of voices and instruments. Network radio made live performances of many kinds of music much more accessible: NBC would create the NBC Symphony Orchestra for conductor Arturo Toscanini in 1937. Dance orchestras routinely broadcast from hotel ballrooms: Benny Goodman's midnight broadcasts from New York found eager listeners in Los Angeles. Early sound systems opened up new venues—Marian Anderson would sing in front of the Lincoln Memorial to a crowd of seventy-five thousand in 1939—and professional opportunities for new kinds of performers; sound systems made Bing Crosby's career as a crooner possible. Films made musicals available to the masses.

Cumulatively, these developments revolutionized the consumption of music. It was now easier to become acquainted with music, from songs to symphonies, by listening to it rather than reading it. Sheet music sales peaked in the 1910s and have been in decline ever since. No other set of developments has had as transformative an effect on the mode and ease of access to music; that it happened so quickly only added to its impact.

Early Electronic Instruments. Even as radio and recordings were changing the ways music reached its audience, another application of electrical technology was beginning to change the sounds themselves. Three kinds of electronic instruments were developed: purely electronic instruments; instruments that were electronic counterparts, or analogs, to acoustic instruments; and electronic apparatus that

Léon Theremin plays his namesake instrument.

LISTEN FURTHER

Hear the eerie sound of the theremin in the YouTube playlist.

MIDCENTURY TECHNOLOGICAL INNOVATIONS

The middle of the century saw technological innovations on several fronts. Among the most far reaching were the development of the magnetic tape recorder, the emergence of commercial television, and electronic sound synthesis.

Magnetic Tape Recording. Among the technologies confiscated by the Allies at the end of World War II was the Magnetophone, an early magnetic tape recorder developed in Germany during the 1930s and kept secret from the rest of the world during the war. It became the prototype for the Ampex tape recorders that revolutionized recording and broadcasting in the postwar decade. Among the significant changes in the recording process eventually made possible by tape recording were much longer recordings, easier on-site recording, record editing, and improved sound quality.

With magnetic tape recorders, the length of a recording jumped from three or four minutes on a 78-rpm disc to thirty minutes or more. This in turn enabled prerecording of radio broadcasts and spurred the development of the long-playing record. Tape recorders were more portable and easier to use than previous generations of recording apparatus, which made live recording in any context considerably easier. Because the recording was preserved on a thin strip of magnetic tape, it became possible to edit the recording simply by splicing: slicing the recordings at appropriate points and taping the ends together. Among the fruits of this new technique were sound collages made up of sounds from a variety of sources, not all of them "musical"; "perfect" recordings by classical performers; and electronic compositions. Sound quality improved rapidly, with the advent of multitrack recording and stereo playback. Multitrack recording made it

amplified acoustic instruments. The first was an all-electronic instrument.

In 1919, Léon Theremin, a young Russian inventor, created the first electronic instrument, which featured two antennae, one to regulate pitch, the other to regulate volume; it bears his name. The **theremin** is unusual in that performers don't actually touch the instrument; instead, they alter both pitch and volume by moving their hands in relation to the antennae.

Two electric analogs to existing instruments appeared in the 1930s. One was the Hammond organ, designed as a more portable and less expensive alternative to the pipe organ. The first Hammond organ appeared in 1935; it was soon standard equipment not only in churches but also in radio studios, cocktail lounges, and arenas. It would ultimately become a popular instrument in jazz and rock groups and was the first of what would become a flood of electronic keyboard instruments. The other was the Rickenbacker solid-body steel guitar, first introduced in 1931. The instrument was the forerunner of the numerous solid-body instruments that appeared after World War II, most notably Les Paul's electric guitars for Gibson and the electric guitars and basses of Leo Fender.

Electronics were also used to amplify the sound of acoustic instruments. The first amplified instrument to come into common use was the electric guitar, which soon found a home in country music, blues, and rock and roll. Beginning in the late 1950s, companies offered pickups for other string instruments, then wind instruments.

theremin
The first electronic instrument, which featured two antennae: one to regulate pitch, the other to regulate volume

possible to assemble a recording in stages rather than all at once. Tape recording would remain the preferred method until the 1980s.

Television. Television, which exploded as a commercial enterprise after World War II, brought sound and image into the home. Millions watched Elvis and The Beatles on *The Ed Sullivan Show*, as well as Leonard Bernstein's *Young People's Concerts*. The 1985 broadcast of the Live Aid concert had an estimated global audience of 1.5 billion. Significantly, television replaced radio as the all-purpose mass medium; as a result, radio had to redefine itself as the more important outlet for music of all kinds.

Image courtesy of The Advertising Archives

Television, which exploded as a commercial enterprise after World War II, brought sound and image into the home.

Synthesizers. In current usage, a **synthesizer** is an instrument capable of generating sounds electronically. Early synthesizers like the Mark II were huge, cumbersome devices that composers needed to program; they weren't capable of live performance. In the 1960s, transistors replaced vacuum tubes, which reduced the size of the device and made it easier to use. The best known of the synthesizer developers was Robert Moog, whose work became known first through Walter/Wendy Carlos's recording *Switched-on Bach* (1968). Moog soon developed the Minimoog, a portable synthesizer designed for live performance. These early synthesizers were called **analog synthesizers**, because they generated sound by varying voltage. They would soon be replaced by digital instruments.

synthesizer
Instrument capable of generating sounds electronically

analog synthesizer
Electronic musical synthesizer that generates sound by varying voltage

DIGITAL TECHNOLOGY

The digital revolution, which began in the 1970s and continues into our own time, has profoundly reshaped our musical world. In digital technology, an electrical signal from a microphone, input, or playback device is converted into digital information by sampling the waveform at an extremely high rate. Alternatively, computers can generate digital models of the waveform directly. This in turn enabled the following technological advances:

- Unlimited reproduction of the original sound source without deterioration
- **Sampling**, the transfer of a recorded sound from its source into another recording
- **MIDI (Musical Instrument Digital Interface)**, the protocol that enables communication between digital instruments and devices
- Audio workstations and computer software capable of manipulating any sound through a wide array of effects

From this have come such new developments as these:

- Sound editing so sophisticated as to be aurally undetectable
- A host of digital instruments—not only keyboards but also drum machines, wind controllers, and the like, each of which can produce an almost unlimited spectrum of sounds: a keyboard can sound like a harp, a flute, or almost any other imaginable sound

© Jack Robinson/Hulton Archive/Getty Images

Robert Moog with his massive invention

- Nondestructive mixing and application of effects, which allow unlimited revision of the musical original
- The ability to adjust one parameter of music without changing others: change pitch without changing tempo or switching timbres
- The ability to deliver audio over the Internet

We are now in a postliterate musical world. Music literacy—the ability to read and write music—was until recently considered an essential qualification for those who created music, or at least music of some sophistication. However, the advances in digital technology have made it possible to completely bypass notation during the creative process. Indeed, contemporary musicians have the best of all worlds, because of music notation software that has multiple ways of entering data, plays back compositions, and prints publishable scores; and because of videos that capture musicians in performance.

The advances in electronic music technology over the last half century, especially since the digital revolution, have created an alternative musical world. In this world, the recording is the document; it can be completely detached from live performance. Recordings of this kind are as disparate as electronically generated compositions, like Babbitt's *Ensembles for Synthesizer,* and pop artists' "perfect" recordings. What they have in common is the fact that the results are impossible to replicate in live performance with acoustic instruments.

At the beginning of the twenty-first century, we are in the enviable position of having all these options for the creation and transmission of musical ideas. The barriers imposed by time and distance have largely dissolved. We have unprecedented access to the music of the past and present.

LO2 Commerce, Culture, and Art

Around the turn of the twenty-first century, a fun-loving academic wrote a revealing parody of a music department search committee's recommendation. In its supposed letter to the dean, the committee argued against hiring Mozart as a colleague, in part because of his prodigious output as a composer (so much quantity must certainly mean poor quality), his lack of familiarity with early music, his inability to obtain foundation support, his frequent appearances as a performer of his own compositions, his irresponsible lifestyle, and—above all—his lack of interest in earning a doctorate.

The parody underscores how different musical life had become two hundred years after Mozart's death. The part of the musical world that keeps Mozart's music alive—academia, established musical institutions, and record companies—might well have seemed stranger to him than the world of high-level pop, rock, and jazz. In both his world and the contemporary world of pop, rock, and jazz, musicians play their own music, improvise, and depend on the marketplace for their living even as they pursue their art. By contrast, those who understand themselves as continuing Mozart's tradition—contemporary "classical" composers and the performers of their music—rely almost exclusively on institutional support: universities, foundations, and governments.

The committee argued against hiring Mozart as a colleague.

Music grew into a massive business during the twentieth century. The shift in support from church and court to the marketplace, which began in the eighteenth century and gathered steam in the nineteenth, was largely complete by the beginning of World War I. The explosion of mass media in the 1920s and their continuing development through the course of the century confirmed and expanded the commercial basis of much music production and drove the ongoing realignment of the musical world.

The major musical developments during the twentieth century were the emergence of popular music as the dominant commercial force in musical life; the fragmentation of the classical music world and the relentless search in all directions for new sounds

sampling
Transfer of a recorded sound from its source into another recording

MIDI (Musical Instrument Digital Interface)
Protocol that enables communication between digital instruments and devices

THE GROWTH OF POPULAR MUSIC

To gauge the magnitude of the transformation of popular music, compare these three songs: "The Star-Spangled Banner," "Take Me Out to the Ball Game," and "Thriller." At the turn of the nineteenth century, the melody of "The Star-Spangled Banner" was already familiar as a British drinking song; Francis Scott Key simply put new words to it. "Take Me Out to the Ball Game" (1908) was the work of lyricist Jack Norworth and songwriter Albert von Tilzer. Most of the revenue from the song came from sheet music sales: the most popular arrangement was voice with piano accompaniment. The first popular recording of the song, also from 1908, featured strong-voiced Harvey Hindermyer accompanied by a band. For much of 1982, Michael Jackson collaborated with producer Quincy Jones to produce Thriller, the best-selling album of all time (110 million and counting). "Thriller," the title track from the album, was among the music videos that helped Michael Jackson break through MTV's color barrier.

Someone transported from the early nineteenth century to the early twentieth would have had no trouble comprehending "Take Me Out to the Ball Game." It speaks the same musical language as "The Star-Spangled Banner" and reached its audience in much the same way: via sheet music or simply by listening and singing along. The big novelty would have been the recording.

By contrast, "Thriller" would probably have sounded familiar to early twentieth-century listeners only at the most basic level. They might have been aware that the song was on a record. However, the mode of delivery—CD, radio, or music video—would have been completely outside the realm of their experience. For them, films were silent, phonographs were cumbersome contraptions, and recording wasn't yet the primary method of disseminat-

At the turn of the twentieth century, most song revenue came from sheet music sales.

ing popular music. None of the key instruments used in the recording—from drum kits to digital synthesizers—had been invented. Moreover, the idea of a rhythm section—a diverse group of chord, bass, and percussion instruments providing consistent rhythmic and harmonic support—would become an essential component of popular music only in the 1920s. The sound system—on video and in live performance—would have been comparably unfamiliar. Even the very identity of the song is fundamentally different. "Thriller" is what is on the recording; no sheet music version can begin to convey what the song is about.

THE FRAGMENTATION OF CLASSICAL MUSIC

In 1958, an article by the American composer Milton Babbitt entitled "Who Cares If You Listen?" appeared in *High Fidelity* magazine. In it, he argued passionately for the composer's right to follow his muse no matter where it led, even if he ended up alienating most of his potential audience. Babbitt, a pioneer in electronic music, was a professor at Princeton, so he didn't have to rely on income from performances and sales of his music to survive. Universities and other secular institutions had become the new sponsors of classical music; their support liberated composers from having to please a specific patron or a general audience. Babbitt's attitude was a radical departure from the composer/audience relationship of previous generations and one of the products of the fragmentation of the classical music world in the twentieth century.

From the late seventeenth century through the end of the nineteenth, European music and the music from the Americas that was derived from it had shared a common musical language. There were numerous dialects and levels of sophistication—contrast the songs of Schubert, Schumann, and Brahms with the minstrel-show songs of Stephen Foster, for instance—but there seemed to be a collective understanding regarding what music was and what it should express: from the use of common practice harmony and the organization of rhythm through regular meter through the choice of instruments and how they should be played. Even the then-futuristic music of Wagner and Strauss used these assumptions as a point of departure.

All such assumptions came under assault throughout the twentieth century. The bold departures from conventional practice heard in the music of such early twentieth-century composers as Schoenberg, Debussy, Stravinsky, Bartók, and Ives set the tone for the century. For the "modern" composer, innovation became the overriding virtue; the highest distinction among a composer's peers was membership in the avant-garde.

For much of the century, composers suffered under the burden of novelty. Novelty trumped accessibility, artistry, and other elements of musical appeal as a source of status among peers, although it did not guarantee regular performances in the established concert world. Most of the innovators in early twentieth-century music drew on the world around them, crafting these available materials in strikingly new ways. However, as the century progressed, the most prestigious modes of composition, at least among the avant-garde, were those completely divorced from vernacular traditions and the language of eighteenth- and nineteenth-century music. Over time, a compositional pecking order took shape. Those who rejected the musical past and present in the interest of moving forward, most notably the Austrian composer Anton Webern and those who built on his legacy, enjoyed the greatest prestige, at least among high-minded artists and intellectuals. More musically "conservative" composers, such as the Finnish composer Jean Sibelius, and early "crossover" classical/popular composers, such as George Gershwin, were much lower down. This trend peaked in the years following World War II, as composers such as Stravinsky embraced new genres like serialism and a new generation of composers created music that was often conceptually stimulating but challenging even to musically sophisticated audiences. The continuous striving for innovation broadened the gap between the avant-garde and the general public. This in turn all but stopped the assimilation of new music into the standard repertoire. Even at the beginning of the twenty-first century, very little of the music composed since 1945 in the most popular genres—operas, choral works, ballets, orchestral music, chamber music, songs, and solo piano music—has received regular performances.

New directions, many inspired by rock, world music, and reclamation of the classical past, have begun to reverse this trend. It is as if those composers who created this music were now saying, "Yes, we do care whether people listen to our music."

A WORLD OF MUSIC: FOLK TRADITIONS IN THE TWENTIETH CENTURY

Beginning in 1905, the Hungarian composers Béla Bartók and Zoltan Kodály traveled throughout Hungary collecting the songs and dances of peasants in rural areas. They used primitive recording equipment to preserve these folk materials. Eventually, Bartók would travel throughout eastern Europe in search of folk music of diverse cultures. Bartók and Kodály were not alone: throughout the century, musicians and folklorists traveled throughout Europe and the Americas collecting folk music of all kinds. Improvements in travel, mass communication, and sound recording made music from around the world—East India, Africa, the Middle East, Southeast Asia—increasingly accessible; sound and video recordings preserved this music for future generations. Indeed, **ethnomusicology**, the study of music within particular cultures, is largely a twentieth-century discipline.

Bartók recording ethnic music in Slovakia (1907)

The study and preservation of folk music of the world have shaped musical life in the twentieth century in several important ways. The diligent work of folk researchers has made available a body of music that many have found inherently interesting. Because it often builds on quite different assumptions about the nature and function of music, it has helped expand our view of what music is. And because it has so often been an integral part of daily life, it can provide insight into different cultures. Collectively, its influence on twentieth-century music has been pervasive, touching all but the most abstruse styles.

The embrace of folk traditions and the music that they helped shape has been the counter-

ethnomusicology
The study of music within particular cultures

point to the cold exclusivity of avant-garde music. Even more than the growth of popular music, it undermined the hierarchy of musical status that Western culture inherited from the nineteenth century. Assumptions of relative musical worth that seemed to be unquestionable at the beginning of the century were scrutinized and challenged during the course of the century: jazz, a music profoundly influenced by a folk tradition, was seen as a corrupting influence in the early years of the twentieth century; by the end of the century, it had become "America's art music." Jazz's dramatic rise in status was a consequence not only of its musical development but also of a shift in cultural attitudes toward musical worth: "art" in music no longer depended on its coming from Europe.

Beyond Category: Dissolving Musical and Cultural Boundaries

When one considers characteristic sounds and contexts, the distinctions among classical, popular, and folk music during the first few decades of the new twentieth century seemed as sharply defined as the differences among the three primary colors. The distinctions among audiences seemed just as clear: classical music was upper-class music, popular music served the ever-expanding middle class, and folk music belonged to the rural working classes.

However, such distinctions simply describe tendencies, not mutually exclusive categories; the boundaries between these differing types of music were not impermeable. Guardians of "musical decency and moral rectitude" fought a losing battle against the irrepressible advance of ragtime, then blues and jazz. Indeed, blues singer Bessie Smith became the darling of New York sophisticates during the 1920s. And Scott Joplin would receive a posthumous Pulitzer Prize in 1976 for his opera *Treemonisha*.

The cross-pollination among classical, popular, and folk goes back centuries: our first encounters came in medieval dance music and Josquin's use of "L'homme armé." Two early twentieth-century developments significantly altered the relationship among these traditions. The more pervasive of these was the impact of sound recording. It preserved music of all kinds and, over time, made authentic versions more widely available. This in turn facilitated interactions among musical traditions.

The other development, more specific and particularly American, was the creation of music that effectively dissolved the boundaries between traditions. Gershwin's opera and orchestral music; the musical theater works of Leonard Bernstein and Stephen Sondheim; and the film music of John Williams: all inhabit their own musical worlds, which draw on multiple traditions but—from a purely musical perspective—do not belong primarily to any one.

If the classical, popular, and folk traditions are analogous to the three primary colors, then the products of their interaction are comparable to the millions of color combinations available on computer displays. The extraordinary diversity of musical life at the end of the century was literally unimaginable at the beginning. This diversity has cultural, geographical, and temporal dimensions—we have music from all over the world, from all strata of society. Moreover, through scrupulous musicological research, we have far better access to the music of the past: we can access more of the music of Bach's time than Bach could.

LO3 What Is Twentieth-Century Music?

It was possible to describe the changes in musical style from the eighteenth to the nineteenth century—from Classical to Romantic—as an evolutionary process: Romantic music proceeded directly from Classical music, although it would soon project a very different set of values. But just as the idea of such musical evolution was gaining widespread acceptance in Western culture (even Wagner's "music of the future" assumed that music evolves), the revolutionary developments of the early twentieth century rendered it invalid. The eighteenth and nineteenth centuries' most basic assumptions about music are overturned, non-European musical traditions blend with the European, and a relentless quest for novelty begins.

Fragmentation, not continuity, is the hallmark of twentieth-century music. To give some sense of the magnitude of the change, we highlight twentieth-century innovations in the elements of music.

Sound: New Instruments, Sounds, and Sound Combinations

The expanded sound world of the twentieth century came from a host of innovations: new instruments, new vocal and instrumental sounds, new combinations of instruments, even a broader understanding of what constitutes a "musical" sound.

Most of the instruments whose sounds were new to twentieth-century European and American ears came from technological innovations or non-European cultures. The only section of the orchestra that would grow significantly in the twentieth century was the percussion section, which often incorporated instruments from around the world. However, the most significant new percussion instrument was the drum kit. The instruments were not new, but when assembled into a unit that one person could play, it enabled a drummer to create rhythms virtually impossible to coordinate among several players.

A host of new vocal sounds also appeared throughout the century. Some involved finding a middle ground between speech and singing: Schoenberg's *Sprechstimme* (speech voice) and rap have this in common. Others evolved in response to new or newly popular genres and new technologies: crooning in popular singing and belting in musical theater; the moaning of the blues singer and the twang of country vocals; nonverbal vocal sounds used in avant-garde music; screaming in heavy metal and punk.

Musicians coaxed new sounds from conventional instruments in a variety of ways. Jazz and popular saxophonists invented new timbres far removed from "classical" models. Jazz trumpeters and trombonists did the same and added even more variety through the use of mutes such as the toilet plunger. John Cage and others produced sounds from the piano by strumming the piano strings directly or altering the sound by putting bolts, erasers, and other objects between the strings. Guitarists created a new, more vocal sound on their instrument by using the neck of a beer bottle. "Found" sounds ranged from the washboards used as a percussion instrument through much of the American South and the cowbells and gourds used in Cuban music to the everyday sounds recorded for some compositions.

© iStockphoto.com/DNY59

Jazz trumpeters and trombonists sometimes used mutes such as a handleless toilet plunger.

Harmony: New Modes of Pitch Organization

From the beginning of recorded musical history to the beginning of the twentieth century, the most basic assumption about pitch organization was that music is organized around a tonic, or home key. We encountered it first in Hildegard's antiphon and then in every subsequent example; even our Native American and Afro-Cuban examples suggest a pitch organization derived from scales focused around a tonic. The development of polyphony would eventually lead to an even stronger way to convey a sense of key. Common practice harmony had been in use for about 150 years by the time Lowell Mason promulgated his scientific approach to composition. However, by the beginning of the twentieth century, Mason's scientific harmony had become the stalest and most conventional of several approaches to pitch organization. Its most common outlets were conservative church music, children's song accompaniments, and the blander sort of popular music. Far more exciting were novel modes of pitch organization, which appeared almost simultaneously during the first few decades of the twentieth century.

The most obviously radical new approach was **atonality**, the principle of avoiding both the tonic and its corollary: organizing harmony and melody so as to move away from and return to the tonic in a coherent fashion. In practice, it took several forms. After two decades of experimentation, Arnold Schoenberg developed serial composition, an approach based on maintaining a strict sequence in presenting the twelve different pitches within the octave.

Less jarring but just as revolutionary were approaches that still focused around a tonic pitch but used differing methods to establish, move away from, and return to the tonic. In some instances, this involved using familiar harmonies in unfamiliar ways, in settings as diverse as the blues and the music of Debussy, Stravinsky, and Bartók. Other approaches included adapting different scales, such as the modal scales of English folk music and the pentatonic scales of African and Chinese music, and building harmonies from them. Even more radical approaches, including dividing the

atonality
The principle of avoiding both the tonic and its corollary; organizing harmony and melody so as to move away from and return to the tonic in a coherent fashion

octave into exceedingly small intervals and abandoning pitched sounds entirely, began to appear in the 1920s and 1930s. By midcentury, it was hard to imagine any option for pitch organization that hadn't been explored. More significantly, there was no dominant harmonic practice, as there had been in the previous centuries. An ever-increasing range of possibilities coexisted, sometimes creatively, sometimes uneasily.

MELODY

Melody was at the heart of nineteenth-century music. There were few successful works that didn't have an appealing, singable melody. Even Wagner, who largely avoided tuneful melodies, nevertheless built his works around memorable melodic material. And in vernacular music, popular song was king.

As with the other elements, a proliferation of new or radically altered options emerged in the twentieth century, from simple repetitive motives to angular, wide-ranging melodic lines that were difficult, if not impossible, to sing. Moreover, there was a large body of music that had no discernible melody, from some of the experimental music composed in the middle of the century to techno and rap.

What also changed was the idea that melody should be the expressive focus of a composition. With the development of new rhythmic approaches, especially from Afrocentric cultures and the relentless search for—and delight in—new sounds, it was no longer necessary, or at times even desirable, for melody to be the main focus. Continual improvement in sound recording and playback supported this shift in balance away from melody toward rhythm and sound.

Conventional melodies, in popular song, folk music, and classical compositions, still found a large and receptive audience. But these had become a few among many options.

RHYTHM

The changes in rhythm from the nineteenth to the twentieth century were just as revolutionary and far-reaching as those in pitch and sound, but for a different reason. The most extreme changes, such as the extension of serial procedures to rhythm and the reliance on chance (as in Cage's *4'33"*), completely removed the rhythms of a musical work from its origins in regular movements like those of dancing, marching, or walking. However, the far more pervasive change was the emergence of a new rhythmic paradigm, which blended the metrical structure of European music with an African rhythmic conception. This new rhythmic approach entered the mainstream musical world through ragtime; its gradual accretion of African features would drive the evolution of popular music and also influence classical music. Other rhythmic approaches from outside the central European world typified by Strauss's waltzes also gained traction among classical music composers—for example, the irregular rhythms of eastern Europe inspired Bartók and others.

Characteristic of virtually all of these innovations in rhythmic organization was an increase in complexity. The precisely timed events in electronic music; the improvised interplay of jazz musicians; the pulsing and propulsive rhythms of Stravinsky, Bartók, and Copland; the complex, irregular, and syncopated rhythmic layers of salsa—these and so many other trends in music reflect the rhythmic sophistication of twentieth-century music.

Rhythm, largely subordinate to melody as a source of musical interest in the eighteenth and nineteenth centuries, became more prominent in twentieth-century music; many times, it was the dominant element.

Rhythms in the music of the eighteenth and nineteenth centuries organized musical time hierarchically, much as our system of measuring time organizes it into seconds, minutes, and hours. The emergence of other rhythmic conceptions from Africa, India, eastern Europe, the Americas, and Asia made it clear in retrospect that the comparatively simple metrical hierarchies of European music were the exception among the musics of the world.

FORM: WHERE IS IT?

As they listened to the sonatas and symphonies of Mozart, Haydn, and their contemporaries, eighteenth-century audiences could generally tell where they were in the music. Convention dictated the number and sequence of movements, as well as the sequence of events within a movement. Even spontaneous events, such as the cadenza in a concerto movement, occurred within a carefully scripted framework. Performers and listeners expected that a movement or piece would begin and end decisively in the home key, with milestones along the way clearly defined by cadences. It was always easy to keep one's bearings.

The idea that a movement or work should be a coherent, clearly defined musical statement came under attack in the nineteenth century: the spooky beginning of the last movement of Berlioz's *Symphonie fantastique* is a familiar instance of this. More progressive composers expanded the frame and blurred its edges: Wagner's *Tristan and Isolde* begins with a famously ambiguous motive and chord and doesn't resolve to the tonic chord until the very end of the opera, several hours later. Nevertheless, for the most part composers did not abandon the idea that a musical composition meant a coherent narrative developed from a central idea.

By the turn of the century, this formal edifice was riddled with cracks; radically different methods of organizing music soon reduced it to rubble. In classical music, several new conceptions of form emerged in the first two decades of the twentieth century. Some—Ives's collagelike forms, Debussy's cinematic forms, Stravinsky's cubist-inspired forms—challenged the essentially linear progression of events. Atonal music removed the harmonic underpinnings from form, dissolving the framework that had previously been so crucial in shaping form. Afrocentric vernacular music, especially blues and jazz, adapted conventional variation form into a modular, open form.

Even more radical approaches to form emerged during the century, especially after World War II. In the music of some avant-garde composers, form could be predetermined by something as rigorous as a mathematical formula or left largely in the hands of the performer—or the environment. Both options challenged the very idea that a musical work was a self-contained entity with a beginning and an end. A parallel trend developed in vernacular music during the rock era. Fade-out endings, open-ended opening vamps, and internally extensible forms (heard in almost any James Brown live performance) also undermined the idea of a rigid framework. Post-disco dance tracks went further, breaking down the idea of a song as a discrete entity; typically, they became part of a much longer mix. Some genres still used the closed forms of the eighteenth and nineteenth centuries, but they had become only one option among many.

Twentieth-Century Music: New Concepts, New Attitudes, New Sounds

Billboard magazine, founded in 1894, began covering the entertainment industry in 1900. In 1936, it began to chart the popularity of popular songs by noting how frequently the top songs were performed on the three big radio networks. Its first chart for record sales appeared in 1940. By the end of the century, *Billboard* featured over twenty different charts (the number typically varied from issue to issue), including charts for "classical," "classical crossover," and "world" and several Latin music charts. Because these charts consider only genres with relatively substantial sales, they don't even fully represent the diversity of musical life at the end of the century. At the beginning of the twentieth century, only the most forward-seeing thinker could have imagined the variety of today's recordings, their quality, and the ease with which they can be obtained and played back.

It would take an even more prescient individual to predict the major developments of the twentieth century: the pervasive impact of technology, the rise of popular music and the growth of the music business, the new developments from almost every corner of the musical world that challenged the most basic assumptions about music. Those who have grown up in the digital age have inherited a musical world quite different in every respect from that of a century ago. What seems normal today was revolutionary at midcentury and all but unimaginable at the beginning of the twentieth century. The radical developments in thinking about, creating, performing, and listening to music have produced a musical world without precedent.

UNIT 18

"ISMS": EUROPEAN CONCERT MUSIC IN THE EARLY TWENTIETH CENTURY

Learning Outcomes

After reading this unit, you will be able to do the following:

LO1 Describe the traits of expressionist music and atonality through an understanding of the music of Arnold Schoenberg.

LO2 Become familiar with impressionism in the arts, specifically in the music of Claude Debussy.

LO3 Learn about the emergence of film and its influence on Debussy's music.

LO4 Hear how composers such as Igor Stravinsky embedded "primitive" elements in ultramodern settings.

© The Metropolitan Museum of Art / Art Resource, NY

IN THE NINETEENTH CENTURY, the suffix "-ism" was increasingly used to identify a particular belief system or set of principles: both "Classicism" and "Romanticism" were nineteenth-century terms. So were more focused developments, such as nationalism, realism, and even Wagnerism.

Around 1900, a wave of new "isms" rattled the foundations of the classical music world: the expressionism of Schoenberg and Berg, the impressionism of Debussy and Ravel, and the primitivism of Stravinsky developed at more or less the same time. These composers abandoned such fundamental aspects of nineteenth-century music as common practice harmony and regular meter; with the disappearance of those practices, the idea of coherent, comprehensible music based on them also disappeared. These composers spoke different musical languages, and their work challenged long-held ideas about what music could say and how it could say it. Their strongest common bond was what they were not: conventional continuations of what had gone before.

CHAPTER 37

Expressionism

"Art belongs to the unconscious!"
—*Arnold Schoenberg*

I n a letter to the painter Wassily Kandinsky early in 1911, composer Arnold Schoenberg asserted, "Every formal procedure which aspires to traditional effects is not completely free from conscious motivation. But art belongs to the unconscious!" At age thirty, Kandinsky (1866–1944), a Russian by birth, had declined a law professorship, moved to Munich, and begun studying art. Over the next fifteen years, Kandinsky's art would become increasingly abstract. By the time he met Schoenberg, his work was almost completely abstract, bearing little relationship to objects in the real world.

On January 2, 1911, Kandinsky attended a concert of Schoenberg's music in Munich. The experience sparked two responses. One was an abstract painting

Did You Know?

Well before rap came Arnold Schoenberg's *Sprechstimme,* a method of vocal delivery that is more than speech and less than singing.

entitled *Impression No. 3 (Concert).* The other was an enthusiastic letter to Schoenberg in which the artist stated, "In your works, you have realized what I . . . have so greatly longed for in music. The independent progress through their own destinies, the independent life of the individual voices in your compositions, is exactly what I am trying to find in my paintings."

Kandinsky's letter sparked a lifelong friendship between the two, which was particularly intense during the three years before World War I. It was a mutual admiration society in which both men crossed artistic boundaries. Kandinsky the painter had studied piano and cello and was enthusiastic about new music. Schoenberg the composer painted prolifically during this time, studying with the Austrian painter Richard Gerstl (who committed suicide after Schoenberg's wife, Mathilde, broke off an affair with him to return to her husband). Kandinsky, an adept organizer as well as an avant-garde artist, organized Der Blaue Reiter (The Blue Rider), a group of like-minded artists, later in 1911 and invited Schoenberg to show his artwork in the group's first exhibition.

LO1 Arnold Schoenberg, Musical Expressionism, and Atonality

Expressionism was a late nineteenth- and early twentieth-century movement in the arts that sought to convey, to *express*, the deep emotions that lie under the surface of—and are often obscured by—objective reality. Expressionist artists often achieved this by portraying scenes of intense emotion or grotesque images using

Wassily Kandinsky, *Impression No. 3 (Concert)*

distorted and exaggerated gestures. In Kandinsky's painting, there is a suggestion of the lid of a piano and of audience members, but the bold gestures and the strong opposition of colors represent his response to Schoenberg's music. In effect, the painting inverts the relationship between the subject and its representation. In a representational painting, the goal is to represent the subject as accurately and precisely as possible. The elements of art—line, color, texture—are all in the service of this goal. Here, however, the message lies in the elements themselves—most strikingly, in the bold patches of color. The subject is simply a medium for these emotions expressed through these elements.

Color was an important component of Schoenberg's music as well during the years before World War I. Indeed, the third of his five pieces for orchestra, composed in 1909, is entitled "Farben" ("Colors"). Vivid tone colors would become one component of his approach to musical expressionism. Another was atonality, as he mentioned frequently in his correspondence.

ARNOLD SCHOENBERG

Arnold Schoenberg was born and raised in the Vienna of Brahms and Johann Strauss Jr. His hunger for learning overcame his family's lack of financial resources and background in music; he received much of his training in music from like-minded friends rather than through formal study. In his early years, he moved back and forth between Vienna and Berlin in an effort to find work that would allow him to compose. He managed to scrape by through teaching and various musical odd jobs—orchestrating operettas and working at an avant-garde cabaret; he received far less income than notoriety for his compositions.

Schoenberg's first important compositions show the overwhelming influence of Wagner. As his music evolved, he came to view atonality as an inevitable continuation of Wagner's innovations. Schoenberg proclaimed the "emancipation of dissonance" in theory (in *Harmonielehre*, his 1911 textbook on harmony) and practice, in music that evolved from the lush late Romantic style of his early works to the freely atonal music that he composed just prior to the outbreak of World War I.

Arnold Schoenberg

Fast Facts

- *Dates:* 1874–1951
- *Place:* Vienna, Austria
- *Reasons to remember:* One of the leading avant-garde expressionist composers of the early twentieth century; a pioneering composer of atonal music

© CNAC/MNAM/Dist. Réunion des Musées Nationaux / Art Resource, NY

SCHOENBERG THE MUSICAL EXPRESSIONIST

In a 1909 letter to the Italian composer Ferrucio Busoni, Schoenberg wrote:

> I strive for: complete liberation from all forms
> from all symbols
> of cohesion and
> of logic
> Thus:
> away with "motivic working out."
> Away with harmony as
> cement or bricks of a building.
> Harmony is expression
> and nothing else.

© iStockphoto.com/Duncan Walker

He goes on to note that "it is *impossible* for a person to have only *one* sensation at a time. One has *thousands* simultaneously." He concludes by saying that his music "should be an expression of feeling, as our feelings, which bring us in contact with our subconscious, really are, and no false child of feelings and 'conscious logic.'"

Schoenberg's letter was in essence a manifesto for musical expressionism.

"It is impossible for a person to have only one sensation at a time. One has thousands simultaneously."

© iStockphoto.com/Bayram TUNÇ

Schoenberg's letter was in essence a manifesto for musical expressionism. He makes clear that he wants his music to be a gateway to the psyche. His interest in the subconscious was in step with the most advanced thinking of the era. And it was very much part of his world: at the turn of the century, Vienna was home to Sigmund Freud as well as Schoenberg, and Freud's writings had attracted widespread interest.

Three years later, Schoenberg composed *Pierrot lunaire*, a setting of twenty-one poems for voice and small ensemble. Particularly in these works, which feature a solo voice supported by an instrumental ensemble, Schoenberg explored the psychological underpinnings of musical expressionism. He conveyed the "thousands of sensations" mainly through two complementary strategies: the intensification of what had been, in the works of earlier composers, mainly coloristic elements and the abandonment of tonality.

SCHOENBERG AND ATONALITY

Atonal music is music that is not tonal, in that it does not organize pitches around a tonic, or home key. The first atonal music in Western culture app eared just after the turn of the twentieth century, most notably in the compositions of Schoenberg. In abandoning tonality of any kind, Schoenberg left behind a musical tradition that reached back more than a millennium; his was the most radical change in pitch organization in the history of music. What made it seem even more radical was that it was both a consequence and a negation of the most sophisticated mode of organizing pitch in human history up to that point: common practice harmony.

Tonality and Structure, Atonality and Expressiveness. Common practice harmony has been the most sophisticated method of pitch organiza-

tion in history because it is the only one that makes syntactic musical organization possible: by the early eighteenth century it had acquired a sense of predictability that parallels syntax in language. So, just as syntax makes it possible for us to organize words into phrases, sentences, paragraphs, chapters, and books, common practice harmony makes it possible to organize music hierarchically into coherent statements. The statements can range in length from a minute or two to more than an hour.

As Schoenberg noted in his letter to Busoni, harmony can be both structural and expressive. The familiar progressions of common practice harmony give musical statements coherence but do not necessarily convey deep feeling. Conventional two- or three-chord accompaniment patterns, such as those used to harmonize simple songs, are easily grasped but emotionally neutral. Expression in harmony comes from defying the expected. Emotionally charged works such as Beethoven's Fifth Symphony use basic structures only as a framework; their power comes in part from elaboration, disruption, and expansion of structural conventions.

During the nineteenth century, even as everyday music (popular song and dance, hymns, parlor music, children's songs, marches) stayed harmonically "scientific," classical composers broke away from these conventions in search of more powerfully and individually expressive music: we heard this particularly in the music of Berlioz and Wagner, who stretched tonality to its limits. However, neither they nor any other significant nineteenth-century composer completely abandoned tonality.

Atonality, as presented in Schoenberg's music, abandons any sense of key, and with it all those conventions associated with tonal music that help orient the listener. As a result, much of the musical meaning arises from more elementally expressive aspects of the music: the shape of the melodic line, the flow of the rhythm, the register within which a voice or instrument operates, and fluctuations in dynamics. This corresponds to the expressionist focus on line, color, texture, and other elements in painting at the expense of realistic depiction of the subject. By closing the door to tonality, Schoenberg opened the door to new, more intense forms of expression.

Given the course of nineteenth-century art music, atonality was, in a way, historically inevitable. Indeed, we will shortly encounter atonal music in works by Debussy, Stravinsky, and Ives as well. But no composer embraced it as fully as Schoenberg, who came to atonality gradually and painstakingly. That he chose to do so even as he became deeply immersed in painting suggests that atonality was one dimension of a broader effort to adapt the expressionist aesthetic to music. Its complement was the intensification of the most basic musical elements.

Atonality abandons any sense of key.

INTENSE COLORS AND EXPRESSIVE EXTREMES

In his early atonal works for multiple instruments, such as *Pierrot lunaire*, Schoenberg heightens the coloristic qualities of his music through strong timbral contrasts and unusual timbral effects. *Pierrot lunaire* requires six performers: a vocalist and five instrumentalists who play flute or piccolo, clarinet or bass clarinet, violin or viola, cello, and piano. The timbres of the instruments contrast rather than blend; the doubling effectively extends the range of each instrument's particular timbre. The most striking of the timbral effects is the vocal style, which Schoenberg called **Sprechstimme**, "speech voice." Although Schoenberg notated both pitch and rhythm, the vocalist must cultivate a sound that lies somewhere between speech and singing. The instruments, particularly the string instruments, produce unusual sounds: in "Nacht," one of the *Pierrot* poems, the cellist must bow the string virtually at the bridge, which produces an ethereal sound. The strong contrasts in timbre high-light the emphasis on extremes found in virtually every element. That they are compressed into a short time span makes them even more powerful, as we hear in an excerpt from *Pierrot lunaire*.

Pierrot lunaire

Pierrot lunaire is a chamber work for voice and instruments. At the time of its premiere in 1912, it was very much in the avant-garde, but its inspiration traces back to a centuries-old theatrical tradition: *commedia dell'arte*.

COMMEDIA DELL'ARTE

The Pierrot (French, perhaps derived from the name Peter) of Schoenberg's work is one of the stock characters in **commedia dell'arte**, "comedy of the artists," a type of improvised theater that developed in Italy during the fifteenth century. In *commedia dell'arte*, troupes of professional actors traveled from town to town, portraying stock characters by wearing masks and costumes and acting out familiar story lines. Several of the characters—Harlequin, Columbine, Pulcinella, and Pierrot—became symbols of particular types of behavior. Pierrot is typically either foolish or lovesick, or both. *Lunaire*, like *lunatic*, comes from *luna*, the Latin word for "moon." Both refer to the myth that blames a full moon for moments of temporary insanity or foolishness: those who are "moonstruck" seem to lose their minds momentarily, usually because of romantic infatuation.

Commedia dell'arte soon became popular throughout Europe, and its characters and conventions infiltrated the culture. For example, the word *slapstick* originally referred to slapping two pieces of wood together; it was one of many comedic devices used by *commedia dell'arte* clowns. Over time, it has come to refer to any physical humor based on clumsy actions. Harlequin, the clown who typically slapped the sticks, wore a costume featuring diamond shapes in varying colors; the word *harlequin* can now also refer to an irregular color scheme.

Beginning in the latter part of the nineteenth century, artists, writers, and musicians rediscovered *commedia dell'arte*, not so much as an entertainment per se but as part of a larger movement that used patently unreal characters to explore the disconnect between appearance and reality. Petrushka is a Russian puppet who comes to life in Igor Stravinsky's 1911 ballet of the same name. Ruggero Leoncavallo's 1892 *verismo* opera

Sprechstimme "Speech voice"; vocal style between speech and singing required in Arnold Schoenberg's music

commedia dell'arte "Comedy of the artists [of improvisation]"; a type of improvised theater that developed in Italy during the fifteenth century

Pagliacci (*pagliacci* means "clowns" in Italian), which involves characters in a *commedia dell'arte* troupe, predates Schoenberg's *Pierrot lunaire* by two decades. In each case, the composition portrays the emotions hidden below the surface—whether the character is a puppet or a clown.

FROM POEMS TO MUSIC

The source of the text for *Pierrot lunaire* was a group of fifty poems by the Belgian writer Albert Giraud; Schoenberg encountered them in a translation from French to German by Otto Erich Hartleben. Giraud's poems stimulated Schoenberg's imagination. In his diary, he noted, "read the foreword, looked at the poems, am enthusiastic," and he completed the work in less than three months. From the fifty poems, Schoenberg selected twenty-one, which he organized into three groups of seven. Schoenberg's subtitle to the work is "Three Times Seven Poems by Albert Giraud."

Giraud subtitled his group of poems *Rondels bergamasques*. A rondel is a strict poetic form. In the rondel "Nacht," for instance, the opening is repeated halfway through and at the end, creating a form similar to musical ABA form:

Obscure, black giant moths
Killed the sun's splendour.
A closed book of spells,
The horizon settles—hushed

From the mists of lost depths
Wafts a scent—remembrance murdered!
Obscure, black giant moths
Killed the sun's splendour.

And from the sky earthwards
Sinking on heavy wings
Unseeable the monsters (glide)
Down into the human hearts . . .
Obscure, black giant moths.

The combination of such strict form with such grotesque imagery seems to have appealed to Schoenberg's compositional aesthetic. Schoenberg knew he was a revolutionary, but he also saw himself as an evolutionary composer. In some of his most revolutionary works—not only *Pierrot* but also his later piano suite—he makes use of traditional forms and genres, as if to counterbalance the more radical elements of his music. "Nacht" is his take on a passacaglia, a centuries-old variation form.

Like the poems themselves, the individual movements of *Pierrot lunaire* are short, because the vocalist declaims the text using Schoenberg's distinctive Sprechstimme. No movement takes more than three minutes to perform, and the entire work amounts to only about thirty-five minutes of music. We consider "Nacht," the first poem in the second group and the eighth movement overall.

Expressionism in Music

Schoenberg's emphasis on bold melodic lines, distinctive and sharply contrasting tone colors, and extremes in virtually every element is comparable to expressionist artists' highlighting color and gesture over representation. Similarly, his abandonment of tonality is akin to abandoning language at moments of great intensity: a scream is exactly such a nonverbal sound. In *Pierrot lunaire* and many of his other important works, Schoenberg relies on the text for coherence. In this instance, the text is coherent only in a syntactic sense; what it portrays is nightmarish. Using tonal harmony—even the richly chromatic harmony of Wagner and Schoenberg's earlier works—would have introduced a sense of normalcy that would be at cross purposes with the intent of the poems and with Schoenberg's expressive intent.

Expressionist music, as realized by Schoenberg in *Pierrot lunaire*,

Sally Burgess (mezzo soprano) as Pierrot

Expressionist music seeks to portray the turmoil of a troubled psyche.

successful during and immediately after its premiere, despite the hostility of many critics. It remains one of the most admired and influential works of the early twentieth century.

After composing *Pierrot lunaire* in 1912, Schoenberg went through an eight-year creative crisis brought about by the war (he was in and out of the Imperial Army because of his poor health) and by his need to develop a method of organizing the dissonance that he had recently emancipated. His twelve-tone method, first presented in a series of works composed during the early 1920s, would become the most influential new direction in the avant-garde for the next half-century.

seeks to portray the turmoil of a troubled psyche by intensifying the most elemental aspects of music—pulse, tone color, pitch, dynamics—and disorienting the listener by avoiding tonality. Both were radical developments that succeeded in *Pierrot lunaire*. The work was largely

---

CHAPTER **38**

Impressionism and Beyond

"I love pictures almost as much as music."—Claude Debussy

In 1911, the French composer Claude Debussy remarked to his colleague Edgard Varèse, "J'aime presque autant les images que la musique" ("I love pictures almost as much as music"). At the time he made this remark, Debussy was known throughout Europe as one of the most innovative composers of the new century. He had been labeled an "impressionist" composer for almost twenty-five years; members of the

Did You Know?

In 1999, the avant-garde pop group Art of Noise released the album *The Seduction of Claude Debussy.* They described it as "the soundtrack to a film that wasn't made about the life of Claude Debussy."

Institut de France first used the term in reference to his music in 1887. Debussy himself vacillated between using the term to describe his work and complaining of its inaccuracy. "Impressionism" can succinctly describe some of Debussy's music, but the term limits and misrepresents his output as a whole.

Claude Debussy, *"Musicien parisien"*

For a visually oriented composer like Debussy, Paris was the ideal place to be. It was a hotbed of artistic activity and a major center for a newly emerging film industry. Debussy would find inspiration in both.

Born in a town just outside Paris, Debussy was enrolled at the age of ten in the Paris Conservatoire, where he studied piano and composition. Aside from a two-year stay in Rome (the result of winning the Prix de Rome, the Conservatoire's most prestigious award for young composers), pilgrimages to Bayreuth in his mid-twenties (like many other young composers of the time, he was briefly under the spell of Wagner's music; he would soon move away from it), and occasional trips to England (Debussy and his music were well received in England, and he was an ardent Anglophile), Debussy spent his life in and around Paris.

Turn-of-the-century Paris was an extraordinarily fertile artistic environment, one that embraced all the arts: the music of Debussy and his fellow composers; several new trends in painting; the sculpture of Rodin; the symbolist poetry of Verlaine and Mallarmé; and the first wave of important films, such as George Mèliés's much-viewed 1902 science-fiction fantasy, *A Trip to the Moon*.

A rocket hits the man in the moon in the eye in *A Trip to the Moon* (1902).

Debussy was a regular visitor at the salons of the artistic elite, where he shared ideas with painters and poets alike. He was an avid fan of the cinema. For Debussy, films were not only an exciting new entertainment medium but also a source of national pride. French filmmakers were at the forefront of this new medium until World War I.

Debussy took in the world around him. And, likewise, the world came to him, or at least to Paris; three "universal expositions," in 1878, 1889, and 1900, gave him the opportunity to hear Javanese gamelan music

Claude Debussy

Fast Facts

- *Dates:* 1862–1918
- *Place:* France
- *Reasons to remember:* One of the most innovative composers of the early twentieth century and the leading impressionist composer

Claude Debussy, c.1908 (b/w photo), Nadar, (Gaspard Felix Tournachon) (1820-1910) / Private Collection / The Bridgeman Art Library International

and other exotic sounds. He explored cultural life at all levels and brought his experiences into his music.

Although he never exhibited publicly as a visual artist—as Schoenberg did—Debussy was arguably the most visually oriented of the major composers. He channeled these influences into a musical aesthetic that in his mind embodied those qualities that are distinctively French: toward the end of his life, he referred to himself as *musicien français*.

Debussy composed successfully in most genres: opera (*Pelléas et Mélisande*), ballet (*Jeux*), numerous songs, chamber music, orchestral music including the groundbreaking *Prelude to the Afternoon of a Faun*, and a wide range of piano music.

LO2 Painters in France: Impressionism and Beyond

It isn't unusual for technology to open up new possibilities within an art form. However, it's unusual for technology to establish a new art form that in turn

For visual artists in the latter part of the nineteenth century, the camera was a tool of liberation.

liberates an established art. For visual artists in the latter part of the nineteenth century, the camera was a tool of liberation. Before the camera, the most common way to preserve an image in two dimensions was to draw or paint it. Accordingly, for centuries, the first obligation of European artists had been to represent the subject of their artwork with some accuracy.

Like drawings or paintings, the camera could also capture images in two dimensions, and it did so much more quickly and with superior accuracy. Thus, when it emerged as a viable medium during the middle of the nineteenth century, the camera freed painters from the obligation to portray their subjects precisely.

Inspired especially by the English landscape painter J. M. W. Turner, a group of French painters, including Claude Monet, Pierre-Auguste Renoir, and Camille Pissarro, created paintings that focused on representing the perception of light and color rather than forms. Monet's work, for example, includes several series of paintings that show exactly the same scene—a cathedral, a haystack—at different times of day. This revolutionary new direction inverted the relationship between the subject and its portrayal. Previously, painterly techniques had sought to represent the subject as artfully and expressively as possible; the focus was on the subject. For **impressionist** painters, the subject wasn't so much the focus as the vehicle for exploring elemental aspects of painting, especially light and color. The movement took its name indirectly from a Monet painting, *Impression: Sunrise*, which was part of the group's first exhibition in 1874. A critic reviewing the exhibition used the title of Monet's painting to identify the work of these artists. Although the critic used the term derisively, the group gave it a positive spin by adopting it to

For impressionist painters, the subject wasn't so much the focus as the vehicle for exploring light and color.

© iStockphoto.com/AVTG

refer to their work. They continued to exhibit together until 1886; after that time, the artists elected to pursue different directions.

The impressionists freed all artists from both traditional subjects and conventional ways of representing them. The numerous postimpressionist directions in France (the pointillism of Georges Seurat, the proto-cubism of Paul Cézanne, and Henri Toulouse-Lautrec's vivid portrayals of Parisian decadence) and throughout Europe (the German expressionists, the abstract art of Kandinsky, the Spanish painter Pablo Picasso's numerous shifts in style) all used the new aesthetics of impressionist art as a point of departure.

Claude Debussy was the French musician who was most responsive to these new directions in art. Along with Maurice Ravel, Debussy would create a musical analog to impressionist art. However, for both composers, impressionism was one option among many. In particular, the music of Debussy is extraordinarily varied in inspiration and realization.

Nowhere is this more evident than in his music for the piano. In part because he was a fluent pianist with a real affinity for the instrument, Debussy composed more extensively and more experimentally for the piano than for any other medium. His output for the instrument spans his entire career; it includes several multimovement sets, plus two books of twelve preludes and twelve etudes. In keeping with his visual inclination, Debussy gave most works descriptive titles: indeed, two sets are entitled *Images*. In these pieces, Debussy presents an extraordinarily varied range of subjects and moods. There are landscapes and seascapes, personal portraits, musical still lifes, action movies, and much more. Some have slapstick humor; others are emotionally neutral. We sample Debussy's multifaceted musical personality in two of his preludes for piano. In "Voiles," we encounter the musical impressionist; in "Minstrels," the musical cinematographer.

impressionism
Late nineteenth- and early twentieth-century movement in the arts that favored exploration of elements such as light, color, and sound over literal representation

Debussy the Impressionist

Debussy was still a boy when impressionist painters first exhibited together; he was in Rome when they mounted their last group show. As he matured as a composer, he rejected the oppressive influence of Wagner on French composition. For him, adapting the impressionist aesthetic to music was a way of asserting a distinctively French identity. The composer Erik Satie, who served as a mentor to Debussy early in his career, recalled that he had encouraged Debussy to help develop a music "without any sauerkraut" by following the lead of painters such as Monet, Cézanne, and Toulouse-Lautrec. And just as Monet's painting moved further away from faithful depiction of the subjects, Debussy's impressionist music moved away from the harmonic, rhythmic, and formal conventions of Romanticism toward evocation and color.

Debussy's self-imposed challenge went beyond simply translating image into sound; rather, it involved translating the handling of visual elements into sound. Further complicating this task are two essential differences between art and music. One is that artists use a concrete image—a cathedral, a haystack, water lilies—as a recognizable point of reference. By contrast, music is almost necessarily evocative rather than depictive. The other is that art is static, freezing a moment in time, whereas music is dynamic, unfolding in time. Debussy's affinity for the visual made him sensitive to these differences and guided him in creating music that expressed the impressionist aesthetic.

"Voiles"

"Voiles" is the second of twelve preludes included in Debussy's first book of *Préludes*, which he composed in 1909 and 1910. The title translates into English as "Sails" or "Veils." Debussy's title, placed at the end of the prelude rather than the beginning, leaves the interpretation deliberately ambiguous. The musical evidence suggests sails rather than veils.

Sailboats, particularly a regatta at Argenteuil, a municipality northwest of Paris, were a popular subject for impressionist painters during the 1870s: Claude Monet painted scenes from the regatta twice; Renoir, once. The first series of paintings, by Monet, shows several stages of an Argenteuil regatta. The most familiar shows the sailboats at rest, apparently awaiting the start. At that time, it is a sunny day. The sails reach high into the air and are reflected on the surface of the water. Another painting shows the regatta under way. The day has become overcast and breezy; the ships are leaning with the wind.

Debussy couldn't depict a sailboat in sound. So, to convey a scene similar to the one painted by Monet, he created a musical setting that captured essential features of such a scene: the lazy, hazy day and—more important—a boat that floats. To imply this requirement Debussy adopted a radical strategy: the pervasive use of a whole-tone scale, a scale that divides the octave into six equal segments a whole tone apart. (A whole tone, or whole step, equals two half-steps.) In this respect it differs from the other scales we have encountered: major and minor, modal, and pentatonic—all of which feature asymmetrical patterns of whole and half-steps.

Regatta at Argenteuil, c.1872 (oil on canvas), Monet, Claude (1840-1926) / Musée d'Orsay, Paris, France / Giraudon / The Bridgeman Art Library International

Regatta at Argenteuil, 1872 (oil on canvas), Monet, Claude (1840-1926) / Private Collection / Photo © Lefevre Fine Art Ltd., London / The Bridgeman Art Library International

Monet, Regatta at Argenteuil (1872), two views

In "Voiles," Debussy weaves together short melodic strands drawn from the whole-tone scale at the beginning and end of the prelude; a brief middle section

> **whole-tone scale** Scale that divides the octave into six equal segments a whole tone apart (A whole tone, or whole step, equals two half-steps.)

(high winds) makes use of a pentatonic scale. How does the **whole-tone scale** convey a sense of floating? By avoiding a tonic, and the melodic, harmonic, and rhythmic events that establish and confirm the tonic. Recall that cadences are the musical events that confirm tonics and that the word *cadence* comes from the Latin word *cadere*, "to fall." Because they provide harmonic, rhythmic, and formal orientation, cadences affirm the pull of musical gravity. By avoiding not only cadences but also the scales and chords from which cadences are formed, Debussy defies musical gravity; the music floats from beginning to end. He complements this harmonic floating with rhythms that float over the pulse.

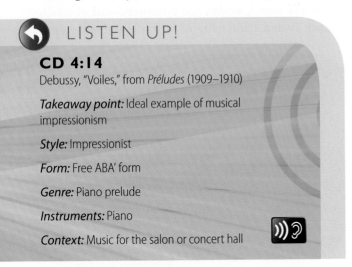

LISTEN UP!

CD 4:14

Debussy, "Voiles," from *Préludes* (1909–1910)

Takeaway point: Ideal example of musical impressionism

Style: Impressionist

Form: Free ABA′ form

Genre: Piano prelude

Instruments: Piano

Context: Music for the salon or concert hall

In this prelude, Debussy follows Monet's lead in his approach to melody. During the course of his career, Monet's art moved away from line toward texture. If we view Monet's later paintings at close range, all we see are dabs of various colors; only at some distance does the image come into focus. Similarly, Debussy's musical impressionism evolved away from the longer melodic lines of his earlier works to fragments—even wisps—of melodic material layered to form rich textures of sound.

LO3 Debussy the Cinematographer

If "Voiles" exemplifies Debussy's musical impressionism, then "Minstrels," the last prelude in Debussy's first book of preludes, shows Debussy creating a film with sound. This prelude is more than a sound track; it is Debussy's attempt to convey in music a filmlike evocation of the minstrel show. This is especially evident in the musical organization, which uses procedures analogous to those used in the first films.

The very first (silent) films were, in essence, animated photographs. A single stationary camera shot the scene as it unfolded; the novelty was simply that the camera captured on film what viewers would experience in real life. However, film editing enabled directors to present an entirely new way of perceiving time and space. Using multiple cameras, directors could show the same scene from different angles, cutting from one to the next as they chose. Through montage, a specifically cinematic process in which discrete sections of film are assembled into a continuously flowing whole, they could compress an extended time span into a few minutes. Specific editing techniques like cuts, fades, and dissolves create a world far different from that of everyday life—a world in which viewers move backward and forward in time and jump from place to place in an instant.

Because we've grown up watching television and films, we readily accept the altered reality that these media provide. But for those living at the turn of the twentieth century, the manipulation of time and space was a startling novelty. For Debussy, the cinema was both an exciting new medium and a source of inspiration. In 1913, he remarked, "There remains but one way of reviving the taste for symphonic music among our contemporaries: to apply to pure music the techniques of cinematography. It is the film—the Ariadne's thread—that will show us the way out of this disquieting labyrinth."

In this case, practice predated theory: Debussy had applied cinematographic techniques to musical

The frenetic pace of "Minstrels," often featuring abrupt shifts from one sound image to the next, captures the high spirits and improvisatory flow of the minstrel show.

composition in his later piano music years before this pronouncement. "Voiles" features dissolvelike transitions in and out of the "storm" section; in "Minstrels," Debussy adapts several different editing techniques.

Debussy's choice of subject—minstrels—was as modern as his compositional technique. The minstrel show was the first distinctively American entertainment to charm European audiences: there, as in the United States, it was a not-very-respectable mass entertainment that attracted a diverse audience. By portraying such a mundane subject, Debussy followed the lead of both filmmakers and painters such as Toulouse-Lautrec, who blurred the boundary between high and low culture by painting scenes of everyday life.

The minstrel show conjures up vivid images, both visual and aural: the minstrels in blackface, strumming a banjo or scraping a fiddle, spouting nonsense or playing practical jokes on the interlocutor, the minstrel show's straight man. In Debussy's portrayal, there is no consistent musical style; instead, there is a collage of styles that ranges from sprightly fiddle tunes and tambourine taps to spooky music and a cabaret-style popular song. The cinematic inspiration is evident in the frequent shifts from style to style. Everything within the prelude is a fragment; there are no self-contained, closed sections. Its frenetic pace, often featuring abrupt shifts from one sound image to the next, captures the high spirits and improvisatory flow of the minstrel show.

LISTEN UP!

CD 4:15

Debussy, "Minstrels," from *Préludes* (1909–1910)

Takeaway point: A cinematic, nonimpressionistic musical composition by the master impressionist

Style: Early twentieth century

Form: Fragmented through-composed form

Genre: Piano prelude

Instruments: Piano

Context: Piano music for the salon or concert hall

"Minstrels" is a modern work, in both its choice of musical materials and the way in which Debussy organizes them. What makes the musical materials modern is their source and Debussy's presentation of them. They don't come from art or folk music; they are inspired by a popular entertainment. And Debussy doesn't try to dress them up, as nineteenth-century composers often did with folk melodies; it sounds as if he has simply adapted them for the piano.

Because its materials are familiar sounding and familiar to Debussy and his listeners, "Minstrels" does not sound as radically avant-garde as Schoenberg's "Nacht." Conceptually, however, the prelude *is* radically avant-garde: the adaptation of film-editing techniques to musical composition was not possible until the beginning of the twentieth century, and the collage-like arrangement of the musical fragments anticipates the visual collages of Picasso and Braque, which appeared shortly after Debussy composed the prelude.

Debussy the Accessible Radical

Throughout much of the twentieth century, it was customary in musical circles to distinguish between "impressionist" composers, such as Debussy and Ravel, and "contemporary," "modern," or "twentieth-century" composers such as Schoenberg, Stravinsky, Ives, and their numerous peers and successors. The implicit message was that musical impressionism was different from Romanticism but not as relentlessly avant-garde as the other contemporary musical styles, because it was "listenable." However, its accessibility disguised its novelty.

Debussy created radically modern music, not by evolving beyond nineteenth-century music but by branching off in a completely new direction. His use of familiar musical materials in works such as "Minstrels" helped make his music accessible, and even the musical materials in his atonal music, such as the whole tone–based "Voiles," sound familiar because the scale is presented mainly through stepwise motion. In this respect, he was not as defiantly avant-garde as other important early twentieth-century composers.

What was most radical about his music, though, was his reconception of the relationship between composer and style. Increasingly, through the nineteenth century and into the twentieth, composers cultivated a personal style through characteristic ways of handling the musical elements: Brahms sounds like Brahms, not like Wagner or Verdi. However, Debussy avoided developing such an individualistic style. In the two books of preludes, there is not a characteristic Debussy sound— that is, music that is the product of certain predilections for harmony, texture, rhythm, or form. Instead,

Debussy often employs existing styles much as an actor would don a costume: he dresses his music in familiar styles to portray such diverse characters as a minstrel troupe, a failed Latin lover, and an English gentleman.

What is novel about Debussy's compositional approach is not the programmatic aspect per se but the extent to which Debussy carries it through. In creating individual sound worlds in each of the preludes, Debussy goes beyond earlier composers of program music in suppressing his musical personality in order to portray the subjects of the preludes more vividly.

Debussy could be an impressionist, as we heard in "Voiles." But he was also capable of far more. The two preludes discussed here hint at the larger picture: taken as a whole, the two books of preludes are the musical counterpart to walking through a gallery containing a cross section of French art from around the turn of the twentieth century: not only Monet and Renoir but also Cezanne, Seurat, Gauguin, and Van Gogh.

In his stylistic adaptability, Debussy anticipated the work of late twentieth-century film composers like John Williams and Danny Elfman. Despite his keen interest in the cinema and his application of film-editing techniques to music, Debussy did not leave an actual film score. Nevertheless, he merits consideration as the godfather of film composers.

CHAPTER 39

Primitivism

"There arose a picture of a sacred pagan ritual: the wise elders are seated in a circle and are observing the dance before death of the girl whom they are offering as a sacrifice to the god of Spring."

On May 29, 1913, a riot broke out in Paris's Théâtre des Champs-Élysées. The occasion was an evening of ballet presented by Ballets Russes, a Russian dance company based in Paris. The evening began innocently enough with a performance of *Les Sylphides*, a traditional ballet choreographed to the music of Chopin. It was the second ballet of the evening, the premiere of Igor Stravinsky's *The Rite of Spring*, that provoked hisses, boos, and catcalls from displeased members of the audience and an equally strong opposing reaction from Stravinsky's supporters. Before the first act had finished, fistfights had broken out between audience members. The police

Did You Know?

Stravinsky's *The Rite of Spring* provided the sound track for the fourth segment of Walt Disney's 1940 animated film *Fantasia*, depicting the birth of the planet.

were called in to restore order, but the tumult in the audience drowned out the rest of the performance.

The riot at the premiere devastated Stravinsky, but Sergei Diaghilev, the impresario who ran Ballets Russes, was reportedly delighted with the audience's reaction: the scandal would be free publicity for his company. Reviews suggest that the most provocative aspect of the work was Nijinsky's choreography. A triumphant concert performance of the work a year later, also in Paris, supports the view that it was the dance, more than the music, that sparked the riot.

Still, Stravinsky's ballet was revolutionary, even for a revolutionary time. It challenged the relationship of contemporary audiences with primitive and exotic cultures and introduced vibrant new sounds, rhythms, and harmonies into musical life.

The Rite of Spring, Howat, Andrew (20th Century) / Private Collection / © Look and Learn / The Bridgeman Art Library International

For impressionist painters, the subject wasn't so much the focus as the vehicle for exploring light and color.

Russia, France, and Stravinsky

The presence of a Russian ballet company in Paris highlights the continuing cultural connection between France and Russia. Ballets Russes, formed in 1909 with dancers brought to France from the Russian Imperial Ballet, was an immediate sensation in Paris. The enthusiastic reaction of the French to the Russian dancers was akin to American Beatlemania, in the sense that the Russian dancers brought a welcome new energy and skill to an art that had originated in France, much as The Beatles reinvigorated popular music in the country that had given birth to rock and roll.

The prominent place of ballet in Russian cultural life was in turn a reflection of the widespread impact of French culture on upper-class Russian society, which was still more focused on the West than on its own homeland. Although nineteenth-century reform efforts had resulted in modest improvements for the rural working class, Russian society remained rigidly stratified through the early twentieth century, with a small elite at the top and an enormous, painfully poor, and largely uneducated peasant class at the bottom. Rich and poor typically coexisted side by side: although peasants worked as servants or farmers for the rich, they inhabited worlds that were, for the most part, mutually exclusive. The economic and social circumstances of Tsarist Russia and the Deep South after the Civil War are parallel in many respects.

Nevertheless, nationalism in music was particularly strong in Russia, where composers such as Mussorgsky, Borodin, and Rimsky-Korsakov (Stravinsky's teacher and mentor) cultivated a national style in reaction to the dominant presence of French culture among the Russian elite. However, with the singular exception of Mussorgsky, Russian nationalist composers presented folk materials using conventional resources. Stravinsky would go well beyond this: he made his reputation by drawing on age-old Russian folk culture and presenting it in increasingly modern settings.

Stravinsky and Nijinsky, in the role of Petrushka, at the ballet's premiere in 1911

Igor Stravinsky

Fast Facts

- *Dates:* 1882–1971
- *Place:* Russia
- *Reasons to remember:* A composer of great imagination and one of the dominant figures in twentieth-century music

© Lebrecht Music & Arts

IGOR STRAVINSKY

Igor Stravinsky was the son of a leading bass singer in the Imperial Opera, based in St. Petersburg. He grew up hearing the music performed at the Mariinsky Theater, which was home to both opera and ballet. His early musical education was typical for the Russian middle and upper class; more intense piano study during his teens would serve him well later in his career, when he toured as a pianist. His calling as a composer came relatively late: he studied law in desultory fashion instead of attending the still-young conservatory in St. Petersburg. Most of his training in composition came from Nikolai Rimsky-Korsakov, with whom he studied privately and who became a mentor and fatherlike figure, especially after the death of Stravinsky's father in 1902.

Stravinsky encountered peasant life and culture most directly at his family's summer home in Ustilug, a small village on the border between Poland and the Ukraine (the Ukraine was part of the Russian Empire at the time). The sounds and images of the villagers' songs and dances would be a major inspiration for the first, Russian phase of his career, which peaked with *The Rite of Spring*.

In 1909, Diaghilev heard a performance of Stravinsky's *Fireworks*, a short orchestral piece, and was sufficiently impressed to commission a ballet from the still relatively unknown composer. Stravinsky's first ballet for Diaghilev was *The Firebird* (1910), which was based on Russian folk tales about a mythical phoenixlike creature. *The Firebird* was Stravinsky's breakthrough work; its success prompted a second commission for the following season: *Petrushka*. Petrushka was a popular stock character in Russian puppet shows; in the ballet, the puppet made of straw comes to life.

Stravinsky left St. Petersburg to attend the premiere of *The Firebird*. By the time he composed *The Rite of Spring*, Stravinsky's wife and child had joined him in Paris. They settled in Switzerland during the 1910s, where two other children were born. He returned to Russia briefly in 1914, just before the onset of World War I; because of the Bolshevik Revolution, he would not return for another fifty years. Ironically, his fascination with the primitive and Russian folk culture enabled him to become the first important cosmopolitan composer, a true musician of and for the world.

LO4 Primitivism and Folk Culture

The Rite of Spring tapped into Europe's fascination with the primitive. The roots of this interest extend back at least to the discovery of the Americas and the subsequent colonization of much of Africa, North America, and South America. The majority of Europeans regarded those whom they colonized as savage, even subhuman: this enabled them to justify the slave trade and still profess their Christian faith. The French Enlightenment philosopher Voltaire, who championed social reform in other areas, articulated the prevailing view by describing blacks as inferior to whites and born to be slaves; not coincidentally, perhaps, he reputedly made a substantial fortune investing in the slave trade.

However, around 1750, Voltaire's contemporary Jean-Jacques Rousseau advanced the idea that humans were inherently good (rather than burdened with original sin) and that civilization had evolved into a corrupt-

The "noble savage" has remained a popular notion in mass entertainment.

ing influence because it had lost touch with nature and natural emotions. This was a seed from which the Romantic notion of living in harmony with nature grew.

With the publication of *Robinson Crusoe* in 1719, the English writer Daniel Defoe introduced into literature the idea of the "noble savage," in the person of Crusoe's companion, Friday. Romantics also expanded on this idea. American writers found it especially compelling, because of the frontier and the ongoing contact with Native Americans: it is evident in writings by Cooper, Thoreau, Poe, Whitman, and above all Longfellow, whose poem *The Song of Hiawatha* was extremely popular in the United States and abroad. Underlying the image of the "noble savage" was the assumption that savages become noble by allying themselves with European culture: Friday converts to Christianity. The "noble savage" has remained a popular notion in mass entertainment: Tonto, the Lone Ranger's Native American sidekick, was a familiar example to those growing up around 1950, and Chewbacca, Han Solo's barely articulate copilot in the Star Wars saga, is a more recent extraterrestrial extension of the idea.

The quest for national identity in folk culture was a homegrown corollary to the "noble savage" idea. Both were concerned with the inferior other: the uneducated, illiterate peasant classes of the homeland vis-à-vis the "savage" but educable members of other races. And in both cases, the "other" was made acceptable by embedding it in the dominant culture. In the nineteenth century, just as savages assumed the trappings of European culture, artifacts of folk culture—stories, songs, dances—were polished for presentation to a sophisticated and literate audience.

In *The Rite of Spring*, Stravinsky and his collaborators took a radically different approach.

The Rite of Spring

After the success of *The Firebird* and *Petrushka*, Stravinsky received a third commission from Diaghilev. For inspiration, he drew on a vision, which he later described in this way:

> There arose a picture of a sacred pagan ritual: the wise elders are seated in a circle and are observing the dance before death of the girl whom they are offering as a sacrifice to the god of Spring in order to gain his benevolence. This became the subject of *The Rite of Spring*.

A contemporary performance of *The Rite of Spring* re-creates the original costume designs, which evoked the world of primitive Russian peasants.

THE RITE OF SPRING: RHYTHM AND THE ASSAULT ON MUSICAL CIVILIZATION

The Rite of Spring was conceived as a radically different kind of dance music. It became a frontal assault on musical civilization, as Europeans in the early twentieth century understood it. At the heart of this assault is an approach to rhythm that is both timeless and radically innovative. It would undercut a practice that had evolved slowly but steadily over the previous three centuries.

The most obvious rhythmic innovation in *The Rite of Spring* is the very prominence of rhythm. Percussion instruments and percussive sounds on pitched instruments are pervasive. Moreover, there are passages where an insistent rhythm, made unpredictable by syncopations and irregular metrical groupings, provides the main musical interest. This alone would set it apart from much nineteenth-century music. However, it is the nature of Stravinsky's rhythmic conception that enables the work to overturn established practice. His use of a repetitive rhythm in which each attack gets the same emphasis connects back to the drumming heard in Native American music (and used for the shamanic journey). In this respect, the rhythm is much more "primitive" than the rhythms of eighteenth- and nineteenth-century music.

However, every other aspect of the rhythm is more modern than in conventional practice. Instead of the regular grouping and division of beats, there are strong

In this work, the Russian folk elements seemed to offer a conduit back to a past before recorded time. He would adapt these sounds to orchestral instruments and weave them into a musical fabric that featured innovative, complex harmonies and rhythms. Working closely with Nicholas Roerich, an artist, folklorist, and spiritual teacher—and the designer of the sets for several Ballets Russes productions, including *The Rite of Spring*—and drawing on his familiarity with the music and dance of Russian peasants, Stravinsky and choreographer Nijinsky created a work that challenged every important convention of ballet: the story, the scenery, the dancing, and the music.

By envisioning a prehistoric Russian ritual, Stravinsky merged the primitive with the folklore of his own culture. What made the work revolutionary in its conception was the willingness of Stravinsky and his collaborators to remove the filter of civilization. The plot of the ballet suggests that they understood how differently prehistoric people valued something as fundamental as life itself. The "wise elders" understand that the sacrifice of the young girl is necessary for the preservation of the tribe. She, in turn, is willing to give up her life for the greater good. This idea was completely incomprehensible to early twentieth-century audiences.

THE LANGUAGE OF MUSIC

STRAVINSKY'S "PRIMITIVE" RHYTHMS

This excerpt from the musical score to *The Rite of Spring* shows the string parts for the opening of the second movement, "Augurs of Spring." The inverted U over each note tells the string players to play each note pair using a down bow (rather than alternating between down and up, which is the usual method of bowing). At this tempo, the marking all but ensures that each attack will receive the same amount of sound as its neighbors.

col legno Violin technique that involves tapping the wooden part of the bow on the strings

syncopations and measures of varying length and grouping. Both undermine the predictability of regular meters. Moreover, he abandons the regular phrase rhythm of nineteenth-century dance music, thus extending the unpredictability into a larger dimension.

To musically sophisticated Europeans, the rhythmic organization in art music had come to be understood as an expression of natural laws: like the beating of one's heart or breathing in and out. However, because he framed conventional practice temporally by including both primitive and modern elements in his rhythmic approach, Stravinsky effectively isolated this purportedly universal rhythmic practice in time and place: it is the product of a particular culture at a particular time in history.

By going beyond a civilized form of musical discourse, Stravinsky undercut both its supposed universality and its status as the most sophisticated mode of rhythmic organization. Through the rhythms of *The Rite of Spring*, Stravinsky opened the door in art music to greater rhythmic complexity, founded on completely different rhythmic assumptions.

LISTEN UP!

CD 4:16–18

Stravinsky, "Introduction," "The Augurs of Spring," and "Mock Abduction," from *The Rite of Spring* (1913)

Takeaway point: Revolutionary rhythms that embed the primitive in an ultramodern setting

Style: Twentieth-century primitivism

Form: Through-composed

Genre: Orchestral work for ballet

Instruments: Orchestra

Context: Music for a dance that evokes prehistory time in a radically new way

LISTEN FURTHER

Watch a re-creation of Nijinsky's choreography of Part I of *The Rite of Spring* in the YouTube playlist.

NEW RHYTHMS, NEW FORMS

Stravinsky's radically old/new approach to rhythm underpinned a new conception of form. Unlike most nineteenth-century composers, who organized form mainly around melody, Stravinsky built his large sections from a series of what might be called "sound panels." As used here, "sound panels" refers to sections of music with a characteristic mix of melodic material, timbres, rhythm, and texture. They are often active, but they are nondirectional and fragmentary. Unlike melodic material in conventional phrases, melodic ideas do not progress toward cadences, nor do they form coherent elements in a hierarchical structure. Instead, Stravinsky arranged the sound panels, which are of varying length, in a sequence. One may follow directly after another, with an abrupt shift, or material from the sound panels may overlap, so that one seems to bleed into the next. In conception and implementation, this was radically different from eighteenth- and nineteenth-century practice.

STRAVINSKY'S REVOLUTIONARY "PRIMITIVISM"

In *The Rite of Spring*, Stravinsky synthesized the ancient and the avant-garde. He embedded the primitive elements in ultramodern settings: dissonant harmonies, irregular patterns and rhythms, melodies without cadences, densely layered textures, instrumentation that exploited new orchestral timbres. In several elements, there is a two-pronged approach to modernity. One path is a new take on existing material, while the other is an approach that is completely new. The following chart offers examples of these two paths.

	Old/new	**Completely new**
Rhythm	"Drumming" chords (complex chords in an ancient repetitive rhythm)	Complex rhythmic textures; irregular meters
Melody	Slavic folk songs borrowed or serve as models and are fragmented and rearranged in asymmetrical patterns	Figuration constructed from atonal materials
Instrumentation	Emphasis on percussion instruments and sounds (string players are asked to play **col legno**, tapping the wood part of the bow on the string); evocation of folk vocal styles in instrumental writing	Expanded orchestra, highlighting of unusual instruments (contra-bassoon) and unusual timbres (high bassoon opening)

THE RITE OF SPRING AND STRAVINSKY'S CAREER

The Rite of Spring was Stravinsky's musical declaration of independence: it served as the catalyst for his musical transformation from Russian to international composer. When he first conceived of the work, he was a Russian. He drew both inspiration and musical ideas from his homeland—not the imported culture of the elite but the Slavic folk traditions found throughout the Russian Empire. However, in the wake of the success of *The Rite of Spring*, Stravinsky increasingly distanced himself from the roots of the music. Almost immediately, he encouraged concert performances of the work. Always a shrewd businessman, he realized that *The Rite of Spring* would receive many more performances as a concert work than as a ballet. And he certainly recognized that it was self-sufficient musically. Musicians soon recognized its stunning originality.

The Emergence of the Avant-Garde

The "isms" music of Schoenberg, Debussy, and Stravinsky represents the cutting edge of the transition from the relatively unified musical world of the nineteenth century to the fragmented musical landscape of the early twentieth. All three began their careers as late Romantic composers. However, by the beginning of World War I, each had moved far beyond this tradition. The impact of their music on fellow musicians and sympathetic listeners made it impossible to suppress their innovations.

What made the new music of the early twentieth century different in kind from the music that appeared during earlier periods of revolutionary change was the fact that the "old practice" was replaced by not one but several new practices, each quite different from the other. Although these composers knew and admired each other's work, neither they nor their peers worked collectively toward a new common style that would replace Romanticism. Rather, they expressed their individuality not by making individual statements within an established style but by making their style individual, or even masking it altogether.

Schoenberg and Stravinsky would become the two most influential composers of the first half of the twentieth century. Their esteem would have two far-reaching consequences for twentieth-century music. First, it established novelty as a primary measure of prestige among composers: to earn the highest respect of one's peers, a composer had to create work that featured concepts and sounds without precedent. This quest for novelty in turn skewed the relationship between avant-garde composers and their audience: their need to, as Schoenberg said, "write what my destiny orders me to write" outweighed the need for acceptance beyond a small circle of the knowledgeable. Inspired by Beethoven's rapid stylistic evolution and Bach's resurrection from obscurity, they comforted themselves that the more sophisticated audiences of the future would eventually appreciate their music. This idea would reach its peak in the decades after World War II.

In America, new kinds of popular music, as notorious in their own way as the avant-garde music of Stravinsky and Schoenberg, also took shape in the early years of the twentieth century. It would become a far more pervasive presence in musical life. We examine its early manifestations and encounter the music of America's first modern composer in the next unit.

UNIT 19
AMERICAN CLASSICAL AND CLASSIC MUSIC IN THE EARLY TWENTIETH CENTURY

Learning Outcomes

After reading this unit, you will be able to do the following:

LO1 Compare the impact of John Philip Sousa's brand of popular music with that of Stephen Foster.

LO2 List the most significant aspects of ragtime's legacy.

LO3 Compare and contrast Sousa's march, Joplin's rag, and Ives's orchestral compositions.

LO4 Recognize the changed dynamic between composition, performance, and musical style through an examination of the African American spiritual.

LO5 Describe the place of classic blues as the first "first-person" music in American culture.

LO6 Be familiar with the role of real jazz and Gershwin's "symphonic jazz" in the evolution of American music.

LO7 Discover the sound of 1920s American popular song and its use in Broadway musicals.

Bandstand (oil on canvas on board), Glackens, William James (1870-1938) / © Butler Institute of American Art, Youngstown, OH, USA / The Bridgeman Art Library International

"IN THE NEGRO melodies of America I discover all that is needed for a great and noble school of music." This pronouncement by Antonín Dvořák during his stay in the United States anticipated a wealth of new and distinctively American music that appeared during the first part of the twentieth century. Much of it was either African American or influenced by African American song and dance, and almost none of it was regarded as "great and noble" when it first became known.

In this unit, we sample a broad range of American music, from a march to a popular song from a Broadway musical. Only one of these works is unqualifiedly "classical," but all are "classic" in the original musical meaning of the term: an exemplary instance of a particular genre. We begin just before the turn of the century.

The Concert Band

"[Theodore Thomas] gave Wagner, Liszt, and Tchaikowsky, in the belief that he was educating his public; I gave Wagner, Liszt, and Tchaikowsky with the hope that I was entertaining my public."
—John Philip Sousa

Did You Know?

John Philip Sousa gave over ten thousand concerts in his career as a concert bandleader.

The World's Columbian Exposition of 1893 was the last of the great nineteenth-century world fairs. It was held in Chicago, mainly in Jackson Park, located on the South Side along Lake Michigan, and on the Midway, a green median that connects Jackson Park with Washington Park, several blocks to the west. Most of the buildings were constructed specifically for the fair; the only one that remains standing is the former Palace of Fine Arts, now the Museum of Science and Industry.

Music was a major attraction at the fair. The most prestigious musical ensemble presented at the fair was the Exposition Orchestra, an augmented version of the newly formed Chicago Symphony, which was conducted by Theodore Thomas. However, concert bands proved to be far more popular attractions—to the point that exposition organizers canceled the last several concerts of the Exposition Orchestra because of consistently poor attendance.

The marquee musical attraction was the band led by John Philip Sousa. The previous year, Sousa had stepped down as conductor of the Marine Band to form his own ensemble, which he called the New Marine Band. Their appearance at the fair was one of their first important engagements; thousands attended each of the concerts.

LO1 The Concert Band

The most popular instrumental ensemble in late nineteenth-century America was the concert band. In an era without radio, TV, and other forms of mass communication, touring concert bands, as well as municipal bands found in almost every city and town, were a primary source of musical entertainment.

Bands had been a part of American life since the Revolution. They performed on most public occasions and gave concerts in season. After the Civil War, some of the bands that had formed in major cities became professional ensembles, playing concerts and dances and enhancing public occasions. The most famous of these professional bands before 1890 was the band of the Twenty-second Regiment of New York, renamed the Gilmore Band when Patrick Gilmore became its director in 1873. Although he initially made his mark as a skilled performer on the cornet (a close relative of the trumpet), Gilmore, an Irish immigrant, was best known for organizing "monster concerts," particularly the National Peace Jubilee of 1869 and the World Peace Jubilee of 1872, which featured choruses of thousands, bands and orchestras of hundreds, plus world-famous soloists. He also raised the level of musicianship in bands by arranging visits of the leading European bands to the United States and by raising the standard of performance in the band that he directed. His band toured annually throughout the United States until his sudden death in 1892. Gilmore's success set the stage for the great era of American bands.

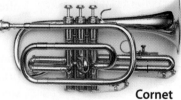

Cornet

The Great Colosseum at the World Peace Jubilee and International Music Festival of 1872

SOUSA'S BAND

From the 1890s through the 1920s, the most popular concert band in the United States was Sousa's New Marine Band. He had established his reputation as a composer and conductor with the Marine Band, which he had directed for twelve years. Sousa formed his own band in 1892, the year of Patrick Gilmore's death. For the remainder of his career, he led his band on annual tours throughout the United States, as well as several tours to Europe and one world tour. Sousa's band was known for its precision and musicianship, as well as for the excellence of its soloists, several of whom subsequently led bands of their own.

Concert bands like Sousa's New Marine Band were large ensembles consisting of woodwinds (including saxophones), brasses, and percussion instruments. For example, the band that Sousa took to Europe in 1900 included sixty-one musicians: flutes and piccolos, oboe and English horn, twenty-two clarinets in four sizes, saxophones, three kinds of high brass (cornet, trumpet, and flugelhorn), French horn, trombones and euphoniums, percussion, and brass bass (named after Sousa as the sousaphone). High brass and clarinets played much of the melodic material; in transcriptions of orchestral music, clarinets most often took over the violin parts.

A typical Sousa band concert included marches, original works for band, solos featuring the band's

concert band Large performing ensemble consisting of woodwinds (including saxophones), brasses, and percussion instruments

march Work for concert band that typically includes four or five melodies or "strains" that are sixteen or thirty-two measures in length, usually written in a duple meter and performed at a brisk walking tempo

virtuoso instrumentalists, arrangements of well-known opera overtures, other classical works, and the popular music of the day, including the latest in syncopated music. In fact, many European audiences first gained exposure to ragtime's syncopated rhythms (see People's Music 12) through Sousa's performances.

The role of professional bands in American musical life around 1900 was much like that of the contemporary pops orchestra. Both feature varied programming: a mixture of popular classical music and popular music, with star soloists. And both direct their programs at a mass audience. Sousa explained why his band drew much bigger crowds than Thomas's Exposition Orchestra: "[Theodore Thomas] gave Wagner, Liszt, and Tchaikowsky, in the belief that he was educating his public; I gave Wagner, Liszt, and Tchaikowsky with the hope that I was entertaining my public."

Sousa and the March

The most popular and memorable music that the New Marine Band performed was Sousa's marches. Although he composed other kinds of works—songs, operettas, and band suites—Sousa made his reputation as a composer of marches. Their popularity earned him the title the "March King" and made him America's best-known composer during his lifetime. Sousa wrote 136 marches between 1876 and 1931. However, most of his best-known marches were written between 1888 and 1900: *Semper Fidelis* (1888), *Washington Post* (1889), and *Hands across the Sea* (1899) are a few.

A Sousa **march** has a modular form; it typically includes four or five melodies or "strains" that are sixteen or thirty-two measures in length. There are two main sections, the march and the trio; the trio is in a different key and typically begins with a lyric melody. Each strain is usually repeated at least once. A march is usually written in a duple meter and performed at a brisk walking tempo.

"THE STARS AND STRIPES FOREVER"

Sousa's most famous march, the National March of the United States since 1977 and probably the most famous march of all time is "The Stars and Stripes Forever." Conceived in 1896 and published the following year during Sousa's peak decade as a composer, it is the quintessential Sousa march. It has stirring and lyric melodies, subtle variation in accompaniment and rhythm, and a rich texture, with several layers of activity.

SOUSA'S LEGACY

Sousa's marches are the instrumental counterpart to Stephen Foster's songs. They share three important

© iStockphoto.com/Keith Bishop

qualities. First, the most famous works by both composers were immediately popular and have remained among the best-known music from the nineteenth century. Second, they are musically significant—the best examples of their genres. Third, they are unquestionably American in character. Together they make up the most important legacy from nineteenth-century American popular music.

Simply because they—and the bands that played them—were so popular, marches by Sousa and others had an impact well beyond the parade and concert venues. The two-step was a popular social dance inspired by Sousa's "Washington Post March." The rhythm and spirit of the march animated popular song, most notably in the patriotic songs of George M. Cohan ("Yankee Doodle Boy," "You're a Grand Old Flag"). Most important for American music, the march and the concert band would also play a seminal role in the development of ragtime, syncopated dance music, and jazz.

 LISTEN UP!

CD 4:19
Sousa, "The Stars and Stripes Forever" (1897)

Takeaway point: Quintessential example of a march for band

Style: Nineteenth-century American popular music

Form: Multisectional

Genre: March

Instruments: Concert band

Context: The march as popular concert music for a mass audience

Ragtime

> "The 'Ragtime Evil' should not be found in Christian homes, according to one writer."

Did You Know?

In 1976, Scott Joplin posthumously received a Pulitzer Prize special award for his contributions to American music.

Among the bigger hits of 1896 was a song entitled "All Coons Look Alike to Me." In our own time, a song with that title would seem to be the work of a white supremacist. However, the end of the nineteenth century was a low point in post–Civil War race relations; in the same year that the song appeared, the Supreme Court's decision in *Plessy v. Ferguson* ratified the "separate but equal" policy that became the law of the land until the 1950s. In this environment, most mainstream Americans seemed not to find derogatory racial terms particularly offensive.

As it happened, the composer of "All Coons Look Alike to Me" was Ernest Hogan, one of the leading black entertainers of the time. His song is romantic: it describes a young man who has eyes for only one girl; other girls "look alike" to him. However, in a climate where the majority of Americans assumed that blacks were inferior, a love song between blacks was not socially acceptable outside the black community. So Hogan found himself with a bitter choice: buy into the stereotypes of the time—even as he tried to undermine them somewhat in the lyric—or fail to get the song published.

Hogan's music is the good news that balances the bad news of the title. In the published version of "All Coons Look Alike to Me," the repetition of the chorus features a "Negro 'rag' accompaniment." This was the first published example of raglike piano style. The first published piano rags, including Scott Joplin's "Original Rags," appeared a year later.

ragtime, rag Syncopated American musical style of the late nineteenth and early twentieth centuries that began as dance music in the bordello districts of New Orleans

LO2 Ragtime

Ragtime first surfaced as an obscure folk-dance music played throughout the Mississippi valley in the last quarter of the nineteenth century. Soon black pianists were playing it in bars and bordellos in the Midwest and along the East Coast.

Toward the end of the century, the terms **rag** and **ragtime** came into use to identify this new style. They were applied to any music with even a hint of syncopation, or "ragged" rhythm. Authenticity was not an issue: it seemed to matter little whether whites or blacks performed it, how much syncopation it contained, or whether it was vocal or instrumental. Among the entertainers most responsible for its popularity was Ben Harney, a white singer/pianist/comedian who was a vaudeville headliner around the turn of the century.

Black pianists began playing ragtime in bars that would later become "juke joints."

Harney's *Ragtime Instructor*, published in 1897, showed aspiring pianists how to "rag" (that is, syncopate) popular songs, classical compositions, and other well-known works. Sousa's band would introduce these syncopated rhythms in Europe: their performance of Fred Stone's 1898 dance, "Ma Ragtime Baby," won a prize at the Paris Exposition in 1900. Only with the publication of the rags of Joplin and others, most notably Joplin's "Maple Leaf Rag" (1899), did "rag" come to refer primarily to the piano music with which we now associate the term.

© Photo courtesy of the Morgan Collection

The sudden popularity of ragtime provoked a powerful backlash from virtually every corner of the establishment, musical and otherwise. In their view, ragtime was immoral, fit only for the saloons and brothels where it was played, and musically inferior, the product of an inferior race incapable of the musical sophistication that Europeans had achieved. Ragtime was also seen as a cause of moral decay. The "Ragtime Evil" should not be found in Christian homes, according to one writer. It is in this environment that Scott Joplin sought to elevate ragtime from a popular style into art.

SCOTT JOPLIN AND THE PIANO RAG

The most enduring music of the ragtime era has been the classic piano rags of Scott Joplin. These have remained familiar, especially since the ragtime revival of the 1970s. Joplin's "Maple Leaf Rag" was the first commercially successful piano rag, and his output of piano rags remains the core of the ragtime repertoire.

A professional musician from his teenage years, Joplin played in saloons and clubs, at first along the Mississippi valley and eventually in Sedalia, Missouri. The "Maple Leaf Rag" is named after the Maple Leaf Club in Sedalia, his place of employment from 1894 until the turn of the century. He also received formal musical training in the European tradition, principally through study at George R. Smith College in Sedalia, and was a fluent composer and arranger in the white popular styles of the day.

In the wake of his success with "Maple Leaf Rag," Joplin devoted most of his efforts as a composer and musician to legitimizing ragtime. This is evident in his and his publisher's insistence on referring to Joplin's rags as "classic" and in his excursions into large-scale classical genres: he composed a ballet, *The Ragtime*

Scott Joplin

Fast Facts

- *Dates:* 1868–1917
- *Place:* United States
- *Reasons to remember:*
  Through ragtime, introduced African American elements into American popular music

© Bettmann/CORBIS

Dance, and two operas, *Treemonisha* and the now-lost *A Guest of Honor*.

The rags that followed "Maple Leaf Rag" are typically more melodious and less syncopated. The syncopated figurations that characterize ragtime are present, but they do not permeate the rags and are somewhat toned down from those found in Joplin's first rags. Moreover, in both his tempo indications for rags and written commentary on the correct performance of ragtime, Joplin constantly admonishes pianists against playing ragtime too fast: for him, ragtime played at a slower tempo gains in dignity.

A Joplin piano rag is, in essence, a march that has been "ragged," played on the piano.

© C Squared Studios/Getty Images

A Joplin piano rag is, in essence, a march that has been "ragged," played on the piano. Virtually all of its musical features come from the European tradition; only the syncopations hint at its African heritage. We hear this in one of Joplin's best-known rags, "The Entertainer."

THE LEGACY OF RAGTIME

Ragtime would have a profound impact on the African American community, on musical life in the United States, on the appeal of American music abroad, and on the relationship between classical and vernacular traditions. These are among the most significant aspects of ragtime's legacy:

CD 4:20

Joplin, "The Entertainer" (1902)

Takeaway point: An elegant example of the classic piano rag

Style: Ragtime

Form: Multisection

Genre: Piano rag

Instrument: Piano

Context: Joplin working to dignify "saloon music"

1. *The music itself.* The classic piano rags of Scott Joplin and other distinguished composers constitute a repertoire of real artistic worth and individuality.

2. *The introduction of an authentic black music to white America.* Because it could be notated, ragtime was the first authentically black music to enter the mainstream.

3. *The blurring of boundaries between classical and vernacular.* Joplin aspired to art; the new syncopated music intrigued important composers of art music, including the American composer Charles Ives, as well as Debussy and Stravinsky.

4. *The transformation of popular music.* Ragtime would play a crucial role in introducing African American elements into popular music.

In all these ways, ragtime was, by example and influence, a catalyst for change—within the world of music and within American society.

CHAPTER 40

Charles Ives: Toward an American Art Music

"You won't get a wild, heroic ride to heaven on pretty little sounds."
—Charles Ives's father

In 1910, a year after he formed the Ives and Myrick Insurance Agency with his longtime friend Julian Myrick, Charles Ives published a how-to pamphlet for his agents. The pamphlet would eventually grow into a substantial publication entitled *The Amount to Carry—Measuring the Prospect.* The publication came to be recognized as one of the first practical guides to estate planning.

Charles Ives led two lives. By day, he was a prominent and innovative insurance executive. By the time he retired from business in 1930, he was a wealthy man. At night and on weekends, he composed feverishly—until one day in early 1927, when he painfully acknowledged that he had exhausted his inspiration.

Unlike most other turn-of-the-century American composers, Ives did not go to Europe for further training and did not pursue a career in music. Instead, by opting for a career in business, Ives provided financial security for himself and his family and liberated himself from the necessity to please the tastemakers in the classical music world. What he sacrificed in time, he gained in artistic freedom. This fiercely independent path was characteristic of the man and his music, and of the environment in which he lived.

Did You Know?

Charles Ives's orchestral sound collages anticipate the sampling of rap pioneer Grandmaster Flash by almost eight decades.

A Connecticut Yankee

New England lives up to its name: it's the region of the United States that is most like England, and it was the center of the movement that would enable the colonies to create a new country, independent of England. It is home to the Handel and Haydn Society, which honors the two most esteemed eighteenth-century composers connected to England. The vast majority of the nation's elite prep schools are in New England. Many of its smaller towns cover a lot of land and consist of groups of villages a few miles apart—all reminiscent of the English countryside.

In cities and towns throughout the six states, one finds memorials to Revolutionary War heroes; in Danbury, Connecticut, there is a monument to David Wooster, who lost his life trying to repel the British. Nearby is the camp where troops under the command of Israel Putnam, one of the heroes of the Battle of Bunker Hill, spent the winter of 1778–1779.

Concord, Massachusetts, would later become the home of the transcendentalists. Charles Ives celebrated them in his *Concord Sonata*: he named the four movements after Emerson, Hawthorne, the Alcotts, and Thoreau. Litchfield, Connecticut, was home to the Beechers, including Henry Ward Beecher and Harriet Beecher Stowe, author of *Uncle Tom's Cabin*. Both were among the prominent abolitionists in the North; so were their not-too-distant neighbors, George and Sarah Ives, Charles Ives's grandparents.

Ives's uncle Isaac was a snake-oil salesman.

New Englanders project seemingly contradictory values. They can be pragmatic, philosophical, or preposterous—P. T. Barnum grew up in Connecticut and lived in Danbury; Ives's uncle Isaac was a snake-oil salesman. They are elitist and populist: Lowell Mason was both, as was Ives. They value tradition, yet their institutions are also hotbeds of innovation; ideas and inventions have poured forth from their universities.

Charles Ives

Few New Englanders embodied these diverse values more fully than Charles Ives. In business, he was pragmatic and populist: his goal was to provide security for as many Americans as possible. Yet these pragmatic objectives were shaped by deep philosophical convictions, which he expressed not only in his writings about his music but also in a long preamble to the nuts-and-bolts aspects of selling insurance in *The Amount to Carry*. His business innovations grew out of traditional New England values: they made money through hard work and did good at the same time. His musical innovations were another matter entirely.

Ives is arguably America's most original composer. His determination to survey uncharted musical territory grew out of his strong sense of time and place, of family going back generations, and of the particular attitudes toward learning and ideas that were characteristic of New England during his formative years.

Charles Ives

Fast Facts

- *Dates:* 1874–1954
- *Place:* United States
- *Reasons to remember:* A truly American musical innovator

Ives's forebears were among the first Europeans to settle in the colonies: William Ives captained a ship from England in 1637, arrived in Boston, and then made his way to New Haven. His descendants settled in Wal-lingford, about fifteen miles north of New Haven; Ives's great-grandfather Isaac was the first Ives in Danbury, arriving there in 1785. The family prospered and acquired a reputation for unconventional, even eccentric behavior. Ives's father, George, was the most

Ives is arguably America's most original composer.

© Neale Osborne/Lebrecht Music & Arts

unconventional of the Iveses. The youngest Union bandmaster during the Civil War, George Ives returned home and assumed direction of the municipal band. Music was sometimes his only work, but he ran a store early in his career and worked at a family bank later.

Many of the most central elements of Ives's musical life respond directly to his father's attitudes and his career as a town musician. Like his son, George had a curious and open mind and remarkable industry. He delighted in unusual sound combinations: on one occasion, he had two bands cross paths to see what they would sound like. He valued substance over style and in amateur music making gave far more weight to the intent than the result. Ives recalled his father's comment about a stonemason's off-key hymn singing: "Look into his face and hear the music of the ages. Don't pay too much attention to the sounds—for if you do, you may miss the music. You won't get a wild, heroic ride to heaven on pretty little sounds." He preferred band music to Mozart, and the fervor of camp meetings to more traditional church services. From this came Ives's familiarity with and delight in the full range of vernacular traditions: marches, gospel hymns, ragtime, popular songs, and the like.

Although Danbury claimed to be "the most musical city in Connecticut" largely on the strength of George Ives's work, many of its influential citizens regarded a musical career as an unworthy profession. Charles Ives detested the more genteel sorts of ladies who gathered in stuffy parlors to listen to sentimental songs and tamer varieties of classical music—these were the same ladies who looked down their noses at George Ives and his music.

Like many of his forebears—but not his father—Charles Ives went to Yale, where he studied under Horatio Parker, one of the most highly esteemed members of the New England school of composers. Ives came to Yale knowing mostly the vernacular music with which he had grown up. Parker led him through more traditional classical literature; Ives's understanding of the Romantic tradition, musically and philosophically, came much more from Parker than from his father. By the time he graduated, he had composed a draft of his first symphony and a string quartet.

Although he was prepared academically for a career in music and had been a professional church organist since he was fourteen, Ives disdained music as a profession. At the same time, his music was Beethoven-like in its boldness and grandness, and it featured a wholesale infusion of vernacular elements. What makes his music even more remarkable is that he heard so little of it performed by anyone other than himself around the time he composed it. The American avant-garde began to perform his music only after he stopped composing new work. The performance history of his orchestral set *Three Places in New England* is all too typical: composition completed around 1914, a first performance as a work for chamber orchestra in 1929, publication in 1935, a full orchestral performance only in 1948. It is now Ives's most popular orchestral work.

LO3 The Music of Charles Ives: *Three Places in New England*

Ives's *Three Places in New England* is true to its title: it depicts the Boston Common, a Revolutionary War site near Ives's home, and a place along a river running through the Berkshires. The three pieces are also about time: in his program notes, he describes the experiences that inspired the works.

In the second movement, entitled "Putnam's Camp, Redding, Connecticut," time and place are specific and close to home: Putnam's Camp is only a few miles from Danbury and even closer to Ives's home in West Redding, which he had built shortly before composing *Three Places in New England*. The movement begins in the present, then drifts back in time. The "present" in this work is a typical Independence Day celebration, circa 1912. The past recalls the winter of 1778–1779. Putnam's Camp was Connecticut's Valley Forge; the winter that year was especially hard. The dream section recounts an incident well known to many Connecticut citizens: some soldiers are thinking of deserting, but Putnam returns to the encampment and gives a stirring speech that persuades them to stay, endure hardship, and fight.

Putnam's Camp was Connecticut's Valley Forge.

Ives uses these events that are so specific in time and place in order to universalize their meaning. The trip back in time serves as a vivid reminder of the underlying purpose of the holiday. It is a tribute to the virtues that made independence possible: courage, perseverance, altruism. It's clear from his writing and his music that these larger themes are central to his outlook on life. Indeed, like the transcendentalists that he so admired, Ives felt the connectedness to all life and the world of the spirit. His most characteristic work may well have been one that he never completed: his proposed "Universe" symphony. Ives's sense of connectedness radiates from his immediate environment: from family, Danbury, New England, and America, to the world. Thus, even as he reaches out to the world, he conveys where he is from and what it stands for.

Ives's self-imposed challenge was to communicate his vision musically. For someone with such a keen sense of place and such deeply rooted populist values, looking to Europe was out of the question, despite Parker's strong influence. European influence is evident only on the most basic level: the use of a symphony orchestra and the intent to present the music in an art-music setting. To achieve this, Ives charted a radically new approach to music.

Ives's music was made up of sprawling American collages.

In effect, "Putnam's Camp" is a sprawling musical collage. Among its most striking features are the snippets of familiar (and familiar-sounding) melodies. Ives "samples" patriotic songs, folk tunes, minstrel show songs, Sousa marches, children's songs, and more. He seldom includes more than a fragment of each song. These are songs that Ives heard growing up in Danbury, and he correctly expected that his audience would also know them. Here, Ives uses these familiar melodies not as the raw material for a larger composition, as Mozart did in his variation sets, but rather for their associative value, much like Berlioz's quotation of the "Dies irae." However, Ives's approach is much more pervasive.

As a result, the simple large-scale ternary form is not defined mainly by melodic material but by the ebb and flow of activity and changes in dynamics. This simple formal model outlines the shift from present to past and back to the present that Ives describes in his program for the work:

A: (present) Once upon a "4 July," some time ago, so the story goes, a child went here on a picnic, held under the auspices of the first Church and the Village Cornet Band. Wandering away from the rest of the children past the camp ground into the woods, he hopes to catch a glimpse of some of the old soldiers. As he rests on the hillside of laurels and hickories the tunes of the band and the songs of the children grow fainter and fainter;

B: (past)—when—"mirabile dictu"—over the trees on the crest of the hill he sees a tall woman standing. She reminds him of a picture he has of the Goddess Liberty—but the face is sorrowful—she is pleading with the soldiers not to forget their "cause" and the great sacrifices they have made for it. But they

↩ LISTEN UP!

CD 4:21–23

Ives, "Putnam's Camp, Redding, Connecticut," from *Three Places in New England* (1914)

Takeaway point: Sprawling orchestral collage that embodies a particular kind of American spirit

Style: Twentieth century

Form: Free ABA'

Genre: Programmatic orchestral work

Instruments: Orchestra

Context: Highly individual orchestral music that rebels against the stuffiness of the "cultivated" music of nineteenth-century New England

march out of camp with fife and drum to a popular tune of the day. Suddenly, a new national note is heard. Putnam is coming over the hills from the center—the soldiers turn back and cheer.

A: (present) The little boy awakes, he hears the children's songs and runs down past the monument to "listen to the band" and join in the games and dances.

Ives: Toward an All-American Art Music

Among the most productive new ideas in mathematics and physics advanced in the latter part of the twentieth century was chaos theory. Chaos theory describes dynamic systems with multiple variables, in which seemingly random events resolve on a larger scale into patterns determined by the initial conditions. Ives's music, exemplified here by "Putnam's Camp," conveys a chaoslike musical intent, in that the seemingly random sequence of musical events resolves into a meaningful larger structure. The impression is that Ives is expressing an idea so powerful that it cannot be realized in conventional musical terms.

Ives's unkempt grandeur—a big statement emerging from apparent disorder—is just one aspect of his compositional art. There are exquisite moments, such as the harmonic haze that ushers in the flashback to 1778 and the haunting oboe melody that follows, and there is the dizzying and dazzling complexity of the work, with so many competing melodies, rhythms, and instruments. Above all, there is the imagination to conceive of something so different from anything that had come before. It is unquestionably important art, although, in its sources and in their presentation, it rejects many of the conventions of the established art tradition.

Ives's art serves his vision of America: it is populist, patriotic, and particular to New England and its long history. Although he composed "Putnam's Camp" for symphony orchestra and derived his sense of grandness from the European symphonic tradition (the movement is longer than the third movement of the Brahms symphony heard in Chapter 33, although the overall form is simpler), he wanted his music to sound homegrown, not imported. He achieved this not only by drawing on the music that was well known to ordinary folk but also by weaving it into a musical fabric that expressed values that he found particularly American—bigness, humor, energy, wildness, honor, enthusiasm—and that rejected those that were in his view not intrinsic to the American character—refinement and sentimentality.

In works like *Three Places in New England*, Ives created an all-American musical tradition, a tradition that was American in concept as well as musical substance. He achieved his implicit objective: to create a uniquely innovative new kind of art music. It is music that is both populist and elite, and a music that far transcended the more conventional musical styles enjoyed by the cultivated members of American society, in Danbury and elsewhere. No other composer discussed in this book conveyed such a specific cultural identity.

Ives's music would not become known until years, even decades, after its composition. As it did, it would inspire a particularly American openness to new sounds. Out of it would come music from composers like Henry Cowell, Lou Harrison, and John Cage.

The Vitality of American Music

Sousa's march, Joplin's rag, and Ives's orchestral canvas, so different in intent and result, nevertheless seem to share several qualities. All have roots in vernacular music, they vibrate with energy, and they help blur the boundary between cultivated and vernacular. Sousa's march is the least overtly American: there is no distinctive feature, like Joplin's ragged syncopation, or practice, like Ives's sound collages of American tunes, that stamps the music as coming from the United States. Yet it sounds American, if only by long association. Sousa, as a composer and bandmaster, helped blur the boundary between high and low art. His marches are, like Johann Strauss Jr.'s waltzes, quintessential examples of a functional music. The performances of his immensely popular band offered a vernacular alternative to the cultivated concert experience. Moreover, Sousa's band and those that followed in its wake contributed significantly to the emergence of the symphonic band as an important twentieth-century ensemble.

In his rags, Joplin strives to elevate the vernacular dance music of an oppressed minority into art by following European practice. Nevertheless, its outstanding feature is the characteristic syncopation. This infused his rags with a particularly American vitality, and the fusion of African-inspired rhythms with European practice invested the music with an elegance that is specific to certain kinds of African American music; we will hear a related instance in the spiritual presented in the next chapter.

Ives's orchestral work is a frontal assault on the cultivated tradition. At the time he composed it, the gap between cultivated and vernacular was still substantial. By the time it was first performed, the gap had shrunk. By the time Ives won the Pulitzer Prize in 1947, the American musical landscape was far more complex and far less divided than it had been at the turn of the century, and American musicians were far more prominent and influential than they had been a half century earlier.

Only Sousa's music was well known and well regarded during the period in which it was created. Ragtime's notoriety far exceeded its popularity, mainly because of its racial origins. The insuperable difficulties Joplin faced in mounting performances of his opera

Treemonisha evidence the low regard in which ragtime and its creators were held. Ives's music languished in obscurity because of its formidable difficulties, its manifold innovations, and the attitude that it conveyed.

All three works exhibit in quite different ways the vitality that would characterize so much American music throughout the twentieth century. This vitality is expressed most directly in rhythmic exuberance: obvious in the Sousa march, restrained but elegant in the Joplin rag, and overflowing in Ives's evocation of a patriotic celebration. This particularly American spirit would resonate through music of all kinds. We will encounter it in popular song and jazz and the jazz-inspired music of George Gershwin, Aaron Copland's populist ballet music, the avant-garde music of John Cage, rock, the minimalist music of Steve Reich, and the eclectic music of later twentieth-century composers Joan Tower and Ellen Zwilich.

CHAPTER 41

Lift Ev'ry Voice: The African American Spiritual

"Music doesn't change laws, but it does help change attitudes."

In 1899, the black poet James Weldon Johnson wrote the poem "Lift Ev'ry Voice," which his brother, J. Rosamond Johnson, soon set to music. The song had its first performance the following year at the Stanton School, an all-black school in Jacksonville, Florida, where both Johnsons had received their primary education and where James Weldon was principal. A 500-voice choir sang it as part of a celebration of Lincoln's birthday.

The Johnson brothers would soon move north to New York, where they joined with fellow Southerner Bob Cole to write for the Broadway stage. They were

Did You Know?

A 1990 recording of "Lift Ev'ry Voice," by black singer Melba Moore and myriad R&B stars, inspired Congressman Walter Fauntroy to have it officially recognized as the "African American National Hymn."

among the most successful black songwriting teams; among their hits was the popular song "Under the Bamboo Tree," which later made its way into the Judy Garland film *Meet Me in St. Louis*. Rosamond Johnson toured in vaudeville, first with Cole, then with others following Cole's death in 1911. Like many other black professional musicians of the time, Rosamond Johnson wore many hats. His professional accomplishments included serving as director of the New York Music School Settlement for Colored People from 1913 to 1919, touring with his group The Harlem Rounders, and singing the role of Frazier in the original production of George Gershwin's *Porgy and Bess*.

James Weldon Johnson would lead a full life as a diplomat, attorney, social activist, educator, and writer. He became one of the leading figures in the

Harlem Renaissance, an outpouring of black creativity in New York City in the 1920s, and in 1922 edited *The Book of American Negro Poetry*. He and his brother would collaborate on two books of Negro spirituals, which were published in 1925 and 1926.

The National Association for the Advancement of Colored People (NAACP), formed in 1909, adopted "Lift Ev'ry Voice" as the "Negro National Anthem" a decade later. During the 1960s, the song was revived as the "Black National Anthem," and in 1990, it entered the *Congressional Record* as the "official African American National Hymn."

© Photo courtesy of the Morgan Collection

When performed literally from the sheet music, "Lift Ev'ry Voice" does not sound "black." That is, it doesn't exhibit musical features commonly associated with African American music, such as the ragged syncopations in Joplin's music. Only in performance by black musicians (and those who emulate them) does it acquire a distinctively black identity. The history of the song and its creators highlights two main themes of this chapter: the suddenly changed dynamic between composition, performance, and musical style; and the role of music in helping to overcome racial and gender prejudice.

LO4 Recording, Composition, Performance, and Musical Style

Contemporary listeners have two quite different understandings of musical style. With classical music, listeners perceive musical style from the choices made by the composers. Multiple recordings of Beethoven's "Moonlight" sonata or Debussy's "Clair de Lune" based on the composer's score will sound much the same; there will be only minor differences from performance to performance. However, since the early twentieth century, listeners have perceived musical style in popular and folk music largely from the choices made by the performers—and those who assist them. Rodgers and Hart's pop standard "Blue Moon" is a "sweet" popular song when sung by crooner Vaughn Monroe, jazz when performed by trumpeter Dizzy Gillespie, rockabilly when recorded by Elvis Presley, doo-wop when recorded by the Marcels, and beyond category when recorded by Bob Dylan in 1970. And the main reason for the rise of performance-based style perception is the *recording*.

For centuries, the most common way to preserve and pass on classical, popular, and church music was through musical notation. Although it grew more sophisticated with each passing century, notation was—and is—a limited tool for transmitting musical information, because it translates sound into visual symbols, which the performer must retranslate into sound. Notation can describe the parameters of performance only in general terms; it cannot easily communicate the fine nuances of performance. For example, notation can indicate pitch more precisely than any other element: midregister pitches notated as A's vibrate at 220 or 440 cycles per second, no matter what. But notation cannot easily indicate subtle inflections of pitch, such as the bent notes of blues singers and guitarists.

The advent of commercial sound recording made it possible to communicate *all* aspects of a musical performance, including those that are difficult or impossible to notate. As a result, listeners could—and did—form impressions of style based on the choices of the performer as well as the composer. This has been especially evident in those musical traditions where performers have had substantial interpretive leeway: to change or choose pitches, rhythms, instrumentation, timbre, and the like.

Recording engineered a paradigm shift in the understanding and perception of style because it changed the basic musical document. Beethoven's symphonies came down to us as musical scores, but the songs of The Beatles came down to us as recordings. Beethoven's music presumes an established performing tradition: the recording of his Fifth Symphony, heard in Chapter 26, lies within that tradition; Walter Murphy's notorious disco version, "A Fifth of Beethoven," does not. But no particular performance—in concert or on record—is inherently better. By contrast, a Beatles recording is the definitive version of a song; any other version is a **cover**—a remake of an existing song.

The African American spiritual provides a special insight into the complex relationship between composition, performance, and musical style, because it exists

Harlem Renaissance
Outpouring of black creativity in New York City in the 1920s

cover Remake of an existing song

simultaneously in two distinct, if interrelated, forms. As a composed music, it is a continuation of the practice of gentrifying folk melodies by providing them with an artful accompaniment. This practice dates from the early nineteenth century, with the setting of Irish and Scottish songs by Beethoven, Thomas Moore, and others. In this form, African American features are embedded within a refined European setting, thus giving the prevailing European art style a gentle regional accent. Concert singers of all races have performed settings of these folk melodies by Harry Burleigh, Roland Hayes, and the Johnson brothers; they were especially popular around the time of their publication in the 1910s and 1920s.

However, the spiritual also exists as a performing style when sung by classically trained African American singers. The style is distinctly and almost inimitably African American. One reason is the culture from which African American vocalists emerged, especially in the years before World War II. It is evident in the singer's diction and in subtleties of inflection and timing. And there are also those indescribable features that seem to come from the spirit.

Marian Anderson and the Spiritual

Before the opening of the Kennedy Center in 1971, concertgoers in Washington, D.C., had to make do with Constitution Hall, a dumpy auditorium that was nevertheless the major venue for concerts in the nation's capital. The Daughters of the American Revolution (DAR), a patriotic society whose membership was limited to direct descendants of those who fought for independence during the Revolutionary War, administered the hall. Although it claimed to promote citizenship and humanitarian service, the DAR had in 1932 put in place a policy banning black concert performers, because some patrons apparently objected to mixed seating among blacks and whites at these events.

"A voice like yours is heard only once in a hundred years."—Arturo Toscanini, to Marian Anderson

© Walter Sanders/Time Life Pictures/Getty Images

In 1939, impresario Sol Hurok attempted to arrange a concert at Constitution Hall for the African American contralto Marian Anderson (1897–1993), whom he had represented since 1935. Anderson, who grew up in Philadelphia, had spent much time in Europe during the 1930s, where she created a sensation. Among her ardent supporters was the famed Italian conductor Arturo Toscanini, who told her, "a voice like yours is heard only once in a hundred years." Despite her success in Europe and considerable acclaim upon her return to the United States, Anderson faced the same discrimination as other blacks: segregated accommodations, dining, restrooms, and travel. And especially in the South, newspapers went out of their way to avoid affording her the same recognition that they would give to a white performer. The DAR's decision was consistent with prevailing attitudes, if not with their professed ideals. However, it outraged fair-minded citizens, including First Lady Eleanor Roosevelt, who promptly resigned from the organization. Mrs. Roosevelt and an ad hoc committee instead arranged for Marian Anderson to perform on the steps of the Lincoln Memorial on Easter Sunday. A crowd of seventy-five thousand people gathered to hear her. On the program were several spirituals.

spiritual Religious folk song sung by both blacks and whites since well before the Civil War

The Spiritual, from Folk to Art

During the nineteenth and early twentieth centuries, spirituals ascended the musical social ladder. They began the nineteenth century as folk music, became popular music

© iStockphoto.com/Gerri Hernández

after the Civil War, and graduated to the concert stage early in the twentieth century. **Spirituals** are religious folk songs sung by both blacks and whites since well before the Civil War. White spirituals date back to the early eighteenth century. The first accounts of black spirituals date from the camp meetings of the early nineteenth century, in which whites came together with free and enslaved blacks to worship. The 1860s saw publication of several collections of black folk music, which included spirituals. The most notable was *Slave Songs of the United States* (1867); the authors, who transcribed the songs from live performances, commented on the impossibility of rendering distinctive features of the performing style in musical notation.

In the wake of these publications, the spiritual became a kind of popular music. Beginning in 1871, the Fisk Jubilee Singers, a group formed to raise money for the newly founded Fisk University, popularized spirituals outside the black community through successful concert tours. Other similar groups soon followed; some came from other newly formed black colleges; others were groups trying to capitalize on the public's enthusiasm for this music.

The Fisk Jubilee Singers (1875)

In the early twentieth century, the spiritual became concert music. Harry Burleigh, who sang numerous spirituals to Antonín Dvořák during Dvořák's tenure at the National Conservatory of Music, published the first set of spiritual arrangements for solo voice with piano accompaniment in 1916. His aim was to provide a classical-style setting for the melodies without suppressing their distinctly African American quality. Other African American composer-performers, including Rosamond Johnson and Roland Hayes, followed suit. Marian Anderson, Hayes, and Paul Robeson were among the black concert singers who regularly programmed spirituals on their concerts.

One might wonder to what extent the emergence of this repertoire and the distinctive way of singing it were a response to the social inequities in twentieth-century America. In the first few decades of the century, a relatively small but active group of blacks sought to define their culture not in opposition to prevailing taste, as rap has done, or largely independent of mainstream taste, as rural blues and early jazz had done, but as an idiomatic variant of the dominant high culture. Scott Joplin's rags were an early example. During the 1920s, the composer William Grant Still (1895–1978) was at work on his *Afro-American Symphony* (1930) even as

LISTEN UP!

CD 4:24

Hayes, "Lord, I Can't Stay Away," performed by Marian Anderson (1961)

Takeaway point: Elegant and distinctively African American rendition of an artfully set African American song

Style: Folk-based art song

Form: ABABA

Genre: Spiritual

Instruments: Voice and piano

Context: The elevation of the folk music of a disparaged minority to concert music

he was arranging music for the Paul Whiteman Orchestra, one of the most popular commercial dance bands of the 1920s. Still, through the singing of Anderson, Hayes, and others, the spiritual became the most familiar and identifiable expression of an African American sensibility within high culture during the first half of the century. We hear a moving example of this genre in Marian Anderson's performance of "Lord, I Can't Stay Away."

It was as if these African American composer-arrangers and singers played the high-culture game and won. They created a style that clearly belonged in a concert setting, yet was uniquely theirs, and that was almost universally liked and admired. White concert singers have seldom programmed spirituals, and fewer still perform them idiomatically. One wonders how clearly concert singers such as Marian Anderson were aware of this unique state of affairs. And one wonders whether, when Anderson sang, she took some pleasure in ownership—whether in her most gracious and dignified way, she anticipated MC Hammer by saying to herself, "U Can't Touch This," and knowing that it was true.

Music and Race: Cause and Effect?

In 1998, VH1 sponsored its inaugural "Divas" concert, an all-star event presented to raise funds for the station's Save the Music Foundation. The concert brought together two rock-era queens—Aretha Franklin (the queen of soul) and Gloria Estefan (the queen of Latin pop)—and three rising stars: Mariah Carey, Céline Dion, and Shania Twain. The Divas concert series ran for six more years; the last concert took place in 2004. The format remained much the same: bring together established stars and new talent; younger invitees included Christina Aguilera, Mary J. Blige, Faith Hill, Jewel, Beyoncé, Brandy, Shakira, and Jessica Simpson.

It is fitting that Aretha was one of the five artists invited to perform at the first Divas concert. Clearly, she was the dominant musical personality, although she only sang with others, and she has been a dominant influence on the vocal style of many of the younger divas—black, white, or Latina—to the extent that the prevailing vocal style of these performers might be described as "Aretha lite." Her influence is evident in the singers' diction, which has something of the intonation and cadence of black speech (and is typically quite different from their conversational speech); in the vocal timbre; and in the forms of expressive nuance, especially the use of melisma. The young divas may have modeled their image and choreography after Madonna, but their musical and vocal conception derives most directly from the soulful singing of Aretha Franklin and her peers.

The Divas concerts make clear that race is a nonissue in contemporary pop. It isn't just that five women of differing ethnic and racial backgrounds teamed up for a stellar fund-raising event. It is that black vernacular singing has become the basis for the prevailing female pop vocal style, irrespective of any particular singer's roots.

© Getty Images

The Divas concerts made clear that race is a nonissue in contemporary pop.

Does society follow music? While it is perhaps too much to assert a cause-and-effect connection between racial attitudes within the musical world and society at large, it can certainly be noted that in the twentieth century, progress in race relations in musical circles have anticipated progress in society as a whole. Before Jesse Owens and Joe Louis, there were Bessie Smith and Marian Anderson, Scott Joplin and Louis Armstrong. Benny Goodman integrated his band a decade before Jackie Robinson integrated Major League baseball and before President Truman integrated the military. Fifteen years of rhythm and blues made Americans of all races more receptive to Martin Luther King's "I Have a Dream" speech.

Music doesn't change laws, but it does help change attitudes. That Aretha Franklin would help celebrate the inauguration of the first African American president was too much to dream for in 1960, when she released her first single on Columbia Records, but it was a reality in 2009.

In this context, we can understand the special place of the spiritual and of its most distinguished interpreters. Before World War II, it was the only African American music that enjoyed broad acceptance by the mavens of high culture. Black jazz was still "illegitimate," confined to speakeasies, uptown venues like Harlem's Cotton Club and Savoy Ballroom, and dingy nightclubs. Blues and gospel were off the radar.

Moreover, Marian Anderson's dignity and her unmistakable artistry forcefully challenged the still-prevalent view of the inherent inferiority of African Americans. Because of her personal and artistic virtues, events like her 1939 concert at the Lincoln Memorial resonated well beyond the seventy-five thousand people who heard her.

The concert settings of African American spirituals now belong to a particular time and place; they are a classical music, with a distinct performing tradition. They were a product of a particular set of circumstances, a response to the pervasive and pernicious racism that infected American life during that time. Indeed, it is possible that if racial prejudice had not been the social equivalent of a barbed-wire fence, Burleigh and others would not have felt the need to preserve spirituals in this particular way. We can be grateful that both the spiritual settings and their performances have been preserved. They remain a silver lining in the dark cloud of bigotry.

Classic Blues

"What ragtime and jazz did for the feet, blues did for the heart and soul."

Among the hottest releases of 1920 was Mamie Smith's recording of "Crazy Blues." The record sold 75,000 copies within a month and reputedly sold around 1 million copies. By the time she recorded the song, Smith was a veteran performer who had starred in Perry Bradford's 1918 production *Maid in Harlem*. Bradford—a key figure in black music in the 1910s and 1920s, and a successful songwriter, arranger, singer, pianist, bandleader, and entrepreneur—was sure that there was a market for a black female singer. He had tried to persuade Columbia and

Did You Know?

Stars from the Rolling Stones to Eric Clapton and John Mayer have been influenced by and have recorded classic 1930s blues such as Robert Johnson's "Crossroad Blues" and "Love in Vain."

Victor, two of the biggest record companies of the era, to record her. Okeh Records, a branch of the German record company Odeon, which was more open to recording music for smaller markets, finally agreed. Her first session did well enough that she returned later to record Bradford's "Crazy Blues." The sensational success of Smith's record got the attention of record companies, who soon began to release **race records**, recordings by black artists aimed primarily at an African American audience.

But Mamie Smith wasn't really a blues singer, and despite its title, "Crazy Blues" wasn't really blues. Rather, it was a blues-influenced popular song that Smith sung in a bluesy, distinctively black singing style. Still, it was a dramatic departure from other kinds of pop singing of the time, and it opened the door for a wave of other female blues singers. They would give America its first taste of real blues style.

LO5 Blues

The **blues** is quintessentially African American music. It has roots in African music, most directly in the stories of griots. **Griots** were the historians and shamans of African tribes, who often sang and spoke their stories while accompanying themselves on a plucked string instrument. Blues also has roots in European music, in its customary use of chords and regular meter. But it is far different from both, and far different from Afrocentric musical traditions in other parts of the Americas. There is no other music that resembles it, although there is much music that has been shaped by it—from early jazz, country, and popular song to hard rock and heavy metal.

---

race records recordings by black artists aimed primarily at an African American audience

blues Quintessentially African American music with its roots in Africa and the Mississippi Delta; created by Southern blacks sometime after the Civil War; characterized by twelve-bar form, call and response between voice and instrument, bent or "blue" notes, and phrases that start high and end low

griot Historian and shaman of an African tribe, who often sang and spoke his stories while accompanying himself on a plucked string instrument

© Sheet Music Collection, The John Hay Library at Brown University

1920s sheet music for an Okeh race record by Mamie Smith

EARLY BLUES STYLES

We know virtually nothing about the earliest history of the blues. We surmise that it took shape as a folk music created by Southern blacks sometime after the Civil War. The field hollers and work songs of slaves and sharecroppers are the most recent ancestors of the blues, although they differ from blues in both musical style and social function. Early anecdotal accounts of blues and blues singing date from shortly after the turn of the century. Down-home **folk blues**—what Paramount Records would call "real old-fashioned blues by an old-fashioned blues singer"—flourished in the rural South, especially in the Mississippi Delta. Shortly after the turn of the century, female blues singers like Ma Rainey began performing blues commercially on the black vaudeville circuit, in tent shows, and in other forms of entertainment.

Folk blues flourished in the rural South, especially in the Mississippi Delta.

W. C. Handy's raglike "Memphis Blues" (1912) was among the first of the printed blues; his "St. Louis Blues" (1914) was the most enduring. These typically used the most conventional form of the blues but only hinted at many essential features of blues style. During the 1910s, both black and white bands performed and recorded these songs; almost all were some distance stylistically from the folk blues of the Mississippi Delta. In the late 1910s, jazz bands began recording instrumental

folk blues Down-home blues that flourished in the post–Civil War rural South, especially in the Mississippi Delta

classic blues Commercially recorded blues

LISTEN FURTHER

"Memphis Blues" (1912)

Takeaway point: Listen to the raglike rhythm of W. C. Handy's early blues in the YouTube playlist.

LISTEN FURTHER

Bessie Smith, "St. Louis Blues" (1914; recorded 1929)

Takeaway point: Listen to Handy's commercial blues performed by "the empress of the blues" in the YouTube playlist.

blues. Many recordings by early jazz bands were instrumental blues; a few featured horn playing that emulated blues singing. However, not until the aftershock of Mamie Smith's "Crazy Blues" did authentic blues style find its way onto recordings.

BESSIE SMITH AND THE SOUND OF CLASSIC BLUES

The most popular and artistically successful of the female blues singers was Bessie Smith (1894–1937), nicknamed "the empress of the blues." By the early 1920s, she had a large following, which prompted Columbia Records to sign her to a recording contract in 1923. Her first record sold over 2 million copies, an enormous number for that time. She would continue to record for Columbia during the 1920s; almost all of the recordings were blues.

Smith's recordings epitomize **classic blues**. They feature Smith's rough, full-voiced singing supported by jazz musicians. The accompaniment varies, from just a pianist to a full jazz band. Most of

This photo, shot when Bessie Smith was about thirty, shows her looking her most elegant and vulnerable. Smith was a big woman with a big voice; other publicity shots show a more rambunctious side of her personality.

her recordings are conventional **twelve-bar blues**, a strophic form with well-established conventions for the lyrics, harmony, texture, and form.

Each complete statement of the twelve-bar blues form—typically called a **chorus**—has three 4-measure phrases. The lyric is a rhymed couplet (two lines of text), with the first line repeated. In "Empty Bed Blues," each phrase begins with Smith singing a line of the lyric to a mournful melody. And in each phrase her singing is answered by trombonist Charlie Green. Regular exchanges between contrasting voices is typically identified as **call and response**; it is a common feature of African music. Pianist Porter Grainger supports the voice and trombone with a somewhat elaborated form of a basic blues progression. A **blues progression** uses the three basic chords of common practice harmony as its foundation: each phrase begins with a different chord and returns to the tonic chord halfway through the phrase. The song as a whole is strophic, with much the same melody setting a series of rhymed couplets.

Following is the opening chorus of "Empty Bed Blues."

	Vocal	Instrumental response
Phrase 1	I woke up this morning with a awful aching head	Trombone
	I chord	**I chord**
Phrase 2	I woke up this morning with a awful aching head	Trombone
	IV chord	**I chord**
Phrase 3	My new man had left me, just a room and a empty bed	Trombone
	V chord	**I chord**

twelve-bar blues A strophic form with well-established conventions for the lyrics, harmony, texture, and form

chorus Each complete statement of the twelve-bar blues form, consisting of three 4-measure phrases

call and response Regular exchanges between contrasting voices, common in African music

blues progression Series using the three basic chords of common practice harmony as its foundation, with each phrase beginning with a different chord and returning to the tonic chord halfway through the phrase

blue note "Bent," expressive note outside the major scale

Smith's classic blues were the first first-person music in American culture. When Smith sings, "I woke up this morning with a awful aching head," we know that she is talking about herself; the events in the song could literally have happened the night before. The lyric swings back and forth between the joys of love and the pains of love lost and love betrayed. For most of the song, she describes lovemaking, sometimes in metaphor ("coffee grinder," "deep-sea diver") and sometimes directly. All of this makes her partner's infidelity even more painful. This emotional range and the intimacy of the subject suggest to us that Smith is singing from the heart, that she is using the blues to talk about *her own* good and bad times—not the feelings of a character in a musical.

What makes "Empty Bed Blues" classic? Three features stand out: the earthy, direct lyrics; Smith's singing; and the use of several blues conventions—the twelve-bar form, call and response between voice and instrument, **blue notes** ("bent," expressive notes outside the major scale), and phrases that start high and end low. The expressive power resides in the words and Smith's singing; the blues conventions are the familiar packaging.

Commercial blues by Smith and other female blues singers were a phenomenon of the 1920s. At the end of the decade, the Great Depression hit America hard, and blacks especially hard. Too few could afford to buy

© iStockphoto.com/Rob Belknap

records or attend the theaters and clubs where these blues singers performed. As a result, the core market for this kind of commercial blues singing had all but dried up by the early 1930s. Despite her earlier popularity, Smith's career nose-dived; mismanagement and her heavy drinking were also contributing causes. She died in 1937 in a Clarksdale, Mississippi, hospital from injuries sustained in an automobile accident.

Nevertheless, through performers like Smith and Ma Rainey and those they influenced, both the idea and the sound of the blues entered the popular mainstream in the 1920s. It reshaped popular song, jazz, musical theater, and even pop-based concert music. What ragtime and jazz did for the feet, blues did for the heart and soul. The music of the 1910s and 1920s was the first generation of popular music to be shaped by the blues. It would not be the last.

CHAPTER 42

The Jazz Age

"Does Jazz Put the Sin in Syncopation?"—Ladies Home Journal, 1921

I n November 1931, the American writer F. Scott Fitzgerald wrote the obituary of the decade he had named. In his essay "Echoes of the Jazz Age," he declared the Jazz Age "the ten-year period that, as if reluctant to die outmoded in its bed, leaped to a spectacular death in October, 1929." For him, "it was an age of miracles, it was an age of art, it was an age of excess, and it was an age of satire." He saw "a whole race going hedonistic, deciding on pleasure," although in fact over 70 percent of Americans lived below the poverty line during the 1920s.

The sound track for the decade was jazz, which "in its progress toward respectability has meant first sex, then dancing, then music." For him, "it is associated with a state of nervous stimulation, not unlike that of big cities behind the lines of war. . . . Wherefore eat, drink and be merry, for tomorrow we die."

For Fitzgerald and most others of his generation, "jazz" meant all the new black and black-influenced music. In retrospect, much of what was called jazz in

Did You Know?

Louis Armstrong's 1964 recording of "Hello, Dolly!" briefly knocked The Beatles from the top of the charts.

the 1920s wasn't what we now consider to be jazz. Al Jolson, who played the lead role in *The Jazz Singer*, the first talking film, was never really a jazz singer. The "symphonic jazz" presented in Paul Whiteman's 1924 Aeolian Hall concert, which featured the premiere of George Gershwin's *Rhapsody in Blue*, was neither "symphonic" nor "jazz" in their most limited meanings, although the influence of both on the work was substantial. But there was plenty of real jazz, by black musicians and by whites who emulated them, and it helped usher in a new, more modern era in American life.

The Modern Era Begins

By the 1920s, America had entered a modern era. To be "modern" in America during the 1920s meant moving and living at a faster pace. It meant believing in progress, especially material progress. It meant moving out of the country and into the city. It meant taking advantage of new technologies, from automobiles and air conditioning to the zippers that were now used on clothing, luggage, and a host of other products. It meant buying into fashionable intellectual ideas and artistic trends. And it meant listening—and dancing—to a new kind of music.

jazz A genre consisting of a group of popular related styles primarily for listening; usually distinguished from the other popular music of an era by greater rhythmic freedom (more syncopation and/or less insistent beat keeping), extensive improvisation, and more-adventurous harmony

During the first part of the century, cities swelled with a flood of immigrants and the migration of Americans from country to city. Large ethnic and minority populations in cities like New York and Chicago helped support their resident musicians and entertainers. Many of the top jazz and popular musicians were black or Jewish: trumpeter-vocalist Louis Armstrong and pianist-composer George Gershwin are two among many. During the 1920s, they found audiences for their music within and beyond their communities, despite rampant and overt prejudice.

Flappers, fast-living young ladies who smoked, drank, "petted," and danced the Charleston throughout the night, seemed to abuse their newfound freedom.

The 1920s was a decade of contradictions. Prohibition banned alcohol; speakeasies served it anyway. Suffragettes fought for and gained rights for women: in 1920, the Nineteenth Amendment, giving women the right to vote, became law. Flappers, fast-living young ladies who smoked, drank, "petted," and danced the Charleston throughout the night, seemed to abuse their newfound freedom. Parents were worried over the financially frivolous activities of their daughters and sons, but many invested their savings in the stock market, then watched it all disappear in the stock market crash of 1929. The decade saw real advances in black music: on Broadway, on records, in clubs, and even on film. But bandstands were still segregated, and many regarded the music and the musicians as primitive and immoral: an article that appeared in a 1921 issue of *The Ladies Home Journal* asked, "Does Jazz Put the Sin in Syncopation?"

LO6 Jazz in the Early Modern Era

Jazz began as an obscure regional black music. It exploded on the music scene in the United States and abroad during the 1910s and early 1920s. It would be recognized as a vibrant and distinctive music by the end of the decade. In its purest form, it stood apart from popular music. Yet it would not only follow its own course but also dramatically reshape popular music during the 1930s and 1940s.

THE ROOTS OF JAZZ

We do know that New Orleans was the birthplace of **jazz**, and that contemporary accounts date its beginnings sometime around the turn of the century. It flourished in the rich cultural mix that was New Orleans: whites of English and French descent, blacks, immigrants from the Caribbean and Europe, plus many citizens of mixed race. Then as now, New Orleans liked to let the good times roll, and music was part of this mix: brass bands for parades, pianists and small groups for the bars, honky-tonks, and houses of prostitution. (From 1897 to 1917, prostitution was legal in New Orleans; it was confined to Storyville, a small area near the French Quarter.)

Throughout much of the nineteenth century, New Orleans had been a relatively hospitable environment for blacks. During the period of slavery, Congo Square (now Louis Armstrong Park) was the only part of the South where people of African descent could legally gather and play drums and other percussion instruments. Over time, New Orleans developed a complex social structure, in which the proportion of European and African blood was the main determinant of social status. "Creoles of color," those with ancestors from France and Africa, enjoyed a higher social standing than ex-slaves. They lived in better neighborhoods, were better educated, and had more freedom. An aspiring Creole musician received traditional classical training, whereas black musicians typically

learned to play by ear. Creoles of color tended to look down on the ex-slaves. They emulated white culture rather than black. That changed with the passage of "Jim Crow" legislation, most notably the *Plessy v. Ferguson* decision that made "separate but equal" legal and reduced race in New Orleans to simply "white" and "colored."

Nevertheless, contact among the musicians who created jazz remained relatively open: jazz would develop from the interaction of blacks, Creoles, and whites. Several lighter-skinned blacks worked not only in black bands but also in the mostly white band of "Papa Jack" Laine, the top white bandleader in New Orleans around the turn of the century. Among the alumni of Laine's band were the five original members of the Original Dixieland Jazz Band. This all-white group was the first jazz band to record; their first discs appeared in 1917, at a time when many white bands in the North refused to play the new syncopated music because of its low-life association. The group's recordings were a novelty success. They put the word *jazz* on people's lips, and a jazzlike sound in people's ears.

JAZZ AND THE SOUNDS OF THE 1920S

The first jazz bands, black and white, were small groups of five to eight musicians. The standard New Orleans jazz band blended the instrumentation of three key popular music genres. From the marching band came the clarinet, cornet or trumpet, trombone, sousaphone, and drum line, now consolidated into a set that could be played by a single musician. From the minstrel show came the banjo, and from the saloons and bordellos came the piano.

© Pictorial Press Ltd / Alamy

The jazz band of the New Orleans Colored Waifs Home in 1912, with a young Louis Armstrong at top center

These instruments were grouped into two distinct units, the front line and the rhythm section. The **front line** (so called because the musicians stood at the front of the bandstand) typically featured three of the band instruments: clarinet, trumpet or cornet, and trombone. A complete **rhythm section** consisted of banjo, piano, brass bass (sousaphone), and drums; many early jazz recordings (including the Armstrong recording discussed later) feature partial rhythm sections. The front line instruments played melody-like lines. The rhythm section had two jobs: to mark the beat and to supply the harmony.

Precedents for the rhythm section date from the Renaissance; the Baroque continuo is similar in many respects. However, the novel features in the jazz rhythm section that distinguished it from earlier practice were the emphasis on percussive sounds, most obviously in the drums, but also in the bass and chord instruments, and the rhythmic conception of the musicians, which was fundamentally different from most European music. This new rhythmic approach was called "swing."

SWING

Swing is the essence of jazz, as Duke Ellington asserted in the title of his 1932 song "It Don't Mean a Thing (If It Ain't Got That Swing)." Here is a succinct definition of **swing**: rhythmic play over a four-beat rhythm. Both the four-beat rhythm and the rhythmic play over it were paradigm-shifting innovations. They were the clearest indications that jazz—and the popular music that it influenced—had embraced a new rhythmic approach, which was the product of an African-derived reinterpretation of European rhythm. The term *four-beat rhythm* is a numerical way of identifying the particular nature of the steady timekeeping that underpins all other rhythmic activity. "Four-beat" refers to the equal emphasis on each beat of a measure with four beats. In Armstrong's

front line The wind and brass instruments (or other melody-line instruments) in a jazz combo; from the position of the players on the bandstand, standing in a line in front of the rhythm instruments

rhythm section The part of a musical group that supplies the rhythmic and harmonic foundation of a performance; usually includes at least one chord instrument (guitar, piano, or keyboard), a bass instrument, and a percussion instrument (typically the drum set)

swing Rhythmic play over a four-beat rhythm

"Hotter Than That," which we hear next, the pianist and guitarist typically play chords on each beat; each receives the same amount of emphasis. This is the typical rhythmic foundation of jazz, although it can be expressed in varied ways.

The black musicians who created jazz kept the metrical structure of European music but interpreted it through an African sensibility. Instead of accenting the first beat of each measure, jazz musicians who marked the beat typically stressed all beats equally. The unvarying emphasis on each beat in jazz was a fundamental departure from nineteenth-century practice: recall the pronounced differentiation among beats in the waltzes of Johann Strauss and Tchaikovsky. So was the rhythmic play over this relentless rhythm.

In isolation, the undifferentiated beats of the rhythm instruments do not produce swing. Swing results from the interplay between the beat and the syncopated accents and irregular patterns that conflict with the steady timekeeping of the rhythm instruments. It is this interplay that makes the rhythm so irresistible and differentiates jazz from all other music of the 1920s and before.

The ease and daring with which a jazz musician played over time was one measure of artistry. Often it was especially infectious because it happened spontaneously, during an improvisation.

IMPROVISATION

Jazz restored **improvisation** to mainstream musical practice in Western culture. In music, to improvise means to create new music in the moment—as one is singing or playing—rather than re-creating someone else's composition. Improvisation in music is comparable to a comedy troupe's creating a skit on the spot from an audience suggestion rather than performing a well-rehearsed and fully scripted routine.

The first generation of jazz musicians began with a melody and supporting harmony, then improvised a series of variations that consisted of new melodies over the underlying harmony. In this respect, they are similar in approach to the Mozart variation sets, which began as improvisations. However, unlike Mozart's variation sets, improvised variations in jazz flow continuously; there is no break between variations.

Improvisation was part of classical music through the early nineteenth century: Bach, Mozart, Beethoven, Clara Schumann, and Liszt were all gifted improvisers. However, by 1850 it had largely disappeared from concert music. It returned with jazz, but in a radically different form, because of the interplay among musicians, instrumentation of the jazz band, the jazz rhythm, and the overall feel of the music. Still, the formal organization (theme and variations) and improvisational approach (new melodies over the same harmony) of early jazz are remarkably similar to European practice.

It is likely that improvisation was customary in popular entertainments, especially those involving black musicians: ragtime and blues can be improvised music. But only with jazz does a sophisticated form of improvisation become an integral component of a new genre. We hear this new approach to improvisation in "Hotter Than That," a recording by Louis Armstrong's Hot Five.

LOUIS ARMSTRONG

In 1922, Louis Armstrong received an invitation from fellow cornetist Joe Oliver to join him in Chicago. During the late 1910s, Oliver led the top black jazz band in New Orleans. He moved them north in 1919, leaving Armstrong behind. Armstrong accepted Oliver's invitation and married Lil Hardin, the pianist with Oliver's band, early in 1924. Soon after, they moved to New York, where Armstrong joined Fletcher Henderson's hot dance orchestra. In New York, Armstrong was a regular in the studio as well as the bandstand, recording with Henderson,

Joe "King" Oliver's Creole Jazz Band in 1923. From left to right: Honore Dutrey, trombone; Baby Dodds, drums; Joe Oliver, lead cornet; Louis Armstrong, slide trumpet; Lil Hardin, piano; Bill Johnson, banjo; and Johnny Dodds, clarinet

a host of blues singers (including Bessie Smith), and the pianist Clarence Williams. Williams, who doubled as Okeh Records' A&R (artists and repertoire) man, noticed that the recordings on which he used Armstrong sold better than others. So in 1925, he offered Armstrong the chance to record as a leader rather than as a sideman. Armstrong, who had returned to Chicago, proceeded to record with what amounted to a studio band of his New Orleans friends, plus Hardin (and, somewhat later, the pianist Earl Hines). Okeh billed them as Louis Armstrong's Hot Five or Hot Seven (depending on the number of players). Armstrong's groups made dozens of recordings over the next four years and made jazz—and music—history in the process.

Louis Armstrong recorded "Hotter Than That" with the Hot Five combo in December 1927. The other band members included clarinetist Johnny Dodds and trombonist Kid Ory—both of whom Armstrong knew from New Orleans—pianist Hardin, and guitarist Lonnie Johnson, an able blues and jazz musician. This recording is unusual in that it features a scat vocal solo from Armstrong in addition to his trumpet playing at the beginning and end. (**Scat singing** is an improvised instrumental-style vocal with no words.)

The harmonic framework for "Hotter Than That" consists of two 16-measure harmonic progressions. Songs containing two 16-measure phrases were common in popular music in the 1910s and 1920s. The performance consists of four variations over the harmonic progressions; each variation is considered a chorus, the term used by jazz musicians to indicate one statement of the form.

Louis Armstrong was the first great soloist in jazz. Every aspect of his playing—his beautiful sound; the

bent notes, slides, shakes, and other expressive gestures; his melodic inventiveness; and above all, his incomparable sense of swing—inspired jazz and popular musicians of the era. His playing became the standard by which other jazz musicians measured themselves.

Recordings like "Hotter Than That" captured an exuberance that is unique to early jazz, in particular to the playing of Louis Armstrong. It comes from the interaction of the relentlessly pulsing beat, the ebb and flow of harmonic tension, and Armstrong's extraordinarily varied and subtle rhythmic play, with its note-to-note variation in accent, timing, and expressive gesture, and it got musicians and listeners moving in time to the music: feet tapping, heads bobbing, fingers snapping.

There is no known precedent for the swing heard in early jazz. No earlier music that has come down to us, not even ragtime, creates a comparably infectious rhythm. Its defining features are far too subtle to commit to notation and seem to elude precise definition. Indeed, when asked to explain swing, Armstrong responded with something like "If you have to ask, you'll never know." Armstrong's influence was pervasive: swing became common currency in the 1930s, when the musicians who followed him absorbed his lessons on how to swing and audiences responded to this vital new rhythm.

JAZZ AND THE NEW SOUNDS OF THE MODERN ERA

Like *ragtime*, *blues*, and *rock and roll*, the term *jazz* initially identified a hot new music, much of which had only a tangential connection with what later generations would consider to be authentic expressions of the style. Musicians and scholars now consider only a small fraction of the music that people called jazz during the Jazz Age to be real jazz. It is in this more restricted body of music that the essential features of jazz are most apparent: its sounds, its swing, and its spontaneous creation (improvisation). These elements would constitute the foundation for subsequent generations of jazz musicians and provide the most important contributions to popular music.

The swing of jazz was one of several new and vibrant rhythms that injected vitality into the music of the 1910s and 1920s. Irene and Vernon Castle brought the Argentine tango and Brazilian maxixe to New York

🔄 LISTEN UP!

CD 5:1

Lil Hardin Armstrong, "Hotter Than That" (1927), performed by Louis Armstrong and his Hot Five

Takeaway point: Hot jazz performed by the first great jazz soloist and his group

Style: 1920s jazz

Form: Theme and variations

Genre: Small-group jazz

Instruments: Trumpet, clarinet, trombone, banjo, guitar, piano

Context: Skilled and swinging musicians at play in the recording studio

by way of Paris in 1913; they were a sensation. They followed it up with the fox-trot, a dance of their own invention. It would soon become the most popular ballroom dance of the modern era; by the 1920s, many hotels had resident dance orchestras. These and other dances would entice Americans to the dance floor and intrigue composers in the United States and Europe. Stravinsky composed three ragtime-inspired works and a tango; the French composer Maurice Ravel worked jazz and blues into his music; and the American composer Aaron Copland composed a jazz-inspired piano concerto in 1926. However, the composer who most successfully fused these new sounds and rhythms with classical practice was George Gershwin.

"Symphonic Jazz"

On January 4, 1924, George Gershwin was shooting pool with his brother, Ira, and Buddy DeSylva, Gershwin's lyricist at the time, when Ira happened to read an article in the *New York Tribune* about an upcoming concert to be presented by bandleader Paul Whiteman, who billed it as an "Experiment in Modern Music."

Paul Whiteman (1890–1967) had begun his professional career as a classical violist, then formed his own dance orchestra in 1919. Within a year, the band had two million-selling recordings; it would become the most popular and most admired dance orchestra of the 1920s. In 1924, Whiteman attempted to elevate jazz to the stature of classical music by offering a concert of "symphonic jazz" in New York's Aeolian Hall. Among the featured pieces on the program would be a "jazz concerto" by George Gershwin.

The announcement in the *Tribune* threw Gershwin into a panic. George had had an informal and rather vague conversation with Whiteman about the project but hadn't imagined that Whiteman took the discussion as a commitment. Working feverishly, he finished the piece, by then entitled *Rhapsody in Blue*, in time for the premiere on February 12. Gershwin's jazz concerto was the highlight of the concert and a critical success.

GEORGE GERSHWIN

Like several top songwriters, George Gershwin began his musical career as a *song plugger*: a pianist who would play (and sing) a publisher's sheet music for prospective buyers. He discovered his passion for music and the piano in 1910, when his family bought a piano. Although his training was brief, Gershwin quickly

developed into an excellent pianist—he and Fats Waller would be the most skilled pianists among the top songwriters of the era. He also received extensive training in classical composition, beginning in 1915. Both skills would serve him well. By 1923, Gershwin was an up-and-coming songwriter. "Swanee," George Gershwin's first big hit, appeared in 1919 and became a best-selling record for Al Jolson the following year. Gershwin was a well-known performer—he accompanied the singer Eva Gauthier in concert in November 1923 in a program that mixed classical and popular vocal music. Gershwin's obvious skills as a composer and pianist and his openness to bringing together classical music with the new modern popular music made him an ideal choice to compose the central work for Whiteman's grand experiment.

George Gershwin

Fast Facts

- *Dates:* 1898–1937
- *Place:* United States
- *Reasons to remember:* Composer-pianist who brought together classical and modern popular music

© Michael Ochs Archives/Getty Images

RHAPSODY IN BLUE

Rhapsody in Blue certainly approaches the symphonic in its scale, length, and sound. A complete performance of the piece typically lasts about fifteen minutes, the approximate length of the first movement of a standard

LISTEN UP!

CD 4:26–28
George Gershwin, *Rhapsody in Blue* (1924)

Takeaway point: A unique and popular fusion of classical and popular music

Style: Pop/classical fusion

Form: Multisectional

Genre: Rhapsody

Instruments: Piano and augmented dance orchestra

Context: A work composed for a concert to make jazz more upscale

piano concerto. (The performance heard here, by Gershwin and Whiteman's orchestra, is an abridged version of the original.) Similarly, Whiteman's good-sized orchestra approaches the sound of a symphony orchestra, but with a popular twist. The string section is, by classical standards, quite small, and Whiteman's orchestra includes three saxophones and a banjo. (A revised orchestration of the work for piano and full symphony orchestra appeared soon after the 1924 premiere.) All this is very much in the classical style, in intent and result.

It's what Gershwin did within this framework that was so remarkable. The piece bubbles over with fresh musical ideas. Almost all of them are stylized reworkings of the sounds, rhythms, and melodies of the ragtime, jazz, blues, and dance music that African Americans had contributed over the prior twenty-five years. Gershwin created rich, distinctive harmonies by blending twentieth-century French harmony with commercial blues sounds. The virtuosic piano writing, however, is Gershwin's own. There are no real precedents for it, not in classical, ragtime, or jazz piano playing.

Rhapsody in Blue is a **rhapsody** in the way it moves from section to section, as if it were cutting or fading between scenes in a film. And it is blue from the first notes—the famous clarinet solo that begins the work takes off from blues-influenced New Orleans jazz clarinet playing.

Rhapsody in Blue was absolutely unique.

Rhapsody in Blue was absolutely unique. It created a new language for concert music, one based on the progressive popular music of the early twentieth century. It inspired many other jazz concert pieces, including several by Gershwin. But none has challenged *Rhapsody in Blue* as the most successful and popular work of its kind. Its premiere was a defining moment in the history of popular music and in the history of twentieth-century music of all kinds.

More than eighty years after its premiere, *Rhapsody in Blue* remains the single most popular work written by an American composer. Given its success, one might expect that its "formula" would have been widely copied. That is not the case. No one, not even Gershwin, has created a work of comparable popularity. Many critics, especially from the traditional classical side, have commented on *Rhapsody in Blue*'s alleged

shortcomings; they have pointed out what it is not—another Beethoven symphony or Mozart concerto. In the process, they have failed to recognize it for what it is: an extraordinarily original, successful, and inimitable piece of music.

The New Classics of the Modern Era

Although they differ in style, genre, and performance context, Gershwin's *Rhapsody in Blue* and Armstrong's Hot Five and Hot Seven recordings share several common features.

1. *They were exemplars of their particular genre.* To this day they remain among the finest examples of "crossover classical" and jazz from their era.

2. *They broke new musical ground.* Gershwin's jazz concerto had no significant precedent. Armstrong's recordings remain the most valued early examples of jazz as a solo art.

3. *They drew on African and European sources for their innovations.* Gershwin fused classical concepts with the new rhythms and sounds of the 1920s. Armstrong's jazz shows its indirectly acquired European provenance in its harmonic and melodic invention and stunning virtuosity, and its African roots in the irresistible swing and expressive nuance.

4. *They remain among the most enduring American music of the 1920s.* Gershwin's rhapsody is arguably the most widely performed twentieth-century classical composition (as of this writing, there are almost two hundred recordings of the work currently available). Scholars, musicians, and enthusiasts agree that Armstrong was the first great soloist in jazz and a seminal influence on its development.

Both Gershwin and Armstrong would continue to be important and influential through the 1930s. Gershwin followed *Rhapsody in Blue* with several other classically oriented compositions, including the tone poem *An American in Paris* (1928) and his 1935 "folk opera" *Porgy and Bess*. He also composed numerous hit

> **rhapsody** Piece of music that moves from section to section as if cutting or fading between scenes in a film

songs for Broadway musicals and films, including *Of Thee I Sing*, a 1931 musical that won the Pulitzer Prize in drama the following year, the first time a musical had received the award.

Armstrong's Hot Five and Hot Seven recordings represent the most exuberantly creative period in his career. They played a decisive role in liberating jazz from the ballroom. By the early 1930s, his playing had become less virtuosic, and his personal style had become established. However, by this time his recordings often included vocal as well as trumpet choruses. He was, if anything, even more influential as a vocalist, because he was among the very first singers to cultivate an expressive personal style. Bing Crosby, the first of the great crooners, was an unabashed admirer; so was the great jazz vocalist Billie Holiday. Indeed, Armstrong's singing and playing influenced—directly or indirectly—virtually every important popular singer of the 1930s, 1940s, and 1950s.

Gershwin and Armstrong helped set in motion a more expanded understanding of art in music. It would take several generations and another revolution in popular music, but it is now widely accepted that musical art does not require a European provenance, that expressive communication through music can come in multiple forms, and that accessibility and art are compatible virtues.

CHAPTER 43

The Broadway Musical and American Popular Song

"The 1920s were the heyday of stage entertainment in the United States."

Did You Know?

Broadway is a street running diagonally through midtown Manhattan. Because many theaters that present musicals are on or near Broadway between 42nd and 53rd Streets, musicals have become identified with it.

In 1926, Edna Ferber published the novel *Show Boat*. Ferber was one of America's most prominent writers, who had just won the Pulitzer Prize in 1925 for her novel *So Big*. *Show Boat* tells the bittersweet story of Magnolia, the daughter of Cap'n Andy and Parthy Ann Hawks.

Among the most enthusiastic readers of Ferber's new novel was the songwriter Jerome Kern, who by 1926 was already a twenty-year Broadway veteran. He had just scored a success with *Sunny*, his first collaboration with lyricist Oscar Hammerstein II, and was looking for a more substantial story. He was convinced that *Show Boat* could be adapted to the Broadway stage.

To get *Show Boat* on Broadway, he first had to convince two people: Ferber and Florenz Ziegfeld. Ferber was concerned that Kern would trivialize her novel; during the 1920s, musical entertainment was lightweight fare. She agreed only after Kern convinced her that he would remain largely true to her novel.

Ziegfeld was an even harder sell. He was Broadway's top producer, had put on his *Ziegfeld Follies* shows annually since 1907, and had recently branched out into musical comedy. As the person responsible for the finances of such a production, he was reluctant to produce a show that would depart too dramatically from other kinds of stage entertainment. Only when Kern and Hammerstein convinced Ziegfeld to bill the production as an "American musical play" did Ziegfeld agree to throw his considerable resources behind its production.

So, sometime after eight o'clock on the evening of December 27, 1927, Paul Robeson, a young African

American actor-singer, stepped into the spotlight of the Ziegfeld Theater in New York to sing a song about a river. Robeson, the valedictorian of his class at Rutgers, a two-time All-America football player, and a graduate of Columbia Law School, had decided to pursue a career in entertainment. His opening number, "Ol' Man River," about as far removed as possible from the parade of chorus girls that usually opened Broadway productions, was a remarkable beginning to a remarkable musical.

LO7 Musical Stage Entertainment in the 1920s

The 1920s were the heyday of stage entertainment in the United States. Vaudeville was still going strong. Revues—series of song and dance numbers held loosely together by a topical story line—were doing well. The most famous of the revues were the *Ziegfeld Follies*, presented annually from 1907 to 1927. Operettas and musical comedies also flourished.

Fred Astaire and Cyd Charisse on the set of the 1946 movie immortalizing the *Ziegfeld Follies*

OPERETTA AND MUSICAL COMEDY

In the early years of the twentieth century, operetta and musical comedy were largely independent forms of stage entertainment. Operettas, composed mainly by Europeans, typically featured long-ago-and-far-away plots, often involving royalty of nonexistent European nations; the most popular were simply lighthearted entertainment, without Gilbert and Sullivan's sophisticated brand of satire. The music drew almost exclusively on European practice; there was little evidence of the new sounds and rhythms that were emerging in popular music.

Musical comedy, with music by American composers such as George M. Cohan, Gershwin, Irving Berlin, and Jerome Kern, was more up to date in story and music and less concerned with dramatic integrity. The plots for musical comedies were lighthearted, comparable in dramatic depth to today's average sitcom. There was a lot of singing, a lot of dancing, and a lot of comedy. These productions were fun—designed to entertain and occasionally to titillate. But they usually didn't go much deeper than that.

THE INNOVATIONS OF KERN AND HAMMERSTEIN

In *Show Boat*, Kern and Hammerstein effectively Americanized operetta and made musical comedy more significant in the process. Their "musical play" featured an American take on the typical long-ago-far-away operetta plot: "long ago," for instance, was the turn of the century. To help convey this, Kern incorporated still-popular hits from that time. And the Mississippi River was, for 1920s New Yorkers, far enough away.

Kern and Hammerstein presented Ferber's controversial interracial story and complex characters with relatively little sugarcoating. Compared to the typical stage entertainment of the era, *Show Boat* was more

revue A series of song and dance numbers held loosely together by a topical story line

musical comedy Lighthearted stage entertainment born in the early twentieth century, featuring a great deal of singing, dancing, and comedy

Paul Robeson as Joe, performing "Ol' Man River" in the movie version of *Show Boat*

serious and substantial; dramatically it was closer to opera than it was to conventional Broadway entertainment. However, it relied musically on the conventions of popular song.

The Modern Popular Song: Style and Form

"Tin Pan Alley" is a stretch of West 28th Street in Manhattan that was home to numerous music publishers around the turn of the twentieth century. These publishers sold only popular songs and marketed them aggressively. They hired **song pluggers**, house pianists who could play a new song for a professional singer or a prospective customer. In the summer, the small rooms where the song pluggers worked got hot. There was no air conditioning, so the pianists opened the windows to try to cool off their rooms. Monroe Rosenfeld, a lyricist and journalist, likened the cacophony produced by dozens of pianists playing popular songs to the sound of tin pans clashing together. Rosenfeld's description caught on, and West 28th Street became "Tin Pan Alley."

TIN PAN ALLEY SONGS

Tin Pan Alley soon referred not only to the publishers' street but also to the songs that they published. The publishers have long since relocated, but "Tin Pan Alley" re-

song plugger House pianist around the turn of the century who could play a new song for a professional singer or a prospective customer

Tin Pan Alley The music publishers' street in Manhattan around the turn of the century, as well as the popular songs that they published from the 1890s to the 1950s

riff Short melodic kernel in popular music that functions much like a motive in classical music but on a more modest scale

mains a generic label for several generations of popular song, from the 1890s to the 1950s. The first big hits were waltz songs (songs in a three-beat meter). Charles Harris's "After the Ball," published in 1892, showed the commercial potential of popular song. It eventually sold 5 million copies of sheet music after Sousa performed it at the Chicago World's Fair in 1893. The 1908 hit "Take Me Out to the Ball Game" remains the most familiar waltz song from the era.

Tin Pan Alley (ca. 1905)

Popular songwriters gradually assimilated elements of the new black styles into popular song. They adapted the syncopations of ragtime, beginning around 1900. During the 1910s, the influence of the commercial blues songs of W. C. Handy and others began to appear. Increasingly, melodies often grew out of **riffs**, short, often syncopated, melodic kernels that functioned much like motives in classical music but on a more modest scale. By the early 1920s, the practice was standard. And as in the blues, the rhythm of the lyric approximated the pacing of everyday speech. By the 1920s, the fox-trot, the dance invented and popularized by Irene and Vernon

Castle and James Reese Europe, the black bandleader who accompanied their dancing, had become the rhythmic foundation of popular song. Virtually all the songs written between 1920 and 1940 were fox-trots. They were performed as vocals and as instrumentals. In the wake of the electrical revolution of the early 1920s, recordings and live performances included both vocals and instrumentals.

POPULAR SONG FORM

The form of the popular song also changed over time, mainly in response to the demands of the marketplace and technological innovations. In American popular music, the overall form of the song—**verse-chorus form**—dates back to the middle of the nineteenth century: whether intended for theater or home use, most post–minstrel show songs featured a storytelling verse followed by a tuneful **chorus**, or refrain. Songs had had both verse and chorus since the minstrel show songs of Foster and others. By the end of the century, both verse and chorus had become longer, and in early Tin Pan Alley songs, the chorus often stood alone. "Take Me Out to the Ball Game" has verses, but they are hardly ever sung; for most people, the chorus *is* the song. During the first part of the twentieth century, the chorus became even more prominent and faster paced. In the wake of the electrical revolution, song and dance merged: performances on radio and recordings typically included both vocal and instrumental statements of the chorus. Moreover, the form of the chorus changed almost overnight, from two parallel sixteen-bar phrases to four phrases in AABA form. This change helped embed the title phrase of the song in listeners' ears; it capitalized on the gradual shift in the dissemination of popular music, from sheet music (which began to decline in the 1920s) to aural sources: radio, recordings, and film.

Among the finest and most experienced songwriters of the era was Jerome Kern. His score for *Show Boat* shows his awareness of the numerous changes in popular songwriting during the early stages of his career.

Jerome Kern's *Show Boat*

It's small wonder that Ziegfeld had reservations about turning Edna Ferber's *Show Boat* into a musical. Compared to the typically lighthearted or satirical Broadway productions, it was heavy fare.

In Ferber's novel, the Hawks run the *Cotton Blossom*, a showboat that travels up and down the Mississippi River putting on theatrical productions. The main actors on the showboat, as well as in a subplot, are Steve and Julie Baker. Julie is part black but light enough to pass for white. However, in Mississippi (where mixed marriages were illegal at the time) her racial heritage is exposed, and she and Steve must leave the *Cotton Blossom*.

Among Julie's important songs was "Can't Help Lovin' Dat Man." In it, Kern and Hammerstein adapted the still-new conventions of popular song to serve the drama.

JEROME KERN AND THE MODERN POPULAR SONG

Jerome Kern was the elder statesman of the great songwriters active in the 1920s and 1930s: he had his first hit song in 1905, the year Harold Arlen (who composed "Over the Rainbow") was born. Moreover, Kern received traditional musical training in New York and Germany and spent much of the 1900s and 1910s traveling between New York and London, where he supplied dozens of songs for shows.

By training, experience, and inclination, Kern, of the major songwriters, was, ironically, the least in touch with the sounds and rhythms of the new black-influenced popular music. Even the songs from late in his career ("The Way You Look Tonight," "All the Things

verse-chorus form
Dating from the mid-nineteenth century, the most widely used popular song form through the late 1950s; featured a storytelling verse followed by a tuneful chorus, or refrain

chorus In verse-chorus songs, that part of a song in which both melody and lyrics are repeated; also called refrain

Jerome Kern

Fast Facts

- *Dates:* 1885–1945
- *Place:* United States
- *Reasons to remember:* The first important American songwriter to concern himself seriously with the integration of music and drama

You Are") favor European values: flowing melodies, surprising harmonies, and rhythms with little or no syncopation. As a songwriter, he was the opposite of Gershwin.

And perhaps because of his extensive experience writing songs for the shows of others, he was the first important American songwriter to concern himself seriously with the integration of music and drama. Between 1915 and 1918, he collaborated with Guy Bolton on a series of operetta-influenced musicals for the Princess Theater, a small venue in New York City. In *Show Boat*, dramatic necessity overrode compositional inclinations, as we hear in "Can't Help Lovin' Dat Man."

POPULAR SONG AS DRAMA

The dramatic function of "Can't Help Lovin' Dat Man" is to suggest Julie's mixed racial heritage. When Queenie, the black cook, hears Julie singing "Can't Help Lovin' Dat Man," she asks Julie how she knows the song, because "Ah didn't ever hear anybody but colored folks sing dat song." In 1927, the most familiar "colored-only" songs were the classic blues of Bessie Smith and others. For numerous reasons—among them the racial climate at the time, the jarring musical contrast it would have created, and Kern's own musical predilections—Kern chose instead to compose a blues-*influenced* popular song, rather than an authentic blues song.

Lonette McKee (left), the daughter of an African American father and a white mother, was the first mixed-race performer to portray the mixed-race Julie on stage or film. Ironically, this did not happen until 1983! Helen Morgan (right), who portrayed Julie on Broadway and in the 1932 film, and who sings "Can't Help Lovin' Dat Man," was white.

"Can't Help Lovin' Dat Man" is an up-to-date song for 1927, in the style of its lyrics, its melodic construction, its use of dance rhythms, and its form. Although their awkward imitation of black speech (downplayed

LISTEN UP!

CD 5:2

Kern and Hammerstein, "Can't Help Lovin' Dat Man," *Show Boat* (1927)

Takeaway point: Characteristic and dramatically effective popular song from the early modern era

Style: Modern popular song

Form: AABA

Genre: Musical theater song

Instruments: Voice and theater orchestra

Context: Julie sings this song, inadvertently revealing her African American heritage.

in Morgan's performance) derives from the minstrel show, the lyrics are typical of the modern era in popular song. The diction, with a preponderance of one-syllable words, is close to everyday speech, and the song is a gentrified blues lament.

Our recording begins with an excerpt from another song in the musical; it is sung just before the point in the musical when Julie is discovered to be part black. It continues with half of the chorus, the verse, then the full chorus.

THE MUSICAL AND MODERN POPULAR SONG

Kern's use of this newly popular form hints at the synergistic relationship between the musical and the popular song during the modern era: musicals (and other forms of stage entertainment—and films in the 1930s) were one of the best ways to get a song to market, and hit songs were in turn a wonderful advertisement for the shows. As soon as a song became a hit, numerous artists—singers, dance orchestras, jazz combos, even just a skilled pianist—would record it. Competing versions, often quite different in instrumentation, harmony, and rhythm, would largely ignore its dramatic function in the musical; performers put their personal stamp on the song, which was often reduced to the lyrics and a recognizable variant of the original melody.

Precisely because so little of the original performance was retained in these differing versions, successful songs quickly achieved a life apart from their source. With the passage of time, the disassociation of the song from the musical has become almost complete. Many of the songs written in the 1920s and 1930s come from stage or film musicals. Most are far more familiar in versions by pop singers such as Frank Sinatra than in their original form. Indeed, many performers and listeners are unaware of, or indifferent to, the source of the song.

Show Boat: A New Kind of Musical Theater

Show Boat was the first of the great modern musicals. It elevated the level of discourse in musical theater, dramatically and musically. Through the example of Show Boat, musical theater became a more elite entertainment, even as vaudeville and the revue disappeared from the stage, casualties of the onset of the Depression and the rise of talking films. Many of the top songwriters on Broadway, including Kern and Gershwin, moved to Hollywood, where they composed memorable songs for film musicals. Those who stayed behind, most notably the team of Richard Rodgers and Lorenz Hart, created musicals that followed the lead of Show Boat in musical sophistication and dramatic substance. However, their musicals enjoyed relatively modest success, and they are seldom revived. Only with the Rodgers and Hammerstein musicals, beginning with Oklahoma! (1943) and extending through The Sound of Music (1959), did the musical enjoy critical acclaim and commercial success comparable to that of Show Boat. Further ripples from the wake of Show Boat include the richly complex music of Leonard Bernstein, as we discover in Chapter 52.

UNIT 20
EUROPEAN CONCERT MUSIC BETWEEN THE WARS

Learning Outcomes

After reading this unit, you will be able to do the following:

LO1 Describe Anton Webern's approach to serial composition.

LO2 Recognize the substantial differences between Igor Stravinsky's early compositions and his later neoclassical works.

LO3 Understand how Mexican composer Carlos Chavez and American composer Aaron Copland became major players in a new kind of musical nationalism that peaked during the 1930s and early 1940s.

LO4 Understand how Béla Bartók and Sergei Prokofiev expressed musical nationalism in both similar and completely different ways that were in tune with current developments in modern music.

© Erich Lessing / Art Resource, NY

THE JOURNAL *MODERN MUSIC*, published by the League of Composers from 1924 to 1946, gave composers and scholars a forum for discussing the compositions and compositional procedures of their peers—American and European. The journal was remarkably inclusive, embracing virtually the entire spectrum of cutting-edge compositional styles, from avant-garde sound experiments to serialism.

Modern music was a term widely used in the first half of the twentieth century to identify the works of forward-looking composers. *Modern* does not represent a common stylistic approach; the works of modern composers were extraordinarily diverse. What linked them—and what made them "modern"—was a rejection of the past and a quest for novelty. The most forward-looking composers of the era sought distinctive identities. Collectively, their innovations touched every musical element and continued the stylistic fragmentation of concert music during the early twentieth century.

Serialism

In 2000, Brilliant Classics, a budget record label based in the Netherlands, began work on a massive project: to issue recordings of all of J. S. Bach's known works in celebration of the 250th anniversary of Bach's death. The boxed set, finally released six years later, contains 155 CDs. By contrast, the CD set that contains the thirty-one works to which Anton Webern (1883–1945) gave opus numbers contains only three CDs: a little more than three hours of music— only about a half hour longer than Bach's *St. Matthew Passion*.

Webern's modest output over a compositional career than spanned almost forty years shows not only the high standards he held for his own music but also the extreme brevity of most of his compositions. The works are short because they are so concentrated; they distill conventional musical gestures into drastically compressed time spans. This sense of compressed energy is one of several innovative aspects of Webern's music. Another is his wholesale adoption and imaginative application of the serialist procedures that he learned from his mentor Arnold Schoenberg.

LO1 Serialism

If you sit down with a guitar, electric bass, or other fret-

ted string instrument, play an open string, then move up the fingerboard one fret at a time, you will reach the note an octave above the open string at the twelfth fret. This activity can confirm experientially the fact that the octave is divided into twelve equidistant half-steps. This consistent division of the octave, known as **equal temperament**, was known and advocated before Bach's time and has been the customary way to arrange the available pitches within the octave since the nineteenth century.

However, in the common practice harmony of the eighteenth and nineteenth centuries, equal distance did not correlate with equal importance. Among the twelve notes within an octave, there is a three-level hierarchy: the tonic pitch, the six other notes of the diatonic scale, and the five **chromatic pitches**, those not in the scale of a particular key.

In Baroque and Classical music, chromatic pitches are most often simply fleeting decorative elaborations. However, they typically played a prominent role in music intended to convey tragic emotions, as we heard in "Dido's Lament" ("When I Am Laid in Earth"). Romantic composers in search of greater expression used chromatic pitches more liberally, as we heard in Chopin's mournful E minor prelude. By the end of the nineteenth century, forward-looking composers such as Wagner composed highly chromatic music. Schoenberg took the inevitable next step.

In emancipating dissonance, Schoenberg discarded the hierarchical arrangement of the twelve pitches. To gain freedom from tonality,

equal temperament Consistent division of the octave into twelve equidistant half-steps

chromatic pitch Pitch not in the scale of a particular key

Schoenberg's goal was to distance his music as much as possible from the trappings of tonality.

he sacrificed order—the well-established framework for organizing pitch that common practice harmony provided. After a flurry of atonal compositions, including *Pierrot lunaire*, Schoenberg struggled for the better part of a decade with the organizational difficulties that his embrace of atonality had caused. However, in the years around 1920, he and composer Joseph Hauer independently developed a system of atonal pitch organization.

In Schoenberg's method, usually called **serialism**, or **twelve-tone composition**, the composer begins by arranging all twelve pitches within the octave in a particular sequence. (The series is often called a **tone row**.) The key relationship in the row is the sequence of intervals—the number of half-steps—between pitches. So long as these remain constant, the composer can alter the starting pitch of any statement of the series to begin with any of the other eleven notes, reverse the direction of the series (the series in reverse order is called a **retrograde**), or invert the series (**inversion**) by reversing the direction of the interval (for instance, the second note is three half-steps lower than the first note rather than three half-steps higher). Collectively, these transformations yield forty-eight possible versions of the original series.

The tone row and its various permutations are the composer's raw material. They are specific to each particular work, rather than patterns common to multiple musical works. We can describe the relationship between common practice harmony and serialism in this way: in a tonal work, the composer invents a statement in an established and familiar language; in a serial work, the composer invents both the statement *and* the language.

It is possible to create a series in which the intervals form familiar patterns. But, more typically, tone rows are formed from dissonant intervals that do not resemble triads, scales, or any other conventional patterns. Indeed, Schoenberg's goal was to distance his music as much as possible from the trappings of tonality.

Webern and Schoenberg: Tradition and Evolution in Austro-German Music

Anton Webern was born in Vienna; his family was on the fringes of the nobility, and his father was a high-ranking civil servant in the Austrian government. Webern obtained a well-rounded musical education, mainly at the University of Vienna, where he earned a doctorate in musicology. However, the decisive event in his musical life was studying composition with Schoenberg. Their association began in 1904, when Webern was among Schoenberg's first private students. Formal training ended in 1908, but their work together would continue throughout most of Webern's life. Although he was less than a decade older than Webern, Schoenberg became for Webern a mentor, friend, and model. They would maintain a close working relationship until Schoenberg's flight to the United States.

Schoenberg, Webern, and Alban Berg, also a student of Schoenberg, formed the Second Viennese School. (Haydn, Mozart, and Beethoven were the first Viennese school.) The three composers were determined to follow their musical destiny from expressionism through serial composition. Schoenberg led the way, but all three composers developed distinctly different compositional approaches. With the support of a small circle of like-minded associates, they worked largely independent of public opinion, which was generally far from enthusiastic. To that end, Schoenberg formed the Society for Private Musical Performances in 1918, which sponsored frequent concerts of contemporary music; only those who subscribed to the society could attend. Webern was on the board of directors. The following year, Webern moved to Mödling, a Vienna suburb, in order to be near Schoenberg, and they spent considerable time together during the period in the early 1920s when Schoenberg was developing his twelve-tone method.

Schoenberg's group viewed their compositions as the most important continuation of the Austro-German

serialism (twelve-tone composition) System of pitch organization in which all twelve pitches within the octave are organized in a series rather than organized hierarchically

tone row In serial composition, the arrangement of all twelve pitches within the octave in a particular sequence

retrograde Reversal of the original sequence of twelve pitches in a serial composition (backward)

inversion In serial composition, reversing the direction of the intervals between pitches of the tone row

Anton Webern

Fast Facts

- *Dates:* 1883–1945
- *Place:* Vienna, Austria
- *Reasons to remember:* A student of Schoenberg; the primary influence on the midcentury avant-garde

© Lebrecht Music & Arts

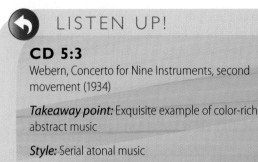

LISTEN UP!

CD 5:3

Webern, Concerto for Nine Instruments, second movement (1934)

Takeaway point: Exquisite example of color-rich abstract music

Style: Serial atonal music

Form: Rounded binary

Genre: Chamber music

Instruments: Flute, oboe, clarinet, trumpet, horn, trombone, violin, viola, piano

Context: Music directed toward a knowledgeable elite made up mainly of avant-garde composers and their supporters

musical tradition, which they valued more than any other. They saw their radical rejection of tonality as the almost inevitable conclusion of the evolutionary path that had begun in the eighteenth century, continued through Beethoven and Wagner, and reached a crisis point early in the twentieth century. They acknowledged their heritage by embracing established genres—suite, string quartet, symphony, concerto—and using traditional forms as a point of reference. Nevertheless, adapting these forms to twelve-tone composition radically altered them, because the structural goals defined by the familiar harmonic progressions of tonal music were no longer present.

Of the three composers, Webern was the most deeply involved, as a performer, with the music of the Austro-German tradition. He derived most of his income from his work as a conductor; his programs focused almost exclusively on this repertoire. Nevertheless, his music moved the farthest away from this tradition. Unlike Webern, Berg never completely abandoned tonality, and Schoenberg reincorporated tonal elements in his later works. It was Webern who committed most fully to serial composition and worked through its implications for other elements: rhythm, texture, dynamics, and timbre. This is particularly evident in his later works, such as the Concerto for Nine Instruments.

Webern began work on his Concerto, Op. 24, in 1931 and completed it in 1934. The concerto is a work for large chamber ensemble, not the usual soloist and orchestra. The ensemble includes three winds (flute, oboe, clarinet), three brasses (trumpet, horn, trombone), two strings (violin, viola), and piano. It contains three movements, in a traditional fast-slow-fast sequence. The form of the second movement, which is discussed later, is also derived from a traditional model: it resembles the rounded binary form used in so much tonal music.

In this movement, Webern's connection to the Austro-German tradition is specifically evident in his meth-

od of creating the tone row. Recall that the practice of building a movement or composition from a simple melodic kernel had been part of Austro-German music since the early eighteenth century and that the melodic material became progressively more individual: Bach built the Brandenburg Concerto movement from a generic three-note motive; Beethoven used a distinctive motive crafted from generic material as the building block for both melodic material and figuration; Wagner saturated his music drama with leitmotifs.

With Webern, the progression from generic to specific ran its course. In this movement Webern constructs his row from permutations of a three-note cell. Thus, every note in the movement—harmony as well as melody—derives from the three notes heard at the outset: the trumpet note and the two-note piano chord. Pitch choices belong specifically and uniquely to this work. There is no apparent connection to the familiar scales and chords of common practice harmony; indeed, the complementary relationship of melody and harmony dissolves in this movement.

The absence of familiar reference points in pitch organization that common practice harmony typically provides brings other elements to the forefront. There is virtually no variation in the rhythmic flow, but there are extreme and frequent fluctuations in tempo—like rubber being stretched and released. The most pronounced tempo changes help articulate the form.

Among the most immediately striking features of the movement are the frequent contrasts in timbre, a procedure that Schoenberg called *Klangfarbenmelodie* (tone color melody). The piano plays continuously throughout. The other instruments typically play only a note or two at a time, like sparkles of different colors against the more neutral background of the piano.

Webern and Abstract Music

Among the major currents in the visual arts during the first part of the twentieth century was abstract art. Abstract artists eschewed representation in favor of work that concentrated on such painterly elements as form, line, color, and texture in and of themselves. The works of abstract artists range from the almost improvisatory paintings of Jackson Pollock to Mark Rothko's studies in color and the geometric compositions of Piet Mondrian, which feature patterns of black, white, and vivid colors.

The familiar rhythmic patterns, melodic procedures, and harmonic progressions of tonal music are like representation in the visual arts, in the sense that both depict "reality" as encountered in day-to-day life. By taking virtually every element to its extreme and divorcing pitch organization from tonality in any form, Webern skewed musical "reality" to the point of abstraction. The musical materials are so far removed from their source that the sense of connection with the tradition that inspired them is obscured by the radical differences. They may be inspired by traditional models, but their transformation by Webern gives them a completely different cast.

Abstract artists eschewed representation in favor of work that concentrated on such painterly elements as form, line, color, and texture in and of themselves.

In particular, the use of serial procedures has the effect of "ungrounding" the music. The tonic note and tonic chord on a downbeat anchor tonal music: they provide a point of departure and a point of arrival. Melodies may soar, but they come to earth at cadences. By contrast, Webern's music seems to float. The effect is analogous to a mobile by Alexander Calder, made up of abstract shapes in contrasting colors, suspended almost invisibly by a thin wire.

Webern's music seems to float.

Webern's music opened a new sound world and introduced a new aesthetic. His wholehearted embrace of serialism and his extreme approach to composition effectively severed the connection with the Austro-German tradition. The signals on which generations of musicians and listeners had relied for meaning were largely absent or distorted beyond easy recognition. In their stead came music with a new kind of beauty: sound objects linked by the consistency of pitch, seemingly floating in space. Despite its debt to the past, Webern's music looked squarely to the future.

Webern's music would prove to be especially influential. Many of the composers active in the two decades after World War II embraced serialism; some applied serial procedures to other elements, such as rhythm and dynamics. Schoenberg may have been the architect of this new method, but Webern's music was, for the more forward-thinking composers, the more widely used model.

The "mainstreaming" of serialism among the classical avant-garde was a decisive moment in the history of music. For the first time since the advent of widespread commercial publishing in the seventeenth century, there was clear discontinuity between everyday music and the music of the most prestigious composers of the day. Twelve-tone composition is a method of pitch organization that is different in kind from tonal music. Listeners unfamiliar with the method would find virtually no common harmonic or melodic ground between serial compositions and other music that they might encounter, such as tonal classical music, popular and folk music, or music for religious services. As a result, avant-garde classical composition became detached from virtually every other kind of music making.

CHAPTER 45

Stravinsky and Neoclassicism

"*No other composer of the era embraced both the old and new dimensions of neoclassicism so fully.*"

Did You Know?

In 1946, Stravinsky composed his *Ebony Concerto* for jazz clarinetist Woody Herman and his big band.

A s 1914 began, Igor Stravinsky's professional fortunes seemed on the upswing: *The Rite of Spring* received two concert performances in Paris in April 1914. This time there were no riots as at the premiere, just adulation. However, his wife was diagnosed with tuberculosis, so Stravinsky and his family relocated to Switzerland, where they lived until 1920. He visited the Ukraine in July 1914, just before the outbreak of World War I. It was his last visit there. The war and the Russian Revolution that followed cut him off from his homeland; he did not return to Russia until 1962. Stravinsky returned to France in 1920 and used the country as his home base until 1939, when he emigrated to the United States as World War II broke out in Europe.

Given the instability of his professional and personal circumstances, one might reasonably expect Stravinsky to have taken the safe course: composing music that mined much the same vein as the three ballets that had established his reputation. In fact, the opposite happened: Stravinsky would never again compose a work similar in style to *The Rite of Spring*. Instead, he brought his unique vision to neoclassicism.

LO2 Neoclassicism

Neoclassicism is any trend in the arts characterized by the revival or reinterpretation of classical values of harmony, clarity, restraint, and adherence to established practices. In architecture and the visual arts, neo-classicism meant embracing these values as embodied in the artworks of Greek and Roman civilization: the Greek Revival buildings on many college campuses exemplify this trend. Neoclassicism emerged as a trend in the visual arts during the Renaissance as one response to reawakened interest in classical civilization. It flourished during the eighteenth century, as an expression of Enlightenment values. For nineteenth-century commentators, the music of the late eighteenth century also embodied these values, hence its designation as the Classical period in music.

The U.S. Supreme Court building, completed in the 1930s, is another example of neoclassicism in architecture.

neoclassicism Any trend in the arts characterized by the revival or reinterpretation of classical values of harmony, clarity, restraint, and adherence to established practices, as embodied in the artworks of Greek and Roman civilization; in music, an umbrella term identifying a body of twentieth-century music that has in common a rejection of Romantic and post-Romantic musical values and a return to, or reworking of, many of the musical features characteristic of eighteenth-century music

In music, *neoclassicism* (as opposed to classicism) serves as an umbrella term identifying a body of twentieth-century music that has in common a rejection of Romantic and post-Romantic musical values and a return to, or reworking of, many of the musical features characteristic of eighteenth-century music. Neoclassical compositions are generally characterized by clear tonal orientation, straightforward rhythms, easily understood forms inspired by traditional models, and modest dimensions. They tend to be emotionally reserved, in contrast with the hyperexpressiveness of late Romantic and expressionist music and the sensuousness of impressionism and primitivism.

The first neoclassical musical works appeared toward the end of World War I. During the 1920s and 1930s, neoclassicism flourished in France: for a decided majority of significant French composers, *this* was the sound of modern music. One reason was the close correspondence between neoclassical values and aesthetic features that they felt were distinctively French. During his years of residence in France, Stravinsky was also among the neoclassical adherents.

NEOCLASSICISM AND STRAVINSKY'S STYLISTIC TRANSFORMATION

Between 1913 and 1930, the year in which he completed his Symphony of Psalms, Stravinsky composed an astonishing amount of music: ballets, operas, choral music, works for large instrumental ensemble, chamber works, songs, works for solo instruments (especially piano), and works that are a genre unto themselves. These new works were remarkably varied in both genre and style. Their most obvious common ground was only that Stravinsky had composed them and that they were unlike the earlier ballets.

His first two important works of the 1920s were Symphonies of Wind Instruments and the ballet *Pulcinella*. The two works are radically different. Symphonies of Wind Instruments is an austere, modernist work, with irregularly formed panels of sound performed by a twenty-four-member wind band. Pulcinella is, by contrast, a reworking of eighteenth-century music. Stravinsky adapted music attributed to the eighteenth-century composer Giovanni Pergolesi so skillfully that it is often impossible to detect where the original music ends and Stravinsky begins.

For Stravinsky, neoclassicism wasn't just a matter of musical style: important works, such as his opera *Oedipus Rex* and his ballet *Apollon musagète*, derive directly from classical Greece. Cumulatively, Stravinsky's neoclassical works are at once deeply indebted to the past and clearly removed from it. No other composer of the era embraced both the old and new dimensions of neoclassicism so fully. The *Symphony of Psalms* continues Stravinsky's neoclassical style but adds a new element: his religious faith.

STRAVINSKY, RELIGION, AND THE SYMPHONY OF PSALMS

On Easter 1926, Stravinsky once again became a communicant in the Orthodox faith. His return to the organized religion of his youth was inspired in part by the Catholic philosopher Jacques Maritain, who was responsible for reviving the philosophy of the thirteenth-century Dominican priest Saint Thomas Aquinas. Through Maritain, Stravinsky embraced the idea of an orderly world in which the artist suppresses his ego in the service of God and the greater good. As he remarked in an interview given two months after the Paris premiere of *Symphony of Psalms*,

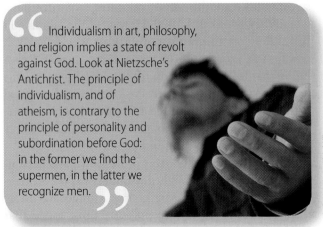

> Individualism in art, philosophy, and religion implies a state of revolt against God. Look at Nietzsche's Antichrist. The principle of individualism, and of atheism, is contrary to the principle of personality and subordination before God: in the former we find the supermen, in the latter we recognize men.

Stravinsky expressed his recently renewed faith most directly through *Symphony of Psalms*.

This remark suggests that Stravinsky's return to organized religion was the spiritual counterpart to the essentially conservative impulse that influenced the music of his neoclassical period. And both reflect not only an important dimension of Stravinsky's personality but also the tenuous life of a composer in a turbulent time. With the success of *The Rite of Spring*, Stravinsky was arguably the most celebrated living composer in the world. However, fame and acclaim did not automatically convert into cash. Commissions and royalties provided only part of his income; more came from his numerous concert appearances as a conductor and pianist. Further, the unsettled circumstances of his personal life—a life divided almost equally between family in the south of France and Paris, and touring with his mistress; the forced separation from his homeland; the poor health of his wife and daughter—may also have motivated Stravinsky to ground himself in a medieval conception of Christianity.

Stravinsky expressed his recently renewed faith most directly through *Symphony of Psalms*, a three-movement work for chorus and orchestra. He composed the work in 1930 to fulfill a commission from Serge Koussevitsky, the conductor of the Boston Symphony. The dedication reads, "This Symphony was composed for the glory of God and dedicated to the Boston Symphony Orchestra on the occasion of its 50th anniversary."

Stravinsky's commission was for a traditional symphony. However, Stravinsky used the commission as an opportunity to compose a work that realized an idea apparently germinating for a while: a symphonic setting of Psalm texts. Stravinsky described the work this way: "It is not a symphony in which I have included Psalms to be sung. On the contrary, it is the singing of the *Psalms* that I am symphonizing."

Stravinsky set verses from Psalms 38 and 39 and all of Psalm 150; he drew the texts from the Vulgate, the Latin-language Bible used by the Catholic Church. The title "Symphony" is used in its more general sense of "instruments (including voices) sounding together" rather than in the more restricted meaning of a four-movement work. The work has three distinct movements, each of which is about twice as long as the preceding movement; in concert they are performed without break. The first movement includes verses 13 and 14 from Psalm 38.

In keeping with the idea that the work symphonizes psalm singing, Stravinsky avoids conventional forms. There is repetition of melodic material, in both vocal and instrumental parts, but the repetition does not resolve into a standard formal pattern.

STRAVINSKY, "NEO" AND "CLASSICAL"

It is a measure of Stravinsky's art that it can be both "classical" and "neo" in a single sound. The chord with which Symphony of Psalms begins is a minor triad, which has been used countless times in tonal music. But Stravinsky's instrumentation and voicing of the chord are unique, and the chord is so distinctive that it immediately identifies the work and presages the particular mix of old and new that permeates it.

It is a measure of Stravinsky's art that it can be both "classical" and "neo" in a single sound.

© Robert Risko/Lebrecht

For Stravinsky, the past is a vast resource that he can cherry-pick for his immediate needs and then transform and embed in a setting that is thoroughly modern. For example, the chorus enters singing in unison a melodic line that barely moves from the opening pitch. Particularly in conjunction with the Latin text that it sets, Stravinsky's melody evokes chant. But unlike chant, the melody has a measured rhythm and is supported by an active accompaniment. The instrumental writing recalls the rhythms of Baroque music (the "classic" in neoclassical embraces *all* the past, not just the Classical style), and much of the accompanying figuration moves in sequential patterns. But the passages do not sound Baroque because the figuration, although consonant, doesn't resemble the patterns used by Bach and other Baroque masters.

One of the most individualistic features of the work is its instrumentation. Stravinsky scored the work for a mixed-voice choir (with the upper two parts sung by a children's choir, if available) and an unusual orchestra: there are no violins, violas, or clarinets, but two pianos. Violins and violas add warmth to the sound of the orchestra in the middle and upper registers. Their absence coupled with the drier sound of the pianos gives the work an austere sound, a kind of instrumental analog to the Latin text and its vocal setting. In turn, the austere sound, along with the unison or homophonic vocal writing and the syllabic setting of the psalm, suggests Stravinsky's hierarchy of importance: words, voices, and instruments, in that order. The melody amplifies the text; the instrumental accompaniment supports and colors the melody.

Stravinsky's Approach to Musical Style

The two samples of Stravinsky's music encountered in our survey contrast strikingly in numerous ways: one depicts a pagan ritual, and the other, a medieval-style

Stravinsky was a chameleon-like composer.

homage to God; one is vivid, colorful, and programmatic, and the other is austere, somewhat dry, and detached; one is rich in complex rhythms and textures, shifts of tempo and mood, and tuneful snippets, whereas the other maintains a steady pulse and is more transparent, and its most memorable melodic material is almost irreducibly simple. There are common features: irregular blocks of sound, active ostinato patterns. However, there is virtually no sense that the *Symphony of Psalms* is the product of the ongoing evolution of Stravinsky's musical approach. Rather, it seems like an abrupt change of direction.

It is possible to view these apparent discontinuities and contrasts as aspects of a consistent musical personality. We know that Stravinsky was an avid consumer of culture during his expatriate years in western Europe. He mingled with artists in all fields and collaborated with several, including Pablo Picasso and the writer Jean Cocteau. He attended concerts, films, and exhibitions and sampled Parisian nightlife. He absorbed new ideas and sounds. His encounter with ragtime in the 1910s led to three rag-inspired compositions. At the same time, Stravinsky had an intense interest in the past. His three early ballets are based on centuries-old material, and almost all his neoclassical works connect back to pre-nineteenth-century sources, both musical and extramusical.

The musical evidence suggests that Stravinsky is a chameleon-like composer: the point of departure for his compositions comes from the world around him. His early works draw heavily on his Russian heritage, several of his works from the 1910s draw on novel and popular vernacular styles, and his post-1920 works reflect musical life in Paris: neoclassicism was primarily a French movement. Stravinsky's extreme responsiveness to outside influences led to radically different approaches to musical style.

In our experience, musical style has typically been the product of musical choices made by a composer (or performer) or a group of composers. For example, we identify a composition as Romantic when we hear a long, flowing melody with distinctive accompaniment. Stravinsky's strategy is fundamentally different. He often uses or adapts established style features not to identify his personal vision but to connect the composition to its inspiration: the parody of chantlike unison singing and the use of medieval modes offer a musical counterpart to the Latin version of the psalm, which dates from the fifth century.

These borrowed style elements disguise the innovative and individual elements of Stravinsky's musical vision, at times to the point of obscuring it. More often, however, Stravinsky's musical personality emerges in his distinctive way of adapting and interpreting these diverse style elements. It is manifest in his highly individual (and difficult to emulate) approach to rhythm, orchestration, tonal organization, and form. These characteristic features continued to influence his music despite the striking surface contrasts from composition to composition.

Stravinsky did not return to Europe until 1951. During his visit, he was disturbed to discover that younger European composers were more interested in the music of Schoenberg and his disciples than they were in his. At the urging of Robert Craft, a conductor, writer, advocate of contemporary music, and Stravinsky's longtime collaborator, Stravinsky gradually adopted serialism. It was the third and final phase of his compositional career.

CHAPTER 46

Art and the People: The Americas

"I believe as you do, that our salvation must come from ourselves and that we must fight the foreign element in America which ignores American music."—Aaron Copland, letter to Carlos Chavez

Did You Know?

In 1977, the "symphonic rock" band Emerson, Lake, and Palmer covered Aaron Copland's often-borrowed *Fanfare for the Common Man*. ELP had previously reworked "Hoedown" from Copland's ballet *Rodeo*.

In a letter dated December 26, 1931, Aaron Copland wrote to his friend and fellow composer Carlos Chavez, "I believe as you do, that our salvation must come from ourselves and that we must fight the foreign element in America which ignores American music." He asked Chavez, who was soon to travel to New York, to bring with him music by Mexican and South American composers.

By 1931, Chavez was the major figure in Mexican art music: its most important composer, conductor of the Orquestra Sinfonica de Mexico, and director of the Conservatorio Nacional de Música. He had first come to New York in 1923 and met Copland, with whom he formed a lifelong friendship, during a return visit in 1926. By 1928, Chavez had invited Copland, one of the most prominent American composers during the 1920s and 1930s, to Mexico. Copland would visit Mexico for

the first time in 1932, where Chavez arranged the first all-Copland concert. In 1936 Copland composed *El Salon Mexico*; Chavez would conduct the premiere with his orchestra the following year.

LO3 Twentieth-Century Musical Nationalism

Both Chavez and Copland would become major players in a new kind of musical nationalism that peaked during the 1930s. Like their nineteenth-century predecessors, this new generation of nationalist composers wished to infuse their music with the character of their homeland. However, the musical results were substantially different because the world in which they worked had changed so drastically in the space of two generations: life in the 1930s was far different from life in the 1880s, musically and otherwise. Among the changes that had a significant impact on their music were these:

1. *The growing political, social, and cultural presence of the working classes.* This presence was manifest in numerous ways, including revolutions that toppled monarchies; the decline of colonialism; the rise of labor unions; migration from rural to

urban areas; and increased visibility of minorities in public life.

2. *A deepened interest in folk traditions and a desire to preserve them against the encroachment of mainstream culture.* In pursuit of this goal, collectors took advantage of new technologies, sound recording being the most significant.

3. *The emergence of a new kind of commercial music.* The African-influenced popular music of the early twentieth century represented the beginning of a new musical tradition. The continuum between art and commercial music that had been part of nineteenth-century musical life all but disappeared.

4. *The fragmentation of style in concert music.* By World War I, Romantic music was an anachronism; in its place was a host of styles, substantially different from one another.

These nationalist composers did not embed folk and vernacular elements in common practice. Rather, they blended vernacular elements from their homeland with innovative elements drawn from concert music to produce works that sounded modern and that acquired over time a national identity. The fact that none of them made use of common practice—even Copland's familiar chords are completely restructured—only sharpened the sense of national identity.

Carlos Chavez: A Mexican Composer

It's hard to imagine anyone doing more for the musical life of his country than Carlos Chavez did for music

Diego Rivera (1886–1957), detail from the mosaic A Popular History of Mexico

in Mexico. Chavez was Mexico's most distinguished composer of the twentieth century; he received commissions from organizations in the United States and Europe. This alone would have represented a significant contribution. However, he also conducted the first professional symphony orchestra in Mexico; served as the director of the national conservatory, where he formed academies to research indigenous music; wrote articles on a regular basis for a major Mexico City newspaper; helped plan the *Instituto Nacional de Bellas Artes* and was its founding director; taught many of Mexico's most talented young composers; and much more.

THE AZTEC RENAISSANCE

In the century following independence from Spanish rule in 1821, Mexico went through a war with the United States in which it ceded over half of its territory (what is now the southwestern part of the United States, from Texas to California); endured a foreign ruler (Emperor Maximilian I, a member of the Habsburgs who was imposed on the country by the French); suffered the thirty-year dictatorship of Porfirio Díaz, who attempted to modernize the country but also catered to wealthy landowners and industrialists; and finally, experienced the Mexican Revolution, which began in 1910 and ended ten years later, after deposing Díaz and laying the foundation for a constitutional republic.

Among the many reforms of the new government were the recognition and support of indigenous peoples. A decided majority of Mexicans, then and now, are mestizos, persons of mixed race, most often Spanish and Amerindian. Much of the remaining population are either full-blooded Amerindian or *criollos*, those who are fully or mostly European. The second article in the Constitution of the United States of Mexico, approved in 1917, acknowledges that Mexico is a "pluricultural" nation based mainly on those who lived in the country before the arrival of the Spanish explorers.

A caste system governed life in colonial Latin America. At the very top were those born in Spain or Portugal. Right below those were *criollos*: to be considered *criollo* or *criolla*, one had to establish "cleanliness of blood." Mestizos and others of mixed European, African, or Amerindian ancestry belonged to lower castes. During the first century of independence, the social order remained much the same. Much of the wealth was concentrated in the land and bank accounts of the criollos, the Catholic Church enjoyed considerable privilege and influence, and the upper classes identified culturally with Europe. Indigenous peoples were marginalized socially, economically, and politically. The wording of the

> "We have found ourselves by going back to the cultural traditions of the Indian racial stock that still accounts for four-fifths of the people."—Carlos Chavez

constitution was one part of a larger effort by the new government to redress centuries of discrimination, repression, and neglect.

One cultural dimension of this heightened awareness of indigenous peoples was the creation of art that drew on preconquest native cultures. Notable works in the visual arts include the Aztec-inspired murals of Diego Rivera. A younger generation of Mexican composers, including Chavez and Silvestre Revueltas, sparked what is commonly called the "Aztec Renaissance": classical music that was distinctly Mexican in theme and style. Chavez summed up their mission in an article written around the time he composed *Sinfonía India*: "We have found ourselves by going back to the cultural traditions of the Indian racial stock that still accounts for four-fifths of the people."

Carlos Chavez

Fast Facts

- *Dates:* 1899–1978
- *Place:* Mexico
- *Reasons to remember:* Mexico's most important composer and musical figure during the middle of the twentieth century

Chavez grew up during the Mexican Revolution; he was on the verge of adolescence when it began and on the verge of adulthood when it ended. He had extended contact with Amerindian music beginning in early childhood. From the beginning of his professional career, he fused nationalistic objectives with the restoration of indigenous culture. His most important early works were two ballets on Aztec themes. Although he established academies for the study of indigenous music, he did not attempt to reconstruct preconquest music in his compositions. Rather, he used Indian musical features evocatively, to affirm its Mexican heritage. He blended them with traditional and modern elements in his music from the 1920s and 1930s, most notably in his second symphony.

SINFONÍA INDIA

In his overtly nationalistic compositions, Chavez sought to bring modernism, nationalism, and accessibility into balance. His approach came most directly from Stravinsky's *The Rite of Spring*: combine the modern (irregular rhythms, fresh harmonies) with the primitive (native percussion instruments, Amerindian melodies, rhythmic repetition) to make a composition sound both modern and indigenous and to cast it in a recognizable version of a traditional form to aid accessibility. In *Sinfonía India*, Chavez's second symphony, he does not turn his back completely on traditional symphonic music. The symphony is a single movement that uses the conventional first-movement form of the nineteenth-century symphony as a point of departure. The symphony has multiple points of entry: energetic rhythms in constantly shifting meters; tuneful Indian melodies, one of which serves as the contrasting theme; prominent percussion instruments, many of them native; and extensive repetition.

Chavez composed *Sinfonía India* in 1935 and 1936, while he was living in New York, and conducted the premiere in January 1936 during a live radio broadcast of the CBS Orchestra. The work features a standard symphony orchestra augmented by extra percussion instruments, including native instruments made from butterfly cocoons and deer hooves. The one-movement

LISTEN UP!

CD 5:5
Chavez, *Sinfonía India*, excerpt (1935–1936)

Takeaway point: Modern symphony with indigenous sounds and rhythms

Style: Twentieth-century nationalism

Form: Sonata (from middle of recapitulation through end)

Genre: Symphony

Instruments: Orchestra with extra percussion

Context: A work designed to assert Mexico's ethnic identity work takes about twelve minutes to perform. The excerpt presented here includes the last third of the work.

THE "MEXICANNESS" OF *SINFONÍA INDIA*

In an article written in 1928, Aaron Copland praised Carlos Chavez as "one of the few American musicians about whom we can say that he is more than a reflection of Europe . . . one of the first authentic signs of a new world with its own new music." In Copland's article, an "American musician" is a musician from the Americas—from what was still called the New World. In discussing Chavez's music, Copland contrasts it with "the Germanic ideals which tyrannized over music for more than a hundred years." The active, asymmetrical rhythms, lucid textures, prominent percussion, and melodic repetition clearly differentiate *Sinfonía India* from nineteenth- and twentieth-century "Germanic" music. However, they do not make it obviously Mexican, if only because the Mexican elements—the folk melodies and percussion instruments—were not widely known. Chavez's music is, in effect, Mexican by assertion: it acquired its national identity only when audiences identified the particular mix of traditional (full orchestra, modified sonata form), contemporary (active rhythms, innovative harmonies), and ethnic (percussion instruments, folk melodies) features as representative of a distinctively Mexican art music.

In retrospect, *Sinfonía India* conveys its "Mexicanness" not only because Chavez largely eschewed "Germanic ideals" but also because the ethnic elements are more than coloristic touches. The consistent presence of percussion, extensive repetition, and open texture was also characteristic of the Native American music presented in People's Music 3. Chavez adapted these characteristic features to an art music environment by varying instrumental color, making the rhythms more complex, and adding harmony and occasional counterpoint. The result is a decidedly different kind of musical nationalism.

Aaron Copland: An American Composer

In 1936, Davidson Taylor, the head of the Music Division at CBS radio, arranged for the commission of orchestral works by six American composers for radio broadcast. Not yet thirty, Taylor was nevertheless knowledgeable enough about music to write for the journal *Modern Music* and make critical suggestions to several of the composers. Among those commissioned was Aaron Copland.

Copland was enthusiastic about the opportunity. For him, "Radio was an exciting new medium—the very idea of reaching so many people with a single performance." He finished the work in the summer of 1937 and submitted it as "Radio Serenade." However, just before the work's radio premiere, CBS radio announced that Copland's new composition would temporarily be identified by the even blander title "Music for Radio" but that it "had a program, or scenario, that not even its composer . . . ventured to interpret." The network and Copland invited listeners to suggest titles, and they received over one thousand suggestions. Copland selected *Saga of the Prairie*; he would change the name of the work to *Prairie Journal* in 1968. For Ruth Leonhardt, the woman who suggested the title that Copland chose, "The music seemed typically American and it reminded me of the intense courage—the struggles and final triumphs—of the early settlers, the real pioneers."

"I visualize a music which is profound in content, simple in expression and understandable to all."
—Aaron Copland

© Julie Lemberger/CORBIS

Copland never "interpreted" the program of *Prairie Journal* directly, but he did acknowledge that he had used a "cowboy tune" (which researchers have not been able to identify), "so the western titles seemed most appropriate." In fact, the work evokes a range of styles heard on radio during the 1930s. Some of this music looks back to Copland's jazz-influenced music of the 1920s, but the "cowboy" and "prairie" elements are the first inkling of Copland's new populist style. In 1940, by which time he had already written the western-themed ballet *Billy the Kid* and two film scores, Copland said, "I visualize a music which is profound in content, simple in expression and understandable to all." This vision would continue to inform his music through the 1940s and, in the process, give America a third regional musical style, one that evoked the West, rather than Ives's New England or Gershwin's New York.

"AMERICANNESS" AND THE WEST DURING THE DEPRESSION

For many Americans, sagebrush replaced the skyscraper as the defining image of America during the Depression years. The stock market crash took some of the luster off the fast-living lifestyle glamorized in the media during the 1920s. The progress toward wealth and material success that seemed inevitable before the crash became a pipe dream for too many Americans in the 1930s. In response, defining images of America seemed to shift from tall buildings, fast cars, busy streets, and full theaters to open spaces, horses, and cowboys with guitars.

Sagebrush replaced the skyscraper as the defining image of America during the Depression years.

In popular culture, the most pervasive expression of this shift was the western. Although western films date from the early silent film era, the genre really took off in the 1930s. Two acclaimed westerns framed the decade: *Cimarron* (1931) won an Academy Award for Best Picture, while *Stagecoach* (1939), featuring a young John Wayne, received several Academy Award nominations, including one for best musical score: the sound track included numerous folk tunes. In between came hundreds of films, including dozens featuring Gene Autry and other singing cowboys.

Westerns presented a simpler view of life: good guys wore white hats; bad guys wore black hats, or headdresses. Frontier justice prevailed: problems were resolved with six-shooters. They glorified the lone hero, even when he flouted the law. Westerns were one manifestation of America's fascination with its frontier heritage. Collections of cowboy songs also became increasingly popular during the 1930s, in large part because of the rise of radio shows that featured country-and-western music, such as the National Barn Dance. Rodgers and Hammerstein's landmark 1943 musical *Oklahoma!* brought the frontier to Broadway. This romanticized view of life in the West contrasted sharply with the brutal present: the Dust Bowl, a decade-long drought that would devastate farmers and ranchers in the Plains and the Southwest, would leave half a million people homeless.

During this same time, folklorists, most notably John Lomax (who published one of the first collections of cowboy songs in 1910) and his son Alan, traveled throughout the South and Southwest recording folk musicians. Their work received support from the Library of Congress; it was eventually added to the Archive of Folk Culture.

Although the Archive included songs of blacks and Native Americans as well as whites, Americans' sense of musical folk roots resided mainly in the songs of whites preserved in collections and presented through the media, and in the recordings and performances of contemporary "folk" performers, most notably Woody Guthrie. This was a retreat from the "melting-pot" ethos that was so much a part of American life through the first quarter of the century. Both the music and the cultures from which it emerged inspired Aaron Copland's cultivation of a distinctively American style.

COPLAND AND VERNACULAR MUSIC

The early careers of Aaron Copland and George Gershwin were remarkably similar in several respects. Gershwin, born two years before Copland, was the Brooklyn-born son of Russian Jewish immigrants; Copland was the last of five children of Lithuanian Jewish immigrants. Both grew up with a keen interest in vernacular music, developed into fluent pianists, and briefly studied classical composition with Rubin Goldmark in the 1910s. Both were great admirers of French music and traveled to Paris to study composition with Nadia Boulanger. Copland stayed three years, from 1921 to 1924. Gershwin traveled to France in 1928 and introduced himself to Boulanger with a letter from Ravel, whom he admired greatly and had met earlier in the decade. She did not accept him, because she felt that he had already found his compositional voice. Both Gershwin and Copland composed "jazz" piano concertos in their mid-twenties.

Aaron Copland

Fast Facts

- *Dates:* 1900–1990

- *Place:* United States

- *Reasons to remember:* America's best-known classical composer; created an accessible style with a distinct American identity

Virtually from the start of his career, Copland had wanted his music to sound American. In his earlier works, such as the piano concerto, he sought this sound by fusing contemporary classical music with jazz. However, by 1930, the American qualities in his most modern-sounding music had assumed a more abstract character. The *Piano Variations* of 1930 features jagged rhythms, dissonant harmonies, clangorous sounds, and sparse textures, all of which support the development of a four-note motive. The work placed Copland in the forefront of modern American composers. During this same period, he had been a tireless advocate of music by composers of the Americas, as his review of Chavez's music attests.

With the *Piano Variations*, Copland had found the essential features of his personal style. Beginning in mid-decade, he composed a series of works, mainly for orchestra, that presented these features in a more accessible form. Copland called this approach "imposed simplicity." He achieved this by replacing the strident dissonances of the *Piano Variations* with the familiar chords and scales of common practice harmony and incorporating folk material and familiar melodies.

Copland had altruistic and pragmatic reasons for simplifying his style. Creating art music for the people was his way of supporting the working class with whom he identified. Moreover, it meant more professional opportunities: commissions for ballets and orchestral music, contracts for film scores, performances, lectures, and the like.

The folk materials that Copland employed in his post–*Prairie Journal* music were one dimension of his "frontier" sound. He frequently quoted cowboy songs, folk melodies, and other thematically appropriate material in his "American" music, most explicitly in his use of a transcription by composer-folklorist Ruth Crawford Seeger of a Kentucky fiddle song called "Bonypart's Retreat" in the ballet *Rodeo*.

However, Copland's music evokes the vast expanses of frontier America mainly through musical choices that are, at best, tangentially related to the use of folk materials. Among the most striking features of his music is the predilection for musical space. He achieves this mainly through his handling of texture, melody, and rhythm: he favors single lines, or widely separated multiple lines, writes melodies with wide intervals, and makes extensive use of silence. We hear Copland's spacious-sounding music in two excerpts from *Appalachian Spring*.

APPALACHIAN SPRING

In 1942, Copland received a commission from Elizabeth Sprague Coolidge to compose a ballet for the dancer-choreographer Martha Graham, to be performed at the Library of Congress. Originally titled merely *Ballet for Martha*, it acquired its title through a suggestion from Graham. His score for the ballet, which premiered in 1944 and won the Pulitzer Prize in music the following year, included only thirteen instruments, due to the small size of the orchestra pit in Coolidge Auditorium. Also in 1945, Copland would rework *Appalachian Spring* as an orchestral suite that included eight of the fourteen numbers in the ballet. It is this version that is most often performed.

FROM BROOKLYN TO THE MOUNTAINS: TOWARD AN AMERICAN SOUND

If much of Copland's American music tapped into one enduring American image by evoking the old West and the frontier, his career tapped into another. Copland was a "melting-pot" success story: the Brooklyn-born son of immigrants who rose to fame and fortune. So there is a delicious irony in the fact that Copland would find his American voice not in the new vernacular music that he heard growing up in New York but in music far removed from his early experience.

Copland's quest for a national style was fundamentally different from Chavez's, because by the time he found his American sound, there were several recognizably American musical styles in the air: among them the music of Ives (which Copland helped promote during the 1920s and 1930s); the numerous black-inspired

LISTEN UP!

CD 5:6–7

Copland, *Appalachian Spring*, first and second sections (1945)

Takeaway point: A fine example of Copland's populist style

Style: Twentieth-century nationalism

Form: Both movements through-composed, but with intermittent repetition

Genre: Orchestral suite

Instruments: Symphony orchestra

Context: Copland composing accessible modern music

styles of the early twentieth century—ragtime, jazz, blues, popular song; and the vernacular/classical fusions of Gershwin and others.

That Copland took the particular musical direction he did seems largely the serendipitous confluence of several developments:

- Fascination with life on the frontier—in the West and elsewhere—expressed in popular culture
- Heightened awareness of the "common man," prompted in part by the hardships of the Depression
- The urgent drive to preserve the folk heritage of the United States before it was lost

- Copland's musical evolution
- The composer's commitment to a "people's music"

Copland's populist style carried over into other works: his film scores, his famous *Fanfare for the Common Man*, the patriotic *Lincoln Portrait*, and his *Symphony No. 3*, composed in 1945. Although his populist style certainly evokes "spacious skies," "amber waves of grain," and "purple mountain majesties," his works from the late 1930s and early 1940s makes clear that the American sound of Copland's music transcends an exclusively regional identity.

CHAPTER 47

Art and the People: Eastern Europe

"These composers turned back to the people, even as many of their peers seemed to be turning their back on a larger audience in the pursuit of their art."

Did You Know?

After Sergei Prokofiev played the well-known children's piece *Peter and the Wolf* for him, Walt Disney promptly secured the rights and later used it as the sound track to an animated film of the same name.

For musicians living in central and eastern Europe during the 1930s, the overriding facts of life were the rise of totalitarian governments and the military aggression of Nazi Germany, the Soviet Union, and Italy, which would lead to all-out war by 1939. Some, especially those of Jewish descent, fled Europe; several ultimately settled in the United States. Schoenberg was teaching in Berlin when the Nazis came to power. He left in 1933 and in 1936 joined the music faculty at UCLA. Among the other Jewish musicians affected by the Nazis were two who ended up near Schoenberg; they were among the European-born film composers working for Hollywood studios. Franz Waxman ar-

rived in the United States in 1935; he would immediately become a top film composer and single-handedly defined music for horror films with his score for *The Bride of Frankenstein* (1935). After shuttling back and forth between the United States and Austria during the 1930s, Erich Korngold returned to the United States in 1938 to compose the film score for *The Adventures of Robin Hood*, just before the Anschluss, which annexed Austria to Germany. He did not return home again.

The Hungarian composer Béla Bartók contemplated leaving his homeland through the latter half of the 1930s but could not leave his mother behind. He left Hungary only in 1940, less than a year after she passed away. By contrast, the Russian composer Sergei Prokofiev (1891–1953) jumped from the frying pan into the fire: he returned to the Soviet Union in 1936 after living abroad for almost twenty years, then had to deal with the Soviet authorities, from Stalin on, for the rest of his life.

In this chapter we consider music by two composers with strong connections to the people. Bartók's connection came from within. He built his musical style on the folk music of Hungary, which he studied in unprecedented depth. Prokofiev's was imposed from above. Upon his return to the Soviet Union, Prokofiev had to contend with the guardians of socialist realism, who required that works of art be accessible to the proletariat so that they could be used as propaganda tools.

LO4 Bartók and a New Kind of Musical Nationalism

While staying at a resort in what was then northern Hungary, Béla Bartók heard a maid named Lidi Dósa sing a song whose title translates as "Red Apple." He learned that it was a folk song from her native Transylvania. He wrote it down and published a setting of it the following year. In 1904, the year of his stay, Bartók was a promising young Hungarian composer and pianist. His compositions to that point were derivative, evidencing the influence of Richard Strauss, Brahms, and what passed for authentic Hungarian music in urban centers. Bartók recognized that his music needed a more distinctive voice, and he wanted to make it sound Hungarian but was unsure how to achieve this.

The encounter with Lidi precipitated a decisive shift in Bartók's compositional focus. He gradually became aware that the path to a recognizably Hungarian personal style lay through the folk music of the peasants who lived in isolated rural areas. He began modestly. As he wrote to his sister at the end of 1904, "Now I have a new plan: to collect the finest Hungarian folksongs and to raise them, adding the best possible piano

"Now I have a new plan: to collect the finest Hungarian folksongs and to raise them, adding the best possible piano accompaniments, to the level of art-song."
—Bartók (fourth from left, recording Slovak folk songs in 1907)

accompaniments, to the level of art-song." As he deepened his involvement with this folk music, he imbued all his concert music—not only songs but also operas and instrumental music—with the melodies and rhythms that he recorded and transcribed during his field trips.

BARTÓK AND HUNGARIAN IDENTITY

During Bartók's childhood, what would become Hungary was part of the Austro-Hungarian Empire—the diminished descendant of the Holy Roman Empire, which had encompassed virtually all of central Europe from the tenth through the eighteenth centuries. The empire had always been a relatively loose confederation of small political entities ruled by kings, princes, dukes, and other royalty. By the late nineteenth century, the empire was a patchwork of numerous ethnic groups, with two governments—one for Austria and the western part of the empire; the other for Hungary and the east. The emperor ruled over both in theory, but not always in practice. Like the division of the empire into two largely independent entities, the emergence of "official" languages throughout the empire as alternatives to German was a further indication of the erosion of central authority.

Nevertheless, Vienna remained the capital, politically and culturally. Its influence was evident throughout the empire, especially in urban centers such as Prague and Budapest. Just as Russians looked to France for cultural guidance, so did the middle and upper classes in provincial capitals follow Vienna's lead. In Budapest, German and Jewish musicians were prominent in musical life; so were the gypsy bands that purported to play authentic Hungarian music.

Bartók was raised on the outskirts of the empire. He was born in a small town that is now part of Romania. After his father's death in 1888, his family moved several times, finally settling in Pozsony—now Bratislava, the capital of Slovakia—where he gave his

Béla Bartók

Fast Facts

- *Dates:* 1881–1945
- *Place:* Hungary/Romania
- *Reasons to remember:* The greatest Hungarian composer in the first half of the twentieth century and a pioneer ethnomusicologist

first public recital. He went to Budapest at eighteen to receive formal training in piano and composition. Musically, he was at first drawn to the works of German composers, particularly the modernist Richard Strauss. The developmental procedures found in eighteenth- and nineteenth-century Austro-German music would remain a prominent feature of his large-scale compositions throughout his career.

Despite growing up some distance from Budapest, Bartók's interest in authentic Hungarian folk music remained latent until his chance encounter with Lidi Dósa. It blossomed almost overnight. The following year he met Zoltan Kodály, a fellow Hungarian composer whose enthusiasm for folk music matched his own and whose training complemented Bartók's. His field trips with and without Kodály over the next several years took him throughout the eastern part of the empire to remote regions of Hungary, into what is now Slovakia, Romania, Bulgaria, and eventually even to Turkey. "Bulgarian" rhythm would become Bartók's term for the asymmetrical rhythms that occur in the folk music of the Balkans, which he would adapt to his own music.

Bartók's fieldwork represented a breakthrough in the collection, preservation, and transformation of folk music. His goal was to locate national identity in this music, so his objective was to distinguish it from more mainstream urban music. He brought to this task his own remarkable musical abilities and a brand-new technology—sound recording. As a result, he was able to transcribe the music he collected with an unprecedented accuracy.

BARTÓK, FOLK MUSIC, AND ART COMPOSITION

The composer's deep immersion in folk music had idealistic, personal, and practical implications. Like oth-er folklorists active in the first part of the century, he felt that by collecting this music, he was preserving a heritage that would soon be lost and providing a firm foundation for a national art music. Sorting through the music that he had collected was an intellectual problem that intrigued him throughout his life and was a task left incomplete at his death. Most significantly, Bartók fully absorbed the music that he studied. From the 1910s to the end of his career, virtually all of his music showed qualities that identified it as the work of an eastern European composer.

No major composer left a more comprehensive record of involvement with the folk music of his homeland than Bartók. His legacy includes field recordings and transcriptions of folk music throughout the eastern part of the empire; compositions that show the full spectrum of possibility when blending folk and art music—from simple settings to abstract compositions; essays on the connection between the two; and his recordings of his own music.

In a 1941 lecture entitled "The Relation between Contemporary Hungarian Art Music and Folk Music," Bartók enumerated five levels of folk influence on art music, which reflect varying degrees of the balance between folk and art elements. The most folklike was presenting the folk melody with a simple, unobtrusive accompaniment. The more artful end of the spectrum involved imitating specific features—such as particular scales or rhythms—or evoking the spirit of the music without referencing folk materials directly. We hear an example of Bartók's individual fusion of folk and contemporary art elements in the second movement from *Music for Strings, Percussion, and Celesta.*

MUSIC FOR STRINGS, PERCUSSION, AND CELESTA

Celesta

Bartók's *Music for Strings, Percussion, and Celesta* was commissioned by Paul Sacher, the conductor of the Basel Chamber Orchestra and an immensely wealthy man who would commission works from several leading European composers, including Stravinsky. Bartók completed the work in 1936; the premiere took place in January 1937. There are four movements, in a slow/fast/slow/fast sequence. The work has an unusual scoring: full string orchestra, divided into two sections that

answer back and forth, plus a large array of percussion instruments, harp, piano, and celesta (a keyboard instrument that produces a bell-like sound). There are no winds or brass.

THE SPIRIT OF HUNGARIAN MUSIC

What's remarkable about works like the *Music for Strings, Percussion, and Celesta,* where the national element is present in spirit only, is how seamlessly the folk elements are integrated into the fabric of the piece. The energetic rhythms, the percussive sound world that enhances them, the catchy motive-based themes, the novel effects, and the frequent—if incessantly varied—repetition invest the music with accessible and interesting points of entry. All reflect the inspiration, if not the direct imitation, of folk music. The music sounds modern, Hungarian, and personal in large part because Bartók did not have to embed the folk elements into common practice. Rather, he was able to use them as a springboard for a unique sound: one with an eastern European identity.

As a result, Bartók *was* Hungarian music to the concertgoing world between the wars, and even more so in the two decades after his death. His music was far better known than his colleague Kodály's and that of every other non-Russian composer from eastern Europe. It remains a stellar example of a nationalistic music from the early twentieth century.

mickey mousing The close synchronization of music with on-screen action

Sergei Prokofiev and the Art of Composing for Film

In the film industry, **mickey mousing** refers to the close synchronization of music with on-screen action. The term came into use because the Walt Disney Studios were the first to coordinate film and sound track with great precision. As early as "The Skeleton Dance" (1929), Disney's first *Silly Symphony,* there was almost flawless integration between the music—which in this instance featured an adaptation of nineteenth-century Norwegian composer Edvard Grieg's "March of the Trolls"—and the movements of the characters. In this respect, Disney was far ahead of conventional filmmakers.

LISTEN FURTHER

"The Skeleton Dance" (1929)

Takeaway point: Watch for the mickey mousing, in this early Disney animation, in the YouTube playlist.

Walt Disney's work was extraordinarily popular in Russia during the 1930s: he was the only American filmmaker honored at the first Moscow Film Festival in 1935. Two Russian artists were among those who had visited the Disney Studios in Hollywood to witness the production process firsthand. The film director Sergei Eisenstein spent time there in 1930. Eight years later, the composer-pianist Sergei Prokofiev also visited and spent a day with Disney at his home.

LISTEN FURTHER

"Peter and the Wolf"

Takeaway point: Watch a dramatization of Disney's meeting with Prokofiev, in the YouTube playlist.

Eisenstein's and Prokofiev's direct contact with the working methods at the Disney Studios would have a profound influence on their first collaboration on a sound film, the 1938 epic *Alexander Nevsky.*

MUSIC AND FILM IN THE EARLY TWENTIETH CENTURY

Music *inspired by* cinema developed more rapidly than music *for* cinema. Although Debussy had predicted in 1913 that "apply[ing] to pure music the techniques of cinematography" would be the "one way of reviving the taste for symphonic music" and clearly followed his own advice in his compositions, he never composed a film score.

During Debussy's lifetime, original film scores by established composers were rare. Far more common were printed anthologies filled with stock musical snippets—either original or borrowed from classical compositions—for common dramatic situations: a villain doing a dastardly deed, a hero riding to the rescue, the romantic moment between the hero and the fair maiden he saved. These were often based on or influenced by music used for melodrama. During the silent film era, theaters engaged pianists, organists, even orchestras to supply this music; typically, they played continuously throughout the film.

Musical backgrounds often disappeared during the action in the first talking films; film musicals were the major exception. One reason was the relatively primitive state of the technology. Initially, music had to be recorded while the scene was being shot, which presented severe logistical difficulties and constrained film editing, because everything had to be planned in advance.

> Music *inspired by* cinema developed more rapidly than music *for* cinema.

Only in the early 1930s did it become possible to dub in sound after filming. Composers quickly took advantage of the new technology. In Hollywood, the trendsetter was Max Steiner. Steiner had emigrated from his native Austria to Hollywood by way of London and New York, where he acquired considerable experience as a conductor and orchestrator-arranger of musical stage productions. Shortly after his arrival in Hollywood, he composed the score to the 1933 film *King Kong*. It was novel and stunningly successful, and almost overnight it became the model for Hollywood sound tracks. Steiner and other European-trained film composers adapted Romanticism—complete with Wagnerian leitmotifs—and impressionism to film scoring.

Film composers in Europe often charted a different, more experimental path. Among the most significant was Sergei Prokofiev, whose collaborations with Eisenstein would prove to be among the most influential film scores of the 1930s and 1940s.

© Image courtesy of The Advertising Archives

Max Steiner composed the score to the 1933 film *King Kong*.

SERGEI PROKOFIEV

Josef Stalin died on March 5, 1953, after almost thirty years of increasingly brutal rule of the Soviet Union. On that same day, the composer Sergei Prokofiev also passed away. It was the ultimate irony in the life of a composer whose career, like his music, was laced with irony. Among the composers of his time, Prokofiev stands apart, because of the complex crosscurrents among personal ambition, patriotism, and political circumstances that shaped his career decisions.

Sergei Prokofiev
Fast Facts

- *Dates:* 1891–1953
- *Place:* Ukraine
- *Reasons to remember:* One of the two greatest Soviet composers during the Stalinist era

© Lebrecht/ColouriserAL

Prokofiev was born in the Ukraine, at that time part of the Russian Empire, and grew up in a relatively privileged environment. He received his musical education in St. Petersburg during a time of political and artistic ferment. Almost from the start of his career, he sought to pursue his own provocative path as a composer and pianist: among his early piano works are his first concerto, which established him as a major talent, a work entitled "Diabolic Suggestion," and a series of several small solo piano pieces called "Sarcasms."

Shortly after the Russian Revolution in 1917, Prokofiev decided to leave Russia, as his initial enthusiasm for the uprising gave way to the realization that the new Russia would not be a congenial place for artists.

Accordingly, he left for the United States the following year, where he met his Spanish-born wife, an opera singer. They moved to Europe in 1922, where they used Paris as a home base, and married the following year. Prokofiev toured frequently as a pianist and composed prolifically, in virtually all genres, including opera, ballet, orchestral music, and piano music.

Prokofiev was dissatisfied with his situation in the West. During his time away from his homeland, he saw himself as professionally overshadowed by the Russian pianist-composer Sergei Rachmaninoff in the United States and Stravinsky in Paris. Reciprocal contact with the Soviet Union, which began around the time of his move to Paris, led to an invitation to perform in 1927, and eventually to his return in 1936.

Prokofiev was aware of the political changes in the Soviet Union, particularly as they affected artists: around the time of his return, he publicly declared that he was simplifying his compositional approach, which would bring it in line with "socialist realism." Patriotic sentiments and homesickness were apparently other factors in his decision. He wrote to friends that he needed to "hear the Russian language in my ears." Perhaps he also saw what he thought was an opportunity to be top dog: Dmitri Shostakovich, the most esteemed Soviet composer during the 1930s, had just fallen out of favor with the cultural bureaucrats.

Whatever his motivation for returning, it is clear in retrospect that Prokofiev's decision to return to his homeland made the last years of his life increasingly difficult. The praise and support given his music during his years abroad diminished dramatically once he returned. He soon relinquished his passport, had performances canceled, and received critical reviews in official publications. After World War II, he lived a nightmare: he had works banned, had to write a public "apology" for straying from the goals of socialist realism, and learned from his sons that Lina, his first wife, whom he had left in 1941, had been sentenced to twenty years in a labor camp. It was a dismal end to a career that had seemed so promising earlier in the century.

Aside from *Peter and the Wolf*, which he composed in 1936, the work of the late 1930s that attracted the most favorable reviews both in and outside the Soviet Union was his film score to *Alexander Nevsky*. It involved a new kind of collaboration between composer and film director.

ALEXANDER NEVSKY

In the face of Hitler's rise to power in 1933 and his escalating hostile threats, the Soviet government commissioned a propaganda film disguised as a historical drama.

Alexander Nevsky celebrates the achievements of Prince Alexander, who saved Novgorod, a city in northwest Russia, by reaching an agreement with the Mongols (who had swept through much of Russia from the east) and defeating two invaders from the West (the Swedes and a crusading band of Teutonic Knights).

The climax of the film is the 1242 "Battle on the Ice," in which an army of foot soldiers defeated the mounted crusaders. The scene, which lasts about thirty minutes, is a thinly disguised allegory. Almost seven centuries after the 1242 encounter, Russians again faced the threat of invasion by a technologically more

Battle scene from *Alexander Nevsky*. "We did it before, and we can do it again."

advanced German enemy. Its message to the Russian people was, in effect, "We did it before, and we can do it again."

The film was released in 1938 and received favorable press within the Soviet Union and in the West. However, when Germany and the Soviet Union signed a nonaggression pact in August 1939, the film was abruptly withdrawn from circulation. It would be re-released about two years later, when Germany invaded the Soviet Union.

In creating the film, Eisenstein and Prokofiev enjoyed an extremely close working relationship, which resulted in unprecedented integration of film and music. Each admired the other's work. Prokofiev stated that

Eisenstein was Russia's finest film director, and Eisenstein, who was knowledgeable about music, commented on how quickly and easily Prokofiev supplied music for recently shot scenes. Prokofiev composed to rough cuts—footage with only preliminary editing—during the shooting of the film, and Eisenstein often synchronized his edits with Prokofiev's music. One product of this working method was a fusion of image and sound, where they combine to largely replace dialogue as the narrative element. This innovative approach is used to great effect in the battle on the ice.

The musical excerpt presented here is the music that underscores the opening of the battle, from the time when the Russian lookouts spy the Teutonic enemy in the distance to the moment they engage. This first part of the battle scene lasts over six minutes. There is virtually no dialogue. Instead, Eisenstein uses Prokofiev's music and his own montage technique (in montage, fragmentary clips are edited together to form a continuous whole) to build almost unbearable tension that is released only with the shouts of the combatants. Prokofiev's music begins ominously with sustained chords spread from extremely high to extremely low. As the camera shifts from the Russians to the Teutonic Knights, Prokofiev parodies medieval chant, first played by horns made to sound ancient, then sung. A relentless rhythm that carries through the final part of the scene accompanies the cavalry as they begin their advance. Several motives, mostly in a low range, add to the suspense: as the forces draw closer, the cuts between shots become faster and the motives pile on top of each other until the music gives way to the thunder of hooves and the sounds of the battle.

This scene dramatically highlights the way in which music and on-screen action work synergistically to convey the emotional impact of the scene. Despite Eisenstein's use of montage to create opposition and tension, the scene falls flat without sound. Although Prokofiev soon arranged the music for *Alexander Nevsky* into a cantata for concert performance, his music has considerably more impact when heard as part of the film. This functional concept has influenced several generations of film composers.

Eisenstein and Prokofiev would collaborate once again during the 1940s on a trilogy about Ivan the Terrible. The first film won the Stalin Prize, and the second film was banned. Eisenstein died in 1948, before he finished the third and final film; most of it was confiscated and destroyed.

From the People, for the People: Twentieth-Century Nationalism

The four musical examples of nationalism considered in this unit highlight both their composers' common ground and differences in approach with each other and with nineteenth-century nationalism. The works connected to each other and to earlier nationalistic music in that all were grounded in some way in the music of peoples within their homeland and concerned with reaching out to those who inspired the music. Yet the composers were also in tune with current developments in modern music, and their music bears evidence of that. All four composers found a balance between modernity and accessibility. The music is innovative, but it contains familiar and appealing features: vigorous rhythms, tuneful motives, restructured common practice chords, and a variety of percussion instruments. In this way, these composers turned back to the people, even as many of their peers seemed to be turning their back on a larger audience in the pursuit of their art.

The progressive nationalism of these and other like-minded composers represented an important new direction in concert music during the 1930s and into the 1940s. However, this trend largely disappeared after World War II, with the increasing influence of serial composition—both Stravinsky and Copland would adopt serial techniques during the 1950s—and the continuing expansion of musical frontiers by members of the avant-garde. We explore several of these new developments in the next unit.

UNIT 21
SOUND FRONTIERS

Learning Outcomes

After reading this unit, you will be able to do the following:

LO1 Explain the place of John Cage and Milton Babbitt in the postwar American avant-garde.

LO2 Describe Krzysztof Penderecki's work in the avant-garde's exploration of alternative pitch constructs.

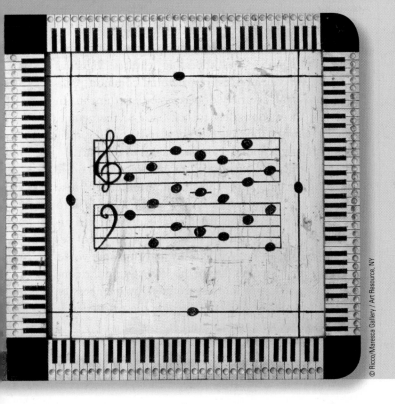

© Ricco/Maresca Gallery / Art Resource, NY

IN 1946, GERMAN music critic Wolfgang Steinecke founded what came to be called the Darmstadt summer courses. They soon became a leading center for avant-garde music, attracting composers, performers, scholars, and critics from both sides of the Atlantic. Although the lecturers who presented at the summer courses over the next two decades represented widely divergent trends, the dominant figures were four Europeans: the Italian composers Bruno Maderna and Luigi Nono, the German composer Karlheinz Stockhausen, and the French composer Pierre Boulez. Known as the "Darmstadt School" (of composition) after a 1957 lecture by Nono, they saw their music as the continuation of the Second Viennese School and were determined to extend serial techniques in inventive ways, including serializing not just pitch but also other parameters, including duration and dynamics.

Serialism, although dominant, was just one of several new directions among the midcentury avant-garde. In this unit, we sample these new directions in three works composed between 1946 and 1964. These works convey some sense of the range of innovation—in sound, pitch, rhythm, texture, and every other musical parameter—produced by the avant-garde during the years after World War II.

CHAPTER 48

The American Avant-Garde after 1945

"It isn't often that one begins preparing a new piano work for performance with a trip to the hardware store."

In an article in the February 1958 issue of *High Fidelity*, Milton Babbitt bemoaned the cultural isolation of those who created what he called "'serious,' 'advanced,' contemporary music." He went so far as to suggest that composers return the favor:

> I dare suggest that the composer would do himself and his music an immediate and eventual service by total, resolute, and voluntary withdrawal from this public world to one of private performance and electronic media, with its very real possibility of complete elimination of the public and social aspects of musical composition. By so doing, the separation between the domains would be defined beyond any possibility of confusion of categories, and the composer would be free to pursue a private life of professional achievement, as opposed to a public life of unprofessional compromise and exhibitionism.

He compared the composer of "advanced" music (of which he was a leading exemplar) to pure mathematicians or theoretical physicists, who explore the frontiers of knowledge without much regard for its practical application. He called on universities to support such composers, just as they support other specialized and advanced areas of inquiry.

Babbitt was part of a musical avant-garde that was extremely active in the generation after World War II. Avant-garde music exploded in all directions,

Did You Know?

Members of the alternative rock band Sonic Youth adapted John Cage's "prepared piano" techniques to guitar and also recorded two of his works on their 1999 double album *SYR4*.

testing the limits and expanding the possibilities of virtually every musical parameter and creating novel combinations of features. Most fundamentally, this meant exploring the extremes of compositional control, from the elimination of the performer (via electronic sound synthesis) to the virtual elimination of the composer, as in Cage's "silent piece" introduced in Chapter 1. However, as varied as they were in methodology, the avant-garde shared a common purpose: to explore and expand the boundaries of musical practice.

LO1 Innovations of the Postwar Avant-Garde

In the *Crystal Reference Encyclopedia*, a 1911 publication that comprised the basic entries for the *Cambridge Encyclopedia*, the definition of music begins like this: "An orderly succession of sounds of definite pitch, whose constituents are melody, harmony, and rhythm." This definition is typical of those found in dictionaries and encyclopedias from the first part of the twentieth century. It would be obsolete a half century later, principally because of the efforts of the postwar avant-garde. We survey some of these boundary-stretching developments next.

New Resources, New Sounds

The most immediately apparent innovations of the postwar avant-garde were an array of new sounds that came from four principal sources:

1. *Innovative performance techniques on conventional instruments.* Some examples of these techniques

multiphonics For wind players, playing more than one pitch simultaneously on an instrument designed to play one note at a time

tone cluster Effect produced by striking the piano keys with a fist or other objects

musique concrète Music created by recording sounds not produced by musical instruments, extracting sound snippets, and subjecting them to various modifications

white noise A broad band of multiple frequencies sounding simultaneously

Composers like Cage "prepared" the instrument by inserting various everyday materials between the strings.

© New York Times Co./Getty Images

are **multiphonics** for wind players (playing more than one pitch simultaneously on an instrument designed to play one note at a time); and **tone clusters** produced by striking the piano keys with a fist or other objects, or guitarlike chords produced by strumming the piano strings. Some of these techniques were not new; composers had made use of them before 1945. However, they became far more common and far more varied in the decades after World War II.

2. *Radical modifications of conventional instruments.* A more extreme version of the previous practice was altering an instrument so drastically that it produced a completely different range of timbres. No instrument underwent more drastic alternation than the grand piano: composers like Cage "prepared" the instrument by inserting various everyday materials, such as nuts, bolts, and spoons, between the strings.

3. *The invention of new instruments.* The most innovative new instrument of the postwar era was the programmable synthesizer, a fully electronic instrument. The first was the RCA Mark II sound synthesizer, which came into use in 1957; it filled an entire room. Rapid technological improvements resulted in a modest-sized instrument that

could be used for performance in real time by the early 1970s. No other sound source developed in the twentieth century has had such a widespread impact.

4. *The use of "found" sounds.* Almost as soon as the tape recorder became a commercially viable product, composers began recording sounds not produced by musical instruments, extracting sound snippets, sometimes subjecting them to various modifications, and combining them. Pierre Schaeffer, the French radio broadcaster who assumed a leading role in developing these procedures, called this process *musique concrète*.

The new sounds that composers asked for or produced themselves represented only one dimension of their exploration of virgin musical territory. They went hand in hand with innovations in pitch, rhythm, and other musical parameters.

INNOVATIONS IN PITCH AND RHYTHM

Avant-garde composers continued to move away from the mainstream in their handling of pitch and rhythm, to the point that they often severed any sense of connection between traditional practice and their work. Here are some of the more radical departures in pitch and rhythm:

1. Dissolving conventional pitch organization through a variety of procedures that included these elements:

   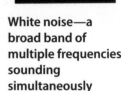

   - The use of **white noise** (a broad band of multiple frequencies sounding simultaneously)
   - The production of sounds with a sense of high and low, but without definite pitch
   - Tone clusters that fill in the gaps between half-steps
   - Continuous pitch change, ranging from rapid glissandi to slow, almost imperceptible movement up or down

   White noise—a broad band of multiple frequencies sounding simultaneously

   © iStockphoto.com/Diane Diederich

2. The use of wide intervals and extreme registral contrast (moving quickly between pitches in a low register and pitches in a high register) to weaken or eliminate any sense of melodic continuity

3. Rhythms so rapid that it is all but impossible to distinguish discrete pitches

4. Rhythms so slow that no underlying pulse is evident

5. Rhythms so varied and nonrepetitive that no underlying metrical organization is apparent

6. Harmonies that are simply the coincidences of pitches sounded simultaneously rather than chords selected from a preexisting or predetermined harmonic language

Other elements also underwent considerable expansion of possibilities: textures ranged from single lines to dense clusters of sound or free interpretation of parts played by performers at their discretion; dynamic change ranged from virtually unchanging to extremely rapid change.

Because of these radical extensions of every musical parameter and because repetition, especially regular repetition, was the infrequent exception rather than the rule, the forms of avant-garde compositions seldom resolve into familiar patterns. Instead, the majority of works seem to be through-composed: music that continuously evolves or changes from beginning to end.

Cage and the Prepared Piano

It isn't often that one begins preparing a new piano work for performance with a trip to the hardware store. However, the score to John Cage's *Sonatas and Interludes* lists the materials required to "prepare" a piano: an assortment of bolts of varying sizes and lengths, screws, plastic, and rubber, to be inserted among the strings. The score also details precisely where these materials are to be placed inside the piano. With this preparation, the sound of the piano was modified so radically by the **prepared piano** technique that it became in effect a different instrument.

JOHN CAGE

In a conversation with Peter Yates, a patron of both Arnold Schoenberg and John Cage, Schoenberg described Cage as "not a composer, but an inventor—of genius." Cage had studied with Schoenberg during the mid-1930s, mostly in classes but also privately on a few occasions. He revered the man as the greatest living composer but realized that his abilities did not align well with Schoenberg's expectations for his students. Cage acknowledged to Schoenberg that he had "no

feeling for harmony," a self-assessment with which Schoenberg concurred. Although he continued to admire him personally, Cage found himself increasingly at odds philosophically with Schoenberg and left rather abruptly to take work in Seattle as an accompanist for dance classes at the Cornish School. There he met Merce Cunningham, a dancer and choreographer, and one of the pioneers in modern dance. They quickly formed a close professional and personal relationship that would last until Cage's death.

Cage's work with dancers, and with Cunningham in particular, stimulated his already active interest in sound and time. Among his early experiments with sound were a percussion ensemble that played "found" instruments like a brake drum; a work for radio broadcast scored for piano, cymbals, and record players playing test tones at varying speeds; and his first experiments at preparing a piano.

John Cage

Fast Facts

- *Dates:* 1912–1992

- *Place:* United States

- *Reasons to remember:* A profound and influential musical thinker who challenged the most basic assumptions about what music is

© Betty Freeman/Lebrecht

In these early compositions, Cage was, in effect, inventing new sounds and new sound combinations—or at the very least, incorporating them into a musical experience. His sonic explorations follow the lead of Henry Cowell, the great American experimentalist whom Cage would describe as "the open sesame for new music in America." Cage had worked with Cowell in the early 1930s; it was Cowell who had suggested that he seek out Schoenberg.

Cage had encountered non-Western music in Cowell's classes; contact with an East Indian musician in 1946 rekindled his interest, which would soon lead to an embrace of Eastern aesthetics and spirituality. This experience introduced him to an ancient idea in both West and East: the purpose of music is to induce a state of tranquility, thus opening the door

prepared piano John Cage's technique of changing the piano's timbre by inserting objects among its strings

to the divine. His major work from the late 1940s, the *Sonatas and Interludes* for prepared piano, expresses this goal. It is a large group of short pieces; a full performance lasts about an hour. We hear Sonata V next.

The purpose of music is to induce a state of tranquility, thus opening the door to the divine.

Cage composed *Sonatas and Interludes* over a three-year period, between 1946 and 1948. The entire work consists of sixteen short sonatas, grouped into sets of four and separated by interludes. Although the individual movements are short, the work as a whole lasts over an hour. *Sonatas and Interludes* was Cage's first work to reflect an alternative conception of the function of music: to quiet and sober the mind.

The piano requires extensive preparation: forty-five notes are prepared, with screws and bolts, plus fifteen pieces of rubber, four pieces of plastic, six nuts, and one eraser. The sounds produced by the prepared piano are more like those of Eastern percussion instruments than like those of a piano.

LISTEN UP!

CD 5:13
Cage, Sonata V from *Sonatas and Interludes* (1946–1948)

Takeaway point: A piano that doesn't sound like a piano

Style: Avant-garde

Form: AABB

Genre: Short piano piece

Instrument: Prepared piano

Context: Cage stretching the sound frontiers of the avant-garde

In its novel timbres, shifting rhythms, absence of harmony, and static forms, Cage's piece represents a radical reconception of music and musical organization. In these respects, it bears more resemblance to a contemporary dance track than it does to the music of most of Cage's contemporaries or predecessors.

CAGE AND CONTEMPORARY MUSIC

Many commentators regard *Sonatas and Interludes* as Cage's first mature work. It also signaled the beginning of Cage's passionate interest in Far Eastern culture, which would in turn directly influence his music. Around the time of the premiere of *Sonatas and Interludes*, Cage began studying Zen Buddhism and immersing himself in Japanese culture. In 1950, he received a copy of the *I Ching*, a classic Chinese text, which inspired him to introduce chance into the performance of his music, which he called **chance music**: he would compose segments, but the order in which the segments were performed depended on coin tossing, according to the method prescribed in the *I Ching*.

Cage would compose segments, but the order in which the segments were performed depended on coin tossing.

Cage's subsequent works and his writings, which were even more influential than his music, challenged the most basic assumptions about music and art. They compelled listeners and readers who took them seriously to expand their minds as well as their ears. Few twentieth-century artists in any field of activity have had a more pervasive impact on American culture than Cage.

Milton Babbitt, Total Serialism, and Electronic Music

Shortly after the time that he ceased studying with Schoenberg, Cage wrote that the music of the future would bear "a definite relation to Schoenberg's twelve-tone system." In the 1940s, he continued to develop this idea, speculating in an article in *Modern Music* that composers would create "sound rows" in a manner analogous to the serial organization of pitches, and finding similarities between rows and Indian ragas as he immersed himself in Indian music. About the same time as Cage's pronouncement, Milton Babbitt (b. 1916) heard a performance of Schoenberg's recently completed Fourth Quartet. Babbitt recalled almost a half century later that the experience "certainly changed my life."

MILTON BABBITT

Babbitt approached Schoenberg's serial music and the system that generated it systematically, not speculatively. By 1946, he had completed a doctoral dissertation entitled "The Function of Set Structure in the Twelve-Tone System," which was not accepted by the music department at Princeton, although it was the first thorough analysis of Schoenberg's methods. He prepared the dissertation with the advice of a member of the mathematics faculty at Princeton. To describe procedures and possible arrangements of pitches, Babbitt frequently borrowed terms from mathematics: the title of his dissertation is evidence of that.

Babbitt's application of mathematical terms and concepts was a natural outgrowth of his inclination and training. His father was an actuary, and Milton had originally enrolled at the University of Pennsylvania intending to major in mathematics. He later transferred to New York University to concentrate on music.

Milton Babbitt

Fast Facts

- *Dates*: b. 1916

- *Place*: United States

- *Reasons to remember*: Composer on the cutting edge of the theory and practice of twelve-tone composition

© Kate Mount/Lebrecht Music & Arts

Babbitt's musical direction in the 1930s represented a drastic departure from his early interests, which were in popular music, musical theater, and jazz. He had grown up in Mississippi, where he played the clarinet, arranged songs for dance orchestras, and wrote his own music: one of his popular songs, written when he was thirteen, won a contest sponsored by a popular bandleader. Although he has remained an enthusiastic follower of musical theater—and was Stephen Sondheim's composition teacher—he chose to follow a different path, one that stimulated his considerable intellect and enabled him to merge his interests in music and mathematics.

TOTAL SERIALISM

In 1947, the year after he submitted his dissertation, Babbitt composed a set of three piano pieces that began applying serial techniques to duration and dynamics. This would ultimately lead to a compositional process usually identified as total serialism.

In **total serialism**, every variable, including but not limited to dynamics, duration, and rhythm—not just pitch—is potentially susceptible to some form of precompositional planning. In an article entitled "Twelve-Tone Rhythmic Structure and the Electronic Medium," published when he began work on *Ensembles for Synthesizer*, Babbitt demonstrated ways in which duration could be organized serially through a procedure, which Babbitt called "time-point sets," analogous to the serial organization of pitch. The possibilities for coordination among the parameters are virtually limitless: the sequence of events in one parameter can dictate the sequence in another; they can unfold at different rates; and they can undergo numerous permutations, individually and collectively.

ELECTRONIC COMPOSITION

Because he applied serial procedures to pitch, dynamics, and duration, Babbitt's music for conventional instruments required such a degree of precision that it challenged the skill of even the most advanced performers. For that reason, and because it offered a virtual orchestra of timbres, Babbitt welcomed the opportunity to work on the newly developed RCA Mark II sound synthesizer, even though creating music on it was an arduous task.

In a 1985 interview, long after the synthesizer had been superseded by much more flexible, powerful, and accessible devices, Babbitt described working on the Mark II:

> What I do is go to this large machine and to a keyboard, but not in the sense of a piano keyboard, in the sense of a typewriter keyboard. I code in my

chance music
Twentieth-century avant-garde music that introduced the element of chance into composition and performance, such as determining the order of performance through the toss of a coin

total serialism Music in which every variable, including but not limited to dynamics, duration, and rhythm—not just pitch—is potentially susceptible to some form of precompositional planning

instructions for every aspect of my music, every single element and dimension of the musical event. I have to tell this dumb machine everything I want by way of the musical result—every aspect, every component of every sound, the pitch, the loudness, the timbre, the envelope, the shape of every single event. It is a long laborious procedure because, remember, I am doing everything. This is a dumb machine. Not only does it not do any composing, but it does less composing than a performer would be obliged to do. When I am through, the sound goes onto the tape, and I record it, on tape, directly from the synthesizer. I also hear it on speakers as I am creating it. And when I walk into that studio with my composition in my hand, I eventually walk out with the finished performance and a tape under my arm.[*]

> *"I have to tell this dumb machine everything I want by way of the musical result."*—Milton Babbitt, on composing on the Mark II synthesizer

Through this arduous process, Babbitt produced music that was revolutionary in every conceivable way. We hear an excerpt from *Ensembles for Synthesizer* next. Like the work as a whole, the excerpt features an extremely active musical surface that changes constantly in every parameter. Melodic fragments (such as the one with which the excerpt begins) occur periodically, but they are not repeated. Indeed, literal repetition is either absent or not readily apparent in Babbitt's music. Similarly, there is no obvious rhythmic continuity, in the form of a steady pulse, nor is there textural consistency. As a result, the excerpt and the work as a whole do not resolve into a familiar, discernible formal stereotype. There are no orientation points; instead, there is a dazzling array of sonic events that stream past the ear.

BABBITT AND THE INTERNATIONAL AVANT-GARDE

Babbitt was in the forefront of a small group of com-

---

* Anne Swartz and Milton Babbitt, "Milton Babbitt on Milton Babbitt," *American Music* 3, no. 4 (Winter 1985): 467–473; available at http://www.jstor.org/stable/3051833.

LISTEN UP!

CD 5:14

Babbitt, *Ensembles for Synthesizer*, excerpt (1964)

Takeaway point: New timbres from a synthesizer

Style: Avant-garde/serialism

Form: Through-composed

Genre: Electronic music

Instruments: Synthesizer

Context: Composition using a synthesizer for unparalleled precision

posers who helped erase the last vestiges of America's cultural inferiority complex. European values continued to shape high culture in the United States through the nineteenth century and well into the twentieth. America's contribution to musical life in the Western world during the early twentieth century was significant and far reaching, but there was one domain where Americans had had little impact: the most prestigious direction of the avant-garde.

In the first half of the twentieth century, Schoenberg was the composers' composer. Even those composers whose music embraced a radically different aesthetic held him in high esteem. As a result, the most prestigious branch of the postwar avant-garde was the group of composers who followed the lead of Schoenberg and his disciple Webern.

In his compositions, writings, teaching, and lecturing, Babbitt has been on the cutting edge of the theory and practice of twelve-tone composition and has led the way in extending its potential for musical organization.

During its gestation period in the 1920s, serialism was centralized in Vienna. However, after World War II, serialism, in its various manifestations, provided "advanced" music an international musical language. Babbitt's stature in this insular but culturally powerful community of practitioners ensured that Americans were no longer second-class musical citizens in any domain. Babbitt is an American composer mainly because he resides in the United States. Unlike the music of Ives, Gershwin, Copland, and even Cage, Babbitt's music shows no obvious evidence of regionalism—nothing of an "American" sound or style. His charter membership in the exclusive community of post-Webern serialists secured American representation in the most "advanced" musical circles during the mid-twentieth century.

CHAPTER 49

The Avant-Garde in Europe

"Penderecki's work provides a direct path to the subconscious."

A top-selling album for most of August and September 1958 was Van Cliburn's recording of Tchaikovsky's Piano Concerto No. 1, recorded with Kiril Kondrashin and the Moscow Philharmonic Orchestra. The previous spring, Cliburn had won first prize in the piano division of the first International Tchaikovsky Competition, held in Moscow and sponsored by the Soviet government. The Soviets were so confident that a Russian pianist would win again that the judges asked Nikita Khrushchev, the Soviet premier at the time, whether they could name Cliburn the winner. Khrushchev asked them whether Cliburn was the best. When they affirmed that he was, Khrushchev said, "Then give him the prize." Cliburn returned to the United States a hero, receiving a ticker-tape parade in New York. *Time* magazine put him on its cover, an unprecedented honor for a young classical musician.

Cliburn's victory came at the height of the Cold War, when tensions between the United States and the Soviet Union were at their peak. With the detonation of the first hydrogen bomb in 1952 by the United States and the subsequent development of the bomb in the Soviet Union, the threat of nuclear annihilation hung over the world like a giant mushroom cloud. Perhaps to channel their aggression into less destructive outlets, the two sides competed in virtually every domain, including the arts.

Culture and the Cold War

Even before the surrender of Germany in May 1945, the wartime alliance between the United States and

Did You Know?

Producer/arranger George Martin adapted avant-garde string techniques for The Beatles' recording of "A Day in the Life."

Western European countries and the Soviet Union had begun to deteriorate. After the war, the Soviet government quickly expanded its sphere of influence over much of Eastern Europe: Poland, Czechoslovakia, Hungary, Romania, and Bulgaria, and the Soviet Zone in Germany, which became East Germany in 1949.

After the Korean War (1950–1953), the Cold War was fought everywhere except the battlefield. The East and West competed in numerous arenas. In technology, the biggest contest was the race to space, and beyond. The Russians won that with their 1957 launch of *Sputnik*, the first satellite to orbit the earth. Beginning in 1952, when the Soviet Union first fielded a team, the Olympic Games were a quadrennial competition for world sports supremacy. The Soviet Union won the medal count in both winter and summer in 1956, 1960, and 1964.

Sputnik

The Cultural War

Culture, especially high culture, was another battleground. Almost as soon as the war ended in Europe, OMGUS—the Office of the Military Government of the United States—took control of German musical life. They restored music by composers whose works had been banned under the Nazis, suppressed composers sympathetic to the Nazis, promoted American music, and helped underwrite the Darmstadt summer courses in new music, initiated in 1946 by Wolfgang Steinecke to foster the teaching of modern composition and promote premieres of new works. The CIA played an even bigger role in the promotion of avant-garde music in the 1950s and 1960s, funding or helping to fund numerous organizations that promoted avant-garde music. As Alex Ross, music critic and contributor to the *New Yorker* magazine has noted, "'Advanced' styles symbolized the freedom to do what one wanted . . . the liberty to experiment . . . to be esoteric or familiar." The most prominent of the CIA-supported organizations was the Congress for Cultural Freedom, which sponsored activity in all the arts. The CIA formed the organization in 1950 as a covert operation to counteract the impression among left-leaning intellectuals and artists that socialism and communism provided better opportunities for artists and thinkers. The involvement of the CIA was revealed only in 1967.

In practice, freedom of expression within the communist bloc in Europe depended to a large extent on distance from Soviet control. Among the most artistically liberated countries was Poland, whose cultural policies adhered to Stalin's socialist realism policy in the early 1950s but opened up after Stalin's death, particularly after the "Polish thaw" of October 1956, which led to a less hard-line government and a loosening of the ties with the Soviet Union. That same month, the Union of Polish Composers presented the first Warsaw Autumn, an international festival of contemporary music, with substantial support from the government. Poland assumed a leading role in promoting artistic freedom in the Eastern Bloc, partly in response to the avant-garde activities in Western Europe. Among the beneficiaries of the more open policies of the Polish government was the composer Krzysztof Penderecki.

The involvement of the CIA was revealed only in 1967.

© iStockphoto.com/Agustin Croxatto

LO2 Politics, Pitch, and Penderecki

According to his friend and benefactor Peter Yates, John Cage complained that "he could see no reason why Schoenberg, having freed music from tonality, should not have gone the entire way and freed music from its twelve notes. If every tone is equal to every other, then any controllable sound is equal to any other or to any tone."

Although Schoenberg and Webern never went that far, some composers who assimilated their ideas did.

Among them was the Polish composer Krzysztof Penderecki, part of a wave of composers active after World War II who expanded the range of pitched sounds beyond the discrete twelve notes within the octave. The practice dated from the early part of the century but became far more widespread after World War II, in large part because of Cage's influence. Indeed the original title of the Penderecki work discussed later is an homage of sorts to Cage. By contrast, its second and final title hints at the influence of politics in the world of the avant-garde, a group that prided themselves on their independence.

Krzysztof Penderecki
Fast Facts
- *Dates*: b. 1933
- *Place*: Poland
- *Reasons to remember*: Avant-garde composer noted for his use of innovative and expressive string sonorities

© Lebrecht Music & Arts

WHAT'S IN A NAME?

Like many composers of his generation, Krzysztof Penderecki initially modeled his music after that of Stravinsky and Webern, then Pierre Boulez, a prominent avant-gardist who, like Babbitt, used Webern's music as a point of departure for the development of more advanced and comprehensive serial techniques. He quickly found a more personal direction, which involved the extensive use of innovative string techniques. The first was *Emanations*, a work for two string orchestras tuned a quarter tone apart (a further subdivision of the standard twelve half-steps within an octave to twenty-four quarter-steps within an octave). Other works for strings, sometimes with other instruments, followed soon after. Among them was a one-movement work for fifty-two stringed instruments originally entitled *8'37"* but soon retitled *Tren (Threnody, for the Victims of Hiroshima)*.

Almost thirty-five years after composing *Tren*, Penderecki recounted why he changed the name:

> I had written this piece, and I named it, much as in Cage's manner, *8'37"*. But it existed only in my imagination, in a somewhat abstract way. When Ian

Krenz recorded it and I could listen to an actual performance, I was struck with the emotional charge of the work. I thought it would be a waste to condemn it to such anonymity, to those "digits." I searched for associations and, in the end, I decided to dedicate it to the Hiroshima victims.

That's one version. A few years later, in a *New York Times* interview, Penderecki commented about the renaming more offhandedly: "Oh, I don't know . . . you know in those days we were surrounded with all this propaganda about the American bomb." Other accounts mention that the director of Polish radio had recommended the change to Penderecki before he submitted the work for the UNESCO prize, a fact that Penderecki does not mention.

> *"Oh, I don't know . . . you know in those days we were surrounded with all this propaganda about the American bomb."*
> *—Krzysztof Penderecki*

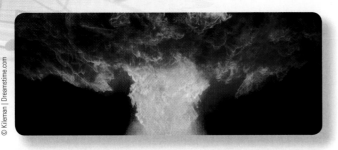

Penderecki's work appeared during the height of the Cold War. Partly in response to the avant-garde activities in Western Europe, governments in Eastern Europe encouraged avant-garde composition and supported composers with publication. Penderecki was one of the beneficiaries of this more open policy.

Tren is a work of truly expressive power. A major source of its impact is Penderecki's handling of pitch. His innovations were part of a larger movement to develop alternatives to equal temperament.

ALTERNATIVE PITCH CONSTRUCTS

At the time of Schoenberg's twelve-tone revolution during the early 1920s, the division of the octave into twelve equal half-steps was, for most musicians and their audience, the closest thing to an immutable law of music. It seemed as permanent and unvarying as the piano keyboards on which one could play all twelve tones. Musicians played "in tune" when the pitches that they played matched precisely the twelve tones within the octave; they played "out of tune" when the pitches did not match one of the twelve tones.

However, as early as the eighteenth century, a few musicians had experimented with other divisions of the octave, particularly on fretted and keyboard instruments. This practice remained a curiosity until the twentieth century, when composers such as Ives composed works requiring quarter tones (twenty-four notes per octave). Ives, Cowell, Bartók, and several other composers also made use of tone clusters: groups of adjacent or nearly adjacent tones struck at the same time. These experiments in fragmenting or blurring the twelve tones appeared in the 1920s, around the time that the first electronic instruments—the theremin and the Ondes Martenot—were invented and composers, most notably Edgard Varèse, composed works mainly or exclusively for percussion instruments. Collectively, these developments represented a far-reaching assault on equal temperament.

The exploration of alternative pitch constructs and the use of sounds with indefinite pitch became more frequent and more varied in the 1930s and 1940s—Cage's prepared piano piece is a now-familiar example. However, challenges to the twelve-tone division of the octave gained even more momentum among avant-garde composers, not only through the use of "concrète" and electronic sounds but also through innovative demands made on conventional instruments. Strings were the instrument family best suited to explore subtle gradations of definite pitch. Because the fingerboard has no frets, it is possible to play the twelve tones within the octave as well as any pitch between adjacent half-steps.

TREN AND AVANT-GARDE EXPRESSIONISM

Among the compositions that exploited these novel sonorities were three works by Penderecki that date from around 1960. The most widely performed is *Tren (Threnody for the Victims of Hiroshima)*. In the excerpt from the work presented here, Penderecki uses an array of devices to blur pitch; among them are quarter tones, **glissandi** (a **glissando** is a continuous, sliding change in pitch), and blocks of pitches so dense that it is virtually impossible to identify individual pitches.

Recall that much of the expressive power in Schoenberg's *Pierrot*

> **glissando** (plural, **glissandi**) A continuous, sliding change in pitch

lunaire came from three pitch-related elements: atonality, *Sprechstimme* (which makes pitch less definite), and the use of extreme registers. By moving away from, then back to, definite pitch and eliminating all rhythms except the entrances and exits of the string players, Penderecki considerably extends Schoenberg's innovations. There is virtually no conventional musical information to process: no distinctive rhythms, no motives, no recurrent patterns. As a result, Penderecki's work provides a direct path to the subconscious. Although it is unlikely that the composer conceived the work programmatically, *Tren* would make a compelling sound track for a documentary of the bombing: the sounds seem to evoke the buzz of the airplanes flying overhead, the explosions, the inarticulate cries of the victims, and desolation in the wake of the bombing.

LISTEN UP!

CD 5:15

Penderecki, *Tren (Threnody for the Victims of Hiroshima)*, excerpt (1960)

Takeaway point: Innovative string sounds to depict the horrors of war

Form: Through-composed

Genre: Orchestral work

Instruments: Fifty-two strings

Context: Avant-garde music with a political message

Sound Frontiers: The Legacy of the Postwar Avant-Garde

It is a measure of the extent to which avant-garde composers distanced themselves from the larger music-making world that none of the works discussed in this unit would have been considered "music" as it was defined in the first part of the century. None has melody or harmony in any conventional sense, and only the Cage piece has a perceptible pulse. After World War II, a definition of music inclusive enough to account for these works would have to be more Cage-like: "music is controlled sound."

THE NEW "COMMON PRACTICE"—AND BEYOND?

As is evident from even this small sample of works, composers bought into the idea that music must evolve: the quest for novelty was the predominant characteristic of this musical generation. For most, the music of the Second Viennese School—Schoenberg, Berg, then Webern—represented the immediately prior stage. As they continued to extend the frontiers of music, avant-garde composers closed ranks, as Babbitt intimated in his article. Their main audience was each other—at festivals, new music concerts, and the like. They sought to please and impress themselves rather than cater to a larger audience.

In their small world, there was a sense of urgency—the excitement of discovery, the pleasure of innovation. But there was a kind of tyranny from within: whereas composers from the Eastern Bloc faced tyranny from without—the state ministries of culture—composers who aligned themselves with the avant-garde faced enormous peer pressure. Serialism was the new orthodoxy, and composers such as Babbitt, Boulez, and Karlheinz Stockhausen were truly the vanguard. Their influence is evident in the widespread adoption of serialism, in varying degrees, not only by a younger generation of composers but even esteemed composers of the prior generation, such as Stravinsky and Copland, who had previously rejected it.

The widespread adoption of serial procedures had the advantage of providing something approaching a common practice for contemporary composition; it remained in force through the early 1970s. However, it had the disadvantage of being a practice that even attentive lay listeners found largely impenetrable. Serial works are inherently difficult to aurally process in real time: the musical information is, by design, unfamiliar, and the amount that listeners must assimilate can be overwhelming. A row contains twelve tones, not seven, in a unique intervallic relationship (which makes it far more difficult to recall, even after several hearings); and the tones do not coalesce via well-established practice into larger units, in a manner similar to the scales, chords, and progressions of tonal harmony.

As a result, little of this music has received broader acceptance. There are, for example, virtually no serial orchestral compositions from the postwar era that have entered the standard repertoire, the way Stravinsky's ballets, Shostakovich's symphonies, or Copland's orchestral music has. In 1999, in explaining the dearth of avant-garde serial works crossing over to a more mainstream audience, Boulez said, "Well, perhaps we did not take sufficiently into account the way music is perceived by the listener."

> "Well, perhaps we did not take sufficiently into account the way music is perceived by the listener." —Pierre Boulez

Serial composition represented increasing amounts of precompositional control over the content of a composition. Those who moved in opposite directions—transferring the result in performance to performers, or even to chance (as Cage did)—enjoyed somewhat more success, particularly if the work had an appealing point of entry or readily imagined expressive intent. Penderecki's *Tren* still receives regular performances. However, here too, the endless search for new sounds worked against broader acceptance, because the unfamiliarity of the innovations and the absence of common ground with established styles made assimilation a challenge.

Thankfully, Babbitt's recommendation for the "complete elimination of the public and social aspects of musical composition" never came to pass—for him or his peers. But the discontinuity between his private world and the public world did exist when he wrote his article, and it still does. It was a problem that he and his peers never satisfactorily resolved.

Mainstreaming the Avant-Garde

Despite the seeming gulf between the avant-garde and the rest of the musical world—classical, popular, folk, and ethnic—and the relatively small audience for their music, the postwar avant-garde has had a substantial influence on the course of music during the latter part of the twentieth century, because many of their innovations were adapted for use in other contexts. For example, Babbitt's pioneering work in music synthesis led to the now-normative practice of bypassing the performer completely: almost any dance track is evidence of this.

Musique concrète–inspired "found" sounds were used in concept albums of the 1960s and 1970s, such as The Beatles' *Sgt. Pepper's Lonely Hearts Club Band*, Frank Zappa's *We're Only in It for the Money*, and Pink Floyd's *The Dark Side of the Moon*. Film composers have mined the music of the avant-garde in an effort to expand their sound palette: almost any horror film makes use of avant-garde-derived effects.

Even as their innovations began to filter into other kinds of music, avant-garde composers faced a dilemma: they couldn't go forward or back. Collectively, their work in the 1950s seemed to explore virtually every musical frontier: it is difficult to imagine music that could evolve much beyond the complexity of Babbitt's synthesizer compositions, and it is even more difficult to imagine anything simpler than Cage's 4'33". Further evolution seemed impractical, if not impossible. However, if they turned away from cutting-edge approaches and novel concepts, they risked censure from many of their peers.

In retrospect, the postwar avant-garde has functioned within the larger musical world much as Babbitt envisioned. Like pure mathematicians and theoretical physicists, avant-garde composers have explored new frontiers, seemingly without much regard for their wider application. Their work is understood and appreciated almost exclusively by a small group of like-minded specialists. And as with their scientific counterparts, their cutting-edge innovations eventually found application beyond the laboratory: without the ideas and compositions of the avant-garde, the sound world of the late twentieth century would have been considerably poorer and far less interesting.

UNIT 22
FROM VERNACULAR TO ART

Learning Outcomes
After reading this unit, you will be able to do the following:

LO1 Understand how jazz evolved in the 1940s from popular dance music to art music for listening.

LO2 Trace the evolution of American musical theater from *Show Boat* to the present.

LO3 Characterize Latin music in the United States through an exploration of a mambo and a tango.

LO4 Describe the rock revolution, using the music of Chuck Berry, the Beach Boys, Bob Dylan, and The Beatles as examples.

CHUCK BERRY, the architect of rock and roll, wasn't afraid to take on the musical establishment in words as well as music. In 1956, he took a good-natured swipe at classical music when he demanded: "Roll over, Beethoven, and tell Tchaikovsky the news!" A year later, he would dismiss both bebop and Latin dance music in "Rock and Roll Music." By 1957, the most "modern" jazz had evolved into a complex, challenging music. In the United States, Latin dances such as the tango and the mambo still belonged mainly on the dance floor. But in Argentina, Astor Piazzolla was transforming the tango into a new, more sophisticated music. Later in the decade, composer Leonard Bernstein would draw on both Latin music and jazz to give greater musical depth to his landmark musical *West Side Story*.

Modern jazz, Piazzolla's "new tango," Bernstein's work, and the rock revolution of the 1960s exemplify an important trend in musical life in the years after World War II: music emerging from vernacular traditions that nevertheless had qualities often associated with art music, such as complexity, originality, and individuality. In this unit, we explore the emergence of art music–like directions in jazz, Latin music, the Broadway musical, and rock.

© iStockphoto.com/FotoAta

CHAPTER 50

Jazz, America's Art Music

"Bebop was the downhill skiing of jazz."

Minton's Playhouse, a small jazz club located on West 118th Street in Harlem, opened in 1938. Its owner, Henry Minton, was a musician; he kept his place open after hours so musicians could get together to play after they had finished their regular jobs. By the early 1940s, Charlie Parker, Dizzy Gillespie, Thelonious Monk, and other like-minded musicians were there, transforming 1930s swing into a new jazz style called bebop.

Did You Know?

Jimi Hendrix, who brought unprecedented virtuosity and imagination to the electric guitar, claimed post-bebop jazz saxophonist John Coltrane as a significant influence.

But their work went largely unnoticed beyond the bandstand at Minton's, because on August 1, 1942, James Petrillo, president of the American Federation of Musicians, called for a recording ban by union musicians. Petrillo was trying to secure additional royalties for recordings that were played on the air. Decca and Capitol agreed to a relatively small settlement about a year later; RCA and Columbia, the two biggest companies, held out for another year. As a result, Parker and his cohorts didn't begin actually recording their music until 1945, so it seemed revolutionary by the time the world at large heard it.

© Prints and Photographs Division, Library of Congress. Reproduction Number LC-GLB23-0628 DLC

Thelonious Monk, Howard McGhee, Roy Eldridge, and Teddy Hill at Minton's Playhouse in New York City (1947)

LO1 Jazz: From Dance Music to Art

From the end of World War I to the end of World War II, the central tension in the professional life of jazz musicians was playing what they *wanted* to play versus playing what they *had* to play to make a living. The jazz of the 1920s and 1930s that jazz fans most value—the "purest" jazz of this period—reveals musicians playing what they wanted. "Hotter Than That" and Louis Armstrong's other Hot Five and Hot Seven recordings are good examples. But most jazz musicians of the era also led or played in dance orchestras. Armstrong and Coleman Hawkins, the most influential tenor saxophonist of the 1930s, were among the numerous important jazz musicians who played in Fletcher Henderson's hot dance orchestras. Paul Whiteman engaged many of the top white jazz musicians of the 1920s, including cornetist Bix Beiderbecke and Joe Venuti, the first great jazz violinist. Duke Ellington led the house band at the Cotton Club, a famous Harlem nightclub, from 1927 to 1930; it was his springboard to stardom.

With the dawn of the "swing era" in 1935, jazz became the hot new music for a new generation. Dancers jitterbugged to the riffs and rhythms of the top swing bands (also called "big bands"), including those led by Ellington, Benny Goodman, Glenn Miller, Count Basie, Tommy Dorsey, and Artie Shaw. The swing era was the one period in the history of jazz where it was truly a popular music.

The expectations for swing-era dance music—particularly an easy-to-find beat that you could dance to and repetitive riffs—left relatively little room for gifted improvisers to explore unfamiliar musical territory. So, during the 1930s and early 1940s, after-hours jam sessions were the most common outlet for jazz musicians. The more adventurous would play in the evening with a dance orchestra, then congregate in the wee hours of the morning to play for each other and a few enthusiastic night owls.

Dancers jitterbugged to the riffs and rhythms of the top swing bands.

© Retro Kitsch / Alamy

Benny Goodman helped bring small-group jazz to a wider audience by leading both a big band and a small combo. In the process, Goodman also broke the color line in jazz—a decade before Jackie Robinson broke it in baseball—by hiring two African American musicians, pianist Teddy Wilson and vibraphonist Lionel Hampton. Goodman showcased the quartet, which also included drummer Gene

bebop (bop) A new kind of jazz, primarily for listening, which evolved during the mid-1940s and featured a rapid tempo and irregular melodic lines that at times sounded like the new style's name

Krupa, on recordings and in the famous "Spirituals to Swing" concerts in 1938 and 1939, which took place in New York's Carnegie Hall.

The music played by Goodman's big band was most often dance music. The music that he performed and recorded with his small groups was primarily listening music, even though it might get listeners to tap their feet in time. It was a prelude to an even more adventurous kind of music: bebop, or simply bop.

Bop, Music of Liberation

© iStockphoto.com/eva serrabassa

Bebop, or **bop**, was a new kind of jazz. Freed from the constraints of the dance floor, it challenged both musicians and audiences. During the mid-1940s, when bop began to explode on the music scene, only a handful of musicians had mastered the new style. Bop musicians performed this new music mainly in small clubs, such as those along 52nd Street in New York.

When bop moved downtown and from there out to the rest of the country, it presented itself as an uncompromising music strictly for listening. It attracted a small but ardent following and also acquired a large number of detractors, black and white, musicians and nonmusicians. Older musicians didn't understand the music and so rejected it. Those jazz fans who were used to the more predictable—if exhilarating—rhythms and riffs of swing didn't know what to make of the music at first.

© Hulton Archive/Getty Images

Dizzy Gillespie (1917–1993; shown here in 1948), who wore a beret and horn-rimmed glasses, and reshaped his trumpet so that the bell projected up as well as out, was a favorite subject of news photographers.

Many found bop musicians' lifestyle as strange as the music: they and their fans formed the first counterculture. For them, night was day. They thought differently, talked differently, dressed differently, and lived differently. Traditional values like steady employment and a stable home life were lower priorities than the chance to make the music and live the life. And like those in the 1960s counterculture, they found a drug to help them escape the day-to-day world. Heroin was their drug of choice, and many became addicts. Both the music and the world in which it flourished were forbidden fruit for mainstream Americans.

THE MUSICAL INNOVATIONS OF BOP

Bop musicians reconceived nearly every parameter of music: rhythm, melody, harmony, and sound. Among the most significant innovations were these five:

1. *Liberation of the rhythm section.* In pre-bop jazz, the main rhythmic function of the entire rhythm section was marking the beat. In a swing band, the guitarist, bassist, and drummer played sounds on every beat. The drummer also used the hi-hat (a pair of foot-operated cymbals) to play a ride pattern and mark the backbeat. With bop, the pianist and drummer were largely liberated from solely a timekeeping role; only the bassist consistently marked the beat. The drummer continued to mark the backbeat and keep the steady ride pattern but also played syncopated accents. Pianists (piano was the chord instrument of choice in most bop combos) "**comped**"; that is, they played chords in intermittent, often irregular and syncopated patterns. As a result, the rhythm section not only laid down the beat but also overlaid it with syncopation and other rhythms that conflicted with it.

2. *Rapid tempos.* Tempo took a quantum leap in bop. Armstrong's "Hotter Than That," an up-tempo song for the 1920s and 1930s, moves at about 210 beats per minute. "Salt Peanuts," the track presented later, moves at about 290 beats per minute, about 40 percent faster. One reason for this dramatic jump in tempo was simply the exhilaration the musicians felt improvising fluently at such daredevil speeds—it was the downhill skiing of jazz. But the brisk tempos were also one way of separating musical wheat from the chaff during the after-hours jam sessions: it was bop musicians' most obvious method of excluding those who hadn't spent enough time developing their skill. There are swing-era performances at lightning-fast tempos, but they were exceptional. With bop, it was part of the style.

3. *Asymmetrical, irregular melodic lines.* Bop-style melodic lines, especially during improvised solos, often consist of a stream of fast-moving notes ending on an offbeat accent. Indeed, the term bebop derives from this practice: a typical bop melody (written or improvised) can be vocalized like this: Ba / doo-ba / doo-ba / . . . / doo-BOP.

4. *Complex harmony.* Bop musicians enriched the harmonic vocabulary of jazz, interpolating new, more complex chords into the relatively simple harmony of blues and popular song. Like virtually every other feature of bop style, noninitiates found this difficult to master.

5. *Aggressive sounds.* Bop horn players cultivated more strident sounds than those of earlier generations of jazz musicians. Parker, in particular, opted for a full but penetrating sound, usually produced with little or no vibrato.

These innovations were the products of the work of a small circle of musicians, including drummers Kenny Clarke and Max Roach, pianists Bud Powell and Thelonious Monk, and trumpeter Dizzy Gillespie. However, the dominant figure in the formation of bop style was a saxophonist named Charlie Parker.

CHARLIE PARKER

Charlie Parker (1920–1955), known familiarly as "Bird" (a shortened form of "Yardbird," a nickname he acquired early on), came of age in Kansas City, Missouri. Except for New York, Kansas City had the liveliest jazz scene in the United States during the 1930s. The town was wide open—the city government was notoriously corrupt—and clubs of all kinds flourished during this time.

Jazz musicians in Kansas City—or those traveling through—played for two audiences. Before midnight, they played for the crowd. After hours, they played for one another. The Kansas City jazz clubs were home to fierce all-night jam sessions. These were competitive affairs called cutting contests, where players would take turns showing how well they improvised. Those who couldn't cut it were mocked and laughed off the stand.

As a teenager, Parker was a regular at the Club Reno, where the Count Basie band was in residence.

comping Jazz pianists' or guitarists' playing chords in intermittent, often irregular and syncopated, patterns

He would sit in the balcony and listen to Lester Young, his idol at the time. One night, when he was sixteen, Parker brought his saxophone along so that he could jam with the Basie band members. Although he had been playing sax for only a year, Parker had worked hard and thought he was ready. He wasn't: when Jo Jones, Basie's drummer, heard young Parker start to play, he was so disgusted that he threw one of his cymbals at Parker's feet. Parker left the bandstand deeply humiliated.

After that, he went in the woodshed—the musician's term for the place where serious practicing gets done—and came out a few months later, well on his way to the bebop breakthrough. He joined Jay McShann's band, one of the top local bands, then moved to New York, where he played in several bands, including those led by Earl Hines (the pianist with Armstrong on several 1920s recordings) and Cootie Williams (a trumpet player and Ellington alumnus).

By 1945, he and his colleagues from Minton's Playhouse were performing together and recording. Parker, who had severe substance-abuse issues, would record frequently until his death in 1955.

© Lebrecht Music and Arts Photo Library / Alamy

Charlie Parker

The Sound of Bop: "Salt Peanuts"

Among the first recordings by the coterie of bop musicians was "Salt Peanuts," a tune written by Dizzy Gillespie in 1942 and first recorded in May 1945. Perhaps because it was written early in the development of bebop, Gillespie's tune retains and reshapes the melodic

cool jazz Post-bop jazz style that kept bop's intricacy but took the edge off, slowing it down and mellowing it out

© iStockphoto.com/JOE CICAK

practice of swing-era jazz. It is in AABA form. The swing connection is evident in the A section, in that like many swing-era tunes, it alternates between two riffs. (The second riff is vocalized later in the track as the title phrase: "Salt Peanuts.") Among the features that bring the tune into bop-era practice are the asymmetrical rhythm of the riffs, lack of steady timekeeping from the rhythm section, breakneck tempo, and extensive syncopation. The rest of the performance, including the complex interludes between choruses and improvised solos, shows characteristic features of bop style: the aggressive timbres of Parker and Gillespie; the rhythmic play within the rhythm section, especially the offbeat chords and accents from the pianist and drummer; the streams of notes in the solos, many of which end on the offbeat; and complex, often dissonant harmonies.

Bop and "Modern Jazz"

Bop was like a shooting star that exploded into view, then trailed away. The intensity and brilliance of the music were difficult to sustain, and the breakneck tempos made the music somewhat one-dimensional. There are numerous recordings by Parker and others of pre-bop popular songs, blues, and other material that feature slower tempos and move away from the angular and asymmetrical melodic streams that are characteristic of bop. However, bop laid the foundation for subsequent jazz styles, which would soon be grouped together under the label "modern jazz."

Bop was a hot music, with aggressive sounds and high energy. The first post-bop style to emerge was **cool jazz**, which kept the intricacy of bop but took the edge off, slowing it down and mellowing it out. One off-shoot of cool was "West Coast" jazz, so called because so many of its players were based in Los Angeles or San Francisco. The keepers of the flame were the hard-bop musicians of the 1950s. More than any other, they built on the legacy of Charlie Parker, even as Parker was wasting away in addiction. Most were African American and lived and worked on the East Coast. Two late 1950s trends, a "return to roots" movement and modal jazz (the use of modal scales and harmonies derived from them in place of jazz-tweaked common practice harmony) presented alternative paths to a simpler starting point for improvisation. But all retained key advances in bop, most notably the greater freedom and rhythmic play within the rhythm section.

Bop: Sound Track for a Social Revolution

In the years after World War II, mainstream America continued to embrace white, Western European values and look to Europe for high culture. Bop challenged the status quo by presenting America and the world with a complex, challenging music for listening that was clearly different from both classical music and the most esteemed popular music. As a result, those who had accepted the pecking order in American musical life were faced with a conundrum: how to reconcile this bold new music with the prevailing view of race and musical value.

Bop was a music that made demands of both performer and audience that were comparable to those of classical music. From the performer it demanded virtuosity, creativity, and passion; from the audience it rewarded attentive listening. Moreover, these qualities had to be realized in the improvisational moment, not after extensive rehearsal. When bop first appeared on records and in the downtown jazz clubs, no traditionally trained classical musicians could play the music competently; the best players from New York's symphony orchestras would have been lost on the bandstand of a dingy jazz club.

Bop went beyond American composers composing American-sounding classical music, as Ives, Gershwin, and Copland did. It went beyond African Americans transforming a vernacular tradition by wrapping it in classical trappings. And it went beyond the classic jazz of Armstrong and Ellington, which for all its artistry still retained a strong connection with jazz's roots as dance music. With bop, America finally had a fully American alternative to the art music imported from Europe and the American music shaped by the European tradition.

Most established critics in the first two decades after World War II viewed modern jazz much as Americans originally viewed sushi: something that came well recommended from a few adventurous and knowledgeable souls but that strayed so far away from traditional expectations that its value was

Critics viewed modern jazz much as Americans originally viewed sushi.

suspect. But bop and the modern jazz that developed from it were the first real chinks in the armor of the cultural elite. The "good music" crowd could dismiss early jazz and swing as popular music, despite their occasional appearances in the concert hall, but they could not dismiss bop and post-bop jazz so easily, despite the bohemian environment that was its customary milieu.

By the end of the 1950s, modern jazz had a toehold in high culture, as numerous jazz/classical syntheses evidenced. These took many forms: among the most noteworthy were collaborations between Dave Brubeck, Leonard Bernstein, and the New York Philharmonic; the third stream music (classical/jazz fusions) involving the Modern Jazz Quartet, Gunther Schuller, and the Beaux Arts String Quartet; and a series of albums by Miles Davis and Gil Evans, who had first worked together to create cool jazz.

The rise of modern jazz in cultural importance opened the door for others to challenge the artistic and cultural status quo. It was a crucial precedent for the art-oriented rock of the 1960s and early 1970s, by The Beatles, The Who, Frank Zappa, and others. Indeed, Bob Dylan was strongly influenced by the beat generation poets, who often read their work accompanied by a combo playing modern jazz.

Further, the reality of bop contradicted the stereotypes of African Americans that were prevalent in American society at midcentury. This was not the product of a race with "natural rhythm," unsophisticated minds, an aversion to hard work, and below-average intelligence. (All were common assumptions in the 1940s.) For the more open-minded members of American society, bop and post-bop jazz offered irrefutable evidence that those who could produce first-class art music did not deserve second-class status.

Jazz is now firmly ensconced at New York City's Lincoln Center, America's cultural capital. The Frederick P. Rose Hall, the home of Jazz at Lincoln Center, contains three performance venues, an education wing, and a display area. Much of what twenty-first-century Americans understand as the normal course of things—multiculturalism, an integrated society, pluralistic conceptions of art—would have been unthinkable at the beginning of the twentieth century. As an art music emerging from African American culture that drew on both African and European sources and was performed by musicians for whom talent trumped race, jazz played a crucial role in effecting these changes. Its value to America and the world goes beyond its impressive musical legacy to include its substantial contributions to a more democratic society.

CHAPTER 51

Musical Theater after *Show Boat*

> "*West Side Story* would serve as the bridge between two eras in musical theater."

Duke Orsino opens William Shakespeare's play *Twelfth Night* with these words:

If music be the food of love, play on;
Give me excess of it, that, surfeiting,
The appetite may sicken, and so die.

These lines, like Feste's song "O Mistresse Mine" (Chapter 12), remind us of Shakespeare's deep affinity for music. It took more than two centuries, but musicians finally responded to Shakespeare in kind. The nineteenth century saw numerous important compositions drawn from or inspired by Shakespeare's plays, now widely available in translation. Most prominent were operas; Verdi composed three: *Macbeth*, *Otello*, and *Falstaff*. There was also instrumental, or mainly instrumental, music. Berlioz was enamored of Shakespeare as well as of a particular Shakespearean actress (recall that he married Harriet Smithson): among his several Shakespearean works was the glorious "symphonie dramatique" *Roméo et Juliette*. Mendelssohn wrote concert music inspired by Shakespeare's *Midsummer Night's Dream*; it includes the famous "Wedding March."

The first important Broadway musical to recast Shakespeare was Rodgers and Hart's 1938 production *The Boys from Syracuse*, an adaptation of the playwright's *The Comedy of Errors*. A decade later, Cole Porter modernized and musicalized *The Taming of the Shrew* in *Kiss Me, Kate*. In 1957, Leonard Bernstein offered an even more radical Shakespeare metamorphosis: *West Side Story* retold *Romeo and Juliet* in contemporary New York, with street gangs replacing feuding families.

West Side Story would soon be recognized as a landmark musical and one of the most effective settings of Shakespeare in any musical genre. Moreover, in its thorough integration of music, drama, and dance; its evocative use of style; and its complex musical settings, *West Side Story* would also serve as the bridge between two eras in musical theater: the "golden era" of the 1940s and 1950s, and the musicals of Stephen Sondheim and other like-minded composers.

Did You Know?

Randy Newman's musical *Faust* brings the timeless Faust legend into the present, with Faust a Notre Dame student. The all-star cast included James Taylor, Don Henley, Elton John, Linda Ronstadt, and Bonnie Raitt.

LO2 American Musical Theater from *Show Boat* to *The Sound of Music*

The three-plus decades between *Show Boat* and the last of the Rodgers and Hammerstein musicals divide evenly into two eras, the sixteen years before the premiere of *Oklahoma!* in 1943 and the sixteen years between *Oklahoma!* and *The Sound of Music*, the last of the Rodgers and Hammerstein musicals. The most outstanding difference between the eras is that we remember the musicals before *Oklahoma!* mainly for their great songs; they are seldom revived as complete shows. By contrast, we remember the best musicals of the 1940s and 1950s because they are great shows that included great songs; the most successful were eventually filmed, and they are frequently revived by professionals and amateurs.

THE MUSICAL AFTER *SHOW BOAT*

Despite critical acclaim and commercial success following its 1927 premiere, *Show Boat* did not spawn a new genre. Instead, talking films and the Great Depression were a one-two punch that brought musical theater to its knees. Broadway became more an elite entertainment, simply because fewer could afford it; film musicals offered a cheaper and more accessible alternative.

Notable musicals that followed the course charted by Kern and Hammerstein include George Gershwin's three political satires in the early 1930s. The second of them, *Of Thee I Sing*, won the 1931 Pulitzer Prize for

Musicals like Cole Porter's *Anything Goes*, produced in 1934, offered escapist entertainment for those who still attended the theater.

best play, one of only a few musicals to do so. Gershwin would follow these musicals with an even more spectacular achievement, his opera *Porgy and Bess* (1935). In its enduring popularity and special place straddling the boundary between classical and popular music, it is Gershwin's vocal counterpart to his *Rhapsody in Blue*. The musicals of composer Richard Rodgers and lyricist/librettist Lorenz Hart from the late 1930s also sought to bring more realism and greater integration of story and song to the Broadway stage; their 1940 musical *Pal Joey* was the capstone of their Broadway career.

The musicals of Gershwin and Rodgers and Hart were the exception. In general, audiences wanted relief, not reality. Musicals like Cole Porter's *Anything Goes*, produced in 1934, offered escapist entertainment for those who still attended the theater. Film musicals, such as those starring Fred Astaire and Ginger Rogers, brought it to the heartland. The 1930s and early 1940s were difficult times for musical theater. That would change almost overnight in 1943.

OKLAHOMA! AND THE GOLDEN ERA OF MUSICAL THEATER

Despite their considerable success, Rodgers and Hart struggled to maintain a successful partnership: Rodgers was a workaholic, and Hart was an alcoholic, whose undependability strained their relationship. They parted professionally when Hart, his health deteriorating, declined an offer from Rodgers to turn *Green Grow the Lilacs* (1931), a play by Lynn Riggs, into a musical. Rodgers then turned to lyricist Oscar Hammerstein II, who had enjoyed great success with *Show Boat* but little since then. Out of their first collaboration came *Oklahoma!* It was the beginning of their long and extremely successful career together; Hart passed away later that year, about eight months after *Oklahoma!* opened on Broadway.

Oklahoma! was a landmark musical, because of numerous innovations and unprecedented commercial success. The musical drew raves from reviewers. As theater critic Stanley Green noted:

> Everything fit into place. . . . Not only were songs and story inseparable, but the dances devised by Agnes de Mille heightened the drama by revealing the subconscious fears and desires of the leading characters.

Audiences loved it even more. *Oklahoma!* ran on Broadway for over five years; its 2,248 performances far exceeded any previous run.

In essence, *Oklahoma!* fulfilled the promise of *Show Boat.* Similarities between the two musicals went beyond their enormous popular appeal and emphasis on dramatic integrity. Both shows drew their plot from existing literature. This practice, a new approach in 1927, had become increasingly common by the early 1940s. Both musicals featured stories set in America, but in a time and place far removed from contemporary New York.

Most important, both incorporated significant innovations in the depth of character development; seriousness of plot; integration of song into the story line; disregard for convention; and in the case of *Oklahoma!* the dramatically purposeful use of dance. The extraordinarily enthusiastic public support for a dramatically credible musical inspired a wholesale shift in values, by both creators and audience.

THE LEGACY OF *OKLAHOMA!*

Rodgers and Hammerstein followed *Oklahoma!* with several more musicals. Most were successful, and many were memorable: *Carousel* (1945), *State Fair* (1947, their only musical written specifically for film), *South Pacific* (1949), *The King and I* (1951), and *The Sound of Music* (1959). Their partnership, the most successful in the history of musical theater, ended only with Hammerstein's death in 1960.

Because of their innovative approach to musical theater and their tremendous critical and popular success—almost all of their Broadway musicals also became extremely popular films—Rodgers and Hammerstein's musicals became the standard by which all other musicals of the time were measured and a major influence on other Broadway musicals. This is reflected in such key matters as the choice and source of subjects, dramatic integrity, and musical language.

Rodgers and Hammerstein musicals offered wholesome family entertainment.

© Magna /20th Century Fox / The Kobal Collection

Among Hammerstein's most important innovations was his willingness to take on difficult social issues. In *Show Boat*, the sympathetic portraits of Julie and Joe and Julie's banishment because of a mixed marriage address racial injustice. The conflict between farmers and cowboys treated in *Oklahoma!* was a real issue in the turn-of-the-century Southwest, often erupting in real life into violence. By any absolute standard, it is treated lightly in *Oklahoma!* ("The Farmer and the Cowman [should be friends]"); still, Hammerstein dares to mention it, and the scene ends in a brawl.

By contrast, the music in the golden-era musical was anything but innovative. Compared with much of the popular music of the time, it was a throwback to the past. Even as rhythm and blues, mambo, bebop, and honky-tonk were bringing not only vigorous new sounds but also strong beats and complex rhythms to American ears, Broadway musicals all but abandoned the innovations of the modern era. Syncopation disappeared; so did the propulsive swing beat that underlay it. Melody reigned supreme. Similarly, performances of musicals often featured singers with classically trained voices singing in a quasi-operatic style. Theater orchestras sounded more like symphonies than like swing bands.

Because of the almost universal conservatism of Broadway—in Rodgers's music, the attitudes of producers, the conventions of the genre, and the expectations of audiences—Hammerstein sugarcoated the controversial issues that he raised onstage and even more in film. In either format, Rodgers and Hammerstein musicals offered wholesome family entertainment. In this respect, they were very much in step with white America's postwar image of itself as portrayed in the media. Not surprisingly, such musicals were also enormously popular. Musicals ran for years; film versions of musicals did well at the box office, as did movie musicals such as *Singing in the Rain*, and Broadway and film sound tracks were among the best-selling albums of the era.

Standing in sharp contrast to this essentially escapist entertainment would be *West Side Story*.

Beyond the Broadway Musical: *West Side Story*

West Side Story grew out of the collaboration of composer Leonard Bernstein, lyricist Stephen Sondheim, choreographer Jerome Robbins, and librettist Arthur Laurents. The key player was Bernstein. By the time he composed *West Side Story*, Bernstein had established himself as one of America's most multitalented musicians of the mid-twentieth century. He had an active career as a conductor, would become music director of the New York Philharmonic in 1958, and had already composed three Broadway musicals, an opera, two ballets, two symphonies, film sound tracks, and numerous other works. He was an excellent pianist, whether performing the classical repertoire or his own compositions. He would become best known to the general public as a commentator on music, through television programs such as the *Young People's Concerts*, which began in 1959. He also wrote several widely read books on music. The breadth of Bernstein's skills and interests—he had strong affinities for jazz and theater music—is evident throughout the musical.

Leonard Bernstein

Fast Facts

- *Dates*: 1918–1990
- *Place*: United States
- *Reasons to remember*: One of America's most multitalented musicians of the mid-twentieth century: composer, conductor, and commentator

© Alfred Eisenstaedt/Time & Life Pictures/Getty Images

West Side Story, staged in 1957 and filmed in 1961, was creative and innovative in its plot, music, and use of dance. Its inventiveness begins with its libretto, which puts a new twist on an old practice: instead of using a long-ago time or an exotic locale, the collaborators took a timeless story—Shakespeare's *Romeo and Juliet*—and set it in contemporary New York.

© Lebrecht Music & Arts

Bernstein and his collaborators turned the Capulets and Montagues into two street gangs: the white Jets and the Puerto Rican Sharks. Tony, a friend of Riff, the leader of the Jets, and a former member of the gang, is the modern counterpart to Romeo. Maria, the sister of Bernardo, the leader of the Sharks, is the modern Juliet. She has just come from Puerto Rico to marry Chino, Bernardo's friend. Tony spies Maria at a dance and immediately falls in love. While Tony and Maria begin their romance, the two gangs plan a rumble (a gang fight). Maria learns of the fight and asks Tony to break it up. Despite Tony's efforts, the fight quickly escalates: Bernardo kills Riff, and Tony, now enraged, grabs Riff's knife and kills Bernardo. Tony visits Maria after she learns that he has killed her brother. In spite of this, they long to escape. They have a brief moment together before Chino shoots Tony, who is carried off by members of both gangs.

Although there are light moments, *West Side Story* is a tragedy: Laurents did nothing to soften the story of Shakespeare's famous star-crossed lovers. That he brought it into the present only made its impact more immediate. No earlier musical had ever approached the realism of *West Side Story*.

"COOL" AND THE INNOVATIONS OF *WEST SIDE STORY*

Among the most innovative features of the musical are Bernstein's music—both the songs and the dance music—and the total integration of dance into the show. In *West Side Story*, Bernstein brought his compositional range to bear in ways that songwriters, even those as skilled as Jerome Kern and Richard Rodgers, couldn't. His musical language is generally up to date. He wrote contemporary jazz for the Jets dance numbers. For the Sharks, he wrote Latin, or at least Latinate, numbers. (There is a mambo, for the dance in the gym, but other music for Puerto Rican characters, like "America," seems derived more from classical music by Latin composers than from Puerto Rican popular music.)

The love songs ("Maria," "Tonight," "One Hand, One Heart," "Somewhere") find a middle ground between Tin Pan Alley conventions and the more extensive development customarily heard in an opera aria. To cite just one example, "Maria" develops from a three-note riff, like a conventional modern-era popular song. But Bernstein soon departs from convention, instead spinning three progressively more intense phrases before dropping to a whisper. Bernstein's more elaborate development of the opening idea positions the song

rock musical Theater work that shows the influence of rock in spirit and style

between Broadway and the opera house.

However, it is in the instrumental writing that Bernstein truly flexes his compositional muscle. In *West Side Story*, dance is functional, not decorative; choreographer Jerome Robbins was a full partner in the collaboration. For dance numbers, Bernstein often shook free of the constraints of popular song and composed extended, complex music that enhanced the expressiveness of the dance.

Among the most dramatically compelling dance scenes is that for "Cool." In the film version, it occurs after the rumble, when the gangs have fled the scene of the stabbings and the Jets have reassembled in a garage after scattering to avoid the police. Some of the Jets are almost boiling over in their urgency to gain revenge on the Sharks, but Ice, the de facto new leader, cautions them to be "cool." In this scene, dance speaks louder than words or song. It captures the repressed emotion of the gang, ready to explode at the slightest provocation and kept under control only by the force of Ice's will. Bernstein supports their nervous energy with a jazz ballet that features an extremely hip fugal section.

To characterize the Jets, Bernstein offers his take on modern jazz. Five years later, he might have used rock and roll, but when he began working on the musical, modern jazz was the "coolest" current music, and it had a distinctly "outsider" association during the 1950s. Bernstein's skillful evocation of modern jazz and Latin music was a distinct departure from the practice of Rodgers and Hammerstein and other golden-era

theater composers, who seldom attempted to use musical style to evoke character or place. It would be one of Bernstein's most far-reaching innovations.

Musical Theater after 1960

As the 1960s began, musical theater seemed to be on top of the popular music world. The 1950s had been commercially and artistically successful. *Fiddler on the Roof* would begin its record-breaking run of 3,242 performances beginning in 1964. Original cast recordings dominated the album charts through the first part of the decade.

However, by the end of the 1960s, film and television had largely supplanted Broadway as a source of hits. Of the fifty original cast albums (recordings of Broadway shows) that made the Top 40 lists between 1955 and 1990, only eight were released after 1965, and only two of these eight after 1975.

Billed as an "American tribal love-rock musical," Hair portrayed the counterculture lifestyle.

© Andrew H. Walker/Getty Images

The musical, like other established genres, had to reckon with the rock revolution. One response was to create **rock musicals**: theater works that showed the influence of rock in spirit and style. The most revolutionary of these was *Hair*, which opened on Broadway in 1968. Billed as an "American tribal love-rock musical," *Hair* portrayed the counterculture lifestyle. To this end, it embodied counterculture attitudes in almost every aspect of its design: the ambiguity and relative insignificance of its plot, the absence of Broadway stars, and the racially integrated cast. Burt Bacharach and Hal David's musical, *Promises, Promises*, adapted from Neil Simon's film *The Apartment*, told the story of a young businessman who let his bosses use his apartment for extramarital affairs in return for job advancement. Bacharach's rock-influenced pop style gave the songs

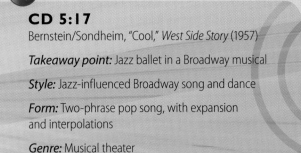

 LISTEN UP!

CD 5:17
Bernstein/Sondheim, "Cool," *West Side Story* (1957)

Takeaway point: Jazz ballet in a Broadway musical

Style: Jazz-influenced Broadway song and dance

Form: Two-phrase pop song, with expansion and interpolations

Genre: Musical theater

Instruments: Voices and theater orchestra

Context: Bernstein's use of jazz to characterize the mood of the Jets and convey the repressed energy of the scene

a contemporary sound. Andrew Lloyd Webber's *Jesus Christ Superstar* (1970) put a contemporary spin on the life of Christ. It would be the first of several blockbuster hits for Webber.

STEPHEN SONDHEIM AND CONTEMPORARY MUSICAL THEATER

Also opening in 1970 was Stephen Sondheim's *Company*. It was the third musical for which he wrote both words and music, and the first since *Anyone Can Whistle*, a 1964 production that closed after only nine performances. Like *Promises, Promises, Company* presented a contemporary story (the plot centered around a single man living in New York who cannot find and keep a partner despite the almost oppressive assistance of several married couples) with a contemporary sensibility (some critics hailed it as the first modern musical) and a contemporary-sounding score.

Sondheim followed *Company* with *Follies* (1971) and *A Little Night Music* (1973). Collectively, the three musicals established his reputation as the major theater composer of his time and offered a retrospective tour of the first part of the century. *Follies* (1971) looks back at Broadway during the heyday of the revue. Its music includes brilliant parodies of the music of the 1920s and 1930s. *A Little Night Music* retreats even further in time, to the turn of the century. To evoke the era, Sondheim set all the songs in waltz time, the most common rhythmic underpinning of popular songs during that period. Sondheim writes in all styles with such apparent ease and authenticity that it's easy to imagine him at home musically during any era prior to 1970.

BEYOND THE MUSICAL

Bernstein's theater music, especially *West Side Story*, foreshadowed a new era in musical theater, which began in earnest with Sondheim's three breakthrough musicals. Their work effectively dissolved the boundary between classical and popular. Both composers capitalized on their ability to change musical style as easily as an actor changes costumes and to seamlessly fuse classical and popular elements. Their musicals are demonstrably more complex and dramatically viable than many operas, yet they have accessible points of entry and melodic processes more characteristic of popular music than of classical music. Their work represents a new middle ground between the golden-era musicals of the postwar era and opera.

CHAPTER 52

Latin Dance Music

"The biggest hit of 1955 was a Latin tune, Perez Prado's 'Cherry Pink and Apple Blossom White.'"

In the 1921 film *The Four Horsemen of the Apocalypse*, Rudolph Valentino portrays Julio Desnoyers, the rakish grandson of a wealthy Argentine landowner. Early in the film, Julio and his grandfather are enjoying a night out in a seedy, smoke-filled bar. They're sitting at a table with two women when a couple goes to the middle of the dance floor and begins to dance a tango, to the accompaniment of a five-piece orchestra. (Viewers see the musicians but don't hear them; it's a silent movie.) Valentino/Julio walks over to the couple and taps the man on the shoulder, demanding to dance with his partner. When the couple ignores him and resumes dancing, Julio yanks the man away from the

Did You Know?

In a memorable scene from *Scent of a Woman*, Best Actor Oscar winner Al Pacino, playing a blind retired army officer, teaches a beautiful girl how to tango.

RUDOLPH VALENTINO 'The Son of the Sheik'

© Image courtesy of The Advertising Archives

Xavier Cugat and his glamorous wife, Abbe Lane

woman, sees the man pull out a stick, then pulls out his own and knocks him down. The orchestra resumes, and Valentino and the woman begin to dance. They move sensuously across the dance floor, and as the dance ends, they share a passionate kiss.

The film was a sensation. It became the top-grossing film of the year, made Valentino a star and established him as the quintessential Latin lover, and reignited America's passion for the tango. That same year, Xavier Cugat formed his first tango orchestra, Xavier Cugat and His Gigolos. Cugat was born in Spain, grew up in Cuba, and was a skilled enough violinist to attempt a concert career. After dissolving his orchestra to briefly pursue a career as a cartoonist, he regrouped toward the end of the decade, again focusing on the tango. However, by the early 1930s, he was well on his way to becoming the "Rumba King." For more than two decades, he and his orchestra represented the only Latin music most non-Hispanic Americans knew. He would appear in more feature films than any other American bandleader, enjoy a string of hit records, and for more than a decade would lead the resident dance orchestra at New York's swanky Waldorf-Astoria Hotel.

Although his band still performed tangos, Cugat stayed on top of the trends in Latin music: the rumba in the 1930s and early 1940s, and the mambo after World War II. His career parallels the history of Latin dance music in the United States: emerging first as an exotic novelty, then gradually integrating with and influencing non-Latin popular styles even as it maintained a distinct identity. In this chapter, we offer

tango Sensuous Argentinian dance

an American perspective on Latin dance music and focus particularly on the quite different paths of the tango and the mambo.

LO3 Latin Music in the United States

The 52nd Grammy Awards in 2010 included thirty fields, among them Pop, Dance, Jazz, Classical, Country, and Latin; the Latin field has seven categories, including Latin Pop, Tropical Latin, and Norteño. The Latin Recording Academy, a nonprofit organization of artists, musicians, and musical professionals based in Miami, has sponsored the Latin Grammy Awards since 2000. For 2010, there were eighteen fields with forty-nine categories, including Salsa, Cumbia, Tango, and Samba, as well as Pop, Rock, Urban, and Christian.

The numerous categories in both the traditional and the Latin Grammy Awards make clear that "Latin" is an umbrella term for a diverse body of music. Its main common ground is its roots in the Spanish- and Portuguese-speaking regions of the Americas. What has been called "Latin music" since the middle of the twentieth century encompasses three broad categories of music:

- Music from a particular region of Latin America, such as the Argentine tango or the Brazilian samba
- Latin/non-Latin hybrids, created by Latin musicians who incorporate non-Latin musical features into their music; for example, tejano music, created by Mexicans living in Texas, which incorporates various non-Mexican styles; Brazilian bossa nova, which combines samba with American popular song and jazz
- Non-Latin music with Latin elements, such as the "Latin" songs of Cole Porter and Carlos Santana's Latin rock

The first Latin styles to gain significant traction in the United States were the tango and the rumba, both of which trace their roots to Cuba.

Latin Music from Cuba

Before 1960, most of the Latin music that attracted a substantial American following and the interest of non-Latin musicians came directly or indirectly from Cuba. The Afro-Cuban habanera entered the United States by way of Mexico, where it had become popular in the 1870s: Scott Joplin subtitled "Solace," a piano piece

Tango

based on the habanera rhythm, as "Mexican Serenade." The rhythms of the habanera were absorbed almost imperceptibly into the cakewalk, a dance popular around the turn of the twentieth century, and into ragtime song.

Musical evidence suggests that the habanera also went south, where it became the rhythmic basis for the **tango**, a sensuous Argentinian dance. In this form, it took a roundabout route back to America. The tango arrived in America in 1913, from Argentina by way of Paris, where Vernon Castle, a British ballroom dancer, and his American wife, Irene, had captivated audiences with their tango dancing. Upon their return to the United States, the Castles introduced the tango in a Broadway show, *The Sunshine Girl*, where it was a sensation. Almost overnight, the tango became the first of the twentieth-century Latin dance fads in the United States, then became a fixture in popular culture, especially in musicals and films.

Maracas

Rumba

Less than two decades later, the rumba, triggered by the overnight success of Cuban bandleader Don Azpiazú's 1930 recording of "El Manisero "(The Peanut Vendor), became the hot new Latin dance. The **rumba** grew out of an Afro-Cuban genre called the *son*. Developing from African and Hispanic elements, the *son* apparently originated in eastern Cuba. It surfaced in Havana around the turn of the century and became popular among all classes with the growth of Cuban commercial radio in the 1920s. "El Manisero" introduced the rhythms of the *son* and authentic Cuban instruments, such as maracas and timbales (Cuban drums), to American listeners.

The Cuban music of Azpiazú quickly gave way to a broad array of Latin/American hybrids. The Latin-tinged songs of Cole Porter ("Begin the Beguine"), Irving Berlin ("Heat Wave"), and others were built on Americanized versions of the rumba rather than the more conventional rhythmic foundation of the fox-trot. In particular, Cugat cultivated an American pop/Latin fusion—Cuban percussion instruments, Americanized Cuban rhythms, vocals in English, sumptuous strings— to broaden the appeal of his music. However, the most far-reaching Latin/American fusion was the mambo.

THE MAMBO

The **mambo** is a musical style created by Afro-Cubans living in New York. Latin musicians cross-bred authentic Afro-Cuban son, as performed in New York by musicians like Arsenio Rodriguez, with big-band horns and riffs. It thrived in New York because of an influx of Cuban musicians and a Latin population that supported them.

The establishment of a Latin district, or *barrio*, in New York dates back to the turn of the century, when, as a consequence of the 1898 Spanish-American War, Spain ceded Puerto Rico to the United States. Puerto Ricans were allowed to immigrate to the United States without restriction. Latinos from

Mambo

rumba Latin dance that grew out of an Afro-Cuban genre called the *son*

son The most common Cuban popular music; literally, "sound"

mambo Musical style and dance created in the 1940s by Afro-Cubans living in New York

other parts of the Caribbean soon followed. New York was the most popular destination. Most settled in upper Manhattan's east Harlem—the "Spanish Harlem" celebrated in Ben E. King's 1961 hit.

By the late 1920s, a substantial community of Cuban musicians resided in the United States. Some appeared in vaudeville or worked in society dance orchestras, but many also played for clubs and recorded for companies catering to Latin communities in the United States and Latin America.

Mambo was born in 1940, when Machito (Frank Grillo [1912–1984]), New York's first important *sonero* (lead singer in a *son* band), formed his own band, Machito's Afro-Cubans, and hired fellow Cuban (and brother-in-law) Mario Bauzá as musical director. Bauzá had worked in black swing bands and wanted to combine Cuban rhythms with the horn sound of swing. Despite the infusion of big-band riffs and (in Machito's music) bebop harmonies, mambo was, at its core, a Cuban music. This is most clearly evident in the prominent place of the rhythmic signature of Afro-Cuban music, the clave rhythm, named after the **claves**, short wooden sticks used as percussion instruments in Latin music.

In Afro-Cuban music, the beat is felt rather than marked explicitly. The most prominent overlaying rhythms move twice as fast as the beat. **Clave rhythm** is the asymmetrical grouping of this faster-moving rhythm. One statement of the rhythm lasts two measures in quadruple meter.

Beat	1	2	3	4	1	2	3	4
Fast overlay rhythm	x x	x x	x x	x x	x x	x x	x x	x x
Clave rhythm	X	X	X		X	X		

The relation of the clave rhythm to the beat and to faster rhythms

claves Short wooden sticks used as percussion instruments in Latin music

clave rhythm Signature asymmetrical grouping of the faster-moving rhythms at the base of Afro-Cuban music

Claves

Clave is to Afro-Cuban rhythm what the backbeat is to American dance rhythms: its most elemental feature and main point of reference. Playing "in clave" is to Afro-Cuban music what rocking is to rock or swinging is to swing. In stylistically authentic Cuban music, other rhythms conform to clave or react against it in a specific way. We hear clave rhythm and other features of Afro-Cuban music in "Carambola," a track recorded by Machito and his orchestra in 1951.

The asymmetrical nature of clave rhythm highlights a fundamental difference between Afro-Cuban rhythm and the black rhythms heard in jazz, blues, and popular song. In American music, the beat is typically marked by a walking bass or a strummed guitar. In Afro-Cuban music, the attention is on the faster rhythms and the clave pattern; the beat is felt but not necessarily kept by any particular instrument.

"Carambola" employs a loosely structured verse/chorus pattern: an extended *canto* (a verselike section featuring the *sonero*) is followed by a coro, which features exchanges between the *sonero* and a group of singers, supported mainly by percussion instruments.

The mambo caught on outside the Latin community shortly after World War II and remained popular through the 1950s: *West Side Story* includes Leonard Bernstein's take on the mambo in the gym scene where Tony sees Maria for the first time. "Carambola" was released in 1951, at the peak of the mambo craze. Machito's orchestra was a big enough attraction that they secured engagements downtown at the Palladium Ballroom, the hotspot for Latin music in the early 1950s, and signed a recording contract with Columbia Records (now Sony).

LISTEN UP!

CD 5:18
Machito, "Carambola" (1951)

Takeaway point: The vibrant rhythms and sounds of an Afro-Cuban/American fusion

Style: Latin dance music

Form: Verse/chorus, with instrumental breaks

Genre: Mambo

Instruments: Vocal, brass, saxophones, piano, bass, Latin percussion instruments

Context: Hot dance music for energetic and skillful dancers

Latin Music at Midcentury

The mambo would be the third and last Latin dance craze before the rise of rock, and the first that was based on music created by Latin musicians living in the United States. During the 1950s, the full range of Afro-Cuban music and music influenced by it included these styles:

- "Uptown" mambos, an Afro-Cuban/American fusion aimed mainly at the Hispanic community in New York
- "Downtown" mambos and other more commercial Latin dance music (Cuban bandleader Perez Prado scored two number 1 mambo hits in the 1950s, and Desi Arnaz portrayed Latin bandleader Ricky Ricardo on the popular television show *I Love Lucy*.)
- Latin/jazz fusions, beginning with "cubop" and continuing into the 1950s
- Latin rhythms in popular song, as an alternative to the prevailing fox-trot and swing rhythms
- Latin novelty numbers by pop performers (Perry Como and Nat "King" Cole recorded a song called "Papa Loves Mambo," which was a million-seller for Como in 1954.)
- Latin rhythms in rhythm and blues songs, especially those from New Orleans

Even as Afro-Cuban sounds and rhythms infiltrated American popular music and jazz, the tango remained largely a novelty in American musical life, watered down in Broadway musicals and parodied in cartoons. However, back in Argentina, a new kind of tango was taking shape.

The New Tango

Carlos Gardel (1890?–1935) arrived in New York on December 28, 1933, to perform on network radio and make films for distribution throughout the Spanish-speaking Americas. Gardel was Argentina's biggest singing star and the person most responsible for broadening the range of the tango. Beginning with his first *tango canción* (tango song) in 1917, the tango became a vocal music, and he was by far its leading interpreter, at home and abroad.

Shortly after his arrival, he was introduced to Astor Piazzolla (1921–1992). Piazzolla was born in Argentina, but his family moved to New York shortly after his birth. Piazzolla's father gave him a *bandoneón* when he was a young child. (The **bandoneón** is a button accordion invented in Germany in the 1840s and brought to Argentina by German immigrants in the latter part of the century. It quickly became the defining sound of the tango orchestra.) By the age of nine, Piazzolla was performing in public; by thirteen, he played well enough to record with Gardel and the NBC Orchestra. Piazzolla became Gardel's translator and guide during the latter's year-long stay in New York. Gardel invited him to join his entourage for a tour through the Caribbean and northern South America, which he had to decline because of his youth. Piazzolla returned to Argentina two years later, where he would become the most famous tango instrumentalist and its most inventive innovator.

As with much Latin music, the defining characteristics of the tango were a sound and a rhythm. It was the rhythm that spread to Europe and North America during the first two decades of the twentieth century; the sound largely stayed home.

The first tango bands were small groups—from three to six players. They included melody instruments, such as the violin or flute; chord-producing instruments, such as the guitar and piano; and the *bandoneón*. The unheard orchestra shown in Valentino's tango scene is characteristic: two violins, guitar, piano, and *bandoneón*.

As the dance gained favor, in Argentina and elsewhere, these small groups grew in size, adding more strings. Gardel's tango songs and the success of the tango abroad raised the social status of the dance and ushered in the tango's "golden age." From the 1920s through the early 1950s, the tango reigned supreme in

> **bandoneón** Button accordion invented in Germany in the 1840s and brought to Argentina by German immigrants in the latter part of the century; the defining sound of the tango orchestra

Astor Piazzolla playing the *bandoneón*

© E Comesana/Lebrecht Music & Arts

Argentina. However, the absence of significant innovation contributed to its loss of popularity after World War II; it remained for Astor Piazzolla to revive it.

PIAZZOLLA AND THE TANGO

Although Piazzolla found work in the top tango orchestra in Buenos Aires soon after his return to Argentina, he chafed at the limitations of tango style. He eventually formed his own tango orchestra and studied with the esteemed Argentinian classical composer Alberto Ginastera. In 1954, he went to Paris to study with Nadia Boulanger, Copland's composition teacher. After looking at his classical compositions, she asked him to play, then assured him that his music spoke most powerfully and personally through the tango. With that, Piazzolla returned to Argentina and began creating what he called *tango nuevo*, or "new tango."

The easiest way to hear the sophistication of Piazzolla's nuevo tango music is to compare the music in this scene from Scent of a Woman with "Chiqué."

© Moviestore collection Ltd/Alamy

From the 1960s on, Piazzolla stretched the boundaries of the tango, not by merging it with contemporary popular styles but by moving it closer to concert music: the influence of both classical music and modern jazz are evident. His reputation grew, first in Argentina, then throughout the world. Toward the end of his life, he enjoyed an international following, with successful and acclaimed appearances in the United States during the 1980s. Among the first fruits of Piazzolla's revolution is "Chiqué," an impassioned tango that Piazzolla recorded with his quintet in 1961.

PIAZZOLLA AND THE TANGO AS ART

In "Chiqué," we hear how Piazzolla mastered the difficult balancing act between tradition and innovation that was the essence of his *tango nuevo*. His quintet consists of violin, electric guitar, piano, double bass (here played with a bow), and himself performing on the *bandoneón*. This continues the traditional instrumentation of the tango ensemble; the double bass, al-

LISTEN UP!

CD 5:19

Piazzolla, "Chiqué" (1961)

Takeaway point: A tango made *nuevo* (new) through the infusion of jazz and classical elements

Style: Latin music

Form: Multisectional

Genre: Tango nuevo

Instruments: Bandoneón, violin, guitar, piano, double bass, güiro (hollow percussion instrument that makes a ratcheting sound)

Context: A tango for listening and (sophisticated) dancing

though not present in the orchestra seen in Valentino's tango scene, became part of the tango orchestra during its golden age.

Piazzolla's innovations touched every musical element. The rhythms use the strong beat marking and habanera patterns characteristic of the traditional tango as a point of departure, but they are more syncopated and far more varied; indeed, there are moments when time seems briefly suspended. The dominant melodic material includes impassioned phrases and running lines that evoke the melodic bursts of bebop. The harmony often suggests a connection to the rich chords heard in French classical music of the 1920s and 1930s, as well as the modern jazz of the 1950s. The textures range from dense contrapuntal webs to block chords over a steady bass—Piazzolla's adaptation of a popular modern jazz sound. The form features three distinct, strongly contrasting sections; the sharp contrasts are another indication of Piazzolla's innovative approach.

Piazzolla's *tango nuevo* evolved by assimilating more sophisticated features, much as bop and post-bop jazz did. At the same time, Piazzolla retained the nostril-flaring passion that is the essence of the tango, just as jazz retained its core-defining swing.

With Piazzolla's "Cliqué," the tango's journey from the slums on the outskirts of Buenos Aires to the international stage was largely complete. Subsequently, Piazzolla's music was incorporated into art films and has been performed by classical and jazz performers as well as tango orchestras. In the sense that it began as a vernacular music among the lower classes and ended as concert music, the tango followed a path similar to that of most of the dances we have encountered. What differentiates this performance from other dance-related art music is Piazzolla's presence as a performer. In this recording, he plays the *bandoneón*, a "people's instrument," as expressively and skillfully as his classically trained violinist colleague. It adds an extra dimension to his tango, which transcends dance music to express the soul of the Argentinian people.

The Acceptance of Latin Music in the United States

For those familiar with the history of twentieth-century American popular music, the accounts of the tango and mambo may well seem like déjà vu. Like ragtime and early jazz, the tango and *son* emerged from the lower classes; were performed mainly in disreputable places; and prompted outrage from "respectable" citizens in large part because the new dances seemed to encourage a wanton and dissolute lifestyle and (except in Argentina) association with blacks. Yet both overcame hostility and prejudice to become the shaping force in the new popular music of its country. By the 1930s, the tango and rumba were as widely accepted in their home countries as the fox-trot was in the United States.

However, for most Americans, authentic Argentinian tangos—the kind that they might have heard in Valentino's film if it had had a sound track—remained an exotic and relatively unfamiliar sound throughout much of the twentieth century. Only in the last quarter of the century did the tango enjoy a mild rebirth, as dance music and as an elegant, expressive, and accessible art music.

By contrast, although the mambo was soon eclipsed by the cha-cha-chá, which was simpler to dance, and then by rock-era dances, its sounds and rhythms have continued to reverberate through popular music in America.

They are most apparent in **salsa**, which is in essence an updated form of the mambo. More generally, elements of Afro-Cuban music became part of the fabric of rock and rhythm and blues. What made the assimilation of Afro-Cuban elements into rock and R&B so seamless was the new rhythmic foundation of rock-era music. In modern-era pop and jazz, each beat was typically divided into two unequal segments, in a long/short pattern. By contrast, the dominant rhythm is the same in Cuban music and rock and roll: both feature activity at twice the speed of the beat. As a result, beginning in the late 1950s, the greater complexity and freedom of Cuban-inspired rhythms became an alternative to rock rhythm: Ray Charles's 1959 hit "What'd I Say" is a noteworthy early example. Moreover, Afro-Cuban percussion instruments, most notably the conga drum, are frequently heard in rock and rhythm and blues: the Rolling Stones' 1969 number 1 hit "Honky Tonk Women" opens with a habanera rhythm tapped out on a cowbell. And even the Latin rock of Santana doesn't represent so much a different rhythmic conception as a different emphasis within the same rhythmic conception.

Although it emanates from the same source, Latin music from Cuba and Argentina has had quite a different history in the United States. There are clear extramusical reasons. Havana is about thirteen hundred miles from New York; Buenos Aires is over fifty-two hundred. The number of Argentinian immigrants is a small fraction of the number of Cuban expatriates and others from Spanish-speaking Caribbean countries.

But the musical reasons have mainly to do with the extent of African influence. Argentina is almost all white—some estimates reach as high as 97 percent. By contrast, it is estimated that about one-third of the population in Cuba and almost half the population in Brazil are either black or mixed race. The differences in sound and rhythm reflect the varying degree of African influence. In the tango, it is confined mainly to the occasional syncopation. Golden-age tango orchestras, such as the one portrayed in Valentino's film, do not include bass or percussion instruments. By contrast, Afro-Cuban music features numerous percussion instruments and complex rhythms.

With the gradual evolution of American popular music toward more African rhythms and sounds, it was just a matter of time before Afro-Cuban music, as realized in the mambo, would mesh with American popular music. We hear the next stage of the evolution of popular music in our discussion of rock.

salsa Contemporary Latin dance that is in essence an updated form of the mambo

The Rock Revolution

"I knew they were pointing the direction where music had to go."
—Bob Dylan, on first hearing The Beatles

To create the cover of The Beatles' 1967 album *Sgt. Pepper's Lonely Hearts Club Band*, designer Peter Blake cut out and arranged more than sixty life-size cardboard images of the band's current heroes. It's a provocative assemblage of famous, once-famous, and not-so-famous personalities: geniuses and gurus; athletes, artists, and actors; writers and comics; and many more. The Beatles appear twice: as wax-museum likenesses (left of center) from their Beatlemania period and "live," dressed in bright band uniforms.

By conflating high and popular culture, past and present, and musicians and nonmusicians—except for The Beatles and ex-Beatle Stuart Sutcliffe, the only musicians on the cover are Fred Astaire, better known for his dancing than his singing, avant-garde composer Karlheinz Stockhausen, and Bob Dylan—Blake's collage signals a new understanding of culture and society. In the postmodern world of the last part of the twentieth century, class distinctions diminished, cultural hierarchies crumbled, and boundaries dissolved. Rock was not only the sound track for these developments but also an agent of change.

Did You Know?

A cardboard image of avant-garde composer Karlheinz Stockhausen, who inspired Paul McCartney, appears on the album cover of *Sgt. Pepper's Lonely Hearts Club Band.*

The *Sgt. Pepper* album cover conflates high and popular culture, past and present, and musicians and nonmusicians.

© Redferns/Getty Images

No other aspect of culture played as significant a role as rock did in reshaping values in Western society. With their openness to new ideas, their unparalleled imagination in integrating the most disparate elements into coherent statements, and their unprecedented popularity, The Beatles played a leading role in a movement that transformed both musical life and Western culture in the last third of the twentieth century.

In this chapter, we focus on rock's meteoric ascent from a teen-themed tangent of postwar rhythm and blues to music of significance and influence. We highlight key stages in its transformation through four examples, by Chuck Berry, the Beach Boys, Bob Dylan, and The Beatles, then summarize its impact on musical life in the latter part of the twentieth century. We begin with rock and roll.

LO4 From Rock and Roll to Rock

In the excellent documentary *Rock and Roll: The Early Years*, there's a clip of a white preacher ranting and raving about the evils of rock and roll. He asks his congregation what it is about rock and roll that makes it so seductive to young people, then immediately answers his own question by shouting, "The BEAT! The BEAT! The BEAT!" thumping the pulpit with each "beat." It was the beat that drew teens to rock and roll during the 1950s.

ROCK RHYTHM

The "beat"—the distinctive rhythmic organization of rock and roll—wasn't entirely new. Boogie-woogie pianists had been pounding it out in bars and barrelhouses since the late 1920s. But delivered on an amplified guitar with backing from bass and drums, it became invasive and, to some listeners, abrasive. Rock and roll had a rhythm and a sound that many teens found irresistibly appealing and their parents found simply appalling.

What made rock rhythm so attractive to teens and so repellent to many of their parents was the fundamental level of activity. Adults had grown up listening to the rhythms of swing, in which the defining rhythms moved at beat speed—the walking bass of jazz—or slower. By contrast, the defining feature of rock is its insistent rhythm that moves twice as fast as the beat. It was this doubling of activity, delivered relentlessly and at what was then considered to be a loud volume, that stimulated teens in the early years of rock. The architect of this sound was Chuck Berry.

Chuck Berry, Architect of Rock and Roll

Sometime early in 1955, Chuck Berry "motorvated" (to use a Chuck Berry coinage) from St. Louis to Chicago to hear Muddy Waters, for years his idol, perform at the Palladium Theater. After the concert, Berry went backstage and asked Waters how he could get a record deal. Waters suggested that he contact Leonard Chess. Two weeks later, Berry was back in Chicago, handing Leonard Chess a demo tape containing four songs. Among them was Berry's remake of a song called "Ida Red," which he entitled "Maybellene." Chess liked the song, Berry recorded it, and Chess released it on August 20, 1955.

"Maybellene" caught the ear of DJ Alan Freed, who promoted the song by playing it frequently on his radio show after negotiating a share of the songwriting credits—and the royalties that went with them. With Freed's considerable help—Freed reportedly

"Are These Our Children?" Rock and roll had a rhythm and a sound that many teens found irresistibly appealing and their parents found simply appalling.

Chuck Berry, architect of rock and roll

played the song for two hours straight on one broadcast—"Maybellene" quickly jumped to number 5 on the *Billboard* "Best Seller" chart.

Berry would have to wait almost a year for his next hit, "Roll Over, Beethoven," to reach the charts in the fall of 1956. In the hits from "Roll Over, Beethoven" to "Johnny B. Goode," Berry assembled the distinctive sound of rock and roll, step by step.

The heart of Berry's new conception was an intensified adaptation of the repetitive accompaniment patterns of boogie woogie, a two-fisted blues piano style popular in the 1930s and 1940s. Berry learned the sound of **boogie woogie** during his long association with pianist Johnny Johnson. He transferred Johnson's patterns to his guitar, gave it an edgy sound, and surrounded himself with piano, bass, and drums. Simultaneously, he developed a lead guitar style that built on the same active rhythm, with frequent double notes and lots of syncopation.

On his classic recordings, Berry advanced this new conception by himself, most notably on "Johnny B. Goode," where he apparently plays both lead and rhythm guitar through **overdubbing**, the process of recording additional sounds on an existing recording. But the other band members—Johnson and the best of Chess Records' house musicians—were still locked into the less active rhythms of swing and country.

However, it didn't take long for Berry's innovation to catch on. Aspiring rock and rollers on both sides of the Atlantic tuned in to Berry's new rhythmic conception. The list of acts that covered Berry's music reads like a Who's Who of late 1950s and early 1960s rock: Buddy Holly, the Beach Boys, The Beatles, the Rolling Stones, the Hollies, and the Kinks. These and other acts covered far more Chuck Berry songs than the songs of any other rock-and-roll artist.

Among the first Beach Boys hits was "Surfin' U.S.A." The song was released in March 1963 and quickly climbed the charts, peaking at number 3. The song wasn't a cover of a Chuck Berry song, but it might as well have been: Brian Wilson, the main songwriter for the group, put new words to Berry's 1958 hit "Sweet Little

boogie woogie Blues piano style characterized by repetitive accompaniment patterns in a low register

overdubbing Process of recording additional sounds on an existing recording

Sixteen." Because Wilson claimed sole songwriting credit, Berry sued, and in response Wilson's father, who was the group's manager at the time, gave Berry full songwriting credit (and the royalties that went with it).

A comparison of the two versions highlights key features of the transformation of rock and roll into rock. One key difference is the Beach Boys' use of electric bass instead of the acoustic bass of pre-rock pop. In 1963, the electric bass was still a relatively new instrument. Leo Fender invented it in 1950, but it was not widely used until the early 1960s. However, it soon became the standard bass instrument in rock because with amplification, it could match the power of the electric guitar.

The other significant change was the use of Berry's innovative rock rhythm by the entire band. Every part in the song—vocal line, rhythm guitar, organ solo, bass line, and drum part—either reinforces this more active rhythm or lines up with it. This development harnessed the energy of rock rhythm so that listeners felt its full impact.

More than any other developments, these two changes transformed rock and roll into rock. The pervasive use of rock rhythm and the replacement of the acoustic bass with the electric bass made this still-new music louder, more active, and more intrusive. We can hear this transformation in a side-by-side comparison of Berry's "Sweet Little Sixteen" and the Beach Boys' "Surfin' U.S.A."

By the time British bands invaded the United States in early 1964, rock had become impossible to ignore.

LISTEN UP!

CD 5:20–21

Berry, "Sweet Little Sixteen" (1958) / Wilson, "Surfin' U.S.A." (1963)

Takeaway point: The Beach Boys' remake of Berry's hit demonstrating the transformation of rock 'n' roll into rock

Style: Rock 'n' roll / early 1960s rock

Form: Modified blues form in melody; strophic/variation form in song as a whole

Genre: Rock 'n' roll / early 1960s rock

Instruments: Voice, electric guitar, piano, bass, drums, lead and backup vocals, electric guitar, electric bass, organ, drums

Context: Both songs directed toward young audience

Beatlemania reinvigorated rock, which had lost much of its momentum in part due to Elvis's induction into the army and Buddy Holly's death in a plane crash on February 3, 1959.

But it was still possible to dismiss rock as mindless music for teens: the original cast album of the musical *Hello, Dolly!* replaced The Beatles' second album at the top of the album charts in June 1964. That would soon change in the wake of a fateful meeting two months later.

Rock of Significance: Dylan and The Beatles

On August 28, 1964, Bob Dylan and The Beatles met face-to-face for the first time. The Beatles were on tour in the United States and staying at the Delmonico Hotel in New York. They had acquired the album *The Freewheelin' Bob Dylan* while in Paris in January 1964; according to George Harrison, they wore the record out, listening to it over and over. John Lennon in particular seemed drawn to Dylan's gritty sound and rebellious attitude. Somewhat later during that same year, Dylan was driving through Colorado when he heard The Beatles for the first time over the radio. Later he would say, "I knew they were pointing the direction where music had to go." Each had something that the other wanted, and perhaps found intimidating. The Beatles, especially Lennon, envied Dylan's forthrightness; Dylan responded to the power of their kind of rock and envied their commercial success. It was Lennon who requested the meeting, through Al Aronowitz, a columnist for the *New York Post*; Aronowitz brought Dylan down from Woodstock to meet The Beatles.

Whatever initial uneasiness they may have felt with one another quickly went up in smoke. Upon learning that none of The Beatles had tried marijuana, Dylan promptly rolled a couple of joints and passed them around. As Paul McCartney later recalled, "Till then, we'd been hard Scotch and Coke men. It sort of changed that evening."

However, there was more to this meeting than turning The Beatles on. It seemed to further motivate both parties to learn from the other. In explaining their musical breakthrough in the mid-1960s, McCartney said, "We were only trying to please Dylan." As for Dylan, the experience gave him additional motivation to go electric, which he did on one side of his next album, *Bringing It All Back Home*, recorded in January 1965.

After that, he never looked back. In retrospect, his years as a folksinger, as important as they were to his career, were simply a prelude to his more substantial career as a rock musician.

We encounter both acts through music from the most significant period in their careers—from the date of their meeting through the release of *Sgt. Pepper's Lonely Hearts Club Band*.

BOB DYLAN

© M&N/Alamy

Highway 61 Revisited and *Blonde on Blonde*, Dylan's first two all-electric albums, brought into full flower the rock-fueled power promised on the electric side of *Bringing It All Back Home*. However, none of his early electric music is typical rock fare. There are no recurrent stylistic conventions, such as a basic beat, harmonic approach, or formal plan. Instead, Dylan invests rock with a freewheeling, anything-goes attitude. Despite their deep roots in rock and roll, blues, folk, country, and Beat poetry, the songs are shockingly original. They juxtapose the sublime and the ridiculous and package elusive and challenging ideas in images that brand themselves in your memory.

Dylan's most far-reaching musical innovation was the evocative use of musical style. He used beats, instruments, harmonies, forms, and the like to create an atmosphere. No one before Dylan had let it penetrate so deeply into the fabric of the music. The varied settings continually recontextualized Dylan's voice. When he sings, it isn't pretty by conventional pop standards, and much of the time his vocalizing is closer to speech than to conventional singing. But it is the ideal vehicle for the trenchant commentary in his lyrics.

Among the most provocative examples of this new approach on *Bringing It All Back Home* was "Subterranean Homesick Blues." The lyric was a stream of obscure references, inside jokes, and stinging social commentary—all delivered much too fast to understand in a single hearing. The density of the lyric and the speed of Dylan's delivery challenged listeners to become engaged; one could not listen to him casually and expect to get much out of the experience.

Dylan embedded his challenging lyrics in a blue-jeans musical setting. His backup band included a full rhythm section behind his acoustic guitar and harmonica. They supported Dylan with a clear two-beat rhythm with a strong backbeat, which derived most directly from **honky-tonk**, the post–World War II country style popularized by such artists as Hank Williams. The ornery mood it set up right at the start was an ideal backdrop for Dylan's words and voice. Dylan delivered his proto-rap lyric as a talking blues, a genre created by Southern rural bluesmen and adapted by Dylan's hero Woody Guthrie.

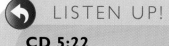

LISTEN UP!

CD 5:22

Dylan, "Subterranean Homesick Blues" (1965)

Takeaway point: Complex, sophisticated lyrics in a down-home musical setting

Style: Rock

Form: Expanded blues form

Genre: Significant rock

Instruments: Voice, harmonica, acoustic guitar, electric guitars, electric bass, drums

Context: Dylan using working-class music as a background for a significant social statement

Dylan's music inverted the traditional pop approach to artistry. Before him, those who wanted to create artistic popular music emulated classical models: George Gershwin's *Rhapsody in Blue* or musical theater productions like *West Side Story*. Dylan's music sent a quite different message: one can be sophisticated without being "sophisticated"—that is, without borrowing the conventional indicators of musical sophistication, such as symphonic strings.

With Dylan, rock grew up. It was no longer possible to mock rock—or at least Dylan's music—as mindless music for teens. His music and the music of those inspired by him not only gave rock artistic credibility and significance but also redefined what credibility was. It democratized popular music while elevating its message in a way that had never

honky-tonk Post–World War II country style popularized by such artists as Hank Williams

been done before: with Dylan, high art did not have to assume high-class trappings.

Dylan's early electric work quickly became the standard by which those who followed him were measured. He inspired others not so much by providing a model that others would copy as by showing through example what could be said in rock. In this way, his influence was profound and pervasive.

For The Beatles, the reverberation from their encounter with Dylan bore fruit about ten months later, when they began work on *Rubber Soul*; the album would be released in December 1965. *Rubber Soul*, the "Dylan album," would make clear the dramatic evolution of their music. The evolution would continue in *Revolver*, released the following year, and most remarkably in *Sgt. Pepper's Lonely Hearts Club Band*.

With Dylan, rock grew up.

THE BEATLES

By the time The Beatles got together with Dylan, they were riding the crest of Beatlemania. Their first three American albums topped the charts; so did numerous singles. Their first appearance on *The Ed Sullivan*

By the time The Beatles got together with Dylan—the very day this issue of *Life* was published—they were riding the crest of Beatlemania.

Show, on February 9, 1964, drew 73 million viewers, and their first film, *A Hard Day's Night*, had just opened in American theaters.

In 1964, The Beatles (John Lennon, Paul McCartney, George Harrison, and Ringo Starr) were young but experienced and versatile, the result of long hours spent performing in Liverpool clubs and strip joints in Hamburg, Germany. In 1962, they auditioned for producer George Martin, who would become their irreplaceable collaborator, and had their first hit later that year. The year 1963 saw a string of hits and growing international recognition, which led to the release of their recordings in the United States and their first American tour.

Their early work built mainly on the work of important American rock-and-roll acts. They typically used the two guitar/bass/drums instrumentation popularized by Buddy Holly, and their first hits were teen-themed songs like "I Want to Hold Your Hand." Before their encounter with Dylan, they had begun searching for qualities that would set them apart: the clangorous chord that begins "A Hard Day's Night" is evidence of that. But even this striking sound hardly prepared their fans for the dramatic evolution of their music over the next three years.

The Beatles' musical growth was unparalleled in popular music; the suddenness with which their music matured remains an astounding development. Like Dylan, they were expanding their sound world, but in a more adventurous, all-encompassing way. Dylan drew mainly on existing popular styles and used them evocatively. By contrast, The Beatles reached further afield, into musical traditions far removed from rock and its roots, such as classical Indian music and string playing reminiscent of classical music. Moreover, they synthesized these nonrock sounds seamlessly into their music; they became part of the fabric of sound behind the vocals.

As their music matured, it became bolder and more individual. The songs are more clearly the work of The Beatles—no one else could have made them—and less like each other. The contrast from song to song had clearly deepened. One can almost reach into a bag filled with song titles, pull out any five, and marvel at the distinctive identity in meaning and sound of each song and the pronounced differences from song to song. These differences reached a peak in *Sgt. Pepper's Lonely Hearts Club Band*, released in June 1967. The most remarkable track on this extraordinary album is "A Day in the Life."

The Sound World of The Beatles: "A Day in the Life"

The Beatles' "style" was an approach to musical choices more than a particular set of musical choices. Their music is almost always tuneful, regardless of its message: McCartney, Lennon, and Harrison were great melodists. More important, The Beatles were among the first important rock-era musicians to write melody-oriented songs that were in step with the changes in rhythm, form, and other elements that were transforming the sound of popular music.

They complemented their memorable melodies with distinctive sound worlds. Settings—instruments, textures, rhythms, even form—were purposeful; their function was to amplify and illuminate the message of the lyrics. Strong contrasts from song to song, and occasionally within a song, as in "Lucy in the Sky with Diamonds" and "A Day in the Life," both from *Sgt. Pepper's Lonely Hearts Club Band*, show the extent of their imagination and musical range. Both imagination and range are clearly evident in "A Day in the Life."

In "A Day in the Life," Lennon creates sound worlds that highlight the contrast between the mundane, everyday world and the elevated consciousness that results from tripping on LSD. They are projected by the most fundamental opposition in music itself, other than sound and silence: music with words versus music without words. The parts of the song with lyrics are everyday life, while the strictly instrumental sections depict tripping—they follow "I'd love to turn you on" or a reference to a dream.

This contrast is made even more striking by the nature of the words and music. The lyric features four vignettes. The first involves a gruesome automobile accident; the second is about a film—perhaps an allusion to the film *How I Won the War*, in which Lennon had acted. The third depicts someone in the workaday-world rat race, and the last one is a commentary on a news article about counting potholes. In Lennon's view, this is news reporting—and, by extension, daily life—at its most trivial: who would bother counting potholes anyway?

The music that underscores this text is, in its most obvious features, as everyday as the text. It begins with just a man and his guitar. The other instruments layer in, but none of them makes a spectacular contribution. This everyday background is opposed to the massive orchestral blob of sound that depicts, in its gradual ascent, the elevation of consciousness. The dense sound,

LISTEN UP!

The Beatles, "A Day in the Life" (1967)

Takeaway point: The greatest song of a great rock band

Style: Rock

Form: Multisectional

Genre: Early art rock

Instruments: Voices, rhythm instruments, strings

Context: The defining track on one of the first concept albums

masterfully scored by George Martin, belongs to the world of avant-garde classical music—it recalls Penderecki's *Threnody for the Victims of Hiroshima* and other works of that type, works familiar to classical music insiders but not well known generally. This creates another strong opposition: well-known versus obscure, and by implication, the unenlightened (not turned on) masses versus those few who are enlightened.

The final chord is an instrumental *om*, suggesting the clarity of enlightenment after the transition, via the orchestral section, from mundane life in the "normal" world. It is a striking ending to a beautifully conceived and exquisitely crafted song, a song that is one of the most powerful metaphors for the LSD experience ever created.

"A Day in the Life" encapsulates the art and achievement of The Beatles as well as any single track can. It highlights key features of their music: the sound imagination, the persistence of tuneful melody, and the close coordination between words and music. It represents a new category of song: more sophisticated than pop; more accessible and down to earth than pop; and uniquely innovative. There literally had never been a song—classical or vernacular—that had blended so many disparate elements so imaginatively. Critics searched for a way to describe the song and the album: they labeled it a **concept album** (an album unified by a particular creative theme) and declared it the rock-era counterpart to the song cycles of nineteenth- and twentieth-century art music.

"A Day in the Life" is less than four years removed from "She Loves You" and the other teen-themed singles of their early years. The Beatles had begun their career by affirming what rock was, in comparison

concept album Album unified by a particular creative theme

to rock and roll and pop. As they reached the zenith of their career, they showed what rock could be.

The Beatles remains rock's classic act in the fullest sense of the term. Their music has spoken not only to its own time but also to every generation since. Their songs are still in the air; they remain more widely known than any other music of the rock era. The Beatles' music is a cultural artifact of surpassing importance. No single source—of any kind—tells us more about the rock revolution of the 1960s than the music of The Beatles.

The Rock Revolution

The rock revolution was sudden and far reaching. In 1959, rock and roll seemed dead. However, less than a decade later, it had captured both market share and mind share: it had become *the* commercially dominant popular music and had begun to redefine both artistic merit and cultural values.

Rock was revolutionary because it changed both the sound of popular music and the messages it communicated. The generational difference might be summarized like this: pre-rock pop typically sought an escape from reality; rock intensified reality. During the Depression and World War II, momentary escape was a welcome, if occasional, antidote to the often-harsh reality of daily life. In the more prosperous postwar era it became as artificial as the lives portrayed in the popular situation comedies that filled TV screens.

By contrast, the best rock was real, in a way that earlier generations of pop seldom were. The message of the song reached its audience directly, because rock-era songwriters usually performed their own songs. Songs were not written *for* something—a musical or a film—so much as to say something. Rock's concern with the present, combined with its direct and often personal communication between song, singer, and audience, elevated the role of the music for many members of that audience from simple entertainment to (quoting noted rock critic Geoffrey Stokes) "a way of life."

Moreover, the rock revolution occurred during the 1960s, a decade of tumultuous social change. Civil rights, protests against the Vietnam War, free love, the gradual empowerment of women, the environmental movement, and a huge generation gap—all challenged the established social order. Rock was not only the sound track for these developments but also an agent of change. The messages embodied in the music and the example of its musicians helped shape attitudes toward minority rights and multiculturalism.

Rock soon gained a presence that the larger musical world could no longer ignore. It influenced virtually all established popular and vernacular genres: soft rock and pop rock, rock musicals, and jazz fusion were important new directions in the late 1960s and early 1970s. Even classical music wasn't above rock's influence. Among the important new trends in the latter part of the twentieth century that were at least tangentially influenced by the openness of rock were more eclectic compositional styles, a return to more accessible concert music, and minimalism. We sample these new directions in the final unit.

{ Test coming up? Now what? }

81% of students surveyed found that 4LTR Press Solutions, like MUSIC, made it easy to study for course exams.

With **MUSIC** you have a multitude of study aids at your fingertips. After reading the chapters and listening to the music at least once, check out these ideas for further help:

Unit in Review cards include all learning outcomes, definitions, Applying Unit Concepts exercises, and a timeline for each unit.

Active Listening Guides walk you through each piece of music step by step and provide additional information and quiz questions.

Online flashcards give you additional ways to check your comprehension of key music appreciation concepts.

Other great tools to help you study include **online quizzes**.

You'll find it all when you visit CourseMate at **www.cengagebrain.com**.

UNIT 23
LATE TWENTIETH-CENTURY MUSIC FOR CONCERT AND FILM

Learning Outcomes

After reading this unit, you will be able to do the following:

LO1 Become aware of the first generation of women composers who have enjoyed status comparable to that of their male counterparts, through the work of Joan Tower and Ellen Taaffe Zwilich.

LO2 Describe the world of the late twentieth-century film composer through an exploration of the music of John Williams and Tan Dun.

LO3 Explain the place of minimalism in late twentieth-century music.

FOR ASPIRING COMPOSERS who came of age during the early rock era, there was a sharp contrast between what they learned in their studies and what they heard outside the classroom. Although most initially followed the trail blazed by the midcentury avant-garde, many reacted against the Darmstadt dogmatists. They drew inspiration from myriad sources: not only classical music composed before 1950 but also East Indian music, African music, jazz, and rock.

The first significant postserial development was minimalism, the antithesis of serialism in almost every respect. It took shape during the 1960s in the work of a small group of counterculture composers. Others took a more eclectic approach, blurring boundaries between old and new, East and West, and high and low culture. They found common ground with new perspectives on tonality, form, rhythm, and musical meaning. The six musical examples presented in this unit hint at the range of these new directions.

© iStockphoto.com/Nikada

CHAPTER 54

Uncommon Women

"The move to unearth women artists, in music as in any other art, is not a neutral act, any more than is their previous neglect."
—Rhian Samuel, 1996

In 1902, Otto Ebel published *Women Composers: A Biographical Handbook of Women's Work in Music.* Ebel's pioneering survey included entries for more than 750 composers. *The Norton/ Grove Dictionary of Women Composers,* compiled by Julie Anne Sadie and Rhian Samuel and published in 1996, discusses almost 900 composers, all born before 1955. More inclusive musical dictionaries, such as Johann Walther's *Musicalisches Lexicon* and Grove's *Dictionary of Music and Musicians,* have also mentioned numerous women composers.

However, despite abundant sources and opportunities for research, many music scholars have until recently given women composers short shrift. Scholars' low opinion of women composers was often implicitly instilled from the start of their training. A case in point: through its first several editions, one leading music history textbook cited more than 450 composers; none was a woman. So it isn't surprising that in the preface of their dictionary, Samuel notes: "The move to unearth women

© Nikolais | Dreamstime.com

Did You Know?

Ellen Taaffe Zwilich was the first woman composer to be awarded the Pulitzer Prize in music.

artists, in music as in any other art, is not a neutral act, any more than is their previous neglect."

Today, women composers no longer work in obscurity. During the last part of the twentieth century, women composers past and present began to receive greater recognition. Several have won prestigious awards for their works, served as composers-in-residence for major orchestras, received substantial commissions for orchestral music and operas, and increasingly populate composition departments at major universities. The playing field in contemporary classical composition may not yet be level, but equal opportunity is much closer than it was a century ago.

Within a larger discussion of such matters as a distinctive "woman's voice" in composition, Samuel identifies "musical eclecticism"—a reconciliation of conflicting styles and cultures—as potentially a defining characteristic of the music of women composers:

> Of all the various trends of the late 20th century, this reconciliation of styles and cultures seems to have found particular favour among women composers. Should this tendency eventually prove to be more pronounced among women than men, the resultant image of the woman composer as Conciliator, or Reaper (of marginalized concerns) seems entirely appropriate, given her parallel social role of Wife/Mother.

In this chapter, we discuss two works: Joan Tower's *Fanfare for the Uncommon Woman* (1986) and Ellen Taaffe Zwilich's *Concerto Grosso 1985.* Their common ground goes beyond the fact that both are works by women composers and that both were composed only a year apart. Both demonstrate in varying degrees the musical eclecticism noted by Samuel, chart new approaches to tonality, and pay homage to Aaron Copland. In these ways, the works highlight noteworthy developments in late twentieth-century concert music.

LO1 Reconceiving Tonality

Among the more active participants in the Darmstadt School during the 1950s was the young German composer Hans Werner Henze (b. 1926). In the late 1940s, Henze embraced serial composition but turned away from it during the mid-1950s. His defection from serial orthodoxy was not well received by his some of his peers. In 1957, Henze's *Nachtstucke und Arien*, a work for soprano and orchestra, was performed at the Donaueschingener Musiktage, a long-running German new music festival. In the audience were three Darmstadt colleagues, Pierre Boulez, Karlheinz Stockhausen, and Luigi Nono. According to several accounts, all three walked out of the performance as soon as they heard a consonant horn melody.

It is possible to write atonal—even twelve-tone—music that retains elements commonly associated with tonal music, such as stepwise motion and consonant intervals. But the most avant-garde of composers disdained the use of these more familiar sounds in the quest for novelty and difference, as we heard previously. Accordingly, in the postwar years, cutting-edge music traded the trappings of tonality for bold new sound worlds that were compelling but not always easy on listeners.

For those contemporary classical composers who turned away from the extremes of serialism to return to more tonal, consonant, and "listenable" music, it was all but impossible to simply turn back the clock. The pressure for novelty was still there, and composers needed to find new modes of expression but use familiar materials. They had as resources the new approaches to tonality in jazz and rock, in addition to alternative approaches to tonality from the first half of the century. Mixing tonal music with atonal music, or even mixing it with sounds without specific pitch, was also an option.

neotonal music
Music composed since the mid-1960s that shares the qualities of (1) orientation around a tonic, (2) heavy reliance on consonant intervals, and (3) motives created mainly or exclusively from consonant intervals, including scale fragments and triads

Among the most widely used features of this **neotonal music** composed since the mid-1960s are these:

1. Orientation around a tonic, which is affirmed by a method other than common practice harmony
2. Heavy reliance on consonant intervals
3. Motives or musical cells created mainly or exclusively from consonant intervals, including scale fragments and triads

We will hear these more consonant approaches to pitch organization in works by Tower and Zwilich—in fact, in all the works discussed in this unit.

Beyond Ceremony: Music for Brass and Percussion

George Lucas's Star Wars series begins not with the famous main theme heard in the next chapter but with an eighteen-second fanfare. The famous film composer Alfred Newman composed it in 1933, and for many years all films from 20th Century Fox began with searchlights scanning the sky around the famous art-deco logo while the fanfare was playing. This film opener fell out of favor during the 1970s, until George Lucas reclaimed it for the Star Wars films. It has since been used in most 20th Century Fox films, occasionally in parody: the film *White Men Can't Jump* begins with a funk/disco version of the fanfare.

© Album/Newscom

 LISTEN FURTHER

Listen to the 20th Century Fox fanfare in the YouTube playlist on the text website.

Fanfares date back to the Middle Ages. Originally, they were short, often improvised pieces performed by trumpets and drums to present royalty during a ceremony or state occasion. Such fanfares were more about noise than music. In his musical dictionary, Johann Walther described its effect in this way: "[a fanfare] indeed makes enough noise and strutting, but otherwise hardly smacks of art."

Toward the end of the nineteenth century and into the twentieth, composers began producing short, ceremonial works for brass instruments—and occasionally with percussion—which they entitled **fanfares**. The most famous is Aaron Copland's *Fanfare for the Common Man*, composed in 1942. Copland's composition is stately and spacious sounding. Its title pointedly democratizes the fanfare: it is for the "common man" instead of a king or queen.

In 1986, Joan Tower composed the first of five fanfares "for the uncommon woman." She conceived of the work as a tribute and a response to Copland's fanfare. Both the Copland and the Tower works are scored for eleven brass and three percussion instruments. Both fanfares are more than ceremonial flourishes; they are short but substantial musical statements. As such, they exemplify a relatively recent trend in musical life: concert music for large ensembles featuring winds and percussion.

CONCERT MUSIC FOR WINDS

Among the major ensembles found in almost every good-sized university music program and many music conservatories is a group composed almost exclusively of woodwinds, brass, and percussion. These groups are typically identified by some combination of the terms *symphonic*, *wind(s)*, and *ensemble*: for example, wind ensemble, symphonic winds, symphonic wind ensemble. These are more prestigious terms for ensembles that evolved from the concert and military bands of the late nineteenth and early twentieth centuries.

The idea of a large ensemble whose repertoire consists almost exclusively of original concert music for winds and percussion took hold only in the latter half of the twentieth century. The driving force in this movement was Frederic Fennell, who formed the Eastman Wind Ensemble in 1952. The name of the group—wind ensemble, not band—reflected Fennell's high-minded approach. This approach distinguished them from the concert bands of the turn of the century, which performed marches, popular music, and transcriptions of the orchestral literature.

In 1952, there weren't many concert works for wind ensemble. The staples of the repertoire were early twentieth-century works by British composers, most notably Gustav Holst and Ralph Vaughan Williams, and individual works for large wind bands by Stravinsky, Schoenberg, and Hindemith. However, a series of innovative recordings by the Eastman Wind Ensemble helped popularize this repertoire, and the wind ensemble quickly became the high-minded counterpart to the concert band in university music programs.

Although there are no full-time resident wind ensembles comparable to symphony orchestras, there are numerous high-level amateur and part-time professional organizations throughout the world, including the Netherlands Wind Ensemble, a part-time professional ensemble made up of musicians from the three major Dutch orchestras, and wind symphonies in Tokyo and Dallas. As a result of commissions and the increased likelihood of performance and recording opportunities, late twentieth-century composers have considerably enriched the wind ensemble literature: the Eastman Wind Ensemble alone has premiered over 150 works.

More generally, the outpouring of music for large groups of wind and percussion instruments brings what used to be "outdoor" music into the concert hall. Much of the wind music composed in the eighteenth century was intended for performance outdoors. For instance, Mozart's works for large wind groups are called "serenades"; according to Walther, a serenade was "an evening piece; because such works are usually performed on quiet and pleasant nights."

In the nineteenth century, band concerts by amateur and professional groups often took place outside: many town squares have bandstands where municipal bands would perform in the summer. Sousa's band performed before thousands at the Chicago World's Fair. By contrast, there are only a handful of nineteenth-century concert works for wind groups, and most are large chamber works mainly for woodwinds, horns, and perhaps double bass.

In the twentieth century, composers have written concert works not only for band and wind ensemble but also for orchestral winds, brass, and/or percussion. The fanfares of Copland and Tower were among the numerous works of this type commissioned by symphony orchestras. These works could just as easily be

fanfare Short, ceremonial work for brass instruments and occasionally percussion

performed by wind ensembles, since they don't require strings; they also contribute to the growing body of music for larger ensembles of winds and percussion.

JOAN TOWER'S *FANFARE FOR THE UNCOMMON WOMAN*

Like many composers of her generation, Joan Tower (b. 1938) began her compositional career as a serialist, and like many of her peers, she abandoned serialism for a more accessible style during the mid-1970s. As she said in a 1993 interview, "I don't trust systems at all. . . . I composed serial music for 10 years, but I've gone totally the other way."

Joan Tower

Fast Facts

- *Dates*: b. 1938
- *Place*: United States
- *Reasons to remember*: Renowned twentieth-century woman composer who abandoned serialism in favor of more accessible music

© Noah Sheldon

Tower has composed almost exclusively for instruments, which reflects her long-standing commitment to performing. A skilled pianist, she was a founding member of the Da Capo Chamber Players, which remains one of the leading contemporary-music ensembles in the United States. Since the mid-1970s, she has been a prolific and popular composer. Her music has received frequent performances, and much of it has been recorded. During the time she composed the fanfare, she was serving as the composer-in-residence of the St. Louis Symphony, and she has been honored with fellowships, commissions, and awards, including three Grammy Awards for *Made in America*.

"I don't trust systems at all. . . . I composed serial music for 10 years, but I've gone totally the other way." —Joan Tower

The character of her music reflects her early exposure to the sounds and rhythms of ethnic musical traditions. Tower's father was a mining engineer, and she spent much of her childhood in South America. She credits that experience with stimulating her interest in rhythm and percussion instruments; much of her mature music is characterized by complex, active rhythms and bold tonal colors.

Among Tower's most widely performed works is the first *Fanfare for the Uncommon Woman*. The work was one of more than twenty fanfares commissioned by the Houston Symphony to celebrate the 150th anniversary of the independence of Texas.

> Knowing Copland's *Fanfare for the Common Man* and being a great admirer of his music, I decided not only to write a tribute to him, but to balance things out a little by writing something for women—in this case, for women who are adventurous and take risks.—Joan Tower

Like many contemporary composers who have written works for large ensembles of winds and percussion, Tower builds harmonies from intervals that are consonant but do not form the triads of common practice harmony. The result is music that sounds largely consonant but defines its own tonality through harmonies that frame the heart of the work: the piled-up harmony that concludes the first brass flourish also serves as the final chord.

LISTEN UP!

CD 5:23

Tower, *Fanfare for the Uncommon Woman* (1986)

Takeaway point: Brief, brilliant work for brass and percussion

Style: Late twentieth-century neotonal music

Form: Through-composed

Genre: Fanfare

Instruments: Full brass (trumpets, horns, trombones, tuba) and percussion

Context: Artful realization of a celebratory musical genre

Tower's fanfare is an exuberant work. Although there are moments of relative quiet, the prevailing impression is of great energy, in the numerous brass

flourishes and percussion barrages. It is also a tightly organized work built from a series of rhythmically active melodic kernels. It is noisy, as a fanfare should be, and it does "smack of art."

Ellen Taaffe Zwilich and Musical Eclecticism

According to the *Oxford American Dictionary*, *eclectic* means "deriving ideas, style, or taste from a broad and diverse range of sources." In music, eclecticism can be a vice or a virtue. Commentators discussing music composed before 1900 often used the term disparagingly to describe composers who simply imitated existing styles rather than found their own creative paths. However, in the twentieth century **eclecticism** has become a widely used compositional strategy, in both classical and vernacular music. Important composers have combined diverse styles evocatively, as we have heard in music by Debussy, Stravinsky, Ives, Gershwin, Prokofiev, and Copland. For film composers, it is an almost indispensable tool, and it has been used increasingly in musical theater since Bernstein's *West Side Story*. Rock, because of its diverse genealogy and inclusive nature, is inherently eclectic.

© Iravanchi | Dreamstime.com

Eclectic means "deriving ideas, style, or taste from a broad and diverse range of sources."

Often a composer's eclectic bent is evident in contrast from work to work, as exemplified by the two Debussy preludes. Less common but more dramatic are works in which the diverse sources commingle. Ives's "Putnam's Camp" and The Beatles' "A Day in the Life" are spectacular instances of this approach. Ellen Taaffe Zwilich's *Concerto Grosso 1985* offers

an even more obvious and focused kind of eclecticism, one that collapses time.

ELLEN TAAFFE ZWILICH

Ellen Taaffe Zwilich was born in Miami and grew up in Florida. She graduated in 1960 from Florida State University, where in addition to composing, she played violin in the orchestra and trumpet in the jazz band, and sang in an early-music group. After graduation, she came to New York to study violin at Juilliard but switched to composition, where she became the first woman to receive a doctorate in composition from the school. It was a 1975 performance of her orchestral work *Symbolon*, conducted by Pierre Boulez, that brought her work to a wider audience. Since receiving the Pulitzer in 1983, Zwilich has earned a steady stream of awards and commissions, including the first Composer's Chair at Carnegie Hall; performances of her works by most major American orchestras and leading chamber ensembles; and numerous recordings, four of which have received Grammy nominations. Her success has enabled her to focus exclusively on composing.

Ellen Taaffe Zwilich

Fast Facts

- *Dates*: b. 1939
- *Place*: United States
- *Reasons to remember*: One of America's most honored composers and among the most distinguished women composers of her time

© Photo by Ray Stanyard and used by permission from Florida State University Research in Review Magazine

Zwilich has commented on the importance of this for her work:

> I think that teaching and playing are wonderful experiences to have had. They are very much a part of a composer's background. But they interfere with your work. Teaching, for example, is very demanding and takes a lot of the same energy that writing does. And the problem with playing is that you are immersed in other people's music. A century ago [the late nineteenth century], when there was only one

style of composition, playing and composing were more compatible. But with today's profusion of musical expression, it's more difficult to have the kind of remove that is probably necessary for a composer.

In 1984, Zwilich received a commission from the Washington Friends of Handel to compose a work commemorating the three-hundredth anniversary of Handel's birth. To fulfill the commission, Zwilich composed Concerto Grosso 1985.

CONCERTO GROSSO 1985

Concerto Grosso 1985 is a five-movement work that lasts about fifteen minutes. The five movements form an arch: the outer movements are comparable in tempo and musical material; the second and fourth movements are fast and rhythmically active; and the third movement, marked "Largo," is the emotional heart of the work. The outstanding feature of the work is Zwilich's quotation of fragments from the first movement of Handel's *Sonata for Violin and Continuo* in D. Handel's work is among the most familiar Baroque solo sonatas, and Zwilich played it in her student days. Zwilich commented, "My concerto is both inspired by Handel's sonata and, I hope, imbued with his spirit."

> *"My concerto is both inspired by Handel's sonata and, I hope, imbued with his spirit."—Ellen Taaffe Zwilich*

Because there are musical connections between the music of Handel and Zwilich, the work brings the past into the present. It is as if Handel's sonata is an old and familiar film, and Zwilich's original music portrays a viewer watching the film, pausing it periodically as she engages in a kind of free association with the earlier music.

This merging of past and present is clearest in the outer movements because they contain direct quotations of Handel. However, throughout the work, Zwilich filters characteristic sounds, textures, and rhythms of Baroque music through a contemporary sensibility. Zwilich's musical language recalls the pre-1950 music of such composers as Stravinsky and Copland, so that the Handel is clearly anachronistic: the sonata is integral to the work yet clearly apart from Zwilich's music. It is a stunning effect.

Women Composers in Contemporary Culture

Tower and Zwilich belong to the first generation of women composers who have enjoyed status comparable to that of their male counterparts, as evidenced by the number and quality of commissions, prizes, recordings, and publications. They are not alone. The Israeli-American composer Shulamit Ran (b. 1949) became the second woman to win the Pulitzer Prize for music, in 1990, and has served as composer-in-residence for the Chicago Symphony. Composer-performers such as Meredith Monk (b. 1942) and Laurie Anderson (b. 1947) have been important innovators. Monk has introduced a wide range of vocal styles; Anderson is known in part for replacing the hair of the violin bow with magnetic tape. Barbara Kolb (b. 1939) and Pauline Oliveros (b. 1932) are among the leading composers of electronic music.

However, they don't have much company. The achievements of Tower, Zwilich, and other twentieth-century women composers are exceptional. Despite greater activity, greater awareness, and greater professional support, women still lag well behind men in the customary measures of acceptance—performances, awards, teaching positions in composition. As several commentators have noted, parity in the profession is still a work in progress. Still, the door has been opened; the successes of Tower, Zwilich, and others should be a prelude to greater opportunities and recognition for women composers.

CHAPTER 55

Music and Film

"One problem that filmmakers don't have when filming composer biopics is music for the sound track."

In explaining why film biographies of classical composers so often present a distorted view of their lives, actor Simon Callow, who portrayed Handel in the acclaimed 1985 film *Honor, Profit and Pleasure*, wrote:

> The reason for this is pretty simple: composing as such, like most artistic activities, is drudgery, and—unlike painting—one that is hard to represent on the screen or stage. To watch even a genius compose is like watching paint dry—with the difference that once the paint has dried, one has something to look at.

Callow's acid observation about what he calls the "Great Dead" underscores the central issue of filming a biography of a composer: composing, the least interesting aspect of composers' lives from a dramatic perspective, is the very reason we most remember them—and why they are central characters in films in the first place.

To address this issue, filmmakers often seek out a dramatic hook and build their narrative around it. Those who approach the task conscientiously research the composer's life and times. Still, in the interest of telling a good story, they often opt for historical plausibility—what *could* have been—rather than historical probability. A case in point is the 1994 film *Immortal Beloved*, which uses the great unsolved mystery of Beethoven's life as a focal point. In a famous unsent letter found among his effects, Beethoven pours out his heart to an "immortal beloved," whose identity cannot be established with absolute certainty. The resulting biographical portrait of Beethoven gives far more weight to the composer's relationship with this mystery woman than is warranted by the historical account.

Did You Know?

Tan Dun composed his *Internet Symphony No. 1* "Eroica" for the YouTube Symphony Orchestra, a Google-sponsored ensemble whose members were chosen via auditions uploaded to YouTube.

One problem that filmmakers *don't* have when filming composer biopics is music for the sound track. They draw freely on the composer's works, not only in scenes where the composer performs and conducts but also as background music. However, for most other films, they must engage a composer to create music for the sound track.

The life of the film composer is far different from a composer's life on film. Beethoven would likely have found the rules and requirements of film composition maddeningly restrictive.

LO2 So You Want to Be a Film Composer . . .

Composing for films presents a unique set of challenges. They begin with the most fundamental: artistic control. In every other genre that we have studied, the creator has had the final say on the musical work. There may be patrons to please, librettos to set, or choreography to accompany, but the composition typically reflects the composer's artistic vision.

Not so with film. In most cases, the film composer's conception must be subordinated to the person who has artistic responsibility for the project. Typically, this is the director, but it may be the producer or even the executive producer. Indeed, the composer must work with a large team of decision makers; the ability to work well with others is an essential requirement for any successful film composer. And this is only the first of several constraints within which composers must work. In *On the Track*, their definitive guide to film composition, Fred Karlin and Rayburn Wright describe in exhaustive detail nine stages in the process of creating music for a film: composing doesn't arrive until the sixth stage!

The process of creating music for a film begins with a first encounter with the film and those responsible for it, sometime after the film has been shot and editing has begun. As a rule, the composer typically meets with the director and other parties, mainly to ascertain the director's vision for the film, then views a preliminary version of the film. In subsequent meetings the director may make his vision more specific by providing musical excerpts, often culled from his own music collection, called "role models." If a role model is cued into the film, it becomes a "temp" (for temporary) track. From these initial experiences, the composer begins to form his musical response to the director's conception.

© iStockphoto.com/ Marcela Barsse

The life of the film composer is far different from a composer's life on film.

The next stage in the process is **spotting**, which involves viewing the film and determining—"spotting"—those scenes where music will enhance the on-screen events. This is typically a collective decision on which the composer consults with the director and others. In the process, the composer learns how much music must be composed: the team provisionally decides the "in" and "out" points of each musical segment. Music rarely runs throughout a film. More

Actor Anthony Hopkins, composer J. Peter Robinson, and director Roger Donaldson at a scoring session for *The World's Fastest Indian*

© Marsaili McGrath/Getty Images

commonly, music accompanies anywhere from 30 to 70 percent of on-screen action. With these decisions made and a budget from the studio, the composer then schedules the recording sessions: the composer must determine the number of musicians required for each musical segment of the film and the number of hours needed to record the music.

At this point, composers often begin formulating a concept that will carry through the entire film. It may reflect the dominant idea of the film, a main character, or perhaps a location. It may be expressed in a melody, a sound, or a rhythm, or some combination of these: the main theme of *Star Wars*, discussed later, is a memorable instance of defining the message of the film from the outset.

At this point, composers begin to work out the math, matching the speed of a click track, which will set the tempo for the segment, to frame-by-frame events in the film. This is a tedious process, but when it's complete, the composer has the time framework within which he must express his musical support for the onscreen drama. Only then does he actually begin to compose, and he will have only a few weeks to prepare the finished score.

The successful film composer must be an imaginative and skilled musician, a diplomat, and an effective communicator and collaborator. The composer must be able to work under extreme pressure, massage egos and calm anxious directors, and subordinate his musical personality to the requirements of the film with great specificity: for example, "This cue lasts 1 minute and 35 seconds." It's about as far from the Romantic idea of the composer as solitary genius or Babbitt's contemporary composer ignoring his audience as a composer can get.

In this chapter, we consider music from two acclaimed films: *Star Wars*, with music by John Williams, and *Crouching Tiger, Hidden Dragon*, with music by Tan Dun. Their scores exemplify two different approaches to film composition.

John Williams and *Star Wars*

In 1941, science fiction writer Bob Tucker coined this definition of space opera:

> Westerns are called "horse operas," the morning housewife tear-jerkers are called "soap operas." For the hacky, grinding, stinking outworn spaceship yarn, or world-saving for that matter, we offer "space opera."

For several decades, "space opera" retained its pejorative connotation. However, around the time that the first Star Wars episode was released, the term began to identify a subgenre of science fiction. Its rise to respectability was helped significantly by the popularity of the Star Wars films, which incorporated a number of its conventions.

Star Wars is the grandest of all space operas. The saga unfolds over seven films, released between 1977 and 2005. In its scope and size, it invites comparison with the grandest opera, Richard Wagner's *Der Ring des Nibelungen*. Both are based on a mythical story spanning several generations: one takes place in an indeterminate future, while the other is set in an indeterminate past; and both require about fourteen hours for a complete presentation.

Although the characters speak, rather than sing, in Star Wars, the films owe a large musical debt to Wagner. John Williams, who composed the music for the Star Wars films, adapts two of the most distinctive features of Wagner's music: lavish and varied orchestration, and the leitmotif.

Williams's use of Wagnerian devices, particularly the leitmotif, was all but inevitable. During the 1930s and 1940s, film composers, especially European émigrés like Max Steiner and Erich Korngold, composed sumptuous scores strongly influenced by Wagner's orchestration, harmony, and use of leitmotifs. Williams's scoring of Star Wars is at once a throwback to Wagnerian-influenced film scoring and a modern adaptation of it.

John Williams is the great emulator. He is at home in a dazzling array of compositional styles: his music may evoke Wagner, Schoenberg, Debussy, Stravinsky, Prokofiev—even Duke Ellington. Williams came by this facility by talent, inclination, and experience. During the 1950s, he led a triple life as a student of classical music in composition and piano, including study at Juilliard; working as a commercial and jazz pianist in clubs and on numerous recordings; and orchestrating and arranging for film, television, and the air force during his military service in the early 1950s. His first major success as a film composer came in 1967, when he received an Academy Award nomination for his score to the film *Valley of the Dolls*. In 1974, he began his long association with director

John Williams

Fast Facts

- *Dates*: b. 1932
- *Place*: United States
- *Reason to remember*: Preeminent film composer of the late twentieth and early twenty-first centuries

Stephen Spielberg; this led to his work for George Lucas and the Star Wars films. For his score to *Star Wars: A New Hope*, the first of the films to be released, he received an Academy Award in 1977.

The opening music for the film provides a glimpse of Williams's compositional modus operandi. After the 20th Century Fox fanfare, there is silence as a message on the screen reads, "A long time ago in a galaxy far, far away ..." Fanfarelike music sounds as the *Star Wars* logo appears on the screen; the triumphant main theme follows as scrolling text sets the stage for the opening action in the film. This segment lasts just over a minute. As the on-screen narrative recedes, the music turns suspenseful by becoming delicate and tonally ambiguous; a piccolo plays a whole-tone melody after Wagnerian strings. Shortly before two spacecraft appear on-screen, the music abruptly shifts to an ominous, warlike character. The rapidly shifting brass chords clash with the pedal tone that runs throughout this section. The dissonances mix with martial rhythms and sounds to create a sense of impending disaster even before the spacecraft come into view.

In the space of just over two minutes, Williams establishes three distinct and stylistically unrelated sound worlds, connecting the first two with a skillful transition and moving abruptly into the third. As this excerpt demonstrates, Williams doesn't project a consistent individual compositional personality, as Prokofiev did in *Alexander Nevsky* and as we'll see that Tan Dun does in his music for *Crouching Tiger, Hidden Dragon*. Instead, he calls on his vast knowledge of musical styles to cherry-pick those that can anticipate and amplify the on-screen events, then tweaks them to make them specific to the film.

The main theme shows how Williams imbues an existing style with a distinct identity. The stirring melody and richly orchestrated, brass-dominated accompaniment evoke the heroic music of the nineteenth century. But Williams places it squarely in the twentieth century through such features as the rhythmic organization of the theme: instead of presenting a four-measure phrase in a conventional quadruple meter, Williams creates measures of 5, 4, 4, and 3 beats. This asymmetry gives the theme a more modern sound while still retaining its connection with the heroic music of the past.

LISTEN UP!

CD 5:25

Williams, "Main Title/Rebel Blockade Runner," *Star Wars Episode IV* (1977)

Takeaway point: Memorable music by a masterful film composer

Style: Eclectic

Form: Through-composed

Genre: Film music

Instruments: Full orchestra

Context: Music amplifies on-screen events: scrolling text, chase scene

Williams's score for the rest of the film follows much the same path: astonishing stylistic variety, with modifications that elevate the music above mere imitation. It has been a winning formula, for Williams and for the many successful films that he has scored.

Tan Dun and *Crouching Tiger, Hidden Dragon*

The film *Crouching Tiger, Hidden Dragon* (2000) grew out of a collaboration among director Ang Lee, composer Tan Dun, and cellist Yo-Yo Ma. The three had been friends for about a decade when they began working on the film in 1996. All three exemplify the synthesis of East and West. Ma, the son of Chinese musicians, was born in Paris and came to the United States when he was five. After establishing himself in the top rank of classical cellists, he began to branch out in numerous directions; among the most far reaching has been his Silk Road project, a musical collective that nurtures interactions among the cultures along the venerable Silk Road from Eastern Europe to China.

Originally from Taiwan, Ang Lee received his film training in the United States: at NYU, he was a classmate of fellow director Spike Lee. He has established himself as one of the leading contemporary directors, winning an Academy Award in 2005 for his direction of *Brokeback Mountain*. *Crouching Tiger, Hidden Dragon* was his "roots" project, an opportunity to connect with the classical Chinese culture he had studied so deeply as a child.

Tan Dun grew up in southern China, and as a young man he spent several years planting rice on a commune. After joining a Beijing Opera troupe and relocating to Beijing, he enrolled at the Central Conservatory of Music. After occasional conflict with the government, Tan came to the United States to pursue doctoral studies in composition at Columbia University. Since completing his studies, he has accumulated a steady stream of honors and commissions, and his major works—operas, orchestral compositions, and chamber works—have been recorded and performed widely. Among them are a commission for a symphony celebrating the return of Hong Kong to China in 1997 and a setting of the *St. Matthew Passion* to honor the 250th anniversary of Bach's death.

Tan's formative musical experiences range from oserving shamanic rituals and learning traditional

Tan Dun

Fast Facts

- *Dates*: b. 1957
- *Place*: China/United States
- *Reasons to remember*: Distinguished and popular Chinese composer whose music often fuses East and West

© LEE CELANO/AFP/Getty Images

 LISTEN FURTHER

Hear Tan and Beethoven in *Internet Symphony No. 1* "Eroica" in the YouTube playlist on the text website.

Chinese instruments in the village where he worked, to encounters with leading classical composers such as Hans Werner Henze and Toru Takemitsu and study with Mario Davidovsky, a leading composer of electronic music. He drew deeply on these experiences for his score for *Crouching Tiger, Hidden Dragon*, for which he won an Academy Award.

The Chinese counterpart of the westerns of American fantasy fiction and the European tales of chivalric knights is a genre known as *wuxia* (pronounced wooshya). The main characters in all of these genres are lone warriors who adhere to a code of honor and fight for right. In *wuxia* novels, martial arts weapons are the counterpart to the six-shooter of the gunslinger and the lance and sword of medieval knights.

Although the themes of *wuxia* novels date back hundreds of years, the genre flourished only in the early twentieth century. The Chinese Communist Party suppressed *wuxia* beginning shortly after they took control of the government after World War II until the 1980s, but the genre remained popular in Hong Kong and Taiwan. Wuxia novels typically blend martial arts and romance. Among the best-known examples is the five-novel *Iron-Crane* series by Wang Du Lu. *Crouching Tiger, Hidden Dragon*, the fourth novel in the series, served as the basis for the screenplay for Lee's film.

Lee turned to Wang's novel in an effort to produce a martial arts film with what Tan called a "human touch." The story intermingles stunning fight scenes, including one on a bamboo forest, with two bittersweet romances.

Tan, Lee, and Ma began working on the film four years before its release. The relationship between Lee and Tan was similar to that between Eisenstein and Prokofiev, in that the music influenced the shooting of the film. As Tan noted, "The musical idea, if you can set it up at the beginning of the film process, benefits the director when he's shooting the film. It helps set up the contrast between the characters, and bridge elements together."

Tan is the quintessential East-West eclectic. For his score for the film, he employed four kinds of sounds: Chinese percussion instruments; traditional Chinese pitched instruments, including the **erhu** (the "Chinese violin") and flutes; the symphony orchestra; and the cello playing of Yo-Yo Ma. Tan blends these elements seamlessly: indeed, both Ma and the orchestral strings emulate Chinese performance styles. He took a similar approach to pitch organization by building the most memorable melodic material around the pentatonic scale, which is frequently used in Chinese music, and supporting it with modal harmony. Thus, the music is

often not only tonal but also diatonic—a far cry from the unrelenting dissonance of much twentieth-century concert music.

Because of his extensive experience in classical composition, Tan was, in his words, "exercising the power of the structure" in conceiving the score. Accordingly, the music is economical melodically and harmonically: most of the music is in one of two keys, and melodic motives, which are fully realized in the love music that ends the work, appear in various forms and fragments throughout the film. This gives Tan's score a consistency that emphasizes the broad themes in the film rather than moment-to-moment events. Ma's role is central: his solo line lends a personal touch, especially in the love music.

"The music can't be just attached to the picture." —Tan Dun

© Photos 12 / Alamy

Tan's music for *Crouching Tiger, Hidden Dragon* is both an integral part of the film and apart from it. Since the release of the film, the music has gained a life of its own. The sound track includes versions of the music that are different from those in the film. The love theme was recast in a pop song version: "A Love before Time," released in both Mandarin and English versions. Tan also created a concert version of the score, which was published as the Crouching Tiger Concerto for cello and chamber orchestra.

In the sound track version of "Farewell," the music that underscores the hero's profession of love as he is dying, Tan brings together the four sound groups. Ma states the melody, accompanied by drums and orchestral strings. An erhu (not heard in the film version) plays an achingly beautiful obbligato above Ma's cello melody: it is the feminine counterpoint to Ma's masculine voice. The track ends (while the credits are rolling) as enigmatically as the film, with a slow trill that dissolves over a sustained note that is not the tonic.

The beauty of Tan's music is in large part the

erhu "Chinese violin"

product of the seamless blending of the different sounds and the sophisticated use of simple musical materials. It is a superb example of the work of a composer with a truly global vision.

LISTEN UP!

CD 5:26

Tan, "Farewell," *Crouching Tiger, Hidden Dragon* (sound track version; 2000)

Takeaway point: Expressive fusion of Chinese and Western musical traditions

Style: East/West fusion

Form: Varied repetition of a short phrase

Genre: Film music

Instruments: Cello, erhu, Chinese percussion, orchestra

Context: The final statement of the love music in the film

Philosophies of Film Composition

In his foreword to Karlin and Wright's *On the Track*, John Williams writes, "I wish this book had been available when I started in the film industry in the 1950s." Karlin and Wright's book represents the most widely used approach to film scoring—applying music from a palette onto the canvas of film—which Williams's music consistently exemplifies. Tan opposes this method. He says, "Typically, the director will shoot a script and then during the tight post-production period, they will come up with musical ideas and see what they can develop. I really don't like that. The music can't be just attached to the picture." Williams would probably disagree.

The two brief musical examples presented here represent sharply contrasting approaches to film scoring. Williams's is the more common by far, given the structure of the Hollywood-based film industry and the relatively slight importance given to film music by the industry as a whole, despite its substantial impact on the final product. Because of their long-standing friendship and shared vision, Lee, Tan, and Ma could conceive of their film organically so that Tan's music was a *component of* the film rather than a *response to* it. The difference in approach is evident in the excerpts: there is considerable stylistic contrast in Williams's music and stylistic consistency in Tan's, which is also characteristic of the score as a whole.

The contrasting approaches reflect the professional lives of the two composers. Williams has made his compositional reputation as a film composer; his music in other genres has been less successful. As we listen to his music, we do not sense a personal style so much as his ability to personalize existing styles in the service of the story. By contrast, Tan is a composer who has composed film scores. Although he simplified his compositional approach to make his music more accessible and appropriate to the narrative, the music has the clear imprint of his personal style.

CHAPTER 56

Minimalism

"[The avant-garde was] a wasteland, dominated by these maniacs . . . who were trying to make everyone write this crazy, creepy music."—Philip Glass

M anhattan is an island borough of New York City. It's just under twenty-three square miles: about thirteen miles north to south and just over two miles east to west at its widest point. It has a small area: more than twenty Manhattans would fit inside the Los Angeles city limits, with room to spare. And it's densely populated: almost 2 million people live in the borough.

Partly because it's such a compact and populous area, it has supported a dazzling range of musical activity, which is associated not just with the city or the borough but also with particular places (and times) within the borough itself. Consider just the music that we have encountered: a stretch of Broadway, between 53rd and 42nd Streets, has been home to musical theater for more than a century. Adventurous New Yorkers during the late 1920s and 1930s traveled uptown to hear Duke Ellington at the Cotton Club, on 142nd Street in Harlem. Modern jazz fans frequented the clubs along 52nd Street in the postwar years. If they wanted to mambo, they could go up a street and up a flight of stairs to the Palladium Ballroom, located on 53rd Street. Milton Babbitt composed electronic music at the Columbia-Princeton Electronic Music Center, located on the Columbia University campus at 125th Street.

Did You Know?

Minimalist composer Philip Glass based his Symphony No. 1 ("Low") on David Bowie and Brian Eno's 1977 album *Low*.

"Uptown" Manhattan is the part of the borough above 59th Street, the southern boundary of Central Park. Columbia University and the Juilliard School are situated in the uptown part of Manhattan. "Midtown" Manhattan includes the area between 59th Street and 14th Street. "Downtown" Manhattan reaches from 14th Street to the southern tip of the island. The north end of downtown includes the more bohemian areas of the borough: Greenwich Village, Soho, the Lower East Side.

In *The Rest Is Noise*, Alex Ross uses geography to demarcate a sharp division—philosophical and musical—between two groups of composers who were active during the 1960s and 1970s. "Uptown" composers were those who taught at major universities and conservatories, in New York and elsewhere. Because they were the apostles of atonality, they did not attract large audiences. However, on campus, they were the tastemakers: there was enormous pressure on their students to conform to the composers' nonconformist orthodoxy. Not all of their students did: a few turned their back on the training they received, in search of a decidedly different direction. Many of them gravitated to the art scene downtown.

LO3 Minimalism and the "Classical Music" Counterculture

During the rock revolution, when university composers were at the height of their influence, a small group of American composers, most notably LaMonte Young, Terry Riley, Steve Reich, and Philip Glass, created a new kind of contemporary music. Their new style,

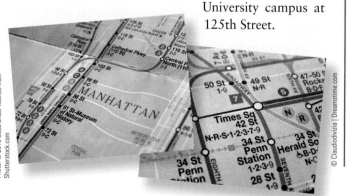

soon called "minimalism," was a comprehensive rejection of serialism and the European tradition from which it came. As Glass said some years later, the avant-garde was "a wasteland, dominated by these maniacs, these creeps, who were trying to make everyone write this crazy, creepy music." Instead, the minimalists sought inspiration in non-Western music and in jazz and rock: Reich immersed himself in African music; Glass and Riley studied with East Indian musical masters. Both Riley and Reich had a strong connection to jazz—especially bebop and the post-bop music of John Coltrane—and, later, rock. The interest was reciprocal. David Bowie and Brian Eno (who worked with Bowie in the 1970s and would later become the mastermind of U2's expansive sound) were in attendance at a London performance of Glass's *Music with Changing Parts;* it would lead to several collaborations. John Cale worked with LaMonte Young before forming the Velvet Underground with Lou Reed.

> *Minimalist composers represented the "classical music" branch of the 1960s counterculture.*

Minimalist composers represented the "classical music" branch of the 1960s counterculture. Reich and Glass lived in downtown Manhattan, below 14th Street. Rather than seek out university teaching positions, they worked odd jobs outside the music field. Like rock and jazz composer-performers, both eventually led their own groups: both the Philip Glass Ensemble and Steve Reich and Musicians were touring ensembles. They performed in a variety of venues—wherever they might attract a crowd. Composer David Schiff recalls attending a Steve Reich concert in 1974 at a dreary auditorium on the Columbia University campus. At the outset, there were only a few people there, and several of them left.

However, many of those who left returned with friends; by the end, the hall was full, of students and other like-minded listeners.

Drugs played a central role in the composers' creative and personal lives: marijuana and mescaline were the drugs of choice. In these and other respects, minimalist composers had much more in common with rock and jazz musicians of the 1960s and 1970s than they did with the classical avant-garde.

ROOTS OF MINIMALISM

Minimalism is an umbrella term used to describe a diverse body of music with little activity or little change in activity. Commentators borrowed the term from the visual arts: it had come into use to describe the work of visual artists such as Frank Stella, Sol LeWitt, and Richard Serra. Minimalism began as an American music. Its two main sources were the American experimentalist composers of the 1930s, 1940s, and 1950s, as well as music from the vernacular countercultures, especially bebop and rock.

The American experimentalists were a diverse group. They shared an interest in new sounds, especially percussive sounds, and they typically looked to the Far East, rather than Europe, for new ideas. Among the most influential were Henry Cowell, Lou Harrison, and John Cage (whose *4'33"* is the ultimate minimalist work). An even stronger influence was Morton Feldman, whose quiet, spare works often left pitch choice up to the performers. The San Francisco Bay Area and downtown New York were the two main nodes of activity for the minimalist movement.

The composer who served as the bridge between Cage and Feldman and the minimalists was LaMonte Young. Young was a superb jazz saxophonist during his high school and college years; he received much of his training as a composer at UCLA, working with an assistant of Schoenberg, before moving to the Bay Area for graduate study. He relocated to New York in 1960, where he became active in the art scene, ingested and dealt drugs, and revamped his compositional approach, often stripping it down to cryptic sets of directions. The entire score of his *Composition 1960 #10* asks the performer simply to "draw a straight line and follow it." Another consists of two notes "to be held for a long time." Young and Terry Riley, whose 1964 composition *In C* put minimalism on the cultural map, never developed a following. Glass and Reich did.

STEVE REICH AND AMERICAN MINIMALISM

In 1969, the German bassist Manfred Eicher started ECM Records to make available the music of Keith Jarrett, Chick Corea, and other important contemporary jazz musicians: Jarrett's ECM recording of a 1975 solo piano concert in Köln, Germany (released as *The Köln Concert*), remains one of the best-selling jazz recordings of all time. In 1978, Eicher expanded the musical range of his label by adding to ECM's catalog Steve Reich's recording of *Music for 18 Musicians*, a work that Reich composed between 1974 and 1976.

Reich's recording was an extension of Eicher's catalog, rather than a departure from it, because of the affinity between Reich's music and that of ECM jazz artists. *Music for 18 Musicians* features motoric rhythms, slowly changing harmonies that were consonant but not commonplace, percussive sounds, and syncopated riff-like figures that are repeated relentlessly. For jazz fans, the materials were familiar, but Reich's handling of them opened up a completely new sound world.

Steve Reich

Fast Facts

- *Dates*: b. 1936
- *Place*: United States
- *Reason to remember*:
  Pioneer of minimalism

© Laurie Lewis/Lebrecht Music & Arts

Steve Reich's musical affinity with ECM artists was a consequence of experiences gained during the latter part of his traditional training. Reich majored in philosophy at Cornell but took several music courses. After graduation, he studied composition, first with classical composer–jazz pianist Hall Overton, then at Juilliard, and finally at Mills College in Oakland, California, where he worked with the Italian avant-garde composer Luciano Berio. After graduating from Mills, he remained in the Bay Area, where he listened to jazz intently—he was particularly drawn to the music of John Coltrane—studied African drumming, and worked at the San Francisco Tape Music Center, where he accidentally happened on a process that would point his music in a new direction. While manipulating a recording of a black street preacher, he discovered that two identical tape loops would go out of phase, creating a unique echoing effect. He soon applied this technique— playing the same phrase on two musical instruments, in slightly different tempos (called, appropriately enough, **phasing**)—to live performance, then adapted features of it, notably the extensive repetition of short melodic ideas, to a richer instrumental setting.

> **phasing** Technique, popularized by Steve Reich, of playing the same phrase on two musical instruments, in slightly different tempos, to achieve a unique echoing effect

The work that epitomizes this phase of Reich's career is his *Music for 18 Musicians*. He began composing the work in 1974 and finished it two years later; the official premiere was in 1976 in New York's Town Hall. Like many important early minimalist compositions, *Music for 18 Musicians* is a long work: there is an opening section that presents eleven chords; eleven sections, each built on one of the chords; and a reprise of the opening. A complete performance lasts about an hour. Moreover, the music is continuous, with no pauses between sections.

The scoring of the work is idiosyncratic: four female singers, a violinist and cellist, two clarinetists doubling on bass clarinet, and ten instrumentalists who move between piano, pitched percussion instruments, and maracas. It bears no resemblance to traditional ensembles in either classical music or jazz. Moreover, the singers perform without words, as if they are instruments.

The instrumentation is one of several innovative features. Most prominent is the rhythmic approach that simultaneously connects to the most basic rhythms in human history even as it rejects the more recent

 LISTEN UP!

CD 5:27

Reich, *Music for 18 Musicians*, Section IIIA (1974–1976)

Takeaway point: Kaleidoscopic, hypnotic musical minimalism

Style: Minimalism

Form: Multisectional

Genre: Large chamber ensemble

Instruments: Piano, pitched percussion instruments, violin, clarinets

Context: One section of a nonstop minimalist work lasting more than an hour

rhythmic approaches within the classical tradition. We get some sense of this from the excerpt here.

Reich built his music on the undifferentiated marking of time heard in African music, Afrocentric music, and "primitive" music and was able to recontextualize European-derived elements to enrich the sound world. His music includes familiar sounds that connect to the vernacular tradition—rich chords, percussive sounds, riff-like melodic material. But they are embedded in a musical fabric in which change happens at an extremely slow pace, despite the incessant activity. As a result, his music seems expansive: we are not so concerned with measuring time as with immersing ourselves in the moment-to-moment experience of the familiar, yet different, sounds. In this way, Reich at once reconnected "concert music" with the vernacular tradition and helped chart a distinctly different musical direction.

The music of Reich and Glass inspired younger American composers, most notably John Adams, to follow a similar path. It also influenced a small but important group of European composers whose music took a related but distinctively different form.

ARVO PÄRT AND "SACRED MINIMALISM"

Among the more surprising platinum recordings of the 1990s were a 1994 recording of Gregorian chant by the Benedictine monks of Santo Domingo de Silos and a recording by the London Sinfonietta, featuring soprano Dawn Upshaw and conducted by David Zinman, of the Polish composer Henryk Gorecki's *Symphony No. 3*. At the turn of the twenty-first century, best-selling classical recordings were rare enough; what was even more surprising was that this music was not only classical but among the most unfamiliar classical music genres: chant and contemporary composition—Gorecki composed the symphony in 1977. The common ground between the two recordings begins with their spirituality and the enthusiastic response to it. As Gorecki remarked, "Perhaps people find something they need in this piece of music. . . . Somehow I hit the right note, something they were missing. Something, somewhere had been lost to them. I feel that I instinctively knew what they needed." The statement could as easily apply to chant.

Sacred Minimalism. Gorecki, the English composer John Tavener, and the Estonian composer Arvo Pärt are the most prominent of a small group of European composers who have sought to express their religious faith through music. Pärt, Gorecki, and Tavener have enjoyed success far beyond that of most contemporary composers. Manfred Eicher recorded Pärt's music on ECM; Tavener's *Celtic Requiem* caught the attention of The Beatles, who arranged to have it recorded on their label, Apple Records; and all have had several of their works receive multiple recordings and frequent performances.

Although the three composers have distinctive, and distinct, styles, they share several common characteristics. Among the most significant are these:

- They often set sacred texts, drawn from scripture or the liturgy of a particular religious denomination, and even music that does not use sacred texts may have a spiritual dimension: two of the three texts in Gorecki's symphony are songs to the Virgin Mary.

- They compose extensively for chorus, both a cappella and with accompaniment.

- They have turned to the music of the past, especially the distant past, for inspiration and musical material.

- Their music is mostly consonant, with freshly reconceived modal and tonal harmonies.

- Their works typically unfold expansively, with slow tempos and understated rhythmic activity.

Because of the similarities in intent, resources, and musical practice, some commentators have described their music as **holy**, or **sacred, minimalism**. It is strikingly different from the music of Reich, Glass, and Adams, most obviously because of its sacred subject matter and a radically different approach to rhythm: the rapid, motoric rhythms of the American minimalists versus the slow tempos and halting rhythms of the Europeans. We hear a beautiful example of sacred minimalism in the Kyrie from Arvo Pärt's *Berlin Mass*.

Arvo Pärt. Estonia is the northernmost of the three Baltic republics. For most of its history, it has been under the dominion of foreign powers: Sweden; imperial, then Soviet Russia; Germany during World War II; and the Soviet Union after the fall of East Germany. In its recent history, it has been an independent nation only twice: a brief period between the two world wars and since 1991.

Arvo Pärt

Fast Facts

- *Dates*: b. 1935
- *Place*: Estonia
- *Reason to remember*: A leading proponent of "sacred" minimalism

Estonia's most distinguished composer is Arvo Pärt. Like most composers active after World War II, Pärt explored serialism. Unlike most composers outside the Soviet bloc, he faced official criticism from the Soviet cultural authorities for his serial compositions. Even more provocative was his undisguised profession of faith in *Credo* (1968), a work for chorus, piano, and orchestra. Pärt's work was, in the context of the Soviet Union's active suppression of religious expression, a defiant act. After Credo, Pärt immersed himself in early music, including Gregorian chant. From this study he developed an approach to harmony that mixed centuries-old practice with modern dissonance. Pärt calls this harmonic approach **tintinnabuli** (from *tintinnabulation*, "the ringing of bells"). This characteristic technique involves grouping two or more voices, one singing a modal melody and the others singing the pitches of a chord. The interplay between the voices produces harmonies that vary from completely consonant to slightly dissonant. We hear it throughout the Kyrie from his *Berlin Mass*.

Pärt's *Berlin Mass* relates more directly to the music of Hildegard and Josquin than it does to any other music that we have encountered. There are obvious reasons: like Hildegard's antiphon and Josquin's mass movement, it is liturgical music, to be used to celebrate the Mass. But Pärt goes well beyond that: his style seems to recap-

LISTEN UP!

CD 5:28

Pärt, Kyrie, from *Berlin Mass* (1992)

Takeaway point: Serene, sublime sacred music

Style: Sacred minimalism

Form: ABC (corresponds to three-part prayer)

Genre: Mass

Instruments: Chorus and string orchestra

Context: Music for a liturgical service

ture the rapture that the earlier music conveys. It is a world that evokes the past yet is unmistakably modern.

Minimalism, the Past, and the Twentieth Century

Three qualities of minimalism evident in the music of Reich and Pärt reconnected the past with a vibrant present: consonance, an expansive conception of time, and a return to spirituality.

Like many of their peers working in other directions, minimalist composers restored consonant harmony without turning back the clock. There are, of course, connections with the past. Reich's static, vibrating chords are pleasing sound objects in themselves. In this respect, Reich is following the lead of Debussy, Stravinsky, and generations of jazz musicians. Pärt mixes familiar chords in unfamiliar progressions with his "tintinnabulized" harmonies; the effect is simultaneously old and new. Both bring a fresh perspective to familiar sounds.

Minimalists also reconceived the way music presents time. Among the significant achievements of eighteenth-century musicians was the hierarchical organization of musical time. Their accomplishments in this domain are comparable to those of clockmakers, whose products enabled people to perceive the passage of time with unprecedented precision. In minimalism, the intent is just the opposite: to free listeners from marking the passage of time at comfortable intervals. Reich achieves this goal by laying fast, undifferentiated rhythms over musical events that change slowly; in Pärt's music, *everything* moves slowly.

The slowly changing harmony, open-ended rhythm, and anonymity of the performing resources—there are no soloists in either work, just choirs of voices and strings in Pärt's work and teams of musicians keeping time or playing riffs or oscillating chords in Reich's—help project a sense of connection to something beyond the self that is essentially spiritual. The spiritual dimension of Reich's music is nondenominational; Pärt's *Berlin Mass* universalizes a specifically Catholic expression of the mystical. Each in its own way connects to the spiritual impulse that

tintinnabuli Arvo Pärt's characteristic technique that involves grouping two or more voices, one singing a modal melody and the others singing the pitches of a chord, to produce harmonies that vary from completely consonant to slightly dissonant

inspired much earlier music: shamanic drumming and chanting; the liturgical music of the Middle Ages and Renaissance; the *santería* music of Afro-Cubans seeking to communicate with their *orishas*. In the two examples considered here, minimalism has restored the spiritual dimension of music in a decidedly innovative way.

More than any other development in concert music during the latter part of the twentieth century, minimalism reconnected concert music with the larger musical world. One can hear both works discussed in this chapter as part of a contemporary soundscape that also includes music as diverse as electronica, rap, punk, and New Age music. Indeed, one can argue that a DJ's mix at a dance club, with the endless and undifferentiated thump of a digital bass drum, is different only in degree, not in kind, from the motoric rhythms in Steve Reich's music.

As the numerous interactions between contemporary pop artists and minimalist composers exemplify, minimalism holds the promise of restoring a sense of continuum between diverse levels of musical discourse that existed in the eighteenth and nineteenth centuries but that largely disappeared during the first two-thirds of the twentieth century.

Musical Life in the Twenty-first Century

On December 31, 1999, the BBC's television program "2000 Today" broadcast the dawn of the new millennium around the world. Over a period of twenty-eight hours, almost a billion viewers worldwide saw the sun rise in country after country. The sound track for the program was Tan Dun's *A World Symphony for the Millennium*, which merged symphony orchestra and choir with sounds from around the world, from low-pitched throat singing in the chanting of Tibetan Buddhist monks to the steel drums of Caribbean calypso. The music shifted in step with the shift from location to location.

Tan's score suggests how radically musical life had changed in just half a century. The insularity of the 1950s—when the avant-garde kept largely to itself and more familiar music was valued according to a widely accepted pecking order, with classical music at the top and rock and roll toward the bottom—gave way to a more open and inclusive attitude. In his *World Symphony*, Tan embraced literally a world of music by drawing on musical traditions from almost every continent. In the process, he dissolved the temporal, geographical, cultural, and stylistic boundaries that seemed immutable only a few decades earlier.

Many musicians working in the last third of the twentieth century shared the attitude exemplified by Tan's work. They challenged long-held assumptions about musical worth and saw the serial music of the midcentury avant-garde as an evolutionary dead end. They opened themselves up to music from other cultures, as well as to all the music of their own. They drew their cue from the rock revolution. The Beatles' *Sgt. Pepper* was a seminal expression of this attitude. And all the works discussed in this unit in some way reflect this unprecedented openness: Tower's indoor concert work for an outdoor ensemble; Zwilich's skillful integration of old and new; Williams's lightning-fast stylistic shifts; Tan Dun's East/West instrumental resources; Reich's African- and jazz-influenced groove; and Pärt's evocation of the serenity and spirituality of chant and Renaissance polyphony. During the first part of the century, such works would have been unimaginable; toward the end, they were increasingly commonplace.

We live in a time when seemingly anything in music is possible. We lack the comfort of a common practice but have a world of music and more than a millennium of documented musical activity to draw on, along with technology that makes it all accessible. It is a time filled with great challenge and great promise. The future directions in musical life are more uncertain than they have been in a millennium. The linear, evolutionary progressions in concert and commercial music have run their course. The closest thing to a certainty is that imaginative and innovative musicians, and perhaps their artificially intelligent counterparts, will continue to forge new creative paths. We look forward to encountering them in the years ahead.

KEYS TO TWENTIETH-CENTURY MUSIC

Key Concepts

Stylistic fragmentation. The relentless quest for novelty in concert music, the continuing evolution of popular music, and the embrace of new music-related technologies resulted in stunning stylistic diversity that increased dramatically during the course of the century.

Key Features

Despite the stylistic diversity of twentieth-century music, there are trends and developments that cut across stylistic boundaries. Among the features that distinguish twentieth-century music are these:

1. **New sounds.** Among the most distinctive new sounds of the twentieth century were an array of percussion instruments; electronic sounds of various kinds and electronically amplified instruments; "found" sounds—natural and man-made sounds not associated with traditional music making; and extended techniques on conventional instruments.

2. **Novel sound combinations.** In both concert music and vernacular styles, three trends stand out: the small mixed-timbre ensemble; an emphasis on percussion instruments; and the use of electronic sounds, alone and in combination with acoustic instruments.

3. **New modes of pitch organization.** New approaches to pitch organization included dialects of common practice; harmony and melody based on modes and pentatonic scales; tonal music that eschewed common practice; free and serial atonality; and in extreme cases, the abandonment of the twelve discrete pitches within the octave.

4. **Diverse rhythms.** New rhythmic approaches included rhythms that immersed listeners in rhythms with a compelling, undifferentiated beat; irregular meters; and rhythms so complex, unpredictable, or slow to unfold that a consistent pulse was not apparent.

5. **Nonlinear forms.** Nonlinear forms, including music for or inspired by film, through-composed forms in concert music, and extensible forms in popular styles from blues and jazz to techno, became common alternatives to the closed forms inherited from nineteenth-century music.

Key Terms

1. **Serialism.** A structured approach to atonality in which the twelve pitches within the octave are presented according to a predetermined order

2. **Rhythm section.** Rhythm sections have provided the rhythmic and harmonic foundation in popular music since the 1920s.

3. **Musique concréte.** Music composed from recordings of natural or man-made sounds not associated with traditional music

4. **Avant-garde.** Those who depart most radically from tradition

5. **Modern music.** Umbrella term widely used in the first two-thirds of the twentieth century to identify music that rejected the values and materials of nineteenth-century music

Music Concept Check

To assist you in recognizing their distinctive features, we present an interactive comparison of Romantic and twentieth-century style in CourseMate and the eBook.

Entries in boldface
are key terms

CourseMate brings course concepts to life with interactive learning, study, and exam preparation tools that support MUSIC. CourseMate for MUSIC includes an integrated eBook, interactive teaching and learning tools, and Engagement Tracker, a first-of-its-kind tool that monitors student engagement in the course.

Here's your user's guide to making the most of the integrated eBook, streaming music, and Active Listening Guides!

Working with the eBook

Your students can read MUSIC wherever and whenever they're online by paging through the eBook on their computers. But they can do much more than just read. The eBook also contains live links to all of the music included in the text and its optional CD set, and more.

Click on each kind of link to access …

Active Listening Guides, which guide students through each piece of music *as it plays* directly from the eBook page. They can pause and replay at any point, click on a Profile for a summary of the elements of music in the piece, check the Key Points for its key features, or take an interactive quiz to test their comprehension.

Streaming versions of full selections and additional musical examples

Interactive demos of key musical concepts; iTunes, Rhapsody, and YouTube playlists; websites; and more

The eBook also features easy page navigation, different page views, highlighting, note taking, a search engine, a print function, and a user's manual (at top right, under the "Help" question mark).

Working with the eBook

Listen Up! cues throughout the book offer checklists of features for music selections. In the eBook, clicking on the *Listen Up!* icons links students directly to online Active Listening Guides and streaming music.

LISTEN UP!

CD 1:10

Monteverdi, "Possente spirto," *Orfeo* (1607)

Takeaway point: Dazzling vocal display
orchestral accompaniment and interplay

Style: Early Baroque

Form: Strophic, with variation

Genre: Opera aria

Instruments: Voice, continuo, violins, trumpe

Context: Brilliant vocal writing charms Charo
so that Orpheus can enter the underworld

CAMPBELL

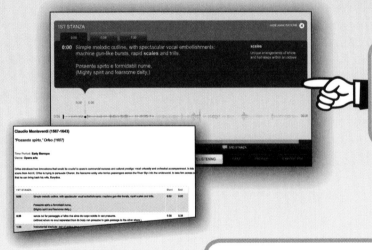

Active Listening Guides guide students through each piece while it plays. If they want a printed listening guide, they simply click on Export PDF to print one out for studying.

Red icons in the eBook link directly to online music demos and the iTunes, Rhapsody, and YouTube playlist items listed on your Instructor Prep Cards.

Music Concept Check

Review and listen to all the instrument families in Britten's *Young Person's Guide to the Orchestra*, on the text website.

Learning Outcomes

LO1   Describe and recognize the basic properties of musical sound.

LO2   Identify the elements of music.

LO3   Define dynamics in detail.

LO4   In the context of understanding instrumentation, compare the tone color of a piano with that of an orchestra.

LO5   Learn the musical meanings of rhythm, beat, and tempo.

LO6   Understand the relationships between beat and meter.

LO7   Define melody and describe how to construct one.

LO8   Understand the uses of scale and tonality.

LO9   Describe the use of phrase in melody.

Terms

Chapter 1	pianissimo, *pp*	orchestration	Chapter 4	pentatonic scale
music	crescendo, $<$	tone color	melody	chromatic scale
dynamics	decrescendo		contour	sharp (#)
decibel (dB)	(diminuendo), $>$	**Chapter 3**	interval	flat (♭)
duration	sforzando, *sf*	rhythm	unison	staff
pitch	instrumentation	beat	octave	clef
timbre	symphony orchestra	tempo	step	key
element of music	strings	meter	leap	tonic (keynote)
	double	duple meter	half-step	tonal
	pizzicato	triple meter	scale	atonal
Chapter 2	woodwind	quadruple meter	tonic (keynote)	phrase
fortissimo, *ff*	brass	measure (bar)	diatonic scale	
forte, *f*	mute	accent	major scale	
mezzo forte, *mf*	percussion	time (meter) signature	minor scale	
mezzo piano, *mp*	instrument	syncopation	mode (modal scale)	
piano, *p*				

Multimedia

Listening Guides

Active Listening Guides with streaming music are available in CourseMate and in the eBook for the following:

Chapter 2

Beethoven, Symphony No. 5, fourth movement (8:27)
p. 8, CD 3:4–8

Music Concept Checks

Demos or streaming music are available in CourseMate and the eBook for the following:

Chapter 1

Blast of the shofar, p. 5
Sound of *om*, p. 6
Shamanic drumming, p. 6

Chapter 2

Britten, *Young Person's Guide to the Orchestra*, p. 9
Mozart/Tchaikovsky, hybrid compilation of "Unser dummer Pöbel meint" and *Mozartiana*, p. 14

Chapter 3

Mozart, Twelve Variations on "Ah, vous dirai-je Maman"
Variation 6, p. 16
Variations 2 and 12, p. 17
Variation 11, p. 18

Chapter 4

Sound of an octave, a leap, and a step, p. 22
Major and minor scales, p. 23

The Language of Music

Chapter 2

Dynamics, p. 9

Discussion Questions

1. **Consider a favorite musical selection. Why do you like the piece?** Listen to it with the musical elements in mind. How does awareness of the elements affect your listening experience?

2. **What is music?** Listen to a musical selection without melody, such as rap. Also, listen to a selection that in your opinion has a beautiful melody. Does music without melody qualify as music? If so, how?

Assignments

1. **Write a critical review suitable for publication in your school newspaper of a live performance of your choice.** Address the performance as a whole as well as use of basic music elements.

2. **Do you like sports?** While you're at a school football game, check out the marching band's halftime show. What instruments do you hear? Now listen to CD 3:4–8, Beethoven's Symphony No. 5, fourth movement, and notice the instruments you hear in that piece. What differences do you notice?

Beyond the Class

For Further Listening

This additional musical selection may be found in the iTunes and Rhapsody playlists:

Chapter 3

• Sugarhill Gang, "Rapper's Delight"

For Further Viewing

These additional video performances may be found in the YouTube playlist:

Chapter 1

• Experience *4'33"* by John Cage as performed by David Tudor. Check out the different blasts of the shofar.

Chapter 2

• Hear a *koudi*, an ancient Chinese bone flute.

Chapter 4

• Hear "Take Me Out to the Ball Game" in its entirety.

A selection of materials may also be found in the Instructor's Manual and PowerLecture.

WHAT'S INSIDE Key topics in this unit:
Chapter 5, Harmony and Texture: Harmony; Texture
Chapter 6, Form: Form; Recognizing Form; Comparing Sections; Examples of Form; Why Bother Understanding Form?
Chapter 7, Style: Musical Style; Listening for Style

Learning Outcomes

LO1 Understand harmony as the simultaneous sounding of two or more tones and the complement of melody, and describe a chord progression.

LO2 Discuss the meaning and function of a cadence.

LO3 Define texture and the roles of part, line, and voice in texture; distinguish between density and independence in texture.

LO4 Define musical form and describe how we recognize musical form through musical punctuation (cadences) and pattern.

LO5 Describe the use of repetition, contrast, and variation in music.

LO6 Differentiate some basic musical forms.

LO7 Describe what we mean by musical style and important considerations in identifying it.

Terms

Chapter 5
harmony
chord
arpeggio (broken chord)
block chord
chord progression
tonic chord
cadence
texture
part (line; voice)
doubling
density

textural independence
monophonic (*n.* monophony)
polyphonic (*n.* polyphony; contrapuntal, *n.* counterpoint)
round
homophonic (melody and accompaniment; *n.* homophony)

Chapter 6
form
repetition
contrast
variation
binary form
rounded binary form
variation form (theme and variations)
strophic form

Chapter 7
style

Multimedia

Listening Guides

Active Listening Guides with streaming music are available in CourseMate and in the eBook for the following:

Chapter 7

Hildegard of Bingen, "Nunc aperuit nobis" (1:52) p. 40, CD 1:1

Music Concept Checks

Demos or streaming music are available in CourseMate and the eBook for the following:

Chapter 5

Arpeggios and chords, p. 30

Cadences, p. 31

Texture: monophony, homophony, polyphony, p. 33

Chapter 6

Structural similarities and differences, p. 36

Chapter 7

Sample Listening Guide, p. 41

Discussion Questions

1. **Listen to a selection of your choice and note the texture.** Does it change or remain constant throughout the piece?

2. **How does texture affect the listening experience?** Listen to Handel's Hallelujah Chorus from your CD set (CD 1:28) for texture. What do you hear? How do the texture changes affect your listening experience?

3. **After listening to Handel's Hallelujah Chorus, compare it with "Hotel California" by the Eagles.** How are texture and punctuation used in "Hotel California"?

Assignments

1. **Check out the Rolling Stones.** How does the use of texture and style affect the success of their music?

2. **Look for opportunities to attend live performances.** Notice the style of the music. What does the music reveal about the composer, the performers, the listeners, and the community?

Beyond the Class

For Further Viewing

These additional video performances may be found in the YouTube playlist:

Chapter 5

- Watch as Arthur Rubinstein plays Chopin's Etude, Op. 25, No. 1. Listen for the broken chords throughout this selection.

- Notice the monophonic texture in the Gregorian chant *Circumdederunt me*.

- Check out homophonic texture in Mozart's *Ave verum corpus* or in Elvis Presley's "Love Me Tender."

- The complexities of polyphonic music can be heard in the aria and first few variations of the Goldberg Variations by Bach as performed by Glenn Gould.

A selection of materials may also be found in the Instructor's Manual and PowerLecture.

Musical Life, 1000–1700

WHAT'S INSIDE Key topics in this unit:

Chapter 8, Medieval, Renaissance, and Early Baroque Music:
Musical Trends and Developments, 1000–1700; Music and Technology; Musical Communication; Looking Ahead

Learning Outcomes

LO1 Understand the significance of the growth of secular music.

LO2 Describe and understand the importance of the development of polyphony and common practice harmony.

LO3 Understand the use of instruments during the Middle Ages, the Renaissance, and the early Baroque.

LO4 Explain the evolution of music as a profession.

LO5 Grasp how technology came to shape musical life.

Terms

Chapter 8
secular music
vernacular
chanson
chant
organum
tenor
heterophony
guild

Discussion Questions

1. **What roles do sacred music and secular music play in modern life?** Are there stylistic differences? Does sacred music or secular music better reflect our culture?

2. **How does technology affect musical style?** Is there a correlation between technology and style?

Assignments

1. **Keep a journal of the music you listen to for one week.** Do you listen to primarily sacred or secular music? How are they different? Do you think your listening choices are comparable to those of your classmates? Initiate some discussions and find out.

2. **Interview a music professional to find out exactly what the musician does and how, why he or she chose a music career, and the type of clientele the musician serves.** Research the person's particular role as a musician. If a similar position existed in an earlier period, compare and contrast the two positions.

Beyond the Class

For Further Viewing

These additional video performances may be found in the YouTube playlist:

- Technology is having a tremendous impact on music today. Check out the theme music for *Dr. Who*, 1963.

- We often assume that technology refers to computers. Many modern musicians are literally looking "outside the box" and creating new sounds from traditional instruments and objects along with the computer. Listen to some excerpts from NIME, New Interfaces for Musical Expression.

A selection of materials may also be found in the Instructor's Manual and PowerLecture.

WHAT'S INSIDE   Key topics in this unit:

Chapter 9, Chant and Hildegard of Bingen: Monastic Life in the Middle Ages; Chant; Hildegard of Bingen; Summary

Chapter 10, Secular Song and Dance in France: Secular Culture in France; Minstrels and Troubadours; Guillaume de Machaut and Secular Song; The Emergence of Instrumental Music; Summary

People's Music 1, "L'homme armé": "L'homme armé"; Summary

Learning Outcomes

LO1   Describe monastic life in the Middle Ages.

LO2   Define chant and its three forms of text setting.

LO3   Recognize the style of an antiphon through Hildegard of Bingen's "Nunc aperuit nobis."

LO4   Become more familiar with the emergence of secular culture during the late Middle Ages.

LO5   Understand more about minstrels and troubadours, the most important secular musicians of the time.

LO6   Describe the life, poetry, and music of Guillaume de Machaut, an important fourteenth-century composer.

LO7   Analyze an example of the earliest dance music that has come down to us.

LO8   Recognize "L'homme armé," a popular song from the fifteenth century.

Terms

Chapter 9
Divine Office
plainchant (chant)
Gregorian chant
syllabic
neumatic
melismatic
antiphon
drone

tonal
modal scale

Chapter 10
chivalry
courtly love
minstrel
troubadour
rondeau

mensural notation
estampie

People's Music 1
cantus firmus
ABA form

Listening Guides

Active Listening Guides with streaming music are available in CourseMate and in the eBook for the following:

Chapter 9

Hildegard of Bingen, "Nunc aperuit nobis" (1:52)
p. 53, CD 1:1

Chapter 10

Guillaume de Machaut, "Puis qu'en oubli" (1:35)
p. 59, CD 1:2
Anonymous, "La uitime estampie real" (1:29)
p. 60, CD 1:3

People's Music 1

Anonymous, "L'homme armé" (0:29) p. 63, CD 1:4

Music Concept Checks

Chapter 9

To assist you in recognizing its distinctive features, we present an interactive demo of medieval music in CourseMate and the eBook.

Discussion Questions

1. **How did life in a monastery differ from secular life?** What effect did monastic life have on music composed by the clergy?

2. **Considering the lifestyle in a monastery, how does chant reflect life in the Middle Ages?** How do you think the general public reacted to chant? In your opinion, would they have reacted primarily to the text or to the music? How do you react to chant?

3. **Compare and contrast secular and sacred music in the Middle Ages.** Now, consider music of today's world, both sacred and secular. How have the roles and traditions of secular and sacred music changed over the centuries?

Assignments

1. **Syllabic and neumatic textual settings are very common in children's music.** As we age and listen to more complex music, we hear more use of melisma. Listen for syllabic style in your favorite music and notice the effect. Do the different approaches support the text? Do they change your reaction to the music?

2. **Listen to "L'homme armé" in the same way you listen to your favorite music today.** Noting that it was, in today's terms, a huge hit, how do you think it reflects the medieval public? Does it reflect the Middle Ages in ways that today's music reflects society? Why do you think "L'homme armé" was so popular for so long?

3. **Let's dance!** Listen to "La uitime estampie real" and try dancing to it. Is it difficult? Dance music has changed drastically over the centuries, of course. Compare medieval dance music with dance music from the early 1960s in a vintage video of Chubby Checker.

Beyond the Class

For Further Viewing

This additional video performance may be found in the YouTube playlist:

Chapter 10

- Have you ever heard a viol or a recorder? Listen and watch a recorder and viols playing thirteenth-century medieval music.

A selection of materials may also be found in the Instructor's Manual and PowerLecture.

Learning Outcomes

LO1 Recognize the main features of Renaissance polyphony.

LO2 Understand the function of sacred music—in particular, polyphonic music—in the late Middle Ages and early Renaissance.

LO3 List the parts of the Catholic Mass that are typically set to music, and hear a mass movement set by Josquin des Prez.

LO4 Understand how, during the Protestant Reformation, Martin Luther connected to Christian believers by adapting secular song for religious purposes.

LO5 Describe the madrigal, its history in Italy and England, its sound, and its social function.

LO6 Understand Elizabethan solo song, the instrument that typically accompanied it, and the use of song in theatrical productions.

LO7 Identify the sounds of Renaissance instruments and their roles within a chamber ensemble.

Terms

Chapter 11	Chapter 12	idiomatic
imitation	ayre	composition
proper	madrigal	
ordinary	a cappella	
ABC form	text painting (word painting)	
People's Music 2	course	
Meistersinger	strophic song	
chorale	obbligato	
strophic form	consort	

Multimedia

Listening Guides
Active Listening Guides with streaming music are available in CourseMate and in the eBook for the following:

Chapter 11
Josquin des Prez, Kyrie, from *Missa l'homme armé sexti toni* (3:38) p. 70, CD 1:5

People's Music 2
Luther/ Walter, "Ein' feste Burg ist unser Gott" (3:00) p. 73, CD 1:6

Chapter 12
Wilbye, "Adew, Sweet Amarillis" (2:40) p. 76, CD 1:7
Morley (attributed), "O Mistresse Mine" vocal (1:35) p. 78, CD 1:8
Morley (attributed), "O Mistresse Mine" instrumental (2:02) p. 80, CD 1:9

Music Concept Checks

Chapter 12
To assist you in recognizing their distinctive features, we present an interactive comparison of medieval, Renaissance, and Baroque music in CourseMate and the eBook.

Discussion Questions

1. **Martin Luther wrote chorales to use for religious music.** How do his chorales reflect changes in religious traditions resulting from the Protestant Reformation?

2. **Compare the madrigal, a secular song, with religious music of the Renaissance.** How do they differ stylistically? In what ways are they related stylistically?

3. **How does the use of music in theatrical productions in the Renaissance compare with music in modern musicals?**

Assignments

1. **Compare and contrast the music of Hildegard and Josquin. How conducive to worship is this music?** Would you describe it as relaxing? agitating? meditative? exciting? Think about daily life in the Renaissance and imagine going into a cathedral and hearing this music.

2. **Have you ever heard a lute?** or a hurdy-gurdy? How about a serpent? or a lizard? Check out more Renaissance instruments at http://www.music.iastate.edu/antiqua/instrumt.html and compare them with modern instruments at http://www.datadragon.com/education/instruments/

Beyond the Class

For Further Viewing
This additional video performance may be found in the YouTube playlist:

Chapter 12
- Enjoy hearing an Elizabethan consort and watching Renaissance dance.

A selection of materials may also be found in the Instructor's Manual and PowerLecture.

WHAT'S INSIDE Key topics in this unit:

Chapter 13, Monteverdi and Early Opera: Opera Is . . . ; The Beginnings of Opera; Monteverdi's *Orfeo*; The Orchestra; Summary

Chapter 14, Henry Purcell and Middle Baroque Opera: The Growth of Opera; Henry Purcell's *Dido and Aeneas*; Looking Back, Looking Ahead

Learning Outcomes

LO1 Understand what opera is, the particular challenge of setting drama to music, and the usefulness of developing musical gestures that can depict feelings and moods.

LO2 Understand the revolutionary impact of the first operas in Europe.

LO3 Recognize the importance of Claudio Monteverdi and the sound and vocal style of his opera *Orfeo*.

LO4 Recognize a large ensemble, as well as new ways of composing for instruments.

LO5 Understand the growth of opera, including musical and dramatic changes, during the seventeenth century.

LO6 Recognize an early example of the use of recitative and aria, as well as the expressive capabilities of common practice harmony, in Henry Purcell's "Dido's Lament."

Terms

Chapter 13
opera
recitative
aria
score
basso continuo

Chapter 14
libretto
semi-opera
ground
   (ground bass or
   basso ostinato)

Unit 6 Outline

Multimedia

Listening Guides

Active Listening Guides with streaming music are available in CourseMate and the eBook for the following:

Chapter 13

Monteverdi, "Possente spirto," *Orfeo* (5:06) p. 90, CD 1:10

Chapter 14

Purcell, "Thy Hand, Belinda / When I Am Laid in Earth," *Dido and Aeneas* (3:58) p. 94, CD 1:11–12

The Language of Music

Chapter 13

A clip demonstrating continuo is available in CourseMate and the eBook.

Discussion Questions

1. **Opera was the beginning of combining drama and music. What impact has opera had on modern music?** Compare Baroque opera with contemporary musical theater, addressing the role of the orchestra and dance.

2. **Discuss the evolution of the lead singer of an opera as a "star" and how this impacts the music and theater world today.**

3. **Notice the use of language in music. Does the music support the meaning of the text?** Do you need to understand the text in Purcell's "Thy Hand Belinda / When I Am Laid in Earth" to feel the singer's emotions?

Assignments

1. **Notice the size of the orchestra and the period instruments as Montserrat Figueras sings "Dal mio permesso"** from *Orfeo*, in the YouTube playlist. How do the size and sound of the orchestra compare with the orchestra used in contemporary music theater?

2. **Compare the use of dance in Monteverdi's *Orfeo*,** in the YouTube playlist, with dance in Bernstein's *West Side Story*, also in the playlist.

Beyond the Class

For Further Viewing

These additional video performances may be found in the YouTube playlist:

Chapter 13

- See the overture to *Tommy* as performed by The Who.
- Experience an excerpt from Peri's *L'Euridice* using period instruments.
- See Montserrat Figueras sing "Dal mio permesso" from *Orfeo*.
- See dance from *Orfeo* compared with dance from *West Side Story*.

A selection of materials may also be found in the Instructor's Manual and PowerLecture.

WHAT'S INSIDE Key topics in this unit:

People's Music 3, Native American Ceremonial Music: Ceremonial Music of the Plains Indians; Plains Indians War Dance, 1958; Connections and Continuations

People's Music 4, Afro-Cuban Music: Middle Passage: Music from Africa to the Americas; Connections and Continuations

People's Music 5, Anglo-American Folk Song: The Anglo-Celtic Folk Ballad; Connections and Continuations

People's Music 6, Anglo-American Folk Dance: The Jig; Newfoundland, Canada, 1982; "Boston Laddie": A Jig from Newfoundland; Connections and Continuations

Learning Outcomes

LO1 Know the sound and cultural function of authentic Native American music.

LO2 Hear the sound of an African musical style from the Americas and understand its use in a religious practice that integrates elements of the Catholic and Yoruba religions.

LO3 Know Anglo-Celtic folk song and its influence on other kinds of music

LO4 Hear authentic Anglo-Celtic dance music and understand its dissemination in Europe and North America.

Terms

People's Music 3
vocable

People's Music 4
santería

People's Music 5
ballad

People's Music 6
jig

Unit 7 Outline

People's Music 3, Native American Ceremonial Music
Ceremonial Music of the Plains Indians
Plains Indians War Dance, 1958
Connections and Continuations

People's Music 4, Afro-Cuban Music
Middle Passage: Music from Africa to the Americas
Africans in the Colonies
From Africa to Cuba
Santería
Connections and Continuations

People's Music 5, Anglo-American Folk Song
The Anglo-Celtic Folk Ballad
Connections and Continuations

People's Music 6, Anglo-American Folk Dance
The Jig
Newfoundland, Canada, 1982
"Boston Laddie": A Jig from Newfoundland
Connections and Continuations

Multimedia

Listening Guides

Active Listening Guides with streaming music are available in CourseMate and the eBook for the following:

People's Music 3

Plains Indians War Dance (1:42) p. 98, CD 1:13

People's Music 4

Anonymous, Song for Odudua (2:07) p. 101, CD 1:14

People's Music 5

Anonymous, "Barbara Allen" (2:34) p. 103, CD 1:15

People's Music 6

Guinchard, "Boston Laddie" (1:42) p. 106, CD 1:16

Discussion Questions

1. **Compare the Native American Plains Indians War Dance with Hildegard's "Nunc aperuit nobis."** Do both create a meditative spirit? How effective are they at contributing to spirituality?

2. **Dance plays an important part in human culture.** Compare/contrast the use of dance in Native American and Afro-Cuban traditions.

Assignments

1. **Consider the effect folk music has had on American music in the last fifty years.** Consider how music like "Barbara Allen" influenced Bob Dylan and the Beatles.

2. **Using the Internet and databases available in your local library, find examples of different types of dance music.** The jig is an example, as are the waltz and the hula. Note the differences in the music, especially in tempo and meter.

Beyond the Class

For Further Viewing

These additional video performances may be found in the YouTube playlist:

People's Music 3

- Documentary on the Plains Indians War Dance

People's Music 4

- Notice the call and response of Obatal Santería Yoruba baba.

People's Music 5

- "Barbara Allen" from *Songcatcher*

A selection of materials may also be found in the Instructor's Manual and PowerLecture.

WHAT'S INSIDE Key topics in this unit:

Chapter 15, From Baroque to Classical: The Growth of the Music Business; Major Developments in Eighteenth-Century Music; Music and Musical Styles: From Baroque to Classical

Learning Outcomes

LO1 Understand the growth of the music business in the eighteenth century.

LO2 List the major developments in eighteenth-century music.

LO3 Contrast the two main styles of eighteenth-century music, Baroque and Classical.

Terms

Chapter 15
pianoforte
common practice
harmony
Enlightenment
Baroque
Classical style

Discussion Questions

1. **The music business as we know it traces its roots back centuries—public performance, instrument making, publishing, music instruction, composition, and writing about music.** Which of these components are still viable today? Are there other options available to musicians today? If so, what are they?

2. **Regarding the growth of music making, how has it changed over the centuries?** Is today's public as musically literate as in the past? Is music making a part of home life in today's society? Why or why not?

3. **Common practice harmony was the musical language of the eighteenth century.** It was used in the Baroque era to convey a single emotional state and in the Classical era to present and bring into agreement contrasting moods. How do both uses compare with the use of music to express emotions and ideas today?

Assignments

1. **The ancient Greeks believed music had power over human behavior.** Visit a restaurant or a store and notice the background music. What type of music do you hear? Is it rock, classical, religious, folk? How does the music affect your dining or shopping experience? How does the music affect the way you feel?

2. **By the end of the eighteenth century, Vienna was the main center of musical activity.** Today, there are many important centers of music in the world. Try searching the Internet for concert schedules of operas, symphonies, musicals, and rock concerts to identify these centers.

Beyond the Class

For Further Viewing
These additional video performances may be found in the YouTube playlist:

Chapter 15
- Vladimir Horowitz, before his death, was a master of the piano. Listen to his interpretation of the Mozart Sonata in C major, K. 330, and notice contrasting elements within the piece. This concert took place in Vienna, a leading center of music during Mozart's life.

A selection of materials may also be found in the Instructor's Manual and PowerLecture.

WHAT'S INSIDE   Key topics in this unit:
Chapter 16, Sonata and Suite: Baroque Instruments; The Baroque Sonata; The Baroque Suite; Baroque Aesthetics and Style in Instrumental Music
Chapter 17, The Baroque Concerto: The Orchestra during the Baroque Era; The Concerto; Bach's Brandenburg Concertos

Learning Outcomes

LO1   Understand Baroque instruments and ensembles, as well as idiomatic use of instruments.

LO2   Recognize the sound of the Baroque chamber sonata through the music of Arcangelo Corelli.

LO3   Become familiar with the Baroque suite through the music of J. S. Bach.

LO4   Review the prevailing Baroque musical aesthetic and style.

LO5   Understand how the orchestra evolved during the Baroque era.

LO6   Become acquainted with the Baroque concerto through Vivaldi's *The Four Seasons*, a famous early example of program music.

LO7   Gain insight into Bach's fascination with instruments by listening to his Brandenburg Concertos.

Terms

Chapter 16
harpsichord
plectrum
continuo
canzona
sonata
movement
church sonata
   (*sonata da chiesa*)
chamber sonata
   (*sonata da camera*)
solo sonata
trio sonata
ritornello

opus
figured bass
suite
allemande
courante
sarabande
gigue
Doctrine of
   Affections

Chapter 17
concerto
solo concerto
concertino
concerto grosso

tutti
ritornello
program music

Unit 9 Outline

Chapter 16, Sonata and Suite
Baroque Instruments
   The Violin Family
   The Harpsichord
   Basso Continuo: The Baroque Rhythm Section
The Baroque Sonata
   Corelli and the Baroque Sonata
   Solo and Trio Sonatas
   The Ritornello
   The Sound of the Baroque Violin Sonata
The Baroque Suite
   The "Classic" Baroque Suite
   Johann Sebastian Bach
   Bach and the Suite
   Bach's Gigue and the Suite
Baroque Aesthetics and Style in Instrumental Music

Chapter 17, The Baroque Concerto
The Orchestra during the Baroque Era
The Concerto
   The Design of the Baroque Concerto
   Vivaldi's The Four Seasons
   Program Music
   "Spring"
Bach's Brandenburg Concertos
   Bach's Different Path
   Bach's Third Brandenburg Concerto
   Bach and Baroque Style

Multimedia

Listening Guides

Active Listening Guides with streaming music are available in CourseMate and in the eBook for the following:

Chapter 16

Corelli, Sonata in C major, first and second movements (4:55) p. 118, CD 1:17–18

Bach, Gigue from Orchestral Suite No. 3 in D major (2:57) p. 121, CD 1:19

Chapter 17

Vivaldi, Violin Concerto in E major ("Spring" from *The Four Seasons)*, first movement (3:42) p. 125, CD 1:20

Bach, Brandenburg Concerto No. 3, first movement (5:33) p. 127, CD 1:21

Discussion Questions

1. **How does Baroque instrumental music compare with modern instrumental music?** Compare and contrast musical elements such as melody and bass line. In Baroque music, the basso continuo was very important. Is this true of today's music?

2. **Bach is referred to as the bridge between old and new.** Explain this. Which elements of his music lean toward the old, and which lead to the new? What music today might be functioning as a bridge? Where does it come from, and where do you think it is leading?

Assignments

1. **Corelli is the first composer to be well known for his instrumental music.** Think about composers of instrumental music today. Are they writing music for similar occasions? Is instrumental music for entertainment as well as worship being composed today? If so, how does it compare to Corelli's? Can you determine, by listening, what type of occasion it was written for?

2. **Analyze your listening experience of the two concertos from Chapter 17 (Vivaldi's "Spring" and Bach's Brandenburg Concerto No. 3) in terms of relating to the music.** Is one easier to follow and understand than the other? If so, why? Does Vivaldi's program help or hinder your experience? Although the program offers you a focal point, does it also inhibit your own creativity as a listener?

Beyond the Class

For Further Viewing

These additional video performances may be found in the YouTube playlist:

Chapter 16

- The lute was a popular instrument during the Baroque era. Listen to the gentle sound of the lute in Bach's Prelude in D minor, BWV 1008.

Chapters 16 and 17

- The harpsichord and the piano are very different, even though they are both keyboard instruments. Notice the difference in the sound as you listen to Bach's Keyboard

Concerto No. 1 in D minor, first movement with piano and third movement with harpsichord. Each movement of the concerto exemplifies the Doctrine of Affections, having one affect that is consistent throughout the separate movements.

A selection of materials may also be found in the Instructor's Manual and PowerLecture.

Learning Outcomes

LO1 Understand the changes in Baroque opera from Monteverdi to Handel.

LO2 Become familiar with recitative and aria in Baroque opera through Handel's *Giulio Cesare*.

LO3 Encounter excerpts of a famous early example of truly popular music in John Gay's *The Beggar's Opera* and understand why it can be considered popular music.

LO4 Understand how Bach integrated familiar hymns into his music for the Lutheran liturgy.

LO5 Get acquainted with the Baroque oratorio, its importance to Handel's career, and Handel's most successful oratorio, *Messiah*.

LO6 Experience the coming together of sacred and secular music in the late Baroque.

Terms

Chapter 18
opera seria
da capo aria
castrato
broadside ballad

Chapter 19
church cantata
cantata
chorus
chorale
oratorio

Multimedia

Listening Guides

Active Listening Guides with streaming music are available in CourseMate and in the eBook for the following:

Chapter 18

Handel, "E pur così" and "Piangeró," from *Giulio Cesare in Egitto* (7:09) p. 131, CD 1:22–23

Gay and Pepusch, "I'm Bubbled," "Cease Your Funning," and "How Now, Madam Flirt," from *The Beggar's Opera* (3:14) p. 133, CD 1:24–26

Chapter 19

Bach, "Und wenn die Welt voll Teufel wär," from Cantata *Ein' feste Burg ist unser Gott* (3:14) p. 136, CD 1:27

Handel, Hallelujah Chorus, from *Messiah* (3:33) p. 138, CD 1:28

Music Concept Checks

Chapter 19

To assist you in recognizing their distinctive features, we present an interactive comparison of Renaissance and Baroque style in CourseMate and the eBook.

Discussion Questions

1. **The Arcadian Academy reformed opera as developed by the Camerata.** What changes did they make? What was their intent, and did they accomplish their goals?

2. **How does early popular music, as exemplified in John Gay's *The Beggar's Opera*, compare with popular music today?** Do they perform similar functions? Is popular music more or less effective than classical music at presenting a slice of life?

3. **How does the use of a chorale as a basis for a cantata enhance the effectiveness of the music as a worship tool?**

Assignments

1. **Originally, the Bach cantatas were a regular part of the Sunday church service.** In what venues are the Bach cantatas performed today? How has the performance status of Bach cantatas changed and why?

2. **Handel is known for his use of contrast while maintaining continuity of affect.** As you listen to the Hallelujah Chorus, notice the contrasting elements. Are there contrasts in use of melody, instrumentation, and texture? Notice that Handel uses homophony, monophony, and polyphony in this chorus. With all of these contrasts, how does Handel follow the Doctrine of Affections, maintaining one affect?

Beyond the Class

For Further Viewing

These additional video performances may be found in the YouTube playlist:

Chapter 18

- Hear the voice of Alessandro Moreschi, "the last castrato," in the YouTube playlist.

Chapter 19

- In this clip from the movie *Farinelli: Il Castrato*, Farinelli is singing "Lascia ch'io pianga" from Handel's opera *Rinaldo*. Notice the liberties taken in the repeat of the A section in this da capo aria.

A selection of materials may also be found in the Instructor's Manual and PowerLecture.

WHAT'S INSIDE Key topics in this unit:

People's Music 7, National Anthems: The First National Anthems
People's Music 8, Revolutionary Song: Songs of the American Revolution

Learning Outcomes

LO1 Identify two well-known anthems and learn about the historical context in which they emerged.

LO2 Know about America's first memorable composer and become familiar with his most famous song.

Terms

People's Music 7
national anthem

Multimedia

Listening Guides

Active Listening Guides with streaming music are available in CourseMate and in the eBook for the following:

People's Music 7

Anonymous, "God Save the King" (0:55) p. 144, CD 1:29
Haydn, "Gott erhalte Franz den Kaiser" (1:10) p. 144, CD 1:30

People's Music 8

Billings, "Chester" (2:15) p. 146, CD 1:31

Explorations
People's Music 8

Check out the Songwriters Hall of Fame, p. 145

Discussion Questions

1. **Compare and contrast "God Save the King" and "The Star-Spangled Banner," considering the text as well as the music.** What do they reveal about their respective countries? Do they adequately and accurately reflect the spirit of each country?

2. **There is often a correlation between melodic style and political stance with hymnlike melodies relating to the establishment and martial melodies to the revolutionaries.** Is there music today that follows this trend? Can you name some examples and explain the relationship between style and political leanings?

Assignments

1. **How does Brian May's version of "God Save the Queen," recorded at Buckingham Palace for Queen Elizabeth's Golden Jubilee in 2002, compare to the hymn version?** Is one more inspiring than the other? Why or why not?

2. **Compare William Billings's "Chester" with vintage footage of Bob Dylan singing "The Times They Are A-Changin'," noting how both reflect their respective cultures.** Can you identify other musicians who are composing and performing songs reflecting the current social and political climate?

Beyond the Class

For Further Viewing

These additional video performances may be found in the YouTube playlist:

People's Music 7

- Listen to Jimi Hendrix playing "The Star-Spangled Banner" live at Woodstock in 1969.

A selection of materials may also be found in the Instructor's Manual and PowerLecture.

The Classical Style

WHAT'S INSIDE Key topics in this unit:

Chapter 20, Classical Sonata and String Quartet: The Emergence of the Classical Style; Sonata Form and Classical Style; Mozart and the Piano Sonata; The String Quartet; Classical Music: Form and Style

Chapter 21, The Classical Symphony: The Orchestra in the Late Eighteenth Century; The Classical Symphony; Haydn, the Symphony, and Classical Style: Something for Everyone

Chapter 22, Mozart and Opera: The Development of Opera during the Eighteenth Century; Mozart, Opera, and *Don Giovanni*; Mozart's Music for *Don Giovanni*; Mozart, Classical Music, and Opera as Drama

Chapter 23, The Classical Concerto: The Concerto in Eighteenth-Century Cultural Life; Mozart and the Classical Concerto; Mozart's Concerto in C Minor and the Classical Concerto; Mozart's Music as Drama and a Preview of Romanticism?

Learning Outcomes

LO1 Recognize Classical style and sonata form through exploring a movement from a Mozart piano sonata.

LO2 Discover the sound of the string quartet, the main chamber ensemble of the Classical era, through a string quartet by Franz Joseph Haydn.

LO3 Be familiar with the Classical symphony, as exemplified by Haydn's Symphony No. 94.

LO4 Describe the changes in opera during the late eighteenth century, as evidenced in two excerpts from Mozart's *Don Giovanni*.

LO5 Understand the form and style of the Classical concerto.

Terms

Chapter 20
sonata form
introduction
exposition
transition
development
modulation
recapitulation
coda
K.
string quartet

Chapter 21
symphony
scherzo
rondo

Chapter 22
opéra comique
opera buffa
Singspiel

Chapter 23
concerto
cadenza

Unit 12 Outline

Multimedia

Listening Guides

Active Listening Guides with streaming music are available in CourseMate and in the eBook for the following:

Chapter 20

Mozart, Sonata in F major, K. 332, first movement (6:35) p. 154, CD 2:1–3

Haydn, String Quartet in C major, Op. 33, No. 3 ("Bird"), first movement (6:59) p. 157, CD 2:4–6

Chapter 21

Haydn, Symphony No. 94 in G, first movement (9:39) p. 160, CD 2:7–10

Chapter 22

Mozart, "Là ci darem la mano," *Don Giovanni* (2:59) p. 165, CD 2:11

Mozart, "A cenar teco," *Don Giovanni* (5:15) p. 166, CD 2:12–13

Chapter 23

Mozart, Concerto No. 24 in C minor, K. 491, first movement (12:56) p. 171, CD 2:14–18

Music Concept Checks

Chapter 23

To assist you in recognizing their distinctive features, we present an interactive comparison of Baroque and Classical style in CourseMate and the eBook.

Discussion Questions

1. **Many changes occurred in the transition from Baroque to Classical style.** Two of the most striking are the change from relatively little contrast, to express one affect per movement, to frequent contrasts within movements and a preference for more homophonic textures. How do these changes affect your listening experience?

2. **Classical style included dynamic contrasts, varied rhythms, and melodic contrasts to increase tension in music.** Do composers today use these same techniques to increase tension and highlight sections of their music?

Assignments

1. **How does form affect your listening experience?** After listening to Haydn, Symphony No. 94 in G, first movement in sonata form, listen to the second movement in theme and variations. Does one movement hold your attention more than the other? If so, which one and why?

2. **Baroque opera functioned as drama through music with *opera seria*.** In the Classical period, there is more flexibility with *opera buffa* and *Singspiel*. Discuss the differences between these styles of opera. Include the use of language, drama, and contrast.

3. **How does the soloist in a Classical concerto compare with soloists in rock bands?** After listening to the cadenza in the Mozart Concerto No. 24 in C minor, first movement, listen to an Eddie Van Halen solo. What similarities are there between the two solos? How does each performance reflect its culture?

Beyond the Class

For Further Viewing

These additional video performances may be found in the YouTube playlist:

Chapter 20

- Do you know the French song "Ah, vous dirai-je Maman?"
- Listen to Haydn's Sonata in A flat, No. 43 played on a restored Cristofori piano originally built in 1720. The Metropolitan Museum of Art in New York has a 1720 Cristofori piano in its collection.

A selection of materials may also be found in the Instructor's Manual and PowerLecture.

WHAT'S INSIDE Key topics in this unit:
Chapter 24, The Romantic Era: The Expanding Musical Life; Romanticism and Nineteenth-Century Music; The Stratification of Music and Musical Life

Learning Outcomes

LO1 Chart the development of diverse trends in nineteenth-century musical life: music publishing, music education, musical instruments and technologies, and entertainment.

LO2 Describe the characteristics of Romanticism.

LO3 Discuss the increasing stratification of musical life, particularly in the latter part of the nineteenth century.

Terms

Chapter 24
musicologist
Romanticism
virtuosity
etude
atonality
Gesamtkunstwerk

Unit 13 Outline

Discussion Questions

1. **A transition allowing professional musicians to obtain income from the marketplace rather than from church or court patronage occurred in the Romantic era.** What effect do you think this had on musical style? Which method of deriving revenue is more limiting professionally?

2. **Socioeconomic changes in Europe in the 1800s had a huge effect on the music world.** What were some of these changes, and how did they affect musicians? Did music publishing reflect these changes? If so, how?

3. **Music publishing had an enormous impact on the music world, giving more people access to music.** How has music publishing fostered the growth of music as a career and the availability of music to all people in the nineteenth century and the present? What has the impact of publishing been from a historical view?

4. **The tradition of music education in the public school began in the nineteenth century.** Is this trend continued today? Are public schools effective in teaching music today? Should music be an important part of a child's education? Why, or why not?

5. **The study of music history, or musicology, developed into a discipline in the nineteenth century.** How does the study of music history affect the listening experience?

Assignments

1. **Many instruments were improved or created during the nineteenth century.** Can you name two and describe how they were used in the nineteenth century versus how they are used today?

2. **Sound recording was invented in 1877 by Thomas Edison.** What impact has sound recording had on the music industry? How has it evolved, and how has the sound quality been affected?

3. **The Enlightenment valued humanity and rationality, and Romanticism valued subjectivity and inspiration.** Compare and contrast these two philosophies. What were possible inspirations for these two viewpoints, and how do they reflect their respective cultures?

4. **Virtuoso performers seem to have superhuman abilities.** The greatest, such as Paganini and Liszt, are still legendary figures. Can you name a virtuoso performing presently? Describe a performance. What was your reaction? Were you impressed?

Beyond the Class

For Further Viewing
These additional video performances may be found in the YouTube playlist:

Chapter 24
- Watch as Lang Lang, a virtuoso pianist, plays Chopin's Waltz, Op. 34, No. 1.

A selection of materials may also be found in the Instructor's Manual and PowerLecture.

WHAT'S INSIDE Key topics in this unit:

Chapter 25, Beethoven and the Piano Sonata: Beethoven the Revolutionary; Beethoven and the Piano Sonata

Chapter 26, Beethoven and the Symphony: Beethoven and the Symphony; Beethoven's Fifth Symphony; Beethoven and the Nineteenth Century

Learning Outcomes

LO1 Understand the revolutionary qualities in Beethoven's music that set it apart from the music of other composers.

LO2 Describe Beethoven's radically different approach to the piano and the piano sonata.

LO3 Understand Beethoven's conception of a four-movement symphony as an integrated musical statement.

LO4 Grasp the impact of Beethoven and his music on nineteenth-century culture, and gauge his influence on other composers.

Terms

Chapter 26
scherzo and trio

Multimedia

Listening Guides

Active Listening Guides with streaming music are available in CourseMate and in the eBook for the following:

Chapter 25

Beethoven, Sonata in C minor, Op. 13 ("Pathétique"), first movement (7:53) p. 192, CD 2:19–23

Chapter 26

Beethoven, Symphony No. 5 in C minor, first movement (7:35) p. 196, CD 2:24–27

Beethoven, Symphony No. 5 in C minor, second movement (10:00) p. 196, CD 2:28–29

Beethoven, Symphony No. 5 in C minor, third movement (5:29) p. 197, CD 3:1–3

Beethoven, Symphony No. 5 in C minor, fourth movement (8:27) p. 197, CD 3:4–8

Discussion Questions

1. **How does Beethoven contribute to the transition to Romantic style?**

2. **Beethoven was considered a radical in his time. Who are some radical musicians today?** How does their music compare with Beethoven's in spirit, vitality, and representation of current culture?

Assignments

1. **Based on your own listening experience, how does Beethoven's Fifth Symphony reflect struggle and triumph?**

2. **Compare and contrast the music of the Classical era with Beethoven's in terms of "emotional message," addressing the difference in expressive power.**

Beyond the Class

For Further Viewing

These additional video performances may be found in the YouTube playlist:

Chapter 26

- Check out the Trans-Siberian Orchestra playing Beethoven. Listen for clips from Beethoven sonatas and symphonies as well as Mozart's requiem.

A selection of materials may also be found in the Instructor's Manual and PowerLecture.

UNIT 15 PREPCARD

Vocal Music in the Nineteenth Century

WHAT'S INSIDE Key topics in this unit:

Chapter 27, Schubert and the Art Song: Song and Singing in the Nineteenth Century; The *Lied*, a Romantic Genre; Franz Schubert; The Art Song after Schubert
People's Music 9, Stephen Foster and Popular Song: The Parlor Song; Minstrelsy; The Birth of American Popular Music
Chapter 28, Spiritual Music: The Requiem: Religion, Deism, and Spirituality; The Requiem in the Nineteenth Century; Johannes Brahms and His Requiem
People's Music 10, Protestant Hymn: A Conflict in Spiritual Styles; The Protestant Hymn in Nineteenth-Century America
Chapter 29, Operetta and *Opéra comique*: Operetta: Gilbert and Sullivan's *The Pirates of Penzance*; *Opéra comique*: Bizet's *Carmen*; The Best of Times, the Worst of Times: The Diversity of Late Nineteenth-Century Opera
Chapter 30, Opera and Music Drama: Giuseppe Verdi and the Resurgence of Italian Opera; Richard Wagner and Music Drama; Verdi and Wagner; The Stratification of Musical Life

LO1 Describe the flowering of song in the nineteenth century.

LO2 Recognize the art song, through the *Lieder* of Franz Schubert.

LO3 Describe the emergence of popular music in America, its audience, and its relationship to the art song, using songs by Stephen Foster.

LO4 Reexamine the musical and social boundaries between sacred and secular, and religious and spiritual, through an exploration of Brahms's *Requiem*.

LO5 Relate developments in European spiritual music to Protestant music for worship in nineteenth-century America.

LO6 Recognize the implications of the development of operetta in the nineteenth century.

LO7 Differentiate *opéra comique* from other types of nineteenth-century opera.

LO8 Describe how Giuseppe Verdi reformed Italian opera.

LO9 Recognize how Richard Wagner changed music and opera.

Terms

Chapter 27
Lied (plural, *Lieder*)
art song
Schubertiade
through-composed
  form

song cycle

People's Music 9
parlor song
minstrelsy
songster

American popular
  music

Chapter 28
deism
requiem

Dies irae

People's Music 10
shape-note (fasola)
  notation
descant

Multimedia

Listening Guides

Active Listening Guides with streaming music are available in CourseMate and in the eBook for the following:

Chapter 27
Schubert, *Erlkönig* (4:01) p. 205, CD 3:9
Schubert, *Gretchen am Spinnrade* (3:48) p. 205, CD 3:10

People's Music 9
Foster, "Jeanie with the Light Brown Hair" (2:54) p. 208, CD 3:11
Foster, "De Camptown Races" (2:41) p. 209, CD 3:12

Chapter 28
Brahms, "Wie lieblich sind deine Wohnungen," from *Ein deutsches Requiem* (5:24) p. 214, CD 3:13–15

People's Music 10
Adams/Mason, "Nearer, My God, to Thee" (1:21) p. 216, CD 3:16
Newton, "Amazing Grace" (2:31) p. 217, CD 3:17

Chapter 29
Gilbert and Sullivan, "I Am the Very Model of a Modern Major-General," *The Pirates of Penzance* (2:54) p. 220, CD 3:18
Bizet, "L'amour est un oiseau rebelle," *Carmen* (3:02) p. 224, CD 3:19

Chapter 30
Verdi, "Dite alla giovine" and "Morrò! Morrò!" *La traviata* (9:15) p. 229, CD 3:20–24
Wagner, Act 1 conclusion, *Die Walküre* (8:09) p. 232, CD 3:25–29

Chapter 29	Chapter 30	
operetta	*bel canto*	motive
patter song	*verismo*	leitmotif
habanera	music drama	
contradanza	reminiscence	

Discussion Questions

1. **How does Schubert's art song compare with songs you hear today?** Is the interplay that occurred between voice and accompaniment in the Romantic era important now?

2. ***Ein deutsches Requiem* by Brahms is sometimes referred to as humanistic.** Explain why this requiem reflects humanism as opposed to religion. Can you name examples of music you have heard that reflect humanity from a spiritual but not necessarily a religious perspective?

3. **How are songs today used as social commentary?** Does music today showcase the text as well as Gilbert and Sullivan did?

4. **Stephen Foster's minstrel songs were the first American popular music and represent a huge cultural revolution.** Give examples of rock bands that have either represented or created a cultural revolution.

Assignments

1. **Compare and contrast Gilbert and Sullivan's "I Am the Very Model of a Modern Major-General" with your favorite Beatles song.** Are there similarities in subject matter and musical elements?

2. **A *Gesamtkunstwerk*, a total artwork, consists of all venues of artistic expression.** Has this trend died out, or is there evidence that it has continued and has had an effect on music performance today? If so, can you name examples of performers today who incorporate other art forms with their music?

3. **Operettas offered the audience escapist entertainment.** What are some examples of escapist musical entertainment today?

Beyond the Class

For Further Viewing

These additional video performances may be found in the YouTube playlist:

People's Music 10
- Enjoy Elvis Presley singing "Amazing Grace" and Mahalia Jackson singing "Nearer, My God, to Thee."
- Watch a clip from the movie version of *La traviata*.

A selection of materials may also be found in the Instructor's Manual and PowerLecture.

WHAT'S INSIDE Key topics in this unit:

Chapter 31, Early Romantic Piano Music: Pianists and Pianos in the Nineteenth Century; German Romantic Piano Music: The Schumanns; Chopin's Piano Music

Chapter 32, The Romantic Orchestra and Program Music: Berlioz and the Orchestra; *Symphonie fantastique*; Berlioz's Legacy

Chapter 33, The Symphony and Concerto in the Romantic Era: Orchestras and Their Audiences; Brahms and the Romantic Symphony; Tchaikovsky and the Romantic Concerto; Tchaikovsky, German Greatness, and a Question of Value

Chapter 34, Music and Dance: The Waltz: Dance in Nineteenth-Century Life; Social Dancing: The Waltz; Tchaikovsky and the Ballet; Rhythm, Dance, and Art; The Rise of Dance

Chapter 35, Nationalism: Nationalism in Nineteenth-Century Music; National Dances and Nationalism

Learning Outcomes

LO1 Explain how the piano became the most common vehicle for the first generation of star soloists during the nineteenth century.

LO2 Describe the conservative approach of early Romantic piano composers Robert and Clara Schumann, and Felix and Fanny Mendelssohn.

LO3 Contrast the conservative approach with the more progressive approach of Paris-based piano composers Frédéric Chopin and Franz Liszt.

LO4 Understand Hector Berlioz's transformation of the orchestra through an exploration of his *Symphonie fantastique*.

LO5 Through an examination of one of Brahms's symphonies, describe how the Romantic symphony expanded on the tradition of Haydn, Mozart, and Beethoven.

LO6 Differentiate the more technically difficult, soloist-dominated concerto of the nineteenth century through a look at a Tchaikovsky violin concerto.

LO7 Grasp the changing role of dance and dance music in the nineteenth century.

LO8 Recognize the conscious nationalism exemplified by Dvořák's music as an important trend in European cultural life during the latter half of the nineteenth century.

Terms

Chapter 31	**Chapter 32**	**Chapter 33**	downbeat
romance	idée fixe	absolute music	ballet
prelude	program symphony	rondo	
two-phrase parallel	tone poem		**Chapter 35**
period		**Chapter 34**	nationalism
		waltz	

Multimedia

Listening Guides

Active Listening Guides with streaming music are available in CourseMate and in the eBook for the following:

Chapter 31

Clara Schumann, Romance in G minor, Op. 21, No. 3 (3:54) p. 240, CD 3:30

Robert Schumann, "Aufschwung," from *Fantasiestücke* (3:15) p. 242, CD 3:31

Chopin, Etude in C minor, Op. 10, No. 12 ("Revolutionary") (2:28) p. 243, CD 3:32

Chopin: Prelude No. 3 in G major (0:53) p. 243, CD 3:33

Chopin: Prelude No. 4 in E minor (1:35) p. 244, CD 3:34

Chapter 32

Berlioz, "Songe d'une nuit de sabbat," *Symphonie fantastique*, fifth movement (9:47) p. 248, CD 4:1–4

Chapter 33

Brahms, Symphony No. 2, third movement (5:14) p. 253, CD 4:5–6

Tchaikovsky, Violin Concerto in D major, third movement (8:13) p. 256, CD 4:7–9

Chapter 34

Strauss, *The Emperor Waltz*, excerpt (4:00) p. 260, CD 4:10

Tchaikovsky, Waltz, from *The Sleeping Beauty* (4:34) p. 263, CD 4:11

Chapter 35

Dvořák, Slavonic Dance in G minor (4:07) p. 268, CD 4:12

Music Concept Checks

Chapter 35

To assist you in recognizing their distinctive features, we present an interactive comparison of Classical and Romantic style in CourseMate and the eBook.

Discussion Questions

1. **The virtuoso pianists dazzled their audiences, creating a fan base.** Compare the virtuoso pianist of the Romantic period with the guitar virtuoso of today. Is the audience affected in similar ways?

2. **Consider conservative versus progressive tendencies of Romantic music.** How do the two approaches differ? Do you see those same trends in today's music?

3. **The use of melody evolved from the Classical to the Romantic period.** What changes do you notice? How does the use of melody in the Romantic period compare with the use of melody in rock music?

4. **How did Brahms use Beethoven as a source of inspiration?** What characteristics of Beethoven's music are evident in Brahms's music?

Assignments

1. **The orchestra evolves as we move from the Baroque through the Classical to the Romantic period.** Does the evolution of the orchestra through these three periods in any way compare with the evolution of the rock band since the 1950s?

2. **Berlioz was very concerned with telling a story in his *Symphonie fantastique*.** Did he accomplish this in the fifth movement? Do musicians today tell stories by using only instruments? If so, name some examples.

3. **Nationalism and exoticism are very evident in Romantic music.** How does this music reflect the culture of the time?

Beyond the Class

For Further Viewing

These additional video performances may be found in the YouTube playlist:

Chapter 31

- Compare and contrast the difference in sound between the Erard piano and the Pleyel piano.

- Notice the ease with which Lang Lang performs Chopin's Etude, Op. 25, No. 1.

Chapter 34

- Enjoy a clip from the 2009 traditional New Year's Concert of the Vienna Philharmonic Orchestra in the Musikverein, Vienna, Austria.

- Experience a little magic watching the Sugar Plum Fairy from *The Nutcracker* by Tchaikovsky.

A selection of materials may also be found in the Instructor's Manual and PowerLecture.

Musical Life in the Twentieth Century and Beyond

Learning Outcomes

LO1 Recognize the widespread impact of technology on every aspect of music in the twentieth century.

LO2 Describe the major musical developments during the twentieth century.

LO3 Paint a picture of the fragmented sound world of the twentieth century in terms of changes in the musical elements.

Terms

Chapter 36
theremin
synthesizer
analog synthesizer
sampling
MIDI (Musical
    Instrument
    Digital Interface)
ethnomusicology
atonality

Unit 17 Outline

Discussion Questions

1. **The recording industry exponentially increased the availability of music.** How did it affect society in the early twentieth century? Compare and contrast live performances versus recordings. What are the advantages and disadvantages of each?

2. **How has digital technology influenced music performance and recording?** Does digital technology open new windows for musicians or allow musicians to be lazy, relying on technology rather than on talent and skill?

3. **Musicians are becoming less reliant on notated music with the development of software that does not require use of notation.** Do you think notation will change or disappear? What future use might there be for notation?

Assignments

1. **As we enter the twentieth century, we will hear music using dissonance differently than in previous periods.** Dissonance will no longer be used to create momentum and tension and then resolve to consonance. Dissonance will be used for the dissonant sound alone. Can you identify any current music that uses a lot of dissonance? What is your response to extensive use of dissonance?

2. **What factors contribute to ethnomusicology being largely a twentieth-century discipline?** How does the study of ethnic music contribute to our understanding of a culture? How does music today reflect our culture?

Beyond the Class

For Further Viewing
These additional video performances may be found in the YouTube playlist:

Chapter 36

- The eerie sound of the theremin.

- Listen to the sound quality of "Listen to the Mocking Bird" being played on an Edison cylinder phonograph and an 1895 Emile Berliner recording of "Sidewalks of New York" played on a George J. Gaskin Victor II Gramophone. George Gaskin is the singer. Berliner is the inventor of this technology.

- Check out a scene from *The Jazz Singer*, including a recently released deleted scene.

A selection of materials may also be found in the Instructor's Manual and PowerLecture.

WHAT'S INSIDE   Key topics in this unit:

Chapter 37, Expressionism: Arnold Schoenberg, Musical Expressionism, and Atonality; *Pierrot lunaire*; Expressionism in Music

Chapter 38, Impressionism and Beyond: Claude Debussy, *"Musicien parisien"*; Painters in France: Impressionism and Beyond; Debussy the Impressionist; Debussy the Cinematographer; Debussy the Accessible Radical

Chapter 39, Primitivism: Russia, France, and Stravinsky; Primitivism and Folk Culture; *The Rite of Spring*; The Emergence of the Avant-Garde

Learning Outcomes

LO1   Describe the traits of expressionist music and atonality through an understanding of the music of Arnold Schoenberg.

LO2   Become familiar with impressionism in the arts, specifically in the music of Claude Debussy.

LO3   Learn about the emergence of film and its influence on Debussy's music.

LO4   Analyze how primitivist composers such as Igor Stravinsky embedded "primitive" elements in ultramodern settings.

Terms

Chapter 37	**Chapter 39**
expressionism	*col legno*
Sprechstimme	
commedia dell'arte	

Chapter 38
impressionism
whole-tone scale

Multimedia

Listening Guides

Active Listening Guides with streaming music are available in CourseMate and in the eBook for the following:

Chapter 37

Schoenberg, "Nacht," *Pierrot lunaire* (2:13) p. 288 CD 4:13

Chapter 38

Debussy, "Voiles," from *Préludes* (3:25) p. 292, CD 4:14
Debussy, "Minstrels," from *Préludes* (1:58) p. 293, CD 4:15

Chapter 39

Stravinsky, "Introduction," "The Augurs of Spring," and "Mock Abduction," from *The Rite of Spring* (7:39) p. 298, CD 4:16–18

Discussion Questions

1. **Expressionism is a movement in art and music that searches for a deeper reality.** How do expressionist music and art encourage delving into one's subconscious? What musical and visual elements were used? How did Freud influence expressionist music?

2. **Compare impressionist art and music in terms of musical elements.** Artists were concerned with color and light, not the object or form. What corresponds to color and light in music? How did composers convey images through music?

3. **Stravinsky is often referred to as a truly international musician.** Explain why Stravinsky merits this designation. Are there other composers you think worthy of being considered musicians of and for the world?

Assignments

1. **Schoenberg described his music as the "emancipation of dissonance."** His music also represents liberation from previous approaches to form and harmony. How do you perceive these changes? Can you relate to the music?

2. **Early twentieth-century music is characterized by atonality.** Compare and contrast the accessibility of atonality among impressionist, expressionist, and primitivist music.

3. **Stravinsky was a genius at combining the primitive with the ultramodern.** Notice how he uses various musical elements to achieve this combination. Listen to music of today and note any similarities. What kind of music do you consider to be ultramodern today?

Beyond the Class

For Further Viewing

These additional video performances may be found in the YouTube playlist:

Chapter 38

- Listen to "Il pleure" from *The Seduction of Claude Debussy* from the 1999 album by Art of Noise.

- Enjoy *Asmarandana* performed by the group Marsudi Raras on gamelan.

Chapter 39

- Check out Nijinsky's choreography, as re-created by the Joffrey Ballet, for *The Rite of Spring*, Part I, Part II, and Part III.

A selection of materials may also be found in the Instructor's Manual and PowerLecture.

UNIT 19

American Classical and Classic Music in the Early Twentieth Century

WHAT'S INSIDE Key topics in this unit:

People's Music 11, The Concert Band: The Concert Band, Sousa and the March

People's Music 12, Ragtime: Ragtime

Chapter 40, Charles Ives: Toward an American Art Music: A Connecticut Yankee; Charles Ives; The Music of Charles Ives: *Three Places in New England*; Ives: Toward an All-American Art Music; The Vitality of American Music

Chapter 41, Lift Ev'ry Voice: The African American Spiritual: Recording, Composition, Performance, and Musical Style; Marian Anderson and the Spiritual; Music and Race: Cause and Effect?

People's Music 13, Classic Blues: Blues

Chapter 42, The Jazz Age: The Modern Era Begins; Jazz in the Early Modern Era; "Symphonic Jazz"; The New Classics of the Modern Era

Chapter 43, The Broadway Musical and American Popular Song: Musical Stage Entertainment in the 1920s; The Modern Popular Song: Style and Form; Jerome Kern's *Show Boat*; *Show Boat:* A New Kind of Musical Theater

Learning Outcomes

LO1 Compare the impact of John Philip Sousa's brand of popular music with that of Stephen Foster.

LO2 List the most significant aspects of ragtime's legacy.

LO3 Compare and contrast Sousa's march, Joplin's rag, and Ives's orchestral compositions.

LO4 Recognize the changed dynamic between composition, performance, and musical style, through an examination of the African American spiritual.

LO5 Describe the place of classic blues as the first first-person music in American culture.

LO6 Be familiar with the role of real jazz and Gershwin's "symphonic jazz" in the evolution of American music.

LO7 Discover the sound of 1920s American popular song and its use in Broadway musicals.

Terms

People's Music 11	Chapter 41	blues	blues progression
concert band	Harlem Renaissance	griot	blue note
march	cover	folk blues	
	spiritual	classic blues	**Chapter 42**
People's Music 12		twelve-bar blues	jazz
ragtime, rag	**People's Music 13**	chorus	front line
	race records	call and response	rhythm section

Unit 19 Outline

Multimedia

Listening Guides

People's Music 11
Sousa, "The Stars and Stripes Forever" (3:11) p. 303, CD 4:19

People's Music 12
Joplin, "The Entertainer" (3:34) p. 306, CD 4:20

Chapter 40
Ives, "Putnam's Camp, Redding, Connecticut," from *Three Places in New England* (5:22) p. 309, CD 4:21–23

Chapter 41
Hayes, "Lord, I Can't Stay Away," performed by Marian Anderson (2:13) p. 314, CD 4:24

People's Music 13
"Empty Bed Blues," performed by Bessie Smith (3:02) p. 318, CD 4:25

Chapter 42
Lil Armstrong, "Hotter Than That," performed by Louis Armstrong and his Hot Five (3:03) p. 323, CD 5:1
George Gershwin, *Rhapsody in Blue* (8:52) p. 324, CD 4:26–28

Chapter 43
Kern and Hammerstein, "Can't Help Lovin' Dat Man," *Show Boat* (3:05) p. 330, CD 5:2

Terms (cont.)

swing	**Chapter 43**	Tin Pan Alley
improvisation	revue	riff
scat singing	musical comedy	verse-chorus form
rhapsody	song plugger	chorus

Discussion Questions

1. **It is said that Scott Joplin introduced authentic black music to white America.** How do you think Scott Joplin's music influenced blurring of racial lines? Can you see a connection between Joplin's music and today's?

2. **How does the music of Charles Ives reflect his feelings of spirituality and connectedness to all life?** How is this reflected in "Putnam's Camp"?

3. **Blues contains elements of rag and African music.** Describe them and how they are used in recent music.

4. **The African American spiritual began as pure folk music but has crossed the boundaries into classical and popular music.** Evaluate the advantages and disadvantages of these differing approaches to performance. Include your thoughts on the spiritual as it relates to racial inequalities. Is one approach more successful at expressing racial tension than the others?

5. **Even though improvisation has been in use for centuries, we typically associate it with jazz.** How does the use of improvisation today compare with previous uses?

6. *Show Boat*, **an example of early musical theater, is a convergence of opera, musical theater, and popular song.** Trace the evolution of vocal music style that leads to this music. Do you see a relationship between this vocal music and current popular vocal music?

Beyond the Class

For Further Viewing
These additional video performances may be found in the YouTube playlist:

People's Music 12
- Scott Joplin can still perform by pianola roll, as he does in a video of the "Maple Leaf Rag."

People's Music 13
- Listen for the roots of the blues in a video of African griots.
- Listen to the raglike rhythm of Handy's "Memphis Blues."
- Listen to Handy's more traditional blues, "St. Louis Blues," performed by Bessie Smith.

Chapter 42
- Watch a tribute to Irene and Vernon Castle, innovators of ballroom dance.
- Enjoy Anna Moffo singing "Summertime" among scenes from Part 1 of *Porgy and Bess*.

Chapter 43
- Enjoy Paul Robeson singing "Ol' Man River" from the 1936 version of *Show Boat*.
- Enjoy a scene from *Show Boat* (1936), featuring Helen Morgan singing "Can't Help Lovin' Dat Man."

A selection of materials may also be found in the Instructor's Manual and PowerLecture.

WHAT'S INSIDE Key topics in this unit:

Chapter 44, Serialism: Serialism; Webern and Schoenberg: Tradition and Evolution in Austro-German Music; Webern and Abstract Music

Chapter 45, Stravinsky and Neoclassicism: Neoclassicism; Stravinsky's Approach to Musical Style

Chapter 46, Art and the People: The Americas: Twentieth-Century Musical Nationalism; Carlos Chavez: A Mexican Composer; Aaron Copland: An American Composer

Chapter 47, Art and the People: Eastern Europe: Bartók and a New Kind of Musical Nationalism; Sergei Prokofiev and the Art of Composing for Film; From the People, for the People: Twentieth-Century Nationalism

Learning Outcomes

LO1 Describe Anton Webern's approach to serial composition.

LO2 Recognize the substantial differences between Igor Stravinsky's early compositions and his later neoclassical works.

LO3 Understand how Mexican composer Carlos Chavez and American composer Aaron Copland became major players in a new kind of musical nationalism that peaked during the 1930s and early 1940s.

LO4 Understand how Béla Bartók and Sergei Prokofiev expressed musical nationalism in both similar and completely different ways that were in tune with current developments in modern music.

Terms

Chapter 44
equal temperament
chromatic pitches
serialism (twelve-
   tone composition)
tone row
retrograde
inversion

Chapter 45
neoclassicism

Chapter 47
mickey mousing

Unit 20 Outline

Multimedia

Listening Guides

Active Listening Guides with streaming music are available in CourseMate and in the eBook for the following:

Chapter 44

Webern, Concerto for Nine Instruments, second movement (2:34) p. 335, CD 5:3

Chapter 45

Stravinsky, *Symphony of Psalms*, first movement (3:23) p. 339, CD 5:4

Chapter 46

Chavez, *Sinfonía India*, excerpt (3:27) p. 343, CD 5:5

Copland, *Appalachian Spring*, first and second sections (5:57) p. 346, CD 5:6–7

Chapter 47

Bartók, *Music for Strings, Percussion, and Celesta*, second movement (7:02) p. 350, CD 5:8–10

Prokofiev, "Peregrinus expectavi" ("The Foreigners Are Expected"), *Alexander Nevsky* (6:21) p. 353, CD 5:11–12

Discussion Questions

1. **It is said that expressionist composers sacrificed order in exchange for freedom from tonality.** After listening to this music, do you agree or disagree?

2. **Stravinsky's genius is evident in his ability to create music that was representative of both "neo" and "classical."** How does Symphony of Psalms reflect neoclassicism?

3. **What political, societal, and cultural elements led to nationalism in America in the twentieth century?**

Assignments

1. **Stravinsky is often referred to as a chameleon-like composer.** How did his personal life contribute to the variety of his compositions?

2. **Copland's music reflects the American West, whereas Ives's reflects New England, and Gershwin's, New York.** Discuss the similarities and differences of these styles and how they all reflect American culture in different ways.

3. **This unit focused on composers' use of folk music with a modern approach, with the intent of reflecting a particular country or culture.** Of the composers studied in this unit, which composer of folk-inspired music do you think is the most successful? Why?

Beyond the Class

For Further Viewing

These additional video performances may be found in the YouTube playlist:

Chapter 45

- Listen as Igor Stravinsky conducts the Woody Herman Orchestra performing the Ebony Concerto.

- Check out an excerpt of Stravinsky's *Pulcinella*.

Chapter 47

- Watch for the mickey mousing in the early Disney animation "The Skeleton Dance."

- Watch a dramatization of Disney's meeting with Prokofiev concerning "Peter and the Wolf."

- Enjoy a clip, preparing for battle in the year 1241, from the film *Alexander Nevsky*.

A selection of materials may also be found in the Instructor's Manual and PowerLecture.

UNIT 21 PREPCARD
Sound Frontiers

Learning Outcomes

LO1 Explain the place of John Cage and Milton Babbitt in the postwar American avant-garde.

LO2 Describe Krzysztof Penderecki's work in the avant-garde's exploration of alternative pitch constructs.

Terms

Chapter 48
multiphonics
tone cluster
musique concrète
white noise
prepared piano
chance music
total serialism

Chapter 49
glissando (plural,
   glissandi)

Unit 21 Outline

Multimedia

Listening Guides
Active Listening Guides with streaming music are available in CourseMate and in the eBook for the following:

Chapter 48
Cage, Sonata V from *Sonatas and Interludes* (1:27)
   p. 358, CD 5:13
Babbitt, *Ensembles for Synthesizer*, excerpt (1:49)
   p. 360, CD 5:14

Chapter 49
Penderecki, *Tren (Threnody for the Victims of Hiroshima)* (2:06) p. 364, CD 5:15

Assignments

1. **In the twentieth century, music changes into something that would be unrecognizable for someone time traveling from the past.** Having the privilege of being a time traveler from the future, how do you perceive this music?

2. **"Well, perhaps we did not take sufficiently into account the way music is perceived by the listener."** Boulez's 1999 quote is revealing of the general public's reaction to avant-garde music. Explain the context. Were composers too focused on their own art? What political and societal conditions contributed to the composer's lack of interest in public reaction?

Discussion Questions

1. **Schoenberg, Webern, and Berg are considered the Second Viennese School of composers. Identify some composers they influenced, and describe their impact.**

2. **John Cage's interest in Eastern spirituality influenced his music.** He believed that music had the power to induce tranquility and open humanity to a divine experience. Does music alter your mood? Do you think John Cage's Sonata V creates a sense of tranquility?

3. **Babbitt's creation of sonic events ensured America's status as a home of serious musicians, even though it did not reflect America in the way that Copland's and Ives's music had.** How has his music influenced the music of today?

4. **John Cage's music often creates a sense of tranquility, whereas Penderecki's seems to go beyond conscious thought to the subconscious**. Listen to Penderecki's music, and describe your experience. Try journaling your thoughts as you listen.

Beyond the Class

For Further Viewing
These additional video performances may be found in the YouTube playlist:

Chapter 48
- John Cage performs "Water Walk" on the TV show *I've Got a Secret*.
- Watch a 1981 interview of John Cage and Merce Cunningham discussing their unique collaborations.
- Experience one of Cage's and Cunningham's collaborations, "Variations V."
- Experience Milton Babbitt's "Occasional Variations" realized on the RCA Mark II Sound Synthesizer, 1968–1971.

Chapter 49
- Listen for the use of avant-garde string techniques in The Beatles' "A Day in the Life."

A selection of materials may also be found in the Instructor's Manual and PowerLecture.

WHAT'S INSIDE Key topics in this unit:

Chapter 50, Jazz: America's Art Music: Jazz: From Dance Music to Art; Bop, Music of Liberation; Bop: Sound Track for a Social Revolution

Chapter 51, Musical Theater after *Show Boat*: American Musical Theater from *Show Boat* to *The Sound of Music*; Beyond the Broadway Musical: *West Side Story*; Musical Theater after 1960

Chapter 52, Latin Dance Music: Latin Music in the United States; Latin Music at Midcentury; The Acceptance of Latin Music in the United States

Chapter 53, The Rock Revolution: From Rock and Roll to Rock; Rock of Significance: Dylan and The Beatles; The Rock Revolution

Learning Outcomes

LO1 Understand how jazz evolved in the 1940s from popular dance music to art music for listening.

LO2 Trace the evolution of American musical theater from *Show Boat* to the present.

LO3 Characterize Latin music in the United States through an exploration of a mambo and a tango.

LO4 Describe the rock revolution, using the music of Chuck Berry, the Beach Boys, Bob Dylan, and The Beatles as examples.

Terms

Chapter 50
bebop (bop)
comping
cool jazz

Chapter 51
rock musical

Chapter 52
tango
rumba
son
mambo
claves
clave rhythm
bandoneón
salsa

Chapter 53
boogie woogie
overdubbing
honky-tonk
concept album

Unit 22 Outline

Chapter 50, Jazz, America's Art Music

Jazz: From Dance Music to Art
  Bop, Music of Liberation
  The Musical Innovations of Bop
  Charlie Parker
  The Sound of Bop: "Salt Peanuts"
  Bop and "Modern Jazz"
Bop: Sound Track for a Social Revolution

Chapter 51, Musical Theater after *Show Boat*

American Musical Theater from
  Show Boat to *The Sound of Music*
  The Musical after Show Boat
  Oklahoma! *and the Golden Era*
    of Musical Theater
  The Legacy of Oklahoma!
Beyond the Broadway Musical:
  West Side Story
  "Cool" and the Innovations of West
    Side Story
Musical Theater after 1960
  Stephen Sondheim and
    Contemporary Musical Theater
  Beyond the Musical

Chapter 52, Latin Dance Music

Latin Music in the United States
  Latin Music from Cuba
  The Mambo
Latin Music at Midcentury
  The New Tango
  Piazzolla and the Tango
  Piazzolla and the Tango as Art
The Acceptance of Latin Music in
  the United States

Chapter 53, The Rock Revolution

From Rock and Roll to Rock
  Rock Rhythm
  Chuck Berry
Rock of Significance
The Rock Revolution

Multimedia

Listening Guides

Active Listening Guides with streaming music are available in CourseMate and in the eBook for the following:

Chapter 50

Charlie Parker and Dizzy Gillespie, "Salt Peanuts" (3:18) p. 370, CD 5:16

Chapter 51

Bernstein/Sondheim, "Cool," *West Side Story* (4:23) p. 376, CD 5:17

Chapter 52

Machito, "Carambola" (3:06) p. 380, CD 5:18
Piazzolla, "Chiqué" (3:34) p. 382, CD 5:19

Chapter 53

Berry, "Sweet Little Sixteen" and Wilson, "Surfin' U.S.A." (2:48) p. 386, CD 5:20–21
Dylan, "Subterranean Homesick Blues" (2:23) p. 387, CD 5:22
The Beatles, "A Day in the Life," p. 389, *not available on CD set or streaming*

Discussion Questions

1. **There's an obvious connection between jazz and African music.** The United States also has a long history of racial conflict. How did jazz affect racial barriers? When did jazz musicians begin to cross racial lines?

2. **Between the premieres of *Show Boat* and *West Side Story*, conservatism permeated Broadway.** Innovation gave way to pure entertainment and escapism that did not challenge the intellect. How does this change reflect society of that time?

3. **The Beatles' music represents the mundane turned meaningful.** How did they accomplish this? Is the music attempting to communicate something meaningful and enlightening, or is it pure escape?

Assignments

1. **One of the innovations associated with bop was use of rapid tempos.** The degree of skill required ranks with that of the Romantic virtuoso. Compare the impact of the virtuoso in bop and Romantic music.

2. **It is said the rhythm guitar and the electric bass are responsible for rock and roll's evolving into rock.** Do you see this evident in the 1950s and 1960s? Is there evidence of it in rock music today?

Beyond the Class

For Further Viewing

These additional video performances may be found in the YouTube playlist:

Chapter 50

- Enjoy Chuck Berry performing "Roll Over, Beethoven."

Chapter 51

- Watch Bonnie Raitt and Randy Newman perform "Feels Like Home" from Newman's musical *Faust*.
- Note the repressed energy in "Cool" from *West Side Story*.

Chapter 52

- In this clip, Rudolph Valentino dances the tango in *The Four Horsemen of the Apocalypse*. Be sure to turn the sound off to re-create the original experience.

- Compare Valentino's tango with that from *Scent of a Woman*.

Chapter 53

- Chuck Berry performs "Maybellene."
- Enjoy The Beatles' "Sgt. Pepper's Lonely Hearts Club Band" video from the movie *The Yellow Submarine*.

A selection of materials may also be found in the Instructor's Manual and PowerLecture.

WHAT'S INSIDE Key topics in this unit:

Chapter 54, Uncommon Women: Reconceiving Tonality; Beyond Ceremony: Music for Brass and Percussion; Ellen Taaffe Zwilich and Musical Eclecticism; Women Composers in Contemporary Culture

Chapter 55, Music and Film: So You Want to Be a Film Composer . . . ; John Williams and *Star Wars*; Tan Dun and *Crouching Tiger, Hidden Dragon*; Philosophies of Film Composition

Chapter 56, Minimalism: Minimalism and the "Classical Music" Counterculture; Minimalism, the Past, and the Twentieth Century; Musical Life in the Twenty-first Century

Learning Outcomes

LO1 Become aware of the first generation of women composers who have enjoyed status comparable to that of their male counterparts, through the work of Joan Tower and Ellen Taaffe Zwilich.

LO2 Describe the world of the late twentieth-century film composer through an exploration of the music of John Williams and Tan Dun.

LO3 Explain the place of minimalism in late twentieth-century music.

Terms

Chapter 54
neotonal music
fanfare
eclecticism

Chapter 55
spotting
erhu

Chapter 56
minimalism
phasing
holy (sacred) minimalism
tintinnabuli

Unit 23 Outline

Multimedia

Listening Guides

Active Listening Guides with streaming music are available in CourseMate and in the eBook for the following:

Chapter 54

Tower, *Fanfare for the Uncommon Woman* (2:34) p. 396, CD 5:23

Zwilich, *Concerto Grosso 1985* (2:45) p. 398, CD 5:24

Chapter 55

Williams, "Main Title/Rebel Blockade Runner," *Star Wars Episode IV* (2:14) p. 402, CD 5:25

Tan, "Farewell," *Crouching Tiger, Hidden Dragon* (2:25) p. 404, CD 5:26

Chapter 56

Reich, *Music for 18 Musicians*, Section IIIA (3:31) p. 407, CD 5:27

Pärt, Kyrie, from *Berlin Mass* (2:40) p. 409, CD 5:28

Music Concept Checks

Chapter 56

To assist you in recognizing their distinctive features, we present an interactive comparison of Romantic and twentieth-century music in CourseMate and the eBook.

Discussion Questions

1. **Zwilich composed *Concerto Grosso 1985* for the 300th anniversary of Handel's birth, making it an example of eclecticism.** What features are representative of Handel, and what is modern? contemporary?

2. **Composing for film has its own peculiarities and varying approaches.** Composers may be brought in after filming to create appropriate music, or they may be involved in the process. Which do you think is more appropriate?

3. **Minimalism takes music in diverse directions, from ethnic to the sacred. Does minimalist music *reflect* cultural changes, or has it *caused* cultural changes?**

Assignments

1. **The fanfare has a long history from noise in the Middle Ages to legitimate music in the twentieth century.** Compare and contrast Tower's *Fanfare for the Uncommon Woman* and Copland's *Fanfare for the Common Man*.

2. **Notice the music as it relates to the action in a movie.** Do you notice any scenes that represent spotting? Imagine watching the same scene without the music. How does the music affect the scene?

3. **Minimalists rejected serialism and the traditions that created it.** What inspired the minimalists? How did their lifestyle affect their music? How did minimalism influence rock?

4. **What do you think the future holds for music?** What will inspire future musicians? Describe what you think music in the future will sound like. How will the sounds be produced? What will music mean to humanity?

Beyond the Class

For Further Viewing

These additional video performances may be found in the YouTube playlist:

Chapter 54

- Listen to the 20th Century Fox fanfare.
- Laurie Anderson performs from her home in Soho in New York City.

Chapter 55

- Hear Tan and Beethoven in *Internet Symphony No. 1 "Eroica."*
- Watch a clip from Tan Dun's *Water Passion after St. Matthew.*

Chapter 56

- Enjoy *Metamorphosis 1* by Philip Glass.

A selection of materials may also be found in the Instructor's Manual and PowerLecture.